W9-ACQ-101

Europe 1914

0 100 200 300 400 miles

20

Kola

Lake Ladoga

Helsingfors

St. Petersburg

Kirov

Tallin

VOLGA

Gorky

Lake Peipus

Moscow

BALTIC SEA

Riga

Vitebsk

Kaunas

Smolensk

R U S S I A

Minsk

URAL

Warsaw

Brest-Litovsk

VISTULA

Kiev

DNIEPER

Tsaritsin

VOLGA

Ekaterinoslaf

Astrakhan

Budapest

DNIESTER

Kishinev

Rostov

CASPIAN SEA

-HUNGARY

RUMANIA

PRUT

Odessa

Sea of Azov

Sevastopol

Baku

Belgrade

Bucharest

DANUBE

BLACK SEA

Batum

Tiflis

PERSIA

MONTE-NEGRO

SERBIA

Sofia

BULGARIA

Constantinople

ALBANIA

Salonika

Angora

T U R K E Y

GREECE

Smyrna

(OTTOMAN EMPIRE)

Athens

MENDERES

Aleppo

EUPHRATES

TIGRIS

Bagdad

CRETE

RHODES

CYPRUS

Homs

Beirut

Damascus

ARABIA

Contemporary Europe: A History

Contemporary Europe: A History

H. Stuart Hughes
Harvard University

third edition

Prentice-Hall, Inc., Englewood Cliffs, New Jersey

LIBRARY OF CONGRESS
CATALOG CARD NUMBER: 74-138474

PRINTED IN THE UNITED STATES
OF AMERICA
13-169763-3

Current printing (last digit):

10 9 8 7 6 5 4 3

PRENTICE-HALL INTERNATIONAL, INC., London
PRENTICE-HALL OF AUSTRALIA, PTY. LTD., Sydney
PRENTICE-HALL OF CANADA, LTD., Toronto
PRENTICE-HALL OF INDIA PRIVATE LIMITED, New Delhi
PRENTICE-HALL OF JAPAN, INC., Tokyo

For Sandra and Kenneth
and David

Other Books by the Author

An Essay for Our Times   (1950)

Oswald Spengler: A Critical Estimate   (1952)
revised edition (1962)

The United States and Italy   (1953)
revised edition (1965)

Consciousness and Society: The Reorientation of
European Social Thought, 1890–1930   (1958)

An Approach to Peace   (1962)

History as Art and as Science   (1964)

The Obstructed Path: French Social Thought in the
Years of Desperation, 1930–1960   (1968)

PROFESSOR HUGHES HAS EDITED:

Teachers of History: Essays in Honor
of Laurence Bradford Packard   (1954)

History of the Kingdom of Naples
by Benedetto Croce   (1970)

Preface

This book is quite personal in organization and conception. It is based on the conviction that the past half century of Europe's history requires a less detailed and more sharply pointed treatment than has characterized most general studies of the era. Hence I have not hesitated to express opinions and to pass judgments; I believe that the historian should make his views explicit—if the reader disagrees, at least he knows what he is differing with. For similar reasons I have restricted the readings at the end of chapters to the more readable and recent interpretations, and I have omitted readings for Chapters 16 and 20, where book and periodical citations would have been too scattered and specialized for the general reader.

Several people have given me help and counsel at critical stages of this book's composition. I am particularly indebted to Richard Hofstadter, Richard Pipes, Stephen A. Schuker, Avery D. Weisman, and Suzanne Dworsky. My two older children, to whom the book has been dedicated from the start, have supported my flagging spirits with their enthusiasm for the work afoot, while my youngest child, whose name has now been joined to theirs, has been responsible for many joyous interruptions.

In two successive processes of revision, my wife, Judy, has been both a meticulous detector of factual errors and a constant source of fresh insights and helpful suggestions.

Contents

Contemporary Europe: A History

Europe
in
Chapter One
1914

I

THE UNIQUENESS OF EUROPE

The primacy of Europe was still taken for granted at the beginning of the twentieth century. Nearly all Europeans—and most non-Europeans as well—assumed that this little continent would continue to play the leading role in world affairs, as it had during the preceding four centuries. Very few suspected that the end of Europe's global supremacy was already on the horizon. The past half-century marks the end of the European age. But to reduce the history of Europe in the last fifty years to an impersonal, external record of decline and fall is to ignore an enormously rich and complex segment of human experience: the internal aspect of history. In the decades after 1914, Europeans were only rarely conscious of the historical fate that was overtaking them. They continued to live their lives *as Europeans,* absorbed in national and ideological struggles and in the maintenance and extension of their cultural heritage.

The origins and sequels of the two great European wars that became world wars—and the abiding menace of a third—bring into focus the problems that Europeans considered peculiarly their own: national rivalries, the struggles of the economically discontented, and the rise of ideologies claiming the total obedience of the citizen. These problems were never really "solved." Some became less acute; others lapsed into obsolescence as, after the mid-century, Europeans began to seek a new equi-

*The funeral procession of
King Edward VII arrives
at Westminster Hall.*
COURTESY PHOTOWORLD, INC.

librium. Here lies the final paradox: in the second half of the twentieth century, the Europeans are achieving a new balance and self-confidence. Their former claims to world supremacy gone, their concentration on internal affairs now sanctioned by both old preference and new necessity, the Europeans of today are settling into a more modest role of social and cultural example, of experienced pace setters for the rest of mankind that has been in such a hurry to overtake them.

The European Cultural Heritage

"A little cape on the Asiatic continent," exclaimed the French poet Paul Valéry, struck by the disparity between the small geographical size of his own cultural community and its enormous influence on world history. What was it, people like Valéry wondered, that had given Europe its pre-eminence? Why had the Europeans alone, of all the peoples in all the world's history, succeeded in achieving universal domination?

The most obvious answer lay in Europe's technological superiority. Of all the great civilizations only modern Europe had created a sustained dynamic of technical change: the Chinese—even the ancient Romans—were satisfied with a modest improvement of the technological achievements of their ancestors, but modern Europeans were driven to accelerate improvement, to speed growth from generation to generation in science and in techniques based on scientific method. Along with their scientific and technical bent, Europeans developed a new kind of business enterprise. Like modern technology, modern capitalism, with all its complex financial and industrial devices, was a unique creation of the European spirit.

Europeans were not content to rest their claim to historical uniqueness on power and wealth alone. They found a major source of strength and self-confidence in their distinctive cultural tradition. As they compared their arts and learning, their philosophies and religions with those of other civilizations, they were struck above all by the *variety* of the European scene, and by a culture that mirrored the landscape, presenting the same picturesque contrasts as the continent's heavily indented coastline and sharp changes of scenery. In contrast to the vast sameness that China and India—and later the Americas—presented to the European eye, the geography and culture of that little continent concentrated in a restricted space an infinite succession of achievements and possibilities.

The key to understanding this variety lay in the very origin of modern Europe. The European civilization that crystallized in the early Middle Ages sprang from two distinct sources: the one was Mediterranean and classical, Greek and Roman; the other was northern and Germanic. The two had been fused together by the influence of the church, but in this fusion the original contrast remained, reflected in the two language groups—Latin and Germanic—that accounted for most of the tongues of Western and Central Europe. In the sixteenth century, the split be-

tween Catholic and Protestant Christianity repeated (save for exceptions such as western and southern Germany) the old linguistic cleavage.

In general, Europeans regarded their dual cultural tradition as a source of strength and vitality. But a third aspect of their world could not be so neatly accounted for. In the tense yet tidy division between Mediterranean and northern, Latin and Germanic, Catholic and Protes-tant, where did Eastern Europe belong? Overwhelmingly Slavic in speech, Christianized mostly from Byzantium rather than from Rome, employing a different alphabet and governed by different social tradi-tions, could the eastern part of the continent be considered European at all? All through the nineteenth century, debate had raged as to the his-torical role to be ascribed to Russia and the Slavic world. The Russian Revolution of 1917 and the Communist regime that resulted from it were to revive this old controversy in an unexpected and inordinately acute form.

The Concept of the Nation-state:
Language and Race

One other historical generalization regularly recurred among Europeans seeking to account for their own uniqueness: the similarity of the Euro-pean continent with the geographical and cultural configuration of ancient Greece. Again one found—greatly magnified—the irregular and extended coastlines, the outlying islands closely linked to the mainland, the mountain ranges clearly demarcating natural territorial units that had characterized the Hellenic world. Modern Europe, like ancient Greece, was characterized by political disunity. In other parts of the world that had progressed beyond the level of mere tribalism, vast em-pires had usually developed. In classical Greece and in Europe, such unity had been fleetingly and incompletely achieved. As Athens, Sparta, and Thebes had once attained hegemony over the Greek world, so, in the centuries after the Middle Ages, Spain, France, and Britain in turn took the European lead. But each held a pre-eminence always contested, never surely established. After the collapse of the medieval ideal of a universal empire paralleling a universal church, the independence of the individual territorial units of Europe became the tradition. Europe, like Hellas, was primarily a *cultural* concept. No political organization for-malized its spiritual and social community.

Here again Europeans saw virtue in their very failings. The political disunity of ancient Greece, they argued, had maintained her cultural vitality and enabled her to influence and assimilate alien societies; this great culture drew strength from its own contrasting and competing sub-cultures. Athenians and Spartans might fight each other constantly, but they agreed on a fundamental point: the superiority of all Greeks. In modern Europe, the French and the Germans, leaders of the two great European cultural traditions, although constantly at each others' throats, took pride in a common inheritance of law and education, religion and economic practices. Optimistic Europeans considered national competition healthy and "life-giving." For the most part, they overlooked its dangers and failed to anticipate the catastrophes to which such conflict would lead.

This tradition of European disunity found its final expression in the concept of the nation-state. For several generations, Europeans (and Americans as well) have taken the nation-state for granted, assuming the normal form of political organization to be a fairly large territorial unit, inhabited by a people who consider themselves in some sense homogeneous and claiming the exclusive loyalty of its citizens. The present dominance of this political model has obscured its comparatively recent origin and the large variety of alternative possibilities that were gradually eliminated through the course of time.

The nation-state was a European invention. Although in this century it has been imitated all over the world—often with bizarre results—its origin lies in Western Europe, in the period between the sixteenth and the eighteenth centuries. First England, France, and Spain organized themselves around a common core. In the nineteenth century, Germany and Italy overcame their more stubborn disunity and emerged as nation-states. By the twentieth century, the nation-state had become the norm throughout Western Europe. In the central and eastern parts of the continent, the multinational Austrian and Russian Empires remained as relics of the past. But these Empires, too, were sovereign and allowed their subjects no higher allegiance.

This undivided loyalty was the great political novelty of the late nineteenth century and early twentieth. Formerly, there had always been narrower allegiances—to municipality, guild, feudal lord, or the like—to compete with and divide the national loyalty of the individual. At the other end of the scale, there had been wider allegiances—to the Holy Roman Empire, to a universal church, to the solidarity of an international aristocracy—to split a man's political devotion. By the third quarter of the nineteenth century, these older political loyalties were either dead or in decay. In the whole of European history, only in the years from 1866 (the dissolution of the German Confederation) to 1919 (the establishment of the League of Nations) did there exist not even a vestige of an international political organization. As the twentieth century opened, the nation-state claimed exclusive and total allegiance.

Here lay an obvious danger, for the new exclusiveness of national loyalties intensified old hatreds and awakened new rivalries. More particularly, the tendency to define a nation as consisting of those people who spoke the same language brought disastrous consequences: it dramatically oversimplified an enormously complex question, and it encouraged conflicting claims that were impossible to reconcile. Actually, national sentiment was only partially linguistic in origin. Trilingual Switzerland, for example, possessed an extremely strong national consciousness. Tra-

dition and history were as important as language in making several million people inhabiting a certain geographical area feel that they were a
nation. Religion, too, might inspire national feeling—as witnessed the
difficulties that the Protestant British were having in keeping within
their fold the English-speaking but Catholic Irish.

As nineteenth-century Europeans tended to make the prevalence of a
common speech the criterion of nationality, so they equated language
with race. Actually these two criteria for distinguishing human beings
are almost entirely distinct. Race is a biological fact, language is a cultural product of history and human experience. The child must *learn* his
language; move him to another place and—whatever his "race"—he learns
another language just as easily. It is almost impossible to discern the
racial divisions of Europe, which seldom coincide with the continent's
linguistic boundaries. Nearly all Europeans are "white" but anthropologists cannot agree on the subraces or "stocks" into which this group
should in turn be divided. Obviously a great many Swedes are blond
and most Spaniards are swarthy—but beyond this truism one can offer
little that is precise. Certainly the chief peoples of Europe present a
bewildering and inextricable combination of origins. Indeed, in physical
type, the average German is indistinguishable from the average Frenchman.

In 1914, however, the average European was almost totally ignorant
of the findings of modern anthropology. His knowledge about race was
almost entirely misinformation, but this was enough to poison the atmosphere. The notion of racial difference led naturally to the idea of
innate national qualities, and these characteristics were in turn transformed into signs of inborn superiority. Nothing in the decades before
1914 did more to break the fragile but still perceptible links of European
cultural unity than widespread and uninformed "theories" of national
and racial differences.

The Perils Ahead

By the opening years of the twentieth century, the whole concept of
European civilization—the unique, infinitely precious product of a thousand years of growth—was in desperate peril. Yet curiously few Europeans were aware of the dangers in the disappearance of supranational
or local loyalties and the steady intensification of national hatreds. Beyond these lay other dangers that in the early part of the new century
were only beginning to darken the horizon.

The inadequacy of Europe's territorial base was becoming apparent.
In the approaching age of large-scale endeavor—economic, technological,
and military—Europe stood at a disadvantage. Its scale was too small,
its national markets too restricted, its traditions of performance too painstaking. Its early strengths became its present weaknesses. Europe had

developed technology in careful, artisan fashion. In a world of mass production, the advantages lay with new powers—the United States and Japan, and the still unexploited potential of Russia and China. In these vast areas, mobile populations, brutally shaken out of old traditions, could quickly learn European skills, overtake their teachers, and then turn these skills against their inventors.

By 1914, it should have been apparent that the world would not much longer continue to pay economic and cultural tribute to Europe. But most Europeans gave only passing heed to the two brief and surprising wars which had marked the turn of the century—the conflict of 1898 in which the United States had emerged as a world power by depriving Spain of its last relics of Caribbean and Pacific dominion, and the war of 1904 in which imperial Russia had been decisively beaten by a resurgent Japan.

A few European diplomats realized the significance of these events, but the majority were too absorbed in the intricacies of their own alliance systems. These diplomats had been guided throughout most of the nineteenth century by the tenuous but still very real notion of a "Concert of Europe"—a general European interest which was to be safeguarded by periodic congresses of representatives of the Great Powers. By 1914, the idea of a Concert of Europe was all but dead. The German capital of Berlin in the year 1878 had witnessed the last time that the foreign ministers of the powers assembled to reach decisions that concerned the entire European community.

The obsolescence of the international gentleman was but part of a much wider social change. Until just before the First World War, European diplomacy was almost exclusively conducted by members of the aristocracy—a caste that had only partially adjusted itself to the modern concept of the nation-state. Europe's aristocracy was prenational in origin, and in some respects it remained international until the First World War. The leading noble families—like the royal families—had uncles and cousins scattered throughout Europe, and they still had an international language—French—in which they could converse. In 1914, French was still the language of diplomacy, but the image of the "good European" that this common language embodied had very nearly disappeared. An aristocrat of the old school might find it natural and proper to put the welfare of Europe before the interest of his own country. To the new democracy of the nation-states, such an attitude was incomprehensible, suspect—or even treasonous.

By the first years of the twentieth century Europeans had come to take their civilization for granted. They had forgotten how unique and wonderful that civilization was—how slowly and painstakingly it had been built up through a millennium of labor—and they failed to notice how vulnerable it had become. The significance of these attitudes is apparent in the record of the two vast and infinitely destructive wars in which the Europeans all but committed cultural suicide.

II

THE PROMISE OF THE NEW ERA

In the first decade of the twentieth century sober optimism colored the prevailing mood in the more "advanced" countries of Western and Central Europe. Indeed, the expectations of the average man had never been so high. For the past century mankind—particularly European mankind —seemed to have been advancing steadily. And as they peered into the coming era, Europeans tended to project this past progress into an indefinite future. On the basis of the record of the last hundred years—in which the dominant notes had been peace, prosperity, and the democratization of political and social life—there seemed no reason to imagine that movement would not continue in the same direction forever.

Technology and Science

The great Paris exposition of 1900 was the climax of a quarter-century of such displays and fittingly ushered in the new century. These expositions had been primarily devoted to the triumphs of modern science and technology: achievements of which Europeans were most proud and which formed the basis for their own optimism about the future.

In most countries of Western and Central Europe, the nineteenth century had been the era of what is called in very general terms the Industrial Revolution. Sometime in the years between 1800 and 1900, great nations like France, Germany, and Italy, and smaller ones like Belgium and Sweden had equipped themselves with the machinery of a modern industrial society. Faithfully copying English accomplishments of the latter part of the preceding century, they had built factories and roads and notably improved their agricultural methods. Machine production had characterized this initial phase of the Industrial Revolution; textiles first, and later iron and steel had been the pace setters of mechanization. And in the second and third quarters of the nineteenth century, the railroad and the steamship had similarly revolutionized land and water transport.

These extraordinary economic changes brought about a vast growth of cities which in turn produced far-reaching social and political alterations. Three aspects of the Industrial Revolution of the nineteenth century deserve comment. First, these social and economic changes did not affect all areas and classes of the European population. Although they transformed old cities and created new ones, they left much of the countryside nearly undisturbed. They profoundly altered the character of the urban middle class and brought into being a whole new class of factory workers, but they affected the peasantry much less markedly. In Southern and Eastern Europe particularly, by far the larger part of the population still lived in a preindustrial world scarcely touched by the breath of modernity. People in the country and in small towns shared only to a slight extent in the new cult of material progress; they remained conservative and traditionalist, skeptical of the novel ideas bred in the cities. The significance of this contrast between rural and urban ways of life, and the fact that they could exist simultaneously and side by side, will recur again and again in the analysis of the social and ideological conflicts of the twentieth century.

Secondly, the new century was bringing with it another and even more far-reaching industrial revolution. The age of coal and iron was about to give way to the age of electricity, light metals and plastics, and the internal combustion engine. By 1900, electric lights and telephones were becoming widespread; the automobile had just been invented; the airplane, the radio, and the motion picture were shortly to make their appearance. The Industrial Revolution of the nineteenth century had been a grimy, sooty affair: men thought of Blake's "dark satanic mills," a picture of dirt and ugliness. The new industrial age promised to be cleaner, brighter, tidier. Already the vast differences between owners and workers that had marked the society of the mid-nineteenth century were diminishing; in clothing, in cleanliness—even in physique—the gap between them was narrowing. Here also Europeans could find reason for optimism about the future.

Finally, the triumphs of European technology in the nineteenth century had greatly enhanced the popular prestige of science and scientific or pseudoscientific explanations. The Industrial Revolution and its sequels were the outcome of applied scientific knowledge; the inventors had linked the world of abstract science with the world of business. In the last decades of the nineteenth century, Europeans had become science-minded. By 1900 the man of ordinary education had discarded a large number of his traditional beliefs: for the explanations of the universe and of human affairs that religion or folk wisdom offered, he had substituted the neater and clearer explanations of modern science. Or at least he thought so. He thought that to reason scientifically meant to seek a single, simple "cause" for every phenomenon and to prefer a materialist or determinist explanation to one that stressed mystery or the "spirit." The Frenchman or German of 1900 who prided himself on his "scientific" thinking had a rather inaccurate notion of what science actually was.

At the very least, his idea of science was out of date: it reflected the certainties of an earlier scientific age. The paradox of the popular scientific beliefs of the first part of the twentieth century was that they bore so little relation to the actual thinking of the more advanced scientists of the era. Just at the time that the older and simpler explanations were winning the allegiance of the general public, they were losing the faith of the scientists themselves. The new men of science were beginning a radical revision of their earlier ideas, particularly in physics: here the notion of plural and even contradictory explanations produced the most perplexing results (*see* Chapter Seven, I). The vast changes in scientific thinking that have taken place in our time offer not the least of the reasons for referring to the past half-century as a time of almost constant revolution.

Human Welfare

Never before in human history had the average man lived so well as he did in the more advanced countries of the Western world at the opening of the twentieth century. Poverty and disease still existed, of course. But the enormous progress already made in eliminating them aroused hopes that these, like so many other scourges that had once plagued humanity, might eventually become no more than an evil memory.

In reviewing the century just past, Europeans could point to accomplishments that would have staggered the imagination of earlier ages. The last vestiges of serfdom and of feudal dependence had been abolished. Nearly everywhere—with the notable exception of Russia—administrative and police methods had become infinitely more humane and less arbitrary: torture, for one thing, was universally frowned upon and was believed to have been eliminated. Similarly, medicine and hygiene had made more progress in one century than in all the rest of human history put together. Surgery and anesthetics had been vastly improved; no longer were hospitals chambers of horrors which one entered only to suffer and to die. Infant mortality had been cut to a fraction of its earlier toll; at the same time the span of human life was being steadily extended. The population of Europe continued to grow in the decades after 1900, not because the birth rate remained high (on the contrary, the number of births was falling in all the more advanced countries), but because doctors and public health officials each year succeeded in saving tens of thousands of additional lives.

In brief, the humanitarian hopes of the philosophers and publicists of the eighteenth century had in the century following become sober reality. And along with this new respect for human life went a new consciousness of the importance of health and physical well-being. By 1900, the city people of Europe were everywhere trying to get outdoors; the twentieth-century cult of sport and the open air had already begun. Decoration and manners reflected the change: the heavy, overstuffed, ornate furniture of the mid-nineteenth century was giving way to lighter and simpler styles, and social conventions were beginning to lose their stiffness and formality. The first signs of the twentieth-century revolt against "Victorian" middle-class morality were clearly in evidence.

These social and intellectual changes were most completely summed up in the spread of literacy. By 1900, the countries of Northern and Western Europe were sending their whole populations to school. Britain and France, Germany and Switzerland, Scandinavia and the Low Countries had virtually wiped out the enormous handicap of illiteracy. Italy and Austria-Hungary lagged behind, but here too a universally literate population had become a practical possibility for the near future. Only on the periphery of Europe—in Spain and Portugal, the Balkan countries, and the vast exception of tsarist Russia—was illiteracy still accepted as normal. But these were also the countries that had made small progress toward political democracy. The coupling of the two deficiencies was obvious: literacy was the prerequisite to the democratic forms of political life that were confidently riding the wave of the future.

The Peace Movement

By 1914, Europe had gone so long without a major war that the very idea was becoming dim in men's minds. For more than forty years—the longest such span in modern history—the Great Powers had been at peace with one another. Since the War of 1870 between France and Germany, conflicts had been limited to engagements in the Balkans and to overseas struggles such as the Spanish-American War, the Russo-Japanese War, and the Boer War of 1899–1902, in which Britain had subjugated the South African republics of the Orange Free State and Transvaal.

In the major nations of Western and Central Europe a whole generation had come of age without knowledge of warfare between equals. The long freedom from intra-European conflict had produced the illusion that it would never recur. People began to argue that mankind had become too civilized for such barbarian pursuits. More concretely, this sentiment—and general humanitarian feeling as well—had manifested itself in the growth of organized pacifism. The pacifist movement had steadily gained adherents since the last decades of the nineteenth century. France and Britain, Switzerland and Scandinavia all had vigorous propagandists for peace; Germany alone was a significant exception.

The pacifists did not rest their case on humanitarian grounds alone. They also argued that under modern conditions war simply did not pay. Moreover they found that the organization of the business world itself precluded war between the Great Powers. In the early years of the twentieth century, vast interlocking cartels had been organized throughout the Western world. In banking and shipping, in textiles and chemicals and tobacco, the international cartelists had strung almost invisible nets binding the economies of potentially enemy states. War would not occur, the argument ran, because the directors of the cartels would not allow it. And the cartelists themselves, under heavy attack for their monopolistic position, found it to their interest to encourage such illusions.

Yet all the agitation for peace had produced but minuscule achievement. Two international conferences had assembled, but these had accomplished very little. The Hague Conference of 1899, called on the initiative of tsarist Russia (which was beginning to feel the strain of the arms race), had immediately run into uncompromising German resistance

to any real disarmament. The Conference succeeded only in adding a
few new provisos to the traditional rules of war and in setting up a panel of judges to which the nations might resort for arbitration, if they so desired. Another Hague conference, eight years later, accomplished still less.

Indeed, the failure to produce any sound arbitration procedures gave clear evidence of how little substance lay behind all the talk about peace. From 1903 on, the nations of Europe had been busily signing arbitration treaties with each other. But all of these (except for two negotiated by Denmark, a country which threatened nobody) contained escape clauses that made them meaningless. The promise to submit to arbitration did not apply when a nation considered its "vital interests" or its "honor and independence" to be threatened.

It is fitting that a discussion of the promise of the new century should end with the "pipe dream of peace." For here the gap between promise and performance, between aspiration and reality, was widest and produced the greatest subsequent disillusionment.

III
THE IDEOLOGIES OF PROGRESS

The over-all view of the world embodied in the early twentieth-century confidence about the future may be called *an ideology of progress*. The nineteenth century had been the first great age of ideology, and it was in this period that the word first came into general use.

Ideology and Conservatism

Ideology lies somewhere between abstract political and social philosophy and the practical activities of parties and pressure groups. Indeed, it provides the link between the two. An ideology is a general concept of the actual or ideal nature of society that gives meaning and direction to the lives of large groups of people. In one aspect, it is a theory of history, charting the "inevitable" course of human affairs and assuring its adherents that the future lies with them. It is no accident that it was the historically minded nineteenth century that first began to think in this fashion. From another standpoint, ideology is linked to class, rationalizing and endorsing the aspirations of one social class and attacking those of its enemies. Finally, it may be viewed as a secular cult with its own saints and martyrs, its own creed, and its own system of missionary work, propaganda, and indoctrination.

Ideology may be either implicit or explicit. In the United States, the dominant ideology of middle-class democracy is usually only incompletely expressed. In Europe, these matters are far more explicit—for one reason, because there is less of a political consensus and ideological competition is keener.

The French Revolution of 1789 marked the beginning of the age of ideology. In breaking the cake of custom, it called all traditional arrangements into question and opened the way to competing definitions of what constituted a proper society. Similarly—and rather paradoxically —it produced for the first time a conscious ideology of conservatism. Under the old regime, conservatism had been spontaneous and implicit: as the expression of things as they were, it did not need justification or a coherent political ideology. After the revolutionary era of 1789–1815, the situation changed. The conservatives, restored to power after the fall of Napoleon, were no longer so secure. They needed to explain and to justify their attempted return to the past. The Revolution, by attacking conservatism, had in fact created a conservative ideology.

By 1900, conservatism seemed to be declining nearly everywhere. Even many conservatives felt that their days were numbered. The first half of the nineteenth century had been more promising for them. For a generation after 1815 the alliance of "throne and altar" had held firm; the religious justification of conservative rule had kept the mass of the European populations in check. But the Revolution of 1848—renewing and extending to the rest of Western and Central Europe the French tradition of 1789—ended all that. Despite the defeat of the revolutionary movements and the return of the conservatives to power, the victory of reaction was an illusion. In the next half-century, conservatism steadily retreated; from decade to decade, progressive-minded leaders conquered quietly and without bloodshed one after another of the positions which their fathers had tried to overwhelm in one great rush as they manned the barricades of 1848.

By 1900, the conservatives had become defeatists: they saw their own political labors as little more than delaying actions, doomed to be submerged in longer or shorter time by the rising flood of democracy. They had lost confidence in their own traditionalist and mystical ideology which, in an age of science, no longer sufficed. The ideologists of progress had set the new rules of political debate, rules which at least purported to be logical and scientific, and the conservatives were supinely allowing themselves to be enmeshed in subleties which at heart they detested.

European conservatism was not to recover its nerve and self-confidence until it learned how to break the rules of the game—and with this knowledge gained another generation of grace.

Liberalism

Conservatism constituted the Right of the European political spectrum —so called because the conservative deputies had become accustomed in the course of the nineteenth century to seat themselves on the right of the semicircular halls in which European parliaments usually met. In the center and on the left sat the ideologists of progress: liberals, radicals, and socialists.

Liberalism by 1900 was roughly equivalent to the political Center. In nineteenth-century Europe this term meant something far different from what it does in America today. In the United States to be a liberal means to be considerably to the left of center—something more than a democrat, with a definite predilection for the welfare state. In nineteenth-century Europe, liberalism was a predemocratic faith and usually distrustful of democracy; it had no smell of socialism about it. It was a doctrine of political moderation.

For European liberals the three key terms were *freedom, law,* and *representative institutions.* Their first and most passionate belief was in the freedom of the individual. It was chiefly the efforts of liberals that brought about the enunciation and codification of the basic Western liberties—the fundamental rights which no state power must be allowed to violate. Such principles as freedom of speech, of the press, of assembly, and of religion, embodied in the first ten amendments to the American Constitution, regularly formed the preambles to European constitutions drafted under liberal auspices. Other articles of these constitutions confirmed the further principles that liberal agitation had won from reluctant sovereigns: a guarantee of the regular processes of law, including the equality of citizens before the courts, and the powers of the parliamentary chambers which claimed exclusive responsibility for legislation and taxation and which were gradually to wrest executive authority from the monarch himself.

To liberals these principles of liberty, law, and representation were the sum of progressive aims. They were interested in going no further in the direction of change and reform. Democracy rather frightened them. The characteristic liberal leader was a man of wealth and education, a member of the upper middle class or, even more typically, an enlightened aristocrat. Liberals usually did not wish to deprive the king of all his power or reduce him to the mere figurehead that he is in contemporary European monarchies. They saw hereditary monarchy as a stabilizing force and felt that the king, as head of the state, should retain a certain amount of independent initiative, particularly in the field of foreign affairs. Another conservative safeguard favored by liberals was an upper house of parliament—a senate or house of peers, either hereditary or appointed by the king. For the elected lower house—the chamber of deputies or house of commons—liberals advocated a restricted suffrage; they thought it monstrous for the ignorant masses to have an equal vote with men of property and education. The constitutional arrangements that conformed most closely to their ideas were those of Britain after the Reform Act of 1832 or the July Monarchy in France after the Revolution of 1830.

European liberals were usually frank elitists: they were convinced of the virtues of their own class, and although they were often forced to compromise with democracy, they believed that little good could come of it. Like the conservatives, they were eventually reduced to delaying tactics; by the end of the nineteenth century, European liberals were finding it impossible to halt the onrush of reform as they confronted an ever wider electorate. But at the same time their philosophy of skepticism and distrust had hidden strengths that only time would reveal. Nineteenth-century liberals, unlike their political competitors to the left, saw the future dangers implicit in democracy, particularly in areas where it might be introduced too rapidly to a population that was psychologically unready for it. As men of culture, liberal leaders cited Aristotle on the inevitable degeneration of democracy into tyranny. The fascist experience of the twentieth century would show how far-sighted they had been.

Radicalism

Pure electoral democracy of the type represented for more than a century by both American political parties lies halfway between European liberalism and the political ideology known as *radicalism*. Actually, few European leaders of the moderate Left called themselves democrats. Democracy was a utopian abstraction rather than the watchword of an organized political movement. In Europe, the democratic forces tended to group themselves to the left of center under the banner of radicalism —something more militant and intolerant than simple faith in majority rule.

Here again differing terminology confuses the issue. To an American, a *radical* means a firebrand, very likely a revolutionary of some sort. To a European, *radicalism* means a political allegiance rooted in the struggles of the nineteenth century. Today, radicalism is rather tame; a half-century ago, however, it was a fighting faith, for the introduction of democracy into Europe was far more difficult than it had been in the United States. Europe had too many relics of the past—privileged bodies of all sorts which the liberals generally were ready to leave intact or to reform but slightly. The churches, for instance, the traditional mainstays of constituted power, were usually treated with respect by the liberals, but violently attacked by the radicals. Hence the European radical was something more than a democrat—that is, something besides a citizen who advocated an equal vote for every man (but not for every woman!) and the abolition of all remaining vestiges of class distinctions. He was also, at least in Catholic countries, an anticlerical: he believed that the church had far too much power in public life and that stringent measures were required to curb the overweening pretensions of the priests.

This was also the stand of European Masonry, and on the European continent radicalism and Masonic affiliation frequently went together. Here too a marked difference exists between American and European attitudes. In the United States, Masonry is chiefly a matter of civic-mindedness and good fellowship. In Europe it has been a lay church, militantly dedicated to the secular values of progress, science, and democracy.

In general, then, European radicals were more "advanced" than the liberals. The tide of the future seemed to be running in their favor, and by the first decade of the twentieth century, they were riding the crest of the wave. In one respect, however, they were often untrue to broader democratic values: they believed passionately in equality, but their devotion to liberty was less certain. In their attitude toward organized religion, they were frequently intolerant of their enemies, real or imagined. European democracy was not to assume its final form until it had fused the liberal love of freedom with the radical insistence on political equality.

Moreover, radicalism had intrinsic weaknesses that were only just becoming apparent as the new century opened. Like the liberals, European radicals stood for the economic principles of free enterprise: they were reluctant to sanction government intervention in the operation of the economy. True, electoral competition from the socialists gradually forced them to modify this attitude. By the first decade of the twentieth century, most French radicals were beginning to call themselves Radical Socialists, and the British radicals (who formed the left wing of the Liberal party) under Lloyd George's leadership were advancing a broad program of social legislation. But these new measures were largely a matter of expediency; they went against the grain. The characteristic European radical was a member of the lower middle class or of the middle bourgeoisie—a small businessman, a landholding peasant, a lawyer, or a doctor. Although on occasion he used inflammatory language, he was in no sense a revolutionary. He thought of himself as a "little man," economically independent, and in every moral and intellectual respect the equal of the great. His vision of the good society was a shopkeeper's paradise in which small enterprise held the field against monopolists on the one hand and the forces of collectivism on the other.

Thus, like most Americans—to whom of all the European ideologies radicalism was the most congenial—the radicals of Europe disliked the very idea of discussing politics in terms of class conflict. Such talk seemed to violate the basic principle of the equality of the citizen. But more and more European politics *was* being talked about in these terms, and this would be even more true after the First World War had taken the fat off the European economy. Similarly, a collectivist economic philosophy was steadily gaining adherents. These changes of sentiment caught radicalism unprepared—as did the still newer tendency to stress and exploit irrational motivations in political struggle. There was something sentimental and psychologically shallow about traditional radicalism: it had too simple a faith in the goodness and rationality of man to cope with the politics of desperation.

self had accordingly organized an international association of working-men which lived a precarious existence from 1864 to 1876, when it finally succumbed to its own internal divisions. This small and fragile organization is known in socialist history as the First International. The Second International, formed in 1889, was far more robust. A federation of the socialist parties of Europe, its delegate congresses paralleled in unofficial form the state diplomacy of the Great Powers.

The congresses of the International resounded with peaceful protestations from delegates of potentially enemy nations. Indeed, its activities offer a final explanation for the widespread illusion that war would not occur. But the actual accomplishments of the Second International were almost as insubstantial as those of the Hague conferences. The one resolution with teeth in it—a pledge to call a general strike to forestall future threats of war—never won a majority, more particularly in the stronger socialist parties like the German and the British, for the average European socialist leader was a solid citizen, with a stake in the existing order of society. He was far less revolutionary and far more patriotic than he professed to be. It should have surprised no one when in August, 1914, the socialist parties of Europe declared in overwhelming majority for support of their countries' war efforts.

IV
THE TRIUMPH OF
PARLIAMENTARY DEMOCRACY

By 1914, parliamentary government had become the European norm. Deviations were ascribed either to the special conditions of small countries or to a "backwardness" that must eventually succumb to the forces of progress.

Parliamentary Government in Practice

The United States is the only major democracy which has not operated under the parliamentary system. Its "presidential" constitution provides for a strict separation of powers: executive authority is vested solely in the president, Congress restricts itself to legislative functions, and the president remains in office even when his party loses its majority in Congress. This type of constitution has had little appeal in Europe. In 1914, the only state that operated even approximately on a presidential basis was the federal state of Switzerland—oldest and smallest of the three European republics then in existence.

Elsewhere separation of powers did not exist. According to the parliamentary model that had developed in the eighteenth century in Great Britain and in the early nineteenth century in France, the effective executive was in fact a committee of the legislature or parliament. The theoretical head of state—the king or (in France) the president—had gradually become a figurehead. Besides performing ceremonial functions, his chief duty was to appoint a prime minister who, along with the colleagues whom he gathered about him to constitute a cabinet or ministry, actually managed the business of state. The king or president could use a certain amount of discretion in naming the prime minister; sometimes the choice was obvious, at other times leadership was unclear and it might be necessary to try out alternate combinations. But the chief criterion was always the same: could the proposed prime minister command a majority in the House of Commons or Chamber of Deputies? For if he failed to do so, or if he lost his majority, he and his cabinet must resign. Thus the ministry—or "government," as the French put it —would fall, a far less catastrophic event than it seemed to American readers of the daily newspapers.

This procedure had grown up hit or miss as precedents gradually became established. It was nowhere codified in written constitutions (Britain did not even have a written constitution), and in practice it took two rather different forms. In Britain, where political life was dominated by two or three relatively stable parties, the cabinet rather than Parliament held the whip: as leaders of the majority party in the House of Commons, the prime minister and his colleagues kept a firm hand on their followers and were seldom overthrown by an adverse vote. On the Continent, more particularly in France and Italy, the situation was reversed. Here parliaments were supreme. Since parties were numerous and ill disciplined, the ministry—which usually represented more than one party—could never be sure of its majority. Because it stood at the mercy of the defection of even a small group of supporters, its tenure was usually brief. In France, for example, the maximum term was three years, the average much shorter. Throughout the Continent the lives of ministries were almost bound to be short unless (as in the case of Italy's Giovanni Giolitti) there emerged a majority-monger of genius, adept at satisfying all the wants of 300-odd deputies and their constituents.

Originally the parliamentary system had been a contrivance of liberal inspiration; later the radicals had adapted themselves to it and turned it to democratic ends. By 1914, even the socialists were beginning to settle down happily within the parliamentary framework.

The Aristocratic Remainders

In 1900, no major European country—with the possible exception of France—could be considered a democracy in any effective sense. Fourteen years later, when the war broke out, at least three had virtually completed the evolution from aristocratic to democratic rule.

Late nineteenth-century European society was frankly aristocratic. The old nobility, constantly reinforced by promotions from the upper bourgeoisie, was far from a spent force. Although feudal privileges were a thing of the past (in legal terms, except in Russia, all citizens were equal), the less tangible elements of a regime of status remained.

Nearly everywhere the nobility held vast tracts of land, and in many places they still exerted an informal dominance over the whole political and social life of the countryside and played a leading role in government. The German chancellor was invariably an important nobleman, and as late as the 1890's, both the Conservative and the Liberal parties in Britain furnished a peer as prime minister. At the top of the government hierarchy, cabinet ministers were more likely to be upper bourgeois than aristocratic in origin, but just below the top the nobility were entrenched. They were strong at the royal courts, in the elite corps of the civil service, in the upper houses of parliament, and, more particularly, as diplomats and army officers, positions which they almost monopolized in some countries. Even in republican France a large proportion of the ambassadors and military chiefs were of noble origin.

The more public-spirited aristocrats and the leading members of the upper middle class together constituted the "notables" of the national or local communities. The prosperous middle class—business and professional people—tended to dominate the lower houses of parliament and to manage domestic affairs, as opposed to the aristocratic role in military and foreign affairs. Many of them were linked to the nobility through business or marriage. Indeed in countries like Britain and Germany, there existed an informal alliance between the two. This understanding was based on the tacit agreement that the aristocrats would hold command over the more showy and impressive manifestations of the national life, while the bourgeoisie stood modestly to the rear, possessing the reality of power, but content to restrict themselves to practical affairs and to the direction of the economy.

Underlying this informal alliance, of course, was the brutal fact of an enormous difference in wealth and in manner of living between rich and poor. Such distinctions were far more visible in the Europe of 1914 than they were to be a half-century later. In the early twentieth century, Europeans with money and position enjoyed their privileges openly and saw no reason to apologize for them; a democratic simplicity of manner had not yet become the style. Wealth and its accompaniments were what most clearly set apart aristocracy and upper bourgeoisie alike from the rest of the population—this and access to a superior education. In Western Europe the best schools might often be run by the state—indeed, on the Continent such was usually the case—but they were elitist in character nonetheless. The "public" schools of England, the *lycées* of France, the *gymnasia* of Germany were in fact if not in theory the preserves of the privileged classes. Here the sons of the wealthy and well-born, plus a scattering of talented recruits from the lower orders, received the classical education that was almost universally supposed to fit them for the positions of responsibility they would later occupy. Such an education was heavily weighted toward literature and rhetoric; it was weak in science, economics, and technology. But it produced future leaders

who spoke and wrote with ease, fluency, and correctness, who understood each other's literary allusions, and who carried themselves with a confidence deriving from a sense of superior talent. This solidarity in manners and education, perhaps even more than their wealth, made the leaders of Europe's upper classes formidable antagonists when the spokesmen of democracy and the trade unions began to challenge their ascendancy.

Thus the system of shared authority between aristocracy and upper middle class worked fairly well almost to the outbreak of the First World War; not until then did the European aristocracy finally lose its grip. After 1918, the upper middle class remained nearly alone as the proponents of conservative values. And they must often have regretted the demise of their aristocratic allies. The latter alone had dash and distinction enough to persuade the public of the merits of reactionary policies. In the postwar years, when political leaders of business origin had to act for themselves without aristocratic support, they stood pitiably exposed to charges of egoism and self-seeking.

The Progress of Democracy

Since parliamentary government was originally aristocratic in inspiration, its extension to the newly formed states in the Balkans produced a scarcely concealed situation of class rule. But in countries of greater political maturity parliamentary government had in it the seeds of democracy. The lower houses—which soon became the key pins of the system —were elective rather than hereditary or appointed bodies, and as the suffrage was gradually extended, these houses of commons or chambers of deputies, and with them the system as a whole, were progressively democratized.

The years 1900 to 1914 were the golden age of European radicalism. In this period, electoral democracy triumphed in country after country. France had enjoyed universal manhood suffrage since the Revolution of 1848; it had been a republic since 1870. But not until the early years of the twentieth century did French democracy become a militant reality. The injustice done to a single army officer of Jewish origin—the celebrated Captain Dreyfus—eventually mobilized the forces of French radicalism in a vigorous assault on political reaction and the church. The elections of 1902 and 1906 were radical landslides. And in 1905 the radical and radically minded majority in the French parliament brought to a climax a half-decade of legislative warfare against church influence in education and politics by severing all connection between the Catholic clergy and the French state.

In Britain, periodic extensions of the suffrage in the half-century from 1832 to 1885 had given most adult males the vote. But here, as in France, it took another generation for this democratization to sink into the national consciousness and alter the voting habits of the average citizen. In 1900, the House of Commons was still aristocratic in composition— still the "best club in Europe." Its attention was directed toward imperial and foreign affairs, and it had a crushing Tory majority. Six years later, all this was reversed: the Liberals—more particularly their radical wing —scored a stunning electoral triumph and proceeded to democratize with a vengeance. Under Lloyd George's eloquent leadership, reform followed reform in dizzying succession: social legislation, income and inheritance taxes, and finally, drastic limitations on the powers of the hereditary House of Lords. By the outbreak of the war, England, like France, in all important respects, could be considered a democracy.

A third great power, Italy, crossed the democratic watershed in the same period. A monarchy like Britain, but in other political respects more closely resembling France, Italy had had a highly restricted suffrage based on property qualifications. The election of 1913 swept away these restrictions. The vast majority of Italian men, some still illiterate, were able to vote for the first time. Although few contemporaries realized it, Italy had entered a period of revolutionary change that was to continue, in one form or another, for more than a generation.

The smaller countries of Northern and Western Europe by 1914 had also evolved toward the parliamentary democratic model. Unlike Switzerland—the cradle of European republicanism—all of them were monarchies. The Low Countries—Belgium and the Netherlands—and the three Scandinavian nations of Norway, Sweden, and Denmark had the reputation of being well-run and peace-oriented states. On the whole, their populations were more prosperous, better educated, and more democratic in manners than the citizenry of the major European nations. In Sweden and the Netherlands, traces of aristocratic privilege lingered, but these were little more than picturesque variations on the dominant tone of triumphant democracy.

The Exceptions

Europe as a whole, however, offered far graver and more threatening exceptions. In the countries of the Iberian Peninsula, democracy was scarcely even an aspiration. Economically and educationally backward, Spain and Portugal vegetated outside the mainstream of European events and influences. The former was in theory a constitutional monarchy; the latter became a republic in 1910. But in both countries real power was held by corrupt and selfish cliques of army officers and landholders.

A similar situation prevailed in the newer but equally backward states of the Balkan Peninsula—Greece, Bulgaria, Serbia, Montenegro, and Rumania. Unlike Spain and Portugal, the Balkan countries were not isolated from the major pressures of European international politics: they were the clients and potential enemies of great powers. The three east-

ern Empires—Germany, Austria-Hungary, and Russia—were deeply embroiled in Balkan rivalries.

These three Empires, as opposed to the three democratized powers of
the West, still stood firm for imperial prerogative and class rule. For a
century they had been the citadels of European conservatism. All had
evolved to some extent in a parliamentary democratic direction, but in
1914 they still lived under curious, hybrid institutions that hovered in a
limbo between autocracy and constitutionalism.

On the surface, Germany looked much like a Western democracy. The
constitution with which Bismarck had crowned its unification in 1871
bore a deceptive resemblance to the Western norm. Its chancellor seemed
to perform the role of prime minister; its Reichstag tried to behave like
a chamber of deputies. True, the Reichstag was elected by universal
manhood suffrage. But its legislative authority was incomplete, it had
virtually no control over the army budget, and the chancellor was not
responsible to it—that is, he was not obliged to resign if he lost his
Reichstag majority. With all its faults, however, the imperial constitution
was less defective from the democratic standpoint than the constitution
of the federal state of Prussia. It was also less significant. Prussia, which
was larger and more populous than all the other German states put together, was the wheel within the wheel that ran the whole machine. Its
king was the German emperor; its prime minister was usually imperial
chancellor also. It ran the army and most of the internal administration of
the whole country. Prussia's constitution was frankly aristocratic. Through
a complex system of three-class voting, its parliament (or Diet) was
dominated by a permanent conservative majority, devoted to its king-
emperor and to the military values that he exemplified. At the very least,
the future democratization of Germany would require making the chancellor responsible to the Reichstag and, still more important, abolishing
the Prussian three-class voting system.

Nor was Austria-Hungary the parliamentary state it seemed. Although
the constitutions under which it lived conformed more closely to the
Western European norm than did the institutions of Germany, the problem of national minorities in the Austro-Hungarian Empire dominated
everything else and made a mockery of the constitutional arrangements
existing on paper.

The Compromise of 1867 with the Hungarians had split the old Austrian Empire into two separate countries linked by a common sovereign
and by common ministries for finance, war, and foreign affairs. Both
halves of the Empire had parliamentary constitutions, and there was
even a rudimentary joint parliament consisting of "delegations" to which
the three joint ministries reported. But in each half, the ruling nationality was outnumbered by the sum of its national minorities; these latter
grew more militant each year, and normal operation of parliamentary
institutions became impossible. In the western or "Austrian" half of the
country—a collection of separate provinces with no traditional name—the

German Austrians ruled with a slipshod tolerance. In 1906 they had introduced universal manhood suffrage, thus producing an influx of minority deputies, particularly from the politically experienced and well-educated Czechs, whose obstructionism paralyzed the functioning of parliament.

In the eastern half—the kingdom of Hungary—no such behavior was tolerated. As opposed to the loosely joined assemblage of territories that made up "Austria," Hungary was a closely knit state, with a thousand-year tradition of its own. And the Hungarians (or Magyars) did not mean to grant any other nationality the parity with the German Austrians that they had so recently won for themselves. In Hungary, voting was public and based on a high property qualification; electoral districts were ruthlessly gerrymandered. Thus the Hungarian aristocracy kept a firm grip on power and held to a minimum the number of minority representatives who reached the halls of parliament in Budapest.

Finally, there was Russia. In name, the Russian Empire was still an autocracy. But it had changed more in the first decade of the new century than any other of the Great Powers of Europe. The revolution of 1905 had produced a constitution and a parliament (or Duma). This body was chosen by a complex system of indirect voting, and its powers were narrowly limited, but it still represented an epoch-making innovation for a country that as late as 1900 had possessed no semblance of a constitution. In the early twentieth century Russia was commonly held to be the enigma of Europe—a half-awakened giant with enormous and rather frightening potentialities for the future.

V

THE DANGER SIGNALS

As the second decade of the twentieth century opened, it was understandable that European democrats should dismiss as mere anachronisms the vestiges of autocratic and aristocratic rule in the three empires of the east. These should be shrugged off as relics of a vanishing past. But the same progressive-minded citizens were less justified in their neglect of certain newer symptoms of undemocratic behavior that had about them the aura of a most disconcerting modernity.

Imperialism at Home and Abroad

In 1885, on returning to the British foreign ministry which he had relinquished five years earlier, the Marquess of Salisbury told his fellow peers: "I do not exactly know the cause of this sudden revolution. But

there it is. It is a great force—a great civilizing, Christianizing force."
He was referring to the sudden scramble for colonial dominion that in
half a decade divided the greater part of the African continent among
the European powers.

Thus began the era of high imperialism which extended for a single
generation from the 1880's to the First World War. In this period, the
Europeans in one final spurt completed their domination over the rest
of the world—through direct colonial possession in the case of Africa
and the Pacific, through indirect economic and diplomatic pressures in
Asia and the Near East. What is most surprising in retrospect is how
recently all this occurred, and how shortly thereafter followed the present-day movement for colonial liberation.

With Japan rapidly modernizing itself and India firmly in British
hands, the Ottoman Empire and China remained as the most enticing
objects for European exploitation. In both areas, the Great Powers had
wrested from weak, bewildered emperors economic concessions and ex-
traterritorial privileges that drastically curtailed the rulers' sovereignty.
But in words, at least, the two great Empires of the Near East and Far
East remained independent. In Africa, such diplomatic niceties were
superfluous. Here the Europeans divided vast stretches of territory among
themselves, either as colonies or as "protectorates" in which the local
ruler was left a shadow authority. Most of the continent went to Britain
and France: the British dominated the south and east, the French the
north and west, including nearly the whole Sahara desert. The Germans
and Italians, latecomers to the colonial game, picked up relatively un-
profitable lands, while the Belgians—favored by the astuteness of their
businessman king—acquired the enormous potential riches of the Congo.
This latter dominion was relinquished in 1960, leaving the two territories
that Portugal had taken over in an earlier age as the most durable of
European possessions on the African continent.

By 1902, when the white settlers of the Boer republics succumbed to
the overwhelming power of the British Empire, only four areas in all
Africa remained even technically independent: the Arab-speaking country of Morocco in the far northwest, which the French were already
coveting; the similarly Arab land of Egypt, which was "occupied" and
dominated by the British; the eastern mountain empire of Ethiopia, which
had repulsed the Italians in 1896; finally, the small west coast republic
of Liberia, whose independence was supervised by American rubber
interests.

So far as Europeans at home were concerned, three aspects of this new
wave of imperialist activity were of decisive importance for the future.
First, as Lenin, among others, was to emphasize, the colonies helped to
keep the fat on the European economy: they contributed heavily toward
a standard of living that Europe could not have achieved on its own.
Secondly, colonial rule was a standing reproach to the democratic pro-

fessions of the Europeans; however they might try, the colonial powers could not square the prevailing radical ideology with their domination over non-white peoples.

The issue was, of course, most acute for France and Britain, for these were the greatest colonial powers and the most democratic of the major nations of Europe. Both made brave efforts to find a scheme of reconciliation, and both failed. The British formula of a self-governing dominion worked in Canada and Australia, where whites soon outnumbered the aborigines. But when in 1910 it was applied to South Africa—in a generous gesture of reconciliation with the Boers—the results were far less satisfactory, although another generation had to pass before this was generally recognized. For in South Africa, as in the rest of the continent south of the Sahara, the blacks far outnumbered the whites, and there was no foreseeable possibility that further white settlement would ever substantially alter this situation. To the black masses, self-government for white settlers was no solution at all.

The French formula initially seemed more promising. For the French did not draw a color line and aimed at complete assimilation; they offered the chance to become equals, *as Frenchmen,* to the "elites" among the blacks south of the Sahara and among the Arab-speaking peoples to the north. These chosen individuals were to receive a full French education and to become French in speech and sentiment. In numerous cases, the technique worked admirably: many Africans did in fact find acceptance in French society and did come to behave like Frenchmen. But assimilation applied only to a select minority; here again, the black masses remained unaffected. After the Second World War, when the masses began to awaken, the assimilated elites had no alternative but to move with the new current and to proclaim themselves African rather than French in their allegiance.

Finally, the late nineteenth-century wave of high imperialism enormously encouraged sentiments of national and racial superiority already latent in the European populations. Ruling tens of millions of blacks was a heady business, and it naturally attracted the more adventurous and ruthless spirits. Cecil Rhodes—the founder of modern South Africa—offered a model for empire building, and Rudyard Kipling rationalized the process in popular verse. Here a note of irony or of national guilt sounded under the confident proclamations about taking up "the white man's burden": the British conscience was periodically troubled by the brutal treatment of the natives that imperial rule entailed. Other Europeans were less squeamish. From 1904 to 1908 the Germans waged a war of near-extermination in their colony of Southwest Africa. In the Congo, before its formal annexation to Belgium in 1908, King Leopold II's business colleagues literally worked hundreds of thousands of natives to death in the newly developed mines and plantations.

Such conduct blatantly contradicted the central democratic principle that "all men are created equal." But few democratic-minded Europeans at the turn of the century made the obvious comparisons; they followed a double standard: one kind of behavior for home, another for the colonies. This at least was true in Western Europe. In Central and Eastern Europe the new emphasis on racial superiority took a more virulent form. The three great Empires of the east shared only partially in the final wave of imperial expansion: Austria-Hungary acquired no colonies at all; Germany arrived in Africa too late; Russia confined its expansion to the vast stretches of Siberia, Central Asia, and the Caucasus, which were contiguous to the Russian landmass, and whose nomad or Moslem populations could hence be dominated directly from the center. In these three Empires there was no such sharp cleavage as in the West between democracy and colonial practice, between conduct at home and conduct abroad. The German and Russian ruling classes were not democratic in sentiment, and they were quite accustomed to ruthless behavior in ruling their own national minorities.

Thus a continental, home-grown imperialist ideology expressed itself in Pan-Slavism and, still more characteristically, in Pan-Germanism. The "pan" movements were true to current fashion in teaching the superiority of one's own linguistic group. But they went beyond this in calling for the union of vast masses of people. Uniting all the Slavs (under Russian leadership), or uniting all Germans wherever they might be, in Germany, in Austria, or in the numerous German-speaking clusters scattered through Eastern Europe, would shatter existing boundary lines; in the three Empires of the east, German and Slav lived inextricably entangled. To preach the superiority of either meant to demand the subjugation of the other. Pan-Slavism and Pan-Germanism were intolerant, explosive, destructive forces. The former eventually succumbed—like so much else in Russia—to the revolutions of 1917. But Pan-Germanism went on to inspire the youthful Adolf Hitler and to provide nazism with the rudiments of an ideology and with some of the most fanatical of its recruits.

Popular Militarism

To the middle-class mind, war and military service have traditionally been hateful. The military ethic is the very negation of the bourgeois virtues of rationality, toleration, and peace. Similarly, for socialists, war, fully as much as capitalism, was a curse to be wiped out forever. The ideologies of progress, then, were clearly antimilitary. Their triumph seemed to imply the destruction of militarism, as one more relic of a barbarous past.

Yet paradoxically, during the first decade and a half of the twentieth century and alongside the rising tide of pacifism, war and military service suddenly became popular. One of the first signs of the change came in Britain during the Boer War; Liberal speakers denouncing this imperialist conflict found themselves shouted down by angry crowds. A few years later, the naval-building race with Germany aroused similar popular enthusiasm; the British sporting instinct was stung by the threat of being overtaken by an upstart competitor, and German nationalists, spurred on by their emperor, responded with massive support of the navy's program for challenging the traditional mistress of the seas.

Of all the ramifying conflicts that contributed to the origins of the First World War, the Anglo-German naval race seems the one that might most easily have been avoided. On any rational grounds Germany did not need a big navy, for it was basically a land power, guarded by the finest army in the world. Nor did even the most sanguine of Germany's naval propagandists claim that its fleet could reach parity with Britain's in any reasonably near future. When Admiral Tirpitz launched Germany's new building program in 1897, his purpose was to create a fleet that would annoy the British and make them hesitate about going to war; in his own words, his navy would make war too great a "risk." Thus during the seventeen years preceding the outbreak of world conflict, the naval race embittered relations between Britain and Germany without fundamentally changing the balance of military power.

In Germany, the navy was a bourgeois affair. Far more than the army, which remained an aristocratic preserve, the German fleet drew its officers from the prosperous middle class. Hence it offered an ideal means for canalizing the new martial enthusiasm of the bourgeoisie. Elsewhere in Europe, middle-class nationalists began to rally to similar causes as the second decade of the century opened. In France, they supported the three-year army law of 1913—a desperate effort to keep up with Germany's growing population by adding another year to the term of military service. In Italy, they found an outlet for their enthusiasm in the successful campaign for the conquest of Tripoli in 1911.

Italy, more than any other country, dramatically suggests the new prestige of the martial life. And it also typifies the way in which early twentieth-century militarism was a movement of youth, closely linked with "irrationalist" innovations in literature and the fine arts. In Italy, as elsewhere, young people were bored. They knew too much of peace and nothing of war. They were tired of the policy of caution which their country had followed, except for a brief era of imperial adventure in the late 1880's and early 1890's. To be sure, that policy had preserved the weakest of the Great Powers from harm. But Italy's impatient youth had nothing but scorn for such prudent considerations. They were deaf to the counsels of the wise old statesman Giolitti; they listened rather to their poets: to the "futurist" Marinetti, and to Gabriele D'Annunzio, who was to lead the interventionist campaign of 1915. Their creed (the words are Marinetti's) was direct and simple: "We want to glorify war, the world's only hygiene—militarism, deed, destroyer of anarchisms, the beautiful ideas that are death-bringing, and the contempt of woman."

If the European Left was traditionally devoted to peace, it also had potentialities that paralleled the new cult of violence among the spokesmen of the Right. There was, for example, the Jacobin tradition—the memory of revolutionary France, a nation in arms against a host of invaders and ruthlessly resorting to terror at home to curb suspected traitors in its midst. This memory never failed to mobilize a substantial segment of the French radicals in support of military measures. It suggests why the old radical Clemenceau could eventually prove so tough a war leader.

Farther to the left, and also drawing on revolutionary memories, was the new movement known as *syndicalism*. Syndicalism, which was particularly strong in France and Italy, was an ideology of direct action. It preached the doctrine of the revolutionary general strike that would deliver the mines and factories of Europe into the workers' own hands. And in so doing it taught the working class to distrust its self-constituted spokesmen, the socialist parliamentarians and intellectuals. Indeed, in its tone and manner it expressed a deep-seated anti-intellectualism: it felt no need for a coherent philosophy of economics or politics. In this respect it broke far more sharply than had Marxism with the main tradition of European public life.

The great days of syndicalism came during the first decade of the twentieth century. Then French society in particular was shaken by a series of tumultuous strikes that took on an almost revolutionary character. After 1910, the movement—which had always been characterized by an anarchical lack of central direction—began to break up. Workers grew discouraged, as it became apparent that all the syndicalist agitation had accomplished nothing.

During the war and in the postwar years, the former syndicalists went in two contrasting directions. One group joined Benito Mussolini and his fascist emulators—thus swelling the forces of irrationalism and direct action inspired by the advocates of imperial glory and popular militarism. The other element went to the newly founded Communist parties.

Only after the Bolshevik Revolution of 1917 did communism become an organized reality in European politics. Yet on the eve of the war the makings of future Communist parties already existed in European socialism. For more than a decade before 1914, Lenin and his intellectual associates had constituted an outspoken left minority within the Second International. Lenin, like the syndicalists, believed in ruthlessness and the revolutionary recourse to violence. Like them, he was disgusted with the parliamentary caution of the dominant figures within European socialism. But he expressed these views with an intellectual coherence and penetration that left the syndicalists far behind. Where they had failed, Lenin was to succeed.

VI

THE ORIGINS OF THE
WORLD CONFLICT

The First World War was produced by the confluence of two explosive pressures: the aspirations of the national minorities in Central and Eastern Europe and the dynamic of the rival alliance systems among the Great Powers. Either one of these had in itself an enormous war potential; together they brought about a steady drift toward armed hostilities that in retrospect seems irresistible.

The Nationalities Problem

The question of national minorities was almost exclusively a Central and Eastern European concern. In the west, most boundaries were of long standing and followed recognized lines of national allegiance. Indeed, in the whole western half of the Continent there were only three areas where serious inequities seemed to exist. Between France and Germany lay the provinces of Alsace and northern Lorraine—the former speaking a Germanic dialect, the latter nearly exclusively French in speech. These had been wrested from France after the War of 1870 and had remained French in sentiment. Also under German rule were the Danes of northern Schleswig—a minority that caused little trouble, since Denmark itself was too weak and too pacific to make difficulties about them. Finally there were the "unredeemed" areas inhabited by Italians—the mountains of the south Tyrol and the Adriatic seaport of Trieste, both of which were growing increasingly restive under Austrian rule.

Obviously, Austria-Hungary had the most serious minority problems, and the Dual Monarchy was often referred to less as a nation than as a mere conglomeration of nationalities. In Germany, the overwhelming majority of the inhabitants spoke German and felt themselves to be Germans (its Polish population constituted the outstanding exception). Even in the Russian Empire, the Great Russian nationality formed the central core of the state and easily dominated the others. For Russia, the chief problem lay in the western borderlands, where the Finns, the small Baltic peoples, and, most important, the Poles, all had standing complaints of one sort or another against rule from St. Petersburg.

In the partitions that destroyed the independence of Poland in the late eighteenth century, Russia received the largest share. The rest had gone to Prussia and Austria. Hence from the very start, the Polish problem had involved all three eastern powers. All three had an interest in the maintenance of the *status quo*, while Austria followed a calculated policy of giving its own Poles the position of a favored minority within the state.

Austrian policy dealt otherwise with two other branches of European

Slavdom. The Czechs and the South Slavs looked to Russia for deliverance, and they had it in their power to rend the whole Austrian state
asunder. The Czechs of Bohemia and Moravia had long ago lost their
separate national existence: like the Poles, they lived on hopes and historical memories. The South Slavs, though culturally less advanced than
the Czechs, were closer to independence. Part in and part out of the
Austro-Hungarian Empire, they were in a position that naturally aroused
maximum awareness of every national injustice.

In 1903 the Serbian monarchy had reverted to the ambitious and Rus-
sian-oriented Karageorgevich dynasty. An aggressive anti-Austrian policy
was the result. The Serbian leaders longed to have their country assume for the South Slavs the role that nineteenth-century Prussia had
played for the Germans and Piedmont for the Italians—the core around
which unity would be achieved. To fellow Serbs just across the border,
and to the Croats and Slovenes farther west, Serbia promised the liberation of all the South Slavs within the confines of the Austro-Hungarian
Empire. This pledge had taken on greater urgency since 1908 when—to
the intense indignation of the Serbs—Austria annexed the South Slav
provinces of Bosnia and Herzegovina, which had been technically still
under Turkish suzerainty.

The Bosnian crisis of 1908 was one of the periodic international crises
which in the years after the turn of the century brought the powers closer
and closer to war and which were usually Balkan in origin. The great
exceptions, of course, were the two crises over Morocco in 1905 and
1911, which eventually resulted in French acquisition of that promising
domain. The year following the French triumph, however, international
attention returned to the Balkans, and it remained riveted on Balkan
problems until the outbreak of the World War itself.

In 1912 and 1913, the small nations of this area went to war, first to
deprive Turkey of nearly all its remaining European territory and subsequently to quarrel over the spoils. The Turks had been the oppressors
of the Balkan peoples for more than five hundred years; the Balkan drive
for national liberation, which began in the early nineteenth century, was
completed in the First Balkan War of 1912–1913. But independence
settled nothing. No Balkan nation was satisfied with its boundaries of
1913. Each had fellow nationals living within its neighbors' borders.
Bulgaria had been humiliated in the Second Balkan War (June–July
1913), when the others had banded together against her. Greece coveted
long stretches of Bulgaria's and Turkey's Aegean seacoast. Rumania
sought the liberation of Transylvania from Hungarian rule. And Serbia
—the most ambitious of the lot—stood in a particularly difficult position,
with a Bulgarian minority inside its borders while it looked north and
west in an attitude of unreserved hostility toward the Austro-Hungarian
oppressors of its "blood brothers." It was obvious to any astute observer
of the Balkan scene that the settlement of 1913 was no more than an
uneasy truce.

Although the Concert of Europe had all but disappeared, the system of European alliances worked reasonably smoothly in the period from 1870 to 1890. Britain continued in its traditional detachment; the French nursed their grievance over the loss of Alsace-Lorraine; and Austria-Hungary and Italy moved into a defensive alliance with Germany. The new German Empire held the center of the stage. Its chancellor, Prince Bismarck, kept insisting that Germany was now a satisfied power. By reassuring Russia and isolating France, he held apart the only two powers that could possibly threaten the *status quo* in Central Europe.

With Bismarck's dismissal by the young Emperor William II in 1890, international relations moved into a graver phase. Within four years, Russia and France had signed a military agreement. By 1900, the German alliance with Italy had virtually become a dead letter. The British, alarmed by their isolation among the Great Powers that the Boer War had revealed, reached a "cordial understanding" with France in 1904. In 1907, the new alliance system was completed when Britain and Russia achieved a similar settlement of past differences.

In theory, then, the Powers stood three against three: a Triple Alliance —Germany, Austria-Hungary, and Italy—faced a looser Triple Entente—Britain, France, and Russia. In reality, the situation was rather less neat. Germany and Austria could no longer count on Italy. Within the rival coalition, only France and Russia were bound by a true alliance. Moreover, during the period 1890–1907, the balance had turned heavily against Germany. Although the Germans were probably the strongest single nation in the world—as their war record was to prove—they felt "encircled" by the united hostility of the second, third, and fourth European powers.

In 1914, the merits of this contention were far from obvious. Each nation was absorbed in its own internal difficulties. For the second decade of the century had brought a break in economic prosperity and in the prevailing mood of optimism. Everywhere, the political militants were on the move. In Germany, the Reichstag elections of 1912 had made the Social Democrats the strongest party in the state. In Britain, the attempt of the Liberal government to grant home rule to Ireland had occasioned a mutiny among the army officers and a stalemate in civil-military relations. In Italy, the Socialists had taken a sharp turn to the left and in June, 1914, engaged in a week of local rioting. France alone remained calm. Indeed, with radical influence weakened, with the passage of the three-year service law, and the election of the nationalist Raymond Poincaré as president, France seemed stronger, more confident, and more united than it had been at any time since the defeat of 1870.

The Outbreak of the War

The assassination at Sarajevo on June 28 rudely shook the statesmen of Europe out of domestic absorptions. In view of the tense relations between Serbia and Austria-Hungary in 1914, no one in Europe should have been surprised that the fuse which set off the great explosion was lighted here. Far from being—as journalists phrased it—an "obscure corner" of Europe, the capital of Bosnia was as likely a place as any for the great war to begin. The heir to the Austro-Hungarian throne, the Archduke Francis Ferdinand, might have known that he took his life in his hands when he ventured to pay a state visit there. No act was better calculated to stir Serbian resentment, and it was natural that the assassin should be a young Bosnian heated to fever by Serbian propaganda.

From this point on, individual national responsibilities for the great conflict unrolled with an iron logic. Serbia had only an indirect complicity in the assassination. Although its prime minister knew in a general way what was afoot, the slayers of the archduke were in no sense the agents of the Serbian government that the Austrians claimed. Moreover, when the Austrians followed up the assassination with a severe ultimatum, the Serbs agreed to nearly all their terms. They drew the line only at the unprecedented demand that Austro-Hungarian officials participate, *within Serbian territory,* in the investigation of the crime. It was the Austrians, rather, who bore the prime responsibility for the ensuing conflict in that they purposely made their requirements unacceptable in order to settle once for all—by war if necessary—with their upstart neighbors to the south. Next to them came the Germans, who in effect gave the Austrians a "blank check" by promising unlimited support to the nation which they correctly regarded as their only reliable ally, and by pressing it to act quickly against Serbia so as to split apart the Triple Entente.

The original Austro-German policy was predicated on the assumption that the war could be "localized." What made it a Europe-wide conflict was the Russian decision to support the Serbs. This brought the whole alliance system into play; for if Russia went to the aid of Serbia against Austria-Hungary, she also had to be prepared to face the German Empire. Still worse, the Russian military machine was slow and cumbersome, and if the country was to mobilize at all, technical considerations obliged it to do so fully and against *both* its potential enemies. Thus when the Russians were ostensibly doing nothing more than offering to protect their Serbian "brothers" against Austria-Hungary, it looked in Berlin as though they were also threatening Germany itself. In the frenzied weeks between the assassination and the outbreak of the conflict, it was the Russians who began the process of "escalation" by mobilizing prematurely; but it was the Germans who bore the responsibility for precipitating matters by declaring war on both France and the tsarist Empire.

In this succession of events, French responsibility was minimal. It has been argued that the French did not act with sufficient energy to restrain their Russian allies. But in reality they were kept in the dark about what the Russians were doing; the latter deceived them about the extent of the mobilization until it was a *fait accompli*. The French government accepted the fact of war with resolution and confidence; but it did nothing to bring it about. Indeed it took up arms not so much in fidelity to its Russian ally as in defense of a European equilibrium which appeared threatened by German hegemony.

Even the British did not wholly escape responsibility, for they kept the Germans guessing up to the very last as to whether they would intervene —thus encouraging the war party within the Reich—and they justified their final decision not on its true ground (their secret military commitments to France) but on the ground of the German invasion of Belgium, which made a better impression on the British public.

Thus the melancholy sequence unfolded: Austria-Hungary threatened Serbia, Russia supported Serbia, Germany supported Austria, France supported Russia, Britain supported France. Italy alone remained aloof. On August 4, 1914, the armies started to move. The First World War had begun.

Readings

For a general interpretation of the changed position of Europe in the twentieth century, see Hajo Holborn, *The Political Collapse of Europe* (1950). A more pessimistic view, drawing on a rich array of cultural examples and reflecting the author's Spanish origin, is Luis Diez del Corral, *The Rape of Europe* (1959). The best general interpretive history of the last decade of the nineteenth century is to be found in Carlton J. H. Hayes, *A Generation of Materialism, 1871–1900* (1941).

For the struggle of ideologies in the late nineteenth century, see John Bowle, *Politics and Opinion in the Nineteenth Century* (1954). A more specific and detailed account of international socialism is contained in G. D. H. Cole, *The Second International, 1889–1914*, 2 vols. (1956). For the origins and perversions of nationalism, see Boyd C. Shafer, *Nationalism: Myth and Reality* (1955), and Hannah Arendt, *The Origins of Totalitarianism* (1951).

The best general account of the diplomacy of the half-century preceding the outbreak of the First World War can be found in A. J. P. Taylor, *The Struggle for Mastery in Europe: 1848–1918* (1954). Sidney B. Fay, *The Origins of the World War*, 2 vols. (1928–1930), Bernadotte E. Schmitt, *The Coming of the War 1914*, 2 vols. (1930), and Luigi Albertini, *The Origins of the War of 1914*, 3 vols. (1952–1957), are the standard treatments of the crisis leading to the war itself. The first tends to favor the Germans; the second, the French; the third, by a leading Italian liberal publicist, is the most detached from partisan polemics. *Germany's Aims in the First World War* (1967), by Fritz Fischer, presents new evidence on the German effort to cut a larger figure on the world scene.

The First World War

Chapter Two

I

THE CHARACTER OF THE CONFLICT

To the generation of the 1920's and 1930's, the First World War was the overwhelming catastrophe that dominated their epoch. A generation later, after the Second World War had been fought, the earlier conflict seemed dwarfed by its vaster successor. It receded into the background, apparently less important and less interesting than the war that followed twenty years later. With the further passage of time, however, the perspective has altered. The First World War now appears fully as important as the Second—indeed, in certain respects, still more decisive in its effects.

It was the first of the world conflicts rather than its successor that fundamentally altered the character of European society. It was the first war that made it impossible to reconstruct the European community on the old basis. This war "stacked the cards for the future"; it created a situation in which men could not maintain domestic and international stability, a situation where a further war eventually became unavoidable.

The Early Illusions:
the Strength of the Powers

When the war started in August, 1914, nearly all Europeans were convinced that it would be brief. The general staffs had made their plans on that basis, and civilians had agreed that the delicate economic ar-

Equipment of allied
soldiers bogged down
in mud in France.
COURTESY BROWN BROTHERS.

rangements of an advanced industrial society could not stand the wear and tear of a protracted conflict. Among other things, the nations would run out of cash—and almost no one foresaw that a bankrupt power could go on fighting merely by printing more and more paper money. Similarly in respect to human resources, even the wildest imaginings of contemporaries did not grasp the millions of casualties that the reality of war was to produce. Again, it seemed unthinkable that the privileged sons of an advanced society should be called on to suffer far more and far longer than their ancestors of ruder ages. As one German officer put it: "No one would have dared at the beginning of the war to expect from the soldier what he afterward had to endure for years as a constant necessity." *

The illusion of a brief war was, of course, matched by the corresponding illusion of a quick victory. Each side believed it had the secret of sure success; neither realized how evenly the two coalitions were matched. Since the strength of the powers varied from department to department within the military establishment, it was impossible to compute what each factor would weigh in the final reckoning. How did one balance Russian manpower against German technical excellence? Or British dominance of the seas against the continental communications system of the Central Powers?

To a superficial observer, the Entente powers—Britain, France, and Russia—might appear the stronger. Russia was by far the most populous of the powers. Britain was mistress of the seas, with all the resources of the Empire to draw on, the arbiter of world trade, outclassed only by the United States and Germany in industrial equipment. France, with the second-best army in the world, enjoyed a happy balance between industry and agriculture that gave it a unique position of self-sufficiency among the European powers. But the advantages of the Entente were more apparent than real; they were potential rather than fully mobilizable at the outbreak of hostilities. The strength of the Entente was scattered through the extremities of Europe and into all the corners of the globe and its fighting effort rested on far-stretched and perilous lines of communication. Everything depended on whether Britain could continue to supply itself with food and raw materials from abroad, on whether a steady flow of equipment from the west would prove adequate to maintain the primitive economy of the Russian Empire.

At the start, then, the fate of the Entente powers rested primarily with France. Distance and bureaucratic inefficiency made the Russian army the slowest to mobilize of all the major land forces—hence the Russian decision to act even before war became inevitable. Russia's army, like the country, was vast, but it was poorly led, ill-equipped, and only feebly supported by the home government; its peasant soldiers could scarcely

* Quoted in Alfred Vagts, A History of Militarism: Civilian and Military, rev. ed. (New York: Meridian Books, 1959), p. 283.

comprehend the technical job of the modern soldier nor did they know
why they were ordered to fight. Britain had a well-trained professional
army, but it was only a small elite force; nearly two years were needed
to bring the country's manpower to bear on the decisive battlefields.
Thus France was left to face the German onslaught virtually alone. To
the French themselves, however, this prospect was not as depressing as
it appears in retrospect. Although they knew that the Germans would
eventually outnumber them, they were convinced that they were their
enemies' equals in military technique and superiors in offensive "doctrine." Moreover, they were justly proud of their new 75-millimeter gun,
which was, in fact, the best field piece in existence. The French did not
appreciate their inferiority to the Germans in machine guns and heavy
artillery: weapons that were to prove decisive in the first weeks of the
conflict.

On the side of the Central Powers, Germany and Austria-Hungary,
the strength was almost entirely Germany, the source of weakness, almost always Austria. In this respect, the Dual Monarchy resembled
Russia; it looked stronger than it was. In technical efficiency, it lay somewhere between backward Russia and the three heavily industrialized
powers, Germany, Britain, and France. Indeed, at some points in the
war on the Eastern Front, the military decision seemed to depend largely
on which was more inefficient and demoralized, Austria or Russia. But
in addition, the Austro-Hungarian empire suffered from a special weakness—perhaps half its army, drawn from the discontented nationalities,
could not be fully relied on: Slavic units seemed so likely to desert to
their Russian "brothers," that the Austrian command hesitated to send
them to the Eastern Front.

As the war went on, Austria-Hungary became more and more the
junior partner, fully subjected to German over-all direction. By the
middle of the war, the Central Powers had achieved a unity of command
that the Entente was to attain only in 1918. The Central Powers had a
second military advantage. They constituted a compact land mass: they
enjoyed excellent "internal" lines of communication and hence could
readily shift troops from one front to another. But to speak of this solid
continental situation is also to suggest a position of peril. Although Austria was self-sufficient in food, Germany was almost as dependent as
Britain on imports from overseas. And at the start of the war—that is,
until the submarines really began to take a toll—Britain was in a better
position than Germany to starve out its enemy. Furthermore, the Central Powers' "internal" situation meant a two-front war—a war in which
Germany must bear the burden on both fronts. On both of these—even,
at first, in France—the Germans would be outnumbered; hence the essence of German strategy was to knock out the enemy to the west before
the enemy to the east could fully mobilize.

Moreover, although Germany had gone further than any other power
in the technical perfecting of its armed forces, it still did not use its

potential resources to the full. The aristocratic survivals in German society were a heavy drag on its efficiency as an industrial state. Thus field commands were often given to crown princes or important noblemen whose qualifications for such posts were only mediocre, and the total number of officers was limited by undefined but well-recognized criteria for promotion. Both Germany and France—in contrast to Britain's tradition of a small professional army—in theory demanded military service of every able-bodied male citizen. But in practice France called up a larger proportion of those eligible to serve—thereby partially balancing the disparity in population between the two countries, which was about three to two in Germany's favor. The French were able to do this because of their lack of prejudice in the appointment of reserve officers to command their fighting masses in wartime. In France, almost any man with a higher education could become a reserve officer, and promotion from the ranks was not impossible. In Germany, Jews and men of humble origin or advanced political opinions were systematically excluded from the corps of reserve officers, and the promotion of an enlisted man was nearly unknown. Aristocratic prejudice thus erected an intangible but very real barrier to the indefinite expansion of Germany's armed forces, and helps explain why, in the opening weeks of the war, France was able to field two more fighting divisions than the invading enemy.

Beyond merely technical considerations, French democracy was an asset that became increasingly apparent as the war dragged on. Not only in a military sense, but also in the wider context of national morale, the anachronisms and inequities within German society exerted a profoundly depressing effect. Once Russia had left the war—and President Wilson had redefined the conflict as a war for democracy—it became clear that nearly all the psychological advantage lay on the side of the Entente.

The Failure of Strategy and of Military Technique

The wars of Napoleon, Bismarck's "lightning" wars from 1864 to 1870 —even the Second World War—showed generals in control of the weapons at their disposal and competent to carry out the operations they had planned. The First World War was quite different. It demonstrated a failure of strategy and of military technique on a gigantic and unprecedented scale. In its bungling, infinitely wasteful character, it was more like the American Civil War than like its predecessors or successor among European conflicts. And, like the Civil War, it soon became a war of attrition which, after four long years of slaughter and discouragement, finally came to an end only because one side gave out of men and materiel, overwhelmed by the numerical and industrial superiority of its adversary.

Here is Winston Churchill's retrospective verdict: "Events passed very largely outside the scope of conscious choice. Governments and individ-

uals conformed to the rhythm of the tragedy, and swayed and staggered
forward in helpless violence, slaughtering and squandering on ever-increasing scales." By the end of 1914 the campaign in the west had become a war of position—a hopeless deadlock in which, despite the loss of hundreds of thousands of lives, the front did not shift in either direction by more than ten miles in three years. The failure of the military mind was patent. Although official propaganda made frenzied efforts to conceal it, by 1917, this failure had become clear to nearly everybody. Only in 1918, when the end was already in sight, did the generals begin to show that they were learning the new realities of their profession.

The great surprise, of course, was trench warfare. The defense had proved so much stronger than the attack that the war had turned into a colossal siege. But this new turn in strategy should not have been totally unexpected: it had been predicted as early as 1902, in an article published in a Swiss military journal. In the Russo-Japanese war, the campaign in Manchuria had bogged down in just this fashion. But the European military refused to heed these portents of the future. They dismissed the conflict of 1904 as a squalid Asiatic struggle and clung to their illusions about a war of movement.

The French rather than the Germans were the more deceived. During the early years of the century, their staff training fell into the hands of a group of "young Turks" who put their faith in an offensive of unbridled fury. The most important of the group was Colonel Ferdinand Foch—later to redeem his reputation as supreme Allied commander at the end of the war. Foch and his colleagues taught what was less a military than a mystical doctrine. It could be summed up in one word—"attack"—always and everywhere. As one of these enthusiasts declared, "The victorious army will be the one which, scornful of reserves and fortresses, will first jump at the throat of the enemy and will at once obtain the moral superiority that forces . . . events. . . . It is necessary that the concept of the offensive penetrate the soul of our nation."

This was the doctrine behind the French war plan for a rapid advance through Lorraine into central Germany. The plan failed utterly. Not until—as Foch put it—the French military leaders had forgotten what they had taught and learned before 1914 did they reach a true understanding of what they were about. The German war plan was less feckless. Indeed, it almost succeeded. But once it too had failed, the German generals, like the French, had to buckle down to the painful business of relearning their profession from scratch.

Psychological Shocks and the Attrition of Morale

The illusion of a short war vanished, and with that went the thoughtless enthusiasm with which so many of the combatants on both sides first went into battle. The reality was infinitely more grim and less glamorous than anyone had imagined. A vast disillusionment ensued—a psychological revulsion that gripped millions of men in uniform.

This was particularly true in France, which had the misfortune of being the main theater of combat. France, moreover—along with little Serbia—suffered the highest rate of casualties in proportion to the nation's total available manpower. True to their doctrine of the "furious" offensive that would sweep all before it, the French generals squandered lives on a reckless scale. The desperate position of an army fighting deep within its own frontiers seemed to justify such waste and in the first sixteen months of combat, France suffered roughly half of all its war casualties. Two-thirds of a million men were killed—a total without precedent in history. The next three years were less bloody, but by this time an attitude of infinite grief and hopelessness had settled on men's minds.

During the first year of the war, nearly half the families of France received one of the dreadful telegrams which in clipped, patriotic prose announced the death of a husband or son. The conflict had run only a quarter of its course, and already the whole nation seemed in mourning. The French themselves, of course, had no idea how long the war would go on. In their matter-of-fact, logical fashion they made their computations: reckoning from what they knew of the toll of lives, they concluded that eventually *every* husband or son in the trenches would be either killed or mutilated.

The case of France is the clearest and most dramatic, but nearly as great a tragedy occurred in Germany, where the end rather than the start of the war brought casualty lists which the nation could no longer endure. Even Britain, after its new army went into battle in 1916, suffered only slightly less than the major adversaries on the continent. Everywhere, the loss of human life on an unimagined scale inflicted a psychological shock that was also without precedent. It produced a vast crisis of confidence, shaking men's minds to their depths and calling into question all the optimistic assumptions with which the century had opened. It spared nothing—leaders, governments, society itself. To quote Churchill once more: "Injuries were wrought to the structure of human society which a century will not efface." *

In the end, Britain and France held firm; their institutions and way of life stood the test. But they were victors, and victory helped to ease the strain. Vanquished Germany, on the other hand, plunged into years of social and political turmoil; it never returned to "normal." Austria-Hungary disintegrated. And Russia turned to communism. Nor is it without significance that Russia had squandered lives most recklessly of all. With infinite cynicism, the Russian generals calculated that their endless supply of men would compensate for a disgraceful shortage of arms and materiel. In certain battles on the Eastern Front, it was literally true that as one Russian soldier fell, an unarmed comrade picked up his rifle

* Winston S. Churchill, *The World Crisis, 1911–1918*, I (New York: Charles Scribner's Sons, 1923), 1–2.

and stumbled on. These stolid peasant soldiers, their officers thought,
would endure anything. They did not envision a day when the long-suffering peasants would simply drop their rifles and start walking home, to claim as their own the factories and farms of Russia.

II

THE WESTERN FRONT
FROM THE MARNE TO VERDUN

The Schlieffen Plan and Its Modifications

The basic German plan of attack had been devised in 1905 by the military chief of staff, Count Schlieffen. It called for a vast wheeling movement through Belgium that would roll up the French army to the east of Paris and end the war in the west at one stroke. To be sure, this plan violated the neutrality of Belgium, which had been guaranteed by the Great Powers shortly after that country had won its independence in 1830, and thus entailed the danger (which in fact occurred) of bringing Britain into the war on the side of Germany's enemies. But in the German military mind this risk was more than balanced by the advantages of surprise and concentration of forces that the Schlieffen plan possessed. Germany's only hope, the generals calculated, lay in knocking France out before the Russian mass began to move. Only thus could the nightmare of a war on two fronts be avoided. And in order to destroy the French armies quickly it was essential to bypass the strong forts on the northeastern frontier and to advance through the more lightly defended northwest.

Schlieffen's bold concept, then, was to strip down to skeleton forces not only the troops defending Germany against Russia but also the left wing of his attack against France. In both cases he ran a risk: he exposed East Prussia to Russian invasion and the area from Alsace to Frankfurt to invasion by the French. And although these risks bothered him, he failed to give the emperor and chancellor adequate warning of them. Everything depended, he thought, on maintaining overwhelming pressure on the right wing of his main attack. His dying warning was supposed to have been, "Make the right wing strong."

Schlieffen's successor, Helmuth von Moltke the younger, quite correctly convinced that he could not stake his nation's future on a single desperate gamble, modified the original plan in two crucial respects. Because he feared the impact on morale of an invasion (or invasions) of Germany, he weakened the right wing by providing for a secondary offensive to the left, in Lorraine. Subsequently—when the campaign was already in progress—he sent off two army corps to strengthen the defenders of East Prussia.

Initially, however, all seemed to proceed according to plan. While the French attack was stopped dead and then thrown back in Lorraine, the German advance through Belgium went off on schedule. A million and a half men organized in seven armies advanced on the Belgian fortresses. The greatest of these—Liége—fell in eleven days, overwhelmed by the unexpected power of the German heavy artillery. With this major obstacle out of the way, the attack continued steadily through Belgium. On August 20, the German First Army entered Brussels in triumph. The battle for France was about to begin.

In the meantime, the British Expeditionary Force under the command of Sir John French had landed at Le Havre and begun to take up positions on the left wing of the defending armies. Compared to the German or French forces, the British contribution was small—five divisions totaling less than 100,000 men—but it was a professional army, undiluted by masses of hastily summoned reservists. Simultaneously, the French had suffered the most stunning reverses. By the end of August, the "Battle of the Frontiers" had turned into a near rout. France paid a bitter price for its blind doctrine of the offensive. The French troops had advanced with reckless courage right out in the open, almost as on parade, and the German machine guns had mowed them down. On the frontiers, the French lost nearly one-quarter of their soldiers engaged—300,000 men. And then the great retreat began. In the twelve days following the Battle of Charleroi (August 21–24), the whole front to the west of Verdun gave way. The road to Paris lay open.

Then occurred the most surprising reversal of fortunes. The Germans began to make mistakes, and the French began to recoup their earlier errors. Moltke kept his headquarters too far back: he lost touch with the reality of events on the fighting line and permitted Kluck, commander of the First Army, to move ahead too rapidly, thereby breaking off contact with the Second Army on his left. A dangerous gap opened between the two. This sudden stroke of luck was not lost on the French commander-in-chief, Joseph Jacques Joffre, who began to revise his plans accordingly.

The First Battle of the Marne

Portly and imperturbable, Joffre now rose to a quiet greatness. Undaunted by the total collapse of his plans, undismayed by the fashion in which the facts of war had shattered the French offensive doctrine, he gathered together the remnants of his armies and improvised a new strategy. Nothing disturbed Joffre's calm: legend has it that he never lost a night's sleep even during the most desperate hours of the great retreat.

Thus he allowed the retreat to go on, waiting for the proper moment to strike back, refusing to commit his reserves prematurely. He was quietly gathering a reserve army to the east of Paris and he turned a deaf ear to his subordinates' anguished pleas for reinforcements. On September 6 came the moment for which he had been waiting. The Ger-

man right wing, which had wheeled east before Paris, was stretched
dangerously thin. At the decisive point Joffre had his adversaries outnumbered four to three.

The success of the French counterattack along the line of the Marne
wavered in the balance for two days. At some points the situation looked
desperate, but French morale was high—the soldiers knew that their
country's fate depended on them—and many German units were worn
out by their long advance. Around the Battle of the Marne a host of
legends have gathered. Along with the defense of Verdun, it is the proudest memory in the French annals of the war. Typical is the telegram that
the dashing Foch, by then an army commander, sent to his chief: "My
left is giving way, my right is falling back . . . I am ordering a general
offensive, a decisive attack by the center."

By September 9 the German First and Second Armies were in full
retreat. For four days they reeled back. Then on the 13th they called a
halt along the Aisne, the best defensive line in northern France. Joffre
had won a great victory. But just as the Germans had failed to destroy
him, so had he failed to throw the invaders out of his country. It was
now clear that the war would continue at least into the following year.

"The Race for the Sea"
and the Stabilization of the Front

October and early November were occupied by the series of battles mis-
leadingly referred to as "the race for the sea." It was rather a series of
local engagements, following the German stand on the Aisne, in which
each army in turn tried to outflank the other. The result was a steady
extension of the line toward the west. Finally the armies reached the
sea—the English Channel—which brought all flanking operations to
an end.

At all costs, the British and French wanted to hold the Channel ports,
for these alone could assure direct communications between the two
allies, particularly after the great Belgian seaport of Antwerp fell to the
Germans on October 9. Following the fall of Antwerp, almost all Belgium
was in German hands, subject for the entire war to the rigors of a strict
occupation. Only a tiny corner by the sea, saved by the opening of the
dikes, remained under the control of the Belgian government, which had
taken up quarters in exile at Le Havre.

This little piece of free Belgium represented the northernmost ex-
tremity of the fighting front. The British resolve to hold on to the whole
French seacoast stretched the line in a northerly arc through Flanders
—the most depressing terrain of all those over which the armies were to
fight for the next four years. A densely populated, highly industrialized
plain, it was dotted with mines and slag heaps, low-lying and subject to

GREAT
BRITAIN

North Sea

NETHERLANDS

RUHR

London

Ostend

Bruges

Antwerp

Düsseldorf

Ghent

Cologne

Lys

Schelde

Meuse

Calais
Passchendaele

Brussels

BELGIUM

GERMANY

English Channel

Lille

Mons

Liége

Namur

RHINELAND

Coblenz

Charleroi

Arras

Frankfurt

Maubeuge

Somme

Cambrai

Moselle

Amiens

St. Quentin

ARDENNES

LUX.

Rhine

Le Havre

Rouen

Noyon

CHEMIN DES DAMES

Sedan

SAAR

Laon

Luxemburg

Saar

Compiègne

Oise

Aisne

ARGONNE

Soissons

VIMY RIDGE

Reims

Verdun

LORRAINE

Marne

Chateau Thierry

Versailles

CHAMPAGNE

Saint-Mihiel

Strasbourg

Paris

Toul

Nancy

Seine

FRANCE

VOSGES

ALSACE

Scale of Miles

Belfort

0   50   100

Basel

SWITZERLAND

FIRST WORLD WAR

Western Front

▲▲▲	Farthest German penetration
▬▬▬	Winter, 1914-1915
●─●─●	Hindenburg Line
▮▮▮	Summer, 1918
◀ ▰▰▰	Armistice Line
⫽⫽⫽	German occupation
▦▦▦	Allied occupation

floods, a vast quagmire in the rainy seasons. Its focal points were Lille
and Ypres, the former on the French side of the border and in German hands, the latter on the Belgian side and guarded by the British. Ypres —or "Wipers," as the soldiers called it—was to be the most bitterly contended city on the entire front. Although it jutted out as an almost untenable salient, the British would never give it up. Here the British Expeditionary Force fought its first major battle—and the last engagement of 1914. Through most of November the British held off a series of massed German assaults. In the defense of Ypres, the old professional army met its death. It lost 50,000 men—about half its effectives. In 1915, the British were to field a new citizen army, which was already drilling through the length and breadth of the home country.

At the end of November, the onset of winter brought active fighting to a close. From Switzerland to the Channel, the front had been stabilized along approximately the course it would follow for the next three years. South of Flanders it ran through the chalk uplands of Artois, then past Vimy Ridge, which the Germans held, to the city of Arras, which remained in French hands. From Arras to Noyon it continued almost due south across pleasant, open farm country. At Noyon it changed its course, now running west to east until it reached Verdun. Noyon, only 60 miles from Paris, was the closest point to the capital the Germans held. Each day on the front page of his own newspaper the old, indomitable Clemenceau—radically dissatisfied with the whole conduct of the war—ran the banner headline, "THE GERMANS ARE AT NOYON," never letting his fellow citizens forget for one moment the peril in which their nation stood.

From Noyon the line ran along the Aisne until it reached Reims and the chalk region of Champagne. Then came Verdun, the great fortress standing out as a bold French salient, and southeast of it a similar German salient at Saint-Mihiel. At Verdun began the quiet sectors of the line, which extended south and east to the Swiss frontier. Although this portion accounted for nearly half the whole front, it was only lightly held on both sides. The terrain was woody and rugged, and there seems to have been a tacit agreement that it was unsuitable for large-scale operations.

Even here, however, the opposing armies were installed in regular trenches. Ever since the Germans had dug in along the Aisne in mid-September, each attack or repulse had eventually been reduced to static trench warfare. The result was the colossal novelty of an almost unbroken line of improvised fortifications extending for more than 300 miles. Sometimes the two lines ran as much as five miles apart; sometimes they were so close that the opposing troops were within shouting distance of each other. Indeed at Christmas in this first winter of the war, a spontaneous, informal truce was declared in certain sectors, and the soldiers advanced without fear into no-man's-land to fraternize and

exchange gifts. The following year no such scenes occurred, for the
drabness and horror of life in the trenches had dulled men's souls—the
boredom broken only by the sudden danger of a sniper's bullet, the anxious waiting before an attack, the cold, the mud, wet and swollen feet,
and the dread moment of fear as the order came to go over the top.

The Germans at least had the illusion of victory as they stood deep
within the enemy's frontiers. But more and more, they were troubled
about the purpose of the war. The French did not need to ask themselves
such questions, for theirs was the simple imperative of holding fast and
of liberating the territory that the enemy had occupied. This amounted
to almost one-tenth of France, including a large part of its major industry, four-fifths of its coal, and nine-tenths of its iron resources. The year
1915 was dominated by the illusion that the moment of liberation was
at hand.

The Year 1915: the War of Attrition

The central reality of trench warfare was simple: the defense had nearly
all the advantages. Originally the trenches had been crude and make-
shift, but during the winter of 1914–15 they became increasingly complex, as barbed wire and communication trenches were added and
protected dugouts installed to the rear. Fieldworks such as these could
survive a terrible pounding from the artillery. Once the barrage lifted
and the attackers went over the top, the machine gunners could quickly
get back into position and mercilessly strafe the advancing columns.

These lessons sank into the German mind more quickly than into the
French and British. The Germans had a new chief of staff, the young
and attractive Erich von Falkenhayn, who had replaced the ailing
Moltke, completely shattered by his failure on the Marne. Falkenhayn
himself wanted to make a major effort in the west, and indeed in April
and May of the new year he launched a massive offensive against the
British bastion of Ypres, which barely failed of success. In this battle
—for the first time in the war—the Germans used poison gas; but they
used it in insufficient quantity and wasted its surprise effect.

After his failure before Ypres, Falkenhayn was obliged to yield to
the overwhelming pressure exerted by the German eastern command,
the redoubtable team of Hindenburg and Ludendorff. He had to give up
offensive plans against France for the rest of the year, and concentrate
on trying to knock out the Russians. Thus the military initiative in the
west passed to the French and British. The French, of course, were still
the dominant partners in the alliance. The British had ready the first
contingents of their new volunteer army, but the bulk of it would not
go into action until 1916. Until then, the French strategic view prevailed.

Joffre and his colleagues had still not cast off all their earlier illusions.

They still believed in massed frontal attack, to which they now added
the notion of an artillery preparation exceeding anything previously known in history. The French were justly proud of their artillery tradition, and in the long winter of waiting, their guns, like their men, had been dug in and all possible targets registered with deadly accuracy. Joffre at least no longer believed that one great attack would end the war. In its stead he planned a succession of partial attacks, which would gradually wear down the enemy. This the French called the "war of attrition."

In line with this altered strategy, Joffre devised a series of offensives which ran from May through the autumn. The first, in Artois, was an initial success. It achieved a breakthrough of three miles, and for a few hours victory seemed to be in sight. But then the Germans closed the gap, and when the fighting finally died down at the end of June, the French came to the sickening realization that they had lost 400,000 men, and gained nothing. The same thing happened in September, when the main blow fell to the east in Champagne. This time the French did not dare reveal their losses (which totaled around 145,000). And the year ended with the front almost unchanged.

Everywhere the story had been the same. The artillery preparation had been massive (in Artois the French calculated that eighteen shells would fall on every yard of the front line), but such long preparation had eliminated the possibility of tactical surprise and had given the Germans the chance to mass their reserves where they would be most useful. Usually there was a breakthrough at some point. But then the attackers found themselves advancing over unfamiliar terrain, where the defenders knew every available shelter or strong point. Eventually the Germans would seal off the hole in the line, and the French would continue to hammer away, unable to cut losses by admitting their failure. Finally, they would be left with no more than a tiny salient, which simply lengthened their own line and made it harder to defend.

The ghastly truth was gradually becoming clear to a few Frenchmen. One deputy brutally summed up the events of 1915: "The war of attrition is working against us."

The Preparations for 1916

Thus as the third campaigning season of the war opened, the Central Powers were apparently in a far better position than the Entente. They had won brilliant victories over the Russians. The extension of the conflict to new theaters had on balance proved to their advantage. The time had come for the Germans to turn west again and inflict a mortal wound on the French. And for the decisive blow Falkenhayn and his advisers—with an astute regard for French psychology—chose the great symbolic fortress of Verdun.

III

THE WIDENING OF THE CONFLICT

The Eastern Front: Tannenberg to Vilna

The war on the Eastern Front always differed from the war in the west. Although at times the forces engaged on each side were nearly as great in the east as in France, the fighting in Austria and Russia never reached the same level of intensity nor did it so fire the imagination of contemporaries. For one thing, it was more like an old-fashioned war. True, both sides regularly dug trenches, but these were neither continuous nor fully developed as on the Western Front. Similarly the general level of materiel and troop training—at least among the Austrians and Russians—was lower and the morale of the soldiers poorer. The armies in the east were subject to sudden and surprising waves of depression or confidence, and the front mirrored the mood of the soldiers. It ranged back and forth over hundreds of miles: in erratic succession, victory followed discouragement, and the decisive blow that was always expected never materialized.

The vast plains of Poland and Russia devoured men and dwarfed the efforts of the generals. As Napoleon had discovered in 1812 and Hitler was to learn in 1941, in these great fields and marshes and forests victory could never be complete. No matter how much Russia might be knocked about, the results could not decide the war as a whole. The real decision —as the Germans gradually learned to their sorrow—could come only in France, and there the front was apparently immovable. Once the Germans had failed on the Marne, then, they were left with no realistic prospect of defeating their enemies: they could only fight the war to a draw. In this sense, they had lost a four-year conflict in its first six weeks. Condemned to fight on two fronts, they could do nothing but pursue the will o' the wisp of victory through the endless stretches of Russia. After three years of fighting, Russia did indeed finally collapse. But by then it was too late: the number of Germany's enemies had become overwhelming and the nation's reserves of manpower were close to exhaustion.

The war in the east began, as expected, with a Russian invasion of Germany's most exposed territory, East Prussia. Something like panic followed, and desperate measures seemed called for. In this hour of peril, Germany found inspired leadership. Quietly and undramatically, in a north German railroad station, the ablest team of commanders that the war was to produce shook hands and began their celebrated collaboration—Field Marshal Paul von Hindenburg, already old, enormous in bulk, taciturn, and with an iron integrity that inspired confidence wherever he went; and his chief of staff, General Erich Ludendorff, sharp, hard-driving, an organizer of genius. When they first met, they

were both unknown to the public; a week later they won the victory that
made them figures of legend for the duration of the war.

The elements of the victory of Tannenberg had already been prepared when Hindenburg and Ludendorff arrived on the spot. The Russians had blundered, and the fashion in which this blunder came about explains a great deal of what was wrong with the whole Russian conduct of the war. Their commander, Samsonov, had led his army in reckless fashion too far into enemy country. Its supply train was improvised, its soldiers weary, unfed, and demoralized. By August 26, it was scattered over a 60-mile front in a dangerously exposed position. To make matters worse, the commander of the Russian relief army, Rennenkampf, tarried to the rear. He had hated Samsonov ever since the two had quarreled during the Russo-Japanese war, and he himself—as his name and origin suggested—was suspected of pro-German sympathies. Whatever the reason, he refused to move to Samsonov's aid.

As a result, Hindenburg and Ludendorff had three days of grace in which to concentrate their forces, and they did it with extraordinary skill. By the end of the month they had Samsonov in a trap. The exhausted Russians surrendered in droves—120,000 out of an army of 200,-000—while their commander stole away in the darkness and put a bullet through his head.

Coming, as it did, one week before the Battle of the Marne, Tannenberg gave the Germans a welcome consolation. As a purely *military* triumph, Hindenburg's victory was more complete than Joffre's, and it was followed by the liberation of East Prussia, as Rennenkampf's reserve army was pursued deep into Lithuania. But scarcely was this task accomplished than the German command had to turn elsewhere: the Austrian allies were in trouble. The Russians had driven them back into Austrian Poland—the great province known as Galicia—and it was up to the Germans to bail them out.

Such was to be the pattern of the war in the east: Austrian reverses, followed by a German-led counteroffensive. This first time the Austrians had taken only a month to get themselves into serious danger. Lemberg, the capital of Galicia and the fourth city of the Empire, had fallen to the Russians. And to the south—caught in a minor version of the two-front war—the Austrians had failed in the first of two attempts to knock out Serbia.

The Germans took two months to assemble their forces, but when help came, it was swift and decisive. Ludendorff planned to relieve pressure on the Austrians by advancing to the north against Warsaw. In mid-November the attack began to roll, and in two weeks the Russians had been driven back to the industrial center of Lodz. Here they turned and made a stand. The fighting was desperate: winter had set in, and the wounded froze to death by thousands. In early December, Lodz fell. But the German advance had been blunted. The fighting season ended with the Russians securely dug in 35 miles to the west of Warsaw.

Meantime in the south, the Austrians had supported the German invasion by gaining some minor victories in the passes of the Carpathian Mountains. Thus they forestalled the worst and saved the great grain-producing plain of Hungary from invasion. But against the Serbs they had failed once again. The "punitive" force sent in early December to chastise their troublesome neighbor fell into a disorderly rout. Serbia was safe for nine more months.

The year 1915 saw still greater victories of the Central Powers over the Russians. The field commander was August von Mackensen, a handsome, ruthless figure, who had the art of charming even the touchy Austrians. He soon became famous as master of the lightning attack that surprised and utterly destroyed the enemy. With a new army of eight divisions transferred from the Western Front, Mackensen was instructed to attack to the south of where the German blow had fallen the previous November. By relieving the pressure on the Carpathian passes, he hoped to penetrate and roll up the whole Russian line.

He succeeded brilliantly. On May 1, a perfect spring day, the artillery barrage opened with stunning effect, and the attack began. Two weeks later the Germans had advanced 95 miles. By June, the Russians were out of Galicia, and the Austrians had retaken Lemberg. Then the advance slowed and it was not until August 4 that Warsaw fell. But the Germans and Austrians continued to push on. The Russians were in appalling straits: morale was extremely bad, and the half-armed, under-fed, and ragged soldiers continued to surrender by the tens of thousands.

At this moment of crisis, the tsar himself assumed personal command. It was only a symbolic gesture—its military significance was nil—but it was one in the relentless series of errors that finally led to the fall of the Romanov dynasty. It was not this gesture that gave the Russians a respite, but the slowing down of the German armies as their communications lines became too far extended. Their last great victory was the capture of the Lithuanian city of Vilna in mid-September. By that time, the Russians had retreated so deeply into their own country that it was impossible to pursue them farther. The Central Powers had pushed back the whole front on an average of 200 miles. All Poland was in their hands —a possession nearly as perplexing and embarrassing as Belgium. Outnumbered by almost half a million, they had captured more than twice that number and inflicted an equal toll of additional casualties. Nowhere in the course of the war was the military record of either side to be more brilliant. The Germans had won great victories—but *victory* itself, complete and decisive, had eluded them.

The Entrance of Italy

Just after the great spring offensive of 1915 took off against the Russians, the unfortunate Austrians were forced to confront another enemy. On May 23, Italy declared war.

The Italians had originally decided to remain neutral. This seemed the most prudent course. Technically they were still in alliance with the

Central Powers. More realistic considerations, however, inclined them toward the Entente, for it was Austria that held the "unredeemed" lands for which Italian patriots longed.

The bulk of the Italian people—to the extent that they were politically conscious at all—undoubtedly favored a neutral course. Such was the view of the chief Catholic leaders, of the Socialists, and of the motley majority in the Chamber of Deputies that looked to Giolitti for guidance. But the master of Italian politics was temporarily out of power. The more conservative and nationalist Antonio Salandra was serving as prime minister; in charge of foreign affairs, was Sidney Sonnino, who was part English. These two responded wholeheartedly to the pressure for intervention on the side of the Entente—a pressure relentlessly exerted by the royal court, the nationalists, army and navy leaders, even a minority of democrats with emotional ties to England and France.

Giolitti believed that Austria would pay a good price to keep Italy neutral, and events confirmed his opinion. Grudgingly and only after persistent German prodding, the Austro-Hungarian government promised to turn over to Italy not *all* the Empire's territory inhabited by Italians but at least the largest area and the one about which Italians cared most—the Trentino; and it agreed to local autonomy for the seaport of Trieste. But the final Austrian offer arrived too late. Salandra and Sonnino had come to a far more favorable agreement with the British and French. The secret Treaty of London of April 26 promised Italy additional stretches of Austro-Hungarian territory—which had a large population of *non-Italians*—plus further acquisitions to be made at the expense of Turkey.

In return, the Treaty of London stipulated that Italy should declare war within a month. But how was this to be done? How was intervention to be managed when a majority of the deputies had expressed themselves against it? Salandra, the generals, and the king were relieved from their embarrassment by a series of street demonstrations that overawed the deputies. With the poet D'Annunzio leading the agitation, the frightened chamber was forced to vote for war.

Actually Italian intervention did not alter the course of the war very much. Although it forced the Austrians to divert a number of divisions from the Eastern Front, it did not seriously threaten the Austro-Hungarian state. In eleven successive battles on the mountainous Isonzo front, the Italians never succeeded in advancing more than 12 miles. Not until the autumn of 1917 did the Italian theater suddenly become of crucial importance.

Balkan Involvements:
Turkey, Bulgaria, Rumania, Greece

In November, 1914, Turkey declared war on the side of the Central Powers. This was only to be expected, in view of the predominant influence that Germany had exerted over Turkish economic and military

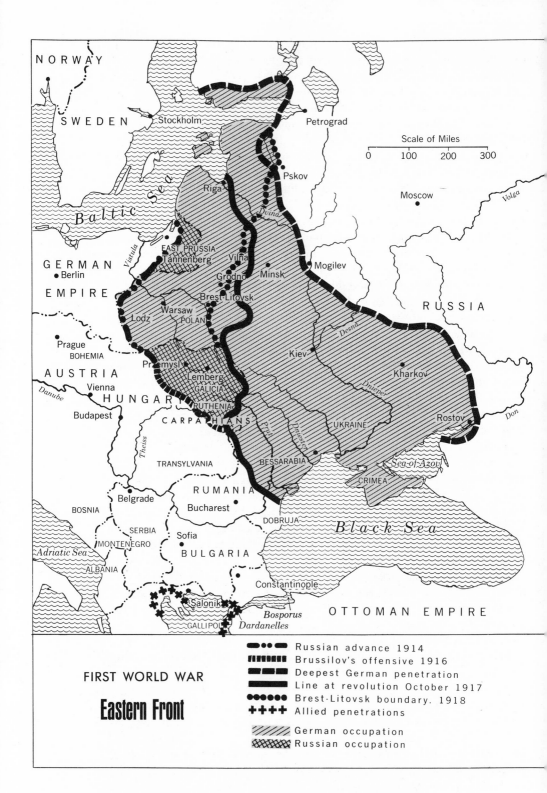

FIRST WORLD WAR

Eastern Front

Russian advance 1914
Brussilov's offensive 1916
Deepest German penetration
Line at revolution October 1917
Brest-Litovsk boundary. 1918
Allied penetrations
German occupation
Russian occupation

policy in the immediate prewar years. The involvement of the other
Balkan countries, however, was less certain. It came later in the war, and only as a result of the same sort of bargaining and realistic calculation that had gone on in the case of Italy.

In September, 1915, the Bulgarians signed a military alliance with Germany and Austria providing for extensive territorial gains at Serbia's expense. Here again the decision was logical in terms of Bulgaria's fierce antagonism toward Serbia and of Bulgaria's humiliation in the Second Balkan War. But still the Bulgarians wanted to wait until they were sure that the Serbians would be unable to retaliate. By the autumn of 1915, the Central Powers were at last ready for their knockout blow. Once again the Germans felt obliged to usurp strategic direction from their faltering Austrian allies. Mackensen—fresh from his victories over the Russians—directed the campaign, and carried out his assignment with his customary speed and thoroughness.

In early October, the armies of the three allied nations converged mercilessly on Serbia. The Serbians fought desperately, but they were overwhelmed by numbers. In six weeks, the campaign was over, and the terrible retreat over the mountains began. In mid-November came a heavy fall of snow, in which tens of thousands of soldiers and civilian refugees froze or died of typhus. Fewer than 100,000 of the Serbian army finally fought their way through to the Adriatic. Here they were rescued by the British and Italian navies and transported to safety on the island of Corfu.

Serbia, like Belgium, had simply been swallowed up in battle. But its sufferings under occupation were to be far more intense. Of all the belligerents on either side, Serbia endured the heaviest casualties, both military and civilian.

A year later it was Rumania's turn. The year 1916 had begun with a deceptive series of Entente successes. The French held off the Germans at Verdun, the British staged their first great offensive along the Somme, and the Russians suddenly came to life and struck back at their enemies with astonishing results. In June and July, under the command of a new and talented general called Brussilov, the Russian armies advanced all along the line. In the end, however, Brussilov gained nothing. Victory eluded him, as it had Hindenburg and Ludendorff and Mackensen the year before. Brussilov lost more than a million men; another million quietly deserted; the spirit of the Russian armies was broken.

The Rumanians, however, anxiously searching the skies for portents, did not realize this. All they saw was that a propitious moment had arrived to enter the war on the side of the Entente. And their choice—like Bulgaria's—was comparatively easy: the major goal of Rumanian expansion was Transylvania, which formed part of Hungary. On August 28, 1916, Rumania declared war. But this calculated decision came a couple of months too late: Germany had already surmounted the threat from Brussilov and the British pressure along the Somme.

Hence it meant nothing that the Rumanians advanced 50 miles into Transylvania almost unopposed. Their success was completely illusory; the formidable Mackensen was already plotting their destruction. Three armies converged on the hapless Rumanians. By the end of the year they had lost three-quarters of their country and were all but out of the war.

The final Balkan intervention—that by Greece—is a complex affair, and one that does no credit to Entente diplomacy. In Greece, as contrasted to Bulgaria or Rumania, the national leaders were hopelessly divided: King Constantine, whose wife was German, inclined toward the Central Powers; his prime minister, Eleutherios Venizelos, was ardently pro-Entente. Venizelos had a clearer view of the national interest, for the lands that the Greeks had marked out for future annexation belonged to Germany's new allies, to Turkey and, to a lesser extent, to Bulgaria. The Entente powers, moreover, whose navies dominated the Mediterranean, were in a far better position than Germany and Austria to bring pressure on the wavering Greeks.

For two full years, Britain and France gradually nudged Greece into the war—first by establishing a vast fortified camp around Salonika on Greek soil, secondly, by supporting Venizelos in his intrigues against the king. Finally there came a military showdown. An Anglo-French navy appeared off the coast near Athens. Entente agents stirred up a minor civil war. By early 1917, King Constantine had been forced to abdicate, and Greece had formally joined the Entente.

The Dardanelles Expedition

The Greek involvement in the war forms part of a larger pattern of Entente action against the Turkish Empire which had begun in earnest in early 1915. At that time, with the front in France stabilized, a number of the more imaginative British and French leaders—among them Winston Churchill, the youthful first lord of the admiralty—had begun to argue for diversionary operations against the Turks. Why continue to butt one's head against a stone wall, they reasoned. Why go on with these costly assaults in France that accomplished nothing? It was far better to swing around the flank—to attack the Central Powers where they were weakest, in what Churchill a quarter-century later was to describe as the "soft underbelly of Europe." Turkey was in fact a weak power. To be sure, a national revival had been evident during the six years before the outbreak of war, and its German-trained soldiers were vigorous and efficient. Nevertheless, the Ottoman Empire, like the Austrian, was a ramshackle affair. As in Austria-Hungary, its ruling nationality was outnumbered by its minorities: the Greeks and, still more important, the Arabs of the Levant, Mesopotamia, and the Arabian peninsula.

The major stumbling block of the 1915 expedition against the Turks was that no clear decision was ever taken either for or against this diversionary strategy. The British and French high commands were both skeptical, but they did not veto the idea entirely. They did worse—they consented grudgingly to an expedition that was to prove totally inadequate for its task. Originally, it was planned to seize the Gallipoli peninsula alongside the Dardanelles and thereby dominate the focal points of the Turkish state, Constantinople and the straits joining the Black Sea to the Mediterranean. At first, the planners believed that a naval squadron could do the job alone. Later they added ground forces, notably Dominion troops from Australia and New Zealand. But at no time did they provide what was required for a really decisive blow.

When the invading force scrambled ashore on April 25, it found little initial opposition. Success seemed assured. But then Turkish resistance hardened and the attackers were pinned to the ground. The same thing happened three and a half months later when reinforcements were sent and new landings attempted. By this time it was August, and the British Empire troops were suffering from heat, lack of water, flies, and dysentery. The coming of autumn added further hardships. By December there was nothing to do but evacuate the exhausted British soldiers. This operation, at least, was highly successful: losses were light, and that achievement gave a bleak consolation to a disappointed British public.

The French had meanwhile decided to establish a fortified camp on the Aegean at Salonika in support of the Serbians. By the time they had done this, however, it was too late: all was over with Serbia. But the Salonika position remained—inactively, it is true—as a token of Entente pressure on the Balkans. Nearly three years were to pass before this force broke out of its encampments and advanced triumphantly toward the Danube.

There was a third eastern area in which the British began to operate in the year 1915: the Arab world. Where they had failed at Gallipoli, here—in a much wider sphere—they were to succeed brilliantly. First in Mesopotamia, later in Palestine, finally among the Arab nomads, where the almost legendary Colonel T. E. Lawrence stirred up something resembling a holy war, the British pushed ahead and worked on Arab sympathies. In the end, they succeeded in freeing the entire Arab world from Turkish rule. The Ottoman Empire, like the Austrian, simply dissolved.

The War at Sea: Jutland

In the decade and a half preceding the outbreak of the war the Germans had tried to challenge the British mastery of the seas. This effort failed of its purpose: far from making war too much of a "risk" for Britain, the

German naval-building program, by embittering relations between the two powers, led them closer to the brink.

In the years of intense naval competition, the British aim had been to keep at least a three to two lead over the Germans in the total number of ships in service and to exceed them in technical efficiency. In the first respect, they substantially succeeded. But in technical excellence, the Germans frequently triumphed. This was particularly true of battle cruisers, submarines, and lighter craft of all sorts.

The latter threat, however, took two years to become apparent. In the early phases of the war, the British quite clearly had the upper hand. They confined the main units of the German navy to its home bases, and they set about systematically rounding up the German overseas colonies and the German cruisers and raiding ships that were preying on commerce. By the end of 1914, this task was essentially accomplished. Throughout the seven seas, the only remaining challengers to British mastery were the neutral navies of the United States and Japan.

Yet a real threat persisted: fast units of the German fleet could always break out and do extensive damage. Once, at the end of 1914, they raided the peaceful seaside resort of Scarborough. Four times in all, the German battle cruisers sallied forth, looking for a fight. The fifth foray, on the last day of May, 1916, led to the one great naval battle of the war. For a day and a night, in the North Sea off Jutland, the two navies met in a confused and blundering fight. At first, the battle cruisers alone were engaged. Toward evening, the main fleets of battleships suddenly and rather surprisingly made contact. At this point, the Germans realized their peril: with the heavy guns of the British battle fleet bearing down upon them, they turned and made for home. Darkness favoring them, they escaped almost untouched.

To this day debate has raged as to who "won" the Battle of Jutland. From the standpoint of seamanship and gunnery, the honors belong to the Germans. They shot more accurately, and they sank nearly twice the tonnage the British did. More particularly, their battle cruisers proved distinctly superior. In fact, the defects revealed in British battle-cruiser construction were the greatest lesson of the whole battle: at least two of them had blown up in combat because of internal defects. At which the bluff battle-cruiser commander, Sir David Beatty, had cried out in bewilderment: "There seems to be something wrong with our damned ships today!"

In a wider sense, however, the British were the victors. Britain's ultimate fate depended on its navy and Sir John Jellicoe, the British commander in chief, was thus, as contemporaries put it, the only man "who could lose the war in an afternoon." Far from doing that, he saved his fleet, and he chased the Germans home. They were never to emerge in such force again. After Jutland, the German fleet moldered in port, and the nation turned to put its whole reliance on the new and deadly weapon of the submarine.

THE ECONOMICS OF WARFARE

The war began, as the British expressed it, in an atmosphere of "business as usual." Economic life would go on just as before, and only the fighting men would suffer directly from the war's upsets. These illusions lasted only a few weeks. By the end of 1914, it was already apparent that this war would be different from all its predecessors in the way it caught whole civilian populations in its grip.

Blockade versus Submarine

Both Germany and Britain, as the two most highly industrialized of the great European powers, depended on overseas imports of raw materials and, more particularly, of food. Hence it was logical that each should try to starve the other out.

The British method was blockade, which they had used a hundred years earlier against Napoleon with only mediocre results. The law of the seas had since been codified by international agreement: the Declaration of Paris of 1856 gave legal force only to an *effective blockade*—a close control over the enemy's ports by ships stationed just offshore—and guaranteed the rights of neutrals to carry goods to all belligerents, except for specific categories of armaments defined as contraband. Beginning in 1914, the British violated both these provisions: properly apprehensive of Germany's mine fields and shore defenses, they maintained a remote rather than a close blockade and systematically interfered with neutral commerce.

The first violation concerned only the Germans and hence caused no particular trouble. The second violation, however, antagonized a host of neutral nations, among them the United States. The British contended that the 1856 list of contraband articles bore no relation to the realities of modern warfare, since it excluded such essentials as rubber, cotton, oil, and copper. They drew up their own list, therefore, and enforced it as thoroughly as they could: they opened mail, they published a blacklist of neutral firms that traded with the enemy, and they halted and led into port suspicious vessels, confiscating their cargoes when necessary. All this was done with a characteristically British combination of firmness and politeness, and gradually the neutrals grew used to it. As the United States slowly moved away from neutrality, it became apparent that the American government regarded the British violations of the laws of war as no more than vexatious: they hindered trade, but they did not entail loss of life. It was far different with the chief weapon of German economic warfare, the submarine.

"Necessity knows no law," the German chancellor had declared, in justifying to the Reichstag the invasion of Belgium. He might have said the same of submarine warfare. It was ruthless, it was cruel—but after the British rounding up of the German commerce raiders, it offered almost the only means available for a beleaguered continental power to strike at its maritime adversary. The character of the weapon dictated the manner of its employment. Except in rare circumstances the submarine could not follow the traditional procedure of searching and seizing a merchantman carrying contraband. Its crew was too small to man another ship, nor could it take the risk of trying to lead such a vessel into a German port, for a submarine on the surface was an extremely vulnerable target. Hence as the war progressed, it became more and more the practice to sink a ship on sight without bothering to inquire whether it was an enemy vessel or a neutral that might or might not be carrying contraband. Naturally, the neutrals were outraged.

Two limitations on submarine warfare, however, had curtailed its ravages in the earlier phases of the conflict. First, the Germans began using their new weapon too soon. In 1914, they could keep only six or seven submarines at sea at one time; hence they gave the British ample warning of what was to come. The latter were quick to work out countermeasures. For the first two years of the war, such devices as patrols and mines kept within bearable limits the total of tonnage sunk. Not until the autumn of 1916 did losses of merchantmen take a sudden spurt that threatened the very survival of Britain.

By that time, the American declaration of war was only a few months away. This suggests the second factor that had limited the submarine menace—the vigorous protests of President Woodrow Wilson as spokesman for the leading neutral power. The sinking of the *Lusitania* in May, 1915, had sent a wave of indignation throughout the United States. This great British liner had been torpedoed without warning off the coast of Ireland and more than a thousand lives had been lost, including a hundred Americans. As a result of the *Lusitania* tragedy and its sequels, Wilson finally wrested from the German government a pledge that in the future merchant ships would not be sunk without warning. But the German promise contained an escape clause: the Imperial Government reserved to itself "complete liberty of decision" in the event that the United States should not exert equally successful pressure on the British to stick to the rules of war. In early 1917, the Germans availed themselves of this "liberty of decision"—with results that were to prove fatal for the final outcome of the conflict.

The Home Fronts

As the war ground on into a second year and then a third, the lives of civilians at home became steadily grayer and more drab. The inexorable casualty lists brought gloom and despair into millions of homes. Daily living became more regimented, as shortages both of goods and of manpower grew ever more severe.

Of the major Western belligerents, France went through the war with the least regimentation. The French prided themselves on their balance between industry and agriculture and the country's near self-sufficiency in foodstuffs. France did, of course, suffer from an acute shortage of military manpower, and a large part of its industrial resources lay under enemy control. But the French tended to work out these problems—as they financed their war—by improvisations. Britain and later the United States supplied a steady stream of industrial products, and the labor of women, foreigners, and prisoners helped fill the manpower gaps.

In Britain, rationing and manpower allocation were stricter than in France, but not so severe as in Germany. It was the beleaguered Reich, rather, that set the model for war controls and supplied the example that was to be followed by nearly all the belligerents a generation later. The Germans had started the war in surprisingly poor economic shape. In strictly military terms they were the best prepared of the Great Powers, but they had neglected to take the most elementary economic precautions. They had done almost no stockpiling, for example, and as the British blockade began to take effect, shortages appeared almost everywhere.

Once alerted to their danger, the Germans responded with vigor and imagination. As "Organizer of German Trade and Industry" the chancellor appointed the talented and visionary industrialist Walther Rathenau. Rathenau's methods, as unorthodox as his own personality, brought good results. He began to organize the different branches of economic enterprise into compulsory cartels under mixed state and private control; his successors in office ruthlessly "combed out" uneconomic small business and set up a system of block cooperative purchasing from neutrals. To replace essential goods which had formerly been imported from abroad, German chemists—pioneers in synthetics—developed all kinds of *ersatz* products or substitutes, particularly in fertilizers and food.

Simultaneously manpower controls were imposed, culminating at the end of 1916 in the Auxiliary Labor Law which, in theory at least, mobilized for war service all German males between the ages of seventeen and sixty. The date of the new law was significant: it marked two major changes that drastically affected the German home front—the dictatorship of the team of Hindenburg and Ludendorff, who had demanded the law in peremptory terms, and the onset of the coldest winter that Europe had experienced in twenty years.

V

THE END OF OLD EUROPE

The Bloodletting of 1916: Verdun and the Somme

Falkenhayn had chosen well in picking Verdun for the site of the great offensive that would induce France to sue for peace. In itself Verdun possessed no particular military significance: it jutted out from the

French line as an awkward salient whose loss might even have been an advantage. Joffre, with arrogant self-confidence, had systematically neglected its defenses, but once the Germans began their attack, he saw no alternative but to hold on at all costs. The defense of Verdun became a symbol. Once more, as on the Marne, the French command, trained in offensive doctrine yet unable to advance, awakened an intense national response through its desperate resolve to retreat no farther.

On February 21, the German attack opened. Its commander was the imperial crown prince, whose victory was intended to buttress an already threatened dynasty. The attack had been preceded by the greatest bombardment yet known in human history, as two million shells rained on Verdun and its outer ring of forts. Four days later, the Germans took the first of these, Douaumont, the key to the city on the northeast, and the fall of Verdun itself seemed at hand.

Its savior, however, was already on his way to take command. Henri-Philippe Pétain had been only an elderly colonel when the war broke out, but as he proved himself in combat, he had risen rapidly until he found the assignment that exactly suited his temperament. As calm and reserved as Joffre, Pétain had far more human warmth and he did not suffer from the old illusions about the offensive. It was in defense, rather, that he was at his best, for here he could bring into play his systematic powers of organization and his ability to inspire affection and confidence among his men.

Pétain's success at Verdun was chiefly due to these two talents: his organization of supply and his considerate treatment of his soldiers. The supply problem he solved by improvising a substitute for the railroad that had been cut. The "sacred road," as the French called it, was reserved solely for military traffic and kept in constant repair as a steady stream of trucks, regularly spaced, plied day and night up to the fortress and back. This procedure, which was to become standard in the Second World War, was a novelty in the First. As for his men, Pétain tried to spare them in every possible way. As opposed to the German insistence on keeping their units in the line until they literally dropped of exhaustion, Pétain set a two-weeks' maximum for front-line duty. He made possible this system of rotation by drawing in reserves from all other sectors of the front until he had more than half a million men at his disposal. Thus the defenders were able to hold on: week after week they suffered and died in shellholes and improvised trenches, week after week they stopped successive waves of German attackers. By April 10, when Pétain issued the famous order "Courage! On les aura," * both he and his soldiers knew that Verdun would be held.

Yet one more ordeal was in store for them. In early June, the Germans launched a last great effort. After a week of desperate fighting they took a second of the protective forts, Vaux, whose defenders, trapped and

---

* "Courage! We'll get them."

without water, struggled underground at close quarters until the last.
Once again the way to Verdun seemed open. With Pétain very nearly at
the end of his nerve, the commander in chief, Joffre, stepped in. He knew
that the British were about to open their greatest offensive of the war.
Once more the defenders of Verdun received the order to hold at all
costs. By mid-July the crisis was over; the Germans were now on the
defensive everywhere.

The great attack along the Somme brought the supreme moment that
the British had been awaiting for two years. Their new army, launched
for the first time en masse, was now to prove its mettle under a new
commander, Sir Douglas Haig, who had succeeded Sir John French in
December, 1915. The Somme offensive had originally been planned as a
joint Franco-British effort, but the defense of Verdun both delayed it
and reduced the contingent that the French could supply. Thus when
the time came, Joffre could put only twelve divisions into the line, and
the Somme became mainly a British show. As such, it reflected the Anglo-
Saxon emphasis on meticulous preparation and weight of materiel. The
outcome was to prove that these were far from enough to assure success.

On July 1, after a week's cannonade, the attack opened on a 25-mile
front. From the start nearly everything went wrong: the soldiers were
too heavily laden and they were assaulting an enemy who held higher
ground and was dug into some of the strongest and most elaborate
trenches of the entire front. By the end of the first day the failure was
manifest. The British had lost nearly 60,000 men, including more than
half the officers engaged—the worst rate of casualties on either side in
the whole war.

Thus it availed nothing that the French, attacking to the south of the
river, had scored a relative success. Nor did it help that the fighting front
was narrowed to a mere six miles. Such an offensive had to succeed on
the first day if it was to keep moving at all. And so this battle—like all
previous ones—bogged down into a heartbreaking succession of bloody
local engagements. By the end of September, the Germans had plugged
the gaps and withstood the storm. It was time to reckon up the losses of
this apocalyptic year.

At Verdun casualties had been about even—each side lost 350,000 men.
The Germans, intending to bleed their enemies white, had done the
same to themselves. The Somme had added half a million German casualties, 410,000 British, 190,000 French. Human imagination could not
grasp such a fearful toll. And for nothing: at the end of the year, the
front ran only a few miles from where it had stood at the beginning.

These terrible facts at last began to sink into the minds of the men at
the front. On neither side was morale the same after 1916. The British
knew that the flower of their new army had been sacrificed in one reckless gamble. Before Verdun, the Germans had begun to surrender in
large numbers for the first time; the Somme had convinced them that
they were materially outclassed by their enemies. Even the French, inspired though they were by the defense of the great fortress, realized

that the victory was not worth the cost. France would never again be able to make such an effort: the new recruits were different from their elders, already tired and defeatist before they had ever seen battle.

Verdun and the Somme marked the climax of the war. The year 1917 was to usher in a new war—and a new Europe.

The "Turnip Winter" and Its Consequences

The spirit of the men at the front had been broken. The ordeal of the civilians was to follow. During the bitter winter of 1916–1917 morale at home snapped. As misery settled over every household, people began to ask themselves, at first in whispers, then more openly, whether it was worth going on, whether there was not some way to stop this cruel bloodshed before European civilization perished utterly.

Germany suffered most. An early frost had spoiled the potato harvest; people grew thin on a diet of turnips and synthetics; the canals froze; transport was bogged; coal ran short; cold and drabness and hopelessness blighted men's souls. The French ate better and were warmer—but they were mourning the losses they could never replace. The British now knew what war really was. The Italians were in a state of smouldering discontent. The Austrians and Russians were at their last gasp.

Gradually it was borne in upon men's minds that Europe would never again be the same. Too many had died; too much that was gentle and rare had been destroyed. Everywhere the elite had been ruthlessly cut down. In theory, losses should have been distributed evenly through all classes of the population—except in Britain, which did not introduce conscription until the beginning of 1916—since universal military service was the rule. In practice it worked out otherwise: the aristocracy and the young men of education were by far the hardest hit. In Britain the reason was obvious: such people had been the first to volunteer. Yet even in the other countries, elite units were thrown into combat first; boys of good family volunteered while still under age, and the proportion of losses among officers was higher than among enlisted men. Everywhere, then, the European aristocracy went under, stubbornly, blindly, through a pathetic combination of heroism and ineptitude in command.

With it, went into limbo the whole tone of life that the aristocracy had tried to set. After 1916, although nobilities continued to exist, their parts were played out; they were leaders and exemplars no longer. The old elegance had gone; the other classes no longer cared to imitate courtly manners. They preferred the slack and the sloppy. No longer did people know or much care what good manners or good breeding meant. All that seemed remote and irrelevant. To the "lost generation," the old precepts rang hollow and meaningless. With half their number dead or maimed, the rest felt burned out and adrift, no longer sure of the significance of their own lives or of the society in which they lived.

In one sense, then, the great change that first became noticeable during the winter of 1916–1917 strengthened the democratic currents that had already been running so strongly in Europe in the years just preceding the outbreak of the conflict. Mass suffering at home and in the trenches made the First World War the first great democratic war. A common slaughter, a common drabness effectively leveled all classes. But this was democracy in its most primitive and negative meaning. In their more refined and subtle manifestations, democratic values suffered almost as much as did those of the aristocracy. The new equality of suffering not only leveled the classes; it also further embittered relations between them, as the remaining injustices and anomalies stood out ever more starkly. And as democratization advanced, disillusionment followed: the parliamentary governments of Britain, France, and Italy all proved themselves incompetent in directing the war, and they shamelessly lied to their people in an effort to cover up their mistakes.

This deception, more than anything else, was responsible for what has been called the wartime "decadence of democracy." Governments everywhere enforced censorship in both a stupid and a capricious fashion. Still worse, they tried to "organize enthusiasm"—to drum up excitement and jubilation for the ghastly failures of their generals—to conceal losses and to falsify communiqués. All these things sickened the men at the front from whom the truth could not be hidden. Particularly in France, the fighting men were outraged by the patriotic "brain-stuffing" that went on behind the lines. It was no wonder that a British journalist, for four years unable to report what his own eyes had seen, entitled his postwar book of wartime experience *Now It Can Be Told*.

The campaign of 1917 opened on a changed Europe—a fact that became almost immediately evident on the battlefields.

Ludendorff versus Nivelle

As a result of the failures of 1916, both sides changed their high commands. At the end of August—when the fortunes of the Central Powers seemed at their lowest—the Eastern Front team of Hindenburg and Ludendorff replaced Falkenhayn. Four months later, Joffre, who had been so recklessly confident about Verdun, was also eased out. For the "hero of the Marne," the last two years of his command had been an anticlimax and a disappointment. But he was a national symbol nonetheless, and a face-saving device was found by reviving for him the old title of Marshal of France, which had never before been awarded under the Republic.

Joffre's successor was General Robert Nivelle. Young, eloquent, and far more congenial to parliamentarians than the aloof and dictatorial Joffre, Nivelle appeared to be a man of infinite promise. He had distinguished himself in the later phases of the defense of Verdun, where he had replaced Pétain in local command and mounted two brief offensives that were models of careful preparation and economy in manpower. Nivelle soon had the French politicians eating out of his hand, for he promised the combination that everybody wanted, and which the cooler military heads knew to be impossible: a new type of offensive that would entail few losses but bring decisive results.

Scarcely had the French and British governments agreed to Nivelle's plans than they began to be shaken by doubts. Nivelle himself seemed to have lost confidence: he became fussy and irritable and his planning less careful. One by one, things went wrong. Nivelle talked too openly about his projects: the Germans captured a full plan of the coming offensive. The rain fell ceaselessly. Finally, and most important, only a month before the attack was to open, Ludendorff foiled his adversary by new dispositions which meant that the great blow would fall largely in a void.

When Hindenburg had assumed command the previous summer, with Ludendorff, his one-man brain trust, in the newly established office of first quartermaster-general, both immediately saw that Germany's military effort was dangerously overextended. In 1916, as in 1914, the German army had been obliged to fight major battles on at least three fronts. This could not happen again: Germany, only slightly more slowly than France, was reaching the end of its manpower reserves. In 1917, then, Hindenburg and Ludendorff resolved to concentrate on knocking Russia out of the war while restricting operations in the west to the most economical defense possible.

In carrying out this decision, they resorted to a stratagem that Nivelle had dismissed as impossible. They drew back their army in France an average of 25 miles to a new and shorter line that could be held with thirteen fewer divisions. All through the winter the Siegfried (or Hindenburg) Line was prepared with characteristic German thoroughness. Then in early March the carefully phased withdrawal began. The French and British were caught almost completely by surprise. Suddenly between them and the enemy there stretched a wide zone of desolation, systematically laid waste by the retreating Germans.

When the French went over the top in Champagne on April 16, they found an enemy better entrenched and farther away than they had expected. Once again, as had happened so often in the past, the first day was enough to predict nearly total failure. Nivelle had promised to break off immediately if this should happen, but now, faced with the reality, he fell into the old trap: refusing to admit defeat, he continued to hammer away. This time, however, his soldiers had had enough. They had been deceived too often; the bitterness of nearly three years of futile losses finally overflowed. Unit after unit refused to go over the top. By May, a large part of the French army was in a state of mutiny. Obviously Nivelle had to go. And the choice of his successor was equally obvious —Pétain, the "hero of Verdun," the only general in France who could possibly face the storm and restore confidence to a demoralized army.

Pétain went about his painful task with his characteristic combination of firmness and humanity. He visited ninety divisions in turn, observing, listening to complaints, and preaching lessons of patience. While he sought to restore discipline, he also tried to satisfy the soldiers' legitimate grievances; food, rest, furloughs were improved. Moreover, he tempered severity with mercy; in the end no more than twenty-three mutineers were executed.

In terms of strategy, Pétain merely decided that France could do no more. He demanded a year's respite for his troops and left it to the British to mount whatever further attacks they should propose. The results were what might have been expected: at Passchendaele near Ypres in Flanders, the tragedy of the Somme was repeated on a smaller scale. For sheer misery and horror, both British and Germans regarded this battle as the worst of the whole war; rain, mud, and the new weapon of mustard gas brought an intensity of suffering that was never to be surpassed.

By the summer of 1917, then, the British and the Germans had joined the French in longing for the war to end. Peace without victory, peace without annexations or indemnities, became the slogans of this new or reawakened revulsion against the ceaseless slaughter. The French mutinies of the spring had not been an isolated phenomenon. They gave tangible evidence of a war weariness and even defeatism that were rapidly spreading among French civilians and were openly voiced by a number of Socialist or Radical Socialist parliamentarians. Similar sentiments found expression in England on the left wing of the Labor party and in an open letter published in the *Daily Telegraph* by the Conservative elder statesman Lord Lansdowne. Finally in Germany, the advocates of a peace of compromise temporarily obtained a majority in the Reichstag and sought to impose their will on the Imperial Government. The Peace Resolution of July 1917 called in what sounded like unmistakable terms for a settlement that would leave neither side the victor.

The diplomats were equally active. In late 1916 and early 1917, all sorts of intermediaries, official or semiofficial, were scurrying about Europe, trying to establish contact between the belligerents. In December, 1916, President Wilson made a final effort to get the warring powers to formulate clear aims on which negotiation could begin; from February to June of the next year, the young Austrian emperor, convinced that only an early peace could save his throne, maintained secret contact with the French and British governments; in August, the Pope, who had constantly pleaded for peace and was particularly concerned about preserving Catholic Austria, made his last and supreme effort to induce the powers to come to terms. None of these attempts even remotely approached success. All would-be peacemakers received evasive or ambiguous responses. By the autumn of 1917, it was clear that the war would go on. A whole year of flagging war sentiment and nearly constant efforts for peace had come to nothing; the belligerents girded for renewed combat.

The peace "offensive" failed because of its hopeless lack of coordination. Neither side was ever ready to talk when the other was. When one coalition faltered, the other plucked up hope. Indeed, any hint of willingness to make peace was interpreted by the enemy as a sign of weakness and a reason to go on fighting all the harder. After more than two years of war, each belligerent had settled into ineradicable distrust of its enemies, and the vicious circle was impossible to break. Moreover, the warring coalitions either failed to specify their war aims or insisted on territorial changes that their enemies could never have accepted. Thus the Germans refused to give an unambiguous pledge to restore the full independence of Belgium, and the French and British added to their war aims a demand for the liberation of the subject nationalities of Austria-Hungary.

Perhaps the clearest case in point was the failure of the Reichstag's Peace Resolution of July. In its demand for a peace without annexations, the Reichstag undoubtedly voiced the longings of the great majority of the German people. But the Reichstag lacked real power, and what power it did have, it did not know how to use. It forced the resignation of the chancellor over the peace issue, but then it acquiesced in a successor who, on this issue, was worse than his predecessor. When the new chancellor declared that he accepted the Peace Resolution, "as he understood it," he meant that he was not accepting it at all. And in this he reflected the views of the true ruler of Germany, Ludendorff, who in the past year had established an effective dictatorship, both military and civilian. Ludendorff opposed the Reichstag majority on two counts: he was dead set against democracy, and he was dead set against a peace of compromise. Indeed, until only six weeks before the end of the war, Ludendorff stubbornly exemplified and held out for the irreducible program of the German ruling classes: large annexations in both east and west, unrestricted submarine warfare, and uncompromising resistance to democratization at home.

Thus the Peace Resolution was effectively buried. And, as a final irony, when autumn brought a new turn in Germany's favor, even its sponsors forgot the resolution and fell back into their annexationist dreams.

VI

THE YEAR OF DECISION

The New War: Russia and the United States

The spring of 1917 saw two events that were to change the whole character of the war, breaking the deadlock and bringing renewed hope of victory to both camps: the first step in Russia's defection from the En-

tente and the entrance of the United States on the French and British
side. The military implications of neither of these events were properly realized at the time: temporarily they even intensified the drift toward a negotiated peace. Only in the autumn did the military potentialities of the new situation become fully apparent. Only then did it become clear that the final period of the war was opening and that in this climactic phase each side in turn would have a chance to win.

The first Russian Revolution of March, 1917, gave brief comfort to the French and British, for there seemed to be hope that under its new democratic government the Russian people would fight more enthusiastically than before. But the morale of the Russian army had sunk too low to be revitalized by a sudden injection of democracy. After one last summer's effort, the nation's military resources collapsed. Even before the second revolution, in November, the Russian army was in full dissolution (*see* Chapter Three).

The American declaration on April 6 had brought into the war a new and potentially stronger ally to compensate for the loss of Russia. President Wilson's decision to ask Congress to go to war was not a simple act; it took him a long time to reach that resolve. Various factors had to be weighed: ties of democratic sentiment that linked the country to the British and French and the more tangible but probably less influential ties of massive wartime loans. The immediate and precipitating cause of Wilson's decision, however, was a still more tangible act on the part of the Germans. In January, 1917, Ludendorff and the other military chiefs induced the emperor and the chancellor to resort to unlimited submarine warfare.

This also had been a desperately debated decision, and the German civilian authorities held out against it until the last. What finally persuaded them was the military men's assurance that even if the submarines did bring the United States into the war, American troops would never be able to reach Europe in time and in sufficient numbers to affect the outcome. Here, of course, the Germans were disastrously mistaken. But even the Allies—as the French and British now began to be called—were almost equally skeptical about the American contribution. It would take at least a year to materialize, and in the meantime the defenders of France would have to face the German storm alone.

The Lloyd George and Clemenceau Governments

In girding for the expected crisis, the British and French had the advantage of new and stronger leadership. Within eleven months of each other, the Allies changed prime ministers, bringing to power the leaders who would put their characteristic stamp both on the final war effort and on the making of the peace.

Britain had started the war under the Liberal government of Herbert H. Asquith, which had already been in power six years. It had long outlived its original reforming mandate, and it was riven by internal dissensions. More important, its leader was not fitted by temperament or experience to mobilize the energies of a nation at war. Tolerant, judicious, urbane, Asquith hated war and the uncivilized behavior that went with it. Only grudgingly would he consent to even the most obvious emergency measures. Hence, as it became apparent that the war would be a long one, authority passed by successive stages to Asquith's most energetic subordinate, the former radical David Lloyd George. First, in May, 1915, when the government was enlarged to include the Conservatives, Lloyd George became minister of munitions. A year later he took over as secretary of state for war. Finally, at the end of 1916, he replaced Asquith as prime minister.

From this new ministry, most of the Liberals were absent. Lloyd George ran a paradoxical coalition government in which the chief figures, aside from himself, were all Conservatives. But this sort of inconsistency did not bother Lloyd George at all. He had lost his earlier ideological bent and, along with it, his allegiance to the Left. Now he was interested only in winning the war as swiftly and as effectively as possible. Hence he consorted with "war lords and profiteers," paid little or no attention to Labor, and ran his own war in a personal and capricious fashion.

France had gone into the conflict under the leadership of the moderate left government of René Viviani. In the first flush of war enthusiasm, the ministry had been enlarged into a "Sacred Union" of all the parties, and it was with this formula, under a succession of chiefs, that France had stumbled along during the next three years. In the spring and summer of 1917, however, the crisis of defeatism tore the Sacred Union wide apart. If the war was to continue at all, the conservatives and superpatriots could govern no more in coalition with the Socialists and left Radicals. France had to make a choice; it could no longer get along on improvisations. Again the choice was obvious—Georges Clemenceau, the old Jacobin patriot, the implacable critic of his country's war effort.

When Clemenceau became prime minister in November, 1917, he changed the whole tone of the government. It became abrupt, peremptory, dictatorial. He effectively silenced the defeatists by jailing some and frightening the rest. He rode roughshod over the Socialists. He whipped and threatened his weary people into one last effort until victory was achieved.

The Lloyd George and Clemenceau governments had much in common: both were led by former radicals who had ceased to be such; both were semidictatorial and impatient of opposition; and both frankly rested on conservative and military support. In this respect, they revealed how different the final year of the war was from its earlier phases. During the first two years of the fighting, the great Western European democracies had enjoyed a true national unity. In the third year of the war, they had undergone a profound crisis of conscience. The last year ostensi-

bly saw the restoration of the earlier unity, but this was more apparent
than real. Part of the nation remained outside the consensus: the political Left hovered in limbo, skeptical and disaffected. The new "unity" actually cloaked the dominance of the leaders of old-fashioned nationalism. This leadership knew precisely what it wanted: victory and the attainment of narrow national aims.

Caporetto, Cambrai, Brest-Litovsk

The last months of 1917 were marked by three events that set the stage for the final campaigns of the war: the battles of Caporetto and Cambrai and the armistice on the Eastern Front leading to the Treaty of Brest-Litovsk.

For two and a half years the Italian and Austrian armies, both riddled with discontent, lay gripped in weary stalemate in impossible mountain terrain. Time after time the Italians had hammered away along the Isonzo River northwest of Trieste without achieving any substantial results. As each successive offensive failed, the soldiers grew more and more disaffected: most of them had no idea why they were in the war at all—their priests and their Socialist leaders kept telling them that the whole thing was a mistake—their officers treated them harshly, and they enjoyed far fewer rear-area comforts than the other Western combatants.

On October 24, 1917, the unexpected happened. The Austrians, reinforced by picked German units and favored by low-hanging clouds, advanced in a massive attack. The Italian mountain positions were overwhelmed. Retreat turned into rout as tens of thousands of deserters swept along with them in blind panic the troops to the rear. Then, when it had left the enemy far behind, the vast flood of men slowed down and grew good-humored: an army of 400,000, sick of war, was simply going home. Under these circumstances, with discipline almost gone, it is amazing that the Italian command was able to save the situation at all. For two weeks, they stemmed the retreat as best they could, in the vain hope of making a stand at each successive river line. Finally, on the Piave, only twenty miles short of Venice, the line held. The crisis was over.

Caporetto, as the great defeat was called, taught the Western Allies an essential lesson. Up to this time, disappointed by the Italian war effort, the French and British had scorned the Isonzo front as unworthy of their attention. Now they began to realize that a disaster on one front was bound to have repercussions elsewhere. The war was all of a piece; a failure in one sector, no matter how minor, could have grave effects on the alliance as a whole. Hence, after the brutal awakening of Caporetto, the French and British quickly despatched help to their hard-pressed ally and took the first steps toward the unified command that they were to achieve the following spring.

Meantime in Flanders, the British were preparing an attack which was to establish a novel pattern for the final phase of the war. On November 20, before Cambrai, the newly invented tanks first appeared in mass formation. They had been tried out a year earlier in the Somme offensive and, rather unaccountably, the Germans had failed to profit by this premature disclosure. The Central Powers made only half-hearted efforts to build their own tanks, leaving the systematic exploitation of this new weapon to their enemies. At Cambrai, the Germans were taken almost completely by surprise; a substantial breakthrough followed. The British success was merely local—but it gave a foretaste of what would happen when the Allies regained the initiative and could at length bring to bear on the Germans their crushing numerical superiority.

Cambrai showed that the generals were finally catching up with the tactical possibilities of the new weapons at their disposal. At last, after three years of blundering, they had relearned their trade. Of the new military contrivances developed during the war, gas alone had disappointed the hopes of its inventors: an almost foolproof gas mask soon protected the Allied soldiers, and the prevailing winds were found to work more often against the Germans than in their favor. In the use of aircraft, both sides made rapid progress. What at the beginning of the war had been merely a risky novelty was eventually applied to the most varied purposes: reconnaissance, attacks on supply dumps, the strafing of troops, and the direction of artillery fire. A final use, however, was almost completely German in inspiration. The terror bombing of large cities—that central feature of Second World War strategy—made its appearance only at the end of the first war. In September, 1917, the Germans staged a full week of night raids on London. They treated Paris more lightly, but even here the famous long-range cannon "Big Bertha" shelled the city at irregular intervals with deadly results.

To match the Allied tanks, Ludendorff developed his own new strategy of shock troops. Such units, which had first proved their worth at Caporetto, were to be the mainstays of the great German offensives in 1918. Small, tightly knit, with a high ratio of officers to enlisted men, these elite detachments incarnated Germany's last hope. They were light and mobile and included a large variety of arms. Their officers were young and fanatical; their men received all sorts of special privileges. The task Ludendorff set them was to infiltrate the enemy's lines, disorganize his rear, and keep the whole battle fluid as the main body of reserves advanced.

Thus both sides had learned how to break the trench stalemate and to fight a war of movement. The Germans were to strike first. But Ludendorff could not move until he had finally accomplished what he had attempted in vain in 1915—the elimination of Russia from the war.

After the March revolution the Russians made one last military effort. Under the stimulus of Alexander Kerensky, minister of war in the provisional government, they pulled together a force of 200,000 men to attack the Austrians in Galicia. The attack ended in rout. It was now the Germans' turn to advance and, almost without resistance, they cut deep into Russia. By August their drive toward Petrograd * had reached the outskirts of Riga. Throughout the early autumn Ludendorff kept up a merciless pressure: he was in a hurry to begin shifting his troops to the west. On November 7, the Bolsheviks seized power. One of their first acts was to sue for peace.

With the eastern armistice concluded on December 15, the peace negotiations at Brest-Litovsk began. When the Germans presented their terms, even the hardened Bolsheviks caught their breath. For Germany demanded the annexation, open or masked, of all Russia's western provinces. The Bolshevik negotiators struggled helplessly for better terms. In February, they even broke off the negotiations entirely. The German reply was to take up arms and to advance to within a hundred miles of Petrograd. Faced with this brutal reality, the Soviet negotiators finally accepted Lenin's reasoning that Russia had no recourse but peace at any price. The final terms of the Treaty of Brest-Litovsk, signed on March 3, 1918, were even harsher than those originally presented.

Meantime, a constant stream of German military trains had been traversing the Reich from east to west. By early March, when the troop transfers from Russia were completed, the Germans had an over-all superiority of 10 per cent and far more fresh divisions than their adversaries on the Western Front.

The Last German Offensives

Ludendorff had decided to risk everything on one last gamble. Beating down the moderates who argued that Germany should take advantage of its favorable military position to reach a compromise peace, he persuaded Hindenburg and the emperor to make a final drive for victory in France. No one had any illusions as to what the decision meant. By summer, Germany would have no reserves left. Failure would mean total defeat. Ludendorff was staking all his country had on a desperate wager that he could beat France and Britain before American help could arrive.

He came very close to doing it. For four months he kept up an almost constant series of attacks, with dizzying effect. First he struck at the rail junction of Amiens, to drive a wedge between the British and the French. The attack began on March 21, in thick fog which limited visibility to as little as twenty yards. The first day saw gains of several miles. Five days later, with the British driven back 40 miles and the fall of Amiens imminent, the French and British leaders held a desperate council of war. Poincaré presided; all the great chiefs were there; never had suspicion between the two Allies been so intense. Haig accused Pétain of

* As St. Petersburg was renamed, in more Slavic fashion, after Russia declared war on Germany.

stinginess in sending reinforcements and feared, correctly, that the French commander intended to concentrate his forces for the defense of Paris. Pétain in turn, skeptical and cautious as ever, thought that the British were interested only in saving their own army (as was in fact to prove the case in 1940). Faced with an almost complete breakdown of mutual confidence, the civilian leaders of both countries decided for extreme measures. The makeshifts of coalition warfare, they realized, could be tolerated no longer. Hence they agreed to appoint as "coordinator" of the Allied forces Clemenceau's military adviser, Foch, the most brilliant of France's soldiers. Three weeks later a similar conference raised Foch at last to the supreme command.

At first—for all his dash and confidence—the new commander in chief could do little more than parry Ludendorff's repeated blows. He held Amiens, it is true, but only after a heavy toll of prisoners had been taken. The next German thrust came in April to the south of Ypres; here Ludendorff broke through again, but his reserves proved insufficient for full exploitation of his success—a forewarning of what summer would bring. With the British finally holding, he threw his main weight to the east against the French. At the Chemin des Dames along the Aisne the third of the great German attacks caught Pétain frighteningly off guard: on May 27 the Germans advanced 13 miles—the greatest progress made on a single day since the stabilization of the front nearly four years before. On May 29, Soissons fell. Next day, the Germans were again at the Marne only 37 miles from Paris, and the disheartening process of evacuating the capital had begun once more.

This time, however, Paris was in no real danger. Although the French did not know it, Ludendorff was already reaching the end of his resources. His last two offensives showed signs of bafflement and uncertainty. He had taken too long about his victory: his enemies now had ample reserve forces from the United States. On June 4, to bolster the French along the Marne, the Americans had gone into action for the first time at Belleau Wood near Château-Thierry. It was only a small engagement, and the American tactics had been amateurish, but the French were indescribably heartened to see that the moment so long hoped for had at last arrived.

In the second week of June, Ludendorff struck against Compiègne. Then he paused for a month to regroup for his fifth and final offensive. This was advertised to the German people as the *Friedenssturm*, the supreme effort that would bring peace at last. Never had a nation been more cruelly deceived. The *Friedenssturm* could not possibly have brought peace. It was a last gasp, a great diversion, no more. Ludendorff knew it, and so did his enemies. Foch and Pétain and Haig and the new American commander, John J. Pershing, were already planning their final march to victory.

And so when Ludendorff struck once more along the Marne west of Reims, Foch was ready for him. The Germans briefly crossed the river, but that was all. On July 18, Foch ordered a counterattack; nine American divisions took part. The Second Battle of the Marne, like the first battle four years earlier, was a great Allied victory. From this time on Foch never lost the initiative. On August 8, "the black day of the German army," the whole front began to roll back.

The Allied March to Victory

From early August the outcome of the war was no longer in doubt. The only question was whether the fighting would be over in the autumn. Nearly everybody, even on the Allied side, thought it would continue into 1919; no one quite realized how close the Germans were to collapse.

Some credit for the early victory, however, must also be conceded to Foch's leadership. The electric little Frenchman, who had been straining at the leash during three long years of combat, now at last had found the assignment that suited his talents—as Joffre had found it on the Marne, or Pétain at Verdun. With the Germans on the run, the doctrine of the attack finally came into its own. Foch's strategy was to keep the enemy off balance—to maintain unrelenting pressure, now here, now there, until the whole front reeled back under the accumulated shock. For it was no longer necessary to save men or materiel. Tanks were available in masses that staggered and demoralized the Germans, and the Americans were arriving at a rate of 250,000 a month.

The British led off before Amiens, where they advanced eight miles on the first day. The Americans followed with their first big assignment, the reduction of the Saint-Mihiel salient southeast of Verdun. The French had meanwhile kept up pressure in the center; by mid-September, they had forced the Germans back to the Hindenburg Line. From here Foch mounted a great pincer movement: the British were to advance over the old battlefields of Flanders—now a mass of desolation—while the Americans were to attack farther east through the Argonne Forest. Both these attacks stalled: Foch was bitterly disappointed as the inexperienced Americans, despite their reckless courage, bogged down in difficulties of transport and supply. But the advance ground slowly on. By early October, the British were taking town after town in Flanders, and the Americans were regaining momentum.

On September 29, Ludendorff's nerve had broken: only an immediate armistice, he told his incredulous emperor, could save Germany now. Five days later, the liberal Prince Max of Baden was appointed chancellor, and the long-delayed democratization of the Reich began.

At this point news began to arrive from other fronts that shook the Germans still further. In mid-September, the Allied army in Greece—quiescent for years—broke out of its Salonika encampments. Under its new commander, Franchet d'Espérey, it quickly overawed Bulgaria, advanced to the liberation of Serbia, and threatened Hungary from the rear. On September 30, Bulgaria concluded a separate armistice, to be followed a month later by Turkey. Franchet d'Espérey—soon to join Joffre and Foch and Pétain in the pantheon of France's marshals—was advancing in triumph to the Danube. The Central Powers' whole Balkan position had collapsed—and worse was to come.

In late October, the Italians at length pulled themselves together and took revenge for Caporetto. Crossing the Piave in force, they defeated the Austrians at Vittorio Veneto. Then came total breakdown. The Austro-Hungarian army dissolved into its component parts, as the different national units struggled to board trains for home, and even the Hungarian minister of war ordered his own troops to lay down their arms. On November 3, Austria signed an armistice. Southern Germany lay open to invasion.

In this desperate situation, the Germans on the Western Front could not hold out for long. By the end of October, although they still stood on French soil, they had only one reserve division left, and overall they were outnumbered by 40 per cent. In less than three months they had lost almost 300,000 prisoners; the remains of thirty-two divisions had simply been broken up.

At home, morale had already cracked. Revolutionary defeatism was sweeping the country. On November 3, the German fleet at Kiel mutinied: refusing to put out to sea on one last great raid, the crews seized control of their ships and of Kiel itself; from here the mutiny spread to the other seaports of northern Germany. Four days later, revolution broke out in Bavaria, which was directly exposed to invasion from the south. On November 8, a German armistice commission met Foch for the first time. The ninth saw the emperor's abdication and the proclamation of a German republic. On the tenth, the emperor fled to the Netherlands. Meantime the German delegation had accepted Foch's armistice terms. On the eleventh hour of the eleventh day of the eleventh month, 1918, the First World War came to an end.

The Balance Sheet

Altogether, between ten and thirteen million men had been killed in the four years and a quarter of the conflict. Germany lost nearly two million, Russia a million and three quarters, France almost a million and a half, the British Empire just under a million. Italian deaths were less than half a million, American just over 100,000. About twenty million in all had been wounded.

A great swath of France lay devastated—some of it, apparently, so blasted that it could never be put under cultivation again. In Germany and Austria, the Allied blockade had taken a fearful toll: Vienna, Berlin, and countless other cities were reaching the last extremities of hunger. In Eastern Europe, millions of civilians were dead or dying: influenza, typhus, cholera—disease raged everywhere. And throughout Central and Eastern Europe social revolution was either enthroned or threatening. For a by-product of the war—and the one with the most far-reaching consequences—had been the Bolshevik Revolution of November, 1917.

Readings

For the gradual militarization of Europe in the years before 1914, see Alfred Vagts, *A History of Militarism: Civilian and Military*, rev. ed. (1959). There are two good one-volume accounts of the war itself, C. R. M. F. Cruttwell, *A History of the Great War, 1914–1918* (1934), and Cyril Falls, *The Great War* (1959). The first gives more detail and is more critical of the high commands; the second is briefer and tries to rescue a few damaged reputations. A longer account which has become a classic is Winston S. Churchill, *The World Crisis, 1911–1918*, 3 vols. (1923–1927). The way the powers blundered into the conflict and its opening battles are narrated in spirited fashion by Barbara W. Tuchman in *The Guns of August* (1962).

For the economics of the war, see Frank P. Chambers, *The War Behind the War 1914–1918* (1939). For the internal politics of the major belligerents, on France there is Jere C. King, *Generals and Politicians* (1951), and on Germany, Hans W. Gatzke, *Germany's Drive to the West* (1950), Henry Cord Meyer, *Mitteleuropa in German Thought and Action* (1955), and J. W. Wheeler-Bennett, *Brest-Litovsk: The Forgotten Peace* (1939).

Three useful biographies, all of them at a high literary level, are Geoffrey Bruun, *Clemenceau* (1943), Thomas Jones, *Lloyd George* (1951), and J. W. Wheeler-Bennett, *Wooden Titan: Hindenburg in Twenty Years of German History* (1936).

The Russian Revolution

Chapter Three

and Its Consequences

I

IDEOLOGY AND THE WAR

At its start the First World War was neither an ideological struggle nor in a real sense a world conflict. It was an old-fashioned European quarrel—the last and greatest of a succession of such quarrels dating back nearly three centuries to the Thirty Years War. Essentially it was fought for national, imperial aims. In the origins of the conflict, ideological goals figured scarcely at all. At the start, at least, the men in the trenches had little sense of fighting to preserve a specific form of government or even a more vaguely realized "way of life." They thought almost solely in national terms. The French and British, for example, felt very simply that they were defending their countries rather than fighting to preserve or extend an abstract principle like democracy. It was only a minority of Italian democrats who, before the United States entered the war, saw the conflict as a struggle of Western democratic society against autocracy and, in consequence, argued that their country should go to the aid of nations whose institutions resembled its own.

This lack of ideology was only natural. The warring coalitions were separated by no clear difference of political principle. The two great democracies, it is true, were fighting alongside each other. But they were also in alliance with tsarist Russia, the most reactionary of the powers. Hence at the start of the war, the Entente had no real ideological cohesion. Its adversaries, rather, were the more closely linked by ideologi-

Last photograph taken of Tsar Nicholas II of Russia before he was killed by revolutionaries while a captive. COURTESY BROWN BROTHERS.

cal ties: both Germany and Austria-Hungary were qualified autocracies or semiparliamentary states. In the ideological spectrum, the Entente occupied the two extremes, and the Central Powers lay somewhere in between. If Russian autocracy could be thought of as canceling out Anglo-French democracy, then there was little to choose between the two coalitions. Indeed certain Germans even argued that it was *they* rather than their adversaries who were fighting for democracy. The German Social Democrats, for example, soothed their Marxist consciences with the claim that by defending their country against Russia they were keeping "Asiatic" despotism out of Central Europe and thus preserving Germany for the democracy that was bound to come.

In the crucial year 1917, all this changed. With the entrance of the United States, the conflict in truth became a *world* war. And with the first Russian Revolution, only a month before, the Entente attained an enviable ideological unity. Now that Italy and America had been added to the coalition—and Russia had cast off its exhausted despotism—five great democracies were ranged in one camp. For a few brief months, this illusion persisted. President Wilson shared it: in his war message to Congress he clearly linked the recent revolution in Russia with the new course on which his own country was embarking. "Does not every American," he asked, "feel that assurance has been added to our hope for the future peace of the world by the wonderful and heartening things that have been happening within the last few weeks in Russia?"

The Bolshevik Revolution destroyed such hopes. Once more the Entente was ideologically riven asunder, as Russia under its new leaders deserted the coalition and proclaimed a novel international role of its own. The brief idyl of Russo-American cooperation was at an end. Ideological competition took its place. Just as the war had been converted into an ideological struggle in 1917 by the two great semi-European powers—Russia and the United States—so the final year of the conflict was to be dominated by the competition between them for the allegiance of the European masses.

The International Opposition

At the start of the war the Socialist parties of Europe forgot their internationalism and rallied to support their countries' war efforts. In France, in Britain, in Germany, the Socialists fell into line almost without a murmur. Everywhere a truce between political parties prevailed: what in France was called the Sacred Union, in Germany took the ancient name of *Burgfrieden*—the peace within the beleaguered fortress. For the first time, moreover, in France and Britain, Socialist ministers entered the government and shared in the direction of the war effort.

This decision did not pass unquestioned. Everywhere there remained a pacifist minority, which was either silenced through party discipline or exiled from party councils. But for the first two years of the war Social-

ists of this opinion were impotent. The tide of patriotic unity was running too strongly against them. In Italy alone, the Socialist party was
to maintain a consistent antiwar stand: first it opposed intervention, and
subsequently, after Italy had joined the Entente, it took a position of
passive nonsupport of its country's war effort.

By the end of 1916, this attitude was beginning to win favor elsewhere.
Socialists and pacifist radicals were coming to have second thoughts
about the war. Not only did the bloody stalemate on the Western Front
seem to make a mockery of the patriotic slogans under which the war
was being fought; the Socialists also began to realize that they had made
a bad bargain by consenting to serve in coalition governments. They
had found that their ministers possessed little real power: they served
chiefly as window dressing, to keep labor at home in line while the conduct of the war remained in conservative and nationalist hands. More
particularly, they had almost no influence on the formulation of war
aims. Hence what had begun as a minority protest within European
Socialism had become, by 1917, something of a mass movement. Through
a series of international congresses, the antiwar Socialists had established
a modest but increasingly effective organizational framework.

The first conference was a small-scale affair. In September, 1915, forty
Socialist delegates met at the little Swiss town of Zimmerwald to draw
up a manifesto calling for peace "without annexations or indemnities."
The initiative came from the Swiss, the Italians, and the Russian Social-
ists in exile, but individual Frenchmen and Germans also were present.
The second conference was larger and more militant in tone: at another
Swiss resort, Kienthal, in April of 1916, the delegates demanded that all
Socialist parties refuse to participate in governments or to vote war
credits.

The internationally minded Socialists planned their largest effort for
the following year. Stockholm, the Swedish capital, was to be the seat
of a much more representative assemblage which would include not
merely the delegates of a pacifist minority but qualified spokesmen of
the official Socialist parties of Britain, France, and Germany. The preparations for the Stockholm conference formed an important part of the
diffused "peace offensive" of the spring and summer of 1917. At this
point, quite naturally, the belligerent governments took alarm. More
particularly the British and French feared that their Socialists would
accept the views of the German Social Democrats and accused the latter
of using the conference to support their own country's peace efforts.
Hence, the Entente governments refused passports for Stockholm. The
conference lost its meaning: when it finally met, in September, 1917, it
was weak and divided.

The denial of passports for the Stockholm conference was a decisive
turning point in the ideological history of the war. It marked the final
alienation of the French and British Left from the war effort, and the
radicalization of both the French Socialists and the British Labor party

as the pacifist minority began to gain ascendancy. In France, it helped to break up the Sacred Union; in Britain, it brought about the resignation of the most prominent Labor minister from the coalition government.

Something similar was happening in Germany but at a very different pace. The internationally minded left wing of the Social Democratic party—disgusted by the conformist attitude of the majority—had split off in April, 1917, to form the Independent Social Democrats (USPD). Their call for a peace without annexations or indemnities found an eager response in a population just emerging from the rigors of the "turnip winter." Indeed, it was partly to compete with the Independents that the other democratic parties in the Reichstag voted the Peace Resolution of July. The Peace Resolution was stillborn; the parties that had voted it lost their enthusiasm for a peace of compromise as the fortunes of war began to favor the German army again, and they even swallowed the conqueror's Treaty of Brest-Litovsk. Once more, the Independent Social Democrats were left as the sole consistent advocates of peace without victory. Only at the very end of the war—when all hope of victory was gone—did the Independents rally the majority Social Democrats to their point of view, and the two emerged together as the spokesmen of Germany in her hour of desperate need.

Wilson versus Lenin

By mid-1917, then, the notion of "peace without victory" was growing popular everywhere. The phrase was originally Wilson's—he had used it in a speech to the Senate in January—and the American president was associated in people's minds with the idea of a settlement in which there would be neither victors nor vanquished. But this was while the United States was still neutral. The American declaration of war changed all that: it brought subtle but decisive alterations in the tone of Wilson's utterances. His appeal was still for a peace of justice, but it was now based on the presupposition of Entente victory. The war must be fought to a finish. International justice was not to be reached through a compromise settlement: it would be *imposed* by the victors on the vanquished.

The need to continue the war limited the force of Wilson's idealistic appeal—except where it could be harnessed to the propaganda of subject nationalities struggling for independence. Wilson was unable to keep Russia in the war. He could do little to reinvigorate the war-weary in Britain and France. The Italian masses continued as disaffected as before. Furthermore Wilson now had a competitor who offered what he did and more—a peace of justice, but an immediate peace and one arrived at through social revolution. This was V. I. Lenin, the Bolshevik leader and, since November, 1917, the master of the Russian state. The competition between the two was not lost on contemporaries. A Swiss writer observed, "It is certain that mankind must make up its mind either for Wilson or for Lenin." [*]

Lenin, as a revolutionist living in exile in Switzerland, had already taken a prominent part in the Zimmerwald and Kienthal conferences. Indeed, he had been partly responsible for the more leftist tone of the Kienthal manifesto. He and a tiny left minority within international socialism kept pressing for an end of caution and an unequivocal demand for a cessation of hostilities. Once back in Russia—helped on his way by the Germans, who correctly foresaw that he would undermine the country's war effort—Lenin was able to put these precepts into practice. Almost the first act of the Bolshevik government was to issue, on the day after its assumption of power, a "Peace Decree" which called on the warring nations to lay down their arms.

To understand this appeal, it is necessary to trace the succession of events in Russia that had brought Lenin and his companions to power.

II
PREREVOLUTIONARY RUSSIA

In 1900, Russia was the only true autocracy left in Europe. The authority of the state did not rest, as in Western Europe, on parliamentary institutions but on a complex, routinized bureaucracy and a potent secret police. Yet it would be wrong to imply that Russia had made no political progress during the previous century. The contrary was true: despite periodic checks and reactions, there had been a slow but steady liberalization. Just after the middle of the century the serfs were freed, and the period immediately following saw the installation of a new judicial system and the establishment of representative institutions on the local level.

At the Imperial Court, however, scarcely anything had changed. Tsar Nicholas II, who ascended the throne in 1894, lived in a world of illusions. Both weak-willed and stubborn, he was surrounded by reactionary advisers and dominated by his superstitious German wife. Into the sickly, hothouse atmosphere of the court, it was impossible for the breath of reality to penetrate.

The Revolution of 1905

Suddenly, revolution broke up this unnatural calm. Touched off by the defeat of Russia in the war of 1904 with Japan, a series of strikes and popular outbreaks in the major cities forced the tsar at last to pay some regard to his people's complaints. This brief revolution revealed how

[*] Quoted in Arno J. Mayer, *Political Origins of the New Diplomacy 1917–1918* (New Haven: Yale University Press, 1959), p. 393.

much Russia had changed in the past decade. Industrialization had come swiftly: a systematic policy of state aid had brought the results that might have been anticipated—large concentrations of "proletarians," sometimes working more than eleven hours a day, and living in the wretched conditions that throughout Europe had uniformly accompanied the first stages of the Industrial Revolution.

Although this new industrial working class had borne the brunt of the revolutionary fighting, it was middle-class liberals who primarily profited from the concessions with which the tsar had calmed the storm. The October Manifesto of 1905 had promised true parliamentary government, with universal manhood suffrage, ministerial responsibility, and a full array of individual liberties. But the actual constitution—or "Fundamental Laws"—of the following May was less liberal. Ministerial responsibility was dropped, and a year later a system of indirect voting replaced equal universal suffrage. As it finally worked out, the parliament, or Duma, was a fairly tame, conservative body, in which the poorer classes of the population were most inadequately represented.

The Policy of Stolypin

In the period from 1907 to 1911, however, the Duma was able to achieve a few constructive results. More specifically it turned its attention to the gap that was now opening between city and countryside in Russian society. The cities were rapidly being modernized; the country remained in its primitive state, hardly touched by change. Indeed, in certain respects the emancipation of the serfs in 1861 had brought a retrogression to an earlier agrarian order. Specifically, it had extended a traditional institution, the *mir*—a peasant commune controlling the village land and periodically reassigning it among the individual families. A large landowner, if he happened to be enlightened, could modernize his estate and make it an economic enterprise. A community of freed serfs was trapped in the old routines and old methods of cultivation.

Now the Duma majority which followed the lead of the vigorous, somber prime minister, Peter Stolypin, proposed to modernize Russian agriculture by permitting individual peasants to leave the *mir* and establish their own farms. Stolypin hoped in this fashion to build up a class of self-reliant landholding peasants who would support the Russian state much as a similar class had proved to be a prop to the French Republic. Hence, he systematically favored the peasants who wanted to contract out of the *mir;* in the decade 1907–1917 more than two million households availed themselves of this opportunity.

The social effects of Stolypin's agrarian reform have been much debated. Some declare that it produced excellent results and that if Russia had only had a decade or so more of peace, it would have developed into a modern democracy. Others stress that this policy increased social antagonisms in the countryside by widening the gap between rich and poor. One thing, however, is certain: as the Bolsheviks were eventually to discover, small-scale peasant farming was no answer to Russia's needs; only a system of large-scale cultivation could provide an adequate food supply for the newly swollen population of the cities.

With Stolypin's assassination in 1911, the era of reform came to an end. The three years preceding the outbreak of war were a period of drift and of an ominous false calm.

The Revolutionary Parties:
Social Revolutionaries and Bolsheviks

The leading parties in the Duma were the moderate Octobrists—who accepted the reforms of 1905–1906—and the more progressive-minded Constitutional Democrats, or Cadets. Both were respectable middle-class parties; the distinction between them corresponded roughly to the Western Europe cleavage between liberals and radicals.

Both, however, lacked adequate contact with reality, for they thought in terms that were only partially applicable to Russia's actual situation. They had the attitudes of nineteenth-century Western European reformers and were convinced that the institutions which had proved their worth in Britain or France would work equally well in Russia. But Russia in the period just preceding the war was still very different from Western Europe: most of its population lived in pre-nineteenth-century conditions; the rest was being hustled into the twentieth century at a dizzying pace. In this respect, Russia in 1917 resembled the countries of Asia today. There was old traditionalist order on the one hand; on the other, the new order of forced industrialization based on monopoly and state favors. Between the two, free-enterprise capitalism scarcely existed. This, of course, was the form of economy that had provided the basis for Western European liberalism and radicalism in the nineteenth century. Without it, the corresponding parties in Russia lacked adequate support. The deeper longings of the Russian people were expressed in the traditional, mystical worship of "Holy Russia" and the tsar and newer doctrines of social overturn and revolutionary violence.

The Social Revolutionaries constituted the strongest party in Russia in 1917. They were distinctively Russian—they had no. Western European counterpart. Their formal organization dated only from 1901, but their origins extended deep into the nineteenth century—to the terrorists of the 1880's, and beyond them, to the *narodniki*, the idealistic intellectuals of the previous decade, who hoped that by "going to the people" they might share and improve the lot of the peasants. The Social Revolutionaries spoke for the rural masses: this association was a source both of strength and of incoherence. As a peasant party, they had by far the largest potential following in Russia, but their peasant affiliation also accounted for their tumultuousness and lack of a clear program. In these failings, the Social Revolutionaries accurately reflected the political inexperience of their constituents. Perhaps the only coherent proposal they made was summed up in the slogan, "the land to the peasants." This

apparently simple goal was susceptible to the most varying interpretations, and the consequent misunderstanding between the right and the
left wings of the Social Revolutionaries was to prove decisive in the
weeks immediately following the Bolshevik seizure of power.

The other revolutionary party, the Social Democrats, was split by a
far deeper division that by 1917 had made them in effect two separate
parties. The Russian Social Democrats were an offshoot of the Marxist
socialism of Western and Central Europe. In theory, they were just another European Socialist party, but in fact they were very different from
their Western counterparts. Three peculiarities of the Russian situation
had given them a highly eccentric character.

First, since late nineteenth-century Russia was a police autocracy rather
than a constitutional state, it was difficult for the Russian Social Democrats
to evolve toward democratic, legalist methods as most of the Western
European parties either had done or were about to do. With the electoral road to power cut off, their very situation condemned them to conspiracy and subversion. They renounced assassination as a weapon—they
thought it childish—but although they castigated the Social Revolutionaries as terrorists, they shared with them a propensity for constant and
feverish plotting.

Second, until the late 1890's, Russia had almost no industrial proletariat. In the seedtime of Marxist ideas in Russia, the prerequisites for a
working-class movement were almost entirely lacking. At its inception
Russian Social Democracy was an affair of the intellectuals, who were
quite free to spin complex webs of theory, untroubled by a mass base or
a responsible trade-union movement.

About 1900, this situation changed radically. An urban working class
appeared, and alongside it the social evils that go with rapid industrialization. But the new Russian working class also was somewhat different
from the corresponding social category in the West. It had no strong
craft or artisan tradition to give it a conservative bent. It consisted rather
of uprooted peasants, whose patterns of thinking inclined them rather toward inarticulate protest and revolutionary violence than disciplined
trade-union activity.

Along with this new social situation appeared the third great anomaly
of the Russian scene: the towering figure of Lenin. Vladimir Ilyich
Ulyanov—to use his real name rather than his revolutionary pen name
—was something new in the world, a "professional trained revolutionist,
who marshaled his troops with the science of a general, backed his procedure with the learning of a scholar, and kept up the standards and
discipline of his calling with the stringency of a Medical Association." *
The son of an ennobled director of schools, Lenin had passed a serious,
scholarly, idealistic youth. Shocked by the death of his elder brother,
who had been hanged for terrorist activities, he had turned to Marxist

* Edmund Wilson, *To the Finland Station* (Garden City, N.Y.: Doubleday & Company, 1940), p. 396.

studies and to revolutionary propaganda. As nearly always occurred in such cases, he had been caught by the police and exiled to a desolate place in Siberia. He passed his three years there in study, in writing, in plotting. He was only thirty when he emerged in 1900, but he was already a seasoned revolutionist, prepared to challenge the older leaders of the party in a ruthless struggle for power.

Three years later Lenin nearly succeeded. At the 1903 congress of the Russian Social Democratic party, held abroad, first in Brussels and subsequently in London, Lenin temporarily won over a majority to his point of view. He and his followers forced through a party constitution providing for a tight, disciplined organization. From this point on the Leninists within the Russian Social Democratic party called themselves Bolsheviks—from the Russian word for *majority*. Their opponents naturally came to be called the Mensheviks—the *minority*. Actually the position of the two factions was soon reversed. Lenin's opponents regained their predominance, and they kept it right down to the outbreak of the war. But Lenin, with his characteristic tenacity, refused to give up the Bolshevik label: he fully appreciated the psychological advantage that the term *majority* gave him.

In reality, Lenin cared almost nothing for majorities. His mind was severely practical: although he was a master of the subtleties of Marxist theory, he was interested in such abstractions only when they could be used to further his own program. And this program was very simple: to build up in Russia a Marxist party that would be radically different from the tolerant, legalist Socialist parties of the West—a new type of party dedicated solely to revolution. Lenin knew that economic conditions in Russia contradicted all Marxist principles: in terms of orthodox theory, his own country, whose industrialization was just beginning, was not "ripe" for a socialist revolution. But that did not trouble him. He was convinced that by organizing around himself a tight core of professional, trained revolutionists, who would look to him alone for guidance, he could eventually succeed.

And so he bullied and browbeat his party comrades into submission, dominating them, as one complained, by literally *living* the revolution twenty-four hours a day. Nearly all these followers were intellectuals: no one else had time or desire to lead the stern existence that Lenin demanded of them. But for such people, the Bolshevik way of life often had a deep appeal: it accorded with the yearning for conspiracy and self-dedication that had been characteristic of the Russian intelligentsia during the whole latter half of the past century.

By 1914, however, Lenin's faction had fallen on evil days. By his insistence on iron discipline, he had in effect split the party into its two constituent parts. In Russia itself—both in the Duma and in the trade unions—the Mensheviks were by far the stronger of the two; already legalist by inclination, they were rapidly turning themselves into a regular Social Democratic party on the Western model. In contrast, the Bolsheviks were almost powerless. They had become the laughingstock of the Duma when their chief spokesman there was discovered to be a police agent; they were literally reduced to highway robbery to obtain funds; and only a few leaders remained who were neither in exile nor alienated by Lenin's autocratic control—among them the faithful but intellectually limited Georgian who had just chosen the revolutionary nickname of Stalin. Lenin himself was in Switzerland, consumed by frustration at his own impotence. At home, he was still almost unknown. If a popular hero did exist, it was not Lenin but Trotsky—a dynamic, driving, imaginative figure who refused to join either the Bolshevik or the Menshevik faction. As a very young man, the eloquent Trotsky had become the popular tribune of the Revolution of 1905, in which Lenin had played scarcely any part.

One of the reasons for Lenin's triumph in November, 1917, was to be his dramatic alliance with Trotsky. But that could come about only after the miseries of war had reduced Russia to a state in which even a tiny revolutionary faction like the Bolsheviks had a chance for success, if only it were sufficiently determined in its bid for power.

Russia at War

Russia succumbed to war weariness earlier than any of the other belligerent powers. The country's primitive economy could not support a long war: even food ran short as the transport system proved completely inadequate. Under the best and most efficient of governments, Russia would have had a bitter struggle to survive. Under the government it had, the country's war effort was doomed from the start.

In the supply of war materials, corruption and profiteering were commonplace. At court, pro-German sentiments were openly paraded: the tsarina herself encouraged them. And she in turn fell under the spell of a disreputable faith healer, Gregory Rasputin, whose influence with the imperial family became a public scandal. In December, 1916, a group of conservative nobles murdered Rasputin, but his death made no more real change than had the tsar's action of the previous year in assuming military command. Nothing apparently could stop the drift to economic and psychological collapse.

The failure of Brussilov's offensive in the summer of 1916 destroyed what was left of military morale. The terrible winter of 1916–1917 did the rest. By the spring of 1917, the Russian people had had enough.

III

FROM THE MARCH TO THE NOVEMBER REVOLUTION

The first of the two Russian revolutions of 1917—the March revolution —was both incoherent and incomplete. Its basic causes were war weariness and distrust of the pro-German faction in the government and the

Imperial Court. More immediately, what toppled the tsarist regime was a series of almost spontaneous strikes and riots in Petrograd, climaxed by a mutiny of the troops garrisoning the capital. In these events, the revolutionary parties played almost no part. If any group had guided and canalized the agitation, it had been the constitutional parties in the Duma, the Octobrists and the Cadets. Hence, it was logical that these should predominate in the provisional government formed on March 12.

Four days later, with a double abdication by the tsar and his brother, the Romanov dynasty disappeared. Russia thus ceased to be a monarchy; its future regime was left open, pending the election of a constituent assembly. Abroad, most people in the Entente camp agreed with President Wilson; they assumed that Russia was now firmly set on a liberal, constitutional course—that it had become a middle-class democracy like its great Western allies. But this was far from the truth. The March revolution had settled nothing.

The Provisional Government and the Soviets

For eight months, the provisional government struggled to rule Russia. At the end of that time it was overthrown by the Bolsheviks with absurd ease. The explanation of this failure is simple—the provisional government had not done the two things for which the people were clamoring: it had not taken Russia out of the war, and it had not satisfied the land hunger of the peasantry.

Lenin, with his relentless logic, had grasped almost from the start that these would be the two crucial issues. On his return from exile in April, he immediately set about to exploit the difficulties with which the provisional government was contending. He did not wait a moment: the very night of his arrival at the Finland station in Petrograd he explained to the cheering throng that greeted him the substance of his "April Theses": immediate peace, the nationalization of the land, and all power to the soviets of workers' deputies.

These soviets were the great novelty of the Russian revolutions. Their name was the Russian word for *council*, and that is what they were—informal bodies speaking for the urban workers, and in some localities, for the peasants and soldiers also. They had originated—almost spontaneously—in the tumults of 1905 and had left behind them a popular revolutionary memory. Hence, it was natural that they should be revived in 1917. This time, however, their role was much extended. Shortly after the March revolution, the chief of them, the Petrograd Soviet, began to act as a shadow government, paralleling and challenging the acts of the provisional government itself.

Within the soviets, the Bolsheviks were only a minority: both the Mensheviks and the Social Revolutionaries were stronger. But Lenin correctly surmised that this situation might be only temporary. If the Bolsheviks offered a program with sufficient revolutionary appeal, they could gradually infiltrate the soviets and gain control over them. Thus they would finally have in their hands the sort of weapon they had always lacked before: truly popular bodies that would capture the imagination of the urban masses. Lenin, therefore, set out to win over the majority in the local soviets. He outflanked the Social Revolutionaries by stealing their agrarian program: land for the peasants. The Mensheviks, and even his own followers, he astounded and disconcerted by calling for a second, or proletarian, revolution. Before Lenin's arrival, Russian Marxists of both varieties had been following a cautious, orthodox course. They had accepted the "bourgeois" revolution that had already occurred and had agreed to wait for the long-term ripening of economic conditions before launching a second revolution. This, Lenin sharply told them, would not do. The second revolution must come at once.

Above all, Lenin outmaneuvered everybody on the issue of peace. He alone declared in unequivocal terms that the Russian army should lay down its arms immediately. With this demand, he hit the provisional government at its weakest point. For with each month that passed, it became more evident that the country would not follow its new leaders in their policy of continuing the war on the side of the Entente.

By May, the war issue had already caused a shift in the provisional government toward the left. The outstanding figure in the old ministry —Professor Paul Milyukov, leader of the Cadets and minister of foreign affairs—was obliged to resign. Milyukov had been the chief spokesman for the policy of loyalty to the Entente, and his departure clearly signified the failure of this course. The new government included two Social Revolutionaries and two Mensheviks. Initially this seemed to give them an advantage over their Bolshevik rivals, but events proved just the opposite: the two more moderate left parties steadily lost ground through their involvement in the continued unpopularity of the provisional government.

This was particularly true of the leading figure in the reorganized ministry, the right-wing Social Revolutionary Alexander Kerensky. Kerensky was even younger than Lenin and Trotsky and, like them, a dynamic organizer and forceful orator. But, as minister of war and later prime minister, he had the misfortune to represent in the popular mind the policy of continuing the war, and it was this association that eventually destroyed him. The new ministry had tried to moderate the war policy as much as it could: it had declared for a peace without annexations or indemnities. But in the summer of 1917 it was proving impossible to get the warring nations to agree on such a solution. All peace efforts had failed, or were about to fail. Kerensky was vainly trying to steer a compromise course between Milyukov's loyalty to the Allies and Lenin's demand for a separate peace with the Central Powers.

Thus with the failure in early July of Kerensky's last despairing offensive on the Galician front, the provisional government began a slow decline. Ten days later, the Bolsheviks—reinforced by the adhesion of Trotsky, whose revolutionary militancy now coincided almost exactly with Lenin's program—made their first attempt to seize power. It came too early. The provisional government crushed it, and Lenin was obliged to take refuge in Finland. In the succeeding weeks, however, Kerensky's difficulties increased: his government could reach no decision on the crucial question of land reform, and the peasants in consequence began to take matters into their own hands; still worse, a right-wing military conspiracy forced Kerensky to turn to the Bolsheviks for support; in the field, the armies were breaking up as the soldiers drifted back to their homes; in the factories and in the Petrograd garrison, Bolshevik propaganda was steadily winning converts.

By October, the Bolsheviks had a majority in the Petrograd Soviet. Trotsky was elected its new chairman. The time had come, Lenin decided, for the supreme bid for power.

The Bolshevik Revolution

The revolution was almost bloodless. In late October, the Bolshevik leaders had organized themselves as a "military-revolutionary committee" to coordinate preparations for the rising. On the appointed day— the early morning of November 7—the revolutionary forces of soldiers, sailors, and Red Guards carried out their assignments with speed and precision. Seizing the key points of the capital city, they imprisoned or drove to flight the members of the provisional government. By afternoon, Lenin was able to announce victory to a meeting of the Petrograd Soviet. In the evening, the second All-Russian Congress of Soviets—with whose meeting the revolution had been timed to coincide—received full power from the Petrograd Soviet, which it delegated in turn to the local soviets of workers', soldiers', and peasants' deputies.

Before adjourning, the congress did two further things: it issued its basic orders, the Peace Decree, already mentioned, and the Decree on the Land, to satisfy at last the clamor of the peasantry; and it appointed a Council of People's Commissars to govern the state.

Thus informally did the new *de facto* constitution of Russia come into effect. In theory, Lenin had done what he had promised: he had won all power for the soviets—the shadow government had become the real government. In fact, something rather different had occurred. The Bolshevik leaders, in their new guise of people's commissars, had seized power for themselves. They subsequently accepted certain left-wing Social Revolutionaries as associates, but final authority continued to rest with Lenin, Trotsky, and their party colleagues. The party dictatorship had been established that has ruled Russia ever since. In no sense could the Bolsheviks be said to speak for the Russian people. Although they had won a majority in the Petrograd Soviet, in the local soviets they were still outnumbered. This was to become abundantly clear with the long-deferred elections to the Constituent Assembly.

The election of an assembly to draw up a new constitution was a customary liberal-democratic device in countries that had just undergone a revolution. It had occurred at least three times in France, and throughout Western Europe it had provided the traditional method for giving legal sanction to a revolutionary change of regime. Hence it was natural that the provisional government—whose inspiration was liberal-democratic and Western—should have followed this same procedure. But it had postponed calling the elections, and the date it finally set fell two and a half weeks after the Bolshevik seizure of power. Thus the elections were held in a setting quite different from that in which they had been planned. They were held under an authority that was no longer liberal-democratic, but rather represented a disciplined, fanatical minority that openly scorned the principle of majority rule.

The elections produced, as might have been expected, a clear majority for the Social Revolutionaries. The Bolsheviks obtained slightly less than a quarter of the seats. The Mensheviks and the Cadets figured scarcely at all. These results obviously embarrassed the new rulers of the Russian state. The popular verdict was difficult to explain away. But Lenin, always fertile in expedients, found a suitable subterfuge. The Social Revolutionaries, he explained, no longer existed as a party. By throwing in their lot with the Bolsheviks, the left-wing Social Revolutionaries had in effect dissolved their party. "The people," Lenin triumphantly concluded, "voted for a party which no longer existed."

When the assembly met in mid-January, then, its proceedings unfolded in a world of unreality. It elected a president and engaged in a desultory debate. But as soon as the Bolshevik deputies found themselves outvoted, they simply walked out, followed after a little while by the left Social Revolutionaries. At this point, the Bolshevik high command decided to shut down the assembly. "The sailor in command of the military guard . . . announced to the president of the assembly that he had received instructions to close the meeting 'because the guard is tired.'" *

Thus ended the brief and foredoomed experiment in Western constitutional government. The third All-Russian Congress of Soviets, which the Bolsheviks were now able to dominate, assumed the functions of the Constituent Assembly. The Bolshevik dictatorship had come to stay.

* Edward Hallett Carr, *The Bolshevik Revolution 1917–1923*, I (New York: The Macmillan Company, 1950), 112, 119.

Its power, however, was not to be consolidated for more than three years. From December, 1917, until November, 1920, the Bolshevik regime was engaged in a life-and-death struggle for its very existence.

At first, the new revolution encountered a stunned acceptance. People had suffered too much to be prepared to take up arms once again; and the transfer of power to the local soviets frequently did not mean much of a change, since in the larger cities, these had already been exercising a *de facto* authority. In the more remote districts, moreover, the change of regime in Petrograd made scarcely any difference: communications had so deteriorated that the central government was physically unable to make its will prevail. Many country people continued to live their lives almost as if nothing had happened.

In no sense, then, did Russia leap from capitalism to socialism overnight. On the contrary, the new rulers of the country were perplexed to know what to do with their power. In putting socialism into practice, they had almost no precepts to guide them. Marx had scorned this sort of planning as "utopian," and even the more practical-minded Lenin had focused his attention so exclusively on how to seize power that he had hardly had time to think about what should be done with that power once it was in revolutionary hands. The first acts of the new Council of People's Commissars bore all the marks of haste and improvisation.

Peace and land reform were the first and easiest matters to deal with. The two original decrees of the All-Russian Congress of Soviets had already established the broad outlines of future settlement. With the Central Powers, Lenin and his colleagues eventually signed the humiliating and ruinous Treaty of Brest-Litovsk. So far as the land was concerned, the original decree, by abolishing private property, in effect invited the peasants to seize it from their landlords—thus ratifying a process that had actually been going on for several weeks. A subsequent decree of February, 1918, tidied up this procedure by reserving title to the state. But the peasants had actual possession of the land, and they simply divided it up among themselves. The method of partition varied from area to area: where the Social Revolutionaries predominated in the local soviets, the criterion tended to be capacity to work the land—which favored the more prosperous peasants; in Bolshevik areas, it tended to be the number of mouths to feed in each family, a procedure obviously devised to win favor with the poor and the landless.

So far as other branches of the economy went, the Bolsheviks were hesitant in the extreme. In general, they seem to have assumed that major enterprises would continue under their old management, with no more than a general supervision to assure that they were run in the people's interest. Only when certain branches of industry proved recalcitrant did the government resort to nationalization. In these cases, the Bolshevik leaders soon got themselves into further difficulties, for it was not clear whether the factories in question should be run by the workers themselves—which seemed the more popular course—or by professional managers—which was obviously more efficient. Not until June, 1918, and under the threat of massive German penetration of the Russian economy, did the Council of People's Commissars finally decree the nationalization of basic industry.

The Generals in Arms: Allied Intervention

In the meantime, a number of tsarist military leaders had taken arms against the new regime. To the south—in the Ukraine and in the Caucasus—the revolt was led at the start by General Kaledin and subsequently by General Denikin and Baron Wrangel; in White Russia and the Baltic region, General Yudenich threatened Petrograd; and in Siberia, Admiral Kolchak, the most persistent of the insurgent military chiefs, proclaimed himself "Supreme Ruler of Russia" and eventually succeeded in dominating most of the country east of the Ural Mountains.

For three years, the Bolshevik government strove desperately to ward off these multiple threats. Time after time, it seemed that the new regime was about to succumb. For no sooner was one general beaten in one part of the country than another raised the standard of revolt many hundred miles away. Month after month, the battles ebbed and flowed in a crazy tangle of local engagements. At the height of the civil war, the authority of the central government extended no farther than old Muscovy, the region surrounding the major cities of Moscow and Petrograd. Still the Soviet regime managed to hold on. In November, 1920, with the final defeat of Baron Wrangel, the Bolsheviks had won the civil war.

What accounts for this surprising victory by a regime that seemed to have almost nothing in its favor? How is the Bolshevik success to be explained? First, by the genius of Trotsky: as commissar of war, the dynamic revolutionary leader transformed himself into a military figure; by skillfully combining the enthusiasm of proletarian volunteers with the indispensable technical knowledge of former tsarist officers, Trotsky created a new Red Army. Secondly, the lack of coordination among the insurgent generals worked in the Bolsheviks' favor: each was thoroughly independent and jealous of the authority of his rivals; moreover, all of them were operating at long distances from each other on the periphery of the vast Russian landmass, while the Red Army, through its control of the center of the country, had the advantage of internal lines of communication.

In addition to these technical considerations, the Bolsheviks had the intangible asset of appearing to be on the "people's" side. Initially, the balance of popular appeal had been more equal: a number of the insurgent chiefs had taken a moderate stand and had promised to restore the constitutional liberties that the Bolsheviks had violated. But as fighting continued and atrocities multiplied on both sides, hatred and bitterness produced an impassable gulf between them. The generals and the "White" armies they commanded became associated in the public mind with a restoration of the old regime. In the areas they controlled they behaved at least as despotically as the Bolsheviks. The decisive factor, however, was the conviction among the peasants that a White victory would mean abrogation of the revolutionary land settlement.

Finally, the White generals were also associated with foreign intervention—with the Germans in the Baltic States, with the British in the northern ports, and with the Japanese around Vladivostok on the Pacific. The German armies had lingered on after the Peace of Brest-Litovsk to exploit their newly formed dependent states. The Japanese were fishing in troubled waters in the hope of territorial gain. The British purpose in Russia was less clear. The protection of military supplies was the official explanation, but it was also apparent that ideological considerations were involved. The Western Allied governments detested the Bolshevik regime and wanted to help overthrow it. They gave both material aid and moral encouragement to the White generals. But they went about it in a blundering and hesitant fashion. The British expeditionary force in Russia was not on a sufficient scale to accomplish anything; it was withdrawn in the autumn of 1919 after the Labor party in Parliament had exposed its absurdities. Yet it had stayed long enough to give the Russians a permanent distaste for foreign armies and for those who associated with them, and it had cast the Bolsheviks in the novel and paradoxical role of patriotic defenders of the motherland.

Dictatorship, Terror, War Communism

The experience of civil war immeasurably strengthened the trend toward party dictatorship. On December 20, 1917, a week and a half after the fighting began, the Council of People's Commissars set up a special body called the Cheka (later renamed GPU) to combat "counterrevolution and sabotage." Thus was founded the secret police that was to play so prominent a role in subsequent Soviet history. The following July, the left Social Revolutionaries followed their right-wing party colleagues into the limbo that had swallowed up the Mensheviks and the constitutional parties. On a charge of terrorist and treasonable activities, the leaders of the left Social Revolutionaries were arrested and their newspapers suppressed. This act ended the fiction of a coalition government. The same Congress of Soviets that had suppressed the Social Revolutionaries concluded its labors by approving a constitution which in effect sanctioned the rule of a single party, whose committees paralleled and gradually came to dominate the regular organs of the state.

A week later, the tsar and his family were shot, and in the month of

August, Lenin himself gave orders for "an unsparing mass terror." Thereafter, although a few oases of liberty remained, opponents of the regime lived a precarious and harassed existence and left the country in wave after wave. While Lenin lived there was always a brake on the worst excesses of police terror. But the institutions had already been founded that were to make it a major weapon of state policy after his death.

The same was true in the economic realm. The necessities of civil war greatly accelerated the process of collectivization and dictatorial control. This was particularly true of labor and the peasantry. Urban workers were subjected to a "militarization" policy that enrolled them in labor battalions. The peasants had to submit to forced requisitions by workers' detachments and "committees of the poor." Only by such drastic means were the Bolsheviks able to keep the economy functioning at all and to provide the cities and the Red Army with a minimum ration of food.

Such were the desperate expedients of what came to be called *war communism*. In rough and brutal fashion, war communism may have accomplished something: it may have staved off the very worst. But it was no better than a jumble of emergency improvisations. It bore as little resemblance to socialist theory as it did to laissez faire capitalism. When the smoke of the civil war had cleared, Lenin and his colleagues found themselves obliged to reformulate their economic policies almost from scratch.

If Russia had been exhausted in 1917, at the end of 1920 it was prostrate. The three years of civil war had been still worse than the corresponding period of international war. Wide stretches of the land lay desolate; communications were disrupted everywhere. Industrial producation had fallen to only 16 per cent of its 1912 level. Still worse, the prerequisities for recovery were lacking: the larger cities had lost more than a third of their population as urban workers dispersed to the countryside in search of food. Regular trade had almost ceased to exist: what exchange of goods there was largely depended on "bagmen" who, like the peddlers of old, went between farm and town carrying on their backs the precious goods that brought exorbitant prices. The official channels of trade were empty: since industrial products scarcely existed, the peasants saw no point in bringing their crops to market. Meanwhile, tens of thousands of disbanded soldiers were roving the countryside in search of food. The Russian economy was caught in a series of vicious circles from which no escape seemed possible. Both people and government were too crushed and weary to find any way out of the morass.

Two events of 1921 revealed the urgent need for drastic action. In March there was a mutiny of the sailors of the Kronstadt naval base near Petrograd. The very units whose aid had been so important in the success of the November revolution now turned against the regime they had helped to install; among their grievances figured a plea for a more understanding treatment of the peasantry. That spring and summer, for the second successive year, there was a drought in the Volga Basin. The wheat crop failed; starvation took a dreadful toll. For the next two years eastern and southern Russia lay in the grip of a great famine in which three million people perished.

Gradually it became clear that the peasant was the key to the situation. The peasantry—whom Marxist theory had always neglected—was the only force which could possibly break through the vicious circle. As Lenin put it to the tenth congress of his own party: "Only an agreement with the peasantry can save the socialist revolution in Russia."

The Pacification:
NEP and the Nationalities Settlement

Thus the core of the New Economic Policy (NEP), which Lenin launched in March, 1921, was an effort to conciliate the peasantry. It aimed to start the economy moving by providing inducements for the peasants to bring their crops to market. And the only way to achieve this end that the Bolshevik leaders could see was restoring many aspects of a capitalist economy. Not only did the peasants receive the right to dispose of their surplus crops as they chose. The "Fundamental Law" of May, 1922, also gave them security in land tenure: both private property in land and the old village community or *mir*—plus a number of mixed or intermediate types of tenure—received official sanction; and in addition, peasants were permitted to sell or lease their land and to hire labor to work it, just as they desired.

Similarly in the commercial field, private enterprise won official recognition. What a later generation was to call the *black market* now became a legal market. The disreputable "bagmen" of the civil war period transformed themselves into "Nepmen," who soon grew prosperous and respectable as they started trade flowing again. In industry, small private enterprise enjoyed an equal freedom; recovery started earlier here than in the large industries, which remained nationalized. Even in the field of finance, capitalist principles prevailed, as the foundation of a new state bank, or "Gosbank," restored orthodoxy in financial practice, and the issue of a new unit of currency brought a galloping inflation to an end.

The retreat from socialism seemed complete. But the Bolshevik rulers of Russia had not changed their purpose: they had merely improvised once more to meet a desperate emergency. Lenin assured his party followers that it was sometimes necessary to take one step back in order to advance two steps forward. Furthermore, the economic structure of the revolution had not been completely dismantled. What Lenin called the "commanding heights" of the economy—heavy industry, the transport system, foreign trade—remained in state hands. Socialism was still no more than a distant mirage. But the *prerequisites* for a socialist policy had been retained. The implications of this situation of socialism held in reserve were not to become apparent until seven years after the institution of NEP, when Lenin's successor, now politically and economically secure, launched a decade of heroic and brutal effort to transform the Russian economy from top to bottom, and thus at last to make the real and decisive break with the past.

In July, 1923, two years after NEP began, another official action completed the pacification of the country: the provision of a constitution for the Russian state, now renamed the Union of Soviet Socialist Republics (USSR). With it, the internal nationalities question found the solution that in substance has been maintained ever since.

The nationalities problem put the Bolsheviks in a most embarrassing position. In theory, Lenin and his colleagues believed in complete self-determination for subject peoples. Immediately after the November revolution, it seemed likely that the nationalities would be left free to go their own way, and that Russia would be reduced in size to the two-thirds of its area where roughly half the people spoke the Great Russian language. And this in fact happened in the western borderlands. First as subject states dependent on Germany, subsequently as new nations protected by the victorious Allies, Finland and Poland and the three Baltic states of Lithuania, Latvia, and Estonia won complete independence.

But when subject peoples farther east tried to do the same thing— when the Ukrainians and the three main nationalities of the Transcaucasus * also declared themselves free—the Bolsheviks reconsidered their position. They cast aside doctrinaire principles and began to think and act as rulers of the Russian state. In fact if not in public profession, they set about reconquering the formerly subject peoples. The victory of the Red Army over the Whites in the civil war was also a victory of the Great Russians over all the minor nationalities.

For two years thereafter, the relation of these non-Russian territories to the central government remained unclear. Obviously it was impossible to restore the old situation of bureaucratic or quasi-colonial control. Yet the grant of full autonomy to non-Russians would mean a renewed threat of secession. In this dilemma, Lenin—disregarding the advice of his specialist on nationality problems, the russified Georgian Stalin— produced an astute solution: a federal state. On paper, its constitution resembled that of the United States or Switzerland: a Council of Nationalities, in which the constituent republics had equal representation, balanced the Council of the Union, in which representation was based on population. In reality, however, the new Soviet constitution stood closer

* Georgians, Armenians, Azerbaijani Turks.

to that of imperial Germany. In the Soviet Union, as in the German Reich, one single state had more weight than all the others put together.

This dominant state, of course, was the Russian Republic (RSFSR), which included most of European Russia and Siberia too. Its capital was the same as that of the Union: since 1918, the old metropolis of Moscow. Its government departments and leading personnel tended to overlap and blend with the corresponding administrative organs and individuals in the Union. Furthermore, the Russian Republic was itself a federation within a federation: its smaller nationalities were not set up as constituent states of the Soviet Union; they enjoyed more limited rights as autonomous republics or areas within the RSFSR. When the Soviet Union was founded, only three major republics were granted even technical parity with the Russian Republic—the Transcaucasian, the White Russian, and the Ukrainian.

Of these, the last was by far the most important. The largest of the former subject nationalities, indeed the second most numerous of all the Slavic peoples, the thirty million Ukrainians offered the great riddle of Eastern Europe. Were they a true nationality and so deserving of independent status? Or were they simply an intermediate people, caught between the Poles and the Russians under whose successive rule they had passed their whole modern history? The Ukraine was far from being a clear national unit. Its language closely resembled Great Russian. Its urban working class was largely of Great Russian origin. The dominant political sentiment among its peasantry frequently seemed to be nothing more than a murderous hatred of its vast Jewish minority. Only its educated bourgeoisie had been much affected by the nationalist teaching of its professors. Thus the Bolsheviks could offer all sorts of explanations for denying independence to the Ukraine. Beyond these national considerations, however, the new rulers of Russia found compelling realistic reasons for keeping the Ukraine at all costs: as the richest area of the Union in agricultural and industrial resources, it seemed essential to the very survival of the Soviet state.

The settlement of 1923 proved far from satisfactory to millions of Ukrainians. Elsewhere in the Union—in the formerly colonial areas of the Transcaucasus and Central Asia—Soviet rule could bring visibly beneficial effects in the form of modernization and social equality. The Ukraine, however, as an area that was *already* among the most advanced, stood to gain little from the new regime. Hence it was natural that the Ukraine should be the focus of discontent among the nationalities during the whole interwar era.

The 1923 constitution—like so many Soviet institutions of this period—was still subject to change. But like the other post-civil war acts of settlement, it served to give the Bolshevik regime a breathing space, a pause for consolidation in a Europe where revolutionary hopes had been disappointed everywhere and which was now hardening into an attitude of unreserved hostility toward the whole Soviet experiment.

V

THE INTERNATIONAL FAILURE

The Bolshevik leaders had never imagined that at the end of six years in power they would find themselves isolated in a hostile world. They had assumed that the revolution would spread to other parts of Europe. Moreover, they took it as axiomatic that unless the revolution triumphed in at least one of the advanced industrial states of Western and Central Europe, it could not possibly survive in Russia. Their expectations proved wrong on two counts: the revolution failed to spread to the countries that were "ripe" for it, and it entrenched itself in Russia, where on all theoretical counts it should not have been able to survive at all.

These are facts that tend to be forgotten today. Communism has come to be thought of almost exclusively as an ideology of Russian origin. So closely is Bolshevism or communism associated with Russia that it no longer seems strange for the two to have come together, and it is difficult to imagine how their history could possibly have been different.

Had the Bolshevik Revolution never occurred, communism would still almost certainly have come into existence both as an ideology and as an international movement. The name *communist* had long been in common use on the left wing of international Social Democracy; as a fighting label, it evoked memories of Marx's original *Manifesto* published in 1848. The differences between the dominant Right and the revolutionary Left within the Second International were already so great, even before 1914, that a secession of the minority might well have occurred even without the experience of war and revolution.

It was this left wing which throughout Western and Central Europe rallied to the support of the Bolshevik experiment and sought to imitate it elsewhere. It was this faction which reconstituted itself as international communism. But the fact that Russia was the only country in which the revolution was successful gave the whole movement a new orientation. By making Russian dominance almost inevitable, it changed the character of communism, placing on it the stamp that it has borne to this day.

The Third International

The wartime revival of international socialism which had found expression in the Zimmerwald, Kienthal, and Stockholm conferences at first seemed to play into the hands of the Bolshevik leaders. The wave of war weariness that was everywhere driving Socialists toward the left apparently put Lenin in an excellent strategic position. By a systematic appeal to the yearning for peace, the Bolsheviks hoped to lead the European masses toward general revolution and social overturn. In this fashion, they believed, the axis of the movement would be displaced farther west, where it would come to rest at last on a secure proletarian base.

Thus it would lose its eccentric Russian character and settle down where
it belonged—in the advanced industrial society of Western and Central Europe.

In this international viewpoint, in this subordination of Russian interests to the revolutionary needs of Europe as a whole, the original Bolshevik leaders were quite sincere. By experience and sympathy, they were internationalists: they had lived long years of exile abroad, they knew foreign languages, they were intimately acquainted with their ideological partners in other countries. Among them Stalin alone—a most significant exception—was provincially Russian and had scarcely traveled. The rest would almost certainly have concurred in shifting the headquarters of the revolutionary forces farther west—perhaps to Berlin —if circumstances had permitted; they would have been happy to shed their specifically Russian character and join with their German comrades in leading a truly international movement.

It was in this spirit that the Third International, or Comintern, was founded. At the outbreak of the war, the old Second International had collapsed—its constituent elements had gone their separate ways as patriotic Socialist parties. Nor was it possible to revive it at the war's end. The differences of attitude toward the Bolshevik Revolution that had developed in the meantime had become too great to be bridged. Hence only those European Socialists already sympathetic with the Bolshevik experiment gathered in Moscow in March, 1919, to constitute themselves as a new International.

The crucial question was already clear: would individuals and groups who were merely sympathizers be allowed to join or would all be obliged to submit to the rigid discipline that Lenin had already imposed on his own party? The issue hung in the balance throughout the first year of the Comintern's existence. And its final solution had a disastrous effect on a revolutionary movement that, in the meantime, had been encountering unexpected resistance nearly everywhere.

The Revolutionary Stirrings:
the German Revolution

When the war ended in November, 1918, most of Europe seemed ready for revolution. The sufferings of the mobilized workers and peasants in the trenches had made it appear only just that the common people of the warring countries should never return to their old situation of social and economic discrimination. Factory workers had gained new confidence from high wages and their indispensability to the war effort; the example of the Bolshevik success had inflamed imaginations everywhere. At the very least, European labor was militant and on the march. At the most, the active leaders of the proletariat were prepared to bring down the whole structure of capitalist society.

The great nations of the West—Britain and France—which had the two advantages of being already political democracies and of emerging victorious from the war, were naturally least shaken by social unrest. In these countries, the postwar disturbances did not extend beyond strikes and political demonstrations. But even here the strike wave of the years 1919 and 1920 had revolutionary overtones and was marked by frequent manifestations of sympathy with the Soviet Union.

Italy came much closer to revolution. As a people who were just beginning the experiment of political democracy and whose war record had been far from brilliant, the Italians had countless reasons for postwar dissatisfaction. In the elections of 1919—the first under universal manhood suffrage—Italian socialism emerged as the strongest party in the country. But this was socialism of a curious sort: it was neither moderate and legalist nor did it resemble Lenin's communism. It called itself *maximalism*—meaning that it stood for a maximum program of immediate socialization. Yet it was unwilling to do anything concrete and realistic to bring this great change about. Lacking discipline and a clear sense of direction, it simply *talked* revolution. Italian maximalism offered the classic case of a movement which, although sympathetic to the Bolsheviks, nevertheless found it impossible to follow Lenin's revolutionary precepts. The most it could achieve was a dramatic but ineffective occupation of the north Italian factories in the autumn of 1920. From this point on, its decline began: for the next two years, revolutionary enthusiasm in Italy was steadily on the wane.

Central Europe, of course, offered the greatest revolutionary opportunities and those that concerned the Bolsheviks most. At the end of 1918, the German Reich and the Austro-Hungarian domains showed all the indications of readiness for revolution: defeat, hunger, sickness of war, and burning social resentment. The old order had failed utterly: the new order still had not appeared. It seems no mere coincidence that the two areas where Bolshevism did have a brief success were both in Central Europe: Hungary, where a soviet republic under Béla Kun survived for four months in the spring and summer of 1919, and the southern German state of Bavaria, where a similar regime led an even more fleeting existence.

But these were minor victories and minor defeats for the revolution. Berlin was the real target; here the fate of Bolshevism in Central Europe —and with it the future of communism as an international movement— was to be decided.

Although Germany was declared a republic two days before the war came to an end, the German revolution bore a curious and artificial character. The real changeover to parliamentary institutions had come a month earlier under the chancellorship of the liberal Prince Max of Baden. Prince Max, called to power in Germany's supreme crisis when Ludendorff's nerve failed, took the essential steps toward democracy: he made his own ministry responsible to the Reichstag, and he introduced legislation for equalizing the Prussian voting system. With these goals accomplished or about to be accomplished, there seemed to be no urgency about going on to declare Germany a republic. There was no great popular pressure for such a move. The pressure came, rather, from President Wilson, who refused to agree to an armistice so long as the emperor was on the throne.

The monarchy still might have been saved, however, under a younger member of the house of Hohenzollern. The declaration of a republic was finally prompted by the fear of left-wing demonstrations in Berlin. With leftist agitators shouting for a soviet republic, it seemed safer to the moderate Social Democratic ministers who were trying to ride the storm to declare Germany an ordinary constitutional republic. And this is what Germany actually became. After five years of repeated social disorders, the German Reich settled into the framework of middle-class democracy. The next six years, from 1924 to 1930, gave Germany a brief period of equilibrium under institutions modeled on those of Britain and France.

Again and again, however, in the years from 1919 to 1923, the German Communists had attempted to seize power. The first effort came only two months after the end of the war, in January, 1919, in the form of an immense demonstration in the streets of Berlin. In the reprisals that followed, there perished the most talented leader of the German Left, Rosa Luxemburg, whose vision of communism was far freer and more spontaneous than Lenin's, and who, ironically enough, had advised against a revolutionary rising. The last effort came in the autumn of 1923, in Saxony and Hamburg, just a month before Hitler was to make his first bid for power. Between the two major attempts, there had been an almost continuous series of minor revolutionary episodes. But these had gradually changed in character. At first they were genuinely popular risings, almost without official party direction, in which left-wing Independent Social Democrats stood shoulder to shoulder with regular Communists. As the years passed, such movements became more and more contrived and conspiratorial: spontaneity passed out of them, as the Independent Social Democrats and other free spirits fell away. At the end, a narrow party bureaucracy was trying, without success, to direct the whole revolutionary effort under Moscow's supervision.

This great change of temper and tactics shows better than anything else what happened in the years 1919 to 1923 to international communism as a whole. The final failure of the revolution in Germany, the Bolsheviks saw, meant its wider failure as an international movement. This defeat was partly their own fault; it was partly the result of circumstances over which they had no control. The mistakes of the Communist leaders and the changed circumstances of the years after 1920 blasted all revolutionary hopes for a full decade of European history.

The Reasons for the Failure

In the summer of 1920, the second congress of the Comintern took the fateful decision that had been debated during the whole year past. It decided to impose "iron discipline" on its constituent parties. The "Twenty-One Conditions" required for affiliation to the Third International demanded more than disciplined obedience; they also specified that the party in question must expel its "reformists" and engage in illegal agitation.

These were conditions that no democratic-minded Socialist could accept. Now all European leftists had to make their choice—either for or against the Leninist doctrine, Bolshevik, Soviet, or Communist, however it might be called. As a result every European Socialist party split. The majority stuck to legalist, democratic principles and kept the old party names of Socialist, Social Democratic, or Labor. The minority established themselves as Communist parties and affiliated with the Third International. Only the Italian Maximalists tried to straddle the issue —professing their sympathy with Bolshevism while at the same time refusing to accept the Twenty-One Conditions. In the end, they, too, regretfully decided that they could not join the Comintern.

In the meantime, economic conditions had suddenly turned against the working class. The two years immediately following the war were a period of boom and labor shortage in which organized workers felt themselves strong and confident in pressing their demands. At the end of 1920, the situation changed: a sharp depression threw hundreds of thousands out of work. With unemployment and a labor surplus now threatening, European labor lost its militancy. And simultaneously its more conservative leaders, who had been overwhelmed in the immediate postwar period, began to regain their old control.

This was true of the trade-union leadership, which had vainly tried to check the irresponsibility and tumultuousness of its followers in 1919 and 1920. It was also true of the Socialist parties. These not only survived the secession of the Communists; they even temporarily profited by it, since they emerged from the crisis with new cohesion and clarity of purpose. Moreover, they were gaining additional constituents to replace the ones they had lost. Middle-class recruits flocked to them in large numbers, for in the perspective of 1921 and 1922, the record of the European Socialists was very reassuring. In the war they had steered between the two extremes of chauvinism and defeatism: they had behaved like patriots without being deceived by the propaganda of the superpatriots. And as a postwar policy they were trying to combine resistance to Communist revolution with steady insistence on social reform and a profound belief in international reconciliation.

Thus by 1921 the Socialist parties were emerging as a great force for order and stabilization in Western and Central Europe. Socialism, more than anything else, was holding the discontented workers in line. All intermediate positions had disappeared: a European leftist must now be either a Socialist or a Communist, and the distinction between them was crystal clear. The former internationalist Socialists—the men of Zimmerwald, Kienthal, and Stockholm—had had to make their choice. There was no longer any room for halfway stations.*

In the Communist camp, a Muscovite discipline reigned. With the final failure of the revolution in Germany and the death of Lenin three months later, the international spirit vanished from the Comintern. It was thereafter to be run in Russian interests, as a new and eccentric arm of Soviet foreign policy. How could a non-Russian Communist object? Was it not the first duty of every Communist, whatever his nationality, to preserve the revolution in the one country where it had triumphed? Thus international communism succumbed to bureaucratic control from Moscow. The life went out of it. Its leadership became routine and unimaginative. Not until the 1930's—in the new situation of fascism and the Great Depression—was communism to regain its ideological flexibility and its ability to inspire party members and large numbers of sympathizers alike.

Readings

For the ideological aspects of the First World War and the propaganda duel between Wilson and Lenin, see Arno Mayer, *Political Origins of the New Diplomacy* (1959).

The best interpretation of Russia on the eve of the revolution is contained in Sir John Maynard, *Russia in Flux* (1948). For the major protagonists in the revolution itself, Bertram D. Wolfe's *Three Who Made a Revolution* (1948) gives an account of the complex personal relationships among Lenin, Trotsky, and Stalin, and Louis Fischer's *The Life of Lenin* (1964) traces the career of the chief leader.

The two standard accounts of the revolution itself are William Henry Chamberlin, *The Russian Revolution*, 2 vols. (1935), and Edward Hallett Carr, *The Bolshevik Revolution*, 3 vols. (1950–1953). The former is anti-Bolshevik in tone and is particularly useful for the civil war period; the latter is more favorable to Lenin and his colleagues, drawing on much recently published documentation. For the origins of Bolshevik nationalities policy, see Richard Pipes, *The Formation of the Soviet Union: Communism and Nationalism, 1917–1923*, rev. ed. (1964).

The spreading effects of the revolution, particularly in Central Europe, are traced in Arthur Rosenberg, *The Birth of the German Republic* (1931), Ruth Fischer, *Stalin and German Communism* (1948), and Franz Borkenau, *The Communist International* (1938). For a brilliant interpretation of why the Bolsheviks failed outside Russia, see Joseph A. Schumpeter, *Capitalism, Socialism, and Democracy*, 3d ed. (1950).

* In 1920, the chief of these intermediate parties, the German Independent Social Democrats, broke up, part going to the Social Democrats and part to the Communists.

The Settlement of 1919–1923

Chapter Four

I
THE WILSONIAN VISION

Nationalism and the War

Nationalism was a force that European Marxists had always underestimated. Lenin, in his appeals to the peasants and workers in the trenches to lay down their arms, ruled out the possibility that the proletarians in uniform might actually believe in the justice of their respective national causes. But in 1917 and 1918 nationalism in Europe was far from dead. One indication of its tenacity had been the response of the Socialist parties to the original declarations of war. Another was the fact that even in the bitter year 1917 the armies of the Western and Central European belligerents—drained though they were by defeatism and war weariness —had fought on. And the final year of the war—the year of the Allied march to victory—seemed to vindicate nationalist war leaders like Lloyd George and Clemenceau who had urged their people to hold out to the last. When the war ended, nationalists of one sort or other were ruling both the victorious nations of the West and the new or enlarged states that were springing up in East Central Europe. Their control—and the substantial popular support they enjoyed—suggests a final and decisive reason for the failure of Lenin's international revolutionary hopes in the years 1919–1923.

Paradoxically enough, Woodrow Wilson himself contributed mightily

Georges Clemenceau
and French generals.
COURTESY BROWN
BROTHERS.

to this strengthening of national sentiment in the final year of the war. In his ideological competition with Lenin, the American president suffered because he did not promise immediate peace. This was indeed a handicap so long as the defeatist spirit of 1917 persisted, but when the morale of the warring peoples had been remobilized for the final effort of 1918, the handicap began to turn into an advantage. Once it was clear that tangible national gains might be won from victory, Leninism began to lose its appeal. Furthermore it soon became apparent that Lenin could not carry out what he had promised. He could continue to urge immediate peace, but he could do nothing to win it; he could preach the liberation of subject nationalities, but he could not help in their struggle for freedom. This became evident after the Treaty of Brest-Litovsk revealed the weakness of the Bolshevik regime and its humiliating subjection to German armed force.

Wilson, in contrast, had behind him the enormous resources of the United States, whose potentialities gradually unfolded with the progress of American mobilization in the latter half of 1917 and the first months of 1918. By March of 1918—when Brest-Litovsk was exposing the extent of Lenin's weakness—Wilson was just coming into his full strength. American troops were pouring ashore in France by the tens of thousands, and a bottomless reservoir of additional strength lay behind them. Lenin had nothing of the sort to help him. The Bolshevik leader's only weapon was revolutionary subversion: Wilson could bring into play the unlimited resources of the strongest nation on earth. This lesson was not lost on the nationalist leaders of East Central Europe, the spokesmen of the Poles and the Czechs, the Rumanians and the Yugoslavs, whose ambitions were to prove decisive for the character of the peace settlement reached in 1919.

Nationalists, realistically calculating their chances in the last year of the war, correctly concluded that they would gain most from Wilsonianism. And so they rallied to it—at least in words. But in fact they altered the Wilsonian appeal, gradually molding it and interpreting it in directions that the president had never intended. In the end, they converted it into something far more crudely nationalist than it had originally been. Thus Wilson became the prisoner of the forces of old-fashioned nationalism he had earlier opposed. This was to be the final irony of the peace settlement of 1919.

Wilson's Aims: the Fourteen Points

The American declaration of war changed Wilson's aim from "peace without victory" to a peace imposed by the victors on the vanquished. The president himself was not entirely aware of how great the shift actually was. He did not fully appreciate the contrast between his earlier, almost pacifist pronouncements and the ringing appeal he delivered on April 6, 1918, to mark the first anniversary of American intervention:

"Force, Force to the utmost, Force without stint or limit, the righteous and triumphant Force which shall make Right the law of the world, and cast every selfish dominion down in the dust."

Three months earlier Wilson had issued his Fourteen Points to clarify him own aims and, if possible, to rally sentiment in the Allied nations behind them. The timing of the declaration was significant. For, once again, the ideological competition with Lenin was the crucial consideration. From the negotiations at Brest-Litovsk the Bolshevik leaders had been issuing pronouncements calculated to rouse the hopes of subject peoples everywhere. Wilson's answer was to draw up a formal list of war aims which would prove to all the world that the Western Allies were willing to go as far as Lenin in their search for a peace of justice. The Fourteen Points address "was not an idealistic program of peace aims made in a political vacuum but primarily a tactical move in psychological warfare, made up in a pragmatic fashion from varied sources and suggestions." *

Nearly all Wilson's points dealt with political, military, or territorial issues. Besides laying down such general aims as freedom of the seas, disarmament, and an international association to guarantee the peace, the American president made a number of concrete proposals for settling the nationalities question: Belgium, Serbia, and Rumania were to be restored; France was to regain Alsace-Lorraine; Italy was to have its frontiers adjusted "along clearly recognizable lines of nationality"; an independent Poland was to be set up, "with free and secure access to the sea"; finally, "the peoples of Austria-Hungary, whose place among the nations we wish to see safeguarded and assured, should be accorded the freest opportunity of autonomous development."

The only economic proposal in the whole list was a vague statement on the removal of trade barriers. Nor did Wilson seem in any way to recognize that national questions were often intertwined with social issues of bewildering complexity. He showed no awareness of the situation —so frequent in East Central Europe—in which the landlord class was of one nationality and the peasantry of another. The possibility that the land hunger of the peasants might be a deeper longing than the desire for national self-determination likewise escaped him. In brief, he failed to understand that much of Europe did not have the type of society that could support the democratic settlement he advocated. He seemed not to know that through most of the wide belt of territory lying between Germany to the west and Russia to the east democracy had never existed and was still a completely unfamiliar way of life.

In Wilson's vision, the self-determination of peoples offered the key to international peace and progress. For self-determination suggested two things: redrawing boundaries in a fair and just fashion and democratiza-

* Victor S. Mamatey, *The United States and East Central Europe 1914–1918* (Princeton, N.J.: Princeton University Press, 1957), p. 172.

tion *within* the new boundaries thus established. Once each people was in control of its own destinies, Wilson believed, the way to international concord would be open. This faith was not unfamiliar to Europeans. It had been held by most radical thinkers in the middle of the nineteenth century. But the faith had waned since then: the extremes to which popular nationalism had proceeded in the quarter-century before the outbreak of the war aroused doubt whether democracy and nationalism always went together, or, if they did, whether this was necessarily good. A tempered skepticism had replaced the earlier trust in the democratic virtue of national feeling.

But Wilson was not a European. Although he was a political scientist, a professor, and an intellectual, he was insufficiently familiar with Europe's history and the complexity of its problems. Indeed, he expressed frank impatience with all these complications. In this, he reflected the characteristic American preference for quick and simple solutions. It is not true, as his detractors have asserted, that Wilson was merely a dour Puritan, rigid and inflexible. Actually he proved himself both a seasoned politician and a skillful negotiator. But he was an old-fashioned political *radical*, with all the virtues and all the limitations that the term implies. In his exclusive trust in merely political solutions, in his neglect of economic and social issues, in his lack of sense for historical tradition, in his addiction to clear and simple formulas, Wilson was true to the purest of the ideologies of progress. It was as the last great exponent of radicalism that Wilson was to try to impose on his hesitant allies his own version of a just and lasting peace.

II
THE LIBERATION
OF EAST CENTRAL EUROPE

Point Ten of the Fourteen Points, the one dealing with "the peoples of Austria-Hungary," had a calculated ambiguity. It could be read either as reassuring the two dominant nationalities, the German-speaking Austrians and the Hungarians, that the Allies did not intend to destroy their respective positions, or as supporting the claims of the subject peoples in their struggle for liberation. And this evidently was precisely what Wilson intended. As late as January, 1918, when he announced the Fourteen Points, he had not yet decided what to do about the Austro-Hungarian Empire. He could not fail to take a stand for fairer treatment of the subject nationalities. But he had yet to be convinced that this meant full independence and with it the breakup of the Empire as a political unit.

As a cautious transition phrase, then, Wilson offered "autonomous development." If it meant anything, it signified no more than self-government *within* the Empire. But this was not at all what the leaders of the nationalities themselves desired. They would settle for nothing less than full independence. One of the great, if largely subterranean, dramas of the year 1918 was the fashion in which these leaders gradually won the American president to their point of view by facing him with a series of accomplished facts. Wilson has often been accused of willfully breaking up Austria-Hungary at the Peace Conference of Paris. Nothing could be further from the truth. Months before the Peace Conference met, the Austro-Hungarian Empire had *already* broken up, as the leaders of the subject nationalities took matters into their own hands and boldly pushed them to the final solution.

The Role of the Czechs

As the best educated, the most democratically minded, and the most advanced economically of the subject nationalities, the Czechs held the key to the situation. They were also the only ones who could destroy the whole Empire. The other nationalities—the Poles, the Rumanians, the South Slavs, and the Italians—merely formed parts of larger groups the majority of whom dwelt outside Austria-Hungary. These nationalities looked beyond the borders of the Empire for deliverance. The Czechs alone—and the neighboring and less developed Slovaks, whose speech closely resembled theirs—lay entirely within the imperial frontiers. The border nationalities could be peeled off one by one, and still the central Danubian core of the Empire would remain intact. Should the Czechs go, all would be lost: the Hungarians would then have no reason for staying with the German Austrians, and the Empire would simply dissolve.

In retrospect, it seems that the Austrian statesmen should have done everything in their power to conciliate the Czechs before it was too late. At the start of the war, "Trialism," as it was called, might have succeeded —if the Empire had been converted from a dual into a "trial" monarchy by giving the Czech land of Bohemia the same parity with "Austria" that Hungary had earlier received, the Empire might have been saved. But the Austrians seem never to have considered this solution seriously. And while they delayed, there emerged new and talented Czech leaders who drove single-mindedly toward their goal of full independence.

This was a final distinction between the Czechs and the other nationalities—the eminence and skill of their leadership. As the war continued, the Czech propagandists in exile came to recognize as their undisputed chief the scholarly, serene Thomas G. Masaryk. Faithfully seconding him was the more lively and intriguing Eduard Beneš. Together Masaryk and Beneš made the most effective team of national spokesmen in all Europe. Beneš knew every trick of propaganda; Masaryk could speak the lofty, philosophical language that Wilson admired. And they received accidental aid from the way in which their countrymen were calling attention to themselves in a most unusual series of armed engagements.

One hundred thousand Czechs, former deserters or prisoners from the Austrian army who had subsequently been enrolled in the Russian forces, found themselves stranded far from home when the Bolsheviks took Russia out of the war. They determined to leave the country and to make their way to join the French on the Western Front. And so they started east along the Trans-Siberian railroad, gradually becoming involved on the White side in the conflicts of the civil war. This odyssey of the Czechs produced the extremely appealing image of a stubborn people who would stop at nothing in their fight for liberation.

On May 30, 1918, during a highly successful visit of Masaryk to the United States, the Czechs in exile drew up a charter of independence at Pittsburgh. Two and a half months later the British granted them recognition, and in September, ten weeks before the end of the war, the Americans followed suit. Czechoslovakia had become an independent nation.

The Allied Promises; the Pact of Rome

The independence of Czechoslovakia climaxed a series of concessions by the Western Allies that had been gradually mounting for more than three years. First the British and French had promised the Italians their "unredeemed" lands within the Austrian Empire in order to get them into the war. Then the Allies made similar pledges to the Serbs in order to keep them fighting. Finally the Allies held out the bait of Transylvania to the Rumanians, which the latter grabbed for, with the disastrous results already described.

Meantime, it had become apparent that Poland would be reconstituted. Initially the Russians proposed to set it up as a dependent state. Then the Germans actually did so, and held Poland in their grasp until the very end of the war. Polish leaders were long divided over whether they should look to the Entente or to Germany for their freedom. Three things eventually decided them: their "independent" status under German control was proving to be a farce; it was becoming apparent that the Allies would win the war; finally Wilson's Thirteenth Point, with its phrase about "free and secure access to the sea," seemed to promise the Poles nearly everything they desired.

It was still necessary, however, to convince the American president that the Austro-Hungarian Empire should be broken up. The process began in March, 1918, when the Serbian leaders wrested from Wilson permission to tell their parliament—convened in the island refuge of Corfu—that he and his Allies "would meet Serbo-Croat national aspirations as far as possible." It was accelerated the next month by the signature of the so-called Pact of Rome. In this document, the representatives of Austria's subject nationalities, meeting in the Italian capital, pledged solidarity with each other in the common struggle for independence. Then in May came Masaryk's visit to the United States, as the Czech

propaganda offensive began to gain momentum. By the summer of 1918,
it was becoming obvious that Wilson was rapidly being won over and that soon nothing would stand in the way of realizing the nationalities' maximum program.

In general, the British and French let Wilson take the lead. Their earlier pledges to the Serbians and Rumanians had been dictated by the necessities of warfare, and they maintained this attitude to the end. In similar fashion, the Italians were mainly concerned with the aid that the subject nationalities could give them in their struggle against Austria-Hungary—hence their sponsorship of the April meeting in Rome. Such a policy, however, involved Italy in an internal contradiction: to promote the propaganda of the subject nationalities meant to encourage the aspirations of the South Slavs who inhabited some of the same Adriatic lands that Italy had been promised in the Treaty of London of 1915. This conflict seems to have been only dimly understood by the Italian prime minister, Vittorio Emanuele Orlando, who had supported and addressed the Rome gathering. It was transparently clear, however, to the foreign minister, Baron Sonnino, the original negotiator of the Treaty of London. Thus as early as the spring of 1918 there had appeared the outlines of the Italo-Yugoslav conflict, which was to prove the bitterest and most troubling of all the issues with which the Peace Conference had to deal.

The Dissolution of Austria-Hungary

On October 16, 1918, the Austrian emperor issued a manifesto promising to reorganize his dominions as a federal state. The concession came far too late. It satisfied neither Wilson nor the subject nationalities. It merely hastened the process of dissolution.

By the end of the month, it was becoming obvious that even the Hungarians had lost faith in the Empire. The other nationalities quietly drew their own conclusions. On October 28, a Czech National Committee in Prague began functioning as a separate government. The Croatian Diet declared its independence the next day. Meantime the war came to an end, as the disintegration of the Empire continued unchecked. The vanquished Rumanians—who had succeeded in re-entering the conflict just in time—took over Transylvania on the first of December. And on the same day, the prince-regent of Serbia proclaimed the union of his country with the lands inhabited by the Croats and Slovenes. A South Slav or Yugoslav state had at last become a reality. But its birth had been far from effortless. Until the very last, the Croats and Slovenes of Austria-Hungary had tried to obtain assurances of equality from the Serbs which the latter had stubbornly refused to give. Here again the outlines of future conflict were clear: the whole foundation of the Yugoslav state rested on an assumption of Serbian supremacy which the sister peoples were reluctant to accept.

Thus occurred the liberation of East Central Europe. The last nine months of the year 1918, which had seen so many other dramatic events, also witnessed the creation of a continuous belt of small independent nations separating Germany from Russia. The Peace Conference could do no more than ratify a settlement for East Central Europe whose major outlines had already been determined on the spot.

III

THE PEACE CONFERENCE OF 1919

The Armistice

On November 7, 1918, the German Reichstag deputy Matthias Erzberger set out on a forlorn mission. In a modest convoy of three automobiles, protected only by a large white flag, he crossed the line between the retreating Germans and the victorious Allies in search of Marshal Foch and an armistice to end the war. It was unprecedented for a civilian rather than a soldier to be given such an assignment. But it was typical of the way in which the German command—ever since Ludendorff's collapse six weeks before—had been trying to shirk responsibility for its defeat. And if a civilian had to do the job, Erzberger was the logical man to go. As the author of the Peace Resolution of July, 1917, he was already identified in the public mind with a compromise settlement. Nor was he afraid of the unpopularity that his armistice mission might bring down upon him. He gladly accepted unpopular assignments—indeed, he almost seemed to seek them out. (And for this he perished by an assassin's bullet three years later.)

The fashion in which the 1918 Armistice came about was the origin of the famous "Stab-in-the-Back Legend"—the legend that the civilians and the home front had betrayed the German Army while it was still undefeated. And the terms of the Armistice seemed to bear out the legend. Erzberger had hoped that he would be able to negotiate with Foch, but when he actually met the Allied commander in chief in his railroad-car headquarters in the Forest of Compiègne, the latter simply asked his deputy to read off an already prepared list of terms. These were designed to make it impossible for Germany to resume the struggle. They provided for a massive surrender of warships, guns, airplanes, and rolling stock; for the evacuation of the left bank of the Rhine and of bridgeheads opposite its major cities; and for the annulment of the Treaty of Brest-Litovsk, with the relinquishment of Germany's territorial gains to the east. Erzberger obtained a few modifications in the final Armistice which came into effect on November 11, but in essence the Armistice foreshadowed what the peace treaty was to be, a victors' settlement imposed on the vanquished.

One other thing rankled in German memories. Throughout the winter

while the Peace Conference was in progress, the Allies were apparently
maintaining their blockade of the Reich. Starvation and suffering continued, and the Germans accused their late enemies of holding the whip of hunger over them. They did not know, however, that it was not the Allies but German shipowners who were delaying the arrival of food by refusing to donate their vessels for humanitarian purposes. Owing to their stubbornness, it was not until April that relief shipments began to arrive. Thus far from offering further evidence of Allied harshness, the continued hunger in Germany "only proved the weakness of the German government in the face of the German shipping lobby." *

Personalities and Organization: the Big Three

Paris was the natural choice for the site of the Peace Conference. As the capital of the nation that had borne the heaviest burden in the war, it seemed to deserve that honor, and the French insisted on it. The choice of the French capital seriously handicapped Wilson in his efforts to arrive at a peace based on justice and distorted the character of the peace treaties, leaving upon them an imprint of triumph and revenge.

Another fateful circumstance was Wilson's decision to attend the conference in person. This was entirely unprecedented. No American president had ever left the country before; never since has the chief executive been away for so long a time. But Wilson was convinced that he alone could persuade the Allies to make the sort of peace he envisioned. In the final months of the war, he had won the grudging consent of his Allies to accepting the Fourteen Points as the basis for negotiations. And it was on this understanding that the Germans agreed to end the war. But Wilson well knew that the French and British—and, still more, the Italians—were far from prepared to let the central principle of national self-determination govern all the decisions of the conference. All three —and the smaller Allies as well—had their own national aims which they were completely unwilling to sacrifice to the wider goal of a just peace. Wilson had redefined the war as a war for democracy. But this was not the war's original character, and the nationalist leaders who were governing the Allied Powers, great and small, at the end of the conflict, did not naturally think in these terms. They had humored Wilson's ideological eccentricities, since they could not afford to offend the United States: American aid was indispensable to their survival. But once the war was safely won, they felt free to return to their traditional national views.

Thus inevitably, the conference was to be marked by conflict between the old-style nationalism of the European leaders and the new-style nationalism of President Wilson. And the American president could see no alternative but to go himself to Paris to fight for the peace in which

* Klaus Epstein, *Matthias Erzberger and the Dilemma of German Democracy* (Princeton, N.J.: Princeton University Press, 1959), p. 294.

he believed. More particularly, he wanted to fight for the League of Nations, the new association of states that he intended to make an integral part of the peace treaties. The League was Wilson's favorite scheme. He gave it priority in the peace negotiations, and for its sake he was prepared to make sacrifices on what he regarded as minor points.

Here also lay a danger for the future. The French in particular were willing to accept the League since it offered no threat to them and could even be turned to the uses of French security. With tongue in cheek, they could concur in what was still a mere abstraction, trading their consent to it for Wilson's agreement to some of their more realistic national aims. And there was another danger still: the League—with the limitations on national sovereignty that it implied—offered the best ammunition to Wilson's enemies at home, the Republican nationalists who had just won the mid-term election of 1918. The point on which the president insisted most was the one which they liked least. Europeans, unfamiliar as they were with the workings of American politics, did not realize the weakness of Wilson's position in 1919. They regarded him as still the leader of his country. They did not understand that Wilson, having lost his majority in Congress, was in a position which, in a European parliamentary state, would have brought about his immediate resignation.

Finally, Wilson's decision to attend dictated much of the organization and procedure of the conference. It meant, for one thing, that there was a constant time pressure. The American president could not be away from Washington too long—indeed in the middle of the conference he returned to the United States for a full month—and this made it urgent to get on with the work. It also doomed the original plan of quickly drafting a preliminary treaty and then drawing up a final treaty with more deliberation—a plan which was scrapped in favor of pushing through a single document. It meant too that nearly all the work of the conference had to be delegated to smaller groups and that Wilson could not possibly follow in detail the progress of each one of them.

The Peace Conference opened in plenary session on January 18, 1919. This was a pure formality; after that the full meetings of the conference became less and less important. The real work was done in specialized committees. Here the usual diplomatic horse trading went on; here the representatives of the smaller powers, denied the forum of a full meeting, pleaded their special cases, with a vast array of historical data and statistics, nearly all of it shamelessly slanted. The French and British usually appointed experienced diplomats to these committees; Wilson, however, brought with him a large delegation of professors, and their presence on the committees and behind the scenes offered one of the great novelties of the conference. In addition, there was the president's personal adviser and friend Colonel Edward M. House, who was more of a diplomat than his chief and far more inclined to compromise on crucial issues.

Above the "experts" and diplomats towered the real masters of the conference: the heads of government and foreign ministers of the Great Powers. It was at their secret meetings that the final decisions were hammered out. Originally they met as a Council of Ten, which included not only the French and British and Americans but also the Italians and even the Japanese, who had entered the war simply to acquire former German colonies. Later the Japanese and the foreign ministers tended to drop out, as the inner circle was reduced to the "Big Four": Wilson, Clemenceau, Lloyd George, and the Italian, Orlando. Finally, when the Italian delegation left the conference in vexation, the Big Three alone remained. Their deliberations dominated the rest of the proceedings and produced most of the legend and controversy that the Peace Conference left behind it.

In the private meetings of the Big Three, Wilson faced formidable antagonists. Lloyd George was willing to go with him part of the way. But the mercurial little Welshman was slippery and unpredictable, and he was seldom at liberty to follow his natural inclinations toward a democratic peace. Time after time he showed himself to be the prisoner of his own supporters, the British Tory nationalists and the prime ministers of the overseas dominions, who, like the Japanese, were bent on colonial gain. He had, moreover, just won an election—the "Khaki Election" of December, 1918—by using demagogic slogans about a punitive peace. Yet Lloyd George was an easy person to deal with, in comparison with Clemenceau. The French prime minister knew just what he wanted, he stood on home ground, and he refused to budge from his bedrock demands. With half a century of political experience behind him, Clemenceau judged men and events in realistic fashion; he could have been called a cynic were it not for his burning French patriotism. Clemenceau's desire was simple: security from German invasion. He had experienced two invasions in his lifetime and he did not want his country to endure a third. Hence he was skeptical of Wilson's schemes and willing to accept only those which could be made to serve French security interests. And should Clemenceau ever be tempted to forget these interests, Marshal Foch was always behind him, pleading as a soldier with single-minded stubbornness for the ancient French goal of "natural" and defensible frontiers.

This, then, was the balance of policies and personalities as the Peace Conference opened.

The Order of Business: the League, the Colonies, the Rhineland, Reparations

Wilson had given priority in his own mind to the establishment of a League of Nations, and it was with this goal that the conference began its labors. It was not hard to reach unanimous agreement to set up such a body and to appoint a committee to draft its constitution. But the decision to go ahead with the League catapulted the conference into one of its most vexatious problems—the disposition of the former German colonies. Here the opposing viewpoints met head on: the Japanese and the prime ministers of the British dominions wanted outright annexation, whereas Wilson insisted on a trusteeship or "mandate" arrangement.

In view of the fact that Japan and the dominions were already in possession of the spoils, Wilson did not come off too badly. The powers finally agreed on a three-stage mandate system. True, the lowest category of these—Class C—which applied to the islands of the Pacific that had been conquered by Japan, Australia, and New Zealand, was no more than veiled annexation. But Class B—covering most of the African colonies—provided for real supervision by the League to assure that the natives' welfare was respected. Class A—applicable to the Arab lands formerly under Turkish rule—envisaged a fairly rapid evolution toward independence. Five present-day nations of the Near East in fact grew out of Class A mandates, and three of the Class B areas in Africa, Cameroon, Tanganyika, and Togo, achieved independence in the 1960's.

With this comparatively simple problem out of the way, Wilson was free to turn his attention to the central issue of France's claims on Germany. But his fighting spirit had already been weakened by the colonial struggle, and just as the debate with the French was reaching its climax, he was compelled to return home. During Wilson's absence from mid-February to mid-March, the conference seemed to be marking time. Actually two very important things occurred. In the first place, after conferring with Senate leaders, Wilson became convinced that it would be necessary to reduce the supranational features of the League in order to obtain American acceptance. On his return to Paris, the president was obliged to have the Covenant of the League altered to give explicit recognition to the Monroe Doctrine; this shift weakened his position by seeming to cast him, too, in the role of pleader for selfish national goals. The second notable change was a stiffening in the attitude of the French. With Wilson away, the more conciliatory Colonel House had conceded a number of important points; when the president returned, he found it impossible to win back all the ground he had lost.

There resulted the first great explosion of the conference—a rupture of relations between Wilson and Clemenceau, as the American president took to his bed with influenza and ordered his ship to stand by for immediate departure. But after two weeks of crisis, House reconciled the two. Once more, the decisions eventually reached were a compromise. The French gave up Foch's favorite scheme of separating the Rhineland from Germany to form a buffer state and they consented to reduce the demands of their client nation, Poland, on Germany's eastern frontiers. But, in return, Wilson had to agree to the military occupation of the Rhineland for fifteen years, and to an undertaking on the part of the United States and Britain to come to the aid of France "in the event of any unprovoked movement of aggression against her . . . by Germany."

The American president also gave his consent to what was undoubt-

edly the worst feature of the whole settlement—the provisions on reparations. Earlier Wilson had insisted that Germany should be made to
pay only *reparations* in the narrower sense—that is, compensation for
the direct war destruction the German armies had wrought. He had
refused to countenance an *indemnity* to cover the cost to the Allies of
waging the war. But on this issue Lloyd George—bound by his pledges
to the British electorate—joined Clemenceau. He insisted that the Germans must pay the whole bill. And such was the decision of the conference. In deference to Wilson's views, the sums demanded were defined
only as *reparations*, but their size and the categories of payments included in them clearly indicated that this concession to the American
view was only verbal and that Clemenceau and Lloyd George had put
indemnities into the final bill. The French and British leaders, moreover,
steadfastly refused to grant the two points on which the American experts insisted—either a fixed sum of money, or a fixed number of years
for payment. As the reparations bill finally emerged from the conference,
it was both vague and astronomical. And the Big Three had added—
without at all realizing the repercussions it would produce—the clause
that was to infuriate the Germans most of all, the demand that Germany
accept full "responsibility" (or "guilt," as it came to be called) "for caus-
ing all the loss and damage" incident to the war.

The Secret Treaties and the Adriatic Explosion

Wilson asserted that before his arrival in Paris he knew nothing of the
secret treaties between his allies—and more particularly the Treaty of
London by which the French and British had brought Italy into the
war. It would have been more accurate to say that he was resolved to
ignore the secret treaties, which the Bolsheviks had published to all the
world, and that the American press had aided him in this resolve by
keeping strictly silent about them.

Thus when the Peace Conference finally came to discuss the Italian
claims, Wilson insisted that he was not bound by the Treaty of London
or by its successor, the still more generous Treaty of Saint Jean de
Maurienne. For this firm attitude, the American president had several
justifications which had not applied in the case of the French demands
on Germany. Italy's mediocre contribution to victory did not seem to
deserve much of a reward. Furthermore, the Italian claims were not
simply at the expense of a defeated foe, as France's had been, but con-
flicted with those of a new friend, the recently founded state of Yugoslavia. Finally, the Italian leaders overplayed their hand: they not only
insisted on their full pound of flesh; they added to it the Adriatic seaport
of Fiume, which had not been specified in the original treaties.

Wilson was prepared to grant the Italian claims against Austria alone
—the city of Trieste and the South Tyrol (or Trentino and Alto Adige)
right up to the Brenner Pass, which meant that a quarter of a million

German-speaking Austrians would be included within the new Italian frontiers. But he was unwilling to do the like with the Adriatic lands inhabited by Croats and Slovenes. At this, Orlando and Sonnino set up a great cry of betrayal and stamped out of the conference. While they were nursing their grievances in Rome, Wilson appealed directly to the Italian people. The appeal backfired: the more articulate Italians were unimpressed by this effort to play on their presumed sentiments of international justice. But Orlando and Sonnino gained nothing by sulky withdrawal. They finally found themselves obliged to return to Paris and to pick up the broken threads of negotiation.

Wilson still held firm. Continuing to support the Yugoslavs, he would not yield on the Adriatic shore, except in the case of two small strips with a considerable Italian population. When the Peace Conference adjourned in June, the question of Fiume remained undecided.

IV

THE PEACE OF PARIS

The settlement that emerged from the Peace Conference is called the Peace of Paris. The individual treaties that constitute it bear the names of the small towns near Paris where they were signed.

The Treaty of Versailles

Dwarfing all the others, of course, and frequently confused with the whole settlement, was the Treaty of Versailles with Germany. On June 28, 1919, it was signed with great ceremony in the Hall of Mirrors in the palace of Louis XIV—the same hall in which, forty-eight years earlier, the victorious Germans had founded their new empire. This time the Germans were simply handed the treaty on a take-it-or-leave-it basis. As in the case of the Armistice, they had hoped to be able to negotiate on specific terms, but they found themselves faced instead with what they called a *Diktat*. When the news reached home, a wave of indignation swept the country: German patriots clamored for refusal to ratify the treaty. For a few days the constitutional assembly meeting at Weimar toyed with the same idea. In the end counsels of prudence prevailed: Germany obviously could not renew the war. The ministry resigned, the deputies protested, a suitable subterfuge had to be found to obtain a majority for ratification. But the terms of the treaty stood, virtually as the Big Three had originally drafted them.

Although the Treaty of Versailles was undoubtedly harsh, it was not as severe as the Treaty of Brest-Litovsk which the Germans had imposed fifteen months earlier on the vanquished Russians. It left the Reich intact—Wilson had successfully resisted all notions of dismemberment—but seriously reduced in area. Both in the west and in the east its frontiers were contracted. In the west, Alsace-Lorraine returned to France, which also received the right to exploit for fifteen years the industrially rich Saar Basin. Two small strips of land went to Belgium, and northern Schleswig to the Danes. In the east, the reconstituted state of Poland bit deeply into Germany's borders. Indeed, the so-called Polish Corridor —giving the new nation that "free and secure access to the sea" which Wilson had promised—completely cut off East Prussia from the rest of Germany. The only solace granted to German feelings was the separation of the German-speaking seaport of Danzig from the rest of the Corridor as a free city under the supervision of the League of Nations.

The military terms of the treaty were even more severe. In addition to the fifteen-year occupation of the left bank of the Rhine and the de-militarization of a zone 30 miles wide on the right bank, the Allies sought in all possible ways to prevent Germany from ever again becom-ing a major military power. They forbade it to build offensive weapons, such as airplanes and submarines, and they limited the German army to a small professional force of 100,000 men. On the navy they imposed an equally drastic ceiling, and added the provision that Germany surrender by far the larger part of its merchant fleet. The costs of occupation were, of course, to be borne by the Germans themselves.

Finally there were the reparations clauses. In the definitive text of the treaty, the total sum to be paid still remained unspecified. All the Ger-mans knew was that in the next two years they must somehow turn over five billion dollars; at the end of that time, they would learn the final bill. And should they ever question why they were paying these vast sums, there was always Article 231, the famous "war guilt" clause of the treaty, to remind them.

The Minor Treaties:
Saint-Germain, Trianon, Neuilly, Sèvres

The settlements with Germany's allies followed the general pattern of the Treaty of Versailles. They too provided for territorial losses, military restrictions, and reparations payments. In each case, however, there were significant local differences.

Austria and Hungary, now left destitute as small and separate states, signed their own separate treaties. The Treaty of Saint-Germain with Austria dealt with a state that did not want to be a nation at all. With its Empire gone, "Austria" had lost its meaning. It now consisted of no more than its old Alpine and Danubian provinces which had a German-speaking population. These people could see no other recourse than to merge with their neighbors of similar speech by joining the German Reich. But this solution the Allies forbade. They obliged the German Austrians to go their way alone. They added to the Austrian sense of injury, moreover, by leaving within the boundaries of the new state of Czechoslovakia three million German-speaking Bohemians and Moravi-

Europe in 1923

- – – 1923 boundaries
- ········· 1914 boundaries

Scale of Miles

0   100   200   300

Atlantic Ocean

NORWAY

SWEDEN

FINLAND

Helsinki

Leningrad

Oslo

Stockholm

ESTONIA

Baltic

North Sea

LATVIA

DENMARK

LITHUANIA

SCHLESWIG

Copenhagen

Danzig

POLISH CORRIDOR

EAST PRUSSIA

Minsk

GREAT BRITAIN

Hamburg

GERMANY

Berlin

POLAND

Warsaw

Brest-Litovsk

UNION OF SOVIET SOCIALIST REPUBLICS

London

NETHERLANDS

Amsterdam

RUHR

RHINELAND

Weimar

Frankfurt

SUDETENLAND

UPPER SILESIA

Kiev

Antwerp

Brussels

BELGIUM

LUXEMBURG

SAAR

Prague

BOHEMIA

Kharkov

Paris

ALSACE-LORRAINE

Munich

MORAVIA

CZECHOSLOVAKIA

Bratislava

RUTHENIA

BESSARABIA

Odessa

ALPS

Vienna

AUSTRIA

Budapest

CARPATHIANS

TRANSYLVANIA

FRANCE

Bern

SWITZERLAND

Geneva

HUNGARY

RUMANIA

Black Sea

TRENTINO

Milan

Trieste

Fiume

CROATIA

DALMATIA

Bucharest

DOBRUJA

PYRENEES

ITALY

APENNINES

BOSNIA

YUGOSLAVIA

Belgrade

SERBIA

SPAIN

Barcelona

CORSICA

Rome

Adriatic Sea

MONTENEGRO

BULGARIA

Sofia

SARDINIA

Tirane

MACEDONIA

TURKEY

ALBANIA

GREECE

Palermo

Mediterranean   *Sea*

Aegean Sea

Athens

SICILY

ALGERIA

ans. The vast majority of these Sudeten Germans, as they were later called, never reconciled themselves to the rule of a Slavic people whom they considered their cultural inferiors.

In a territorial sense, the Treaty of Trianon with Hungary was the harshest of all, for by conceding the maximum claims of Czechoslovakia, Rumania, and Yugoslavia, it deprived the historic kingdom of Hungary of nearly three-quarters of its area and two-thirds of its inhabitants. During the whole interwar period, the Treaty of Trianon occupied the foreground of the Hungarian national consciousness: "No, no, never" became the patriotic slogan—the refusal for one moment to accept the shame of the most humiliating peace treaty of modern times.

The Treaty of Neuilly with Bulgaria was mild in comparison. It gave Bulgaria's Aegean seacoast to Greece and smaller portions of territory to Yugoslavia and Rumania, thus reducing the country still further from its already contracted borders of 1913. The final peace settlement—the Treaty of Sèvres with Turkey—ratified the liberation of the Arab states, the more important of which simply exchanged one foreign master for another by becoming Class A mandates of Britain and France. This loss the Turks were willing to accept, but when the Allies tried to carry out the terms of their secret treaties by carving up Asia Minor itself—the homeland of the Turkish people—nationalist sentiment rebelled. By the time the sultan, after long delays, finally accepted the treaty in August, 1920, the Turkish nationalists were already in arms against it. From the moment of its signature, the Treaty of Sèvres was a dead letter.

A Critique

The settlement of 1919 has occasioned more debate than almost any other issue of contemporary European history. It has been attacked as a great betrayal of all that Wilson stood for and defended as the best that could be obtained under the circumstances, including by far the fairest delimitation of frontiers that Europe had ever known. Both contentions are justified. For each depends on where one lays the emphasis and on which of the specific terms of the treaties one chooses to focus.

Even a generous historian, however, must make at least one major criticism: the reparations imposed on Germany were both unjust and impossible to collect, and the "war guilt" statement which sought to justify them was a radical distortion of the actual origins of the conflict. This is what the great British economist John Maynard Keynes argued in his masterly polemic *The Economic Consequences of the Peace,* in which he poured out all the pent-up wrath of an expert whose advice had been flouted. The reparations clauses in turn suggest one cardinal fault of the treaties as a whole—their neglect of the economic aspects of settlement and their almost exclusive concentration on national and territorial questions. Thus in their haste to accept the liberation of East Central Europe, the peacemakers of 1919 did not pay sufficient attention to what they were doing to the economy of the area. They forgot that the Austro-Hungarian Empire, despite all its faults, had given economic unity to the Danube Basin, and that if the Empire must end, something must be found to replace it.

It should also be added that although the boundaries drawn in 1919 conformed more closely to the linguistic frontiers of Europe than any before or since, in case of doubt the peacemakers almost invariably resolved the conflict in favor of the victors or their newly created allies. And doubtful cases were legion in East Central Europe, where different nationalities so frequently lived inextricably entangled. In certain disputed regions, Wilson had insisted on plebiscites, for example, in northern Schleswig and in Upper Silesia. But Wilson well knew that in a number of critical areas, such as the South Tyrol and the border rim of Bohemia, he and his colleagues had directly violated the wishes of the inhabitants. For these major injustices—and for all the others that the passage of time might reveal—he relied on the machinery of the new League of Nations as the ultimate corrective.

The greatest disappointment of the whole peace settlement was the failure of the League to fill the place in international affairs for which the American president had intended it. And this was less the fault of the Europeans than of Wilson's own countrymen. In March, 1920, the American Senate refused to ratify the Treaty of Versailles, largely because of the Covenant of the League of Nations which, as Wilson had insisted, formed an integral part of it. He had already had the Covenant substantially modified, and he refused to accept the further amendments that might have saved the treaty as a whole.

With the United States out of the League and withdrawn into the new isolation of the 1920's, Britain and, more particularly, France were left to carry out the terms of a treaty in which they had never really believed. Moreover, the failure of American ratification also removed the guarantee of aid against potential German aggression with which Wilson and Lloyd George had tried to allay Clemenceau's fears. While the British hesitated, the French quite simply went about converting the peace settlement into what they had wanted from the start: they used the machinery of the League of Nations to protect French security; they made military alliances with the new or newly enlarged nations of East Central Europe; and they held the whip of reparations collections over a prostrate Germany.

As finally drafted, the Treaty of Versailles had fallen between two stools—it was neither a peace of iron nor a peace of reconciliation. It was neither severe enough to hold down the Germans forever, as the French had desired, nor sufficiently generous to reconcile the vanquished to their new situation. The same was true of the way in which the terms of the treaty were applied. In the early 1920's, when the French tried to enforce the letter of the Versailles settlement, they received insufficient support from the British; after 1924, when the French shifted over to reconciliation, it was too late to eradicate the resentment that had already become fixed in German minds. Such was the final tragedy of the Treaty of Versailles.

V
THE FINAL LIQUIDATION
OF THE WAR

The Peace of Paris brought the First World War to its official end, but it did not bring stability to Europe. Numerous areas of conflict remained, and local wars and disturbances continued for four more years. Not until the end of 1923 did the Continent reach a new and precarious equilibrium.

The Local Wars: Poland, Turkey, and the Adriatic

The final adjustment of Poland's frontiers involved both formal warfare and sporadic local fighting that continued for nearly three years after the Treaty of Versailles was signed. In Upper Silesia, a plebiscite held in March, 1921, returned a vote of three to two in Germany's favor. At this, the Poles took up arms, German irregular forces responded in kind, and the League of Nations was obliged to step in. There resulted a partition of the area—most of it going to Germany, but the major industrial and mining resources being awarded to Poland.

Meantime the Poles had embroiled themselves in a far more serious conflict with their great neighbor to the east. Poland's eastern frontier had remained unspecified in the settlement of 1919, to which, of course, Bolshevik Russia was not a partner. The Poles themselves demanded a restoration of the eighteenth-century boundaries of the state, including nearly all the Ukraine and White Russia. The Allies, on the other hand, proposed a boundary several hundred miles to the west—called the Curzon Line, after the British foreign secretary who devised it—which ran fairly close to the linguistic frontier. But such a frontier was impossible to establish with any accuracy: in these borderlands, Poles blended imperceptibly into Ukrainians; the landlords tended to be of the former nationality, the peasants of the latter. The Polish government refused to accept the Curzon Line and in April, 1920, attacked Soviet Russia to enforce its claims. This local war in turn became part of the civil war and foreign intervention which were currently wracking the Soviet state. At first the Poles succeeded in occupying most of the Ukraine. But then the Red Army turned on them and advanced nearly to Warsaw. Only the most stubborn resistance, plus the promise of French military aid, saved the Polish capital.

It was now obvious that neither side could impose its will on the other. In the Treaty of Riga of March, 1921, the warring powers resorted to a device that was to become standard after the Second World War: they divided the disputed area along the line at which military operations had come to an end. The result satisfied no one: neither Poland nor Russia recognized the frontier of 1921 as final. And the same was true of the Germans who never, even in the most hopeful days of international reconciliation, were prepared to accept their boundary to the east.

The interwar position of Poland was now established—as a client state of France, exposed to the merciless enmity of its neighbors to the east and to the west. Should French help ever falter, the Poles were doomed. As early as 1922, with the final delimitation of Poland's frontiers, the double threat to its existence that eventually precipitated the Second World War was already fully evident.

Similarly in Turkey, the settlement reached at Paris proved only temporary: the Treaty of Sèvres never came into effect. The nationalist leader Mustapha Kemal (subsequently called Atatürk) refused to accept its provisions. He attacked the Greeks who had already landed in Asia Minor to take over the lands that the Allies had awarded them; he fought off their further advances, driving them back to the Aegean; and he deposed the sultan, whose authority in the meantime had virtually ceased to exist. Thus the wartime Allies, hopelessly divided in their attitude toward resurgent Turkey, were obliged to draft a new settlement. The Treaty of Lausanne, in July, 1923, restored Turkish authority over all Asia Minor and the area around Constantinople. In addition, the Turks and Greeks signed a supplementary agreement for an exchange of populations, thus inaugurating another device for international settlement that was frequently resorted to in subsequent decades. Under its terms more than a million Greeks of Asia Minor—a population that had lived there since antiquity—were shipped to the Greek mainland, and a smaller number of Turks who had resided in Greece took their place.

With the Treaty of Lausanne and the proclamation of a republic that followed, Turkey completed its postwar metamorphosis. It was no longer a decrepit empire, struggling to maintain a hated dominion over far-flung regions of alien speech. It had become a compact national state, bent on rapid modernization and adaptation to Western norms.

Finally there remained the supremely vexing problem of Fiume and the Dalmatian shore. The Italian government tacitly renounced the latter, but kept up a futile annexationist propaganda for the seaport itself. After the question had hung fire for three months, the nationalist poet D'Annunzio, enraged by the indecision of his government, decided to take over Fiume himself with the aid of a strange crew of war veterans and adventurers. For more than a year he governed it in eccentric and dictatorial fashion. Then at the end of 1920 the Italian government, now in less nationalist hands, came to an amicable agreement with Yugoslavia for establishing Fiume, like Danzig, as a free city, and proceeded to expel D'Annunzio from its administration. But this agreement in turn was in effect for only fifteen months before it was overthrown by a Fascist coup. And when Mussolini himself came to power, he formally annexed Fiume to Italy. The Yugoslavs, whom the Great Powers had now forgotten, found no recourse but to accept the inevitable. By the Pact of Rome of January, 1924, they renounced Fiume entirely. For the next decade and a half, the Adriatic question remained quiescent—but it was to explode once more in the Second World War when a revolutionary Yugoslavia found itself at length in a position to challenge Italian primacy.

Germany: Reparations and the Ruhr

Of all the undecided questions that disturbed Europe during the four years following the signature of the peace treaties, the problem of Germany itself was naturally the most important. And the central feature of this problem was the collection of reparations.

At first it seemed as if postwar Germany was settling into a peaceful democratic course. The elections to the constituent assembly, held in January, 1919, gave a crushing majority to the three parties that had sponsored the Peace Resolution of 1917—the Catholic Center, the Democrats, and the Social Democrats. The constitution that resulted from their labors was in the Western democratic mold. But this constitution had been in effect for less than a year when a new period of troubles began. In March, 1920, a rightist coup—the Kapp Putsch—temporarily won control of Berlin, and a few days later the Communists took up arms in the Ruhr.

Threatened as it was from both the right and the left, the government also had to contend with the problem of reparations. After a series of conferences between the Allies and Germany failed to arrive at agreement on the amount and manner of payment, the French took matters into their own hands; in March, 1921, they occupied three industrial cities in the Ruhr Valley. Thus coerced, the Germans accepted the Allied reparations bill—finally fixed in May at thirty-three billion dollars—and proceeded to pay as best they could.

For a year and a half, a coalition government under a Center chancellor struggled to fulfill the reparations terms of the treaty. By the end of 1922, the Germans would bear no more: the government's reluctance to impose restraints on the business community was already inducing a severe inflation of the mark, and the Allies refused to renew a moratorium that had eased the strain for a few months. In December, Germany defaulted. The next month the French and Belgians—this time totally unsupported by the British—proceeded to occupy the entire Ruhr.

The 1923 occupation of the Ruhr marked both the climax and the end of the postwar time of troubles. Initially it awakened a wave of patriotic revulsion. Rallying behind a new ministry of nonparty experts and industrialists, the German people resorted to passive resistance. The French in turn tried to coerce the Germans by operating the Ruhr mines and railroads for their own benefit. In the end, both policies failed. Coercion did not pay, and passive resistance brought on more evils than the occupation itself. The German state almost dissolved, as Communists, nationalist fanatics, and separatists working for the French contended with each other in a confused, many-sided civil war. In more than one area, starvation threatened. And to support the hundreds of thousands whom passive resistance had thrown out of work, the German government printed paper money faster and faster as the mark went into the wildest inflation that the world had yet seen.

By late summer, both sides were sick of the struggle. In September, a new German ministry under Gustav Stresemann called off passive resistance. At the same time the French were coming around to a more realistic assessment of their reparations claims. As the year 1923 drew to a close, the era of postwar stabilization was already in sight.

Readings

The effect of Wilson's policies on the breakup of the Austro-Hungarian Empire is traced in Victor S. Mamatey, *The United States and East Central Europe 1914–1918* (1957). An older account, inspired both by national patriotism and a Europe-wide cultural experience, is Thomas Garrigue Masaryk, *The Making of a State* (1927), by the founder of Czechoslovakia.

For a spirited and scholarly account of Germany in the last phases of the war and the negotiation of the armistice itself, see Klaus Epstein, *Matthias Erzberger and the Dilemma of German Democracy* (1959). Paul Birdsall, *Versailles Twenty Years After* (1941), is the best brief account of the Peace Conference, and Harold Nicolson, *Peacemaking 1919* (1933), the sprightly and revealing diary of a participant. In his *Politics and Diplomacy of Peacemaking* (1967), Arno J. Mayer argues that the Bolshevik menace dominated the conference behind the scenes, while Piotr S. Wandycz, *France and Her Eastern Allies 1919–1925* (1962), traces the alliance system that resulted from this fear. René Albrecht-Carrié, *Italy at the Paris Peace Conference* (1938), Ivo J. Lederer, *Yugoslavia at the Paris Peace Conference* (1964), and Nina Almond and Ralph H. Lutz, *The Treaty of Saint-Germain* (1939), deal with the most perplexing problems relating to the Austrian Empire and the Balkans.

The classic denunciation of the economics of the treaties is John Maynard Keynes, *The Economic Consequences of the Peace* (1920), to which one should add the reply by a French economist, Etienne Mantoux, *The Carthaginian Peace, or the Economic Consequences of Mr. Keynes* (1946).

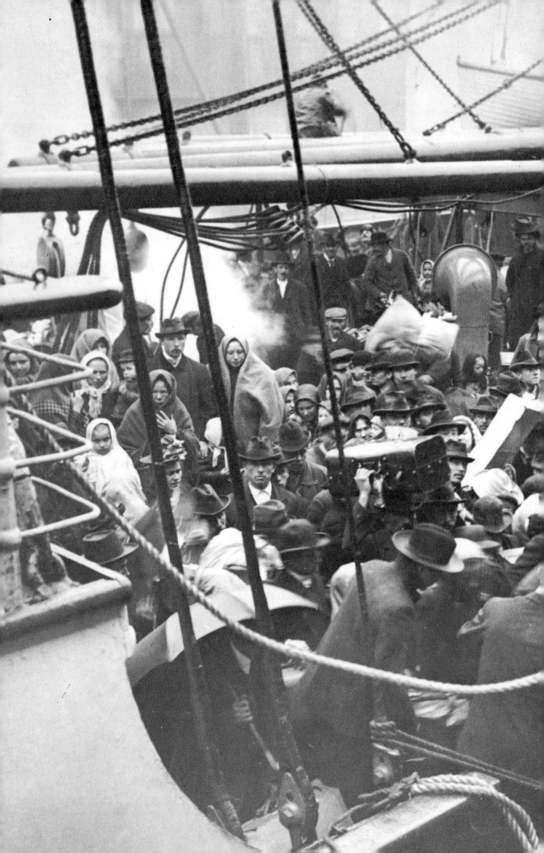

Technology and Society: Between Old and New

The first years of the twentieth century brought with them a second industrial revolution which was to substitute for the nineteenth-century dominance of coal and iron, a cleaner, lighter, and speedier technology typified by the automobile and the airplane, synthetic products and the radio. The earlier technology—with its connotations of dirt and heavy labor—had separated European society into two sharply differentiated classes of proletarians and owners, those who performed the drudgery of industrial production, as against those who managed them and lived on the proceeds of their toil. Under the aegis of the new technology, this division would become less clear-cut: the primacy of heavy industry was to be challenged by lighter and more specialized products, and production itself was to lose its old exclusive importance, as management and distribution absorbed more and more time and manpower. In this new technological and industrial situation, clerks and technicians would begin to take the place of factory hands and heavy labor; a blurring of class lines would naturally follow. And the result would be a *de facto* democratization of life far more real and deep than anything that the radical political leaders of the previous century had been able to bring about. The new society of abundance was also to be a society of substantial equality.

Such was the logic of the situation as Europe emerged from the First World War. But events did not move so logically. In the 1920's, Europe found itself on the threshold of the new society—but unable to take the decisive steps that would have led it securely into the future. The nine-

Some of the many emigrants to the United States after the First World War. They are shown debarking from steerage. COURTESY BROWN BROTHERS.

teenth-century way of life had obviously outlived its usefulness: the twentieth-century way of life seemed unable to come into being. This was to be the tragedy of European society in the interwar period.

I

THE NEW TECHNOLOGY

The Pace of Change

The experience of the First World War greatly accelerated the changes, both social and technological, that were already evident in the immediate prewar era. The necessities of combat and of economic mobilization acted as a spur to invention and to boldness in the exploitation of unorthodox methods. Military requirements first brought the airplane into its own; the British blockade stimulated the development of synthetic products in Germany. Similarly in the case of the automobile: at the outbreak of the conflict, horse-drawn vehicles predominated in the streets and on the highways of Europe; at the end of the war, the reverse was true. The armies had gone into the war almost wholly dependent on horse transport; when the fighting ended, although the artillery was still horse drawn, the success of trucks and tanks and motorized ambulances had convinced even the most conservative that the future lay with the internal combustion engine.

The same speeding-up of development was apparent in the case of technical innovations that had found a less direct application to war needs—electric power and radio, for example, and the newly invented motion picture. The 1920's saw the decisive shift to electricity in field after field. By the end of the decade, an urban building without electricity was considered disgracefully old-fashioned, and the electrification of the countryside had become a major goal of all nations that wanted to be in the technological vanguard. Even Lenin—hampered as he was by the backward condition of Russian society—had proclaimed rural electrification as one of the first tasks of the new Soviet regime. In the case of radio and the motion picture, forms of entertainment that before 1914 had been only rare and exciting novelties were already commonplace by the mid-1920's. No prosperous home was now without its radio set; going to motion pictures had become the usual form of cheap entertainment in all except the smallest towns and villages. And in the second half of the decade the talking picture began to transform still further the range and character of mass entertainment.

Inventions of this sort vastly altered rural living. No longer were country dwellers so isolated—so cut off, as they formerly had been, by a wall of mutual incomprehension, from the ways of the great cities. In the 1920's both new forms of entertainment and new means of communication began to bring the peasantry into unprecedentedly close contact with the metropolis. Rural bus lines linked villages that even the smallest railways had never touched, and year after year the telephone network was extended to ever more remote communities.

The new means of communication also began to reach out across national and continental frontiers. If Europeans were slower than Americans to improve and extend their highways—a country like France, for instance, already had a fine road network well fitted to the first generation of the automobile—they moved faster in developing commercial aviation. As early as 1919, two British pilots made the first transatlantic flight. Only a few years later, regular commercial service was inaugurated between the major European cities. When American flying was still largely limited to military uses and carrying the mails, air travel was becoming a normal mode of transport for Europeans. From 1920—when the Dutch instituted a regular air service between Amsterdam and London—each year saw the opening of some new line linking the European capitals. By the end of the decade, Europeans were inaugurating more remote services to their Asian and African colonies. Only on the eve of the Second World War, however, were Europe and the United States —which had been connected by telephone since 1927—to be linked by a regular air service.

In the United States, the exploitation of the new methods of communication and transport was usually left to private enterprise; competition and independent initiative were the rule. In Europe, on the contrary, the government almost always stepped in, either to run the new service itself or to enforce a monopoly. Thus radio broadcasting, on the model of the BBC, founded in 1922, was nearly invariably monopolized by the state, and commercial aviation was farmed out to individual companies on a noncompetitive basis.

The Rationalization of Production

In the field of production and technology, "rationalization" became the slogan of the decade. From one standpoint, this effort also reflected the war experience, since military exigencies had dictated a search for more efficient solutions and the reconstruction of war-devastated plants and mines had given free scope for innovation. From another standpoint, the drive for rationalization offered further evidence of America's new prestige and influence. For the models of efficiency which the Europeans copied usually derived from the United States—the chain-belt method of mass production first perfected by Henry Ford; the standardization of parts and supplies, which substituted skilled repairmen for old-fashioned artisans; the "scientific" reorganization of work in the factory, usually called "Taylorization," after Frederick Winslow Taylor, its American inventor; and the exploitation of novel machinery, such as the electric furnace, which reduced the cost of producing light metals like aluminum to a fraction of its former level. In nearly all these techniques and in the wide variety of new products that accompanied them—rayon, plastics, nitrates, and special types of building cement, to cite only a few —the United States had taken the lead.

A similar rationalization, but at a much slower pace, was also occurring in the countryside. Here, too, the war accelerated developments already in progress. The peasantry, second only to the aristocracy, had suffered the heaviest war losses. At the end of the fighting, a real shortage of rural manpower began to appear for the first time in history in such countries as Britain, France, and Germany, and with it a pressure to consolidate holdings, introduce farm machinery, and even to abandon the cultivation of marginal land. Moreover, the peasants now had the money to make such improvements, for the food shortages of the war and immediate postwar periods had resulted in high prices for farm goods, and in many areas, small farmers were able to wipe out almost entirely their traditional burden of debt. Meantime, the long-term drift of young people to the cities continued—reinforced, in the postwar years, by the psychological shocks of the conflict itself and the growth of new and attractive types of white-collar employment.

But changes such as these came at a most uneven pace. The agricultural countries of Southern and Eastern Europe were almost untouched by them. Even in the industrialized nations, the process of rationalization affected certain sectors of the economy very heavily while scarcely disturbing the established routines of sectors closely adjacent. In France, for example, the main work of modernization was confined to the areas of war devastation, such as the textile plants of the north and northeast. In Britain, a dangerous gap opened between the newer industries like electricity, chemicals, automobiles, and aircraft, where equipment was up to date and methods of production rationalized, and the older industries based on coal and iron and textiles, which languished in nineteenth-century inefficiency. Even Germany—the European leader in the propaganda for rationalization—carried the work forward in a disorderly fashion. The great inflation of 1923 enormously stimulated the concentration and cartelization of industry. But not all these new combines could demonstrate their economic rationality: if this was true of "vertical" concentrations, such as the steel trust, the Vereinigte Stahlwerke, founded in 1926, or the great chemical combine I. G. Farben, which had been established in the previous year, no argument of utility or efficiency could be made for "horizontal" combinations, like that of the trust-monger Hugo Stinnes, which sprawled octopus-like over the economy, sweeping up such diverse enterprises as chemicals, textiles, forests, and shipping lines along its way.

Furthermore, clear-sighted Europeans well knew that in the race for rationalization they no longer had all the advantages on their side. In this sort of competition, the countries of the New World, more particularly the United States, had a scope for innovation and mass production that Europe could not match. The European market was too small and its economic horizons too narrow—and these handicaps were intensified by a sharp postwar resurgence of economic nationalism. Thus even the countries in the European vanguard were moving forward only within the *European* frame of reference; in the *world* competition, they were falling behind. Germany—to take the outstanding case—by 1928 had recovered its place as second only to the United States in over-all industrial production. Despite the loss of the resources of Upper Silesia and the Saar, it had increased its productive capacity by 40 per cent of the prewar figure. But its *share* of world production, which had been 17 per cent in 1909, had fallen to just over 11 per cent at the end of the 1920's.

Yet it was not merely the unavoidable limitations of the European economy that restricted the process of rationalization and the passage to a new type of society. The economic and social effects of the war itself were also at work. For although some of these had acted to speed the pace of change, more of them, as the 1920's wore on, revealed themselves to be both depressing and conservative in their long-range implications.

II
THE SOCIAL AND ECONOMIC EFFECTS OF THE WAR

Population Movements: Refugees and Emigration

The First World War, hardly less than its successor, churned up and dislocated the civilian populations of Europe. Only in the stable countries of the West did the mass of the people remain untroubled. In Central and Eastern Europe, social revolution and the postwar redrawing of boundaries set millions moving: it is impossible to know how many families, at one time or another, were on the road, driven from their homes by hunger, political terror, or longing to remain with their fellow nationals.

The Bolshevik Revolution produced the most dramatic of these migrations. By the end of the civil war, perhaps as many as a million and three-quarter Russians had left their country, scattering widely throughout the rest of Europe. Subsequently a small percentage returned—but the vast majority remained abroad, the older ones consumed with homesickness and never assimilating with their new environment, the younger gradually merging into the population around them. Paris was the greatest center for this influx and reflected in the arts and in the theater the stimulating innovations that the refugees from Russia brought with them.

In Central Europe, the defeated powers found themselves forced to absorb a mass of refugees who refused to accept the new allegiances imposed by the boundaries of 1919. In the post-Versailles years, Germany experienced a foretaste of a problem it was to face on a far, far greater scale after 1945—the incorporation into a nation with diminished territory of hundreds of thousands whose homes now lay beyond its borders. The vast majority of these—nearly three-quarters of a million —came from the lands awarded to Poland, but there were also more than 100,000 from the minority of Alsace-Lorrainers who had been satisfied with German rule. The absorption of this additional population proved comparatively painless: a great industrial state like Germany was accustomed to internal migrations, and a few years after the war its economic expansion was able to take up the slack. But in the case of small and agrarian Hungary, an added population of 400,000 from its border regions imposed a severe strain. The presence of this undigested mass of discontented refugees suggests a further reason why the Hungarians never accepted their new boundaries as defined in the Treaty of Trianon.

The Greeks and the Turks eventually agreed to a massive exchange of populations. Although this device was copied elsewhere on a smaller scale, it was not able to regularize all the anomalies of citizenship that the war had produced. Many postwar refugees—unwanted in their new homes—never succeeded in achieving secure legal status. Thus the 1920's produced that new and pathetic symbol of contemporary society, the "stateless person," the refugee without a passport, the scarcely tolerated dweller in a foreign land who could be expelled at any moment by the whim of some dictator or petty bureaucrat.

Such were the direct effects of the war and the postwar settlement. Among the indirect effects, the restriction of emigration to the United States was probably the most important. The American quota laws of 1921 and 1924 abruptly halted a process that had become a normal part of Europe's population rhythm. Over the course of centuries, Europeans had become accustomed to seeing the adventurous and the unwanted among them emigrate overseas. More particularly, in poor peasant areas emigration had acted as an essential safety valve on the pressure of population. As this pressure mounted with each passing decade of the nineteenth century, the small streams of overseas migrants grew to a mighty torrent. In 1913, about two million Europeans left for overseas, the greater part of them bound for the United States; subsequently, with the lifting of wartime restrictions on transport, 800,000 more poured into the United States alone.

At this point, the American Congress took alarm. The result was the quota system, which in its final form fixed the number of annual arrivals at 2 per cent of the total residents of each national origin in the United States in 1890. By setting this as the governing date, the law of 1924 favored the countries of older emigration while almost cutting off immigration from Southern and Eastern Europe—for only in the quarter-century before the war had arrivals from these areas reached large proportions. Thus the American quota system worked almost diametrically contrary to Europe's needs: poor lands like Italy and Poland, from which literally millions would have liked to emigrate, found immi-

gration into the United States almost completely stopped; the richer
lands of the West—notably Great Britain—which enjoyed ample quotas,
did not fill their totals.

There remained, of course, the other major areas of overseas settlement—South America and the British dominions. In the decade of the
1920's, Argentina received just under a million and a half immigrants,
and Brazil 840,000. But more than half of these, dissatisfied with their
new conditions of living, returned to Europe, and the million-odd that
remained were only a fraction of those that the United States would
have been able to absorb in the same period. Nor did the British dominions provide an adequate substitute—for these, like the United States,
had begun to restrict immigration in order to favor people of Anglo-
Saxon or northern European origin.

Thus postwar Europe was largely left to cope with its population problem unaided. Fortunately one land of traditional immigration had increased rather than reduced its readiness to receive strangers from
beyond its borders. This was France—the only great country of Europe
which before the war had been notably underpopulated, and whose war
losses left it with a severe shortage of manpower. In the 1920's France's
population was stable and even declining: its birth rate was failing to
keep up with its deaths. Had it not been for the more than a million and
a half foreign workers whom France received in the years from 1920 to
1928—most of them from Italy, Poland, Switzerland, and Belgium—the
country would have been less populous at the outbreak of the Second
World War in 1939 than it had been when it faced the First World War
a generation earlier. And even in its situation of demographic stability,
France found its military manpower decreasing, as the average age of
its people steadily rose.

The interwar situation of France suggests the salient new features of
Europe's population picture: this population had become older, as the
advance of medicine and hygiene lengthened the span of human life;
its chief movements—whether in search of work or of political refuge—
had become intra-European rather than transoceanic; and the countries
where it was growing fastest were those least able to cope with the problems it raised.

Between 1913 and 1928, the population of Europe—despite the losses
of the war—rose from 498 to 534 million, a net gain of 36 million. But
this gain was very unevenly distributed: Germany experienced substantial increases, but Britain and France grew scarcely at all; the largest
share of the increase came in the poor peasant areas of Italy and East
Central Europe. These lands, however, could not cope with their growing populations: unable to industrialize adequately and with emigration
largely cut off, they let their surplus people remain on the farms—with
depressing effects on rural wages, the standard of living, and the whole
morale of the countryside.

In the nineteenth century, the growth of population had acted as a spur to economic initiative. In countries like Britain and France and Germany, the new industries of the cities had drained off the rural excess and mobilized it for production. After 1920, on the contrary, both population stability and population gain seemed to act as social and economic depressants. In the former situation—which was characteristic of the advanced industrial societies of the West, with the notable exception of Germany—a stable population became associated with economic stagnation. In a situation of growth—characteristic of the south and east—the new population could find no suitable employment. Here once again, although the possibilities of progress were present, Europe became snarled in a complex web of short-run difficulties, from which, for the better part of a generation, it could find no escape.

Boom and Bust, 1917–1922

By the midpoint of the First World War, abnormal economic conditions in nations mobilized for combat had begun to change substantially the standard of living and the relative position of classes within the European population. Initially, factory workers had suffered, since wages failed to keep pace with mounting costs. By 1917, however, these discrepancies had largely disappeared. In that year the French cost-of-living index (with 1914 as 100) stood at 180, and wages at 170. On paper, then, there was still a slight gap between the two. But family income had now pulled ahead, since overtime pay had become usual and more members of working-class families found jobs. Thus family take-home pay, including overtime hours and the wages of wives and daughters, was far higher, in real terms, at the end of the war than it had been at the start.

The effect of this change, if it had continued—as it was in fact to do after the Second World War—would have been to reinforce the democratic currents within European society. It had already stimulated the confidence of the working classes in the months immediately following the Armistice. But the postwar boom came to a very rapid end. As soon as the immediate needs of reconstruction and the accumulated backlog of nonmilitary orders had been filled, a short but severe depression set in. The end of 1920 found all the Western nations contending with the same problems: sagging currencies, stagnating production, and massive unemployment.

By 1922 recovery had begun. But it was to be slow and hesitant, and the confident rhythm of the immediate postwar years was never to be regained—as was reflected in the timorousness of European trade-union and Socialist leadership in the years of apparent stability. In rather different fashion, the same tone prevailed among the salaried middle class. One of the threatening and depressing features of the society of the 1920's was that the working classes and white-collar people both were nursing profound economic grievances.

For the salaried middle class, the war brought little but hardship. Like
the workers, people in this group had suffered severely from the price rise in the early part of the conflict but, in contrast to industrial labor, they found no compensation in the later war years. Clerical and professional salaries continued to lag behind steadily mounting prices. Thus in France the pay of civil servants rose scarcely 50 per cent during the war, while the cost of living almost doubled. But this was not all—even the smaller middle-class people, unlike the workers, usually had savings in addition to their salaries. And savings were still more dangerously undermined than were wages and salaries by the economic dislocations of the war.

All the governments except the British had financed their military effort in reckless and haphazard fashion—mostly by printing paper money. With the coming of peace, the bill had to be paid somehow. In the immediate postwar years, governments shifted and tacked and tried to avoid facing up to the inevitable. For a while—at least in the victor countries—the illusion persisted that reparations from Germany would solve the problem. By 1923 this illusion had vanished. One after another the nations of Europe defaulted on their obligations—a few, like Soviet Russia, by simply refusing to recognize the debts incurred by the previous regime, but most by a currency inflation of varying proportions. Inflation on this scale meant paying for the war by a capital levy—a levy falling more heavily on the salaried or pensioned middle class than on any other element of the population. In Britain inflation was minimal, and by the mid-1920's the pound had been restored to its prewar relation to the dollar; in France and Italy three-quarters of the previous value of money was wiped out; in the defeated nations—Austria, Hungary, and Germany —the old currency ceased to exist as the economy plunged into an inflationary crisis that shook European society more profoundly than any other series of events in the entire decade.

The German Inflation of 1923

This vast social crisis brought about a "proletarization" of the middle class. When the French marched into the Ruhr in early 1923, they precipitated a sweeping change in the relationship of Germany's social classes that had been in the making ever since the war ended. The crisis of 1923 shattered traditional German society: it constituted the real German revolution, dividing old from new in a far more profound fashion than had the brief and largely superficial political revolution of 1918.

By the summer of 1923 the mark had become practically worthless. A whole suitcase full of paper money was sometimes needed to settle a small debt, and even this cumbersome fashion of payment soon proved impracticable, as the value of money fell almost from hour to hour. Finally only payment in kind made sense. Durable goods of intrinsic value stood at a premium: people rushed to buy whatever seemed likely to survive the inflation intact. Under such conditions the regular functioning of the economy became impossible: with advance planning out of the question, trade and production were reduced to the most primitive forms of barter and muddling through from day to day.

In November, the new Stresemann government stabilized the mark at the rate of one trillion old units of currency to one of the new. It was obviously the only thing to be done, but its effects were devastating. Such a drastic reconversion had no precedent in history; never since the invention of the modern financial system had the face value of money vanished so utterly. In effect, all promises to pay of whatever sort—bank notes, pensions, savings, mortgages, and bonds—had been wiped out completely. Those who had skimped and saved and trusted in their governments and in the future were left without a penny.

Had everyone suffered equally, these losses might have been easier to bear. But in fact the German population was divided into those who suffered desperately, those who suffered a little, and those who suffered not at all or even profited by the inflation. In the last category were the major industrialists and stock owners in the more solid industrial concerns: as holders of real rather than paper values, these people rode through the inflation untouched and were in a position to buy up the enterprises of their weaker competitors who had been unable to withstand the financial storm. Thus the inflation of 1923 strengthened the tendency toward the concentration of industrial holdings that already characterized the German economy. In the category of moderate sufferers were most industrial workers. Few of these had substantial savings, and most of them were able to return to their previous standard of living once industry began to pay stable wages again. But even they incurred less obvious losses whose results were to become apparent only years later. Among the side effects of the inflation were the abolition of the eight-hour day—which had ranked as one of German labor's major postwar gains—and the almost total loss of trade-union treasuries. Together, these two changes helped intensify that mood of defeat which had settled upon European labor after 1920 and which, a decade later, was to be responsible for the apathy and disunion of the German working classes in the face of the Nazi menace.

The greatest sufferers were the small middle class. In economic terms, the inflation had "proletarized" a large part of them—had reduced them to a level as low (or even lower) than that of the industrial workers. But in psychological terms, the effect was rather different. Indeed, had the proletarization of the middle class been emotional as well as financial, the results might have been healthier. For these people might then have united with the workers in protest against an intolerable social situation and in resistance to the oncoming of fascism. But this middle-class people would not do: they nursed their grievances in isolation, refusing to face the realities of their economic plight.

The truth was that they were more pained by their loss of social status than by their financial disaster: they were troubled more by vast questions about the nature of society than by the day-to-day problem of making ends meet. Whom was one to trust in the future, they asked themselves, now that their government had defaulted on its obligations? And how in this new situation could they cling to their difference from the proletariat, which they felt so deeply but which they no longer had the money to support? The older people simply shook their heads in bewilderment. The young people went their own way without regard for their elders. For the inflation of 1923 inflicted a shock on the traditional authority of the German father from which it never recovered: a head of the family who could no longer either provide adequately for his children or offer them reassuring answers to the problems of life obviously could not play the tyrant at home. Hence both young and old were consumed with dissatisfaction—the elders in passive and pessimistic fashion, the young people in a more activist and militant mood that led them to seek out new political leadership. An examination of the origins of German fascism shows that some of the earliest recruits to the Nazi party were young people of the small middle class, former officers or men trained for the professions who could find no proper outlet for their talents.

Young and old, however, had one thing in common: their passionate nationalism. The old liberal and rational explanations had failed them; the newer Marxist explanations they rejected with scorn. They saw only the nation to fall back on, and in its hour of defeat they identified the national humiliation with their own. The result was what the psychologists call *projection:* "instead of being aware of the economic and social fate of the old middle class, its members consciously thought of their fate in terms of the nation. The national defeat and the Treaty of Versailles became the symbols to which the actual frustration—the social one—was shifted." *

The Limits to Recovery
and the Narrowing of Economic Horizons

By 1924 European society and the European economy seemed to be over the hump. Or, to put it at the very latest, by 1926 when France stabilized its currency and Britain mastered the general strike, things seemed as if they had returned to normal.

In France the most impressive achievement was the reconstruction of the country's devastated cities and farms. At the end of the war France found itself with nearly a million destroyed buildings, 9,000 factories that were similarly blasted, most of its coal and iron mines wrecked or

* Erich Fromm, *Escape from Freedom* (New York: Holt, Rinehart & Winston, Inc., 1941), p. 216.

flooded, 6,000 bridges gone, and 1,000 miles of railway lines put out of use. These losses at first seemed almost as irreplaceable as that of the million and a half young men who had been killed. But in fact the French were able to repair their physical damage rather quickly. In this task they were signally aided by the reacquisition of Alsace and Lorraine. The former territory had a well-developed textile industry. The latter possessed some of the finest iron deposits in the world. With the return of Lorraine to France, the country jumped to first place among the iron-producing nations of Europe.

Toward its citizens whose property had been destroyed, the French state behaved with extraordinary generosity. It compensated them not just for the damage they had suffered—it also paid for the complete replacement of their assets, plus suitable improvements and modernization. The results were highly satisfactory from a technical standpoint and made a notable contribution to the postwar rationalization of production, but in architectural terms most of the new building was undistinguished, and its financing was lamentable. The French had hoped that reparations from Germany would cover the bill in full: in the end these accounted for only 40 per cent of the total. The rest was paid for through inflation—with social and political results that disillusioned and depressed a whole generation of Frenchmen (*see* Chapter Six, II).

Across the Rhine, German industry—with the threat of French seizure no longer hanging over it—resumed its customary brisk pace; in the late 1920's, French patriots regularly lamented the fashion in which the defeated enemy was not suffering sufficiently for past sins and was apparently prospering rather more than the victor nations. But German prosperity was more apparent than real. It was entirely dependent on foreign loans—more particularly from the United States. Even in the "good" year 1927 the country had a foreign trade deficit of nearly a billion dollars. And this prosperity also proved far more beneficial to the great cartels than it did to the public at large. By the end of the 1920's such combines as the Vereinigte Stahlwerke and I. G. Farben effectively dominated the German economy. The former grouped together more than half the country's steel-producing capacity—a capacity equivalent to that of the whole of Great Britain. The latter, with its 300,000 employees, ranked as the largest trust in the world. Through international patent agreements with such companies as Du Pont de Nemours, I. G. Farben gradually established an influence which extended throughout the world.

By 1925, the national incomes of the major countries of Western and Central Europe had returned to their prewar level. During the next four years, this figure rose an average of 30 per cent. But in the conditions of the late 1920's increases of such an order were insufficient: they could not keep up with world competition. For in this crucial half-decade, the newer powers like the United States and Japan were pulling ahead.

Here again, there is a direct relation between the war and a European economic recovery that could not generate a self-sustained advance. In four years of conflict, Europe had consumed its economic fat; it had eaten up its savings. No longer could it produce a large surplus of funds for investment overseas: French overseas holdings were only half what they had been in 1913; Britain, which had invested 160 million pounds abroad in the seven years preceding the war, invested only 45 million pounds overseas between 1920 and 1927. And with this reduction of foreign investments went a corresponding loss of revenue from trade and transshipment. During the war years, the producing nations of Asia and the Americas grew accustomed to dealing with each other directly, rather than resorting to the British or French as middlemen. They began the generation-long process of breaking loose from European financial and commercial dominance. In the 1920's, the total volume of world trade in manufactured products—which had tripled between 1870 and 1913— remained practically stationary; *European* trade had sensibly diminished.

In those same prewar decades, the rate of growth of European industrial production had averaged more than 3 per cent annually; in the 1920's it hovered just over one per cent. Once again, the mental attitude of societies just emerging from the world conflict was responsible. Rather than enlarging the horizons of political leaders and businessmen—as it was to do after 1945—the war experience seemed to have narrowed them; in the 1920's the economic directors of the Western European nations could think of nothing better than to pick up where they had left off in 1914 and go back to the old routines. Thus in Britain, both the government and the Bank of England ranked it as a great triumph when in 1925 the country succeeded in returning to the gold standard; they failed to see that this restoration of financial orthodoxy was a hollow victory which hurt rather than improved Britain's economic situation; by overvaluing the pound in relation to other currencies, thereby raising the price of British goods, the return to gold increased the difficulties with which the country's foreign trade was already contending.

In short, by the mid-1920's the pattern of postwar recovery in the major European nations was already established in a partial and unsatisfactory fashion. Germany seemed to be prospering—but this prosperity was frantic and uneven in its distribution. France and Britain, on the other hand, were threatened with industrial stagnation. In both countries, the older industries were settling into chronic depression. This was particularly true in Britain, which, as the oldest industrial power, had the highest percentage of obsolete equipment and the greatest tendency to fall back on nineteenth-century routines. Long before the onset of the Great Depression of the 1930's, British industry was already running on part time: its total volume of exports rose to only three-quarters of what it had been before the war. Throughout the decade, whole areas of the country in the Midlands, Lancashire, and South Wales remained in a state of permanent depression, and the "depressed areas" became a standing reproach to British political leaders of all parties. Here another new and threatening phenomenon was concentrated—the permanent army of unemployed, which even in the best years never fell below one million, and in most depressed branches of the economy, such as coal mining and textiles, averaged around 16 per cent of the working force. The unemployed and their families eked out a miserable existence on what came to be called the "dole"—the extended insurance payments instituted in the depression year of 1921 and subsequently enlarged into a permanent system.

Stagnation in industry found its parallel in stagnation on the farms. By 1925, the good postwar years of European agriculture were over. Now that they had paid off their debts and improved their holdings, landowners and peasants found themselves once again face to face with their old difficulties. In the late 1920's, with the stabilization of the European currencies, interest rates rose and prices fell. Farmers were caught in the familiar squeeze: overproduction threatened, as the prices of staple crops fell on the world market. In country after country, the agricultural population turned to their government for help. The help, when it came, was grudging and insufficient—not sufficient to finance the renewal of an agrarian rationalization program on a planned and massive scale, but just enough to keep afloat a rural population whose political influence far outbalanced its real economic weight.

To meet the permanent agrarian crisis, the governments of Western and Central Europe could offer nothing better than palliatives—short-term measures to prop up an old-fashioned segment of the economy threatened by technical obsolescence. The favorite expedient was raising tariffs: during the 1920's economic nationalism became increasingly popular, particularly in the new countries of East Central Europe. But even in the West, France and Italy maintained and tightened their traditional tariff policies, while Britain, long the homeland of free trade, was more and more receptive to protectionist propaganda. Such, in sum, was the character of economic policy in the 1920's: patching up, muddling through, insisting on financial orthodoxy whatever the price, hoping against hope that something would break through the stagnation of commerce, the reduced rhythm of industry, and the permanent depression on the farms.

By the mid-1920's, the wiser European economic observers had realized that the Continent would never return to "normal." But they did not yet know what to do about it. The renewal of systematic economic thinking and planning had to wait for the Great Depression of the 1930's to sweep away the smugness and illusions of the previous decade.

III

THE NEW SOCIETY

Nevertheless, the society of the 1920's was significantly different from what it had been before the war. It was less tradition-bound; it was more democratic; and the relics of the past were regarded as quaint anachronisms rather than as patterns of life to be admired and imitated.

Democracy in Practice

By the 1920's, the center of gravity of European society had definitely shifted from the countryside to the city. Even France, the most agrarian of the advanced nations, had experienced a major change, as the prewar percentage of its working population engaged in agriculture, which had been slightly under one-half, fell to just over one-third in 1931. But this new population of the cities was rather different from what Karl Marx had anticipated. It no longer consisted primarily of "proletarians." In fact, the urban working class, as defined in the nineteenth-century sense, grew scarcely at all after 1900. It remained stationary—for although industry expanded, the productivity of the labor force also increased, as new and more efficient machines were introduced, and the same work could be done by fewer men.

What grew, rather, was the new white-collar class. And people in this group—who rejected the Marxian scheme of things—reinforced the more conservative and prosperous members of the old working class, who were also turning away from doctrinaire socialism. White-collar workers and the higher ranks of industrial labor swelled the tide of middle-class democratization. In dress, in manners, in thought, they behaved as bourgeois rather than as proletarians. And between them and the upper middle class the gap had perceptibly narrowed. Even for the rich, the war had simplified life: clothing became less elaborate, servants rarer, and entertaining less opulent. The rich, moreover, were no longer the same persons: many had been impoverished by inflation and high taxes, and their places had been taken by speculators and profiteers, whose manners were more plebeian.

To this new social mobility—to this blurring of class lines in the cities —the postwar style of life notably contributed. Manners had become relaxed, and with them the traditional code of sexual behavior. Almost before anyone was aware of what had happened, Europe had been caught up in the jazz age. Old-fashioned moralists shook their heads as respectable women began to smoke in public and young people demanded and won a freedom that their elders had never known.

The Emancipation of Women

The emancipation of women symbolized the change most dramatically. Through the wartime manpower shortage, European women made more progress toward economic equality in the four years of the conflict than they had in the entire previous generation of feminist agitation. Now a whole range of industrial and professional jobs was open to them which before the war had been strictly reserved to men. Women lawyers, women doctors—even women members of parliament and cabinet ministers—began to appear. With the war's end, in two of the great countries and several of the small, women's suffrage became a reality. Germany took the lead: in the republican constitution of 1919, women received the vote on an equal basis with men. Britain advanced more hesitantly: in 1918 an act of Parliament extended the suffrage to older and more prosperous women, but not until ten years later were all women entitled to vote on the same basis as men. France and Italy made no similar moves. Another generation had to pass before the Latin countries were ready for women's suffrage.

Here, far more than in the nations to the north, the vestiges of women's traditional inferiority of status lingered. Even in democratic France the civil code gave a husband rights over his wife and daughters which had disappeared or were disappearing in the practice of other advanced nations. But provisions such as these were more and more coming to be regarded as anomalies, destined to vanish with the passage of time. In southern Europe, as in the north, large numbers of women were now receiving a higher education, and in a decade or two it seemed likely that they would win the same equality of rights that they had earlier attained in Britain or Germany or Scandinavia. Those who looked optimistically toward the future did not realize that the forces of social conservatism were far from beaten, that in the Mediterranean countries, authoritarian regimes would soon come to power and set back the cause of women's rights for at least a generation.

The Problem of Political Leadership

In this postwar European society that was so rapidly democratizing itself and still seemed unable to advance to a full equality of rights, the problem of political leadership became particularly acute. The old elite had failed in the war—except in a few countries of Southern and East Central Europe, where semifeudal and patriarchal practices still survived, aristocratic government was no longer possible. The new elite of democracy and the career open to talents was only now being formed. Between the old leadership and the new lay a void.

Thus lawyers and businessmen assumed leadership by default. Sometimes—as in Britain, Germany, and Scandinavia—political leaders trained as trade-union executives alternated with them. But all, in varying fashion, tended to be men of mediocre endowment and limited views, cautious, routine-minded, and unimaginative. And they were also old and tired. Again and again in the interwar years, observers of the European scene bewailed the lack of youthful political talent and recalled the potential leaders who had perished in the trenches. Over the whole twenty-year period between the wars—intensifying the atmosphere of depression, economic and psychological—brooded the memory of the millions of young men who could never be replaced.

Readings

For general accounts of the economy, see P. Alpert, *Twentieth Century Economic History of Europe* (1951), and David S. Landes, *The Unbound Prometheus: Technological Change and Industrial Development in Western Europe from 1750 to the Present* (1969). Eugene Michel Kulischer, *Europe on the Move: War and Population Changes 1917–47* (1948), is the standard work on the major alterations in Europe's population during the interwar period.

The specific problems of the individual European countries are dealt with in the following: for Britain, Charles Loch Mowat, *Britain between the Wars 1918–1940* (1955), and A. J. P. Taylor, *English History 1914–1945* (1965); for France, D. W. Brogan, *France under the Republic 1870–1939* (1940); for Germany, W. F. Bruck, *Social and Economic History of Germany from William II to Hitler 1888–1938* (1938), and Alexander Gerschenkron, *Bread and Democracy in Germany* (1943).

The Years of Stability, 1924-1929

Chapter Six

During the twenty-year span between the First World War and the Second, no more than six years could be considered in any sense "normal." This was the period of apparent stabilization that separated the liquidation of the Ruhr crisis at the end of 1923 from the onset of the Great Depression at the beginning of 1930.

The five previous years had been the era in which the military sequels to the war gradually disappeared and the revolutionary threat was checked. In the second half of the 1920's peace finally became a reality, and the stabilization of society provided a basis for at least short-term planning, as opposed to the previous tendency to improvise from month to month and to live by temporary expedients. On the international scene, voluntary pacts replaced settlements imposed by force, as the League of Nations acquired prestige and influence. On the domestic front, conservative government became the rule. This was the classic era of ministries led by businessmen or by political figures in sympathy with the business point of view. In general, these governments remained in the parliamentary democratic mold; indeed, one salient characteristic of the period was the apparent consolidation of democratic practices. But curiously enough, even the countries living under authoritarian regimes—Fascist Italy and Soviet Russia—in this era turned a relatively conservative face to the outside world, reserving their more dynamic activities for the next decade. In Italy, the first ten years of Fascist rule were a period of caution in foreign affairs; in the Soviet Union, Lenin's successor, Stalin, marked time during his first half-decade of power (*see* Chapters Nine, Ten).

Dr. Gustav Stresemann of Germany makes his first speech at a League of Nations Conference.
COURTESY BROWN BROTHERS.

The late 1920's were also characterized by a restoration of financial orthodoxy and of prewar practices in industrial production. In this sense, as in government at home and in foreign relations, the era showed a return to "normal." What marked its economic prosperity likewise proved true of its politics and its international relations: the return to good times was more apparent than real—just under the surface lurked threatening forces that needed only a suitable opportunity to break out again. At the end of the decade, the Great Depression was to reveal how illusory was the optimism of the late 1920's and how shaky were the foundations of economic prosperity and international concord on which it rested.

I
THE SPIRIT OF LOCARNO

History texts of a generation ago gave much attention to the international conferences of the 1920's. They recounted in full detail the cast of characters and agenda of each of them and their record of failure or accomplishment. Today these matters can be dealt with more briefly. In present perspective, the inconclusiveness of these conferences looms larger than their achievements. With the hindsight acquired through the experience of fascism and communism on the march, the Second World War, and the Cold War that followed it, the progress made in the 1920's toward a lasting peace seems small indeed.

Yet if these years were mostly barren of diplomatic results, they were decisive in changing the character of diplomacy itself. They closed the era of international relations in the old sense and ushered in the new era of mass democracy in foreign affairs which has continued until our own day. The social and political changes of the years immediately preceding the war had weakened the diplomatic monopoly of the old aristocracy and, with it, the sense of what it meant to be a "good European." This process was enormously accelerated by the course of the war: both the intensification of national passions that the conflict aroused and Wilson's insistence on a new type of diplomacy responsive to the popular will had worked in a similar direction.

Wilson had pleaded for "open covenants openly arrived at." His condemnation of secret treaties such as the one which had brought Italy into the war permanently discredited these transactions with the European public. The secret treaties of 1915 and 1916 may be considered the last gasp of the old diplomacy. But the new diplomacy which replaced it was in many respects less effective in keeping the peace. It was more open, true, but it was also more amateurish and slipshod in its methods. The preference now went to conferences among heads of government or foreign ministers rather than to long and patient negotiations between professional diplomats. And the results—although fully exposed to the public—were frequently inconclusive and confusing. For the ordinary

newspaper reader, and even for members of parliaments themselves, it
was often next to impossible to learn precisely what a given international conference had accomplished—more particularly since the participants did everything in their power to make their achievements seem greater than they actually were.

In the 1920's, only the less dangerous faults of the new diplomacy were manifest—its carelessness and its tendency to work through amateur negotiators and informants over the heads of those who had been trained for the job. It was not until the 1930's that the more sinister aspects of the postwar situation became apparent. It was only then that the fascist dictators completely subverted the new diplomacy to give it once again the worst features of the old. In the hands of a Hitler the traditional procedures of international relations became meaningless; diplomacy was reduced to a subservient instrument of military preparation and economic and psychological pressure. The decisive influence in foreign affairs passed to the war planners and the commercial strategists —the specialists in armaments and the subtler weapons of economic penetration. This final transformation of the new diplomacy has remained characteristic of international relations down to the present day.

The Phase of Liquidation: the Dawes Plan and the Changed Position of France

In the first postwar years, the foreign ministers of the powers seemed to be in continuous session. Their agenda was almost always the same—the problem of German reparations. This phase in international affairs ended with the French occupation of the Ruhr. The Ruhr crisis, lacerating though it was, marked at least two steps forward in the settlement of the reparations question: first, by substituting the reality of force for the unreality of negotiating with a defeated enemy which had no bargaining power, the French action opened the way to a more honest confrontation of the issue; second, by showing the futility of both coercion and passive resistance, it brought both sides to a more accurate assessment of where each stood, and with that came a new readiness to compromise.

In September, 1923, the German government ended its passive resistance to the Ruhr occupation. Two months later, the French agreed to have the reparations question studied by two international committees. From the resulting deliberations there emerged the plan that for the first time put reparations on a practicable basis—the Dawes Plan of April, 1924, named after the chairman of the committee which drafted it, Charles G. Dawes, who the following autumn was to be elected vice-president of the United States.

The Dawes Plan started Germany's annual reparations payments at 250 million dollars, with the provision that they were to be gradually increased over the next five years. By the end of that time they were to be more than doubled. In addition, the plan provided for a foreign loan, amounting to nearly as much as the first annual reparations installment, which was intended to support the newly stabilized mark and start money flowing for future reparations payments. More than half of this loan was subscribed for by American financiers, who thereby set the pattern of German dependence on American capital that was to characterize this half-decade of illusory prosperity.

When the Dawes Plan came into effect in the summer of 1924, a new era opened in postwar international relations. The first tangible evidence of the change of spirit was the French evacuation of the Ruhr that began the following November. And this action in turn reflected the substantial shift in French sentiment at home which had brought to power a Radical government pledged to a policy of international conciliation. Although contemporaries did not fully realize it, the year 1924 witnessed a major alteration in France's international position. It marked the end of the Indian summer of French greatness for which the unique conditions of the immediate postwar years had provided the setting.

France—once the "great nation" without peer both by patriotic claim and by the reality of its strength and resources—had long ceased to be the arbiter of Europe. The German victory in the War of 1870 had demoted it from first to second position among the continental European nations. In the global rating of the powers, it ranked behind both Britain and the United States, whose immediately mobilizable strength was less than that of France, but whose ultimate potential was greater. Thus at the outbreak of the First World War France stood no higher than fourth among the world powers. Paradoxically, even its eventual victory confirmed this diminished role: whereas France could not possibly have survived and won without the aid of its Allies—and it emerged from the war irremediably drained of its best manpower—Germany was able to hold off a mighty coalition for four years almost unaided and to recover its economic and human strength far more rapidly than its victorious foe.

The settlement of 1919 produced a power vacuum in Europe. One great power—Austria-Hungary—had ceased to exist; two others—Germany and Russia—were in a state of disgrace and international quarantine; a fourth—the United States—had withdrawn from the European scene. Meantime a fifth power, Great Britain, was vacillating between rigor and leniency in its attitude toward its former enemy. This left France alone to police Europe and enforce the peace. The four years 1919–1923 were years of a restored French hegemony merely because no other power was prepared to challenge a position of leadership that had passed to France almost by default.

The Ruhr occupation revealed that even under these optimum conditions France was not strong enough to do the job alone. With the British reluctant to follow, the French were obliged to fall back on alliances with the smaller nations of East Central Europe—primarily with Poland, but also with the three states that were linked by gains made at Hun-

gary's expense, Czechoslovakia, Rumania, and Yugoslavia, which came
to be called the Little Entente. Yet the strength of all these four together did not remotely approach that of a great power. The apparent solidity of the Little Entente derived almost entirely from the temporary weakness of Germany and Russia. Under the new conditions of the middle and late 1920's, France had no recourse other than resorting to the League of Nations to see what could be made of its novel machinery for eliminating international discord and enforcing the peace.

The Phase of Hope: the League and Locarno

As devised by the peacemakers of 1919, the organs of the League of Nations struck a careful balance between the principle of equality among sovereign states and the realities of great-power predominance. The authority of the League was thus divided between the Assembly —in which every member nation had an equal vote—and the Council, on which Britain, France, Italy, and Japan had permanent seats, and four smaller powers (later increased to six), chosen for a fixed term of years by the Assembly, served as temporary members. Originally the membership of the League consisted solely of the signatories of the Treaty of Versailles, but since other nations could be admitted by a two-thirds vote of the Assembly, the League was gradually enlarged to include nearly all the sovereign states of the globe, except the two quarantined powers, Soviet Russia and Germany, and the United States, which had chosen not to join.

The League's Council and Assembly met in the Swiss city of Geneva, and it was there that it had its Secretariat—a body that was able to do much effective work of a technical nature in the interwar period. Beyond such quiet labors as regulating passports and international communications and controlling the traffic in drugs, the main business of the League was to keep the peace. And the effectiveness with which it could do so largely depended on how seriously its membership took their obligations to bring before it all important matters at issue and to abide by the League's decision on them.

From the very beginning there were at least two reasons for skepticism. First, the League's machinery for enforcing its decisions lacked "teeth": it depended on a unanimous vote of the Assembly and on the willingness of the membership to apply Article 10 of the Covenant—the key provision of the whole document—by which each individual member undertook to "respect and preserve as against external aggression the territorial integrity and existing political independence" of the others. Thus the recommendation by the Council and subsequent vote by the Assembly of what came to be called "sanctions" against an aggressor constituted both a doubtful and a cumbersome process. Secondly, the sphere of the League's day-to-day influence was almost entirely restricted to Europe. With the United States and Soviet Russia out, and

Japan uninterested, effective leadership within the League devolved on the former European Allies, Britain, France, and Italy. It is significant that during the only period in which the League was able to make its influence felt at all—the second half of the 1920's—it concentrated on European problems, finding a temporary basis of agreement between the victors and vanquished Germany, and that this period of League influence came to an end with an extra-European crisis, Japan's aggression against Manchuria in 1931.

The changed atmosphere that began to manifest itself in 1924 was particularly associated with the fortunate coincidence that France and Germany almost simultaneously found foreign ministers of an unusually conciliatory turn of mind, both of whom remained in office uninterruptedly for six years. On the surface, the two were extremely different human beings. The Frenchman, Aristide Briand, was a man of humble origin, a former Socialist turned conservative, already seven times prime minister and a master of the parliamentary art, with a quarter-century of political experience behind him—a supple, insinuating debater, who had developed to a fine point the talent for veiling precise meanings in ambiguous but alluring phraseology. Only one thing about him was clear: however often Briand might be accused of hypocrisy and deceit, the genuineness of his devotion to peace was beyond doubt.

His German counterpart, Gustav Stresemann, was a man of sterner stuff. A businessman and the son of a prosperous beerhouse owner, Stresemann had ranked during the war as a leading nationalist and annexationist among Germany's parliamentary liberals. The defeat of 1918 shook him out of his illusions and started him on the slow process of revising his earlier beliefs. Emotionally shattered by the national catastrophe, Stresemann passed the next five years in the political wilderness, gradually working out a new and practical policy which would combine the fulfillment of Germany's treaty obligations with systematic pressure for their revision. Thus in 1923, in his country's hour of crisis, Stresemann stood out as the one man capable of giving a clear lead: the rest were either discredited or dead. After three months as chancellor in the summer and autumn of 1923, Stresemann never again headed the German government. But from that time on until his death in 1929 Stresemann's presence at the foreign ministry was considered indispensable to all cabinets, whatever their political complexion.

Beyond their obvious differences in background and temperament—and beyond their equally obvious concern for peace—Briand and Stresemann had in common the fact that they remained more conservative and nationalist than their public statements suggested. Although in parliamentary and League of Nations addresses they spoke the language of the antiwar Left, in more private utterances they sought to reassure their nationalist supporters. This was no easy game to play, and it was more difficult for the forthright Stresemann than for the more supple Briand. The German foreign minister found it almost impossible to

make his countrymen understand that his policy of "fulfillment" actually
aimed at the revision of the Versailles Treaty—he could not state this in public for fear of offending his new friends in France. And he certainly could not reveal that he both knew and approved of clandestine German rearmament. Briand, in contrast, had an easier time with his own parliament; whenever he was tempted to go too far toward conciliation, he had at his elbow the permanent officials of the French foreign ministry, who, ever vigilant of their country's abiding interests, could always pull him back. Only in 1931, at the very end of his tenure, did Briand get into serious difficulties with the parliamentary Right.

In sum, for all the atmosphere of cordiality that surrounded their frequent and rather vague conversations, neither Briand nor Stresemann ever conceded very much. Each remained acutely aware of his country's national interests and of the line beyond which he would never consent to retreat. Their most substantial achievement—indeed, almost the only substantial achievement in international affairs of the whole decade—was the negotiation of the Locarno Treaty and the entrance of Germany into the League of Nations that followed it. And this was more the regularizing of an existing situation than a bold departure along a new path.

Following an abortive effort by the short-lived British Labor government of 1924 to put teeth into the League Covenant through a provision for compulsory arbitration—known to history as the Geneva Protocol —Stresemann came forward with a more modest idea. His original proposal of February, 1925, for a Rhineland mutual guarantee pact was welcomed by Briand, who began his long tenure in the French foreign ministry two months later and who added to Stresemann's scheme the condition that Germany should enter the League of Nations. The following autumn, after months of quiet negotiation, and with the British foreign secretary, Austen Chamberlain, playing the role of mediator, the foreign ministers were ready for a dramatic display of international concord. In early October, 1925, at the Italian Swiss lakeside resort of Locarno, the statesmen of Europe spent ten idyllic and informal days that were marked by such unconventional diplomatic spectacles as Briand rowing Stresemann around in a small boat. By December, the treaties that resulted from these happy hours were ready for signature in London.

The Locarno agreements included a main treaty guaranteeing the Franco-German and the German-Belgian frontiers—to which, besides the three principal powers involved, Great Britain and Italy adhered as guarantors—and a series of bilateral arbitration treaties. The agreements were followed, as Briand had proposed, by Germany's admission to the League in March, 1926, with its great-power status recognized by a permanent seat on the Council. In effect, the Locarno agreements meant that the Germans had accepted at least part of the Versailles settlement: they had agreed to regard their new western frontier as final (including the demilitarization of the Rhineland) and to renounce all thought of regaining Alsace-Lorraine. In return, their former enemies had recognized their new international respectability by associating them with the existing machinery for keeping the peace.

The general jubilation engendered by the "spirit of Locarno" tended to make people forget what the agreements had omitted. Although the Germans had signed treaties of arbitration with Poland and Czechoslovakia, they had not specifically accepted their frontiers with these two states. No "eastern Locarno" completed the agreements applying to the west alone. As the post-Locarno years passed, it became obvious that the relaxation of tension and new sense of security along the Rhine had no counterpart in East Central Europe, where the old irreconcilable hatreds raged as bitterly as before.

The Phase of Illusion: the Kellogg-Briand Pact, the Young Plan, and Disarmament

Thus in the international field, the era of stability produced its best effects very early. The period after 1926 was to be an anticlimax, marked only by disappointment and illusory success.

The most striking instance of illusion was the Pact of Paris, of August, 1928, usually called the Kellogg-Briand Pact after its sponsors, the ever-active French foreign minister and his American counterpart, Secretary of State Frank B. Kellogg. The product of a revived Wilsonianism joined to Briand's restless search for plausible schemes, the pact provided for a general renunciation of aggressive war. It offended nobody, since no compulsory machinery of enforcement was attached to it; hence the nations rushed to sign: it was rather like declaring oneself against sin. From the start, the Kellogg-Briand Pact signified little more than hopeful aspiration.

The next year saw a more solid achievement. After five years of operation, the Dawes Plan had revealed certain technical defects, more particularly in the transfer of reparations payments from one country to another. The Young Plan of June, 1929—named, as its predecessor, after an American financier, Owen D. Young—established a more efficient machinery for making these payments, scaled them down still further, set a final 59-year limit to them, and ended international control over their delivery. To contemporaries, it appeared that the Young Plan had dealt definitively with this vexing matter and that reparations would trouble the statesmen of Europe no more. They could hardly guess that only three years later, faced with a resurgent Germany caught in a desperate economic depression, some of the same statesmen would be forced to deal with reparations once again and, in effect, to bury them forever.

As early as 1929 the German public was behaving less passively than it had five years earlier when the Dawes Plan was inaugurated. The Young Plan unleashed within the Reich a storm of opposition to accepting the new arrangements. Nearly all the rightist and nationalist groups banded together in a vicious campaign of abuse against Stresemann—a

campaign which quite literally killed him, since he wore himself out in
combating his enemies' lying propaganda. Stresemann's death, coming in the same month as the great Wall Street stock market crash, gave ominous foretaste of what lay ahead.

The decade closed with disarmament occupying the center of the international stage. The Washington Conference of 1921–1922, which had achieved a substantial success in the limitation of battleship building, had aroused hopes that the same spirit of agreement might be extended to other categories of armaments. But such hope proved groundless. In 1927, a conference of the three largest naval powers—Britain, the United States, and Japan—was unable to reach any sort of agreement. Three years later, a larger conference, this time including France and Italy, finally achieved some modest gains—most of which, however, were canceled out by an "escalator clause" to which the powers were permitted to resort if they considered that their national needs demanded it. At the end of 1930, when the preparatory commission of the League of Nations for general disarmament completed its labors, it was quite apparent that the draft convention it had adopted had no consensus behind it and that the major disarmament conference scheduled for fourteen months later could produce only the most profound disagreements.

Meantime the statesmen hovered between trepidation and hope. The Young Plan ranked as a success, and the Germans had received their reward for accepting it: an early evacuation of the Rhineland by the occupying forces. But this single encouraging achievement was far outweighed by what appeared on the negative side of the balance—the weakening of Briand's influence, the death of Stresemann and the revival of German nationalism, the American depression and its threatened repercussions in Europe, the futility of the Kellogg-Briand Pact and the snail's pace of disarmament. All these signified the renewal of the general European crisis, economic, social, and political, that had been held at bay for six years and that now in country after country was returning in full force on the domestic front.

II

THE CONSERVATIVE GOVERNMENTS

In domestic affairs as in foreign policy, the second half of the 1920's was characterized for each of the powers by the personality of a single statesman who put his stamp upon the period. In Britain, it was Stanley Baldwin; in France, it was Raymond Poincaré; in Germany, Gustav Stresemann incarnated the hopes of his countrymen both for domestic stability and for international peace.

A further generalization is in order: the internationalist outlook of the second half of the decade had sprung from the parliamentary Left. It found its first and clearest expression in the policy of short-lived governments led by statesmen with moderate leftist views—who fell from power because of domestic rather than foreign issues—and its most enthusiastic supporters continued to be on the left. But subsequently the conservatives took over the new internationalism from its original proponents. Indeed, successful manipulation of peace sentiment in the late 1920's by the parliamentary Right was a principal reason for the conservatives' long tenure of power.

British Prologue: from the Irish Settlement
to the First Labor Government

Lloyd George's coalition government had emerged from the war with high prestige and an apparently justified confidence in its ability to carry on almost indefinitely. Its first act was to confirm its mandate by the election of December, 1918. Its calculation proved well founded: by playing on patriotic themes and the hope of substantial gains from reparations, it crushed both Labor and the independent wing of the Liberals and brought back to the House of Commons a majority that outnumbered its combined opponents by nearly four to one.

Thus the prospect for the 1920's was a scarcely veiled single-party rule; the Conservatives would allow Lloyd George to continue as prime minister so long as they themselves held the realities of power, and both the coalition Liberals and the parliamentary opposition would be reduced to impotence. For the postwar coalition was even more markedly Tory in character than its wartime predecessor had been, since its Conservative supporters by themselves sufficed to give it a majority. With the Liberals divided between those who followed Lloyd George inside the government, and those who still rallied around Asquith in opposition, the traditional second party of British politics was unable to make its weight count either way: it had gone into a decline which no subsequent change of fortune could arrest. Labor had taken its place as the chief opposition party—but with fewer than sixty seats in the House of Commons, the British Socialists were far from ready to challenge the overwhelming predominance of the Conservatives.

That this situation did not last—that the coalition was to be replaced first by a purely Conservative government, and second, and more fleetingly, by Labor itself—was the result of an accumulation of unforeseen difficulties and mistakes. There were the economic depression of 1921 and British hesitations in international affairs. Above and beyond these there was the revolt of Ireland.

Since the seventeenth century Ireland had existed as a semicolonial dependency of Great Britain. Although the majority of its population was separated by religion and tradition from that of its larger island neighbor, the country had been ruled by a thin stratum of Protestant gentry of English sympathies. In the late nineteenth century, however, after repeated extensions of the suffrage, the Catholic majority finally came into its own; it began to send to the House of Commons a solid phalanx of members single-mindedly pledged to the cause of Irish home rule and prepared to obstruct all other parliamentary business in order to achieve their aims. Thus from the 1880's on, the Liberals had good reason to take up the Irish cause; in this case, ideological devotion to the principle of freedom was reinforced by need for Irish votes. After three decades of futile effort to get a home rule bill through Parliament, the Liberals finally succeeded just on the eve of the First World War.

But the home rule bill of 1914 never came into effect. The one part of Ireland with a Protestant majority—the northeastern region known as Ulster—threatened to defend by force its union with Britain, and in this resistance it enjoyed the support of an influential segment both of the Conservatives and of the army. What the Liberal government would have done if the general European conflict had not supervened is far from clear: the army was mutinous, civil war was threatening, and Asquith was trying to work out a compromise that would avoid coercing Ulster into accepting home rule. The overriding necessities of wartime decided the issue. The government merely shelved the Irish question for the duration. For the next four years, Ireland lived in ominous calm, broken by an abortive rebellion on Easter, 1916, for which fourteen nationalist leaders paid with their lives.

In the election of 1918, however, Irish politics suddenly revived—and with a new virulence added by the four years of waiting. Instead of the comparatively mild "home rulers" of the prewar period, Ireland now sent to Parliament more than seventy members of the new party called Sinn Fein ("We Ourselves"), who were no longer satisfied with mere autonomy and were pledged to a program of complete independence. These people refused to take their seats at Westminster. Instead, they established themselves as an Irish parliament—the Dail Eireann—meeting at Dublin, and in January, 1919, they formally declared Ireland an independent nation.

Lloyd George's government took its time about dealing with this act of open rebellion. Only gradually did it drift into war with the Sinn Fein. But by the autumn of 1919, when the British decided upon full repression, they acted in the most inept fashion possible. They did not send in the regular army to subjugate Ireland in a quick campaign. They merely reinforced the regular Irish constabulary by recruiting a special force of volunteers—the notorious "Black and Tans"—whose discipline was lax and whose methods were unnecessarily cruel.

For more than a year, two irregular armies fought a strange and undeclared war in the city streets and rural byways of Ireland. Both sides were ruthless—the Irish volunteers no less than their British counterparts. Although most of the population went calmly about its ordinary tasks, no one could be sure that violence would not suddenly erupt in the form of ambushes, bomb explosions, arson, torture, or the seizure of hostages.

It was a brutal and sickening struggle—made no better by the increasingly blunt fashion in which a large segment of British public opinion began to question the justice and expediency of the whole policy of repression. Nor did the passage of another home rule bill do any good: the Dail Eireann refused to accept it, and continued to issue its orders as the clandestine government of Ireland.

By the summer of 1921, the pressure on the British authorities to reach a settlement had become overwhelming. Lloyd George summoned the Sinn Fein leaders from their political shadow world to meet with him in London and discuss a compromise. A first series of meetings, in July, produced nothing but deadlock. A second conference in the autumn found a solution: by a regular treaty signed between the Irish representatives and the British government, most of Ireland, under the name of the Irish Free State, became a self-governing dominion on the model of Canada or Australia. Ulster was granted special status: the six Protestant counties of the northeast, which had accepted the home rule act of 1920, were set up as an autonomous region of the United Kingdom, called Northern Ireland, which was both to have a parliament of its own and to continue to send members to the British parliament at Westminster.

The treaty of December, 1921, did not give the Irish Free State formal independence. But it gave the substance, and for moderate-minded Irishmen that was enough. A narrow majority in the Dail accepted the treaty and prepared to put the new institutions into effect, but the irreconcilable nationalist minority, under Eamon de Valera, refused to submit and declared for a continuation of the struggle with Britain. The British, however, would have no more of it: they were sick of fighting. It was left to the new government of the Irish Free State to wage another and still more cruel civil war for an additional year until in the spring of 1923, De Valera and his irreconcilables were finally overwhelmed.

It is hard to say who won the Irish struggle. Temporarily it was the moderate nationalists who had accepted the compromise of 1921. But by 1927, De Valera had returned to the political arena; five years later he was president and undisputed spokesman of his country. Indeed, after the Second World War, Ireland declared itself a republic and severed its remaining links with the British Commonwealth. The nationalist triumph seemed complete. Yet to this day the Ulster settlement remains unchanged: the six counties of the northeast, despite protracted and occasionally violent opposition by propagandists from the south and by their own Catholic minority, have kept their special status as an integral part of the United Kingdom along with England, Scotland, and Wales.

The tragic struggle in Ireland notably undermined the authority of Lloyd George's coalition government. So did the economic depression of the early 1920's and the disputes with France over foreign policy. In the autumn of 1922, the more aggressive Tories decided to cast aside Lloyd George and persuaded the elderly and respected Scotsman, Andrew

Bonar Law, to lead a purely Conservative government. This new Tory
ministry immediately went to the country to confirm its mandate; in the parliamentary elections of November, 1922, it emerged triumphant with a substantial majority over all the other parties and factions combined.

Both wings of the Liberals had continued their decline. But Labor had returned in force, more than doubling its previous parliamentary representation. And this new strength and militancy on the part of Labor was to become still more evident six months later when Bonar Law's ill health necessitated a change of prime minister. The Conservative leaders and the king passed over the outstanding candidate, Lord Curzon—thereby establishing the constitutional precedent that under the new conditions of democracy a peer was no longer suitable to lead the government—and picked instead the comparatively obscure Stanley Baldwin.

Baldwin's first tenure of office was unexpectedly brief. Rashly staking his own and his party's reputation on the untried plank of tariff protection, he called for another election. This time, the Liberals closed ranks and united behind Asquith; Labor continued to gain confidence; and both opposition parties raised havoc with the Tories' new protectionist stand. When the votes were counted, the Conservative party, though still the strongest in the House of Commons, had lost its majority and had unmistakably been repudiated by the electorate.

After the election of December, 1923, Asquith faced a difficult choice. Although his party was still the weakest of the three, it had made a substantial recovery, and it occupied a strategic position between its two larger rivals. The Liberals might have agreed to a coalition either with the Conservatives or with Labor—in either case the new government would have had a solid majority. Asquith chose to do neither. True to the spirit of tolerance and fair play with which he was almost excessively endowed, he declared that Labor, as the second party and the stronger of those which had successfully opposed protection, should be given a chance to govern alone. His decision amounted to political suicide for the Liberals: never again were they to come within striking distance of power. And for Labor it was a curious and not altogether welcome gift. For it meant that the first Socialist government in Western European history was to make its risky experiment under the most unfavorable conditions possible.

Britain: the Baldwin Era

The first Labor government was a flimsy structure from the beginning. Without a parliamentary majority, it could exist only on Liberal sufferance. Even organizing it proved extremely difficult. There were literally not enough Labor leaders in Parliament with sufficient experience and standing to man a full cabinet, and the new prime minister, Ramsay MacDonald, felt obliged to call on a scattering of former Liberals and independents to complete his ranks. Thus the ministry began tamely—and in this it reflected the personality of its leader, who was far more cautious than his public style suggested.

A Scotsman of humble origin, Ramsay MacDonald looked like a born leader. He was handsome, he was eloquent, his whole manner suggested an innate superiority to other men. But on closer acquaintance his followers discovered in him both vanity and hesitation, and in his noble, poetic language a lamentable absence of clear thought. As a moderate pacifist, MacDonald had been under a political cloud during the war, but in 1922 he had returned triumphantly to the leadership of his party. This choice proved fateful for Labor's whole future: in subsequent years many of those who had voted for MacDonald came to regret that they had not cast their ballots for one of the tough-minded trade-union leaders whose views were sharper and closer to those of the party rank and file.

In his ten months of office, from January to November, 1924, Mac-Donald tried to do little more than reassure the country that Labor was not so bad as people had feared. Only in the international field did he take decisive action, with the diplomatic recognition of Soviet Russia and the launching of the policy of conciliation with Germany. Meantime the Tories waited for a suitable opportunity to bring him down.

This came earlier than they had any right to expect. The matter was trivial—the government's failure to prosecute a Communist editor for publishing seditious articles—but it gave the Conservatives exactly the issue they needed to harass the prime minister. The Tories pressed the case relentlessly; MacDonald was inept in replying; finally he made it a matter of confidence, and with the Liberals now voting against him, the first Labor government went down to ignominious defeat.

In the ensuing election, the Conservatives again exploited the "red" danger to the full. The timely discovery, just before polling day, of a letter—probably forged—from Zinoviev of the Third International to his loyal followers in Britain, gave the public the impression that Labor was somehow tainted with communism or, at the very least, was insufficiently alert to the Bolshevik menace. The Tories would probably have won the election of 1924 without the aid of the Zinoviev letter, for the Labor government had been a disappointment, but the discovery of this strange document certainly helped. From the third election in as many years, the Conservatives emerged with the biggest majority of the whole decade; Labor lost a quarter of its seats; and the Liberals received a crushing blow from which they never recovered.

So Baldwin returned—this time for five years—and he proceeded to give the country the "sane, commonsense Government" that he had promised. Like MacDonald, Stanley Baldwin was a cautious mediocrity: his language was vague and moralizing, and he hated to make up his mind. But he was far more successful than MacDonald in inspiring public confidence. He wore his tweeds and smoked his pipe and looked the simple but astute north-country businessman that he was. Above all he seemed "safe"—and this was evidently what a majority of Englishmen wanted after a full decade of upsets and adventures.

Thus he gave the country a carefully measured dose combining basic conservatism and occasional innovation. Most of the time he relied simply on the old English virtue of "muddling through." But in the international field—after quickly withdrawing the hand of friendship that Labor had tentatively held out to the Soviet Union—he was happy to see his foreign minister, Austen Chamberlain, working in harmony with Briand and Stresemann in the League of Nations. Similarly at home, he gave Chamberlain's half-brother, Neville, the minister of health, free rein to undertake a program of widows', orphans', and old age pensions and local government reform which ranked as the only great constructive achievements of the entire half-decade.

The Conservative mandate to govern remained unquestioned for almost five years. But as the decade of the 1920's ended, it became more and more apparent that all was not well in Britain. Baldwin did nothing substantial about the interlocking problems of industrial and commercial stagnation, of the depressed areas, and of permanent unemployment. He postponed action from year to year, hoping that things would somehow take a turn for the better, and in the one major case of social unrest that occurred during his long tenure of power—the general strike of 1926—he behaved in a fashion that intensified the bitterness of class feeling.

The strike had its origins in the languishing coal industry. The government in July, 1925, had conceded the miners' demand that a royal commission be appointed to inquire into their grievances. Yet no one seemed very confident that the commission would achieve success: by autumn both the government and private groups were organizing for emergency action to meet the general strike that the labor leaders were threatening in support of the miners. In March, the commission made its report, which satisfied neither side. But the mine owners proved still more intractable than labor: with the government supporting them, they shut down the pits and defied the trade unions to do their worst.

The general strike went on for nine days in early May. Its scope was unprecedented: two and a half million workers were out. Equally unprecedented were the enthusiasm and efficiency with which the government mobilized volunteers from the propertied classes to run the essential services: Oxford and Cambridge students unloaded ships; there was even the story of a peer at the throttle of a train, who, when rebuked for reaching the station ahead of schedule, replied that he had only just discovered how to stop the engine. Most of the time both sides remained good-humored, and the weather was blessedly fair. But the often repeated anecdote of strikers playing football with the police gives only part of the story. Nobody lost his life in the strike, but there was sporadic local violence and great intensity of feeling.

This was particularly true of the way in which the strike came to an end. After two days of frantic negotiations, Baldwin cajoled the trade-union leaders into accepting a settlement that amounted to unconditional surrender on the miners' demands. The latter felt betrayed, and they continued their own strike, desperately and hopelessly, for six months after the general strike ended. And then—as though the bitterness of labor's failure was not already enough—the government pushed through Parliament the Trade Disputes Act of 1927, which banned sympathetic strikes and severely limited labor's bargaining power. In this undisguised piece of class legislation lay the remote origins of a revulsion of feeling that, two years later, was to end Baldwin's long period of rule and sweep the Labor party into power once more.

France: the Poincaré Era

In France the decade of the 1920's was marked by a double political failure, first by the Right and then by the Left, until in 1926 the country at last attained a precarious equilibrium.

The French parliamentary elections of 1919, like those in Britain a year earlier, produced a conservative and nationalist majority. Indeed the "Horizon-Blue Chamber," as it was called, from the number of war veterans in blue uniforms who sat in it, was the most conservative that France had known since the turn of the century. But the victorious coalition of parties—the Bloc National—did not know how to exploit its success. It repudiated old Clemenceau because he had yielded to Wilson on the Rhineland, and under leaders of lesser stature it embarked on the ill-fated policy of coercing Germany and asserting French hegemony throughout Europe.

The Ruhr failure of 1923 ended this phase of postwar French history. The government's resort to military action had frightened many people at home—conjuring up as it did the specter of renewed warfare—and the resulting wave of pacifist feeling reinforced the general discontent over the high cost of living to carry the Left into power. The Cartel des Gauches which defeated the Bloc National in the election of 1924 consisted of an alliance between the Radicals (since the early 1900's the strongest party in France) and the Socialists, who were just recovering from the secession of their Communist wing. These two could get along admirably when it came to electoral campaigning: for such purposes the old slogans of anticlericalism and "republican" solidarity gave excellent service. But when it came to governing, the two parties were almost immediately at odds.

The ministry led by Edouard Herriot in 1924 was, like its leader, primarily from the Radical party; it had no Socialists in it, but it depended on them for its support. The chief issues it faced were financial—inflation and the related problems of reparations and war debts to the United States. On matters such as these, the laissez faire Radicals and the quasi-Marxist Socialists were poles apart. In addition, Herriot, like most French

statesmen, was more rhetorician than student of economics. He had only
the vaguest notions about financial policy, and his attitude toward the country's economic plight was lax and irresponsible. For a full decade, France had been living beyond its means: its war financing had been the worst of any major belligerent; by 1919, its circulation of banknotes had increased more than sixfold, while taxation had not raised sufficient funds to cover even normal peacetime expenditures; and to all this it had added the enormous expense of reconstructing the devastated areas.

For five years the deputies had played politics as usual with problems of an unprecedented gravity. Then, in 1924, with the previous year's disappointment on reparations, the accumulated errors of a half-decade cascaded on the hapless Herriot. Inflation crept along unchecked, and the government seemed powerless to stop it. After less than a year in office Herriot gave up the struggle. His two sucessors did no better. By the summer of 1926 the franc had fallen to two cents—a tenth of its prewar value—and heroic measures seemed called for.

Once again, as in 1917, France found the right leader. Raymond Poincaré stepped in to form a national union ministry, in which he made a place for six former premiers. Poincaré was not a popular man—but his firmness and rectitude could awaken confidence after twelve years of financial facility. Even Poincaré's faults—his coldness and his narrowness of vision—might rank as assets in this sort of crisis. Moreover, he had learned from earlier disappointments: as wartime president of the Republic, he had felt eclipsed by the more appealing Clemenceau, and as prime minister during the Ruhr invasion he had experienced the realistic limits to nationalist agitation and solutions of force.

It was a temperate and chastened Poincaré, then, who took up the task of "saving the franc." He did nothing very extraordinary to bring this about: he simply behaved like the scrupulous and systematic lawyer that he was, tightening up the administration here and improving the collection of taxes there until the franc held firm and even began to mount on the foreign exchanges. In 1928, it was finally stabilized at twenty to the dollar, the rate it was to maintain for most of the interwar period.

Poincaré's success was more psychological than technical. The French realized that at last they had a "serious" government, one that meant what it said and would save from catastrophe as much as possible of the country's fortune. Indeed, in their gratitude that something at least had been rescued from the financial wreck, many people almost forgot that they had lost three-quarters of their savings. They reacted in a notably different fashion from the Germans, who were overwhelmed with bitterness by their losses.

With this achievement behind him, Poincaré was solidly installed in power. He retained the premiership for three years—an interwar record —and the basically conservative coalition he led won without difficulty the election of 1928. But Poincaré's success, like Baldwin's, was only transitory: like his English counterpart, he dealt with only one of his country's really pressing problems; the rest he pushed under the rug. Both of them profited from a unique period of tranquillity that was soon to come to an end. When Poincaré retired in the summer of 1929, a new era of storms was only a few months away.

Germany: the Stresemann Era

When Stresemann assumed power in the desperate summer of 1923, Germany was almost out of leaders. Public sentiment had turned against the Social Democrats, whose attitude toward the country's late enemies did not seem sufficiently patriotic, and the two outstanding figures among the leadership of the middle-class democratic parties, Matthias Erzberger and Walther Rathenau, had perished at the hands of nationalist fanatics.

Stresemann's three months of power marked the turning point for the republican regime that had been established at Weimar four years earlier. It ended the era of constant uncertainty, in which people scarcely knew from month to month under what sort of authority they were going to live. Through a resort to martial law and firm action against both types of extremists that were threatening the state—the Communists in Saxony and Hitler's National Socialists in Bavaria—Stresemann, like Poincaré three years later, proved the seriousness of his intentions and his resolve that middle-class democracy in Germany should become a reality at last. And this is exactly what happened. When in November Stresemann retired as chancellor—to continue for the next six years as foreign minister—the Weimar constitution had finally come to function in an approximately "normal" fashion.

Germany's republican constitution was the most complete and the most carefully drafted that Europe had yet seen. It was a lawyer's masterpiece which seemed to cover every possible contingency. In its provisions for women's suffrage and a popular referendum on major issues, it went beyond the constitutions of Britain and France.* In most respects, however, it either imitated the common practice of Europe's parliamentary states or continued, in modified and democratized form, the institutions of the old imperial regime. Thus in making the chancellor responsible to the Reichstag, it conformed to the usual parliamentary norm, but in leaving almost unchanged the constituent states of the Reich—including the unwieldy bulk of Prussia—and in providing for an upper house to represent the states' interests, it perpetuated many of the anomalies of the country's earlier federal structure. Even traces remained of the old authority of the emperor himself, for the presidency

---

* The Scandinavian countries were still more advanced: Norway had instituted women's suffrage in 1913, Denmark in 1915, and Sweden was to follow in 1921.

which had replaced the imperial office was rather stronger than the corresponding position in France or in Britain: by the famous Article 48 of the Weimar constitution, the president was empowered to take emergency action in periods of grave national danger.

One legend that has haunted the discussion of Germany's republican institutions deserves to be laid to rest—the assertion that the country's federal structure had an intimate connection with democracy, and that centralization and Prussian influence encouraged antidemocratic forces. Almost the opposite was true. The Weimar regime was more centralized than the old imperial government because a democratized Reich needed to be able to enforce uniformity in such fields as taxation, where previously there had been the widest variations from state to state. Nor did Prussia in itself any longer constitute a reactionary threat. However doubtful the wisdom of leaving intact a state that was more populous than all the others combined, the decision of the Weimar constitution makers not to break up Prussia had no connection with the subsequent collapse of German democracy. On the contrary, throughout the republic's history the Prussian government was more securely oriented toward democracy than was that of the Reich. With the abolition of the old three-class voting system, Prussia's urban masses of the Rhineland and Berlin came to dominate the electorate, and these generally voted for Social Democracy or the Catholic Center. It was rather in one or two of the small states and in Bavaria, the second state of the Reich, that reactionary and antidemocratic forces found the most hospitable reception.

In any event, by 1924 the great majority of the German electorate had at least passively accepted the new republican institutions. It was significant that in the two Reichstag elections of that year the Nationalist party had its first real success at the polls, and that early in the following year it gave tangible evidence of its "domestication" by consenting to serve in the government. Still more symptomatic were the results of the presidential election held in the spring of 1925: on the death of the first president, the Social Democrat and former saddlemaker Friedrich Ebert, a plurality of the nation's voters picked old Field Marshal von Hindenburg, the hero of the nationalist Right, who proceeded to carry out his functions in punctilious accordance with his constitutional oath.

By the middle of the decade, then, German democracy seemed to be firmly established. To the new and rather surprising economic prosperity, there was now added a cessation of domestic strife, a pacification of spirit that made the violence of the previous half-decade—the constant street fights and assassinations—seem only an evil memory. With the three founding parties of the republic—the Democrats, the Center, and the Social Democrats—there were now associated in support of the new institutions Stresemann's People's party, a small group primarily representing business interests, and the Nationalists themselves, who, although they remained irreconcilably monarchist in theory, in practice followed Hindenburg in conforming to the *de facto* situation of republicanism and democracy. Most of them had cut their ties with the direct-action extremists: these, like the Communists, were now languishing in obscurity and banishment from the newly achieved consensus.

But even in the best years of the Weimar regime this consensus was neither as complete nor as solid as it seemed to be. For all its apparent stability, the party system never functioned properly. With six major parties in the field, coalition government was inevitable, and the task of forming such coalitions was still further complicated by the primacy of foreign affairs and the consequent necessity of keeping Stresemann—who alone commanded confidence abroad—in the foreign office, although his own party ranked as the least important of the six. Under these conditions, authority tended to pass from the Reichstag and the ministers to the party machines that made and unmade governments at their own discretion or, alternatively, to the civil servants who alone could assure continuity of policy.

Thus there came to be something flat and uninspiring about Weimar democracy. A creeping paralysis and decay began to affect the parties most intimately associated with it. First the Democrats started to lose votes: in the election of 1928 this party—which typified better than any other the moderate middle-class democracy of the 1920's—made a poor showing from which it never recovered. Then the Center lost its democratic moorings. Since the death of Erzberger, it had lacked decisive leadership, and it gradually drifted into a situation of ideological confusion. As a Catholic party, it appealed to all types of voters from socialist-minded trade unionists to conservative landowners and businessmen, and its central situation in the ideological spectrum made it an indispensable partner in all coalitions, whether of the Right or of the Left. No government ever lacked Center ministers, and the Center provided the chancellor more frequently than any other party. But this political bigamy was bad for the Center: no clear policy line was possible when the same ministers served first in a government of the Right and then in one of the Left—and the confusion was further compounded when the Center was simultaneously participating in a Right coalition for the Reich and a Left coalition for Prussia.

If the Center was thus engaged in a perpetual balancing act, the other great party on which the regime rested, Social Democracy, was succumbing to weariness and ossification. The Social Democrats and the trade unions were hard hit by the inflation of 1923. In subsequent years, they reknit their cadres and tried to carry on as before. But the life seemed to have gone out of them: both the party and the unions found their leadership aging and becoming more bureaucratized and the young people less and less interested in their activities. In the election of 1928, the Social Democrats made a surprising recovery, and for the first time since 1920 they were able to enforce their claim to the chancellorship. But this victory availed them nothing: they no longer knew how to devise and carry out an imaginative social program.

This same election produced other and more threatening symptoms of approaching change. Two million voters cast their ballots for small parties and independent candidates that appealed to discontents and resentments of all sorts, more particularly those of the peasantry. Still worse, the Nationalists came under new leadership: the industrialist and superpropagandist Alfred Hugenberg forced his way into control of the party, brushing aside the three-year-old policy of moderation to form an alliance with Hitler's struggling National Socialists—an alliance that was to vent its full venom in the following year when it waged the campaign against the Young Plan which cost Stresemann his life.

By 1928, the forces of nationalism and reaction that had been in abeyance for a mere three or four years began to come to life again. Only on the surface and in the great cities had Germany changed: deeper down and throughout the countryside, the old imperial mentality lingered on. A decade later, the superficiality and incompleteness of the Revolution of 1918 had become painfully apparent. The consequences of all that the builders of German democracy had left undone now returned to plague them: they had not broken up the great estates of the Prussian nobility, they had not purged the judiciary and the civil service, they had not altered the composition and prestige of the officers' corps. In all these places, reaction remained entrenched: landowners concealed the veterans of extremist bands as farm workers; judges acquitted nationalist terrorists or handed down ridiculously short sentences; civil servants sabotaged the reforming measures of their ministerial chiefs; the army —made still more aristocratic and tight-knit by the restrictions imposed in the Treaty of Versailles—pursued with impunity its goal of clandestine rearmament, reporting not to the chancellor but to President von Hindenburg himself, who cast a cloak of respectability over its illicit activities.

In brief, even before the death of Stresemann and the onset of the Great Depression, German democracy was beginning to reveal its fragility. Like Stresemann's own policy of "fulfilling" the terms of the Versailles Treaty, German democracy had an air of the synthetic and provisional. Indeed, in the minds of many nationalists the republic and Versailles were almost interchangeable ideas: the same assembly that drafted the republican constitution had also accepted the humiliation of the treaty, and the two documents betrayed the irremediable taint of antipatriotism. The reconciliation of 1925–1928 had been transitory and largely unreal. The irreconcilables had never actually abandoned their nostalgia for the past.

In his last months, Stresemann had dreamed of a great new party that would capture the imagination of the disaffected youth of Germany and mobilize it in the service of the nation. Within a half-decade this dream was to come true. But it was to be another than Stresemann, the fanatical corporal Adolf Hitler, who here as elsewhere was to reap what the great foreign minister had sown.

III

THE LURKING NEMESIS

What has just been said about Germany applies to a lesser extent to the other countries of Western and Central Europe. Each of these and all together contained depressing or explosive forces that the prosperity and peace—domestic and foreign—of the "good years" after 1924 barely succeeded in concealing.

The War Debts–Reparations Nexus

In the minds of businessmen, economists, and occasionally even diplomats, the dominating preoccupation of the era was the precariousness of the new-found prosperity. Statesmen and the public usually took it for granted: more farsighted economic thinkers questioned its permanence. For the prosperity of the late 1920's rested on a fragile base—and this was particularly the case in Germany, whose state of health, whether economic or psychological, should have been the crucial consideration for Europeans during the whole interwar period.

To all outward appearances, Germany was booming. Not only was industry expanding; the German municipalities were also adding to their public services, improving city transport, laying out parks and recreation centers, and constructing hospitals, schools, and workers' housing. Many of these buildings were being designed in the new "International Style," which, with its simple masses and clean lines, began to give the cities of Germany an aspect of tidy and efficient modernity (*see* Chapter Seven, IV). Defeated Germany, as the French complained, was becoming the showplace of Europe while victorious France was growing shabbier; almost no architectural imagination had gone into the reconstruction of the devastated areas, which for the most part was ugly and conventional, and elsewhere construction lagged, as French housing slipped into a state of backwardness that was to last for another thirty years.

But the German building boom was expensive, and it was financed in slipshod fashion by excessive issue of municipal bonds. These found ready takers in the United States, which also invested heavily in German industrial expansion. Thus in the 1920's, as in the period after the Second World War, German prosperity was overwhelmingly dependent on American financial aid. But there were two important differences: in the years after 1924, the help came from American private capital rather than from the government, and it was usually in the form of short-term loans rather than of grants extending over a number of years. Hence it was inordinately sensitive to fluctuations in the American economy: the maintenance of German prosperity was impossible unless the postwar boom continued in the United States.

There was a further difference between the two postwar periods. In the 1920's, the United States was not alone, as it was to be after 1945, in its position of economic benefactor. Germany was also involved, through its reparations payments to France, Britain, and a number of lesser powers. These in turn were obliged to pay back to the United States the sums they had borrowed during the war. The question of war debts engendered continual bitterness; for an entire decade it dominated and poisoned relations between France and the United States. The Republican administrations in the United States held the French to the letter of their bond and brushed aside the argument that the Americans, who had lost so few lives in the common cause, might at least recognize the enormous contribution in blood that the French had made, by exercising a corresponding generosity in releasing them from their debts.

The French answered stubbornness with stubbornness. Should Germany ever default on reparations, they claimed, then they, the French, could no longer pay their war debts. Thus the two problems became one, as reparations and war debts were associated in a tight nexus, to which the United States alone held the key. The result was a most curious triangle of transatlantic payments: the Americans lent money to Germany, Germany paid it out to France in the form of reparations, and finally it returned to the United States again as payment of war debts. Everything rested ultimately on American capital—one sign of weakness on Wall Street, and the whole fragile structure would come tumbling down.

The Weakening of Colonial Authority

If the war debts–reparations problem primarily concerned the two former enemies, France and Germany, a second area of interwar weakness, the colonial question, involved France in a common difficulty with its recent ally and rival colonial power, Great Britain.

From one standpoint, 1919 marked the apogee of European colonialism. With the breakup of the Ottoman Empire and the assignment of most of its Arab-speaking areas as mandates to Britain and France, the Europeans had brought under their control an unprecedented extent of territory. But at the same time the reaction against colonialism was already beginning. The Wilsonian innovation of mandates had implied it, and almost constant unrest in some of the more advanced areas of Asia and Africa proved that the lesson of self-determination which Wilson had preached in Europe was finding eager converts in the Europeans' colonies and dependent states.

France's troubles lay in the Arab world. In Morocco, which had never been completely pacified after its acquisition in 1912, revolt flared among the tribesmen of the Riff mountains. In the mid-1920's, the French and the Spanish (who held a smaller Moroccan protectorate over the Mediterranean coast area) were obliged to fight a regular military campaign of subjugation until they finally captured the rebel leader Abd el-Krim. A similar situation prevailed in the new mandate of Syria, where the insurgent Druses resisted for nearly two years. Here once again the French were driven to drastic measures: only after they had twice bombarded Damascus could they recover control of the Syrian capital and put the Druse leaders to flight.

The British sore point was India—the largest and most populous colonial area in the world. The postwar era started badly with the Amritsar massacre: in April, 1919, a local military commander, faced with mob violence, lost his head and ordered his soldiers to fire on the crowd for a full ten minutes, with a resulting loss of nearly four hundred lives. Amritsar was not an isolated incident; it marked the beginning of the alienation of the Indian elite, who gradually grouped themselves into the Congress party, following the teachings of civil disobedience and nonviolent resistance incarnated in the compelling personality of Mahatma Gandhi. Gandhi knew how to dramatize his case: his well-publicized fasts and his march to the sea in 1930 in defiance of the government's salt monopoly made the British look ridiculous; to these subtle acts of rebellion the colonial power could find no better reply than a crude resort to mass arrests.

By 1935 Gandhi's propaganda had won a substantial success. The Government of India Act of that year, by providing for native ministries in the Indian provinces, obviously offered a preparation for full independence. And the framework for India's continued association with Britain had also been made ready with the evolution of the Empire into a Commonwealth of sovereign states. Here the decisive act was the Statute of Westminster of 1931, which completed the transformation of the overseas dominions—Canada, Australia, New Zealand, South Africa, and the Irish Free State—into independent nations, linked to Great Britain only by the symbol of a common crown and by sentimental ties of long association. Through this act—and the settlement with Ireland that had preceded it—the British showed that for all their ineptness in India, they were a full generation ahead of the French in their conceptions of colonial development.

The Decay of Liberalism
and the Authoritarian Undercurrent

The colonial question was particularly embarrassing to liberal and radical parties. Conservatives could frankly assert the superiority of European rule, but the ideologists of progress found it impossible to square the realities of colonial government with the democratic principles they advocated at home.

The colonial dilemma was only one manifestation of the obsolescence of liberalism which became increasingly apparent as the decade of the 1920's wore on. That obsolescence was evident in the dwindling of the German Democrats, in the incapacity of the French Radicals to deal with the financial crisis, in the electoral decline of the British Liberals.

Parties such as these seemed unable to cope with current problems. The
solutions they offered were too literary and rhetorical, too vague, too moralistic—in short, old-fashioned. Although high-minded and tolerant men, their leaders had neither the technical competence nor the toughness of soul needed to deal with the economic stringencies and crude realities of power that were coming to dominate the postwar era.

Conservative, business-oriented leaders—men like Stresemann or Baldwin or the two Chamberlains or Poincaré—could at least make some show of coping with such problems. A military figure or "strong man" could stage an even more plausible performance. And however modest a figure they might cut, "strong men" were never long absent from the scene in the middle and late 1920's.

In 1923, General Primo de Rivera seized power in Spain. Three years later, Marshal Pilsudski set up a similar military dictatorship in Poland —thereby establishing a pattern which each of the new democracies of East Central Europe was to follow until only Czechoslovakia remained in the parliamentary mold. In Eastern Europe the usual formula became a veiled dictatorship in which the monarch himself played the leading role. In 1929 King Alexander of Yugoslavia took over the realities of power—as King Carol was to do after his triumphant return to Rumania in 1930, and King Boris in Bulgaria later in the same decade. These royal dictatorships were not full-fledged fascist regimes; they maintained the form, if not the substance, of parliamentary government. But they prepared for a fascist mentality in East Central Europe by the practices they encouraged or tolerated—police brutality, the training of young people for systematic violence, anti-Semitism, the persecution of national minorities, and the tacit alliance of the wealthier classes with military adventurers.

Meantime the Portuguese had established what has come to be the longest-lived of European dictatorships. In 1926 a military coup had overthrown the country's republican regime. Two years later Antonio de Oliveira Salazar had taken office as minister of finance and the strongest figure in the government. In 1930 a single party was founded on a quasi-fascist model, and in 1932 Salazar became prime minister and the unquestioned ruler of his country—a post which he was to occupy without interruption during the succeeding three decades of tumult and overturn in European political history. Thus by 1930, quite openly in East Central Europe, and just under the surface in the democratic West, rightist authoritarianism was quietly prospering: Mussolini was at the height of his popularity at home, and an increasing number of people abroad, more particularly in Germany, were talking about imitating him.

To date the new authoritarianism had shown a reassuring face. In most respects it seemed to reinforce rather than to undermine the prevailing temper of sober conservatism. But what would happen if it should discard moderation and if its destructive and "demonic" aspects rose to dominance? Here Germany obviously held the key—and it was troubling to observe that German clandestine rearmament had become more brazen and that Soviet Russia, in accordance with an understanding originally reached at Rapallo in 1922, was providing factories and training areas for the German armed forces in return for German technical education. This was the last and worst of the secret nightmares of the 1920's: the Soviet-German understanding, which Locarno had weakened but not destroyed, might one day flower into a true alliance before which the democracies of Western Europe would find themselves adrift and powerless.

Readings

Edward Hallett Carr, *International Relations between the Two World Wars* (1947), gives a clear and hard-hitting account of foreign affairs in the Locarno era. A more detailed and balanced series of interpretations, which draws on material published since the Second World War, can be found in the collaborative volume by a group of American scholars: Gordon A. Craig and Felix Gilbert, eds., *The Diplomats: 1919–1939* (1953).

On the politics of the individual countries, for Britain, besides Mowat and Taylor (*see* readings for Chapter Five), there is D. C. Somervell, *British Politics since 1900* (1950), and for Germany, Arthur Rosenberg, *A History of the German Republic* (1936), Samuel W. Halperin, *Germany Tried Democracy* (1946), and Erich Eyck, *A History of the Weimar Republic*, 2 vols. (1962–1963). Brogan's *France under the Republic* (*see* readings for Chapter Five) is full of political detail, which, however, tends to be confusing and over-allusive; David Thomson, *Democracy in France Since 1870*, 5th ed. (1969), is, in contrast, admirably clear on the long-range trends.

The Culture
of   Chapter Seven
the 1920's

I

THE CULTURAL SETTING

A Decade of Innovation

Although in politics and economics the 1920's were predominantly years of conservatism and caution, in cultural life, these years were marked by bold innovation. In this decade, the "modern temper" finally triumphed, altering the character of science and the arts for a full generation. Yet the change was far from uniform. In each cultural area, words like *modern* or *contemporary* carried very different meanings. In physics, they meant relativity, plural explanations, and indeterminacy; in social thought, they suggested both a cult of the irrational and a meticulous concern for precise meanings; in literature, they conveyed the triumph of symbolic forms of expression; in the fine arts and music, they signified a revolt against sentimentality and an inclination toward sharp tones and hard outlines. But in every instance, twentieth-century styles had a common scorn toward the preceding century: the cultural innovators rejected the lessons of their grandfathers and self-consciously chose new idioms of expression.

Toward the generation of their fathers, however, they frequently showed more respect. Actually, the cultural innovations of the 1920's were not as startling as they seemed to the contemporary public. Many —perhaps most—of them were the logical outgrowths of changes that

Photograph of Paul Cézanne taken by Emile Bernard in 1904 in the artist's studio at Les Lauves. He is seated in front of his "Bathers" (small version), which now hangs in the Barnes Foundation in Marion, Pennsylvania. COURTESY BROWN BROTHERS.

had occurred a generation earlier. The twentieth-century revolution in physics had its origins in the 1890's, as did Freud's theory of psychoanalysis and Schönberg's twelve-tone scale. Indeed, in the last two instances, the innovators themselves found in the 1920's the wider audience that they had earlier been unable to reach. Such experiences were common in the immediate postwar years: ideas or modes of expression that before the war had appeared to be revolutionary or impossibly difficult now began to attract the attention and to win the allegiance of the general educated public.

The war itself, of course, contributed to this increased receptiveness to cultural novelty. The social and psychological shocks that four years of struggle had inflicted disturbed established patterns of thought and expression and prepared men's minds for new ways of looking at the universe. Again and again in the postwar years, men asserted that Europe's traditional culture had failed—that the leisurely cultural traditions of the European upper bourgeoisie no longer sufficed to express the new realities of life—that something sharper and more vital must be created to take its place. The result was a cultural and scientific outpouring of a richness that no other single decade in the century can match.

The Major Centers

In novelty of expression, defeated Germany took the lead. This was perhaps natural since German society was so much more gravely disturbed by the war and its aftermath than were the societies of France or Britain. In Germany, the former ruling classes—and the culture they embodied —had abdicated their authority. The prewar Reich had exuded an atmosphere of stuffiness and self-satisfaction; in postwar Germany, the cultural temper was raffish, tormented, and revolutionary. For a number of years, the young insurgents had the arts almost entirely to themselves, and even when life became somewhat more stable, the cultural atmosphere of Weimar Germany remained incomparably lively and diverse. Only in the quieter university towns did intellectual activity continue much as before. These towns kept their previous eminence—as did the artistic and literary center of Munich. But the great novelty was the sudden emergence of Berlin, modern, untrammeled by tradition, and the largest city on the European continent, as the most experimental and daring center of all.

Paris, however, still eclipsed Berlin in range of cultural activity. The city on the Seine remained what it had been for centuries—the literary and artistic capital of Europe. Indeed, in certain respects Paris increased its earlier lead. In the field of painting it had no rival: the school of Paris drew into its orbit not only the most varied talents from all parts

of France but also the eager and ambitious who poured in from Spain
and Italy, from Russia and America. In the ballet, in the theater, in the novel, Paris enjoyed a pre-eminence that was reinforced by the talents of foreigners. The Russian ballet, the American expatriate novelists like Ernest Hemingway suggest how postwar conditions intensified artists' long-established tendency to seek in Paris the ideal city for cultural creation.

In different ways, then, Berlin and Paris both profited because other centers had apparently become less hospitable to talent. American writers fled to France in revulsion against postwar conventionality and "materialism" in their own country. Austrians and Hungarians, who had become accustomed to life in great capital cities, felt cramped and stifled within the narrow confines to which the settlement of 1919 had reduced their national communities. Tens of thousands of educated Russians fled from Bolshevik tyranny, as did a smaller number of Italians after the establishment of the Fascist dictatorship. Thus the 1920's saw the beginnings of that uprooting of European intellectuals which was to become almost a mass movement in the next two decades.

Two further changes occurred. In England, the decade of the 1920's was characterized by an extraordinary deprovincializing of cultural life. No longer did Britain seem so separated from the Continent as it had once been; no longer were the British themselves so satisfied with their traditional island ways. Now they were much more ready to learn from the French and the Germans, the Russians and the Austrians. Here again the experience of four years of fighting in a continental war doubtless contributed to the change of attitude. Before 1914, the "Bloomsbury Circle," for example, had been a group of very young writers without much influence; now it set the intellectual fashions by quiet but persuasive propaganda for French painting, the Russian ballet, and Viennese psychoanalysis. The Bloomsbury group had grown up in the intense intellectual atmosphere of Cambridge—and the 1920's were also to be the period in which the pre-eminence of Cambridge in physics and philosophy won nearly universal recognition. The twenties likewise saw a form of art, music—that Britain for two centuries had chiefly regarded as an alien importation from the Continent—at length achieving a new status, as major native composers awakened the interest of an alert and educated public.

Finally, in this remarkable decade Spain emerged from its long intellectual isolation. In the philosopher Ortega and the poet Lorca, Spain produced writers whose interests were European in scope and who were read throughout the Continent. In retrospect this intellectual revival in the Iberian Peninsula was to seem tragically futile when, a decade later, it was cut off by civil war and the ensuing dictatorship of General Franco. The war cost Lorca his life and drove Ortega into uncompromising opposition to Franco's repression of intellectual liberty.

II

THE PROGRESS
OF NATURAL SCIENCE

The Revolution in Physics

In the early twentieth century, physics stood out as the dominant natural science—displacing biology and geology, which had held a similar position in the age of Darwin. In both cases the reasons for pre-eminence were the same. In the late nineteenth century, the biological sciences provided the metaphors and ways of thought—positive, determinist, material—that were congenial to the wider intellectual temper and seemed most readily applicable in other fields. In the twentieth century, the more abstract and indeterminate language of physics appealed to a society that was questioning nearly all the old certainties. Furthermore, a spurt of progress resembling that which biology had made in the second half of the nineteenth century was to give physics a special prestige in the first third of the century following.

At its earliest, the twentieth-century revolution in physics can be dated from 1895, when Professor Wilhelm Konrad Röntgen of Munich discovered X rays. Thus began the atomic age, as one revelation followed another in quick succession. A year after Röntgen's discovery, Henri Becquerel's experiments with uranium opened the way to an analysis of radioactivity, on which Pierre Curie and his wife were soon to be working, and in the next year, the identification of the electron as a negatively charged particle suggested an approach to explaining this whole series of new phenomena.

Initially, the explanations were presented in terms that combined the old Newtonian principles of motion with the nineteenth-century concept of electricity. Thus the physicists of the first decade of the twentieth century viewed electricity as the common property of all matter and pictured the atom as a miniature Newtonian solar system, in which the positively charged nucleus held in dynamic tension negatively charged electrons—varying in number from one in the case of hydrogen to ninety-two in the case of uranium I—that were circling in orbits around it. In this fashion, a physicist like Lord Rutherford (first in Montreal and Manchester, subsequently in Cambridge) in 1903 was able to ascribe radioactivity to an explosive disintegration of atoms of great weight—that is, which had a large number of electrons in orbit—and seven years later to make the basic discovery that identified the nucleus of the atom with its positive charge.

Many previously unfamiliar phenomena fitted conveniently into the new explanatory scheme. On the border line between physics and chemistry, it enabled scientists to bring to virtual completion the periodic

table of the atoms by locating several theoretically possible elements
that earlier had escaped detection. Meantime, however, two further
threats to intellectual consistency had appeared. In different forms, the
discoveries of Albert Einstein and Max Planck, both of Berlin, overturned
the newly devised scheme of explanation and opened the major phase in
the physical revolution that is still going on.

Einstein's work bore only tangentially on atomic theory, since it dealt
chiefly with mechanics and astrophysics. As early as 1905, he had suggested that the notion of space and time as absolutes needed to be abandoned, that these were categories derived from metaphysics and should
properly be viewed as always relative to the person measuring them.
During the First World War, Einstein extended his theory to take account of the phenomenon of gravitation. This he explained in terms of a
four-dimension continuum—in which time was the fourth dimension—
and a "curved" universe that made possible the eventual return of light
waves to their starting point. During the eclipse of 1919, Einstein's
calculation of the deflection of light was confirmed by simultaneous
astronomical observations from points on both shores of the South Atlantic.

Even for atomic physics, however, the implications of Einstein's theory
of relativity were already clear: the hard, solid "matter" of traditional
science—which men like Rutherford had dissolved into electricity—
needed to be redefined still further in terms that made its particles no
more than a "series of events in space-time." These conclusions were
confirmed by the more directly relevant theories of Max Planck who,
independently of Einstein, had almost simultaneously arrived at equally
revolutionary conclusions.

Planck originally devised his "quantum theory" in 1901 to take account
of certain jumps and discontinuities which he had observed in radiation
phenomena. According to his new explanation, radiation did not come
in continuous waves but rather in definite units or quanta. Indeed it was
in terms of quanta, Planck argued, that energy in general and changes of
atomic structure in particular should be viewed. At the start, physicists
did not quite realize how novel this theory was, and the efforts of Niels
Bohr of Copenhagen to fit Planck's quanta into the "solar-system" explanation of the atom seemed initially successful. In 1913, Bohr, working
in Rutherford's laboratory, devised a way of combining the English physicist's theory of orbits with a concept of a series of "jumps" of electrons
from one orbit to another.

For twelve years, this reconciliatory theory held the field. Then in
1925, the final and culminating phase of the revolution in physics began
when it was discovered that Bohr's explanations did not account for all
the phenomena observed in the hydrogen spectrum. Soon new theories
of a bewildering diversity and complexity began competing for acceptance. On the one hand, Werner Heisenberg argued for a complete dis-
carding of physical hypotheses such as orbits—which he found unwar-

ranted by the facts—in favor of the more abstract language of differential equations. On the other hand, Erwin Schrödinger turned to the theory of wave mechanics that Prince Louis de Broglie had developed in France. Schrödinger contended that a stream of electrons should be regarded as having certain properties of a wave as well as those of a series of particles. Meanwhile Bohr began to revise his own earlier theories, and a large number of other physicists, British, continental, and American, branched out into still newer hypotheses suggested by the quantum theory.

A theoretical situation of unparalleled complexity resulted. Only on the ground of mathematics—where Heisenberg's and Schrödinger's equations proved to be equivalent—could the new explanations meet. In terms of classical mechanics, unitary theory had broken down completely. Sometimes one spoke of particles; sometimes of waves. Physicists chose between the two on a pragmatic basis as one theory rather than the other seemed to fit particular experimental facts. Discontinuity, indeterminacy, and uncertainty replaced the earlier clear and unilateral explanations. Just as in the first stage of the revolution in physics, Rutherford and his colleagues had dissolved matter into motion and electricity, so in its second and third stages the notion of electricity itself began to break down, as the final explanations of science were resolved into either mathematics or mystery.

Mystery was the first of two contrasting implications that contemporaries drew from the twentieth-century revolution in scientific theory. If the physicists themselves—the acknowledged masters of abstract science —could not agree and were unsure of their conclusions, what was the mere layman to think? How was he to distinguish fact from fancy in the physical world? Thus the ordinary educated man who had picked up something of the new physics tended to turn either to skepticism or to religion. He might choose to live in a state of suspended judgment and philosophical pluralism. On the other hand, he might decide to take a leap into religious faith—if the physical world was ultimately a mystery, that proved how right were the theologians who had always argued that this was so. The new self-doubt on the part of the natural scientists of the 1920's had not a little to do with the return to religion that was to be so striking a phenomenon in the two succeeding decades (see Chapter Eleven, III).

The second implication of the new discoveries was at first less troubling. However bewildering abstract scientific theory might appear around 1930, on the level of practical applications scientists were advancing from triumph to triumph. Two discoveries of the year 1919 inaugurated the period of applied atomic physics—the invention of the mass spectroscope, which made possible the identification of more than two hundred stable isotopes (that is, variant forms of the basic atoms), and Rutherford's initial experiment with controlled atomic transformations. During further experiments of the latter sort, physicists discovered a whole new series of constituent particles of the atom comparable to electrons—

positrons, protons, neutrons, and the like—until by 1944 seven in all had been identified. The most far-reaching of these discoveries was the identification of the neutron by Sir James Chadwick in 1932. It was with particles of this kind which carried no charge and hence could pass freely through the atoms in their paths, that the physicists began the intense bombardment of basic matter which was to culminate during the Second World War in the awesome discovery of the atomic bomb.

Biochemistry and Its Medical Applications

In contrast with the cosmic earthquake that the study of physics underwent in the years before 1930, change moved tranquilly in the fields of biology and chemistry. Indeed in biology most of the work of the 1920's continued along lines already established in the nineteenth century.

In genetics, the key event was the rediscovery in 1900 of the work of the Bohemian monk Gregor Mendel, who, contemporaneously with the later researches of Darwin in the 1860's, conducted the epoch-making experiments with the crossbreeding of peas that were to form the basis of the whole modern study of inheritance. The most significant outcome of Mendel's discoveries was the identification of indivisible and unalterable units called *genes*, through whose infinitely varied combination the process of heredity proceeded. This genetic theory seriously undermined Darwin's principle of natural selection. Some geneticists were ready to discard natural selection entirely, some preferred to retain it in modified form, but there was general agreement that acquired characteristics were not inherited. Mendel's original conclusions were reinforced when twentieth-century geneticists began to extend his work to systematic experiments with the fast-reproducing fruit fly, and to apply the calculus of probabilities to their findings. As a result, by the 1920's the new science of genetics had reached a high level of technical exactitude. Moreover, in treating the gene as a basic and indivisible unit, it seemed to confirm Planck's contention that nature proceeded by jumps and in definite quantities rather than through the continuous and imperceptible processes of change that had been postulated by nineteenth-century philosophers of nature.

Another link between biology and the theory of physics was provided by the new science of biophysics, which, along with the related field of biochemistry, accounted for a large part of the progress made in the study of the human body. Perhaps the most dramatic experiments were those of Sir Frederick Gowland Hopkins in 1912, which became the starting point for the systematic investigation of nutrition and the identification of the basic vitamins. For a long time the chemistry of all the vitamins except D remained a mystery. But in 1929, with the chemical breakdown of Vitamin A, there began a period of rapid progress in the analysis and synthetic production of these substances that continued down to the outbreak of the Second World War.

Closely related to this study was the development of the new science of glands and internal secretions known as *endocrinology*. In the 1920's, the function of hormones began to be understood, and work on the pituitary and thyroid glands proceeded steadily. Discoveries such as these obviously had relevance for medicine. Indeed, a salient characteristic of the decade was that now, for the first time in history, new research in physiology and biochemistry was quickly applied in clinical practice. An astounding advance resulted. In the mid-1920's there began a period of breathtaking innovation that brought more progress in medicine in a single generation than the profession had known in all previous human history.

The discovery of antitoxins, begun in the 1890's, moved on steadily, as did the analysis of the corresponding viruses. By this method, medical research succeeded in eliminating certain diseases almost completely: as smallpox had been routed in the nineteenth century, so the conquest of diphtheria, yellow fever, and tetanus followed in the interwar period. But most diseases resisted this sort of immunization. Although the ravages of tuberculosis, for instance, were enormously reduced, no satisfactory antitoxin was discovered to combat it. In dealing with these stubborn diseases, the development of antibiotics marked the crucial turning point. Beginning with Sir Alexander Fleming's almost accidental discovery of penicillin in 1928, one new drug followed another in a rapid sequence of successful experiments leading to commercial production.

In all these cases, however, there had been a time lag between laboratory research and its clinical application. Not until the Great Depression had focused attention on problems of hunger and want were the new discoveries in the field of nutrition and vitamins fully exploited. Through the necessities of treating vast masses of sick and wounded soldiers in the Second World War, penicillin, the sulfa drugs, and DDT came into their own. These examples suggest the close relationship between social needs and the development of scientific and medical knowledge in our time.

Similarly, in the organization of research, economic and social factors began to exert an increasingly important influence. In the past, the isolated scientist or physician could produce useful and even epoch-making results with the simple equipment of his own home laboratory. By the 1920's, only a well-furnished laboratory or research institute could contribute to the growth of scientific knowledge. With this change, the problem of the organization and financing of research took on a new urgency. In such respects, a large and wealthy society like that of the United States enjoyed obvious advantages; a socialized country, such as the Soviet Union, held potential assets for the future. Thus even as early as the 1920's, men of science in the three countries that together had accounted for most of the scientific progress of the nineteenth century—Britain, Germany, and France—were beginning to wonder whether the economy and the way of life that had yielded such marvelous results a generation or two earlier, would prove capable of dealing with the unfamiliar and pressing demands of twentieth-century mass society.

III
SOCIAL SCIENCE AND PHILOSOPHY

The "Old Masters":
Freud, Croce, Weber, Durkheim

In social thought, the decade of the 1920's can be regarded in two contrasting fashions. On the one hand, it was an era of consolidation, in which an earlier revolution in ways of looking at society began to find wide acceptance and to extend into new areas of knowledge. On the other hand, it was marked by a philosophical revolution of its own, which drastically altered the earlier vocabulary of intellectual exchange, creating a cleavage between English and continental thinking that was never satisfactorily bridged.

At the end of the First World War, a generation of unusually original social thinkers was passing from the scene or turning its intellectual activity in new directions. In Austria, the most influential figure of the whole half-century—Sigmund Freud—had virtually completed the outlines of his psychoanalytic theory. In Italy, Benedetto Croce had attained a position of unquestioned philosophical leadership: the volumes of his *Philosophy of the Spirit* in which Croce defined the criteria of aesthetics and historical study were achieving the position of classic formulations that they retained for the whole interwar period. In Germany and France, Max Weber and Émile Durkheim had put the study of sociology on a more empirical and objective basis, by deriving from specific and manageable problems the principles for the scientific study of society that the nineteenth-century fathers of sociology had tried in vain to formulate at one blow.

Durkheim died during the war; Weber, a year and a half after its close. Freud and Croce lived on for another generation, broadening the scope of their thinking and directing it into novel and unsuspected channels. But the effect on younger contemporaries was the same: alive or dead, the "old masters" continued to dominate the field, and the study of human society remained fixed in the paths that these had marked out for it in the prewar years.

Psychology: Behaviorism, Gestalt Theory,
and the Heirs of Freud

Without doubt, the greatest single change that distinguished the intellectual atmosphere of the 1920's from that of the period before 1914 was psychology's leap into the center of attention. Here again, however, the way had been prepared in the prewar era. The social thought of the decade and a half preceding the outbreak of the war had been markedly subjective in character. In nearly all the major writings of this period, the common element had been an emphasis on unconscious mental processes, on criticism of one's own thinking, and on the doubtful character of knowledge about society. The war experience had further encouraged this tendency toward subjectivity and self-doubt. When all stable values had been thrown into question, the human psyche emerged as the one fixed point in an indeterminate universe.

The Freudian theory of psychoanalysis most clearly exemplified the new trend, but its pre-eminence did not pass unquestioned. The laboratory study of experimental psychology continued on its patient, cautious way, scarcely troubled by the philosophical quarrels of the Freudians and their foes. These latter included the Behaviorists, who followed the American J. B. Watson in stressing the relationship of internal feelings to the observable activities and the physiological structure of the individual—as opposed to the psychoanalytic practice of deducing unconscious thought and emotion from dreams, random remarks, and slips in speech. Behaviorism—in Europe at least—had only a passing influence; a more serious intellectual challenge to the teachings of Freud came from the German Gestalt school. These theorists, who were speculative philosophers rather than clinicians, held that the way to understand an individual mind was through the painstaking delineation of its whole form (Gestalt) in an effort to grasp all the subtle connections linking the complexities and apparent contradictions that constituted a single, unique emotional life.

Nevertheless, it was Freud and his school who aroused the liveliest interest. The great Viennese psychiatrist was a little more than sixty and apparently at the height of his powers when the war came to an end. Four years later, however, he was stricken by a cancer of the mouth that necessitated operation after operation and that finally killed him in 1939, just after the outbreak of the second world conflict. This constant battle with illness severely limited Freud's ability to work—but he continued with stoical resolution in the two main areas of his earlier activity, the clinical practice of psychoanalysis and the publication of books and articles on psychological theory.

Most of Freud's time was devoted to clinical psychiatry, which he had revolutionized a generation earlier with his novel technique of free association. More and more, however, those who lay on the couch in his office and sought his help were not regular patients but fledgling psychiatrists who had come to Vienna to be trained in psychoanalytic method. In the half-decade before the war, psychoanalysis had become an international movement, and although the four years of the conflict checked this development, its growth was resumed after 1918 on a still larger scale. Besides Vienna, which remained the general headquarters,

Berlin, Budapest, London, and New York were main centers of psycho-
analytic teaching and practice. Paris, Rome, and the Latin and Catholic countries in general showed themselves much less receptive to Freudian ideas. It was in the German- and the English-speaking worlds that psychoanalysis became firmly established in the 1920's.

The foundation of new psychoanalytic institutes and the maintenance of contact between them necessitated a great deal of consultation and correspondence on the part of the founder himself. Freud also continued with his theoretical writing, but this began to change in character. The main structure of his theory, which he had begun in 1899, with his *Interpretation of Dreams,* was now finished. In contrast to the volumes which presented and explained the central ideas and the method of psychoanalysis, Freud's later writings were shorter and more speculative, and they showed greater concern for the social and historical implications of his theories. The most influential of these, *Civilization and Its Discontents* (1930), dealt with the restriction of instinctual expression that Freud found inevitable in civilized societies and forecast the inhuman behavior to which the authoritarian states of Europe would very shortly resort. The measured pessimism in this little book was echoed in two brief studies of religion: *The Future of an Illusion,* in which Freud voiced his confidence in a humanist and atheist morality, and *Moses and Monotheism,* his last work, in which he traced the tragic history of the Jews (his own ancestors) to their creation of the concept of a single deity.

Meantime the psychoanalytic movement continued to be shaken by internal splits and struggles which were themselves of an almost religious intensity. Just before the first war there had been two notable defections from the Freudian camp. One of these, led by Alfred Adler of Vienna, had tried to turn psychoanalysis away from its basic emphasis on the unconscious emotions of the individual and to direct it toward questions of conscious participation in group life. Adler's teaching offered a curious combination of stress on the will—a Nietzschean inheritance— and of socialist ideals of Marxian origin. In the 1920's its influence did not extend very far, and Adler's own death in 1937 robbed it of its chief. The real importance of ideas of this sort was to be apparent only a decade later, when the Second World War focused attention once again on the relation between individual psychology and the organization of society.

A more serious challenge came from the Swiss Carl G. Jung, who had once ranked as Freud's heir apparent. In the years following the war Jung diverged further and further from the teachings of his original master. Through his study of Oriental philosophy and religion, the Swiss psychiatrist concluded that there existed a vast "collective unconscious" in which the same myth-symbols kept repeating themselves in widely separated places and ages. By tapping the resources of these great "archetypes," Jung argued, people could reach a higher understanding of their emotional difficulties. Hence, although he did not profess a specific faith of his own, Jung urged on his patients and on his readers the therapeutic value of a return to religion. In this emphasis on the usefulness of faith—which contrasted so sharply with Freud's atheism—Jung made a notable contribution to the wider movement of return to religion in the postwar epoch.

Sociology and Anthropology

During the war and immediate postwar years Max Weber wrote the books that were to rank as the basic documents of contemporary sociology. In his studies of the relation between religion and economic activity, and in his work of synthesis, *Wirtschaft und Gesellschaft* (Economics and Society), Weber tried to apply what he had earlier defined as the "ideal-type" method. This procedure involved the conscious and even arbitrary selection of certain typical or salient features of social and historical phenomena so as to "idealize" them and thus make them comparable to one another.

In 1919 and 1920 Weber's influence was at its height. After two decades of withdrawal from teaching—made necessary by an inordinately severe psychic depression—he had accepted a university chair in Munich. The Bavarian capital was an extremely lively place in these years: a brief phase of left-wing Socialist and Communist rule had been followed by a longer period of nationalist reaction. Extremism of all sorts was flourishing—indeed, the same persons often engaged in both political and artistic experimentation. For all these contrasting tendencies, Weber had understanding and even sympathy. His mind was a tissue of contradictions held in tense equilibrium—he was a fervent nationalist and a doctrinaire democrat, a freethinker and a man fascinated by religion, an unsparing critic of socialist doctrines who held Marx in deep respect. Young people of every ideological allegiance turned to him for political and intellectual guidance—but this he could not give: he was far too shaken by scruples and self-doubt.

Weber's untimely death in 1920 at the age of fifty-six robbed Germany of its leading social thinker. But his students and colleagues continued the study of sociology in the ideal-type framework that Weber had devised and in the close relationship to history that was congenial to the German tradition. In the process inevitable alterations occurred. Among the older generation, Werner Sombart turned more and more to a semimystical interpretation of community spirit that eventually landed him in the Nazi camp. Among the juniors, Karl Mannheim tried to combine Weber's teaching with the analysis of the collective thinking of classes and social groups which the philosopher Max Scheler had baptized the "sociology of knowledge." The result was a shifting, many-layered type of sociological argument which pushed the relativist implications of

Weber's thought to their logical conclusions. Mannheim's *Ideology and Utopia* (1929) constituted a summing up of two generations of political and intellectual debate in Germany on the eve of the National Socialist onslaught.

Italy had produced in the period before the war two great political sociologists—Vilfredo Pareto and Gaetano Mosca—but their influence was limited and perverted in the course of the 1920's. With the advent of Mussolini in 1922, there began an official direction of intellectual life that tried either to suppress social theory entirely or to steer it into support of the regime. Such "steering" proved to be relatively easy with Pareto's writings, which taught a hard, unsentimental doctrine of rule by elites in the tradition of Machiavelli; moreover, Pareto died in 1923 after having given Fascism his qualified support. Mosca, in contrast, had expressed the same Machiavellian inheritance and the same emphasis on a "governing class" in terms of liberalism and constitutional government. His writings were clearly antifascist in tone, and from the floor of the Italian Senate—whose members were appointed for life—Mosca voiced his opposition in measured but uncompromising terms. So did another senator, Benedetto Croce, the dominant figure in Italian intellectual life. Yet Croce was hostile to the study of both psychology and sociology, and under his guidance, Italian social thought remained almost exclusively absorbed with history and philosophy. Not until the 1930's was Croce to expand the range of his historical thinking to embrace a full-scale repudiation of authoritarianism in all its forms (*see* Chapter Eleven, II).

One of the greatest strengths of the work of Émile Durkheim in France had been his combination of sociology and anthropology as a single academic pursuit. After Durkheim's death in 1917, this legacy remained, and the two subjects continued to be linked in the French curriculum. Indeed, of all the social sciences, anthropology made the greatest progress in the 1920's. This had been the last of these studies to be fully defined: in the nineteenth century it had still been largely in the hands of explorers, missionaries, and imaginative amateurs. After the First World War, it became more systematic, as the anthropologists of France, Britain, and the United States elaborated their techniques of field investigation. From France, the heirs of Durkheim applied in the field the lessons that their master had worked out at home; in England, a new generation of anthropologists put almost their whole emphasis on long residence in Africa or the Pacific, with only scant attention to the claims of theory. A notable exception was the Polish-born Bronislaw Malinowski, after 1927 professor of anthropology at the University of London, who tried to test the ideas of Freud by comparing them with the results of his own investigation of the Trobriand Islanders of New Guinea. Malinowski's field work only partially confirmed Freud's theories. But he agreed with the Viennese psychiatrist in stressing unconscious motivation as expressed through tribal ritual. In this respect, the new study of anthropology reinforced the emphasis on the irrational and on the unconscious which dominated the social thought of the whole era.

Philosophy: Irrationalism and Logical Empiricism

In philosophy also, the irrational found enthusiastic exponents. Indeed it was here—at least on the more popular levels of philosophical expression—that the lessons of the previous generation were most seriously misunderstood in the postwar years. Men like Freud had emphasized the irrational only to understand it better, to master it, and to guide it into constructive channels. They were not irrationalists in the sense of being on the side of unreason. Yet in the postwar generation many writers did declare themselves frankly and enthusiastically for "thinking with the blood," and contributed to the advent of fascism in Italy and Germany by giving it a specious veneer of intellectual respectability.

On the more abstract level, the most influential of the irrationalist schools was existentialism (see Chapter Sixteen, I), a philosophy of German origin, as the names of its two chief exponents, Karl Jaspers and Martin Heidegger, suggest. Existentialism found a ready audience among the university students of Germany after 1919—a phenomenon that was to be repeated on a European scale in the years following the Second World War. Not until 1945, however, did the existentialist philosophers achieve their full historical importance by awakening the interest of the general public.

One of existentialism's intellectual antecedents, the phenomenology of Edmund Husserl, shared with it a confidence in the power of human intuition to pierce behind the surface appearances of the physical world. But whereas existentialism went on to indulge in wide-ranging moral reflections, phenomenology limited itself to a careful and exhaustive analysis of the objects and ideas that human beings encountered along their way.

Thus both these philosophies stayed within the major German tradition of idealism—that is, they remained true to the doctrine that ultimate reality lay in the world of ideas and the spirit rather than in sense experience. This was also the position of the Spanish philosopher José Ortega y Gasset. Ortega's writings reflected a characteristic Spanish concern with problems of decline and decadence, and with the situation of traditional European culture in a rapidly changing society. In his most widely read book, The Revolt of the Masses (1930), Ortega warned of the fall in the level of literature and education that the new democratization of life would inevitably entail and propounded a theory of cultural guidance by gifted minorities that was strongly reminiscent of the elitist teachings of Italians like Croce and Pareto.

Ideas of this sort were as conservative from the philosophical standpoint as they were in politics. The new and really revolutionary tendencies in philosophy were embodied in what in most general terms can be called the analytic school. Analytic philosophy had its origin in the work of two Cambridge scholars, Bertrand Russell and Alfred North Whitehead, who in the years 1910–1913 published its founding charter, the *Principia Mathematica.* As its name implied, this treatise sought to recast philosophical prose in mathematical form. Disgusted by the vagueness of traditional idealism, Russell and Whitehead argued that only by using the unambiguous language of mathematics and symbolic logic could philosophy speak with the clarity and precision at which it had always aimed.

In the war and postwar years, these teachings made steady but unspectacular progress in the English universities. On the Continent, however, they impinged with explosive force. Here a number of young Germans and Austrians, inspired by Russell's example, formed the "Vienna Circle" in 1923. Their unofficial leader was Rudolf Carnap, but most people were to associate them with Ludwig Wittgenstein, whose *Tractatus Logico-Philosophicus,* published in 1921, became the most influential philosophical work of the entire half-century. In this terse, intentionally provocative statement, Wittgenstein tried to reduce to nonsense nearly all the major concerns of traditional ethics and metaphysics. Nothing, he argued, that could not be talked about without ambiguity in the language of symbols or of ordinary speech deserved to be treated as philosophy at all. The rest was mere wind—and best be left unspoken.

This new doctrine of logical positivism—or logical empiricism, as it was later called—never won much favor on the Continent. To Frenchmen and Germans, it seemed far too radically destructive: it took away too much of the traditional material of philosophical discourse by reducing it to a set of highly abstract propositions that only a few initiates could understand. Continental philosophers generally refused to make this sacrifice and continued in their loose and speculative ways, but in Britain and the United States logical empiricism gradually became the new orthodoxy. And this receptiveness to the doctrines of the Vienna Circle was reinforced when in 1929 Wittgenstein emigrated to England—where he educated a whole generation of Cambridge philosophers to devote minute attention to the possibilities and pitfalls of ordinary language— and when, a few years later, Carnap went to the United States.

Analytic philosophy had originated in the Anglo-Saxon world, where empiricism and an antimetaphysical attitude had always been at home: its passage through Vienna seems in retrospect rather accidental. By the 1930's—when authoritarian government was stifling free inquiry in the German-speaking world and Austria had ceased to be a major center of thought—there was a complete philosophical cleavage between the Continent on the one hand and Britain and the United States on the other. Between German or French speculation on ethics and metaphysics, and Anglo-American analysis of the narrow problems that alone were compatible with the rigorous methods of logical empiricism, any sort of meaningful exchange had become almost impossible.

IV

IMAGINATIVE LITERATURE:
THE LEGACY OF SYMBOLISM

The Postwar Mood: Expressionism, Dadaism,
Surrealism, the Influence of Gide

In imaginative literature—in poetry, drama, and the novel—the 1920's were the period in which the small groups of antirealistic writers who before the war had constituted an experimental avant-garde suddenly found themselves in control of the field. Yet realist writing of the late nineteenth-century type did not die out completely. In England, for example, Edwardian novelists like John Galsworthy and H. G. Wells continued to publish with great success. Throughout Europe most books remained in the realist vein. But such work was beginning to seem old-fashioned and conventional. The general public went on reading it, but those who considered themselves modern found it dull and turned toward more experimental writing.

The common denominator among these newer writers was a focus on symbolic meaning—on the event or physical detail that unexpectedly tapped hidden depths of esthetic perception and emotion—as opposed to the earlier emphasis on photographic accuracy of description or narrative. In this, the writers of the 1920's were the lineal heirs of the French symbolist poets of the late nineteenth century, whose cult had been spread to the English-speaking world by young writers like Ezra Pound and the Bloomsbury Circle in the period just before the war. In common with the symbolist poets, the postwar writers were interested in extracting from human experience its mysterious essence, often dreamlike in character, which could be conveyed only in images of doubtful but overpowering significance; they were also absorbed with the problem of language, preferring striking combinations in which familiar words suddenly acquired novelty and freshness; and, independently of Freud and Jung, whose theories they later welcomed as confirmation of their own discoveries, they searched out the unconscious anxiety or passion that underlay the apparent senselessness of human actions.

Common interests of this sort, far more than any specific and self-conscious movement, distinguished the postwar literary scene from what had gone before. There was no lack of regularly constituted movements, but these were more prominent during the war and immediate postwar years than in the major phase of the 1920's. In Germany there was Expressionism, which tried to tear away the mask from conventional behavior and—inspired by the horror of the trenches—to show the brutality and perverseness behind. In France there was Dadaism—an explosion of anger against "false values" of all sorts, in philosophy, morality, social

organization, and religion—and its successor, Surrealism, which sought
for a new reality, a "logic of nonsense," beyond the reality of commonplace experience. But once the immediate postwar ferment was over, the rather pretentious manifestos of these movements began to sink into insignificance. What was truly exciting and creative in them was absorbed into the wider perceptions of major writers who gave their allegiance to no single school; the rest was forgotten. A similar experience characterized painting, which in these tumultuous years had been enrolled under the same banners as literature.

Perhaps the outstanding immediate contribution of the young Dadaists and Surrealists to literature was drawing attention to a man of the older generation whom they considered their precursor. André Gide was forty-eight when the war ended. He was known as little more than a coterie writer who prided himself on his "immoralism." Only in the 1920's did he win general recognition as a superb stylist in several genres —the novel, the farcical story, the personal soliloquy, the drama, and the essay—and as a man of unsparing honesty who, despite his frank confession of sexual deviance, retained the rigor of a Protestant conscience. The publication of Gide's autobiography and of his major novel, *The Counterfeiters*, in 1926, established him as France's leading prose writer, a position he held until his death three decades later.

The Novel: Proust, Kafka, Mann, Hesse, Lawrence, Huxley, Forster, Woolf, Joyce

Two other novelists to whom the new receptiveness of the postwar reading public granted a sudden and belated fame were Marcel Proust and Franz Kafka. Both died early—Proust lived just long enough to experience his own triumph, but Kafka died unappreciated, and with the bulk of his work still unpublished.

The first part of Marcel Proust's vast novel *Remembrance of Things Past* had appeared just before the war under the title *Swann's Way*. In its elusive and infinitely elaborated analysis of hidden motives and of the mysterious meaning behind apparently insignificant memories, it seemed tedious and incomprehensible to the general public. But when the second installment appeared in 1919, it had an immediate success. Its author, however, was already near his end. For years he had lived as an eccentric invalid recluse, writing in bed and going out only at night, and it was in this fashion that he worked on at the revision of the final volumes of his great novel until he died in 1922 at the age of fifty-one.

Kafka was twelve years younger than Proust and far less sure of his own genius. Shy, tormented, and inordinately frightened of his father, he passed a miserable existence in the Czech-speaking city of Prague, where he felt doubly alienated from the people around him, first as a German writer and second as a Jew. When he died in 1924, still a young man, Kafka had published very little—notably the extraordinary short story *Metamorphosis*. It was his posthumous novels that were to bring him fame—*The Trial* and *The Castle*, nightmare fantasies of a world of threatening, inexplicable necessity, which left the individual bewildered and helpless, and in which later readers were to discover intimations of the authoritarian practices of the next decade.

In Germany itself, the new temper was exemplified by Thomas Mann and Hermann Hesse. Mann's vast novel of disease, death, and ideological debate in an Alpine tuberculosis sanitarium, *The Magic Mountain* (1924), ranked second only to those of Proust and Joyce in subsequent literary influence. Already a mature writer when the war ended, Mann was to achieve his greatest international fame two decades later, when he became a symbol of literary opposition to Nazi tyranny. The same was true of Hesse, whose distaste for German militarism had prompted him to seek lifelong exile in Switzerland even before the First World War. Hesse's *Demian* (1919) and *Steppenwolf* (1930), with their assaults on bourgeois hypocrisy and their pleas for an individual standard of values, which drew heavily on the author's own psychoanalytic experience with the Jungian school, profoundly stirred the youth of Germany in the Weimar years.

Across the Channel, the break with the prewar era was less sharp. Novelists like D. H. Lawrence, Aldous Huxley, and E. M. Forster offered no radical innovations in technique over accepted Edwardian practice. They were distinguished, rather, by the daring of their themes, which shocked the complacent into recognition of how much society had changed around them. Thus Lawrence reflected the postwar liberation of manners by glorifying natural sexual desire, more particularly in his *Lady Chatterley's Lover* (1928), which most readers knew only in expurgated form; Huxley, in *Point Counter Point* (1928) depicted the brittleness and modish diversity of contemporary intellectual exchange; Forster, by far the most refined literary craftsman of the three, in *A Passage to India* (1924) gave what was to become the classic account of relations between Europeans and Asians in the twilight era of overseas imperialism.

In delicacy of technique, Virginia Woolf was closely related to Forster. She was the one major novelist to come out of the cultural ferment of Bloomsbury, and she was also, second only to Joyce, the major innovator of the period in English fiction. Virginia Woolf converted the novel into a pattern of internal monologues, proceeding in an apparently random succession of images, thoughts, and emotions reminiscent of the psychoanalytic technique of free association. Thus a book like *Mrs. Dalloway* (1925) distilled a wide range of human experience from the reflections and sensations of the heroine on a single decisive day of her life.

With Virginia Woolf, the new stream-of-consciousness technique remained within the bounds of traditional literary language; with her Irish contemporary, James Joyce, the old conventions were broken almost completely. The author of *Ulysses* (1922) was a wanderer by nature;

self-exiled to the Continent, Joyce, like Hesse, was deeply influenced by
contact with Jung. And in the novel that disturbed its generation more than any other—the account of a single day in the streets and pubs and middle-class houses of Dublin—he indulged his literary fancy to the full: word plays and parodies, scraps of recollection, and fragments of foreign languages tumbled one on another in an apparently hopeless confusion whose careful articulations only close study would reveal. Its successor, *Finnegans Wake* (1939), was still more hermetic, and its appearance prompted critics to ask whether Joyce had not led the novel to its farthest limits, beyond which lay only dissolution or a return to more conservative techniques.

Poetry: Eliot, Yeats, Valéry, Rilke, George, Lorca

Poetry too in these years seemed to be straining the powers of its readers to the breaking point. It became tight and involuted, compressed and cryptic. In the English-speaking world the most influential poet was T. S. Eliot. American-born but English by residence and preference, Eliot expressed in *The Waste Land* (1922) the doubt and torment of his whole epoch—the dreariness and desolation of a world of discarded ideals, frayed nerves, and meaningless pleasures. Whereas Eliot's style was characteristically elliptical and sprinkled with learned allusions, that of his Irish counterpart, William Butler Yeats, had a more direct appeal. Yeats combined traditional lyricism with a stoic attitude toward the contemporary world: convinced that an old culture was breaking up, he stuck to his own exacting literary ideals and, unlike Joyce, remained in Ireland, where he came to rank as the most distinguished figure of his country's twentieth-century literary renaissance.

In France, the poet whose influence paralleled that of Eliot in the English-speaking world was Paul Valéry. And the single poem that corresponded to *The Waste Land* in epitomizing the attitude of an entire generation was *La Jeune Parque* (1917), the long meditation with which Valéry marked his return to poetry after twenty years of silence. In the interval, this lineal heir of Symbolism had cultivated his interest in mathematics and abstract philosophy, and even after he took up poetry again, his work continued to be marked by a classic coolness and a severe intellectuality.

Germany lost its greatest twentieth-century poet in the mid-1920's when Rainer Maria Rilke died at the age of fifty-one. Like Valéry's, Rilke's poems expressed a classic repose, but he was not concerned, as was his French contemporary, with intellectual riddles, but rather with intense observation of animals and scenes from nature. In this absorption with the pictorial and the plastic, Rilke remained close to the world of French painting and sculpture, which had originally inspired him to become a poet. Indeed, he was at least as much Latin as he was German in sympathy, and his most discussed volume of poems, the *Duinian*

Elegies (1923), reflected in its strong rhythms and its deep religious feeling the author's sense of harmony with the Italian Adriatic shore.

Far more German was Stefan George, who transmitted and perverted the message of Nietzsche to the postwar world. In brief, cryptic, carefully chiseled poems, George taught a stern ethic to his chosen circle. The poet himself was far from being a Nazi—but in his images of ruthlessness and his idea of a special standard of conduct for the strong, he helped create a cultural attitude in Germany from which Hitler was eventually to profit. Quite the contrary in his range of sympathies was Federico García Lorca, Spain's leading creative writer of the century, whose "surrealist" poems unfolded with warm understanding the passions and sufferings of the Spanish peasantry.

The Drama: Shaw, Pirandello; the Ballet

Lorca also wrote prose dramas, which rose into poetry in their moments of maximum intensity. Of these the haunting *Blood Wedding* (1933) is perhaps most familiar to American readers. Similarly poetic in tone were the dramas of the Irishman Sean O'Casey, who continued into the postwar era his countryman J. M. Synge's effort to restore to the English theater a richness of speech that it had not known since the days of Shakespeare.

Generally, however, playwrights used prose. It was in this medium that the two leading dramatists of the decade—George Bernard Shaw and Luigi Pirandello—cast their long series of plays.

Most of Shaw's career lay behind him when the First World War ended. His wartime and postwar production included only two plays that have regularly held the stage since—*Heartbreak House* and *Saint Joan*. Both were overlong: the master in his old age was growing garrulous. Nor did they add anything novel to dramatic technique; they remained with Ibsen and Chekhov in the prewar world of "realistic" social analysis. But such was their verve and the freshness which they gave to familiar ideas that audiences remained as entranced as ever.

Pirandello was a far more original writer. Little known before the war, he sprang into sudden prominence in 1921, when he wrote the two plays that were to make him famous—*Six Characters in Search of an Author* and *Henri IV*. Unlike Shaw, Pirandello cared nothing for the conventions of the theater. He wanted to portray a reality that was psychological rather than that of common sense, and he resorted to the most extraordinary expedients to arrive at his aim. Thus in his *Six Characters* he brought two sets of players simultaneously on the stage—the members of a family desolated by domestic tragedy, and the professional actors whom they implore to play their personal drama: each offers his own version of the truth; the audience is left to choose and to draw its own conclusions. And so it went in nearly all Pirandello's plays which, although they were billed as comedies, actually dealt with problems of emotional desperation and imposed a severe intellectual strain on their listeners. It is not surprising, then, that the dramas of Pirandello proved more popular abroad than with the more conventional audiences of his native Italy.

France in this period produced no playwright of the stature of Shaw or Pirandello, but it maintained a high standard of writing and performance, marked particularly by the opening of new experimental theaters. Paris was full of young talent—less serious than Shaw and Pirandello, concerned rather with entertainment and pure fun, like the playful surrealist Jean Cocteau. In Paris moreover, the arts collaborated more closely than they did elsewhere: first-rank painters did not scorn to design stage sets, nor composers to write incidental music for individual productions. The outstanding example of this sort of collaboration was the Diaghilev ballet, which in the years before the war had already electrified Paris with a freedom of interpretation previously unknown outside Russia. Cut off from their home country by the Bolshevik Revolution, Diaghilev and his troupe pressed into enthusiastic service much of the youthful talent of the French capital.

V

THE ARTS: THE TRIUMPH
OF THE MODERN

Music: "The Six"; Stravinsky, Prokofiev,
Schönberg; National Music

In music, the most striking novelty of the immediate postwar period and the one closest to the world of entertainment and the ballet, was the emergence in Paris of a group of young composers who came to be called "The Six." Of these, three eventually achieved international recognition: the Swiss Arthur Honegger, a composer of powerful choral works, culminating in the episodic opera *King David* originally produced in 1921; the Provençal Darius Milhaud, who began his career with intentionally shocking experiments in cacophony and "futuristic" effects, but who gradually came to a more sober definition of his art, which he expressed in a memorable series of operas, ballets, and symphonic works; finally, the Parisian Francis Poulenc, a versatile and witty composer, slightly younger than his friends—who were in their mid-twenties at the war's end—and primarily known for his songs and his works for the piano.

Jean Cocteau, who sponsored "The Six," in a manifesto issued in 1918 had called for a new type of music, brief, sharp, and precise, and not afraid to adopt the rhythms of jazz. Cocteau and his friends wanted to shake off the pervasive influence of the master of modern French music and the most influential composer in all Europe in the first decade of the twentieth century, Claude Debussy. Behind Debussy's fluid style and chromatic evocations of emotion, the musical innovators also discerned the legacy of Richard Wagner, who had held a similar position a generation earlier.

The post-1918 revolt against Debussy's Impressionism echoed a similar breaking away from established models in painting. It was characteristic of German music also, and even of a French composer like Maurice Ravel, whose style was often incorrectly confused with Debussy's. Ravel was a half-generation older than "The Six," and most of his work dated from before 1920—the year of *La Valse*, which marked a transition from his earlier and more serene compositions to his postwar experiments with the new rhythms.

Like many an established artist who sees the young pressing hard upon his heels, Ravel tried to keep pace with his juniors. In one respect, however, he had preceded them all: as early as 1910 he had written his *Daphnis and Chloë* for the Diaghilev ballet. Shortly thereafter he had met the Russian composer Igor Stravinsky, whose *Rite of Spring* was shocking Parisian audiences with its barbaric splendors. Stravinsky was already established in the world of ballet, with such popular works as *The Firebird* and *Petrouchka* behind him, and together with Ravel he gave the Diaghilev troupe a distinction that later attracted to it such younger talents as Milhaud and Poulenc and the Russian exile Sergei Prokofiev.

Prokofiev, like the leading members of "The Six," with whom he was almost exactly of an age, enjoyed a musical joke, as he had already shown in his terse, deft *Classical Symphony* (1917). This humor was always breaking out—in his farcical opera *The Love of Three Oranges* and in his children's fairy tale *Peter and the Wolf*. But Prokofiev was also a meticulous musical craftsman, whose clarity and simplicity served as a model to subsequent composers. When he returned to Russia in the early 1930's, his work became still simpler and closer to lyricism and folk themes; in this it reflected the reaction from modernism in the arts that was so marked a feature of the Stalinist era (*see* Chapter Ten, V). Toward his country's new regime, Prokofiev took a different attitude from Stravinsky: the latter, who had already spent a large part of his youth in Western Europe, simply stayed on after the Bolshevik Revolution and subsequently emigrated to the United States, but Prokofiev— at first an exile also and apparently thoroughly "westernized"—could not refuse the call of his homeland, where he became almost a composer laureate, alternately pampered and reproved by the guardians of official Soviet culture.

Paris, with its reinforcement of Russian talent, in the 1920's was unquestionably the most versatile and the liveliest musical community in the world. But its experiments, which seemed so daring at the time, mostly remained within the established tradition of Western harmonics. It was in Germany and Austria, rather, that the great musical revolution took place whose full effects were to become apparent only after the Second World War. This was, of course, the invention and systematic development of the twelve-tone scale, the work of Arnold Schönberg, a contemporary of Ravel, whose string sextet *Verklärte Nacht* had profoundly upset Vienna audiences just before the turn of the century.

The basic idea of the twelve-tone scale was relatively simple. It consisted in using all the notes of the scale—black as well as white—arranging them into a basic pattern, inverting the pattern thus devised, and then going on through progressive transpositions until a musical "datum" was arrived at on which the individual composition could be built. The result was highly intellectual—algebraic and schematic. Its defenders claimed that this "atonal" revolution was comparable to what Johann Sebastian Bach had accomplished at the end of the seventeenth century: just as Bach had substituted for the old church polyphony the modern harmonic style based on major and minor scales, so Schönberg had inaugurated a new era by substituting twelve-note atonality for the tonal style that had characterized the two greatest centuries of Western music. All this seemed plausible enough. But critics pointed out that whereas tonality had developed naturally, through constant experiments with the earlier "modes," atonality appeared suddenly, all of a piece, with its implications fully worked out, and in an abstract form that appealed more to the eye of the expert reader who could fully appreciate the elegance of its construction than to the ear of the uninstructed listener in the concert hall.

In any case, the twelve-tone scale made its way very slowly. But even before the war, Schönberg—who was a hardworking, ultraserious composer and teacher living at various times in Vienna, Berlin, Munich, and finally in the United States—had found two pupils who were themselves to become influential composers: Anton Webern and Alban Berg. The latter is best known for his opera *Wozzeck* (1922), which set a macabre story reminiscent of Kafka in a tightly knit symphonic form, using instead of regular singing what was called *Sprechstimme*—a half-spoken, half-sung kind of dialogue which heightened the eerie effect of the whole.

It would be wrong to imply, however, that atonality in any sense dominated German music in the postwar years. It remained an experimental style, and the vast majority of composers continued to work in more traditional vein. In Germany and Austria, which had dominated nineteenth-century music, the memory of the old masters was close at hand—among them Gustav Mahler, but lately dead, and, of course, Wagner, whose lineal heir, Richard Strauss, was still Germany's best known composer, however old-fashioned he might seem. Elsewhere nineteenth-century styles also lingered on, as in the majestic symphonies of the Finnish national composer, Jean Sibelius.

Other national figures similarly labored in comparative isolation, fitting into no neat scheme of musical succession. Italy, whose orchestral tradition had virtually been obliterated in the ninteenth century by the popular obsession with the opera, after 1900 began to revive its interest in instrumental music. The most popular, if not the most original, of Italian twentieth-century composers was Ottorino Respighi, whose *Fountains of Rome* (1917) and *Pines of Rome* (1924) became standard pieces in the symphonic repertory. Hungary produced Béla Bartók—a collector of folk melodies which he put into a bold modern idiom. In England, Ralph Vaughan Williams represented the older generation and William Walton the younger. Walton's orchestration of the poems entitled *Façade* by the still unknown Edith Sitwell offered another example of the general tendency toward collaboration among the arts. One art offered its aid to another in a common effort to express the mood of the postwar era through startling the public into a new range and depth of esthetic appreciation.

Painting: from the "Fauves" to the Abstract

In painting, as in music, a characteristically twentieth-century style began with a revolt against French Impressionism. Since the 1860's, at the very least, European painting had lived under the dominance of the school of Paris, which had produced its finest flowering in the work of the Impressionists. But then an orthodoxy of the unorthodox had set in. What had been very daring in 1875 looked tame a generation later. To the young painters just after the turn of the century, Impressionism lacked freshness; it seemed superficial—too obvious in its sensual appeal and unclear in its ideas of form and of line.

The great exception they made when they repudiated their elders was Paul Cézanne. The most influential Western painter since Giotto, Cézanne lived on until 1906, working in almost complete retirement in the south of France. From his example, in one form or another, nearly all the new movements of the twentieth century took their start. And these movements in turn had an influence that was to last in some cases for four decades: the generation of painters who were beginning their careers at the turn of the century proved unusually long-lived. Two of them at least were still active as the 1960's opened, still casting their enormous shadow over the work of their juniors.

One can take 1905 as the year twentieth-century painting began. In 1905 a group of young French painters joined together to exhibit their work in the Autumn Salon. A visiting critic, struck by the boldness of their colors and brush work, called them *fauves*—wild beasts—and the name stuck. It suggested what these fledgling artists had in common— clarity of outline; strong contrasts, which at the same time produced an effect of harmony and distinction; and a brilliant palette characterized by such sharp tones as orange, green, and brick red.

The Fauves honored the memory of Paul Gauguin, the painter of the natural splendor of Tahiti, where he had died in 1903; they also had much in common with a new artist just slightly older than themselves,

Pierre Bonnard, who in a quieter and less aggressive fashion used colors much as they did. Of the Fauves themselves, the two who achieved the greatest subsequent reputation were Henri Matisse and Georges Rouault. However they later varied their styles and experimented with new techniques, they always remained true to their original Fauve inspiration.

Two years after this first revolution a second occurred. In 1907, another young Frenchman, Georges Braque, along with a recent arrival from Spain, Pablo Picasso, launched the movement which came to be called *Cubism*. Deliberately banishing lyricism and bright color from their work, the Cubists concentrated on form, on architectural constructions of a geometrical complexity and abstraction. This sort of austerity did not last long. Soon strong colors returned, and Picasso in particular went on to experiment with a whole range of new styles, which followed each other in bewildering succession for the next half-century. Just before the war both he and Braque tried the technique of *collage*—sticking actual objects like colored paper or bits of fabric on to their paintings— and Braque also became fascinated with work for the theater, including the inevitable designing of sets for the Diaghilev ballet.

The next major change of direction came from Germany. In 1910, a number of young Expressionists in Berlin and Munich constituted themselves as the *Blaue Reiter* ("Blue Rider") group dedicated to "pure form." Very shortly, however, they, like the Cubists, began to split up to develop highly individual styles. In the 1920's, several of them became associated with innovation in architecture also. And the two who were to have the greatest influence—Paul Klee and the Russian-born Wassily Kandinsky—turned more and more toward an abstract style that was to make them the progenitors of present-day nonrepresentational painting.

After Expressionism there followed during the war and postwar years the manifestos of Dadaism and Surrealism. These were movements in literature as much as in art, and their influence on painting was as transitory as in poetry and the novel. Picasso, it is true, went through a surrealist phase—but then Picasso was always something of a showman, eager to keep himself before the public eye by abrupt changes in his artistic credo. None of these literary orientations in painting was to exert as strong a permanent effect as either Fauvism or Cubism.

By 1930, the major innovators of the prewar years had become middle-aged men with established reputations, each cultivating his own style and his own subject matter with little regard for programmatic statements. Bonnard and Matisse had been producing still lifes and interior scenes of a highly decorative elegance; Rouault was specializing in clowns, old men, and prostitutes, whose powerful lines and dark colors reflected his early training in stained glass; Picasso was turning from a classic and almost conventionally pictorial phase to the violent subjects he met with on his return to Spain in 1934—an evolution that was to culminate in "Guernica," his personal reaction to the horror of bombardment during his country's civil war.

Two Italian painters of a slightly younger group likewise remained independent of any constituted movement in the arts. The first, Giorgio de Chirico, became known as a "metaphysical" painter, an artist whose vision embraced landscapes and town scenes of a brooding solitude and desolation. The second, Amedeo Modigliani, had settled in Paris before the war and associated himself with the school of Paris, but in the delicate curves with which he outlined his figures, he remained true to the Italian linear tradition. After 1908 he produced an extraordinary series of nudes and portraits—until in 1920 he died, still under forty, his life destroyed by dissipation and hardship.

Since the influence of the established masters remained predominant, the years after 1925 saw far less innovation than had the two preceding decades. One tendency that was steadily gaining, however, was that of abstract or nonrepresentational art. This sprang both from the principles of Cubism and from the work of the German *Blaue Reiter* group. Indeed, its origins go back as far as paintings by Kandinsky in 1910 and by the Dutch artist Piet Mondrian in 1914. The latter, more than any other, became the father of contemporary abstract painting. In the essay he published in 1920 on what he called "neoplasticism," Mondrian laid down the rules of a rigorous abstractionism—a technique of carefully plotted lines and segments of primary colors, whose greatest influence was to come only after the experience of fascism and the Second World War had scattered and regrouped the world of art more thoroughly than any other catastrophe of modern times.

Architecture: the International Style of Gropius and Le Corbusier

In architecture the 1920's witnessed the establishment of the "International Style," primarily through the work of Walter Gropius in Germany and Le Corbusier in France—the two founders, along with their predecessor and rival Frank Lloyd Wright in the United States, of contemporary construction and contemporary design.

The origins of modern architecture lay in the realization on the part of a few pioneers in the late nineteenth century that the new world of vast cities and of the machine demanded a wholly new conception of building. Not only had requirements changed: factories and offices, railroad stations and hospitals had been added to the previously standard demand for churches, town houses, and city halls. It was also true that new materials had revolutionized construction possibilities: steel, glass, reinforced concrete, and plastics gave a freedom from conventional limitations that only slowly sank into the minds of architects and of the public. Similarly the technical complexity of these new types of buildings had changed the role of the architect himself: he could no longer be a mere academic designer of pleasing ground plans and façades; he must now understand something of engineering, sanitation, and electricity, and he must also be a town planner, moving old communities into the new framework that alone would fit the new society.

The most obvious feature of the modern idiom in architecture was its stress on the function of each building. The pioneers of the new style were impatient with the usual practice of copying parts of buildings from the past and adapting them more or less adequately to modern uses. They thought that the design of a railroad station should suggest the purpose it served, instead of imitating a Roman bath or a Renaissance palace. Similarly, they rejected the general tendency to use ornament in indiscriminate fashion. Ornament, they argued, should grow naturally from function; all new styles at their inception had been stark and simple. Thus the severity of line which the public found the most objectionable aspect of modern architecture might be considered a merely transitional characteristic, destined to pass away as the style reached maturity.

Among the precursors of the International Style, the greatest continuing influence was that of Auguste Perret, who as early as 1903 had begun to design in Paris buildings of reinforced concrete which permitted great freedom in the arrangement of individual floor plans; the walls no longer carried the weight of the building—this was borne by a few concrete columns. In Germany also, early experiments with industrial design were proceeding in a similar direction. But the decisive break with the past came in 1911, when the twenty-eight-year-old Gropius was given the assignment of designing the Fagus Works at Alfeld for a client who was in complete sympathy with his views; the result was an elegant, light building, whose clean lines and walls of glass showed it as the prototype of a style in industrial building that after the Second World War was to become almost standard both in Europe and in the United States.

In 1919, Gropius established the Bauhaus—a "high school for creative art" aiming to bridge the gap between art and industry. At Weimar and subsequently at Dessau, the Bauhaus grouped a wide variety of talents including the painters Klee and Kandinsky, for Gropius believed in teamwork, in the union of art and technics, and, unlike his contemporaries Wright and Le Corbusier, he was willing to keep his own personality in the background in order to achieve this result. He was primarily a teacher—the most influential of his whole era. Even when in 1928 he returned to private practice, he produced buildings that again gave a clear direction to future planning. In the lofty, elongated slabs of the experimental housing schemes which he designed for suburban Berlin, subsequent architects found inspiration for some of the best work in city reconstruction in the years after 1945.

The Nazi regime forced Gropius into exile, first in Britain and then in the United States. During the same period, his Franco-Swiss counterpart Le Corbusier was finally coming into his own. Le Corbusier was more of an individualist and a visionary than Gropius. Throughout the

1920's he received no large commissions—his project for the Palace of
the League of Nations was passed over in favor of a more conventional
plan—and he was reduced to house design and to elaborating the principles of construction that he had originally learned in Perret's office.
These included a flat roof; great freedom in planning interior space;
horizontal ribbon windows which sometimes even ran around corners;
and a first floor lifted off the ground by columns, giving the building the
effect of being suspended in air with a garden spreading under it. He
also consoled himself with vast plans for rebuilding the center of Paris
and for a "radiant city" of the future in which tall buildings would stand
widely spaced among ample stretches of green.

In the 1930's when Le Corbusier was at last able to turn from house
design to public buildings, a reaction against the International Style was
already setting in. Nazi Germany denounced it as "decadent," and
France, whose building industry remained in the doldrums throughout
the depression decade, relapsed into a timid semiclassicism. Both Gropius
and Le Corbusier left the Continent—the latter spreading to Brazil the
message of the new architecture that Gropius was teaching in the United
States. Thus it was in the smaller countries and outside Europe that the
International Style continued to advance in the 1930's: Switzerland, the
Netherlands, and Scandinavia became particularly hospitable. Here
younger architects like the Finn Alvar Aalto turned away from the severe
cubic designs of the pioneers to a warmer, more supple and curved style
that was to reach full fruition only after the Second World War. When
this conflict broke out, most new building in Europe, as in America, was
still in one or another of the traditional styles, but the new idiom was
now known everywhere. The triumph of the modern, in architecture as
in so much else, was only a matter of time: the new generation was already growing up that would come to take it for granted.

Readings

For the epoch-making changes in natural science, see the comprehensive,
handsomely produced collaborative work, largely by French scholars, René
Taton, ed., *Science in the Twentieth Century* (1966), and for the single
science which changed most profoundly, Ernst Zimmer, *The Revolution in
Physics* (1936), and E. N. da C. Andrade, *Rutherford and the Nature of the
Atom* (1964).

H. Stuart Hughes, *Consciousness and Society: The Reorientation of European Social Thought 1890–1930* (1958), gives a general interpretation of the
work of the European social thinkers who dominated the 1920's; Ernest Jones,
The Life and Work of Sigmund Freud, 3 vols. (1953–1957), is the standard
biography of the most influential of them. For sociological thought in particular, see Georges Gurvitch and Wilbert E. Moore, eds., *Twentieth Century
Sociology* (1945). Morton White, *The Age of Analysis* (1955), offers a series
of selections from the major philosophers, with useful introductions to each

text. In *Weimar Culture* (1968), Peter Gay analyzes with verve and discernment the precarious zenith of German cultural achievement.

The most stimulating general interpretation of the newer trends in the literature of the period is Edmund Wilson, *Axel's Castle* (1931). Emile Langui, *Fifty Years of Modern Art* (1959), gives a concise account of painting and sculpture, lavishly illustrated with plates and with brief biographical accounts of the leading artists. For the rise of the International Style in architecture, see Jurgen Joedicke, *A History of Modern Architecture* (1959). Two books, both bearing the title *Twentieth Century Music*, treat that subject with discrimination and at a high level of technical competence, the one by Peter Yates (1967), the other a collaborative volume edited by Rollo H. Myers (1968).

The Great Depression, 1929-1935

Chapter Eight

I

ORIGINS AND CHARACTER

In the autumn of 1929 came the catastrophe which so few had anticipated but which in retrospect seems inevitable—prices broke on the New
York Stock Exchange, dragging down with them in their fall, first the
economy of the United States itself, subsequently that of Europe and
the rest of the world. Financial losses of such magnitude had never before
been known in the history of capitalist society, and the ensuing depression was also unprecedented in scope. There had always been business crises; economists had come to take them as normal and even to
chart a certain regularity in their occurrence. But this one dwarfed all
its predecessors: no previous depression had remotely approached it in
length, in depth, and in the universality of impact. Small wonder that
countless people were led to speculate whether the final collapse of
capitalism itself, so long predicted by the Marxists, was not at last in
sight.

On October 24, "Black Thursday," more than sixteen million shares
of stock were sold in panic, and in the next three weeks the general
industrial index of the New York Stock Exchange fell by more than
half. Nevertheless, it was by no means clear at first, how severe the depression was going to be. Previous crises had originated in the United
States—this was not the great novelty. What was unprecedented was the
extent of European economic dependence on America which the crash

*Because of the shortage of houses, the high
rent, and other difficulties, whole families in Berlin
have been forced to live in municipal lodging houses.*
COURTESY PHOTOWORLD, INC.

of 1929 revealed. This dependence varied greatly from country to country. Central Europe was involved first, as American financiers began to call in their short-term loans in Germany and Austria. Throughout 1930 these withdrawals of capital continued, until in May, 1931, the Austrian Kreditanstalt suspended payments entirely. Thereafter, panic swept the Central European exchanges as bank after bank closed down and one industry after another began to reduce production and lay off workers.

Meantime the crisis had reached Great Britain. In September, 1931, the country went off the gold standard, to be followed two years later by the United States and nearly all the other financial powers of the world. The great exception was France: with a balanced economy and relative self-sufficiency, the French held off the crisis longer than anyone else—not until 1932 did its effects become really severe. But late involvement did not help the country in the long run: for France was the slowest and the least successful of the major powers in pulling itself out of the Depression, which left a wound in French society that was far from healed when the Second World War broke out.

The fall in production and the fall in prices everywhere reached unprecedented depths. In Germany—which was hit worst of all—production had fallen by 39 per cent, at the bottom of the Depression in 1932, and prices by only slightly less. In France, which was stubbornly holding to the gold standard, the price level in 1935 was just over half what it had been in 1930. But of all the manifestations of the Depression, unemployment was most grievous and most clearly left its mark on the whole era. In this respect, France was the least seriously affected: the number of those out of work never rose above 850,000. But here as in Italy and in the agricultural nations in general, there was much semi-employment and concealed unemployment in the countryside. In Britain, the jobless numbered nearly three million—between a fifth and a quarter of the whole labor force. And in Germany unemployment mounted to the horrifying total of six million; trade-union executives estimated that more than two-fifths of their members were out of work entirely and another fifth employed only part time. With roughly half the population in desperation and want, it was no wonder that the Germans turned to the extremist leadership that they had so narrowly avoided in the crisis of 1923.

Elsewhere social unrest never reached such grave proportions, but throughout Europe governments and peoples felt themselves on the edge of a precipice, as the turbulent and questioning mood of the immediate postwar years returned with redoubled intensity. As had occurred during the war, a crisis situation evoked state intervention in the economy on a massive scale. Governments found themselves forced to resort to all sorts of measures of which the conservative disapproved. These measures gradually came to follow a common pattern: most countries turned inward, trying to save their own economies without reference to, or regard for, their neighbors, through raising tariffs and setting up schemes for currency pooling and block buying abroad; they sought to relieve the sufferings of the unemployed through extended subsistence payments, on the model of the British dole, and to provide new jobs through vast programs of public works and, eventually, through rearmament.

Most of these measures were mere palliatives, however, undertaken in skeptical and hesitant fashion, and only after years of delay had robbed them of maximum effect. Furthermore, a number of them were of doubtful merit. The turn toward economic nationalism probably did as much harm as good—constricting the volume of world trade and still further reducing Europe's share in it. In Europe, as in the United States, the only policy that brought much lasting benefit was direct provision of new employment by the government. Even this was far less effective in its original form of public works than in its subsequent guise of war production. On both sides of the Atlantic, only rearmament proved a sufficiently powerful antidote to the Great Depression. It is sobering to note that the great power which was the most successful in pulling itself out of the slump—Nazi Germany—was also the one which plunged most wholeheartedly into preparation for war.

Thus, by the mid-1930's, the economic and social struggles of the decade were blending imperceptibly into the origins of the Second World War itself.

II

CENTRAL EUROPE:
THE YEARS OF TURMOIL

Germany: from Brüning to Papen and Schleicher

The first European government to fall as a direct consequence of the Great Depression was the German ministry led by the Social Democrat Hermann Müller. The cause of its collapse was characteristic of a divergence on economic policy that was to split country after country in the ensuing years: the Left wanted increased unemployment relief; the Right argued for retrenchment and a balanced budget. In such a debate the conservatives initially held the stronger cards: they had on their side the weight of economic theory and the orthodox maxim that reduced spending was the proper way to move the business cycle out of depression. The socialists were more hesitant: on problems such as these Marxist theory was of little help, and they were obliged to fall back on arguments of humanitarianism and expediency; the new economics of Keynes and the experience of the American New Deal had not yet taught them to see virtue in deficit financing.

Thus it was a conservative government that came to power in Germany in March, 1930. It rested on that portion of the Reichstag Center and Right—still the larger part—which refused to follow Hugenberg and

Hitler in their propaganda of unbridled nationalism. But the government had no majority in the Reichstag as a whole, nor did its chief inspire general devotion and loyalty. The new chancellor, Heinrich Brüning, was a man of rectitude and disciplined intelligence. As the first to reach political power of the generation which had actually seen front-line service during the war, he might have been expected to appeal to younger voters. But for this he was far too cold and rigid. Even in his own party, the Center, Brüning was not popular.

Yet he managed to stay in office for more than two years. Month after month, he doggedly stuck to his task, as the depression deepened, the army of the unemployed swelled to frightening dimensions, and both the Communists and the National Socialists made steady gains. In one sense, Brüning's might be called Germany's last democratic government of the interwar years; its leader did all in his power to resist the on-slaught of nazism. In another sense, this ministry marked the beginning of the end for German democracy. Lacking a parliamentary majority, the Brüning government felt obliged to resort to the emergency decree powers that the constitution vested in the president, and beginning with the July budget of 1930, it enacted measure after measure by Hinden-burg's fiat.

Meantime, the electoral returns gave mounting evidence of the Nazis' rise. In September, 1930, they increased their seats in the Reichstag from 12 to 107—thus becoming the second largest party in the country and making the Reichstag itself still more unmanageable than before. Eighteen months later, when Hindenburg's term expired, the National Socialists decided on the bold maneuver of running their own man, Adolf Hitler, against Germany's undisputed father figure who, at eighty-five, was ready to do his soldier's duty by standing for re-election. Hin-denburg won—but only because the Social Democrats felt driven to the paradoxical course of voting for a military hero to save what was left of German democracy.

At this point the former understanding between chancellor and pres-ident—which alone had permitted the Weimar system to continue work-ing at all—broke down in unexpected fashion. Hindenburg, who was tied to the Prussian estate-owning class by origin and long association, refused to enact a land-reform decree which Brüning had laid before him. Brüning resigned. His successor was Franz von Papen, in name a member of the Center, but in fact a reactionary aristocrat and schemer who thought himself clever enough to give Germany a nationalist gov-ernment without calling on Hitler for aid.

With the advent of Papen in May, 1932, began the eight-month agony of German democracy. The new "ministry of barons" did not pretend to have the confidence of the Reichstag and relied solely on the support of President von Hindenburg. Its first acts clearly suggested its authori-tarian sympathies: it lifted the ban on Nazi Storm Troop activities which had been imposed two months earlier by the Brüning government and then, under the flimsy excuse that the constant street clashes between Communists and National Socialists made regular administration impossible, it went on to dissolve by police action the Social Democratic government of the key state of Prussia.

Now, if ever, was the time for German democrats to stand up and fight for their liberties. From this point on it would be too late. But nobody seemed prepared to take decisive action. The Democratic party had nearly vanished; the Center was paralyzed by its own internal divisions; the nationalist Right was more and more conniving with the Nazis. The Social Democrats alone held firm, with their electoral strength only slightly reduced. But their fighting spirit had been depleted beyond repair.

In late July, another Reichstag election gave the Nazis more than two hundred seats—thus ratifying their claim to being the strongest party in the nation. Unemployment stood at six million, and street battles between the private armies of the extremists had become almost a daily occurrence. Papen, like Brüning before him, found the ground slipping from under his feet. The Reichstag was completely unruly, and Hindenburg was losing confidence in the chancellor of his own choice. Bewildered and senile, the field marshal had only a few lucid hours a day, and in these was governed by those who were close at hand. Among them was General Kurt von Schleicher, still more of an intriguer than Papen and at least as confident of his ability to outwit Hitler. In early December, Schleicher became the German Republic's last chancellor.

Papen had behaved in office as a frank reactionary; his successor embarked on a more subtle policy. Schleicher decided to try demagogy, hoping to break the power of both the Communists and the Nazis by a pseudoleftist appeal. And he felt that he had reason for optimism because Hitler, for the first time since the onset of the depression, had lost ground in the second Reichstag election of the year, and the economic situation was slightly improved. More particularly, Schleicher decided to investigate the illegal profits that some of the great landowners had made through the agrarian relief measures enacted by his predecessor. At this point conservatives took alarm—an alarm which put within Hitler's grasp the power that had very nearly eluded him (*see* Chapter Nine, II).

Austria: Party Strife and the Accession of Dollfuss

To Austria, which had not wanted to be a separate state, the postwar years had brought less apparent turmoil than to Germany. After a battle with inflation almost as severe as that which the neighboring Reich was about to experience, Austria seemed to settle into relative stability. This impression of calm was reinforced by the fact that the Austrian political situation was far simpler than the German: two great parties, the Socialist and the Christian Social, between them virtually monopolized the field.

This might suggest that Austria had found its way to the two-party system which students of parliamentary democracy—with the Brtiish experience in mind—usually regarded as the optimum. In reality, there was a thoroughgoing difference between Austrian and Anglo-Saxon politics. In Britain, the two parties agreed on fundamentals; and this remained true even after Labor had replaced the Liberals as the second party. In Austria, no such agreement was possible. The divergences between the parties split the national community wide open, reflecting not only the usual cleavage between Right and Left but also the two radically different types of society that the Treaty of Saint Germain, in reducing Austria to its German-speaking provinces, had forced to live together.

On the one hand there was the city of Vienna, which had a quarter of the country's population—a vast metropolis shorn of its imperial function, cosmopolitan, industrial, and freethinking, with a large percentage of its inhabitants of Slavic or Jewish origin. Vienna regularly voted for socialism, which was rather more leftist and militant than its German counterpart. Joined to Vienna in unhappy union were the Danubian and Alpine provinces of the old Empire—Tyrol, Salzburg, and the rest—overwhelmingly rural, conservative, Catholic, and inclining toward anti-Semitism and distrust of foreigners. These naturally voted Christian Social. This was a Catholic party not unlike the German Center, with a tradition of paternalistic reform extending far back into the nineteenth century, but which, by the end of the 1920's, was increasingly tempted by authoritarian solutions.

A federal constitution alone enabled these two parties and the two types of society they represented to live together. For the better part of a decade they coexisted in a state of uneasy truce; the Christian Socials regularly dominated the federal government and the rural provinces, while the Socialists ran Vienna, which had been set up by itself as an urban province. Periodically the tension between the two broke out in vast street demonstrations in the capital—in 1926 and again in 1929, when the federal constitution was modified in a more authoritarian direction. The Christian Socials were scandalized at the fashion in which the Socialists ran Vienna—at high taxes and expensive public housing schemes. The latter contended that such measures were essential to relieve the economic distress of a ghost city which had lost its natural markets and was suffering grievously from the tariff policies of its neighbors. The Socialists had equal reason to distrust the Catholic party, for the Christian Socials were coming under increasingly heavy pressure from their fascist-minded direct-action groups, which by 1930 were beginning to receive secret help from Mussolini's Italy.

The coming of the Depression brought these latent tensions into the open. In 1931, the Austrian fascists made their first local bid for power; the next year the Christian Socials found the "strong man" they needed. With the accession of Engelbert Dollfuss to the chancellorship, a new era opened in Austrian history. The six years 1932–1938 were to be a period of growing authoritarianism, a semifascism which steered a tortuous course between the democracy it had rejected and the ever-present menace of absorption into the Nazi state (*see* Chapter Nine, III).

The International Aspect: the Abortive Customs Union and the End of Reparations

When the union of Austria with Germany finally came about in 1938, it was against the will of both major Austrian parties. Earlier, however, the idea of union, or *Anschluss,* had been very popular—indeed, it was almost the only thing on which Austrians were agreed. One of the failures which had undermined the authority both of Austrian democracy and of the Brüning government in Germany was the veto imposed by the French and their allies on the Austro-German plan for a customs union—an obvious first step toward *Anschluss*—which was broached in 1931. The matter finally went to the World Court, which declared against it in an eight to seven vote whose political motivation was only too apparent.

This marked the last time that the French were to take decisive action against their late enemies. From 1931 on, the trend toward revision of the Versailles settlement became irresistible. The British had always favored modification, and the Americans and Italians, for different reasons, agreed. The French found themselves isolated—particularly since they had chosen to exert their pressure for the dubious purpose of preserving Austria's freedom against the wishes of its own inhabitants.

Thus in international affairs, the years 1930–1932 can be regarded as a transition period between the Stresemann-Briand era and the era of fascist aggression that was to follow. As the depression in Central Europe deepened and hit bottom in 1932, it became apparent that the vacuous optimism of the previous half-decade would no longer suffice. In international affairs, as at home, the battle against the Depression demanded something more substantial than high-sounding declarations of good will. The time of reckoning had come: the tangled knot of reparations and war debts now finally had to be unraveled. In the summer of 1931, on the initiative of President Hoover, the powers agreed to a moratorium on all intergovernmental debts. In effect, the Hoover moratorium suspended both reparations and war debts without distinction —despite the American government's continued insistence that the two problems were not to be lumped together. The following summer, at Lausanne, the powers in fact, if not in theory, canceled German reparations entirely. Simultaneously the payment of war debts came to an end. Although a few token payments were subsequently made—and although the American Congress stubbornly refused to recognize the inevitable —the problem of reparations and war debts had actually been swept away once and for all by the onrush of events.

This, far more than the long-awaited Disarmament Conference, which met at intervals for twenty months and achieved almost nothing, was the real accomplishment of 1932. The reparations nightmare had been lifted from Germany, and the Reich was well on its way to international equality. By now it was quite clear that the Germans were rearming, and that nobody was prepared to stop them. The "fetters of Versailles" were falling off one by one. Ironically, these very fetters were providing Hitler with his most reliable propaganda assets in his drive toward power. The German people failed to understand how much the last chancellors of the Republic—Brüning and Papen—had actually accomplished in strengthening Germany's international position: by the summer of 1932, these two—both nationalists to the core—had *already* set their country firmly on the course of patriotic revival which was later to be the Nazis' proudest boast.

III

WESTERN EUROPE:
THE YEARS OF DRIFT

During the years of crisis when Germany and Austria were shaken by social unrest and moving inexorably toward authoritarian government, Britain and France drifted, safe from threat of revolution, but sure of nothing else. The illusory stability of the era of Baldwin and Poincaré had vanished. Government by businessmen had failed, but no clear alternative had emerged. Hence the rule of the Right continued, without talent and without imagination, until in the decisive year 1936 the people of Western Europe began awakening to the multiple threats, domestic as well as foreign, that were slowly undermining the societies in which they lived.

Britain: the Second Labor Government

In Britain, as in Germany, the Great Depression struck when a socialist government was in power. Here, as in the Reich, the Labor ministry proved incapable of coping with economic problems of such unprecedented dimensions.

The parliamentary elections of May, 1929, returned Labor to power under conditions only slightly better than those that had confronted the party's first effort to govern in 1924. The new ministry certainly had more popular support: taking its cue from the Liberals, it had fought the election on the issue of unemployment and had apparently made good its contention that the Tories were to blame for allowing the economy to languish even in a time of prosperity. For the first time, Labor won more seats than the Conservatives. But it still lacked a majority; it was still dependent on Liberal tolerance; and it still had as its leader Ramsay

The First World War

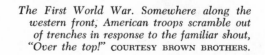

The First World War. Somewhere along the western front, American troops scramble out of trenches in response to the familiar shout, "Over the top!" COURTESY BROWN BROTHERS.

General Ferdinand Foch of France, commander-in-chief of the Allied armies in France from April 14, 1918. COURTESY BROWN BROTHERS.

General Joseph Joffre, marshal of France. COURTESY BROWN BROTHERS.

Georges Clemenceau, nicknamed
"The Tiger," premier of
France (1906–1909 and
1917–1920). COURTESY
BROWN BROTHERS.

Marshal Henri-Philippe Pétain
of France. COURTESY BROWN
BROTHERS.

*Emperor Francis Joseph of
Austria-Hungary.* COURTESY
BROWN BROTHERS.

*Field Marshal Paul von
Hindenburg of Germany.*
COURTESY BROWN BROTHERS.

William II, German emperor.
COURTESY BROWN BROTHERS.

General Erich Ludendorff of Germany. COURTESY BROWN BROTHERS.

The Big Four at Versailles, 1919. From left to right: David Lloyd George of Great Britain, Vittorio Emanuele Orlando of Italy, Georges Clemenceau of France, and Woodrow Wilson of the United States.

The Russian Revolution

*Bolshevik revolutionists are mowed down b[...]
machine gun fire on the Nevsky Prospect [...]
Petrograd during the July uprising (1917[...]*
COURTESY BROWN BROTHER[...]

V. I. Lenin, several years after the revolution of 1917, addresses paraders during a First of May celebration.
COURTESY BROWN BROTHERS.

Leon Trotsky, shortly before his break with Stalin. COURTESY BROWN BROTHERS.

Aristide Briand, foreign minister of France (1925–1932) and co-author of the Kellogg-Briand Pact. COURTESY BROWN BROTHERS.

Ramsay MacDonald, prime minister in the first Labor government of Great Britain (1924 and again in 1929–1935). COURTESY BROWN BROTHERS.

Gustav Stresemann, chancellor (1923) and foreign minister (1923–1929) of Germany. COURTESY BROWN BROTHERS.

Raymond Poincaré, president (1913–1920) and prime minister (1922–1924, 1926–1929) of France. COURTESY BROWN BROTHERS.

Between the Wars

Stanley Baldwin, prime minister of Great Britain (1923–1924, 1924–1929, 1935–1937). COURTESY BROWN BROTHERS.

Max Planck, whose quantum
theory revolutionized the
study of physics. COURTESY
BROWN BROTHERS.

John Maynard Keynes, English
economist, whose theories have
greatly influenced contemporary
welfare state policies.
COURTESY BROWN BROTHERS.

Pope Pius XI, who made a
stirring plea for social reform
in his encyclical Quadragesimo
Anno. COURTESY BROWN
BROTHERS.

André Gide, French novelist and a leader of French free thought. COURTESY BROWN BROTHERS.

Sigmund Freud, founder of the school of psychoanalysis. COURTESY BROWN BROTHERS.

Thomas Mann, German novelist and essayist who exiled himself in protest against the Nazi regime. COURTESY BROWN BROTHERS.

The strength and determination of the Axis powers in 1937 is triumphantly displayed as Hitler and Benito Mussolini review a German labor corps. COURTESY BROWN BROTHERS.

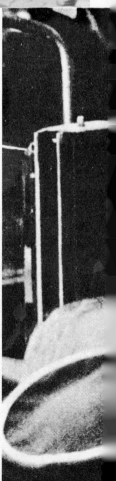

Named chancellor of Germany in 1933, a triumphant Adolf Hitler parades with the aged and ailing Von Hindenburg shortly before the latter's death. COURTESY BROWN BROTHERS.

Prelude to War

*Neville Chamberlain, prime minister of Great
Britain, returning from Munich (1938). The
press dispatch which accompanied this
photograph read ". . . the savior of
Europe. . . ."* COURTESY BROWN BROTHERS.

MacDonald, whom age had made even vaguer and more hesitant than before.

The new government would be judged on how well it handled the crucial issue of unemployment, and here, almost immediately, it entered upon a desperate struggle with the financiers. Labor had been in power only four months when the Wall Street crash occurred. By the next spring, the effects of American withdrawals on the British economy were all too evident. Unemployment, which had stood at a million and a half at the beginning of 1930, by midsummer reached two million, and at the year's end it was two and a half million. Obviously a Labor government could not let these people starve: it must support them somehow, and the only method available seemed to be giving the "dole" to larger and larger numbers of the unemployed.

This was a severe strain on the budget, already weakened by a fall in tax receipts. In the summer of 1931, the chancellor of the exchequer —whose financial principles were blamelessly orthodox—brought in the report of an expert committee on expenditure, which had concluded that the one way to meet the deficit was to reduce unemployment benefits. The somber picture it had drawn of Britain's financial position created a mood approaching panic. From mid-July to mid-August, banks of all sorts experienced heavy withdrawals; at the Bank of England the gold reserve was sinking to the vanishing point. With Parliament on vacation, MacDonald was left alone to deal with the crisis; and for such a position, he was supported neither by his temperament nor by his minimal knowledge of economics and finance.

Recalled in haste from his holiday in Scotland, the prime minister summoned his cabinet on the weekend of August 22–23. He explained that the government and the country could find financial salvation only by accepting the recommendation to reduce unemployment payments. The alternative was bankruptcy. This was made quite clear by a group of New York financiers who refused to extend further loans to Britain unless its government carried out important economies. Half the cabinet refused. With the ministry deadlocked, MacDonald asked for and received the resignations of his colleagues. When the meeting adjourned, the ministers believed that a Conservative-Liberal coalition would replace them.

But this was not MacDonald's plan. He had been to see the king, and the latter had talked to Baldwin. What emerged from these confabulations was a National Government, with MacDonald still prime minister and Baldwin as his deputy.

The National Government of 1931, like Lloyd George's Coalition from 1916 to 1922, was a mere façade for Tory rule. No more than three Labor ministers followed MacDonald into it, and there was only token Liberal representation. The prime minister, like Lloyd George before him, had become the prisoner of the Conservatives. He was beguiled into betraying his own party—by the pressure of financiers both British and American; by the patriotic pleas of the king; and by his own vanity, which could not resist the blandishments of the well-born. It was a crushing blow for Labor: although the party expelled MacDonald and the handful of members of Parliament who followed him, it needed a full decade to recover its strength. For the Liberals—who were entitled to expect a real share in power—it was one more step on the long downward path. For the country, it was a catastrophe parading as salvation: it meant nine years of fumble and muddle, with MacDonald and Baldwin, once political enemies, now pooling their talents for delay and obfuscation, at which they both so notably excelled.

Britain: the National Government: MacDonald, Baldwin, Chamberlain

Presumably the National Government was formed to save the pound. But its first action was to go off the gold standard. This did not prove as catastrophic as the orthodox economists had feared. The pound fell from $4.86 to $3.40 on the international exchanges—and that was all. Simultaneously Parliament swallowed the 10 per cent cut in unemployment benefits at which the Labor ministers had balked.

Thus the financial crisis was surmounted with suspicious ease. Its sudden passing suggests that it had never been so grave as the financiers had pretended and that the Conservatives, as with the Zinoviev letter of 1924, once again were arousing fear in order to oust a Labor ministry. This suspicion was confirmed when the new government went to the country to ratify its mandate. The election of October, 1931, was all too reminiscent of Lloyd George's "Khaki Election" of 1918. Under the guise of a coalition effort, the Conservatives pre-empted the greater part of the joint candidacies, and their electoral propaganda was unashamedly partisan. Consciously striving to create a mood of panic, the Tories threatened national disaster if Labor should win. Their tactics succeeded: the Conservatives emerged with the largest majority of the century—472 seats out of the 556 that went to candidates supporting the National Government. Labor, on the contrary, experienced the greatest debacle of its history—with only 46 members elected, it had lost five-sixths of its seats, including nearly all those held by former cabinet ministers.

The National Government, then, was in a position to rule almost without opposition. Once again, its first act was to ride roughshod over the principles of its Liberal supporters. It revived Baldwin's old program of tariff protection—now sponsored by the more forceful and convincing Neville Chamberlain—which it pushed through Parliament in early 1932. During the summer it went on to make preferential trade agreements with the overseas dominions. Britain, which had always ranked as the citadel of free trade, was following the rest of Europe into economic nationalism. At this point, the Liberal ministers decided that they had had enough. They resigned from the ministry, leaving it an indisputably Tory preserve. This situation was not openly avowed until three years later when Ramsay MacDonald—his eyesight failing and his speeches getting more and more incoherent—yielded the post of prime minister to Stanley Baldwin.

The party that MacDonald had betrayed meanwhile licked its wounds and made what show of opposition it could. Under younger and stronger leaders, Labor reorganized its cadres and slowly began to move away from its pacifist position in foreign affairs. By the autumn of 1935, the party was ready for the election which Baldwin suddenly announced to Parliament on its return from summer recess. Labor's new confidence proved justified: when the votes were counted, the Conservatives had lost nearly seventy seats, while Labor had more than tripled its own. But the National Government still rested on an enormous Tory majority; Baldwin had put both opposition parties at a disadvantage by robbing them of their most appealing planks—internationalism and support of the League of Nations. No one yet knew that within a month the government was flagrantly to abandon these very principles, and that the House of Commons just chosen was to sit longer than any other Parliament of modern times. Its electoral origins long since forgotten, this same body was successively to endorse appeasement, war, and Winston Churchill, until in the moment of victory it vanished unmourned (*see* Chapter Twelve, II).

In the intervening years, economic recovery had begun. After reaching its peak at the beginning of 1933, unemployment fell steadily, until it leveled off in 1936 at a little more than a million and a half. Production rallied in similar fashion: by 1937, it stood 20 per cent above its 1929 level. Yet these figures were less encouraging than they seemed: even before the Great Depression began, Britain had been in a state of semidepression, so that a return to "normal" did not mean what it did in other countries; the plight of men on the dole was not eased and resentment continued to smolder among the working classes in the depressed areas and in the country as a whole.

In undertaking state intervention, the National Government followed a line which was neither the hands-off attitude that a Brüning or a Hoover adopted in the early part of the Depression, nor the active policy later pursued by such sharply contrasting experiments as the American New Deal, the Nazi Third Reich, and the French Popular Front. Nothing done in Britain provided anything like their stimulus to morale, and its absence helps account for the apathy and discouragement that brooded over the country throughout the 1930's. In general, the National Government restricted itself to keeping interest rates low and sponsoring a substantial housing program. And these were largely the work of the one decisive figure in the ministry, the chancellor of the exchequer, Neville Chamberlain.

Chamberlain was never popular, and his association with appeasement and the catastrophe of 1940 has injured his historical reputation. He was stubborn and unimaginative; his rasping voice, his dark clothes, and his perpetual umbrella symbolized all that was unlovable in the

British business classes. But he was an excellent administrator who knew what he wanted and had complete confidence in his ability to carry it out. When Baldwin retired in 1937—having successfully surmounted the crisis of a royal abdication *—there appeared no alternative to making Chamberlain prime minister: he at least stood for *something*—the rest of the cabinet were little more than ciphers.

France: Tardieu, Herriot, and the Election of 1932

When Poincaré withdrew as French prime minister in the summer of 1929, no satisfactory successor appeared. Nobody combined as he did a basic conservatism with a thoroughly "republican" record calculated to reassure the part of the electorate that always suspected authoritarian tendencies on the right. The men who followed Poincaré in office were too young to have such a record, and in the case of the three most important—Tardieu, Laval, and Flandin—subsequent dealings with fascism or approaches to fascism proved these suspicions amply justified.

Poincaré's immediate heir, André Tardieu, was far too intelligent and far too undiplomatic to please most deputies. Originally a protégé of Clemenceau, he resembled the great war leader in his shortness of temper and impatience with opposition. In a time of grave national emergency, the Chamber of Deputies might endure leadership of this sort. But Tardieu could not convince his colleagues that the early 1930's were indeed such a period. The deputies continued in their customarily irresponsible attitude toward the national economy, and refused to listen to Tardieu's warnings that unless they consented to heavy investment in economic improvements, their country was bound sooner or later to be caught up in the worldwide depression. They preferred the leader who alternated in power with Tardieu—Pierre Laval—a sly and slippery fellow, converted from the left to conservatism like so many successful deputies, who summed up in his own person all that was cynical and corrupt in French parliamentary politics.

By 1932, the Depression had in fact struck France, and in the election of that year the Left won easily. This put the Radicals under Herriot back in power for the first time in six years, with the Socialists providing support outside the government, as they had done in 1924. Once again —as had happened then—the Left ministry involved itself in insoluble financial difficulties. Herriot stayed in office half a year; of his four successors, only one remained for more than three months. The last of these —Edouard Daladier—had hardly begun his tenure when the storm broke that was to drown the Radicals in a torrent of well-orchestrated indignation.

---

* King Edward VIII, who had been on the throne for only eleven months, was forced to abdicate in December 1936, owing to his insistence on marrying an American divorcée.

France: the Riots of 1934: Doumergue and Laval

In December, 1933, the police unearthed one of the widely ramifying scandals by which the French Republic was periodically shaken. The details of the Stavisky case are unimportant—indeed, they were never properly explained. They involved a provincial pawnshop, a fraudulent bond issue, and all sorts of unsavory minor details. The really sinister aspect of the case was its exploitation by the authoritarian wing of the French Right. French reactionaries spread reports that a number of leading political figures were involved in the scandal and that the government was concealing their guilt; thus democracy and the Republic itself were discredited in the minds of countless Frenchmen of conservative and patriotic views.

On February 6, 1934, the adherents of the leading rightist and patriotic organizations flocked into the streets of Paris to call for Daladier's overthrow. They failed in their attempt to storm the Chamber of Deputies: the police stopped them with gunfire, and eleven demonstrators lost their lives. But they did succeed in bringing down the government: Daladier had shed the blood of patriots, and Daladier had to go.

Not since the Commune of 1871 had France been so close to civil war. Although the riots of February, 1934, were no more than an uncoordinated succession of street demonstrations, they were symptomatic of a deep-seated *malaise* that was gradually destroying whatever fragile consensus existed within French society. The government of the Left had failed: the Radicals had proved themselves unable to do anything coherent to meet the Depression, and they were hopelessly at odds with the Socialists in their notions of economic policy. More and more the left electorate was turning in disgust toward a new militancy and a near-revolutionary temper. On the right a similar shift was occurring in still more threatening form: weary of incompetent leadership, French conservatives were eyeing with growing admiration the fascist experiments beyond their borders.

And so—as had happened in 1926 and as was to happen once again in 1938—the French Left, after two years in power and with two years of its electoral mandate still to run, found itself bankrupt both financially and ideologically and obliged to hand over power to the conservatives. But the conservatives' attempt to repeat the financial "miracle" of 1926 did not succeed. The old ex-president whom they hoisted into office, Gaston Doumergue, was far from being a Poincaré, and his government failed to produce the anticipated national revival. Even the presence of the hero of Verdun, Marshal Pétain, as minister of defense, could not give it the proper patriotic flavor. Doumergue succeeded only in restoring a minimum of order in the national finances. When the old prime minister stepped down in November, to be succeeded by the dapper Pierre-Etienne Flandin, the country was well on its way back to politics as usual. When Laval replaced him the following June, all thought of national regeneration had long since vanished.

In the last half of 1935, under the rule of Pierre Laval, France touched its lowest point of the interwar period. In foreign affairs Laval inaugurated an uninspiring policy of appeasement. In the economic sphere, the government had nothing better to offer than retrenchment, salary reductions, and a pedantic adherence to the gold standard. The other powers had abandoned gold and were beginning to move out of depression. France alone was holding firmly to a deflationary policy and sinking ever deeper into economic stagnation. Meanwhile, the paramilitary formations of the authoritarian Right were holding their parades with impunity. On the left, a new unity was growing, as anger and frustration mounted at the impotence of French democracy and the spreading influence of fascism. The Socialists had joined with the Communists—while the Radicals limped more hesitantly behind—to forge the Popular Front that in the year following was to lead France into the most tumultuous and decisive period of its entire interwar history (see Chapter Nine, V).

IV

SCANDINAVIA: THE MIDDLE WAY

The Role of the Smaller Democracies;
the Belgian Language Question

From 1919 to 1939, the smaller democracies of Western Europe impinged only rarely on the wider sphere of international and ideological contention. Most of the time, they followed their own course, secure in the conviction of unquestioning acceptance of the democratic way of life by the vast majority of their people. Of the large nations of Europe, Great Britain alone was as firmly settled in the electoral and parliamentary mold as were the Low Countries, Switzerland, and Scandinavia.

Since the mid-nineteenth century Switzerland had lived almost without a history—that is, in the sense of wars, political reversals, and major divisive issues. Split as they were among three nationalities and two religions, the Swiss knew that their survival in unity depended on mutual forbearance. They realized that the only way to hold the nation together was through constant compromise and the maintenance of a delicate equilibrium among the interests of diverging languages and creeds. Thus in Switzerland politics and elections tended to become formalized: their main function was to ensure the national consensus by perpetuating the tacit compromises on which the federal system ultimately rested.

In the Netherlands also, inherent conservatism kept the country in the old political routines, but in neighboring Belgium no similar national

unity prevailed. Like Switzerland, Belgium was linguistically divided.
Roughly half its population spoke French; the other half spoke Flemish,
a local variety of Dutch. But unlike the Swiss, the Belgians had never
granted equality to the different national languages. French had ruled
supreme as the language of the aristocracy and of business, of education,
the law courts, and the administration. Only very slowly and after long
parliamentary struggles was the Flemish-speaking population permitted
to use its own language for all its public concerns.

Between 1922 and 1932 this battle was substantially won. But a minority of the Flemings still remained dissatisfied. Linked as they were by
speech not only with the Dutch but with the Germans directly across
their borders, they began to succumb to the blandishments of Nazi
propaganda. Fascism never won real political power in Belgium—but
here, alone among the small democracies of Europe, it recruited a following which seriously weakened the nation when the Second World
War struck.

The Socialist Record in Norway, Sweden, and Denmark

In the Scandinavian countries to the north, the interest of foreigners was
chiefly aroused by the experience of Socialist government. Here, as opposed to the major countries of Western Europe, where interwar socialism produced little but disappointment and failure, democrats of
Socialist sympathies could point to a record of administrative competence
and substantial success in meeting economic difficulties.

In the 1920's, Socialist parties had attained power for the first time in
all these countries and become used to the responsibilities of office, but
it was not until the Great Depression that they came to dominate political life. During these years they launched a series of experiments which
gradually fused in the public mind with the wider image of a Scandinavian "way."

In the northern countries, socialism from the beginning had more to
build on and was more congenial to local tradition than was true in the
larger nations to the south. For Socialists everywhere the crucial dilemma was reconciling a collectivist economic philosophy with devotion
to democracy and the rights of the individual. In France or Britain, Germany or Italy, these two goals frequently seemed opposed. In Scandinavia there was no such conflict of values. The individualism on which
the Norwegians or the Swedes prided themselves had been accompanied
by a strong emphasis on community action. A severe climate, a relatively
sparse population, and a high degree of social homogeneity had encouraged an attitude which combined in a fashion that was unique in Europe
a robust sense of personal freedom with a talent for working in common.
The result had been the strongest movement of agricultural and con-

sumers' cooperatives in the world—a movement which eventually came to include about half the population of Sweden and more than a quarter of the inhabitants of Norway and Denmark.

In addition, the Socialist parties of these countries—which resembled the British Labor party more than they conformed to any continental pattern—were notably undogmatic. They did not insist in doctrinaire fashion on the nationalization of basic enterprise: they preferred, where possible, to establish some mixed scheme for joint governmental and private regulation of the economy. The same was true of the trade unions. Far from confronting capital with uniform hostility and distrust, labor leaders were accustomed to settling their difficulties with employers through semiofficial procedures of arbitration and conciliation.

Thus, when the Great Depression struck, the Scandinavian nations were better prepared than were the nations to the south to deal in coherent fashion with the economic and social problems it raised. Working from the already existing tradition of common action, the Socialists substantially enlarged the sphere of government intervention in the economy. The Swedes, for example, concentrated from the beginning on maintaining purchasing power—a goal that the major nations of the Western world accepted only gradually, as the orthodox solutions of retrenchment and deflation revealed their inadequacy. The Swedish government was not afraid to borrow heavily in order to maintain jobs and prices; it used monetary policy systematically, as a weapon in economic planning. And throughout Scandinavia, social insurance schemes inherited from earlier years were extended and rationalized during the Depression to cover the hazards of sickness, invalidism, and old age for the entire population.

To observers from Britain, France, or the United States—oppressed by the fumbling of their own governments, by mounting class tension at home, and by the steady advance of fascism and communism abroad— Scandinavia in the early 1930's seemed to offer a haven of competence and good sense. Here governments ensured full employment and protected their people against want; capital and labor composed their differences across a conference table instead of fighting it out in bitter strikes; the economic and psychological barriers between classes were losing their rigidity as the welfare state imposed ruinous taxes on the rich and guaranteed a livelihood to the poor. Even the physical aspect of these countries seemed better: the cities were clean and trim and amply provided with parks and public housing. Indeed, the housing exhibition held at Stockholm in 1930 epitomized the whole trend: building after building reflected the influence of the new "International Style" which, like so many other twentieth-century innovations, had been accepted by the Scandinavians in common sense fashion as the type of construction best suited to the requirements of contemporary life.

No wonder, then, that these observers hailed the Scandinavian course as the "middle way"—the way of pragmatic flexibility, steering between doctrinaire socialism on the one side and doctrinaire free enterprise on the other. It seemed to offer a new and heartening possibility for saving democratic government throughout the Western world. And such a fresh look at democracy was urgently needed: nearly everywhere else in Europe, authoritarian government was confidently advancing, and democratic parliamentarism revealing its pitiable inadequacy.

V

THE CRISIS OF
PARLIAMENTARY DEMOCRACY

By the mid-1930's, the Depression was beginning to lift. In all the major countries except France, the national economy had turned the corner: production was mounting, unemployment was falling. But depression lifted only in the strictly economic sense. In political life and popular morale, the depression psychology persisted. The great democracies of Western Europe seemed sick—and none knew what remedy would cure them. In Italy and Germany, parliamentary democracy had disappeared. In Britain, it was functioning only lamely. In France, it seemed to be wallowing in political squalor. How long, people asked, could such a system maintain itself?

The parliaments of Europe had been caught unaware by problems of unprecedented scope and had failed to deal with them. Before 1914, it was possible for representative bodies to proceed in leisurely and amateurish fashion: the parliamentary practice of engulfing issues in floods of oratory had sufficed when the issues themselves were still of a political or ideological nature which demanded no special expert knowledge. But when the First World War, its liquidation, and the Great Depression raised their acutely complex economic and financial problems, the old political routines proved obsolete. Something else was needed to master a situation in which the role of government itself had increased so vastly: in this respect, as in so many others, postwar Europe never returned to "normal."

National leaders resorted to a variety of provisional expedients. None proved satisfactory: each raised as many problems as it settled. Among these expedients was government by coalition. A coalition of parties was, in itself, a proper and democratic way of setting up a government—that it, when it was honestly managed. In a multiparty state, the alternation in power of two great coalitions offered the only possible way of approximating a two-party system—as in France in 1919 with the Bloc National and in 1924 with the Cartel des Gauches. But this was true only if the coalitions stood for principles—if they were clearly of the Right or of the Left and had some vestige of a common program. When this was not true—as in Germany through most of the Weimar period—coalition government became a travesty; it distorted the verdict of the electorate without providing governmental stability in return.

A similar dishonesty characterized the "national" ministries to which Britain resorted in 1916 and 1931, and France in 1926 and 1934: under the guise of rising above parties and expressing the unity of the nation, such governments proved themselves little more than a device for returning to power the conservatives who had lost the previous election. It was not surprising that the Left railed against these ministries—that the French Radicals, who had been tricked into such a combination in 1926, proved more wary in 1934, and that the British Labor party, which had seen the Liberals sold out during the war by their leader Lloyd George, reacted so violently to MacDonald's similar act of betrayal in 1931; only by reviling him, expelling him from the party, and developing new leaders, was Labor able to escape the fate by which the Liberal party had been overtaken.

If government by coalition might become mere fraud, the other favorite expedient—rule by decree—was even more doubtfully democratic. In the interwar years, Britain succeeded in avoiding this latter practice entirely, but in Germany and France, its general employment contributed heavily to discrediting democracy. When heads of government like Brüning and Doumergue insisted that the only way to cope with a recalcitrant parliament was to issue laws by executive order, it was quite obvious that democratic practices were breaking down. It was equally apparent that the locus of political power was shifting. The authority that was slipping from the hands of parliament was only ostensibly passing to the ministry which derived from it, for the ministers understood no better than the deputies the technical complexities of the issues at stake. Actually, authority was passing to the high civil servants—those anonymous but powerful persons who had always had more permanent positions and greater prestige in Europe than in the United States. They alone possessed the technical competence to deal with inflation and deflation, taxes and tariffs, monetary controls and public works. In general the solutions they favored were conservative and paternalistic; for career public servants customarily came from the propertied classes—indeed, in certain cases they carried into the postwar era the rule of the old aristocracy that had ended in the forum of party politics. Graduates of special schools and with a strong sense of caste, these "technocrats" scorned both public and parliament as mere ignoramuses; from this it was only a step to scorn of democracy itself.

Here, too, the democratic Left felt betrayed. Winning elections did it no good: the "establishment" of the propertied and the well-born always returned to power. Had the result been aristocratic rule in the true sense —that is, rule by the "best"—such defeat might have been less frustrating. But usually, the expedients of the conservatives produced only government by pretentious mediocrities. This was what the fascist leaders pointed to when they vaunted their own "corporative" plan of drawing into the nation's service the best talent from business and the professions. And it was what Soviet spokesmen sneered at when they boasted of how they were raising up a new and technically competent elite from the young men of promise among Russia's toiling millions. Both these authoritarian systems, in their widely contrasting fashions, seemed to have solved more adequately than had parliamentary democracy the problem of finding leadership that could give purpose and direction to the national life.

What were, then, these two systems which by their mere existence and example offered so perplexing a challenge to Western democracy in the depths of the Great Depression?

Readings

For a general account, besides Alpert (*see* readings for Chapter Five), there is H. V. Hodson, *Slump and Recovery, 1929–1937: A Survey of World Economic Affairs* (1938). John Kenneth Galbraith, in *The Great Crash 1929* (1955), gives a spirited account of the beginnings of the Depression in the United States.

Of books on individual countries, besides Mowat and Taylor for Britain (*see* readings for Chapter Five), the following deal specifically with the political and social problems of the Depression: R. T. Clark, *The Fall of the German Republic* (1935), Charles A. Gulick, *Austria from Habsburg to Hitler*, 2 vols. (1948), John T. Marcus, *French Socialism in the Crisis Years 1933–1936* (1958), and Henry W. Ehrmann, *French Labor from Popular Front to Liberation* (1947).

The Scandinavian example during the Depression years is traced in sympathetic fashion in Franklin D. Scott, *The United States and Scandinavia* (1950), and Marquis W. Childs, *Sweden: The Middle Way*, new ed. (1947).

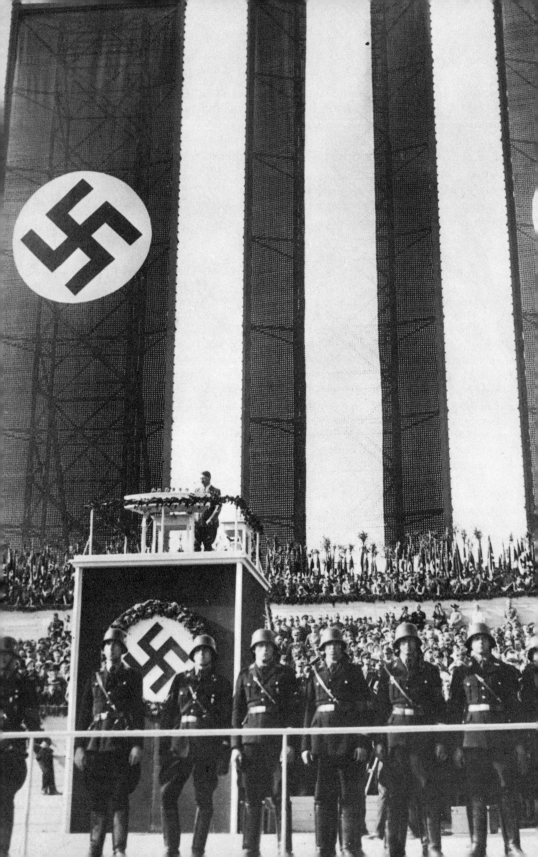

The Fascist Regimes

Fascism was the great political surprise of the first half of the twentieth century. Communism, or something resembling it, had been threatening ever since the European revolutions of 1848; the novelty of communism after 1917 lay not in its ideology but in the eccentric twist given to it by its Russian abode. For the coming of a socialist society in an authoritarian and intolerant form, the European mind was reasonably well prepared, and individual reactions to it followed a predictable course: conservatives and liberals were hostile from the start; democratic Socialists, after an initial period of hesitation, usually swung around to determined opposition. It was not always easy to judge what Soviet Russia intended or was doing, but the main outlines of the system were clear to both friend and foe.

With fascism, it was quite different. In this case there had been no half-century of preparation to warn Europeans of what was coming. To most of them, it appeared quite suddenly and unexpectedly with Mussolini's March on Rome in 1922. There had of course been a few premonitory signs before the First World War: the brutalities of overseas imperialism, the "pan" movements, popular militarism, and the longing for war. These were but the bits and pieces of an ideology. The impact of the First World War was needed to precipitate a true mass movement. For fascism, far more than communism, was a product of war and postwar conditions—and of the sufferings of the Great Depression, which gave it the decisive chance.

Fascism seemed bewildering because it had no clear ideology. It

In front of gigantic symbols of nationalism and Nazi power, Hitler is shown addressing more than two million workmen during a Mayday celebration at Tempelhof Airdrome in Berlin. COURTESY PHOTOWORLD, INC.

spoke the language of socialism—but adopted an economic policy which buttressed the forces of large capital. It stressed its revolutionary origins —but carefully reassured the propertied and the tradition-minded. Did fascism belong on the right or on the left, people wondered: even the seating of its deputies in parliamentary bodies created a problem, although it was usually settled by putting the fascists alongside the ultra-conservatives. Similarly, the most astute students of the phenomenon have concluded that fascism was more reactionary than revolutionary. It was—to cite the best simple definition that has ever been proposed —a "radicalism of the Right." When the old symbols of loyalty—"honor," "nation," and the rest—no longer seemed to bind society together, fascism reinvigorated them by an infusion of brutality and melodrama.

So much for a tentative definition. For all their local variations, the fascist systems bore a considerable family resemblance. Both uniformities and contradictions are evident in the three main manifestations of the fascist phenomenon: Mussolini's Italy, Hitler's Germany, and the "clerical-corporative" regimes in Portugal and Austria.

I

MUSSOLINI'S ACHIEVEMENT

Fascism advanced in three successive waves. First there was the period of postwar turmoil, in which it failed in Germany but brought Mussolini to power in Italy. Second there was the Great Depression, in which it triumphed in Central Europe. Finally there was the Second World War, in which German and Italian arms spread the system—or some facsimile of it—to the greater part of the European Continent.

Ideological Origins and the March to Power

Originally, Mussolini's success seemed an isolated occurrence, in sharp contrast to the ideology of democratic parliamentarianism that predominated in Western and Central Europe in the 1920's. Mussolini indeed had acted in isolation: he had triumphed on his own without help from the outside. And his remained the original fascist regime—the only one called Fascist with a capital F—and the one that even after the advent of Hitler was more admired and imitated than the Nazi model. It is important to remember this when considering the later phases of Fascist history, in which Mussolini found himself overshadowed and humiliated by his German partner.

Benito Mussolini was a true proletarian. Born the son of a blacksmith in 1883, he was a Socialist by family inheritance and a revolutionary by temperament. After a youth of odd jobs, wide but spotty reading, and draft evasion in Switzerland, he early became the most dynamic figure within Italian socialism. When he was not yet thirty, he led the party's agitation against the Libyan War of 1911, and in the following year he succeeded in being chosen editor of the official Socialist newspaper and in expelling the "reformists" from the party's ranks.

Up to 1914, Mussolini's career had followed a fairly usual course. His oratorical talents and his personal magnetism had brought him while still very young to a position of dominance not unlike Lenin's. And he seemed to belong with Lenin on the left or revolutionary wing of international socialism. But then the unexpected happened. A few months after the outbreak of the war, Mussolini changed his stand entirely: he declared for Italian intervention on the side of France and Britain, joining the motley ranks of those who followed the poet D'Annunzio in urging the government to go to war. At the time it seemed an act of political suicide: Mussolini was driven from his editorship and from the Socialist party itself. There was nothing left for him but to prove the reality of his conversion to nationalism by doing military service at the front.

Wounded and invalided out of the army, Mussolini languished in political obscurity. In 1919, when he formed his first "combat groups" (*fasci di combattimento*), from which his movement took its name, only very few answered his call. Not until D'Annunzio had been dislodged from his "regency" over the disputed port of Fiume did Mussolini, at the beginning of 1921, begin to enroll his first important body of recruits from the veterans of that tragicomic enterprise.

From then on, everything seemed to help the new movement. Italy was suffering from the usual dislocations and disillusionments of the postwar period—rendered still more acute by the poverty of the country—and Mussolini was able to draw profit from nearly all of them. In addition, the nation had just embarked on the perilous experiment of political democracy. The new mass electorate of universal suffrage had swamped the Liberal and Radical parties, which before the war had dominated Italian politics. The Chamber of Deputies elected in 1919 had a far different composition from its predecessors: a majority of its members came from two great parties that appealed to the poorer classes—the newly organized Popular party, a Catholic formation not unlike the German Center, and, of course, Mussolini's former comrades, the Italian Socialists. Could these two have worked together, Italian democracy might perhaps have been saved. But of that there was never a real possibility. The Popular party leaders lacked experience, and as good Catholics, they distrusted the Marxist ideology of the Socialists. The Socialists were overflowing with revolutionary enthusiasm but had no coherent program. Their occupation of the factories in the autumn of 1920 had revealed the futility of the Maximalist attitude of simply waiting for the revolution to fall like bounty from the skies.

What helped Mussolini more than anything else, however, was the disappointment that Italian patriots had experienced at the Peace Conference of 1919. Their government, they felt, had betrayed them by failing to obtain the full price for Italy's entrance into the war. This sense of injury swelled to a chorus of indignation as a series of short-lived ministries proved unable to master the new political forces that the postwar turbulence had unleashed. Among these forces the Fascists soon eclipsed all their rivals in the vigor and brutality of their tactics. They beat up Socialists, trade unionists, and adherents of the Popular party; they burned and looted and administered almost lethal doses of castor oil. But to Italian conservatives they began to look more and more like avenging angels sent from heaven to ward off the perils of "bolshevism."

Actually whatever "Bolshevist" threat there had been had disappeared by the end of 1920 with the failure of the occupation of the factories. It was the Fascists themselves who had replaced the revolutionary Socialists as the chief disturbers of law and order. By the spring of 1921, however, both the government and the propertied classes were winking at Mussolini's depredations and even occasionally treating the Fascist armed bands as auxiliaries of the regular police. In this attitude, Italian conservatives were encouraged by the fact that fascism from the start spoke a double language: it talked of revolution and of social leveling, but it also preached national revival and lauded the virtues of martial ardor, of hierarchy, and of discipline. As time went on, these latter themes gradually came to predominate. By the autumn of 1922, Mussolini sensed that it was time to give the conservatives still more specific assurances of good behavior. In early October he formally renounced any intention of threatening the Italian monarchy.

In the next three weeks, Mussolini's black-shirted bands—which already controlled much of the northern countryside—prepared to seize power. In the end this proved unnecessary: the politicians in Rome lost their nerve and refused to fight. When the last prime minister of parliamentary Italy went to the king to ask for a proclamation of martial law, the monarch refused his signature. Instead he called on Mussolini to form a government. Thus the threatened March on Rome never occurred. This event—which was to figure in Fascist history as the foundation of the new regime—was no more than the token occupation of a citadel which had already fallen. As the Blackshirts began their anticlimactic entry into the capital, Mussolini was arriving by sleeping car from Milan to take over the reins of authority.

The Consolidation of the Dictatorship: the Murder of Matteotti and the Parliamentary Secession

The advent of Mussolini at the end of October, 1922, was extraordinary in every respect. Technically it fell within the limits of constitutional procedure, but from the beginning Mussolini had no intention of governing as a parliamentary prime minister. For one thing, he did not have the requisite majority in the Chamber of Deputies. Only thirty-five Fascists had won seats in the last regular elections, held in the spring of

1921, and in order to make up his ministry Mussolini felt obliged to call
on the Nationalists—whose program he had stolen and whose following
he was about to absorb—and on the Popular party, which later regretted
the grudging support it had given him. Besides all this, the new prime
minister made no secret of his scorn for parliaments, elections, and
democracy in general. "A gray and squalid hall" was what he called the
meeting place of the Chamber of Deputies, and he taunted the parliamentarians with the boast that he might well have used it as a bivouac
for his soldiers. To his constitutional functions he much preferred his
party role of *Duce*—or chief—the title by which he was most often called
in subsequent years.

Only gradually, however, did Mussolini impose full Fascist control
over Italian life. For the first year and a half—still unsure of his tenure—
he left a margin of liberty to the press, to the trade unions, and to the
parties in parliament. In this period many Italians of liberal and democratic sympathies adopted a wait-and-see attitude toward the new regime
or even gave it their qualified support. Since fascism was still so new,
they did not know how far it would go; in its favor was the fact that it
had brought order to the country; and moderate-minded people cherished the illusion that by participating in Mussolini's experiment they
could influence it toward milder courses.

This honeymoon came to an abrupt end in the spring and summer of
1924. In April, Mussolini finally obtained a massive majority in the
Chamber of Deputies through a rigged election in which violence and
intimidation were freely employed. Two months later, the Socialist
deputy Giacomo Matteotti disappeared. Matteotti had courageously
spoken out against Fascist acts of terror: it was widely suspected and
later proved that he had been murdered on official orders. In protest
against this crime, some 150 deputies seceded from the chamber; they
included nearly all the remaining representatives of Italian democracy,
from the Socialist, the Popular, and the Liberal parties.

Initially it seemed that the secession would bring Mussolini down. The
Duce, badly shaken by the Matteotti murder, tried to brazen it out
through disavowing his subordinates and imposing a strict press censorship. The secessionists, however, failed to press their advantage. They
delayed and argued and lost precious time. Still more important, they
were unable to persuade the king to dismiss his prime minister. Hence
by the autumn of 1926 Mussolini felt sufficiently sure of himself to strike
back. He accepted responsibility for all that had occurred, and he
ordered the secessionists deprived of their seats in the chamber and
their political parties dissolved. From this point on, the opponents of
the regime had no choice but to keep quiet or to emigrate. The older
and more eminent usually chose to leave. The younger stayed on to
engage in clandestine activity; sooner or later, nearly all of them were
arrested by Mussolini's political police and sent to prison or to forced
detention on some barren island.

By the end of 1926 the Fascist dictatorship had consolidated its authority. The press and the chamber had been brought into line; the Fascist party had received a monopoly of political activity, with its Blackshirts acquiring official status as a militia of volunteers; the indoctrination of Italian youth was proceeding apace, as boys and girls of all ages were enrolled in semimilitary formations which taught fanatical loyalty to the regime.

The Corporate State

One reason why Mussolini felt safe in hitting back at his opponents was that he had finally reached a satisfactory understanding with the business leaders of the country. Most large industrialists had been skeptical of fascism at first; recruits for the new party had come rather from war veterans and the lower middle class, and what moneyed support it enjoyed was provided almost exclusively by the landowners of northern and central Italy. As time went on, however, and it became apparent that Mussolini would remain in power, some of the more farsighted leaders of Italian industry began to see that a mutually advantageous bargain could be struck with the new regime. Long negotiations followed, until finally in the autumn of 1925 an agreement signed at the Palazzo Vidoni in Rome regularized the relations between fascism and Italian industry.

The Palazzo Vidoni agreement was little known outside Italy, and only a handful of foreign observers understood its importance. Essentially it gave organized Italian industry the privileged position of a state within a state in return for its implied promise to support the Fascist regime. The Federation of Italian Industrialists which had negotiated with Mussolini received semiofficial status as a self-governing body for the regulation of the economy. A similar official endorsement was subsequently granted to the organizations of large employers in agriculture and commerce. Labor and the professions, on the other hand, enjoyed no such favors: *they* were compelled to enroll in Fascist-led formations, in which party representatives monopolized authority.

Together these various semigovernmental bodies made up what Mussolini called *the corporate state.* In official theory, they constituted the foundation of the regime, particularly after 1934, when they were reorganized on a much more elaborate basis, and 1938, when the Chamber of Deputies was transformed into a Chamber of Fasces and Corporations. It was similarly part of the theory of corporatism that bodies of this sort reconciled the conflict of classes by bringing capital and labor together under the benevolent auspices of the party-state. But the facts were rather different. In the corporative structure, capital alone enjoyed true self-government. Labor was shackled by the triple authority of the employers, the state, and the party, which usually managed to agree. Denied the right to strike and the right to leadership of their own choice, the workers of Italy might console themselves with a high-sound-ing "Charter of Labor" that was almost devoid of content.

Such was the reality of the corporate state. In the pretentious verbiage with which the regime enveloped it, lurked a great deception. When the rhetoric was stripped away, Italian corporatism stood revealed as little more than an elaborate engine of class rule.

The Church, the Lateran Treaty, and Catholic Action

Mussolini was a forthright atheist. So were nearly all his chief party fol-lowers. But as a realist, he fully appreciated the importance of Catholi-cism in Italian life. Among a people whose vast majority were of one faith, religion, if properly exploited, could serve as an invaluable rein-forcement to national unity. Mussolini also saw that his predecessors, the parliamentary governments of Italy, had lost the support of millions of Italians by their anticlerical attitude and by the conflict with the Vatican that had lingered on for two generations ever since the kingdom of Italy in 1870 deprived the Pope of his territorial dominion over Rome and the surrounding area.

Mussolini had good reason to conciliate Italian Catholicism. Among the other evidences of his turn to conservatism after 1922—paralleling his reassurances to monarchists and men of property—were a series of minor acts of favor to the church. Once sure of his own authority, Mussolini moved on to more important matters; he opened secret negotiations for the settlement of the "Roman Question" itself.

These negotiations—frequently difficult and at one point interrupted entirely—continued for nearly three years. Finally, however, they were completely successful. In February, 1929, Pope Pius XI and the Duce announced that they had reached agreement on all the issues which had pitted church against state in Italy for nearly sixty years. By the Lateran Treaty and the Concordat that accompanied it, the Pope gained his minimum demands: he won territorial sovereignty over a few acres around the basilica of St. Peter's and the Vatican—thus securing that formal independence from the control of any temporal state on which the Papacy had always insisted; he also obtained a privileged position for the church in Italian public education and assurance that Italian mar-riage law would be brought into conformity with Catholic teaching.

The mood of harmony and of national jubilation created by the ac-cords of 1929 did not last long. By 1931, church and state had returned to war. And the reason for the renewed conflict was symptomatic of the basic hostility between fascism and Christianity. Mussolini objected to the youth and university organizations run by the laymen's organization called Catholic Action; they competed, he complained, with his own Fascist formations. The Pope defended Catholic Action with all the polemical vigor at his command and denounced the "pagan intentions" of Mussolini's regime. After a summer of struggle, the two authorities reached a new compromise: the Catholic Action groups would continue to operate but with a strictly limited program. After this, the old cordiality never returned; the relations between the Papacy and fascism remained strained until the outbreak of the Second World War.

Among the general public, however, the happy memory of the settlement of 1929 continued to predominate. This was certainly the most popular thing that Mussolini ever did, and it marked the zenith of his prestige and influence. As the 1930's opened, then, Italian fascism seemed forever established in the affections of the Italian people. Both at home and abroad its authority was virtually unquestioned. At home, Mussolini had brought a new discipline and sense of purpose to Italian life. As the tourists put it, he had "made the trains run on time." Internal opposition had been crushed by the secret police, and the political exiles across the border were consumed with rage at their own powerlessness. Abroad, Mussolini enjoyed general respect as a strong ruler, essentially a moderate despite the regrettable strong-arm tactics of his subordinates. The Duce took care to encourage this impression of respectability by putting restraints on his own love of bluster and by cultivating the friendship of distinguished Englishmen. In return, such Tory worthies as Austen Chamberlain and Winston Churchill said complimentary things about him, implying that democracy might work for Anglo-Saxons but the more childish Italians required a stronger authority.

Only a bold prophet indeed in 1930 would have foretold that within thirteen years the Fascist Duce—his regime in full disintegration and his foreign ventures all come to naught—would succumb to the overwhelming hatred of his own people.

II

THE COMING OF HITLER

Mussolini made his way to power on the first wave of fascist agitation. His German counterpart, Adolf Hitler, had to wait another decade before reaching the same goal. This difference suggests the contrasting experience of German and Italian fascism and the divergent natures of their leaders and of the societies which they would strive to mold in their own image.

From Vienna to the Beer-hall Putsch

Hitler was six years younger than Mussolini and of less proletarian social origins. His father had been a customs official on the Austro-German border with pretensions to middle-class status which Mussolini's father would have scorned. This frontier situation, moreover, meant that Hitler could not take his nationality for granted as the future Duce did;

it was something he had to fight and strive for. Technically an Austrian, Hitler longed for a wider fatherland.

It was natural, then, that when he went to Vienna to seek his fortune he should become a Pan-German, pledged to seek the unity of Austria and the German Reich. Nor was it surprising that, as a bewildered and humiliated young man from the provinces, Hitler should learn to hate the Jews, who symbolized for him all that was cosmopolitan, sophisticated, and "decadent" in the Austrian capital. Hitler's own experience in Vienna was one of uniform failure: he was refused admission to the study of architecture, and he found himself reduced to menial tasks, to unemployment, and to living in dreary flophouses. His acquaintances of those days depict him as a moody, compulsive talker who was devoured by the sense of a mission both vague and vast. Here also there is a contrast to Mussolini. The future Duce made his way early in life; he had a clear, if rather cynical mind and a robust emotional constitution; he knew what he wanted and was never the dupe of his own oratory. Hitler was a drifter and a dreamer; his mind bore the marks of the psychopath; he followed his political instinct, as he himself expressed it, "like a sleepwalker," and in his moments of oratorical exaltation he behaved as though in a trance.

The outbreak of the First World War found Hitler in Munich. Overwhelmed with joy at the news, he fell on his knees in thanksgiving. He enlisted in the German army, in which he served throughout the war, bravely and honorably but never rising above the rank of corporal. Army life suited him perfectly: its comradeship gave him emotional security for the first time in his life, and its discipline supplied him with a sense of direction that he had never known before.

After the war Hitler joined the throng of jobless veterans, artistic bohemians, and political agitators who were making the Bavarian capital so lively a place in which to live. He himself specialized in rabble-rousing speeches with the stress on nationalist and anti-Semitic themes. In 1919, he attached himself to a struggling group called the National Socialist German Workers' Party, which he raised from obscurity by infusing it with his own demonic force. Within a very short time he had become the Nazis' chief—the *Führer*, as he was to be known to history. Gradually he gathered around him the other leaders who were later to achieve fame—among them the corpulent, brutal Hermann Goering, who had been an ace flier in the war, and Josef Goebbels, a small, lame propagandist of burning intensity, who after 1926 ran the northern branch of National Socialism from his headquarters in Berlin. There were also sympathizers who were more loosely attached to the movement—notably old General Ludendorff, the dictator of the Reich in the First World War.

In Germany's years of torment between 1919 and 1923, conditions were at least as favorable for a fascist assumption of power as they were in Italy. Governmental authority wavered from month to month; street battles or assassinations became almost daily occurrences. Indeed, there was rather an excess than a lack of talent of an extreme nationalist and racist variety, whereas in Italy—after D'Annunzio's collapse at Fiume—there was only one fascist movement and one undisputed chief. Thus German fascism or semifascism remained dispersed and divided: its main strength, rather than going toward politics, was thrown into the military activities of the Free Corps—irregular armed bodies of war veterans and young students, who served the government when it called on them in its moments of desperation, who fought Communists and Poles and murdered such democratic political leaders as Erzberger and Rathenau.

The Free Corps rose in the Kapp *Putsch,* the rightist insurrection which, in March, 1920, forced the government to flee from Berlin and was beaten only by a general strike of the German trade unions. The next two years were quieter; democratic authority began to establish itself. But then came the terrible year 1923, with the French occupation of the Ruhr and the runaway inflation. The economic suffering and social dissolution of that year gave Hitler his chance. In November, the National Socialists made their own bid for power. It began with a tumultuous meeting in one of Munich's vast beer halls—hence the name "beer-hall *Putsch*" by which it is derisively known to history—and it ended with a street procession that was intended to turn into a general revolution. But Hitler had waited too long. Had he acted in the summer, he would have had greater chance of success. By autumn, however, Stresemann was in power and resolved on decisive action. The Nazi street demonstration was stopped by police fire: old General Ludendorff, who was marching alongside Hitler, remained standing as he faced the bullets; the future *Führer* fell flat on the street, and two days later he was tracked down at the home of a friend and sent to prison.

From "Mein Kampf" to the Chancellorship

In the period of Germany's apparent stabilization, the Nazi party languished. Hitler was in jail, and nationalist extremism was everywhere on the wane. But these years were not wholly lost. In his prison cell Hitler wrote *Mein Kampf*—"my battle"—a vast, turgid autobiographical reflection that was to become the bible of the movement. And the lean years brought indirect benefit to the Nazis by ridding them of their rivals; as one after another of the extremist formations withered and died, National Socialism was left alone to incarnate the spirit of racial hatred and patriotic revenge.

At the end of 1924, when Hitler emerged from prison, he had revised his thinking about political agitation and concluded that better organization and discipline were required. He recast his movement as a regular political party, in which further putsches were discouraged and the "leadership principle," as he put it, was strictly enforced. By 1928, he

was ready to make the alliance with Hugenberg's wing of the Nationalists that brought such rich returns in the form of joint agitation against
the Young Plan and the chance to hound Stresemann to his death.

But the alliance with the Nationalists was only a temporary expedient
and, with the coming of the Great Depression, Hitler felt strong enough
to strike out on his own. The spread of unemployment finally gave the
Nazis what they wanted—a rich field for the recruitment of desperate
men. Tens of thousands of the jobless enrolled as Storm Troopers in the
brown-shirted party army that corresponded to Mussolini's Blackshirts.
Frequently their officers were former Free Corps men who knew how to
kill and to inspire a rough loyalty among their followers. But their
radicalism was in action rather than political ideology. The Free Corps
had shown little interest in politics. And the National Socialists themselves were gradually forgetting the second term in their party label;
their program was still sprinkled with socialist phrases, but these were
vaguely expressed and it was doubtful how seriously the leadership
took them. One straw in the wind was that in 1930 Hitler expelled from
the party Otto Strasser, who had been attempting to steer the movement
in a leftist direction.

The Nazis' electoral strength and their power in the streets grew
steadily in the early depression years. By the summer of 1932, they were
riding high and sure of their ability to reach power within the very near
future. But then an unexpected catastrophe occurred. In the second
Reichstag election of the year, held in November, the Nazis lost votes.
They were still the strongest party in the country, but they could no
longer pose as an irresistible wave of the future rolling on from triumph
to triumph. Indeed, they might already have missed their historic opportunity. When the results of the voting came in, something like panic
gripped the Nazi leadership. The series of elections following closely
one on another had bankrupted the party treasury. There were literally
no funds with which to pay the Storm Troopers—and this spelled disaster, for it was the promise of a square meal that had brought so many
of these people to nazism in the first place, and the loss of their meal
ticket would soon send them drifting away again.

At this point German business came to the rescue. At a meeting of
Rhine-Ruhr industrialists held on January 4, 1933, in the house of the
Cologne banker Curt von Schroeder, Hitler received a promise to pay
the party's election debts and the wages of the Storm Troopers. In return, the Nazi leaders implicitly undertook to maintain a hands-off policy
toward German industry. And this promise Hitler actually kept.

Now the way was open for the Nazis to grasp power. German conservatives of all sorts were growing nervous over Chancellor von
Schleicher's flirtations with demagogy and financial house cleaning.
Insistently they bombarded President von Hindenburg with advice to
call Hitler to office. On January 30, the old Field Marshal bowed to what
he had come to regard as the inevitable. He appointed Hitler chancellor

with a coalition cabinet in which a majority of Nationalists and nonparty men (including former Chancellor von Papen) was intended to guarantee the preservation of conservative values.

The Gleichschaltung

Hitler accomplished in six months what had taken Mussolini four years. Within that time he had *gleichgeschaltet*—brought into line—nearly every phase of the national life.

First, he consolidated his political authority. A fire which destroyed the Reichstag building—and which many thought had been set by his own henchmen—gave him an excuse to crack down on the Communists and to suspend constitutional guarantees of individual liberty. In the elections that followed, the Nazis used their position in the government to mount a propaganda campaign of unprecedented intensity and to give their Storm Troopers full license to terrorize the electorate. Still they failed to win a majority. The Social Democrats and the Center held firm.

When the new Reichstag assembled, however, Hitler made certain that it would not behave in the unruly fashion of its predecessors. He moved it out to the overawing atmosphere of the Garrison Church at Potsdam, where he staged an impressive ceremony suggesting his own solidarity with the conservative and imperial past. Behind the scenes, he neutralized the Center by a promise to respect the liberties of the Catholic church. Since the Communists were already nearly all in jail, this left the Social Democrats isolated in opposition. Alone they faced the storm of Hitler's abuse, and alone they voted against the Enabling Act which he had imperatively demanded.

The Enabling Act of March 23, 1933, was the cornerstone of the Nazi dictatorship. It gave the government power to rule by decree for four years—a power which Hitler used to the full. Never again until the *Führer's* death was Germany to enjoy even the semblance of political freedom. With this act in his pocket, Hitler turned against the very people who had helped him to power. Papen and the Nationalists were left breathless; the chancellor whom they had intended to use for their own purposes began, on the contrary, to exploit them in ruthless fashion and had soon reduced them to the shabby function of window-dressing for the regime. The Center fared no better: its vote in favor of the Enabling Act was of no avail, and it disappeared along with Social Democracy when all political parties except the Nazis were dissolved the following spring and summer. The trade unions experienced a similar fate; one by one, virtually every independent body in every field of the national life was abolished or *gleichgeschaltet*. By the summer of 1933, Hitler's opponents were either in jail or in hiding, in exile or in concentration camp.

Even the Nazi party did not escape. In the following year came the turn of the dissidents within the movement itself. On the "Night of the Long Knives" of June 30, 1934, Hitler struck down those close to him

who had deviated either to the right or to the left. Among the conservatives who perished in this night of terror was his predecessor as chancellor, Kurt von Schleicher. Among the "radicals" were some of the most
prominent of the Storm Troop and former Free Corps leaders, for the
main purpose of the blood purge was to destroy the independent power
of the Storm Troops, which the army disliked and feared and whose
unruly ways no longer befitted a party that was governing the state.
Hitler's choice of executioners was again fateful for the future: he called
on a newer and smaller body than the Storm Troops, his own elite guard,
or SS. These wore black uniforms instead of brown, they were specially
selected for their "Nordic" qualities and physical fitness, and they were
trained to a dumb obedience that asked no questions. From the summer
of 1934 on, the SS was to play an ever more important role in the Nazi
state.

Five weeks after the blood purge, the eighty-seven-year-old Hindenburg conveniently died. With the passing of this sole remaining link to
the past, Hitler was free to combine the offices of president and chancellor in his own person—a decision ratified by a plebiscite in which
nearly nine-tenths of the German people voted yes. Thus Hitler early rid
himself of the competing constitutional authority that in Italy, in the
person of the king, was to plague Mussolini to the very end.

Racism and Anti-Semitism

As the Gleichschaltung proceeded, it became apparent that of all Germans the Jews were faring worst. Anti-Semitism had been one of Hitler's
favorite propaganda points in his drive to power, and it had behind it a
long history in German popular legend and in sporadic outbursts of
hatred and violence.

At Hitler's accession, the Jews of Germany numbered about half a
million. In numbers and in social situation, the Jewish population of the
Reich lay midway between the norm in Western Europe—where Jews
were few and well assimilated into the national life—and that in Russia
or Poland—where they numbered millions and suffered from periodic
persecution and discrimination. In Western Germany, conditions similar
to those in France prevailed; in Eastern Germany, assimilation had not
gone so far. But in both areas, only in legend did the Jews dominate
economic life. Actually their participation in German industrial leadership was small; it was in retail trade and banking, rather, that they
enjoyed some influence. Their real prominence lay in the professions,
in intellectual life, and in the world of art and entertainment.

Nevertheless throughout the latter half of the nineteenth century and
the first part of the twentieth, German demagogues had regularly depicted the Jews as having a stranglehold on the business life of the
country. Such agitators also described them as racially inferior and
"impure," for along with anti-Semitic propaganda went an insistence on
the racial superiority of the German people. The Germans, the racist

propagandists claimed, were obviously superior, since they were tall and blond and had blue eyes. Even the most casual observer of the German scene might have noticed that this was true of only a minority of the country's population. It was in the Netherlands and Scandinavia, rather, that such "Nordic" or "Aryan" physical traits predominated. But Hitler and his followers apparently believed their own propaganda; they really thought that the "purity" of German "blood" was in danger from Jewish "contamination," and that it was their duty to the race to preserve it from further admixture.

The evidence is overwhelming that a very large part of the German people agreed with them. Little indignation was heard when Hitler began to take discriminatory measures against the country's Jewish population. Before attaining power, the Nazis had been forced to restrict themselves to attacking the Jews in slanderous and obscene language and to beating Jews and occasionally murdering them in the streets. From 1933 on, however, they were able to proceed in a more systematic fashion. The "Nürnberg Laws" of September, 1935, forbade people of Jewish origin—defined as those with one Jewish grandparent—to marry or to have sexual relations with "Aryans." Two months later Jews were expelled from the civil service, and a weeding-out process began that, by 1938, had virtually eliminated them from government, the professions, and cultural life. Then in the summer of 1938, they were required to adopt first names that were easily identifiable as Jewish and to carry special identity papers. Finally in November, 1938, occurred the event that sent the anti-Semitic campaign into high gear: a Jewish boy, crazed by his people's sufferings, murdered a German diplomat called Vom Rath. The Vom Rath murder not only unleashed a storm of indiscriminate violence within the Reich; it also served as a pretext for new legislation forcing Jewish businessmen to liquidate their concerns at a loss and for starting a systematic roundup of the Jews who had not yet left the country.

A large percentage of the German Jews had already emigrated, either to neighboring European countries or to America. After 1938, emigration was much more difficult; those who chose to leave now had to depart almost penniless. The majority remained, still attached to their homes, still hoping to survive in some fashion. They did not yet know that in 1942 Hitler was to decide on the "final solution" of the "Jewish Question," which would bring death to nearly all of them in the holocaust of six million of their coreligionists that ranks as the greatest crime of modern times.

Economic Policy and Preparation for War

In the economic field, *Gleichschaltung* operated most unevenly. Labor was quickly curbed: as the Fascist regime had done in Italy, so in Germany the Nazis forced the German workers into a party-dominated

Labor Front. As organized labor, workers had no real rights; instead, as individuals, they had the organization called "Strength through Joy" which provided free holidays and excursions into the country.

The majority of German workers probably accepted this sort of paternalistic treatment as good enough. They had a more important reason for being grateful to Hitler: within five years, the new regime all but eliminated unemployment through a massive program of re-armament and public works. This remained the bedrock of Hitler's popu-larity—as the depression had brought him to power, so his solution to the problem of unemployment offered the most convincing reason for thinking he should stay there.

The rearmament of Germany was popular not only with the working classes; it also found favor with industrial capital, to which it guaranteed large orders and high profits. Hitler did not have to force German industry into line; it did not cost him very much to keep his implied promise not to tamper with ownership. Generally, the needs of the regime and the needs of heavy industry ran parallel—both had a vested interest in preparation for war. It was simpler for the government to deal with a few large concerns than with many small ones. Thus in prac-tice the Nazis favored the economic concentration which had already been stimulated by the inflation of 1923. They were content to let the larger industrialists dominate the self-governing bodies that ran the vari-ous branches of the economy in corporative fashion; during the Sec-ond World War the government itself contributed to the process by "combing out" small and uneconomic enterprises. The leading indus-trialists were frequently rewarded with high party rank, and the Nazi chiefs for their part acquired large industrial holdings on their personal account—much of it through the plunder of Jewish property which was euphemistically referred to as "aryanization." By the outbreak of the war nearly everyone had some reason to be content: although wages remained low, jobs were plentiful, and the army was taking up what slack remained; industry was booming; and good Nazis enjoyed every opportunity to feather their own nests.

The Struggle with the Churches

Scarcely a promise of Hitler's was more flagrantly broken than the one by which he had undertaken to preserve the liberties of the Catholic church. Initially, however, everything seemed to be going well. The summer of 1933 saw the negotiation of a concordat with the Vatican that met nearly all the church's requirements. But after a brief period of ap-parent harmony, the regime felt secure enough to attack: it launched a vicious propaganda campaign against the members of religious orders, accusing monks and nuns both of smuggling and of acts of sexual im-morality.

The reasons behind these wild charges did not take long to appear.

The *Führer's* target was the Catholic schools and youth organizations, which threatened the monopoly of the "Hitler Youth" into which he was trying to enroll the young people of the Reich. By 1937, he had effectively destroyed the influence of church education: nearly all Catholic schools were closed, and those which remained led a precarious and persecuted existence. There was nothing left but for German Catholics to bow their heads and for the Pope to protest in unmeasured terms. In one of his strongest encyclicals, *Mit brennender Sorge*—"with burning sorrow"—Pius XI condemned the Nazis' racial doctrine and their deification of the state. The papal castigation of fascism, which in Italy had been tempered by understanding, in Germany amounted almost to a declaration of war. Yet a complete break between church and state was avoided. During the Second World War, Pius XI's more diplomatic successor, Pius XII, refrained from speaking out against the horrors of the Nazi extermination camps in a fashion that might have shaken the national loyalties of Germany's Catholic citizens.

Already in the early years of the Nazi regime a few farsighted members of the German church hierarchy had begun to warn their flock of the subtle poisons contained in Hitler's ideology. In his Advent sermons, Cardinal Faulhaber, archbishop of Munich, preached to overflow congregations on the theme of paganism in Nazi doctrine. To the north, Bishop von Galen of Münster spoke out in even sharper terms. The government left these ecclesiastics unharmed; they were the only people in Germany who enjoyed even a limited right of free speech.

Against dissident Protestants, however, Hitler proceeded with greater rigor. As the majority faith, German Protestantism offered opportunities for *Gleichschaltung* and enrollment in the national effort that were lacking in Catholicism, whose minority status and international affiliations limited its usefulness to the regime. Initially Hitler tried to unify and to nazify the Protestants by forcing the church organizations of the individual states into a single Reich church under the rule of a "Reichsbishop." This the majority of Protestant pastors resisted. The Reichsbishop found his authority defied nearly everywhere, and he soon resigned in discouragement. But the nazified church organization remained. So did a number of "intact" churches in states whose bishops were sufficiently astute to avoid *Gleichschaltung;* these tried to keep their organizations out of the political struggle—as did the majority of the pastors of Germany. A strong minority, however, constituted themselves as the "Confessional" church, preaching root-and-branch opposition to racism, the leadership principle, and the association of Christianity with the Nazi state. The most eloquent spokesman among the Confessional pastors was the former submarine commander Martin Niemöller, who in 1937 along with more than eight hundred of his fellows was sent to concentration camp.

Such was the extremely complex situation of German Christianity on the eve of the Second World War. The Nazis had failed in their effort to bring the churches into line. They had succeeded rather better with the

Protestants than with the Catholics—but this was natural in view of the
formers' disunity, the greater pressure put upon them, and German
Protestantism's long record of nationalism and obedience to secular authority. At the same time, in the Confessional pastors, the Protestants
had given the most courageous examples of defiance against the radically
unchristian practices of the Nazi state.

In general, then, the Christian churches were comparable only to
organized business leadership in the limited autonomy they enjoyed
within the confines of German fascism. Hitler would have been well
advised to leave them entirely untroubled. For it was from the ranks of
militant Christian laymen, Protestant and Catholic alike, that the future
resistance to him was to recruit its most devoted adherents.

III

THE CLERICAL-CORPORATIVE STATES

Nothing so clearly distinguished the milder fascist regimes from the German and Italian systems as the privileged position that the church enjoyed under them. These more moderate regimes have quite properly
been called "clerical-corporative," for their two outstanding features
were their clericalism and their corporative organization of economic
life. They existed only in Catholic countries—in Portugal after 1930, in
Austria after 1933, and in Spain (with some qualifications) after 1936
(*see* Chapter Twelve, III).

Portugal under Salazar

The assumption of power by Professor Salazar in Portugal brought order
to a state that had been shaken by unrest ever since it deposed its ruling
dynasty and became a republic in 1910. The Portuguese population was
in economic terms the most backward, and in political terms the most
uneducated, in all Western Europe. To rule it was comparatively simple:
no elaborate ideology or pseudosocialist program was required; a strong
hand alone sufficed.

Hence, although he was an admirer of Mussolini, Salazar restricted
himself to the barest minimum of fascist practices. He did not organize
a private army nor try to whip up the enthusiasm of the populace
through frenetic appeals to national pride. He established a quiet dictatorship, in which the press was severely controlled and his own
National Union enjoyed a monopoly of political activity. By the authoritarian constitution promulgated in 1933, Portugal was defined as a "new
state" resting on the twin pillars of a corporative economic organization
and the Catholic church.

Portuguese corporatism followed the Italian model in curbing the working classes while leaving the employers substantially at liberty to run their businesses as they pleased. Toward Catholicism, however, Salazar's policies diverged markedly from Mussolini's. He went far beyond merely granting the church a favored position in the state. An austere and devout Catholic himself, Salazar sincerely believed that he was carrying out Christian principles in ruling his country as he did, and that such should be the basis of any properly run society. Hence he gave the church a monopoly of education and tried to suffuse all aspects of Portuguese life with the spirit of a Catholicism which he interpreted in ultra-conservative fashion as a doctrine endorsing quiescence and permanent stability in human affairs.

Austria under Dollfuss and Schuschnigg

In effervescent Austria, such an old-fashioned model of rule would not suffice. Engelbert Dollfuss, the authoritarian-minded chancellor of Christian Social origin who came to power in 1932, soon found it impossible to continue governing within the constitutional framework. With the advent of Hitler in January, 1933, it became apparent that sympathy for nazism was spreading rapidly into Austria, and that only a recourse to dictatorial methods could save the state from eventual subversion. The following March, Dollfuss suspended parliamentary government and a few months thereafter dissolved the opposition political parties. This latter measure was aimed primarily at the Austrian Nazis, but it also included the Socialists, who had been the Christian Socials' rivals for power in the years of constitutional rule.

Neither party accepted dissolution without protest. The Socialists were first to act. In February, 1934, goaded to fury by a series of government raids, the Socialist paramilitary formations blockaded themselves in the great housing development called the Karl Marx Hof and prepared to resist by force of arms. Dollfuss' reply was to concentrate his army and police and to bombard the Socialists into surrender after three days of combat. Thus ended the threat from the Left: Austrian socialism was vanquished for a full decade. But the Nazis—backed as they were by the overwhelming strength of Austria's great neighbor—could not be dealt with thus easily. Five months after the Socialist uprising, a band of National Socialist conspirators forced their way into Dollfuss' office and killed him.

This first Nazi bid for power failed. Mussolini concentrated troops on the Brenner Pass and declared himself the protector of Austrian independence. Simultaneously Dollfuss' successor as chancellor, Kurt Schuschnigg, began to act with resolution and authority. A quiet, ascetic, scholarly figure somewhat like Salazar, Schuschnigg proceeded to apply the dictatorial constitution that had been voted just three months before his predecessor's death. Under the new system, a single party, the Fatherland Front—which had absorbed most of the Christian Socials—received the usual fascist monopoly of political influence. Meantime the organization of corporative bodies proceeded only slowly. It was in its clericalism, rather, that the Austrian regime showed where its primary ideological allegiance lay.

For nearly four years, Schuschnigg kept his country from the German and Nazi embrace. Within Austria, life remained deceptively calm: the dictatorship was relatively mild, and the average citizen had freedom to go about his ordinary concerns and to grumble against the government quite openly. Under the surface, however, the situation was far from placid: the Nazis were preparing in secret for the great day of annexation to the Reich, and the Socialists remained bitterly unreconciled. The government could not rely on *them* to help it when Hitler should decide to strike. Thus the regime drew support from a perilously narrow grouping: fragments of old-fashioned conservatism, nostalgia for aristocratic values, and, of course, clericalism. Ultimately what kept it in power was the promise of Italian armed support. Should Mussolini falter, all would be lost. But in 1936, Italian fascism began to align itself with its German counterpart (*see* Chapter Twelve, II). This spelled the end of Austria's freedom and of the moderate version of fascist rule which it had come to incarnate.

IV

THE NATURE OF THE
FASCIST SYSTEM

As one follows the history of the major fascist regimes, there emerge certain similarities and uniformities which may serve to define more precisely this new "radicalism of the Right." It is significant that the two societies in which fascism appeared full-blown—the Italian and the German—had things in common that distinguished them from the societies of France and Britain on the one hand and those of Eastern Europe on the other. In the great Western democracies, middle-class values and the middle-class way of life predominated without question; despite the frequent bitterness of class feeling, there was a real homogeneity within the social structures of Britain and France which made them capable of withstanding the most severe political and ideological shocks. Similarly in Eastern Europe—before communism began its vast effort of economic transformation—there existed the more primitive homogeneity of a traditional agrarian society. Italy and Germany, in different ways, fell between these two norms: an old-fashioned rural or patriarchal society lived alongside and entangled with a modern industrial society; lack of understanding and permanent tension were inevitable when two such different ways of life were condemned to an existence in common.

France and Britain, moreover, won the First World War; Germany lost it. To Italian patriots also—cheated as they felt themselves to be of the spoils of victory—the war seemed as good as lost. Thus the origins of fascism in both countries lay in the disillusionment among returning veterans and in the thirst for action among boys just young enough to have missed the experience of combat. In more general terms, fascism arose out of the frustrations of the lower middle class from which so many of these former soldiers and dissatisfied students had come. Members of this class had particular reason to feel distressed and anxious in the postwar years. Threatened with proletarization—and unwilling to throw in their lot with the Marxists—these people were casting about for a new political movement that would give voice to their sense of profound injustice. Their bitterness appeared in its most desperate form in the great German inflation of 1923, when their grievances made them turn against their own government and blame a newly founded democracy both for their personal sufferings and for the humiliation of the nation, whose fate they identified with their own.

The original fascist leaders came from the ranks of the unreconstructed veterans. Down and out themselves, they appealed to others in similar straits. They prided themselves on their toughness; they disliked what was superior or distinguished or refined; more particularly, they disliked intellectuals—which was perhaps natural since a number of them were would-be intellectuals who had fallen short of their goals (as Hitler had failed in his ambition to be an architect). They were liars, they were bullies, they led disreputable lives—in short, as one shocked conservative put it, they were a collection of juvenile delinquents. And they were filled with resentments of all sorts. Indeed, the most curious feature of early fascism was its combination in the same individuals of the most ordinary petty-bourgeois grievances with absolutely limitless dreams of grandeur.

There was something seedy and even comic about the fascist parties in their early stages. Small wonder that so many people, reactionary and democratic alike, refused to take Mussolini and Hitler seriously. All this posturing and marching, this frantic eloquence, these solemn salutes with outstretched arms—all this seemed too ridiculous. Something more than that was needed to get fascism out of the back alleys of Milan or Munich and to make it a great national movement capable of seizing power.

This additional strength—and the sobering influence that went with it —came when men of property and conservative inclinations began to see in fascism a possible ally in their struggle with the political Left. In the immediate postwar years, when trade unionism and revolutionary socialism were at a high point—and again in the years of the Great Depression —conservatives were frankly frightened: the rising tide of Socialist or Communist agitation might carry to power a militant government of the Left that would deprive them of their property. Faced with this threat, the prosperous and propertied wondered whether their fathers and grandfathers had been right in espousing the cause of liberalism or democracy. If democracy led by inevitable progression to socialism, they reasoned, then perhaps democracy should be destroyed. Perhaps authoritarian rule offered the only solution. And this was exactly what fascism promised.

There was, of course, a great difference in temperament and background between the men of property, with their education and their refined manners, and the demagogues who led the fascist movements. This difference took a long time to bridge, and it was only hesitantly that businessmen and aristocrats began to extend the hand of friendship to people whom they regarded as little better than gangsters. But they had urgent reason for doing so; in a time of crisis, they could not trouble about manners. Furthermore they shared the fascists' hostility to Marxism in all its forms and agreed with the fascist emphasis on national honor and prestige. Those who made the first move or who remained most closely associated with fascism, moreover, were usually the less squeamish of their class—self-made men with new fortunes built on war and inflation, men with shady pasts who had good reason to worry about the legitimacy of their profits. To these a fascist government could give protection from embarrassing questions or parliamentary committees of investigation.

Men with older fortunes followed more slowly and accepted fascism more grudgingly. Some never accepted it at all. But most businessmen both in Italy and in Germany eventually made their peace with the fascist system and prospered under it. From it, they won protection from social unrest and freedom from trade-union pressure: to it, they gave respectability and financial support. It was a profitable bargain for both sides.

This convergence between the fascist parties and the interests of the business class—more particularly the larger industrialists—was the central feature of the fascist regimes in practice. Here lay the crucial distinction between fascism and communism and the reason for not regarding the semisocialist or pseudosocialist statements in the fascist programs very seriously. The union between business interests and demagogy explains how fascism became that paradoxical phenomenon, a conservative regime in revolutionary clothing.

It was not until later, however, that the businessmen and the fascist leaders concluded the tacit pact which gave security to both. In Italy, the chief industrialists held back until *after* the March on Rome; in Germany, the decisive meeting with the Rhine-Ruhr business leaders occurred less than a month before Hitler's appointment as chancellor. Each side was suspicious of the other: neither wanted to commit itself too soon. It is significant, however, that in both countries the fascist leader gave reassurances of a conservative sort just at the point when it seemed essential to him to take power at all costs—in Hitler's case, when the movement had apparently passed its zenith and was going downhill. In Italy as in Germany, despite all the bluster about revolution and the use of force, fascism moved into the seat of government by ostensibly constitutional means.

Yet it is incorrect to assert, as the Marxists have, that fascism was only a mask for rule by monopoly capitalism. In the crucial decisions, the party rather than the business interests had the last word. In both Italy and Germany, occasional spurts of radicalization as well as tough talk from the fascist chiefs showed who was the master. But this happened only infrequently: most of the time the interests of the regime coincided with the interests of the men of property.

Although Mussolini and Hitler governed police states and relied heavily on terror to enforce their will, they did not succeed in remolding Italian or German society in a truly totalitarian form. They did not smash an old organization of society and build up a new one as Lenin and Stalin did. They merely *superimposed* a fascist structure on the existing system, which they left virtually intact. Even Nazi Germany—which went much further toward *Gleichschaltung* than did Fascist Italy—left in being many organizations that had existed before the regime came to power and that were to continue after its fall.

In both cases the authoritarian party did not absorb the functions of the state machinery, as it did in the Soviet Union. The traditional state —the civil service, the diplomatic corps, the armed services, and the judiciary—operated much as before, and its officials not infrequently defied or sabotaged the directives that came down to them from the party. There were also two quite different elements in society that enjoyed a situation of special privilege—large capital and the Christian churches. It is extremely significant that, for all his browbeating of the clergy, even Hitler never dared to mount a full-scale assault against the religious faith of the German people.

There remains, however, a major distinction between fascism in its German and fascism in its Italian form. In Hitler's Reich, the older centers of allegiance—the army, big business, and the church—existed only by the tolerance of the regime. Their situation was precarious, and their power limited. They could not effectively threaten the authority of the *Führer* or of the party he led. When Germany began to lose the Second World War—and when concomitantly more traditional conservatives lost confidence in Hitler—they could not get rid of him. They were reduced to secret conspiracy and to a desperate project to save their country by assassinating its leader. When this assassination attempt failed, they had no choice but to go along with Hitler to the bitter end.

In Italy, on the contrary, the old-line conservatives—including a number of dissidents within the Fascist party itself—threw Mussolini overboard before it was too late. They were able to do this because the monarchy continued to exist, and the king provided an alternative symbol of loyalty around whom the discontented could rally. In broader terms, despite his longer period of rule, Mussolini's tenure had never been as secure as Hitler's. The Italian Fascists had always been more dependent than the Nazis on the conservative elements in society that had originally helped them to power.

Here also lay the crucial distinction between fascism in its fully developed form and the clerical-corporative regimes in Portugal and Austria. Perhaps these ought not to be labeled fascist at all; "authoritarian conservative" may be the description that fits them best. For they never moved much beyond the stage of "fundamentalist" reaction—a return to the old-fashioned values that liberalism, democracy, and socialism had undermined. Fascism always retained this reactionary spirit. It was apparent, for example, in the fascist attitude toward women, reasserting women's traditional inferiority by emphasizing their duties in the home and by restricting their educational opportunities. In Germany and Italy, however, policies of this sort played a minor part in the propaganda of the regime: in Portugal and Austria they were central.

Yet even these two latter countries did more than revert to old verities, for which the rule of a mere "strong man" would have sufficed. They tried —however lamely—to organize a single party and to proclaim a coherent ideology. And this, after all, was the core of fascist ideology: the effort to reinvigorate old values by giving them a new dynamism.

How far, then, did fascism actually extend along the range of this dynamism? In Italy, it did not go very far. The Italian people were too skeptical by tradition to take Mussolini's propaganda at face value; most of them simply shrugged their shoulders and went their own way. The longer the Fascists stayed in power, the more obvious it became that their ranks were full of timeservers and profiteers. Nor did Mussolini for his part behave with the cruelty and thoroughness of Hitler and his henchmen: he organized no real concentration camps, and he embarked on an anti-Semitic policy only in 1938, when the pressure to follow German example had become overwhelming.

In the Nazi Reich, on the other hand, anti-Semitism and the concentration camp together created a demonic atmosphere of torture and frenzy which made Hitlerism unique in modern history. The persecution of the Jews was intensified after the outbreak of the Second World War (see Chapter Thirteen, III). Similarly, during the war the concentration camps frankly became places of extermination. Before then, prisoners were merely worked to death, as undernourishment and privation gradually sapped their strength. No economic rationale lay behind the Nazi concentration camps: they served no productive function. They were simply abodes of torment through which perhaps half a million *Germans* passed, even before the war gave the Nazis the opportunity to round up millions more from the countries they had occupied. Over them presided the black-shirted SS and the secret police, the Gestapo—both headed by the pedantic, meticulous Heinrich Himmler, who looked more like a routine-minded German clerk than Hitler's chief executioner.

These demonic features, however, were not central to fascism. The tendency of historians to focus attention on such horrifying aspects of the system has frequently obscured the less spectacular side of its relationship to the society and the economy which it dominated. Under fascism, the fundamentals of life for most of the population remained unchanged. Fascist rule did far more to shore up an old society than to build a new one. Thus the relatively temperate Mussolini, rather than the psychopathic Hitler, offers the more characteristic model for a fascist control of society. Not until the Second World War thrust Germany to the fore did the Italian image begin to wane: only when the conditions of combat pushed fascism to its final extremities of cruelty did anti-Semitism and the concentration camp loom ever larger until, in the end, they blotted out everything else—leaving the fascist regimes nothing to show for two decades of exertion but heaps of ruins and millions of corpses.

V

THE POPULAR FRONT MENTALITY

Long before fascism advanced to its final phase of systematic horror, European democrats had concluded that it was a force of cultural and ideological destruction that should be resisted at all costs. During the Great Depression, European democracy confronted a double threat: on the one side, fascism, and on the other side, Communist parties whose confidence was growing with the anticipated collapse of the capitalist system, and whose ranks, like those of the Nazis, were swelling month by month with the influx of the unemployed. In this two-front war, fascism presented the more immediate danger. Hitler's Germany was close at hand and was growing more aggressive every day. Stalin's Russia was far away and absorbed in the vast task of rebuilding its own society. In a military sense, it threatened nobody: in the 1930's, the Soviet attitude was almost purely defensive—the basic aim of Russian foreign policy in this period was to prevent an alliance of the Western capitalist countries which, with the new infusion of fascist energy, could overwhelm the Soviet experiment of "socialism in one country" before it was even properly launched.

In its vocabulary and in its aims, moreover, communism seemed far closer than did fascism to the aspirations of European democracy. It talked of human betterment, of the brotherhood of man, and of international concord, while Hitler and Mussolini preached hatred between races and nations. There were, of course, the terrorist and dictatorial aspects of Soviet rule—but in the 1930's European democrats of the Left were inclined to neglect these or to gloss them over as problems that could be dealt with in calmer times. What seemed of overriding present importance was that democracy and communism had a common enemy, before which they should sink their differences and present a united front. Thus the minds of left-wing democrats were prepared for common action against fascism when the Communist parties of the Western countries began to make advances to them in the summer of 1934.

The Origins of the Popular Front

What came to be called the *Popular Front* was originally Communist in inspiration. Indeed, better than anything else this showed that after a decade of sterility and bureaucratization, European communism was again on the march. In the sense of organization and numbers it had been revived by the Great Depression, but in the ideological sense the decisive event was the shock of Hitler's coming to power. Both the Third International and the German Communists had catastrophically underestimated Nazi strength and had never anticipated that Hitler would actually be able to accomplish his aims. Like Papen and the Nationalists, German communism had thought it could use the Nazis for its own purposes and subsequently order them to depart. In the Communist reckoning of the future, Hitler figured as the precursor of a Soviet Germany, the unconscious herald of the new society who would do the dirty work of clearing away the debris of bourgeois democracy and then succumb himself to the true revolution of the people. In line with this strategy, the German Communists in the last period of Hitler's march to power did little to oppose him and even sometimes cooperated with the Nazi Storm Troopers in their street battles with the Social Democrats. To their surprise, they found themselves after January, 1933, treated no better —indeed worse—than Hitler's "bourgeois" and Social Democratic enemies and saw their party completely smashed within a few weeks.

The advent of Hitler precipitated great soul-searching and self-criticism among European Communists, particularly in France, which felt directly threatened by what had gone on in the Reich, and among Italian Communists in exile, who had already borne the iron hand of fascist tyranny. It was the French and Italian Communists who originally devised the idea of common action alongside Socialists and middle-class democrats. It was they who pressed the suggestion on the Comintern, which finally accepted it in 1935 as a major new departure in the International's policy. The Popular Front concept was that very rare thing in Communist history—a spontaneous initiative from a national party that was only later endorsed by Moscow.

France: the Election of 1936 and the Blum Government

In France, a further event had added to the sense of urgency: the French had experienced the riots of February 6, 1934, which had apparently come close to overthrowing parliamentary democracy itself. Actually the peril was not as great as French Radicals and Socialists imagined. The rightist demonstrators of February had neither the intention nor the power to stage a fascist *Putsch*. Indeed, the "Leagues" of war veterans and patriots which appeared to be the French counterparts to the Italian Blackshirts or the German Brownshirts were not nearly so brutal or determined. Most of them were unarmed. Their leaders, moreover, had only the vaguest ideas of how to recast the French state in more authoritarian form. They really never got beyond the stage of "fundamentalist" reaction. French society was still too secure—too solidly bourgeois—for fascism to have a mass appeal. Only the special conditions of defeat in war would give the French fascists their chance.

But in 1934 French democrats of the Left could not be expected to reach so cool an assessment. They knew that in Germany people like themselves had underestimated the danger and they were determined not to make the same mistake. Hence when the Communists proposed a united front, the Socialists joined with alacrity at a special meeting of their national council held in mid-July. The following year the Radicals also joined, and the three parties marked the national holiday, July 14, by staging an impressive demonstration of republican solidarity.

By this time, Laval was prime minister and inspiring no confidence at all in his ability to withstand fascist blandishments. He was followed in January by a stopgap cabinet improvised to tide over the interval until the spring elections—an interval of which Hitler took advantage to effect his decisive breach of the Versailles Treaty system. French prestige and French morale had never been so low as on that day in early May, 1936, when the people went to the polls to cast their votes for a new Chamber of Deputies.

The result was an overwhelming victory of the Left—far more crushing than its previous triumphs of 1924 and 1932. This time the Popular Front added to the old alliance between Socialists and Radicals the new and untested strength of communism, and within the electoral coalition itself the shift toward the left was manifest nearly everywhere. The Socialists displaced the Radicals from their traditional position as the strongest party in the Chamber; still more, the Communists increased their seats from 10 to 73 to become for the first time a major force in French politics.

Thus the Socialists were the logical party to provide the new prime minister—again a departure from the established Socialist tradition of refusal to participate in government except in time of war. The designated leader was Léon Blum—Jewish, cultured, tolerant, humane—a perfect antithesis to Hitler. Yet for that very reason he aroused antipathies on the right which limited his ability to guide the country through a profound social crisis. Blum was a man of undoubted courage—as he showed when he rallied his shrunken party in 1920 after the secession of the Communists, and as he was to show again during the Second World War. But he was not sufficiently decisive to repulse two enemies at once: the open hostility of the French business community, which pursued him

with a hatred to which anti-Semitism added a peculiarly bitter edge,
and the covert hostility of the Communists, who ostensibly supported his ministry but who refused to participate in it and, in fact, made difficulties for it at every turn.

On the very day he assumed office, Blum faced an unprecedented situation. A million industrial workers of the Paris area, inspired by the Popular Front electoral victory and fearing that they would be defrauded of its fruits, as had so often happened in the past, were engaging in sitdown strikes in their shops and factories. This movement—which owed something to the example of the Italian occupation of the factories in 1920—was almost uniformly good-humored: the strikers were scrupulous about not damaging property, and there was scarcely any violence. But in these days of early June the propertied classes sensed revolution in the air: Paris was in a holiday mood which could readily pass over into civil war.

Blum's answer was to call the employers and the trade-union leaders together in his official residence, the Hôtel Matignon, and insist that they reach a settlement forthwith. Within two days these conferences produced the Matignon Agreements that were to be the founding documents of the welfare state in France. The employers made nearly all the concessions: they granted labor the forty-hour week, a minimum wage scale, paid vacations, and the right to collective bargaining.

The first month of Popular Front rule was its best. After June, nearly everything went wrong. Blum's government failed to maintain its reforming momentum. The new social reforms proved expensive, and productivity did not rise to keep pace with them. Then in the autumn Blum found himself forced to go off the gold standard—but here again the measure failed of its effect. The deflationary policy of his conservative predecessors had continued too long; France had sunk into an economic morass from which only strong and coherent economic direction could lift it. The Popular Front offered goodwill and humanitarian sentiments, but these were not enough.

By the spring of 1937, Blum was being hounded by a host of enemies. The conservatives remained entirely unreconciled to the new relations he had established between capital and labor; as soon as they dared, employers started to evade and to sabotage the Matignon Agreements. Meanwhile the Radicals—most of whom had worked with the Popular Front only reluctantly—began to regret that they had ever agreed to share power with the Socialists and returned to their familiar interelection maneuver of evolution toward the right. On Blum's left flank, the Communists continued to take advantage of their strategic situation —half in and half out of the governing coalition—to snipe at the ministry with impunity and to infiltrate Socialist-led trade unions. In June, 1937, after a little more than a year of power, the Blum government succumbed to this combination of hostilities. Its resignation marked the end of the Popular Front era in France. The two ministries which succeeded it still gave lip service to the idea, but by April, 1938, when Edouard Daladier returned as prime minister, the Popular Front concept had vanished without a trace.

Had the Popular Front, then, accomplished nothing? Had it failed in its double aim of pulling France out of the Depression and thus bringing to a halt the advance of fascism? True, despite the enthusiasm and devotion that had gone into it, the Popular Front's achievements were small indeed. The country's economic situation had improved only slightly. Blum's reforms had widened rather than bridged the chasm separating the owners from the laboring classes. He had failed to lead the workers from the marginal situation they occupied in French bourgeois society and to associate them more closely with the national consensus. Still worse, Blum's failure further embittered the workers and made them turn toward Communist leadership that was eventually to ruin both the Socialist party and free trade unionism in France. As for stopping the advance of fascism, in some ways the Popular Front accomplished just the contrary, for French conservatives were so furious at what Blum had attempted to do that they became more than ever susceptible to authoritarian propaganda. To save the country from this Jewish schemer, they reasoned, the Republic itself might have to go— hence the slogan "Better Hitler than Blum" that was to do so much to sap French national morale in the years immediately preceding the Second World War.

Nevertheless the legacy of the Popular Front was not wholly negative. The Matignon Agreements and the legislation that implemented them —despite continued violations—served as a model for succeeding governments. Like the American New Deal, these measures finally brought France abreast of the social legislation that for decades had prevailed in Germany, Britain, and Scandinavia. They provided the foundation on which the French postwar welfare state was to build. And this welfare state emerged from the experience of the wartime resistance to Hitler and to collaboration with fascism which ranks as the proudest French memory in recent history. Indeed, the Resistance itself was to be a militant revival of the Popular Front—as Blum was to be one of its quiet heroes. In the achievements of the Resistance, the Popular Front, for all its weaknesses and failings, was to receive a retrospective rehabilitation as the *only* ideological movement in France in the whole interwar period that held any real promise for the future.

Readings

For discriminating comparative analyses of fascist movements, see Ernst Nolte, *Three Faces of Fascism* (1966), F. L. Carsten, *The Rise of Fascism* (1967), and S. J. Woolf, ed., *The Nature of Fascism* (1968).

The most recent and judicious full-scale biography of the Italian Duce is Ivone Kirkpatrick, *Mussolini: A Study in Power* (1964). Gaudens Megaro, *Mussolini in the Making* (1938), traces in admirable detail his career until

1914, and A. Rossi, *The Rise of Italian Fascism, 1918–1922* (1938), deals with

his march to power. Herman Finer, *Mussolini's Italy* (1935), and Gaetano Salvemini, *Under the Axe of Fascism* (1936), are still the best general studies, although they were written before the fall of the regime. There are no good pro-Fascist accounts to balance the strong anti-Fascism of these two. For an eminently fair history of the vexed church-state issue by a liberal Catholic, see D. A. Binchy, *Church and State in Fascist Italy* (1941).

The Nazi regime still awaits a comprehensive critical account. In its absence, the best general works are Maurice Baumont, et al., *The Third Reich: An International Symposium* (1955), and Franz Neumann, *Behemoth: The Structure and Practice of National Socialism,* 2d ed. (1944), the first by a group of historians from several countries, the second by an *émigré* scholar with a qualified Marxist outlook. For a good narrative, William L. Shirer's *The Rise and Fall of the Third Reich* (1960) makes exciting reading, while for Hitler's biography, Alan Bullock, *Hitler: A Study in Tyranny,* rev. ed. (1964), is thoroughly satisfactory. Robert G. L. Waite, *Vanguard of Nazism: The Free Corps Movement in Postwar Germany: 1918–1923* (1952), deals with one of the major sources of the movement. Eugen Kogon, *The Theory and Practice of Hell* (1950), is the most impressive single volume in the extensive concentration camp literature, while Guenter Lewy analyzes in highly critical vein *The Catholic Church and Nazi Germany* (1964).

For the clerical-corporative regimes, besides Gulick on Austria (*see* readings for Chapter Eight), there is M. Derrick, *The Portugal of Salazar* (1939), a frank apologia.

The Stalinist System

I

THE CONSOLIDATION
OF STALIN'S AUTHORITY

The Problem of the Succession to Lenin

When Lenin died in early 1924, no one knew who would succeed him as leader of both the Soviet Union and international communism. Nor had Lenin left any unambiguous instructions on the subject. This in turn was logical in view of the character of the authority that the founder of bolshevism had wielded. Lenin's dominance had always been extraconstitutional and informal. He had held no high office in the state machinery —indeed, this in itself was a sign of how completely the Communist party dominated the Soviet state. Not until the Second World War did the chief figure in the party, who for a decade and a half had been Stalin, consider it necessary to assume the office of prime minister which Mussolini and Hitler had occupied from the start. In Lenin's day—and throughout the greater part of Stalin's period of rule—dictatorial authority derived solely from a leading position in the party. In Lenin's case, this position was almost entirely informal and personal: he was simply the most persuasive person in the five-man Politburo, which formulated the policy line for the Communist party and through it guided the Soviet state.

In March, 1919, at the same time that the Politburo had been set up,

*One of Stalin's thorniest
problems was the collectivization
of Russia's peasants.*
COURTESY BROWN BROTHERS.

257

the congress of the Communist party had established two further bodies which were intended to handle the more routine questions of party organization and discipline. These were the Organizational Bureau or Orgburo—again a committee of five members—and the permanent Secretariat. By the time Lenin died, Stalin had become the chief figure in both bodies. As secretary-general of the party he controlled the complex network of local and regional party committees; as the leading member of the Orgburo he was in a position to check any effort to review what he had done in the Secretariat. Finally, he was a member of the Politburo itself, and hence authorized to know all the inner secrets of the party.

In the twenty months that Lenin lay incapacitated—from his first stroke in May, 1922, to his death in January, 1924—Stalin was able quietly to consolidate his own authority. At this time, he was far from being the obvious heir apparent. He was a narrow party man, of limited education and with almost no capacity to develop Marxist theory. At least three party leaders seemed to rank higher than he did—Trotsky, of course, and after him Gregory Zinoviev, who ran the Third International, and the subtle theoretician Nikolai Bukharin. But all these had serious counts against them. Trotsky was not an "Old Bolshevik": in the decisive years before 1917, when personal loyalties and associations were first forged, he had been the lone wolf of the Russian Left, and even after he had proved his organizing abilities both by launching the revolution itself and by beating the Red Army into shape, he remained isolated—too much of a visionary for the routine tasks of running a would-be socialist society. Zinoviev, along with his inseparable companion Leo Kamenev, had hesitated in 1917: he had doubted the success of the revolution and this had never been forgiven him. Finally Bukharin—to Westerners the most appealing of the three—was too gradualist in his approach, too much of a "liberal" intellectual to survive in the jungle warfare that Stalin was about to inaugurate in his struggle for supremacy.

In addition to the handicaps of their pasts, these three lacked understanding of how political power actually operated—of what was needed first to acquire power and then to keep it. Apparently they fancied that with Lenin's death control over the party would revert to what it had always been in theory—the rule of a committee—and that on this committee they could share power in a spirit of revolutionary comradeship. This was far from being Stalin's idea. His rivals made their supreme error in underestimating, because he was their intellectual inferior, a man who was to prove himself one of the craftiest and most ruthless rulers of modern times.

The Struggle for Power

Though Stalin's method for reaching his goal was the old and simple one of "divide and rule," it fooled his adversaries, who never thought of combining against him until it was too late. First Stalin joined Zinoviev and Kamenev to form a *Troika* (or triumvirate) directed against Trotsky. Just a year after Lenin's death this tactic achieved complete success: faced with the implacable opposition of a majority within the Politburo, Trotsky resigned as commissar for war. Potentially, this was one of the strongest positions of power in the Soviet Union, controlling as it did the whole organization of the armed forces. Yet it apparently never occurred to Trotsky to rally the Red Army for his own defense: he was too much of a civilian and an ideologue. Also, he was far too loyal to the Communist party to resort to any such putschist tactics. In Trotsky's behavior are evident the beginnings of the attitude of deference and of self-doubt that was to handicap each successive group of Stalin's party opponents. They were so imbued with the notion of ideological solidarity that to oppose the party seemed to them the supreme, the unpardonable crime. They lost sight of the fact that the party was not a platonic ideal but rather what flesh and blood human beings made of it —and that the man who after 1924 was restyling it to his own taste was their personal enemy and the enemy of nearly everything in which they believed.

With Trotsky's power broken, the *Troika* fell apart. Stalin now began to work with the right wing in the Politburo, the outstanding figure of which was Bukharin. At the same time Stalin took care to protect his own interests by bringing into that body three new "center" members dependent on him alone; among them were Marshal Klementy Voroshilov, a military hero of the civil war, and V. M. Molotov, later to become famous in the West as "Old Iron Pants," the foreign minister who never conceded an inch. Zinoviev and Kamenev were thus isolated as the left wing of the party directorate. These two still controlled one citadel of power—the former capital of Petrograd, now renamed Leningrad, of which Zinoviev was party boss. Again nearly a year elapsed before Stalin struck. Finally, at the end of 1925, armed with a massive vote of confidence from the party congress—most of whose delegates were dependent for their positions on him alone—Stalin set out to break Zinoviev's power over the Leningrad machine with the well-tried and infallible appeal for party discipline.

Now at last Zinoviev and Kamenev thought of banding together with the discredited Trotsky. But when they acted, in the spring of 1926, it was too late. On November 7, 1927—the tenth anniversary of the Bolshevik Revolution—the opposition made its last public effort to stem the Stalinist tide: it held parades separate from those officially organized by the party. Retribution descended immediately: both Trotsky and Zinoviev were expelled from the party's ranks. Here their paths diverged. Zinoviev recanted his errors and was given a few years of grace. Trotsky, who refused to bow, was exiled, originally to one of the Soviet Republics of Central Asia, and later abroad. He lived first in Turkey and then in Mexico, where he served as an ideological rallying point for disillusioned Communists—the "Trotskyists" of the 1930's who tried to return the party to its original "purity" of doctrine. And it was in Mexico in 1940 that Stalin's assassin sought him out in his fortresslike abode and slew him in cold blood.

All that now remained for Stalin was to deal with Bukharin and the "rightists," which he did in 1928 and 1929 in connection with his own swing toward the "leftist" economic policy. Like Zinoviev, Bukharin and his associates abjured their heresies. And like him, they were given a few more years to live before the great blood purge of the mid-1930's carried them off with nearly all the others.

"Socialism in One Country"

In one respect, Stalin's triumph was consistent with the basic situation in his country. After the final failure of communism in Germany in 1923, the Soviet regime had turned in upon itself. For a full decade it lived almost in isolation from the rest of Europe: the great nations of the West maintained only minimum relations with it, and the smaller countries which bordered on it served as what the diplomats called a *cordon sanitaire*—a zone of quarantine against contagion. Thus sealed off from Europe, the Soviet Union turned its back on the West and began to interest itself in Asia; Stalin's only foreign adventure in this period was an unsuccessful effort to exploit the revolutionary situation in China. Indeed, Russia as a whole seemed to be reverting to its half-Asian past, and Stalin's enemies saw a grim appropriateness in the fact that the country was being ruled by an "oriental despot" whose methods recalled those of Genghis Khan.

An important reason for the indecisiveness of the various opposition groups in the years after 1924 was their inability to adjust to this new situation. Most of Lenin's Bolshevik comrades believed it impossible for a socialist society to build itself in Russia unless the revolution spread to other and more developed countries. After the failure of 1923, the more sophisticated and internationally oriented of these leaders found themselves at a loss. Obviously they could not give up the struggle: they had to do *something*. Thus Trotsky and his allies continued to insist on keeping up pressure abroad and on pushing ahead with a socialist policy at home in order to maintain the momentum of the movement at all costs.

Stalin, with his simpler and harsher mind, found a clear answer. In the autumn of 1924, he launched the slogan of "socialism in one country." Russia, he proudly asserted, could create socialism alone, without help or support from the outside. Simplifying the issues and twisting them to his own purposes, Stalin depicted Trotsky and people like him as men of little faith and dangerous adventurers besides, who, with their doctrine of "permanent revolution," would lead the country into needless peril. The Soviet Union's vast resources were sufficient, Stalin argued, to overcome all its handicaps of backwardness and to win respect for a regime that already governed "one-sixth of the world." This reassuring doctrine—with its undertone of smugness and its return to prerevolutionary patriotic themes—was well calculated to appeal to the new generation of organizers and managers whom Stalin had raised up in his party machine and who were far less concerned with abstract ideological speculation than was the generation of the Old Bolsheviks.

The Last Years of NEP and the "Scissors" Crisis

The only flaw in Stalin's reasoning was the virtual nonexistence of socialism in Russia. After the disappointing experience with war communism, Lenin had inaugurated the compromise with free enterprise called the *New Economic Policy*. NEP had given the country the minimum that the Soviet leaders had expected of it—a breathing space for consolidation. It had enabled the economy to start moving again after the civil war had brought it nearly to a stop. But once this basic goal had been achieved, NEP began to reveal serious shortcomings. It was very slow in raising industrial production: not until 1926–1927 did industry as a whole reach the level of 1913; in per capita terms, it still remained below that level, since the population had increased by eight million. In addition, Russia's prewar industrialization had been far from adequate to satisfy the minimum demands of a European nineteenth-century society, let alone those of a twentieth-century socialist one. In the countryside, where recovery had proceeded more rapidly than in the cities, NEP had accomplished no more than to return the agricultural population to the situation of 1913. As Stolypin had done in the prewar period, moreover, NEP had encouraged the growth of a class of self-sufficient peasants, or *kulaks*, at the expense of the peasant majority.

The gravest symptom of economic difficulty, however, was the "Scissors" Crisis which first became apparent at the end of the summer of 1923. With agricultural production rising and industry lagging behind, a gap began to grow between the prices that peasants obtained for their crops and those they had to pay for the industrial goods they required. Two years of good harvest followed the famine year of 1921–1922, and with food plentiful at last, wholesale prices for agricultural products fell to just over half what they had been in 1913. Meanwhile the corresponding prices for manufactured goods stood at nearly double their prewar level: industry could not possibly meet the demand. Caught between the blades of these widening "scissors," the peasants began to wonder whether it was worthwhile to deliver their produce to the cities at all. If they could get nothing they wanted in return—or if they had to pay exorbitant prices—they might do better to consume what they grew or to store it until the government agreed to a higher price. Thus from the mid-1920's on, the Soviet Union faced a chronic and growing crisis in feeding its urban population. The *kulaks*, whom NEP had so notably strengthened, were proving themselves the strongest economic force in the nation, since they had it in their power to starve the cities at will.

By 1927 it was apparent that the Soviet economy was caught, as it had been six years earlier, in a series of vicious circles. Ten years after the Bolshevik Revolution, Russia was scarcely closer to socialism than it had been at the start. The state-owned sector of the economy was still too weak to dominate the rest; the government organs of planning and control lacked the power to bring the countryside to terms. Quite simply, what was required was a strong and coherent policy that could cut through all the interlocking dilemmas at one blow: feed the cities, raise the level of industry, and provide new manpower for a new type of society.

At this point, at the end of 1927, Stalin decided to adopt the policy of Trotsky which he had earlier attacked so fiercely and, by utilizing to the full the machinery for economic planning which was already in existence, launch the great changeover to a socialist society.

II
THE GREAT TRANSFORMATION

Stalin, as his name implied,* had nerves of steel. Once he embarked on a policy, he let nothing deflect him from it. So it was after 1927: he had decided upon forced industrialization and the collectivization of agriculture and he moved straight ahead, never permitting himself to be deterred by mistakes, calamities, or the enormous human suffering they entailed. For more than a decade he whipped and drove his people into the greatest and most sustained economic effort ever made by a single nation in the history of modern Europe.

The Collectivization of Agriculture

The first campaign was directed against the power of the *kulaks*. By forcing peasants to merge their holdings in large collective farms, Stalin and his advisers hoped to produce a rural social structure that would be more equalitarian, more efficient, and easier to control than the system of peasant landholding.

Beginning in 1928, teams of party agitators and industrial workers were despatched to the countryside to urge the peasants to collectivize. At first the campaign seemed to sweep all before it. The official reports suggested that the peasants were rushing with enthusiasm to consolidate their holdings, and Stalin himself began to be carried away by the momentum of events. In mid-1929, he decided to speed the tempo of

---

* The revolutionary nickname by which he is known to history was derived from the Russian word *stal'*, meaning "steel."

collectivization. Those who continued to refuse, he insisted, must be forced to comply. In short, what needed to be done was to "liquidate the *kulaks* as a class."

With these brutal instructions, Stalin's agents began to bear down on the still reluctant *kulaks*. They declared class war in the countryside, inciting the poor peasants, who had something to gain from collectivization, against the more prosperous, who had everything to lose. But by American or Western European standards, these "prosperous" peasants were poor folk indeed. They were simply independent and self-sufficient and they saw no reason to give up their land for some dim goal of a socialist society.

The vast majority of *kulaks* resisted. The government overcame their resistance by regular military operations in which recalcitrant villages were forced to capitulate at machine-gun point. In this fashion, two million *kulaks*, who with their families constituted a population of at least eight million, gradually succumbed. Some were killed; many more starved; the greater part were apparently driven off to cultivate as well as they could the remote regions of Siberia that needed to be exploited. Before they left—or before they submitted to joining a collective—the peasants did what they could to wreck the new experiment. They smashed their farm implements, burned crops, and slaughtered their animals. In this way, more than half Russia's livestock perished: by 1933, by Stalin's official admission, the country had lost just over half its horses, 45 per cent of its cattle, and two-thirds of its sheep and goats.

Long before this, government and party had been obliged to call for a pause. In March, 1930, Stalin indirectly conceded the extent of the calamity in the countryside in a statement bearing the curious title of "Dizziness with Success." As in so many Communist pronouncements, the message that was actually conveyed was just the reverse of what it purported to be; it was an admission of failure rather than a hymn to success. In it, Stalin also resorted to the equally well-tried trick of shifting the blame to subordinates who had "misunderstood" his orders. In any case, the practical result was an easing of pressure on the peasants: for the next few months collectivization proceeded more slowly. But in 1932 and 1933 Stalin resumed his campaign, and this time the horrors of famine were joined to those of mass uprooting. A crop failure in 1932, added to the disorganization of life in the countryside that collectivization had entailed, brought starvation on a scale that Russia had not known for a full decade. Again, as in the case of the famine of 1922, it is impossible to say exactly how many perished. But demographers have estimated that the direct and indirect effects of the collectivization campaign together cost the country five million lives.

By the end of 1933 the government had won its battle against the *kulaks*. Meanwhile it had begun to reassure the country people that it was not going to make rural factory hands of them. By the basic statute of the collectives promulgated in 1935, these enterprises were granted their land in perpetuity, and the individual peasant members were permitted to keep a cow or a few goats and to cultivate as their own small garden plots not exceeding a couple of acres.

On this basis, the collectivization campaign continued into the latter part of the 1930's. Thereafter, official pressure was steady and brought results; with the resistance of the *kulaks* broken, the earlier excesses were unnecessary. By the outbreak of the Second World War, about 95 per cent of the Soviet Union's farms had been collectivized. The basic type remained the regular collective or *kolkhoz*, run by the peasants themselves (perhaps with a professional or party manager), varying in size from 1,000 to more than 7,000 acres, and consisting of from sixty to two hundred families. There were also a much smaller number of state farms or *sovkhozes*, which served as models of management to the rest. Finally there were the machine tractor stations, holding a pool of expensive and scarce farm machinery that could be rotated among the collectives in a given area.

The foregoing, however, may give too tidy an impression. In actuality, even at the end of a decade of trial and error, the collective system on the land was still far from perfect. Not one of its goals was fully attained. A greater equality prevailed among the peasants than had been true before, but there was still the contrast between rich and poor *kolkhozes*, between those which were prosperous and efficiently run and those which were little more than a pooling of peasant misery. Moreover, within the *kolkhoz* itself there grew up distinctions between good workers who received a generous share of the community proceeds and the slovenly who were granted the barest minimum for subsistence. Nor did the program fully achieve the goal of feeding the cities: after the terrible experiences of the period between 1928 and 1933, years were needed to rebuild agricultural production and livestock numbers to their earlier levels; and the collectives themselves frequently proved as reluctant as the *kulaks* had been to make deliveries promptly and in the amounts specified. Millions of peasants were sullen and uncooperative, far from reconciled to the collective idea. Throughout the period of Russia's forced industrialization, agriculture was to present a most perplexing problem; along with transport—which was never adequate for the load put upon it—the recalcitrance of the peasants continued to be the chief weakness of the entire Soviet economy.

At the least, however, Stalin had effected an agrarian revolution that broke up the old patterns of life and work in the countryside and began to substitute for them new ways of doing things more suited to an industrial society. In the long run—in the *very* long run—these new ways were also to prove more efficient, for a most important by-product of the collectivization of agriculture was the revelation that Russia—in common with nearly all other undeveloped agrarian societies—had far too much of its population on the land, where it depressed the standard of living and discouraged economic improvement. With collectivization, millions of excess farm hands became available for other employment. By com-bining persuasion and coercion, government and party herded them to the cities, where they joined the ranks of the new working class that was engaged in the gigantic task of building up the country's heavy industry.

The Five-Year Plans

A few months after the decision to collectivize the land, the party leaders determined on a second and related program that was at least as ambitious: the rapid industrialization of the Soviet Union through a systematic and coordinated plan. In so doing, Stalin and his colleagues resolutely repudiated the tolerance for private enterprise that had characterized the NEP period. They decided to utilize to the full the resources of the state planning commission (*Gosplan*), which had existed since 1921, and to make the Soviet Union a strong and truly socialist country at last by building state-owned factories and electric power stations that would rival the greatest plants in the United States.

The First Five-Year Plan, to run from October, 1928, to 1933, aimed to double over-all Soviet production; it put chief emphasis on basic industry, which was scheduled to grow by 300 per cent, and on electrification, which was to increase more than fivefold. At first, carried away by enthusiasm, the planners launched the slogan of completing the work in four years, as sector after sector apparently overfulfilled its quota. Then all sorts of difficulties appeared: planning was still in its infancy, and the officials at the center had not yet learned how to anticipate local bottlenecks and shortages. Moreover, an unanticipated price rise and the continued resistance of the peasants to collectivization made all the original calculations inaccurate. Yet in the end the over-all output of Soviet industry was certainly more than doubled.

The Second Plan, running from 1933 to 1937, and the Third Plan, which was interrupted by the war, were originally intended to shift the earlier almost exclusive emphasis on heavy industry and basic equipment to a more balanced development of the economy, in which the consumer would receive his fair share. But meantime the international situation had changed: with the advent of Hitler, the threat of war, which had already influenced the original decision to industrialize, became acute and immediate. Hence heavy industry maintained its priority, and war preparation, particularly in the years after 1936, began to approach the level of Germany's. By the outbreak of the Second World War, then, Soviet economic development remained unbalanced and one-sided: vast pockets of backwardness still existed alongside industrial complexes that ranked among the most modern in the world.

The Soviet production figures for 1937—the last prewar year in which reliable statistics were published—bear eloquent testimony to the unevenness of economic growth under the first two Five-Year Plans. As compared to a decade earlier, the output of machinery and metal products had increased nearly fourteenfold, while that of coal and of pig iron had more than tripled and quadrupled, respectively. But the production of cotton cloth—a sensitive index of how consumer goods were faring —had risen by only a quarter. The percentages by which capital goods goals had been overfulfilled in the two plans balanced fairly evenly the extent of disappointment in the consumption sector. In the period of the First Plan the Soviet factories turned out 126.7 per cent of the capital goods expected; for consumer goods the figure was 80.5 per cent. At the end of the Second Plan, the favored heavy industrial sector stood at 121.2 per cent, while once again consumer products fell short by nearly 15 per cent.

The essentials, however, had been accomplished. Russia had finally become a major industrial power, pushing Britain out of third place— after the United States and Germany—in over-all production. Furthermore, the transition to socialism had been achieved: by 1939, private industry and commerce no longer had any significance in the Soviet economy. The very look of the land had changed: the vast dam spanning the Dnieper, the factories producing farm machinery at Stalingrad and Rostov-on-Don, the great metallurgical complex at Magnitogorsk—all these had altered the landscape beyond recognition. The last of these—Magnitogorsk—lay in Asia behind the Urals, for one of Stalin's subsidiary aims was to shift the centers of industry toward the east, where they would be less exposed than they had been in 1914 to war destruction and foreign occupation.

In terms of the Soviet Union's situation in 1928, the ten-year achievement had been stupendous. In a mere decade, the country had pulled itself from backwardness and inferiority to the position of a front-rank industrial power. True, outside help had been utilized: thousands of engineers and technicians were recruited abroad, particularly from Germany and the United States. These came as individuals, attracted by sympathy, curiosity, or the hope of gain. The governments of the West had not helped at all: there had been no official program of aid to an underdeveloped nation. Hence the capital for the colossal investment program that the Five-Year Plans entailed had to be squeezed from the Soviet peoples themselves. It was literally on the backs of the suffering Russian masses that Stalin pushed forward to his goal.

The social consequences were what might have been expected. Housing was insufficient, and the swollen population of the cities lived huddled together in dreary, unsanitary quarters. Working hours were long and consumer goods unobtainable. In an economic sense, Russia might be growing more and more socialized, but in terms of human relations, the incentives of capitalism were returning. Piecework replaced daily wages; scales of pay became sharply differentiated according to skill and effort; the national heroes of the Five-Year Plans were the Stakhanovites —the workers capable of exceeding all the regular norms, their prototype the half-legendary Stakhanov, who had mined more than a hundred tons of coal in a single day!

Observers both in the West and in the Soviet Union itself wondered whether it was worth the cost. The question, of course, permits no conclusive answer. To deal with it, even tentatively, requires a consideration of the character of Soviet society as it began to crystallize around 1934 in a form quite different both from what had prevailed before 1917 and from what most Bolsheviks had imagined when they dreamed of the promised future.

III

THE POLITICAL AND SOCIAL IMPLICATIONS

The Constitution of 1936

In 1936—as if to mark the fact that after two decades of Bolshevik rule the socialist society had at last become a reality—Stalin ordered the promulgation of a new constitution for the Soviet Union. On paper, it was—as sympathizers in the West liked to say—"the most democratic in the world." All the usual Western liberties received due attention, and the Soviet constitution makers added a few new ones. They abolished the limitations which earlier had deprived capitalists and aristocrats of the vote. And the roster of Soviet republics—which had already been increased in 1925—was raised to a total of eleven, thereby suggesting that the non-Russian peoples of the Transcaucasus and Central Asia were being given a larger share in the running of the Union. Finally, a change in terminology from "commissar" to "minister" created the impression that in the conduct of government the Soviet Union was going to behave as a parliamentary democratic state rather than as the party dictatorship it had been before.

Very little of this made any difference in practice. The Soviet Union remained a police state—indeed, from this standpoint there was deterioration rather than improvement. The real significance of the new constitution lay elsewhere. First, by ending the era of improvisations, it emphasized the fact that the Soviet regime had hardened into its final form; the abolition of the distinctions that had denied full rights to the former possessing classes most clearly epitomized the change by suggesting that the power of these classes had been broken and that they no longer represented a threat to the regime. Secondly, the new constitution provided excellent propaganda material for Western consumption. It seemed to mark the climax of three years of "liberal" policies that had put the Soviet Union into a light more favorable than any in which it was to appear during the whole interwar period. After 1933—as if to underline the alternative he offered to the new threat of nazism—Stalin relaxed his pressure in the collectivization drive; he took his country into the League of Nations and made it a strong supporter of "collective security" at Geneva; by adopting the Popular Front idea, he seemed to endorse the notion of a "domesticated" communism that would be an acceptable ally to the Western democratic Left. There emerged the image of a strong and confident Russia which was setting out to build a socialist society at the very moment when the capitalist economies of the West lay crippled by the Great Depression. This picture stirred imaginations and led Western European democrats to slur over or conveniently forget the somber aspects of the Stalinist system which in ordinary times might have troubled them very deeply.

Most of these Western sympathizers did not know that at the very time the new constitution was being drafted Stalin had already entered on a phase of intensified terror that was to disillusion nearly all of them.

The Great Purges

In December, 1934, a young assassin struck down Stalin's trusted deputy, Sergei Kirov. For once the man of iron appeared really shaken. He hurried to Leningrad, the scene of the crime, and himself questioned the murderer. The official story which emerged from hours of interrogation was the revelation that an opposition existed within the apparently monolithic Soviet state, that the assassin had belonged to a group of young Communists who bitterly resented Stalin's oppressive rule and who regarded Zinoviev—with whom, apparently, they had no contact—as their ideological guide. Subsequent revelations, however, have brought out the more sinister story that Kirov, who had been popular through his espousal of the new "liberal" line, had been put to death by the secret police itself.

In any event, the master of Russia determined on a complete house-cleaning. In January, 1935, Zinoviev and Kamenev were tried for treason and conspiracy and sentenced to long prison terms. A year and a half later, they went on trial again, and this time they were executed. Meanwhile, the party cadres themselves had experiencd a thorough purge, and the process began to reach into all branches of the government and the national life. In early 1937, another group of high party leaders went on public trial—nearly all of them to receive death sentences—and in the spring and early summer eight outstanding army leaders were convicted and executed in secret. Finally, in March, 1938, came the turn of Bukharin and the old "Right" in the party. Thus by the beginning of 1939, when Stalin officially announced the end of the purge, every possibility of opposition had been destroyed—two or three alternative governments had been eliminated. Only a handful of Old Bolsheviks—all of them loyal to Stalin—remained alive; the heavy hand of party orthodoxy had snuffed out every shred of independent initiative in the Soviet state.

Observers from the West—who were admitted to watch the more important trials—were puzzled by the abject fashion in which defendant after defendant entered the dock and declared himself guilty in the most circumstantial terms. Most of the stories they told seemed pure fabrications; only in the case of the army leaders have subsequent historians admitted the probability of a true plot—and in their case one might argue that the Red Army's long years of clandestine military cooperation with Germany cast doubts on its high command's reliability in defending the country against the Nazi attack that now threatened. So far as the party men were concerned, however, there seems to be no evidence of any concerted opposition to Stalin. These Old Bolsheviks were already beaten and broken men; they had lost the political struggle at least a half-decade earlier and they knew it. They did not like Stalin's methods, and they probably still grumbled against him in private, but they offered no real threat to his authority.

Thus they were easy game for the government interrogators and prosecutors who attacked them. It is doubtful how much they were actually tortured—those who appeared in the dock had evidently not been seriously injured—and physical pressure seems to have played a relatively minor part in their confessions. Psychological pressures of various sorts were probably of much greater importance. Among these was the faint hope of saving their lives if they proved cooperative, as happened with at least two prominent defendants. Perhaps the deciding factor was the weariness and resignation of defeat, coupled with the sense that the verdict of history had gone against them. And this last, in terms of Marxist reasoning, was almost equivalent to an admission of guilt: if in the 1920's they had in fact opposed what proved to be the main course of history—that is, Stalin's rule—then in an "objective" sense, they were guilty of "antiparty" activities. From here, it was only a step to confessing whatever was charged against them.

So much for the defendants. There remains, however, the additional question why Stalin behaved as he did. Why was it necessary for him to kill nearly all his old comrades-in-arms, who were no longer in a position to threaten him? Once again, the answer seems to lie in emotion rather than logic. Just as by the "objective" dialectic of the situation those accused could find themselves guilty *of something*, so could Stalin feel himself threatened by their mere existence. Like the Russian despots of old to whom he was compared both in praise and in condemnation—men like Boris Godunov and Ivan the Terrible—Stalin was possessed by the demon of universal suspicion. As he aged and his crimes multiplied, he feared more and more for his own life and trusted fewer and fewer people—until in the end he was overcome by a paranoia that made his last years a nightmare for all those close to him.

The New Conformism

Beyond all this, men like Bukharin and Zinoviev recalled a past that Stalin wished to have buried and forgotten. They recalled a time when revolutionary comradeship still existed and when, within the confines of the party at least, real freedom of discussion and expression was permitted. Lenin, for all his preaching of Marxist ruthlessness, would never have dreamed of murdering party colleagues.

By the 1930's, Russia was living in quite a different atmosphere—an atmosphere of "oriental" or "Byzantine" despotism. Party congresses had become mere rubber stamps; even the Politburo, which met in almost constant session, consisted solely of Stalin's creatures. The great man himself was virtually deified: he assumed the mantle of Marx and Lenin, arrogating to himself the role of high priest of theory and ideology, although he wrote a flat, tasteless style and his thoughts were notably unoriginal. His most banal statements were welcomed by his sycophants as revelations from on high, and the history books were altered to magnify his deeds in the early days of the regime and to depreciate those of his rivals. Indeed, authors who wished to find official favor were obliged to flatter him shamelessly and even to imitate the way he wrote. In all fields of culture a deadly conformism and sterility settled over Russian life (see Chapter Eleven, IV). There developed too an emphasis on rank and hierarchy, a widening gap in income and standard of living between the mere worker or peasant and the highly paid party chief or factory manager, which suggested that the Soviet Union had left the revolution far behind and had found its own equilibrium of conservatism and stability.

In the background, threatening at one time or another nearly everyone of any prominence in the country, lurked the dreaded secret police. As it had earlier changed its name from Cheka to GPU, so in 1934 it became the MVD—the innocuous-sounding Ministry of Internal Affairs. In fact it remained what it had always been: a machine for government by terror. With the liquidation of the kulaks and the great purges, its functions grew. It herded hundreds of thousands of dissidents into the remote wastes of Siberia where, often in almost arctic conditions, it set up a whole series of forced labor camps. In many respects, these recalled the concentration camps run by the Nazis: they too were places of suffering and despair. But at least they served the clear economic purpose of opening inhospitable areas where Russians would never have settled of their own free will, and outright sadism was apparently less common there than in the camps managed by the German SS. Thus, even in its terrorist institutions, Soviet communism showed some trace of that rationality that regularly distinguished it from Nazi practice.

The New Intelligentsia

Despite terror and hardship and the fear of war, the new Soviet generation was growing up strong and confident. By the time the constitution of 1936 was promulgated, less than half the people of Russia could remember the prerevolutionary era. This was a young population: unlike that of Western Europe, it was growing very fast. Far more than in the

past it was a city population: virtually the entire increase for the years
1926 to 1939 came in the cities alone; in this period, Moscow almost doubled in size, growing from just over two million to more than four million, and some of the smaller industrial cities quadrupled the number of their inhabitants. Of the entire urban population, two-fifths consisted of peasants who had lived in cities for less than twelve years.

The new generation took communism and the Soviet system for granted. The more gifted members found opportunities for advancement that they would never have known under the old regime and that were rare even in the democracies of the West, for newly industrialized Russia was clamoring for technical talent, and it could obtain it in sufficient quantity only by training the sons and daughters of illiterate peasants. During the NEP period, the regime had been obliged to rely on "specialists" from the prerevolutionary intelligentsia whom it had never fully trusted. During the First Five-Year Plan, it welcomed engineers from abroad. But what it really wanted was technicians of its own, and preferably of proletarian or peasant origin. Therefore, in the five years 1933 to 1938 the Soviet Union sent a million young people into courses of higher education. From their ranks emerged a new intelligentsia of engineers and doctors, agronomists, teachers, research scientists, and factory managers. By Western standards, many of them were poorly and hastily trained, but they were enthusiastic, hardworking, and filled with pride in the new society that was theirs to create. It was on them that the regime very rightly rested its faith for the future.

The System on the Eve of the War

What did this new intelligentsia actually think of the system of government under which it lived? How did it reconcile its optimism and Communist faith with the brutal realities of Stalinist rule? In the 1930's, these questions seemed unanswerable: Soviet Russia loomed up in the east as a vast paradox, in which devotion to the task of building a new society went alongside political behavior of a meanness and squalor rivaling that of the fascists.

With the passage of time, however, it has proved possible to detect some connection between these apparent irreconcilables. Study of the Stalinist system has shown that it had within it certain safety devices that made it look like something more than a regime of police terror. Even in the darkest days of Stalin's tyranny, the ideological link with the Leninist past never snapped entirely. Lenin's precepts remained in honor—and the way they were twisted to new uses explains a great deal about how the system actually worked.

Lenin had at least partially realized the danger to liberty that would be entailed by the concentration of so much power in the hands of state and party. To counteract that, he had relied primarily on two devices: "self-criticism," which would ruthlessly ferret out and correct past mistakes, and the system of "democratic centralism," by which each party echelon elected the one above it, thereby ensuring democracy at the base of the political pyramid. Devices of this sort were lacking under fascism, which invariably functioned in authoritarian fashion through orders handed down from the top. Under Soviet communism, although the practice was equally authoritarian, the democratic elements in the theory were never entirely forgotten, and their continued presence does much to explain the greater staying power of the Soviet system.

Under Stalin, these safeguards were thoroughly perverted. State and party elections became only a formal endorsement of a slate of candidates selected from above; thus "democratic centralism" worked almost exactly in the reverse fashion from what had been originally intended. Similarly "self-criticism" never touched the essentials of the system: although there was constant discussion at all levels of the economic and party hierarchy—all the way from "town meetings" in collective farm or factory right up to the deliberations of the Politburo itself—these discussions dealt solely with the technical details of policy; they did not go to the heart of the matter. In essence, the safeguard of self-criticism was gradually altered to perform the opposite function from the one for which it had been devised. It served not to correct the abuses of the dictatorship but rather to strengthen the authority of the top party leaders through directing popular hostility toward the lower bureaucracy and toward specific technical mistakes. Thus criticism was "deflected away from policy itself to the execution of policy," and the central reality of the system that emerged was a "curious amalgam of police terror and primitive 'grass-roots' democracy." *

The democracy in the Soviet system was mostly spurious, and the self-criticism merely formal, but at least they resembled real popular participation in the processes of government and economic direction, and this was more than the fascist systems offered. Furthermore, communism had a theory—in the works of Marx and Lenin—whereas fascism had virtually none, and it was in terms of this body of doctrine that Stalin and his colleagues always felt obliged to explain their actions. Even when they violated Marxist-Leninist precepts most flagrantly—as in the creation of rigid hierarchies in every branch of Soviet society—they rationalized the change as a logical development of Communist theory. Throughout Stalin's period of rule, government and party were periodically shaken by the demand from on high to break the hold of bureaucracy and to get back to the fundamentals of Marxist democracy.

The result was a regularly recurring ritual of self-castigation. In the process certain abuses were in fact corrected, but the main function of campaigns of this sort was psychological: it reassured the people that

---

* Barrington Moore, Jr., *Soviet Politics: The Dilemma of Power* (Cambridge, Mass.: Harvard University Press, 1950), p. 403.

the regime was deeply concerned about making Marxist socialism a
reality in Russia at last.

In a sense, the Soviet system had accomplished this. Despite its perversion of so much of Marxism into a merely ritualistic mouthing of phrases—despite the horrifying methods of its secret police—it had reached two fundamental goals: it had nationalized the means of production and it had constructed an economy that seemed to have eliminated forever the capitalist nightmare of unemployment. For tens of millions of Soviet citizens, these achievements were apparently sufficient to justify their confidence and even devotion: the ordeal of the Second World War was to reveal in Soviet society a solidity that neither its friends nor its enemies had ever properly appreciated.

Readings

The standard and detailed account by Edward Hallett Carr, *A History of Soviet Russia,* vols. 4–7 (1954–1964), of which *The Bolshevik Revolution (see* readings for Chapter Three) forms the first three volumes, goes only as far as 1926. For Stalin's own career, Isaac Deutscher, *Stalin: A Political Biography* (1949), gives the best single biographical account, to which one may add the three volumes on Trotsky by the same author: *The Prophet Armed* (1954), *The Prophet Unarmed* (1959), and *The Prophet Outcast* (1963).

For information on NEP, the collectivization of agriculture, and the Five-Year Plans, see Alexander Baykov, *The Development of the Soviet Economic System* (1946). The theory and practice of the purge are dealt with in Zbigniew K. Brzezinski, *The Permanent Purge: Politics in Soviet Totalitarianism* (1956), and the ideological and psychological elements in Soviet society are treated in Barrington Moore Jr., *Soviet Politics: The Dilemma of Power* (1950), and Raymond A. Bauer, *The New Man in Soviet Psychology* (1952); for the opposition to Stalin, see Robert Vincent Daniels, *The Conscience of the Revolution; Communist Opposition in Soviet Russia* (1960).

Civilization

Chapter Eleven

in Crisis

I

THE SOCIAL CONSEQUENCES
OF THE DEPRESSION AND FASCISM

The Loss of Social Momentum

During the decade of the 1930's, when the Soviet Union was transforming itself from top to bottom, in the West, society and the economy languished. Gripped by depression and the fear of war, countries like Britain and France made little technological progress. They lost the momentum of change that had characterized their history for more than a century; in many areas of national life, they could do no more than to maintain the equipment and procedures inherited from preceding generations. Still worse, much of this equipment lay idle or under-utilized. The depression years stand as a period of pause in the economic and technological modernization of Western Europe. And this decade was to be followed by a further half-decade—that of the Second World War—in which innovation was almost entirely directed to military needs. In their externals, the cities of the West which had been spared war damage did not look much different in 1945 from the way they looked in 1930. When economic progress was finally resumed in the late 1940's it came with explosive force.

The clearest indication of loss of social momentum was a further decline in the birth rate. In the 1930's, it sank to the lowest level known

A scene from The Three-Penny Opera *by Bertolt Brecht and Kurt Weill. A bitter social satire, the play was a big success in postwar Germany before it was banned by Hitler.* COURTESY BROWN BROTHERS.

since regular records began to be kept in Western Europe. Faced with economic hardship and uncertainty, young people tended to postpone marriage and the arrival of children; birth control became so common a practice that governments began to worry about its effect on the strength of the nation. Among Northern and Western European democracies, in the Netherlands alone the figure for births remained significantly above that for deaths; elsewhere they were nearly in balance, with the population growing older. In the fascist countries, as might be expected, the regimes took vigorous counteraction: both Italy and Germany encouraged large families through tax favors and special allowances; whether owing to these measures or to the natural tendencies of their people, both countries experienced a population rise which contrasted sharply with the situation among their neighbors.

Another sign of social stagnation was the near-cessation of population movements in the early 1930's. When these did occur, they often reversed what had become normal in a highly industrialized society—as when city dwellers began to return to the farms, or emigrants to the United States took ship for their old homelands. Nearly everywhere, governments tried to protect their own working population by keeping down the influx of foreigners seeking employment. This was a further manifestation of the turn to economic nationalism reflected in the raising of tariffs and the official control of foreign trade. Even a country like France which had traditionally been hospitable to immigration now began to limit the arrival of workers from abroad: in 1934, it admitted only one-third the number that had entered in 1930. Everywhere the national nightmare was the same—unemployment, the curse of the decade that put its stamp on nearly all aspects of social and cultural endeavor.

The Political Refugees

In one form, however, emigration continued and even increased, particularly in the latter part of the decade. This was the flight of almost 400,000 Germans from political and racial persecution. It was paralleled by a continued trickle of clandestine departures from Italy, which suddenly grew in 1938, when Mussolini imitated his Nazi ally by instituting discriminatory measures against the Jews. Finally in 1939, with the end of the Spanish Civil War, nearly half a million Republican soldiers and refugees crossed over the border into France.

Only at the end of the decade did emigration of this sort begin to reach the proportions of a mass movement. In general, it was an emigration of elites rather than of broad strata of the population, but for that very reason it had a social and cultural importance far beyond its numerical scale. The people who left Italy or Germany tended to be leaders in their fields—scholars and trade-union executives, members of parliament and financiers. Even the emigration of the Jews—although it involved every social class—had an elite character, since members of this faith were, on the average, both wealthier and better educated than the run of the population. Thus the flight from fascist persecution in a very real sense impoverished the countries that drove these people out and enriched those that received them. When Germany lost through emigration its most original composer, Arnold Schönberg (who was Jewish), and its most influential novelist, Thomas Mann (who was not), the national culture experienced an irrevocable loss; indeed, as the departure of intellectuals from Germany continued, it became apparent that the country was suffering a drain of talent which a whole generation could not make good. As cultural levels in Italy and Germany declined, they rose in the countries which opened their doors to the refugees—at first primarily France, where the Italians in particular felt most at home, and later the United States, after the war drove so many *émigrés* to set off on their second move.

If for the mass of the population the fundamentals of life did not change under fascist rule, this was true only of the torpid and conformist majority. For the minority of the free-spirited, the creative, and the "racially" alien, life changed catastrophically. The persecution of the Jews and the denial of free thought under fascism came to rank as the second nightmare of the decade—adding a further note of grimness to the earlier specter of unemployment. The jobless worker and the refugee from fascist oppression—whether Jew or intellectual or perhaps both— became the twin symbols of the 1930's. Together these symbols suggest why in cultural terms the period was one of "engagement"—of protest against injustice and of enrollment under the banners of social reform.

II

THE LITERATURE
OF "ENGAGEMENT"

To writers who found themselves face to face with the two great evils of the time—the Great Depression and fascism—it seemed impossible to maintain any longer the attitude of a detached esthete. Sooner or later nearly all of them were swept up in the drive for social justice. Seeing intolerable conditions around them, even those who had earlier shown no interest at all in the condition of their fellow men began to ask themselves why all this suffering had to exist, and whether mankind could not find a new organization of society that would make life freer and happier. They revived the utopian strain that had figured so prominently in the thought and action of the nineteenth century and put new life into the old ideologies of progress. From this standpoint, the 1930's appear as an Indian summer of the previous century: the decade of despair was also a decade of hope.

Obviously European intellectuals did not discover ideology overnight with the coming of the Great Depression. The previous generation had had many writers whose work either directly or by implication furthered political causes. But most of these were isolated individuals who prided themselves on their freedom from humanitarian prejudices. Like D'Annunzio in Italy, they combined sensualism with a glorification of war and killing. When they did show interest in political action, it was usually in the service of fascist or near-fascist movements. It was against writers of this sort that the French philosopher Julien Benda warned in 1927, when he published his influential polemic *The Betrayal of the Intellectuals.*

In the 1930's, as fascism in practice revealed both its brutality and its intellectual shoddiness, writers who had earlier welcomed it as a movement of protest began to desert it. They turned instead toward restoring human fellowship and rational behavior. Some embattled writers of the 1930's were Marxists; some were "bourgeois" democrats; but they had a common vision of a better society which would end forever the blundering incompetence that had produced the Great Depression and the disappointment of human hope that had led to fascism and the menace of war. This vision of the future was often extremely eclectic: it combined elements both of traditional Marxism and of traditional liberalism; it tried to reconcile them or to go beyond them to a type of society whose outlines were vague but which would express the new realities of the twentieth century more adequately than either of them. Among writers as among politicians there grew a Popular Front mentality.

One further quality these writers shared was a new simplicity and directness. They were profoundly concerned with being *understood*— as had been true neither of the literary forebears of fascism, who had affected a "rich," mannered style and scorned the common herd, nor of the frankly experimental novelists and poets of the 1920's. From this standpoint, the decade of struggle against the Depression and fascism marked a pause in literary innovation or even a step backward: writers seemed to be telling themselves that the times had become too grave for merely technical experiment—what counted now was to transmit a message as sharply and as decisively as possible.

Historical Speculation: Spengler, Toynbee,
Croce, Bloch

As Europe experienced its second great crisis of the century—as depression and fascism added their shocks to the psychological damage that the First World War and its aftermath had inflicted—people began to turn toward historical speculation and to ask themselves in the broadest terms to what end the modern age was moving. This mood of cosmic questioning had already been widespread in the immediate postwar years; the experiences of the 1930's revived it and increased its range.

Just as the First World War was ending, an extraordinarily timely book had appeared in Germany, *The Decline of the West*, by an unknown historian, Oswald Spengler. People rushed to buy it: it was unprecedented for so serious and difficult a work to have so great a sale. The public pounced on it because it seemed to explain the catastrophe that had overwhelmed Germany and to add the comforting reflection that the victors in the war were no better off. Spengler proposed the thesis that Western civilization as a whole had reached its era of decline: by comparing its "life cycle" with that of other civilizations in history, he located to his own satisfaction the stage that Europe was now in— a century beyond its last cultural flowering and on the threshold of an age of iron in which, as in the last centuries of the Roman Empire, a cosmopolitan and "soulless" urban society would passively vegetate under the guidance of "Caesar-figures" who, with ruthless energy, would ward off the barbarians at the gates.

Spengler had devised his theory before the war; only the accidents of publication delayed its appearance until 1918. Yet the conflict itself and Germany's defeat gave it a relevance it would not have had if it had been published earlier, for Spengler implied that the First World War was only the opening engagement of a whole cycle of world conflict; Germany had lost the first battle, but several more such battles were to be fought before Western civilization found the destined "Caesar" who would bring it peace and order. Spengler held out hope that this towering personality might come from his own people; throughout the 1920's, Spengler ranked as a leading publicist of authoritarian conservatism, preaching discipline and the restoration of national strength for the great trials to come. But when Hitler carried out such a program, Spengler repudiated him; like so many German conservatives, he was disappointed by the tyranny he had helped to bring about.

A year after the advent of the Nazi regime, a younger contemporary of Spengler's, Arnold Toynbee, published the first three volumes of *A Study of History*, which was to be completed in 1954. Toynbee's work promised to be far longer than that of his German counterpart; it was less dogmatic and richer in historical scholarship. In its main outlines, however, it was much the same: like Spengler, Toynbee compared the life courses of civilizations and by so doing tried to determine the prospects for his own. In scanning the horizon of the contemporary West, Toynbee, too, concluded that its culture had "broken down" centuries ago. Yet unlike the German, the British historian refused to despair: he rejected any strict determinism and encouraged the hope that his own civilization might differ from all its predecessors in reviving its creative spirit long after it had apparently been spent. It would do this, he thought, by a return to ethical and religious faith. Thus Toynbee mirrored the mood of the 1930's in at least two of his affirmations—in his emphasis on moral values and in his rejection of despair.

Wide-ranging speculations of this sort became part of the staple fare of conversation in the 1930's. Much of it, of course, was mere chatter, based on almost no precise historical knowledge. It is significant, however, that even the most scrupulous professional historians of this period began to enlarge the scope of their investigations and to engage in the sort of generalization or declaration of political allegiance they would earlier have condemned as a betrayal of scholarship. Italy's greatest man of letters, Benedetto Croce, gradually fused into one unified attitude toward human affairs his political opposition to fascism and his abstract theory of historical interpretation. In *History as the Story of Liberty*—his last important work, published in 1938 when he was seventy-two years old—Croce proclaimed his faith that all true history was necessarily "liberal" in character; tyrannies were no more than episodes in history—its guiding thread remained the story of liberty, however faint its traces might become.

Meantime Croce's friendly rival, Germany's senior historian Friedrich Meinecke—whom the Nazis deprived of his influence over the profession but otherwise left unmolested—was similarly widening the range of his historical speculations. Meinecke was a Prussian and a German nationalist. His earlier books had endorsed Prussian leadership and Bismarck's work of unification, but in the study of the growth of historical thought which was the labor of his old age Meinecke quite clearly condemned Hitler and his like as destroyers of the German intellectual tradition. During the war years, the octogenarian historian moved still further to a repudiation of nearly all that German nationalism had stood for during the past century.

In France a group of historical scholars conceived the project of a multivolume collaborative work called *Evolution of Humanity*. It was intended to be a synthesis of the different approaches to historical understanding—economic, social, literary, religious, and the like—which conventional accounts presented as separate volumes or chapters. Perhaps the most impressive individual contribution was that of the economic historian Marc Bloch, whose book on feudal society, published in 1939, offered a model for the imaginative use of varied evidence to produce a unified picture of the past. It is worth adding that Bloch himself eventually became enrolled in the ideological struggle: a responsible leader in the French Resistance to German occupation, he was captured and shot by the Nazis in 1944.

Neo-Marxism: Communist and Social Democratic

The Depression and the Popular Front gave Marxism a crucial importance among European ideologies. Indeed, these events put Marxists in the strongest position they had enjoyed since the early 1920's—when the split between Communists and Socialists weakened both wings of the movement, and the consolidation of parliamentary government under the leadership of conservatives cut the ground from under them. After 1933, this situation was reversed: capitalism was now on the defensive for having allowed the Great Depression to occur and for having encouraged, or at least tolerated, the coming of fascism; Communists and Socialists were militant and self-confident and were beginning to sink their differences in common action against a common foe.

In both cases, however, Marxist doctrine required renovation. Under Stalinist orthodoxy, communism had transformed Marxism into little more than a stereotyped set of principles which could be twisted to justify anything the Soviet Union might choose to do. In the case of Social Democracy, conduct no longer jibed with theory: parties which for a generation had been parliamentary and legalist still mouthed the language of violent class struggle. In the 1930's, each tried to bring theory up to date and both failed.

After Lenin and Bukharin, European communism produced only one important thinker who combined party leadership with theoretical writing—the Italian Antonio Gramsci. Gramsci, however, was arrested by Mussolini's police before he had had time to measure his strength and influence against Stalin's: as the newly chosen chief of the Italian Communist party, he was imprisoned in 1926 and not released until just before his death in 1937. Gramsci's thought and example were expressed not in his party's councils or in those of the Third International but in fragmentary prison writings which were published only after the Second World War. In these, Gramsci put a new stress on the subjective and noneconomic elements in Marxism: he dealt with popular culture and with its relation to the old literary culture of the educated classes and to the new society dominated by the machine; he struggled with the problem of how a Marxist social consensus could be achieved after a successful seizure of power, but he never reconciled his own longing for spiritual freedom with his unquestioning acceptance of the necessity for single-party dictatorship.

Similarly, the other great theoretician of neocommunism, the Hungarian-born and German-educated Georg Lukács, always ultimately bowed to party discipline. Again and again he fell afoul of the official leadership. His own theory, which, like Gramsci's, was primarily cultural and subjective, was based on the idea of a "class consciousness" existing independently of political and economic conditions. It opened the way to an individual judgment of events—which in terms of Communist orthodoxy was the supreme danger. Lukács more than once had to repudiate what he had written; but he stubbornly returned to his favorite themes. As an old man he was to find at last in the Hungarian revolution of 1956 a brief satisfaction for his constantly repressed rebelliousness (see Chapter Nineteen, IV).

Although neither Gramsci nor Lukács had much direct influence outside a narrow circle of the Communist elite, similar ideas gradually filtered down to the party rank and file. This was particularly true during the wartime Resistance period, when thousands of Communists, left to their own devices and thrown into close association with former class enemies, worked out for themselves a more liberal interpretation of Marxist principles, and again, after Stalin's death in 1953, when individual national versions of communism began to gain ground. In the 1930's, however, tendencies of this sort had little chance: one after another they were smothered by the dead weight of Stalinist orthodoxy.

By the 1930's, a number of Socialist leaders had decided that the old and crude slogans of class warfare no longer sufficed. Among them was the French Popular Front chief, Léon Blum, who tried to change Marxism into an inclusive doctrine of humanism and humanitarianism in which all men of good will could recognize their own aspirations. But Blum's formulation of this goal remained vague, and in his day-to-day activities as a political leader he was chained to the traditional routines of his party. On the other hand, Socialist leaders who did succeed in making a clean break with the class warfare dogmas of the past, fell into worse difficulties. The most representative of them, Henri de Man in Belgium and his younger disciple Marcel Déat in France, both moved toward an emphasis on national values and on a corporative organization of society that bore an increasing resemblance to the fascist viewpoint. Both de Man and Déat finally compromised with fascism by consenting to work with the Nazi authorities in the period of wartime occupation.

Thus European socialism failed to renew itself. It found no fresh vocabulary to explain how and why it had become the nondogmatic catchall for European democrats who longed for a more just and efficient organization of society. Nor did it develop a new economic doctrine to replace the Marxist theory in which it only half believed, and the orthodox principles of capitalist finance which it applied most of the time when in office, since it knew no other. The task of devising a fresh theoretical approach fell to an English economist—a non-Socialist and even an enemy of socialism—John Maynard Keynes, the most influential economic thinker of the whole half-century.

The New Economics of Keynes

Keynes was a man of lively and versatile mind who had had a number of careers before the 1930's when he reformulated the principles of economics. He was far from being simply an economist: an associate of Bertrand Russell and Wittgenstein at Cambridge, he had written a treatise on probability which was an early contribution to the new analytic philosophy; he was a member of the Bloomsbury Circle of esthetes, sharing its characteristic enthusiasm for French painting, psychoanalysis, and the Russian ballet; he had been a high-ranking civil servant, an influential figure at the Paris Peace Conference, from which he returned disillusioned and angry, to write *The Economic Consequences of the Peace,* a little book that did much to create the bad conscience of the British about the Treaty of Versailles in general and German reparations in particular.

As Keynes observed the stagnation of the British economy in the late 1920's and its crisis in the half-decade following, he began to reconsider the orthodox principles of economics which he had been teaching. Preoccupied, like most of his countrymen, with the nightmare of unemployment, he came to question nearly all the dogmas of "sound" financing, deflation in time of crisis, and free enterprise at all costs. The result of these re-evaluations, *The General Theory of Employment, Interest and Money,* appeared in that extraordinary year 1936 when so much else in Europe was astir.

Keynes undertook to prove that government could manipulate the economy—through such devices as altering the interest rate, monetary expansion, public investment, and public works—without resort to socialism. Scornful of the orthodoxies of laissez faire, he judged economic policy on the strictly practical criteria of the total output of goods and the volume of employment that it succeeded in creating. Moreover, he added to the classical principles of economics a novel psychological element: these principles, he explained, might be correct in the abstract, but they did not work out in practice, since real human beings often refused to think like the proverbial economic man—trade unionists, for example, stubbornly denied the logic of taking a wage cut in a time of depression and falling prices. In line with this practical turn of thought, Keynes stressed "macroeconomics"—the analysis of interconnections within the economy as a whole, as opposed to the conventional method of isolating individual problems for detailed study. It was also characteristic of him to emphasize short-run considerations, in contrast to the comforting conviction of the orthodox that in the long run all difficulties would resolve themselves. In a crisis like the Great Depression, Keynes argued, there simply was not time to wait for the ineffable logic of the economy to set things right. "In the long run," he said, "we are all dead."

Keynes scorned socialism nearly as much as he did laissez faire. He called it "a dusty survival of a plan to meet the problems of fifty years ago, based on a misunderstanding of what someone said a hundred years ago." The "important thing for government," he further explained, was "not to do things which individuals are doing already . . . but to do those things which at present are not done at all." * Not government ownership, but government intervention at the key points in the economy, was the substance of Keynes' message. Yet despite his hostility to

* "The End of Laissez-faire" (1926), in *Essays in Persuasion,* new ed. (London: Rupert Hart-Davis, 1951), pp. 316–17.

the Socialists, he was to become their teacher; he taught them where they had made their mistakes and what they were really seeking—after they had found Marxian economics inapplicable, class warfare distasteful, and nationalization of basic industry a panacea that was far from sufficient. Had Blum and the leaders of the Popular Front in France known of Keynes' work, they would have had a clear substitute to offer for the deflationary policy of their predecessors, which they knew to be disastrous but whose economic premises they never succeeded in escaping. British Labor was in a more fortunate situation: it came to power only in 1945, when it had absorbed Keynes' teaching and was able to apply large parts of it in the postwar reconstruction of the British economy.

In general, it was in the United States rather than in Europe that Keynes first exerted practical influence. In America, his writings were used to justify theoretically what the New Dealers had been doing by a process of trial and error. Indeed in its simplest form, this was the historical significance of Keynes' work: it provided a sanction of theory for the unorthodox practices that necessity had forced upon governments during the Depression—deficit financing, for example, and the effort to maintain full employment by state action. Along with this sanction went the heartening assertion that it was not necessary to make an all-or-nothing choice between doctrinaire socialism and laissez faire capitalism: both were at fault; both had failed to see how much that was new could be done within the old framework of a private-enterprise economy. Like the Scandinavian governments whose practice had anticipated and paralleled his own theory, Keynes offered the possibility of a "middle way."

Novelists and Poets:
Marxist, Catholic, and Surrealist

In imaginative literature, the tendency of the 1930's toward ideological "engagement" and a new directness of expression appeared both in the work of younger writers who first achieved recognition in this period and in that of established authors who found themselves turning to new themes.

Among the elders, Thomas Mann offered the outstanding example. Even before the Nazis came to power, Mann had begun a series of novels dealing with the Old Testament story of Joseph and his brothers, and it was with the manuscript of the second of these novels that he went into exile, first in Switzerland and later in the United States. Mann's *Joseph* books—which were to be published in succession between 1933 and 1943—set their biblical theme in a contemporary ideological context. In the character of Joseph, Mann conveyed his own image of the bourgeois humanist, wise, tolerant, and efficient—who also had a flavor of the welfare-state administrator. Through this mythical figure presented in modern dimensions, Mann was evidently seeking to restore to honor the humane values that the Nazis had trampled on and to express his personal solidarity with the Jewish people in their years of persecution.

In France, the writing of comparable *romans-fleuves*—long series of novels that flowed along from year to year like a river—became particularly popular in the 1930's. The most ambitious of these was Jules Romains' *Men of Good Will;* this was begun in 1932 and by the outbreak of the Second World War had already reached eighteen volumes with no hint of approaching its end. Romains attempted to convey to his readers the variety and intensity of French life through a number of simultaneous plots—some interlocking, some quite unconnected—with characters drawn from all levels of society and from all walks of life. Through these experiences, the author implied, one could gradually reach an understanding of the fellowship that bound human beings together and the way one man's life was entwined with that of another entirely outside the knowledge or conscious purpose of either. Sometimes Romains failed to achieve this effect, and the result was forced and artificial but, at its best, *Men of Good Will* attained an almost epic quality; this was particularly true of the climax of the series, the volume entitled *Verdun* (1938), which was swiftly acknowledged as France's finest novel of the late war.

A quieter and less pretentious writer than Romains but a better literary craftsman was André Gide's friend, Roger Martin du Gard. The account of a French upper-middle-class family, *The Thibaults,* which Martin du Gard had begun in the 1920's, was interrupted for half a decade. When the author resumed publication in 1936, a change of theme and of tone was immediately apparent. The earlier volumes had dealt with such nonpolitical matters as the relation of a father to his sons, adolescent sexuality, and the practice of medicine. The later volumes were weighted with ideological polemics and suffused with socialist faith and hatred of war. The series ended in 1940 on a note of total despair: the author could find hope neither for his country nor for the West as a whole, which seemed to be entering on its age of iron.

Among the younger men there were Germans like Erich Maria Remarque, whose *All Quiet on the Western Front* (1928) ranked as the most influential of European antiwar novels, and Franz Werfel, whose *Forty Days of Musa Dagh* (1933) gave a stirring and timely account of Armenian resistance to Turkish oppression. But men like Remarque and Werfel never regained their literary force after the Nazis had driven them into exile; unlike the more serene Thomas Mann, they could not function successfully in the unfamiliar conditions of emigration. It was the French and British, rather, who continued and broadened in the 1930's the postwar tradition of the ideological novel. Many of these writers were Marxists, more frequently of Communist than of Socialist affiliation. Notable among the Communists was André Malraux, an adventurer and fighter by nature, who combined surrealist technique with class-conscious attitudes in describing the great ideological struggles of his own time. In *Man's Fate* (1933), he depicted the failure of the first Communist bid for power in China; in *Man's Hope* (1938), the heroism of the Republican forces in the Spanish Civil War.

The Civil War in Spain, more than any other series of events, marked the high point of ideological commitment in the 1930's. It began for European intellectuals on a note of hope—they regarded it as a crusade for social justice and human rights—and, like the decade, it ended in profound disillusion. This disillusion sprang from two related sources—the Communist perversion of the Republican cause in Spain itself and the horror of Stalin's purges within the Soviet Union. One by one, writers dropped away from Communism and from the Popular Front idea: Malraux himself was among them. By the end of the 1930's in both Europe and America the former Communist had become a familiar phenomenon in intellectual circles—a sad figure who had lost his ideological moorings and was looking rather bewilderedly for a new cause.

Almost alone among writers of the Left, George Orwell remained clearheaded and sure of his bearings. In his *Homage to Catalonia* (1937), Orwell gave what was to become the classic account of how a popular revolution had been wrecked for Stalinist ends. Orwell was from the start rather different from the usual intellectual of leftist orientation: he knew poverty and the working class at first hand, and he maintained through his bitterest experiences a tough-minded, undogmatic realism. The postwar reading public was to delight in his anti-Communist fantasies, *Animal Farm* (1945) and *Nineteen Eighty-Four* (1949), which expressed to perfection what most intellectuals had recognized only slowly and grudgingly about Stalinist despotism.

Less numerous than the Marxists, but also characteristic of the new spirit of ethical engagement were the Catholic novelists of France and Britain. Among the French, François Mauriac took the lead; among the British, Graham Greene. Writers of this sort were not religious in the sense of seeking converts through their work. Far from preaching a message of salvation, they were pessimists, whose estimate of human nature was thoroughly disabused. From their novels of adultery and family antagonism emerged the image of a weak and sinful humanity, whose only faint hope lay in the mystery of divine grace.

Even poetry did not remain untouched by the new mood of the 1930's. In Britain, young poets like W. H. Auden and Stephen Spender turned to a simpler and more lyric language and were not ashamed to deal with social themes. In France, the former surrealists Paul Eluard and Louis Aragon were converted to communism; both now conceived of their poetry as a revolutionary force and brought their vocabulary and syntax closer to those of ordinary speech. Although Aragon became involved in political polemics—particularly in the postwar years—to the damage of his art, Eluard remained true to his lyric gifts, to the fluidity and musical quality that made him at his death in 1952 his country's most widely known poet.

III
THE RELIGIOUS REVIVAL

"Quadragesimo Anno" and Its Sequels

In May, 1931, just as the church's struggle with Mussolini over Catholic Action was beginning, Pope Pius XI issued the encyclical *Quadragesimo Anno*. This pronouncement marked the fortieth anniversary of *Rerum Novarum*, the basic papal statement on the nature of modern industrial society, whose central principles it intended to reaffirm and bring up to date. The coming of the Great Depression had given this anniversary a burning topical interest.

Quadragesimo Anno, like its predecessor, severely criticized the capitalist order for its heartlessness and its exploitation of the working classes; it endorsed the intervention of the state to correct intolerable abuses and the association of workingmen in unions for their mutual protection and improvement. In ideological terms, it steered carefully between individualism and collectivism, between traditional liberalism —which "had already shown its utter impotence"—and socialism—which it called "a remedy much more disastrous than the evil it designed to cure." As a substitute for both of these, it advocated harmony between classes. It was more precise about how to achieve this understanding than *Rerum Novarum* had been; among the devices it recommended were profit sharing and the establishment of "vocational groups" within each branch of the economy.

The Pope couched these recommendations in such broad terms that Catholics in diametrically opposed ideological camps could find in his words an endorsement of what they were already doing. Economic conservatives interpreted his statement about "vocational groups" to mean self-governing bodies of the corporative type associated with fascist or quasi-fascist states. Indeed, clerical-corporative rulers like Salazar and Schuschnigg argued that they were building their regimes on the very principles set forth in *Quadragesimo Anno*. On the other hand, Christian Democrats of leftist and strongly antifascist orientation found in the same encyclical support for their own advocacy of militant social action in favor of the laboring classes.

Thus *Quadragesimo Anno* faced in two directions: it served both as an endorsement for the milder forms of fascist rule and as a summons to almost revolutionary activity. At the time, the former interpretation appeared the more justified: by its attacks on liberalism and socialism, the encyclical seemed to add still another powerful voice to the chorus of condemnation of European democracy, which had been so closely associated with both of those ideologies. As the years passed, however, and the shams and deceptions of fascism and corporatism were gradually exposed, the Christian Democratic interpretation came to predominate. Then Catholics began to stress the quiet criticism the encyclical had made of corporatism in practice—of its denial of freedom and its domination by the state. During the war years the principles of *Quadragesimo Anno*, interpreted in this fashion, inspired the Christian Democrats of France, Italy, and Germany who played a militant role in Resistance movements. In the immediate postwar period, these same principles stimulated widespread Catholic support of the welfare state.

Such activity, however, always stopped short of socialist measures, for on one point the encyclical had been categorical: even though it distinguished European socialism from communism as far less dangerous to the proper organization of society, it had still condemned it as a "mitigated" evil. This injunction was to have important effects in the postwar period: cooperation between Christian Democrats and Socialists—the main support on which European democracy rested in the critical years from 1944 to 1948—was always to be grudging and limited. Papal condemnation of the Socialists confirmed their suspicions of Christian Democratic "clericalism." The wall of mutual distrust was never breached—with highly damaging results for European democracy.

The Theological Aspect: French Catholicism
and Protestant Neoorthodoxy

The important place that a papal pronouncement must be given in an account of social and cultural currents in the 1930's suggests the new significance that Europeans in this period began to attach to religious concerns. The ideologies of progress had usually neglected religious values: they either were hostile to religion or regarded it as of little importance to the direction of society and government. After 1930, however, as these ideologies were forced on the defensive nearly everywhere, their adherents were obliged to reconsider their attitude toward religion —or at least to take it seriously into account as a social force they had underestimated. Was it not possible, they wondered, that people were now rushing with religious fervor to embrace fascism or communism for the very reason that this emotion had earlier been thwarted and denied? Were not these militant ideologies themselves a perverted answer to a religious need? The nineteenth-century ideologies of progress had allowed men's souls to atrophy, and in the fourth decade of the twentieth century they began to pay for it.

The religious, both Catholic and Protestant, found their consciences aroused by the human suffering which the Depression and fascism had brought about. They realized more sharply than they had before how closely people had come to associate the Christian churches with the propertied and the well-born and how, as a consequence, the urban working class had fallen away from organized religion. If the unemployed were turning by the thousands to fascism or to communism, it was partly because they felt abandoned by the churches; there were not enough priests or pastors who cared about their fate. The more socially conscious of Europe's religious leaders began to urge a great effort of re-Christianization: they preached the need of missionary activity within Europe itself to fill the spiritual void among the masses and to bring congregations back to the empty churches.

It was characteristic of the temper of the 1930's for a revival of religion to go hand in hand with a strong social conscience. The drive for social reform and the drive to restore theology to honor were often exemplified by the same individuals. This was particularly the case in France, where de-Christianization had gone furthest and where the revival of religious thinking attained the highest level. The separation of church from state in 1905 had been a harsh and vindictive measure but, in impoverishing Catholicism and driving it back on its own resources, both economic and spiritual, it had prepared the way for its rejuvenation. As opposed to the situation in Italy or Ireland, Poland or Portugal, where the church enjoyed official favor and did not need to change, in France both clergy and laity were obliged to reconsider their earlier certainties. In this respect twentieth-century French Catholicism offered a stirring example of what Toynbee called the "virtues of adversity."

Among the French religious thinkers whose influence extended far beyond the confines of their own country, three were outstanding: Gabriel Marcel, an eloquent opponent of the inhuman practices of industrial civilization; Emmanuel Mounier, founder of the left Catholic review *Esprit,* in which he expressed his "personalist" solution for the crisis in European values through reasserting the central importance of human personality; finally, Jacques Maritain, a "theologian of culture," who applied the old categories of Catholic thinking to the new problems of European politics and society. Maritain shared with Marcel an exemplary position as a convert to the Catholic faith; he shared with Mounier the fact that he had become a democrat and a leftist in his social views. These new allegiances suggest the key position of French Catholics on the eve of the Second World War as leaders both in re-Christianization and in reinterpreting the church's message in less conservative terms.

In the theological revival within the Protestant world, Germany and Switzerland took the lead. Here the most influential figure was the Swiss, Karl Barth. Just after the First World War, Barth had startled theologians with his epoch-making commentary on St. Paul's Epistle to the Romans. In 1921, he went to teach in Germany, where he remained for more than a decade until the advent of Hitler drove him back to Switzerland.

Barth's goal was to restore the fundamentals of Protestant doctrine as they had been enunciated in the sixteenth century. He was impatient with the "liberal" interpretation of dogma which more recently had come to dominance in the Calvinist and Lutheran churches. This, he argued, was merely a feeble compromise with Christian truth: it was because the clergy offered such thin fare that their congregations had deserted them. Barth's neoorthodoxy was a trumpet call for a return to first principles. It was also an appeal for the active practice of Christian charity through social endeavor among the de-Christianized working classes. Finally it preached uncompromising opposition to all forms of tyranny: it was indicative of the moral conviction behind neoorthodoxy that the pastors of the Confessional church who resisted Hitler most actively came from among those influenced by Barth rather than from among the "liberal" theologians.

While in the West both Catholicism and Protestantism were renewing themselves, in the Soviet Union the Orthodox church was slowly succumbing to Communist pressure. From the start, the Bolsheviks had set out to destroy Christianity. Militant atheists themselves, they saw nothing but evil in the "opiate" of religion, which tried to console the poor rather than arouse them to revolutionary protest against their lot. The new rulers of Russia persecuted the church; they shut its places of worship, even sometimes turning them into antireligious museums. They taught atheism in the schools and through the Communist party. After a decade and a half, such methods brought substantial results; the Orthodox church itself, whose clergy was frequently corrupt and uneducated and whose close association with the old order had damaged its prestige, failed to arouse among the people the spontaneous response of solidarity that supported Western Catholicism or Protestantism in their periods of persecution. By the mid-1930's, the new Soviet intelligentsia had grown to maturity without religion; the regime was so sure that atheism had come to stay that it even granted the church a grudging tolerance. Orthodox Christianity in Russia had become what it was to remain thereafter —the barely tolerated faith of a minority of women and old people.

IV

THE PEOPLE AND THE ARTS

The Cultural Reaction: Germany, Italy, the Soviet Union

Along with its other retrograde tendencies, nazism spelled reaction in the sphere of culture. Hitler and his henchmen rejected abstract art and experimental music, the modern style in architecture, and such novel practices as psychoanalysis. He drove the Freudians into exile—including, finally, Sigmund Freud himself who, one year before his death, was forced to leave Austria in 1938 on its annexation to the Reich. Hitler derided and hounded abroad Germany's leading architect, Walter Gropius, and such influential painters as Klee and Kandinsky. He imposed on

the country a barren neoclassicism in painting, sculpture, and architecture. This effort was expressed in monumental form when he opened in
Munich in 1937 a colossal House of German Art to contain the painting
and sculpture of which he approved. Across the street, in cramped and
squalid quarters, he ordered displayed as horrible examples the "decadent" art of the 1920's that he had banned. The art-loving citizens of
Munich, however, jammed the "decadent" show day after day and left
all but empty the echoing marble corridors of the official museum.

In Italy there reigned a similar "fascist" style. Cold, formal buildings,
intended to suggest the country's imperial mission, aped the symmetry
of the classical without its grace of proportion and decoration or its
honesty of workmanship. Sham classicism as a cultural manifestation of
fascist rule did not surprise Europeans very much: it seemed of a piece
with the rest of the system. They were more surprised to see the Soviet
Union turning in a similar direction. Here again, architecture took the
lead: in 1931, the competition for the new Palace of the Soviets was
won by a totally unimaginative and tasteless design for a neoclassic sky-
scraper looking rather like a wedding cake.

This turn to artistic conventionality in Russia was one aspect of the
general imposition of Stalinist orthodoxy. Stalin, like Hitler, hated what
was experimental or demanded an effort of understanding; so he laid
down the law that architecture must follow traditional styles, painting
must be pictorial and "realistic," music must be tuneful, and writing
must deal with optimistic themes calculated to inspire confidence in
the workers' state. The guiding principle was "socialist realism"—a formal notion of reality that would further socialist goals, a far cry from
the tolerance or even welcoming of artistic experiment that had characterized the Bolsheviks in their first years of rule. It seemed almost miracu-
lous that works of any merit at all succeeded in emerging from such a
setting. Most of them were esthetically worthless—propagandist novels
and plays, pompous oil paintings of revolutionary incidents, clumsy,
overdecorated buildings. Yet occasionally something first-rate broke
through the official limitations: Prokofiev continued to write witty, lyric
music, and the novelist Mikhail Sholokhov, in *And Quiet Flows the Don*
(1929), produced a work of "socialist realism" that could lay claim to
epic qualities.

The Popular Arts and the Classic Age of the Films

Before cultural blight settled over the Reich, the country had enjoyed to
the full one final fling of splendid popular art. In *The Three-Penny Opera*
(1928), Bertolt Brecht, who wrote the words, and Kurt Weill, who composed the music, adapted the theme of the English eighteenth-century
Beggars' Opera to the contemporary milieu of postwar Germany: it was
bright, it was cynical, it was full of bitter social satire. From Hitler's

standpoint it was certainly "decadent," and after 1933 both Brecht and Weill were to go into exile.

The success of *The Three-Penny Opera*—which was not only a popular triumph but also won "highbrow" acclaim—suggests the new attitude toward art and entertainment which was to become characteristic of the 1930's. During the previous decade, these two worlds had remained separate: art was avant-garde and for the elite—entertainment was conventional and for the masses. In the 1930's, the two tended to come together, as the new interest in the common man implied. While "high" art was becoming simpler and more direct, the popular arts were acquiring greater esthetic standing.

This was particularly apparent in the motion picture. By the 1930's, the cinema had perfected its techniques; it had long since developed into an art form in its own right. The socially conscious temper of the decade encouraged directors to treat large themes and to produce films of both intellectual and esthetic importance. In general, the British film industry remained devoted to pure entertainment—but even here such *émigrés* as the Hungarian-born Alexander Korda after 1933 turned to subjects of wider range. In Germany, Nazi oppression snuffed out a promising art which in the previous era had produced such early masterpieces as *The Cabinet of Dr. Caligari* and *Metropolis*. In Russia, the Stalinist veto on originality descended later on the films than it did in other fields: Sergei Eisenstein had time to create both *Potemkin* and *Alexander Nevsky*—the latter with music by Prokofiev—before the iron hand of the dictator cut off his work in the middle of his slow-moving and turgid *Ivan the Terrible*. It was in France, however, that the cinema of the 1930's produced its greatest triumphs—in René Clair's *A nous la liberté* (1931), with its characteristic fantasy of liberation from the industrial system; in Jacques Feyder's *Carnival in Flanders* (1935); and in Jean Renoir's *Grand Illusion* (1937), one of the most telling, because one of the quietest, of antiwar films. In films such as these, and in the directors who conceived them, Europeans were to discover in retrospect a classic age of the cinema.

Readings

For an understanding of the over-all development of French culture in the period, consult the collaborative work: Julian Park, ed., *The Culture of France in Our Time* (1954), and for an analysis of French social thought, see H. Stuart Hughes, *The Obstructed Path* (1968). Although there are no corresponding volumes covering Britain and Germany, Walter Kaufmann, ed., *Existentialism from Dostoyevsky to Sartre* (1956), gives selections from a number of the most influential German thinkers.

Historical speculation on the European crisis is dealt with in Pitirim A. Sorokin, *Social Philosophies of an Age of Crisis* (1950), Hans Meyerhoff, ed., *Contemporary Philosophies of History* (1958), and H. Stuart Hughes, *Oswald*

Spengler: A Critical Estimate, rev. ed. (1962). For a sympathetic introduction to the work of the leading economist of the period, see R. F. Harrod, *The Life of John Maynard Keynes* (1951).

In the field of imaginative literature, Henry C. Hatfield, *Modern German Literature* (1966), traces the careers of the most influential German writers, and Henri Peyre, *The Contemporary French Novel* (1955), deals with parallel developments in France. The theological revival is covered in a selection of texts with brief introductions by Will Herberg, ed., *Four Existentialist Theologians* (1958).

For the most important of the new popular arts, see Béla Balázs, *Theory of the Film: Character and Growth of a New Art* (1953).

The Road to Catastrophe, 1935–1939

Chapter Twelve

Contrary to the First World War, whose origins were extremely complex and responsibility for which was spread among a number of nations, the Second World War was the work of one man, Adolf Hitler. Of Europe's national leaders Hitler alone brought about the conflict. The only serious controversy among historians has occurred over the question of whether or not he wanted to accomplish his purposes by war and precipitated it at a moment of his own choosing. Certainly Hitler had no clear timetable—the documents alleged to present such a schedule are contradictory both with each other and with the course that events actually pursued—and it seems plausible that (like most statesmen) he would have preferred to get his way without resort to arms. He embarked on his earlier adventures uncertain as to exactly how far he would go and prepared to withdraw if international opposition got too tough. In addition, a gradual abdication of responsibility by the French and a peculiarly inept alternation between conciliation and resistance on the part of the British played directly into his hand.

When all this has been said, however, the fact remains that Hitler's goals at the very least involved the subjugation of three European nations—Austria, Czechoslovakia, and Poland—and that by the time he had gotten to the third of these, the French and British had no idea where he would stop. The *Führer* made no secret of the fact that restless expansion and eventual hegemony over Europe were essential to the Nazi dynamic. And after his initial gambles had succeeded, he was quite frank about stating (both in public and in private) that he would not

Troops of the army of War Minister Ras Moulougete—which had a total strength of 100,000 men—parade and demonstrate their loyalty before the palace of Emperor Haile Selassie in Addis Ababa, Ethiopia, November 1935. COURTESY BROWN BROTHERS.

shrink from war in the future. No other national leader was anywhere near as determined a bully as he. All the others whose aggressiveness or ineptitude encouraged the drift toward war—even Mussolini—were only auxiliaries in the process.

The war was the climax of five years of blundering and bluff, of the irresolute diplomacy of the Western powers pitted against Hitler's demonic force and unswerving dedication to his goal. Its main origins lay in the successive stages of Nazi expansion. Yet the most important single series of episodes was the Spanish Civil War—that tragic prelude to the major international conflict—in which Hitler played only a secondary part and in which the chief actors and sufferers were the Spanish themselves.

I
REARMAMENT AND
THE RHINELAND

The first major act of aggression breaking the false calm of the post-Locarno years did not come from Germany but from Japan in 1931, with the conquest of Manchuria; six years later, this conquest was to expand into an undeclared war against China and eventually to merge into the Pacific phase of the Second World War itself. The failure of the League of Nations to stop the Japanese advance marked the beginning of its decline.

The Vogue of "Collective Security":
Barthou and Litvinov

In the early 1930's, however, the League's weakness was not nearly so obvious as it was to appear in retrospect. Indeed, the three years between Hitler's appointment as German chancellor in early 1933 and the last decisive action in the League's history at the end of 1935 were a period of intense interest in maintaining peace through the collective action of the European powers.

This vogue of what came to be called "collective security" was partly based on illusion: millions of peace-minded people in the democracies of the West hoped that it would be possible to restrain the Nazis through moral pressure alone. It was also based on the fact that Hitler's coming to power required three years to produce its logical results: the new international alignment had not yet crystallized. In 1933 and 1934, the two fascist powers still stood far apart, and the pattern of Nazi expansion was as yet unrevealed. The other European powers did not know how seriously to take Hitler's frantic rhetoric: they still did not realize that he meant quite literally the program for German domination of Europe which he had outlined in *Mein Kampf*.

At the start, moreover, Hitler tried to reassure the statesmen of Europe. However he might bluster at home, abroad his diplomats spoke more suavely, leaving their hearers with the impression that the new German regime would be modest in its demands. True, Hitler's predecessors, Brüning and Papen, had already succeeded in removing the worst of the burdens that the Treaty of Versailles had laid on the German people: six months before the Nazis came to power, reparations had disappeared. When Mussolini proposed that the French and British join with him in a Four-Power Pact with Hitler to maintain the peace, there seemed to be no good reason for refusing. In July, 1933, such a pact was in fact solemnly signed. In retrospect its clauses sound strangely irrelevant. The final text of the treaty merely reaffirmed the spirit of the 1920's by engaging each power to continue to respect its undertakings under the Covenant of the League, the Locarno Treaty, and the Kellogg-Briand Pact. But Mussolini's original concept had been far more "revisionist," and France's Eastern allies were alarmed at the prospect of the Great Powers settling their differences at the expense of the small.

Two months later the Germans cast off the mask. In October, Hitler announced that he was withdrawing both from the Disarmament Conference—whose nearly two years of labor had failed to produce a satisfactory formula for German military equality—and from the League of Nations. These two actions produced a preliminary awakening on the part of Europe's statesmen—the first of a series of brusque shocks that were to punctuate the history of the next six years. In France, Hitler's moves occasioned only passing activity; in the Soviet Union they produced a major policy change.

In Paris, as a side effect of the riots of February, 1934, and the formation of Doumergue's government of national union, for the first time since Briand's retirement there came to power a foreign minister with a clear notion of his goals. Louis Barthou was an elder statesman and a solid republican of conservative views. His foreign policy was simple: to build a wall against Nazi expansion by strengthening France's alliances in East Central Europe. By associating the Poles and the members of the Little Entente still more closely with France's policy, he hoped to convince Hitler that aggression would not pay. Barthou had barely begun this reconstruction of his country's alliance system when he was killed in October, 1934, as he was vainly trying to shield the king of Yugoslavia from an assassin's bullet. His death seriously weakened the policy he had personified: under Premiers Flandin and Laval, the French foreign ministry showed less determination to resist Hitler's international aims.

To the Soviet Union, on the contrary, German withdrawal from the League came as a heaven-sent opportunity to gain international respectability. Germany had not been a year absent from that body when, in September, 1934, partly owing to Barthou's persuasions, Russia joined the organization which in the previous decade had kept it in quarantine.

The moral seemed clear: with Germany out and Russia in, who could doubt which country was the more devoted to peace? The Soviet representative at Geneva, Maxim Litvinov, underlined the lesson by preaching more strenuously than anyone else the doctrine of collective security. Litvinov was an Old Bolshevik of the international type; with an English wife and strong ties to the West, he was ideally equipped to present Soviet policy in a new and attractive guise. This change helps explain the appeal of the Popular Front and the prestige that Russia enjoyed among European democrats in the years 1934–1936.

The First Breaches of the Versailles and Locarno Treaties

In March, 1935, Hitler formally announced that he would no longer abide by the disarmament clauses of the Treaty of Versailles. He restored the system of peacetime conscription which Germany had employed up to 1918 and which characterized such important continental powers as France, Italy, and the Soviet Union. There was a certain consistency in Hitler's contention that he was merely trying to raise Germany to a position of equality with other European nations. By their failure to disarm, he implied, they had themselves made German rearmament inevitable.

Partly for this reason the reaction to Germany's unilateral action was relatively mild. Clandestine German rearmament had been going on for years before Hitler came to power; the only novelty in the 1935 declaration was the reintroduction of conscription. The League of Nations, of course, condemned the action. A week before the League meeting, representatives of France, Britain, and Italy, in a conference at the Italian lakeside resort of Stresa, had agreed on common action against the German menace, but this "Stresa Front" proved as transitory as that other Italian initiative in international affairs, Mussolini's Four-Power Pact. Within a matter of weeks, each of its signatories had gone its own way. France had completed Barthou's design by signing a military alliance with the Soviet Union. Rather more serious, in a vain gesture of conciliation, Britain had made a separate naval agreement with Germany, which permitted the latter to build up to 35 per cent of British strength. It was scarcely surprising that the French felt betrayed.

In the meantime, the third of the Stresa partners, Italy, had continued preparations for the conquest of Ethiopia. By the autumn of 1935, the Stresa Front was shattered. With the powers divided and their attention riveted on Africa, Hitler was in an excellent position to take decisive action once more. On March 7, 1936—scarcely a year after his denunciation of the disarmament clauses in the Versailles Treaty—he sent German troops into the Rhineland cities which the same treaty had demilitarized. They were greeted by delirious crowds: at last Germany seemed to have attained full international equality. Hitler waited, nervously wondering whether his gamble would succeed.

But the French army did not move. Although it was still stronger than the German, its strategy had become exclusively defensive, and it was quite unprepared to march into the Reich. The government, moreover, was weak and hesitant, merely trying to muddle through the remaining few weeks until the May elections which would bring the Popular Front to power. The Italians were alienated—the British were unimpressed—in the end the French and the League of Nations itself were reduced to ineffective protests against this breach not only of the Treaty of Versailles, which Germany had accepted under duress, but of the Locarno Pact, to which the Reich had freely consented.

Hitler's troops stayed in the Rhineland. The first—and the best—opportunity had been lost for nipping Nazi aggression in the bud. After the crucial year 1936 it was too late.

II
THE ETHIOPIAN WAR

Meanwhile, the other fascist dictator, Benito Mussolini, had finally given free rein to the vocation for conquest which he had been talking about for a decade and a half, but which until now he had prudently held in check. No doubt the example of Hitler helped to spur him on. The effect of Mussolini's actions in 1935 and 1936 was certainly to bring about the alignment of his country with Nazi Germany which the British and French had earlier been fortunate enough to avoid.

Italy's Imperial Disappointments

In the scramble for Africa at the end of the nineteenth century, Italy had gained the least. Repulsed by the forces of the emperor of Ethiopia in 1896, the Italians had been obliged to content themselves with two barren strips of coastline in East Africa and the equally barren shore of Libya which they had added in 1911. This was a meager "empire": along with Italy's disappointments at the Paris Peace Conference, the memory of colonial repulses had rankled all through the 1920's in the minds of Italian nationalists.

The continued independence of Ethiopia seemed to stand as a permanent taunt to Italy's martial valor and abilities as a colonial power. The great defeat of 1896—one of the worst that Europeans had ever suffered at the hands of "natives"—clamored for vengeance. Since the French acquisition of Morocco in 1912, Ethiopia had ranked as the only important area in Africa which had never submitted to colonial conquest. What could be more natural, then, than for Mussolini to set out to occupy nearly forty years later the great mountain empire which Italians had so long regarded as rightfully theirs?

The European attitude toward colonial wars, however, had changed. The better part of a generation had passed without further acquisition of colonies. Indeed, the tide had turned: with native nationalist movements springing up in so many parts of Asia and Africa, the problem for Europeans was now to hold what they already had rather than to acquire new territories. Along with increased difficulty in ruling the colonies had come a new guilt about doing so at all; the Socialist parties in particular were turning to a militant anticolonialism. Mussolini was much mistaken when he thought that other Europeans would regard an Italian war of conquest in the 1930's as casually as they would have in the 1890's. Colonial war no longer was what everybody else was doing.

The Hoare-Laval Agreement

At the outset, however, it seemed as if the Duce would succeed. In January, 1935, he had persuaded the French foreign minister (soon to be premier), Pierre Laval, to agree to a free hand for Italy in Ethiopia. But in the summer, as Italy's war preparations became increasingly obvious, the British public began to take alarm; support and sympathy for the Ethiopians were almost universal. In September, the British foreign secretary, Sir Samuel Hoare, gave public assurance before the Assembly of the League that Britain would stand behind it in resisting Italian aggression. Early the next month, after a dramatic debate, the annual conference of the Labor party abandoned its traditional pacifist stand and swung around to support of "sanctions." Finally, in November, the Tory-dominated national government fought the parliamentary election campaign on a platform of internationalism and the League, and won it by depriving Labor of this popular issue.

On October 3, Italy had launched its invasion of Ethiopia. Within little more than a week, the Council of the League had declared Italy an aggressor, and its Assembly had voted economic sanctions in the form of embargoes under the terms of Article 16 of the Covenant. On November 18—four days after the British election—sanctions actually went into effect. In Europe, opinion seemed united against Italy and behind the League, and in Ethiopia the emperor's forces were putting up a stout resistance. But the backers of the League had failed to reckon with the wily Laval. In early December the French prime minister lured Hoare to Paris and persuaded him to accept a plausible-sounding compromise under which, either directly or through veiled annexation, the emperor of Ethiopia would be obliged to cede two-thirds of his land to Italy. Hoare himself was not too hard to convince; the British cabinet, however, might make difficulties. To avoid this, Laval allowed the details of his plan to leak to the French press.

To his great surprise, news of the deal aroused a storm of indignation in both London and Paris. Laval could never understand how his opponents' minds worked, and that there might be other motivations in foreign affairs besides narrow concern for the national interest. Hoare was swept from office on a wave of outraged protest; Baldwin saved his government only by sacrificing his foreign minister and replacing him by the young and handsome Anthony Eden, who had already made a name for himself as British representative at Geneva. The following month Laval himself had to go. It appeared that the forces of international virtue had triumphed all along the line.

The Consequences: the End of the League and the Rome-Berlin Axis

This was not the end of the story. Despite the changes of ministers, Britain and France still refused to impose the one form of sanctions that would really hurt, an embargo on oil. Britain seemed bellicose—at one point its Mediterranean fleet was even put on the alert—but it did nothing decisive. France was even less militant, the French Right arguing quite sensibly that with German power growing, it was folly to antagonize Italy. The sanctions that the League had voted in the autumn proved ineffective, or perhaps even worse than ineffective, since they infuriated Mussolini by denying him much-needed goods, but failed to cripple his war effort. By the spring of 1936, the Italians had broken Ethiopian resistance: on May 5, they marched into the capital, Addis Ababa, and a few days later Mussolini bestowed on his king the new title of emperor.

Such was the first real war that Europe had known since the sequels to the First World War had come to an end in 1922. The Ethiopian conflict introduced four years of alarms following closely one on another until at last the major European powers themselves went to war. More important, it ended one international institution and inaugurated another. It killed the League: the failure of sanctions against Italy was too flagrant to be explained away by the pious phrases of internationalism; after 1936, it was impossible to consider the League seriously as an instrumentality for keeping the peace. Simultaneously with the disappearance of Geneva as a center of influence in foreign affairs, there emerged a new alignment between Fascist Italy and Nazi Germany. Almost overnight, what came to be called the Rome-Berlin Axis took its place as the strongest force in Europe, for the experience of French and British hostility—of being considered one after the other the bad boys of Europe—finally drove the two fascist leaders together. In his conquest of Ethiopia, Mussolini had received understanding and support from Germany alone; similarly, in his remilitarization of the Rhineland, Hitler had found the Italians to be the only ones who accepted his act as natural and inevitable. The Rome-Berlin Axis did not come into effect officially until the following October, but by the summer of 1936 it already existed in fact—as the next great international crisis, the outbreak of the Spanish Civil War, was so amply to prove.

III

THE SPANISH CIVIL WAR

*The Origins: Alfonso XIII and the Dictatorship
of Primo de Rivera*

Spain's twentieth-century time of troubles began with its defeat by the United States in the war of 1898. The Spanish-American War destroyed the last lingering illusions about the country's traditional greatness. It not only stripped Spain of nearly all its colonies and ended what remained of its great-power status; it also revealed how many aspects of the national life were corrupt or decayed or functioning badly.

The war exposed in all its nakedness the selfishness and inefficiency of the small minority of wealthy or aristocratic people who, behind the façade of a constitutional monarchy, actually ruled the nation. The war also became the starting point for mounting revolutionary agitation in three distinct forms. There was first the working-class movement, which came later to Spain than to France or Italy, since Spanish industrialization was less far advanced. Then there was the growing demand for autonomy in areas whose speech and tradition differed from the dominant Castilian, more particularly in the two regions bordering on France, the Basque provinces to the west and Catalonia to the east. Finally there was a marked resurgence of anticlericalism, which directed its attacks against the vast wealth that the church had acquired in the last quarter of the nineteenth century. According to popular rumor, the Jesuits alone controlled one-third of the capital of the country, and although this was unproved, it was undeniable that the association of the church with the upper classes in the minds of the Spanish people made for a falling away from Catholicism and a widespread loss of faith during the early years of the new century.

These three currents of discontent converged in the city of Barcelona, the Catalan capital. Enterprising, modern, oriented toward France—with its speech in fact very close to the ancient language of the southern French—Barcelona epitomized the new or centrifugal energies that were threatening to tear apart the traditional Spanish state. In 1909, the city was shaken by five days of wild rioting and convent burning. Thus a quarter of a century before the Civil War the pattern was already established that would make Barcelona the focal point of autonomist, anticlerical, working-class protest during Spain's years of fratricidal struggle.

Spain avoided involvement in the First World War. But isolation from the rest of Europe during the great conflict intensified its existing difficulties by creating a boom in certain sectors of its economy and a depression in others. The state of military alert in which the country lived notably strengthened the already powerful influence of the army in the national life. This influence was reinforced after the war by the five-year campaign for the subjugation of the Riff tribes in the Spanish zone of

Morocco. It began in 1921 with another great humiliation—Abd el-Krim's victory at Anual, which destroyed the bulk of the Spanish forces stationed in North Africa—and it ended in 1926 only after the French had intervened and sent a powerful army to support Spain's ineffective work of repression.

Meanwhile the military—exasperated by successive defeats and feeling unappreciated by the nation—had seized control of the home country. They were encouraged by the reigning sovereign, Alfonso XIII, who had been a king literally since the day of his birth and who cherished anachronistic ideas of the possibilities of monarchy in the twentieth century. Alfonso hoped that if the parliamentary constitution was destroyed, he himself would become the real power in the country. Hence he did nothing to oppose the military coup d'état that brought General Primo de Rivera to power in September, 1923.

Primo de Rivera, however, was not prepared merely to serve the king: he wanted to rule Spain himself. Unfortunately he had no clear notion of what he intended to accomplish. Aside from aligning the country diplomatically with Fascist Italy, he allowed it to drift; under the surface of a military dictatorship, Spanish life remained as anarchic and invertebrate as before. Finally, the king himself grew tired of his "strong man." In January, 1930, he dismissed him, and the majority of Spaniards rejoiced, but when two months later Primo de Rivera died in Paris, the full consequences of his dismissal descended on Alfonso's head. With the dictator gone and buried, the Spanish had lost the target of their hatred, and they turned on the king instead. Alfonso's effort to rule through another general failed utterly. After a year of hesitation, in February, 1931, he announced the restoration of the constitution and, as an initial token of the return of liberty, he scheduled the election of municipal councillors for mid-April.

The election campaign quickly mounted into a full-scale national consultation. The leaders of the various republican parties—whose strength had grown steadily in the last half-decade—concerted their efforts and converted the municipal elections into an informal plebiscite on the monarchy. When polling day came, they had already won over the cities. While these voted almost solidly for republican candidates, the countryside remained generally monarchist. Yet the vote of Madrid and Barcelona and the other major centers made the greatest impression: shaken by what appeared to be a tidal wave of opposition, the king left the country without abdicating. On April 14, 1931, the Spanish Republic was proclaimed.

The Republic: Azaña, Gil Robles,
and the Election of 1936

It was easier to proclaim a republic than to make it a reality. The Constituent Assembly, or Cortes, which assembled in July was divided at least four ways in its interpretation of what the new regime meant. To the left were those who wanted social revolution; in the center left was the party of Republican Action, liberal moderates who followed the one true statesman whom the revolution produced, Manuel Azaña; then came the scheming and corrupt party of the Radicals; finally on the right were the clericals, who accepted the Republic in their public professions but despised it in their hearts.

For the first two years of the Republic's history, under Azaña's leadership, the new regime seemed to be making some progress in developing a coherent program out of these contrasting tendencies. Azaña's government acted constructively: it curbed the army, granted autonomy to Catalonia and to the Basque provinces, and stimulated popular education. But it failed to take the dramatic action toward breaking up the great estates of the south and the southwest that would stir the popular imagination; during 1932 and 1933, land reform proceeded at a very slow pace. And by their army reforms Azaña's ministers brought down upon themselves and upon the Republic the implacable opposition of the military. A revolt of high-ranking army officers in August, 1932—which the government suppressed without difficulty—gave a foretaste of the far graver threat that was to come four years later.

At the end of 1933, with the dissolution of the Constituent Assembly, the first elections for a regular Cortes returned a conservative majority. There followed the *bienio negro*—the "black" two years of clerical reaction. At first the outlines of this second phase of the Republic's history were far from clear. The most influential leader seemed to be the Radical party chief, Alejandro Lerroux, who steered a tortuous center course. But as the government and the Cortes began to reveal their true colors —as they undid one by one the reforms of the Azaña era—it became apparent that the most powerful man in the country was not Lerroux at all but the clerical leader José Maria Gil Robles. Under Robles' skillful prodding Spain was moving toward the quasi-fascism that already existed in Portugal and that in these very years was being established in Austria.

To stop this threat, the parties of the Left and left Center banded together for the elections of February, 1936. As their counterparts in France were simultaneously doing, they formed a Popular Front which embraced groups ranging from the Azaña type to revolutionary Socialists and Anarcho-Syndicalists. This coalition won a narrow victory. Azaña's friends returned to power. For a moment it seemed as though Spain was merely returning to the situation which had existed before the reaction set in at the end of 1933.

But to think that was to mistake the dynamics of the Popular Front. The electoral campaign had released a great wave of revolutionary enthusiasm, which was not to be stopped by prudent counsels of moderation. The extreme left parties in the victorious coalition had not formed its majority—but they had provided its fighting force. And this was driving toward social revolution. Brushing aside the temperate policies of

Azaña and his like, the Left took matters into its own hands and resorted to direct action. In the spring of 1936, land seizures, revolutionary strikes, and even murder became everyday occurrences; outrages against churches and the clergy grew more and more frequent. Finally, in July, with the assassination of a prominent reactionary deputy, army leaders and the conservatives raised the standard of counterrevolution and began to converge on Madrid.

The Civil War: the Military Aspect

The Spanish Civil War can be regarded from at least three different standpoints. It can be treated as a civil war in the narrower sense—a desperate, bloody struggle which lasted nearly three years and periodically bogged down into a trench stalemate not unlike that which the First World War produced. It can be viewed as an international conflict—a dress rehearsal for the Second World War. Finally it can be seen as a battle of ideologies—a social revolution aborted not only by the forces of military and clerical reaction but also, in paradoxical fashion, by a party which itself professed revolutionary aims, the Spanish Communists and their Soviet chiefs. The Spanish Civil War was each and all of these.

From the military standpoint, the Civil War began on July 17 with the revolt of an important garrison in Spanish Morocco and the arrival of General Francisco Franco from the Canary Islands to take command. The next day, a number of mainland generals took up arms. The insurgent forces rapidly dominated the south and west—the more backward half of the country—and this remained throughout the war the headquarters of their strength. But it was in Burgos to the north that at the end of July they set up their Junta of National Defense, which ten weeks later named General Franco chief (*Caudillo*) of the Spanish state.

Franco himself was a wily man, small, heavy-set, and imperturbable in manner. His leadership of the Nationalist cause had come about somewhat accidentally; the more prominent general who was scheduled to direct the movement had been killed in an airplane accident just at its start. But once installed in power, Franco proved well equipped to bind together the heterogeneous coalition that was assaulting the Republic. With no clear ideology of his own, except for respect for tradition and discipline, Franco was sufficiently skeptical of all ideologies to take his own followers no more seriously than they deserved, particularly the Spanish fascist party, the Falange, which provided much of the drive and enthusiasm behind the Nationalist cause but certainly did not account for the bulk of its strength. The majority of Franco's followers came, rather, from the various monarchist factions, and more generally, from landowners and propertied people and those loyal to the Catholic church.

By November, the Nationalists—who began the war with the great advantage of having most of the regular army on their side—had reduced the defenders of the Republic to approximately the positions they were to occupy for the next two years. The Republicans were holding at bay the forces besieging Madrid, from which the government had fled to the east coast city of Valencia. Farther north along the coast, Barcelona ranked as the third major center of Republican loyalty. A fourth area of strength, but isolated from the others, were the Basque provinces, conservative by tradition, but which had thrown in their lot with the Republic in an effort to preserve their newly won autonomy. The Republican forces were thus on the defensive nearly everywhere, and they held a smaller part of the country than did the insurgents, but in falling back on the triangle Madrid-Valencia-Barcelona they at least derived some benefit from basing themselves on the most modern and industrial part of the nation.

The Republican coalition was as ill-assorted as the one which Franco led. Once the war began—more particularly, once the government decided to arm the workers for its defense—control slipped from the hands of the moderate democrats. In early September, the appointment as prime minister of the left Socialist Francisco Largo Caballero marked the triumph within the Republican camp of the forces pressing for social revolution. But even the revolutionary Left was much divided: besides the Socialists, there were the Communists, the Trotskyite POUM,* and the Anarcho-Syndicalists. The last of these represented the strongest single power among the Spanish people—a force characterized by spontaneous revolutionary enthusiasm and a wild cult of liberty. In Catalonia in particular, the Anarcho-Syndicalist drive reinforced the Catalan autonomist spirit to make the city of Barcelona the focus of revolutionary sentiment on the Republican side.

In this fashion—after the original momentum of Franco's forces had been stopped—the war settled into something approaching a stalemate, in which intervention from outside, and with it the pressure of foreign ideology on both camps, was gradually to change the character of the Civil War almost beyond recognition.

The Civil War: Foreign Intervention

It was obvious from the beginning that the two fascist powers, Italy and Germany, sympathized with the Nationalist insurgents. It was equally obvious that Léon Blum's new government in France sympathized with the sister Popular Front that was defending itself across the Pyrenees. Although Hitler and Mussolini actively aided Franco's cause, the French Popular Front restricted itself to semiclandestine encourage-

---

* *Partido Obrero de Unificación Marxista* (Workers' Party of Marxist Unification).

ment of the shipment of war materials to Madrid and Barcelona. In this
difference of policy lay the crucial difficulty that eventually was to spell ruin for the Spanish Republic.

Italy and Germany scarcely made a secret of what they were doing. Under the guise of "volunteers," Mussolini even sent regular ground troops to swell Franco's forces, although Hitler limited himself to providing aviation and tank units and other specialist personnel—using Spain as a proving ground for testing his new military equipment. Against all this the British protested vigorously. With a conservative government in power and the people profoundly divided over Spain, Britain's leaders tried to steer a strictly neutral course. They pressed for a general nonintervention agreement among the major European powers, and they were particularly incensed over acts of "piracy" in the Mediterranean by unidentified submarines, which were universally suspected to be Italian. After nearly a year of British prodding, the representatives of the interested powers, meeting at the little Swiss town of Nyon, in September, 1937, agreed on a joint Mediterranean patrol; "piracy" abruptly came to an end. International negotiation proved far less successful in limiting the arrival of "volunteers." Mussolini agreed to their withdrawal only toward the end of the war when they had already accomplished their purpose and Franco's victory was assured.

One reason why the French government found it impossible to aid the Spanish Republic was Britain's neutral stand. Secondly, France itself was grievously divided. Indeed, the Spanish Civil War was paralleled by a "cold civil war" among the French people: partisans and enemies of the Popular Front lined up in similar fashion in their attitude toward Spain and found in its armed conflict a projection of their own domestic struggle. Faced with this bitterness and division of feeling among the French people, Blum could take no decisive action. After his fall in June, 1937, his successors were less concerned than he had been for the fate of the Spanish Republic; by its failure to go to the aid of Spain, the French Popular Front had irremediably undermined its own ideological position.

With the default of France, the role of protector of the Spanish Republic devolved on the Soviet Union. The Russians were slower than the Italians or the Germans to intervene in the Spanish Civil War; they did not act until October. But when they did, it was as massively as geographical remoteness and limitations of transport permitted. Like Hitler, Stalin sent no ground troops, but he provided war materials of all sorts, plus technical advisers, pilots, drivers—and political commissars. The last of these, who came from among the leaders of both Soviet and Western European communism, had as their task not only to advise and guide the Spanish Republic but also to indoctrinate the International Brigades which first went into action in November, 1936, in the defense of Madrid.

The International Brigades consisted of volunteers in the true rather than in the Italian sense. Those who enrolled in them were mostly young idealists of democratic or leftist convictions—antifascist *émigrés* from Italy or Germany and also Englishmen and Americans. Just over half were Communists when they enlisted, but since Communists served as the political commissars of the Brigades, a larger number fell under Communist ideological influence during their Spanish service. The historical importance of the International Brigades extended far beyond their strictly military role: their chief significance was in swelling the legend of the Civil War as a struggle for democracy and in sustaining the sympathy for the Spanish Republic among Western European intellectuals which so strongly marked the literary atmosphere of the late 1930's. The legend gathered particularly around the defense of Madrid as it lay under attack from the converging columns of "the four insurgent generals" (in the words of a haunting Civil War song) while a "fifth column" waited to betray the city from within. For Italian antifascists there was also the stirring memory of the defeat they helped inflict on Mussolini's "volunteers" at Guadalajara in the spring of 1937. In the minds of Italians, still more than in those of the French, the Spanish Civil War provided a welcome arena for fighting out domestic quarrels on foreign soil.

On both sides, foreign intervention changed the character of the opposing coalitions. Mussolini's and Hitler's help brought Franco closer to fascism; Stalin's aid to the Republic gave its defense a Communist tone which had been almost wholly absent at the beginning. Influence from abroad operated most unevenly in the two camps. In Franco's case, it was not decisive: despite his dependence on Italy and Germany, the Caudillo kept the Nationalist movement firmly in hand, and its essentially Spanish character remained intact. With the Republic, it was quite different: President Azaña and Prime Minister Largo Caballero found it impossible to resist Soviet pressure. They had no recourse; no other champion had come forward. As they became ever more dependent on Russian and Communist aid, they found their cause perverted and at the last almost completely deprived of its spontaneous Spanish character.

The Civil War: the Ideological Transformation

Soviet intervention in the Spanish Civil War had the contrary effect from what might have been anticipated. It did not strengthen the forces of social revolution. Rather it stopped the revolution in its tracks by sacrificing everything else to the goal of military efficiency.

At the beginning of the war, the workers in a number of areas had taken matters into their own hands by seizing control of factories, landed estates, and even commercial enterprises. This grass-roots socialization had proceeded in haphazard fashion—Republican Spain was far from being a socialist state when Communist influence began to be felt at the end of 1936—but the momentum of the embattled Republic was pushing strongly in that direction, particularly in Catalonia. The arrival of Soviet "advisers" halted all this, for Stalin had decreed a policy of no socialism in Spain in an effort to reassure the Spanish middle class and Western "capitalist" opinion.

Abroad, this pragmatic and even cynical policy failed. The "moderation" that the Soviet Union imposed in Spain was so obviously calculated that it carried little conviction to Western conservatives. It merely disillusioned a number of Republican sympathizers like George Orwell, who returned home bitterly disappointed with the treatment that the Spanish revolutionaries had received. Within Spain, it stimulated the growth of a peculiar sort of communism. At the beginning of the war, the Spanish Communists had been insignificant; they had been far weaker than the Socialists and the Anarcho-Syndicalists. Now, with the possibilities of protection that Soviet aid afforded, large numbers of middle-class people who had been frightened by working-class agitation enrolled in the Communist party. It became an ideological catchall and a refuge for the timorous and the opportunistic.

Meanwhile within the government, some middle-class political leaders began to cooperate with the Spanish Communists against Prime Minister Largo Caballero. For this strange alliance there were compelling practical arguments: the Soviet and Communist organizers were the only people in Spain who could provide the bureaucratic competence and the military discipline that the Republic required if it was ever to survive against its better trained enemies; as the indispensable source of funds and supplies, moreover, Stalin's deputies had an unanswerable argument for getting the last word.

In the early months of 1937, Communist influence spread relentlessly throughout Republican Spain. On the fighting fronts, units of the Communist-trained People's Army began to replace the less disciplined workers' militia. The showdown between the two came in the streets of Barcelona at the beginning of May. After three days of sporadic fighting, the revolutionary formations of the POUM and the Anarcho-Syndicalists were overwhelmed. Later the same month, the able, hard-driving Juan Negrín, who was convinced of the necessity of working with the Communists, replaced Largo Caballero as prime minister. The POUM was dissolved and its leaders imprisoned or killed. The representatives of the Anarcho-Syndicalists were dropped from the government. Thereafter, until the end of the war, the Soviet Union and the Communists were firmly in control: with bourgeois politicians like Negrín cooperating with them, they used their dominance of the army, the police, and the propaganda department to mold according to their own desires the whole Republican cause.

Franco's Victory and the Balance Sheet of Terror

In mid-1938, the Soviet Union decided to abandon the Spanish Republic. The policy of moderation, Stalin realized, was not working; it had not persuaded the great Western democracies to come to the help of Spain.

Hence he determined to cut his losses and to abandon the struggle. Although few realized it at the time, this decision appears as the first sign of Soviet disillusionment with the four-year-old policy of Western orientation, of "collective security" and Popular Fronts, that would lead eventually to a cynical settlement with the Nazis in August, 1939.

With the end of Soviet aid to the Republic, Franco's armies broke the stalemate and began to roll once more toward victory. In December, 1938, they mounted their great offensive against Catalonia: the following January, Barcelona fell; Madrid and Valencia, whose position was now hopeless, fought on until the end of March. With their fall, the Civil War ended. Hundreds of thousands of Republican soldiers and refugees poured over the Pyrenees to a miserable life of internment in France.

Franco had won, and the quasi-fascist government he had established was recognized by the Western democracies. Although France and Britain and the United States bowed to the accomplished fact, within those countries debate over the Civil War continued to rage. Those who had favored Franco spoke of his followers as "Christian crusaders" against "bolshevism." The far more numerous apologists for the Republic depicted the latter's struggle as a fight for democracy, for a legal and popularly chosen regime pitted against the forces of reaction and military tyranny.

Both of these views were gross simplifications. Neither reflected the realities of the Spanish situation, in which the usual categories of Western ideological debate simply did not apply. The legal argument was largely meaningless: the election of 1936 had been very close, and following it the left parties in the Popular Front had made no secret of their intention to break all legal norms by launching a social revolution. Nor, on the other hand, was it realistic to depict as virtuous warriors of the church the soldiers of General Franco who murdered wherever they went. Indeed, on both sides atrocities were sickening. The war was without pity for prisoners or civilians. On the Republican side, the killing of priests and nuns at the start of the war and Communist terror against leftist dissidents at its end, added the horrors of sacrilege and the miserable spectacle of a revolution devouring its own children. But the Nationalists slaughtered more than the Republicans. To the 600,000 who perished during the war itself, Franco added a million more victims whom he threw into prison or concentration camp at its close.

The Spanish Civil War can be described most succinctly as a class struggle in which the rich defeated the poor. The majority of the Spanish people doubtless were only helpless bystanders. Yet it was quite apparent that the Republic had more popular support than did Franco. As evidence one need only point to the fact that despite the aid of the regular army, and the massive help they received from Mussolini and Hitler, the Nationalists needed nearly three years to win. There was ample evidence for another fact: although the Civil War was not a struggle *for* Western democracy, Franco's victory represented a major defeat for democratic values throughout Europe. While the democratic powers had shown themselves weak and vacillating in their attitude toward Spain, the fascist states had stood strong and united. This was to be further demonstrated in the next great international crisis—the German annexation of Austria—which erupted when the Civil War in Spain had run but a little more than half its course.

IV

THE FALL OF AUSTRIA
AND CZECHOSLOVAKIA

The Anschluss of 1938

After two years of deceptive quiet and a steady increase of armed strength at home, on March, 1938, Hitler struck again. He sent his tanks rolling into Austria, which succumbed without a fight. The next day the country was formally annexed to the German Reich.

The *Anschluss* had been preceded by a month of intense pressure on the Austrian government. On February 12, Hitler had summoned Chancellor Schuschnigg to his Bavarian mountain retreat at Berchtesgaden and, after long hours of table-pounding and invective, bullied him into submission. Schuschnigg agreed to an amnesty for imprisoned Austrian Nazis and to appoint a Nazi as his minister of the interior. In short, he was bludgeoned by Hitler's "Trojan Horse" tactics into opening the way to slow absorption of his country by its powerful neighbor.

On his return to Vienna, however, Schuschnigg's attitude stiffened. He reaffirmed his intention of maintaining Austria's independence and began to mobilize public sentiment behind him. The Austrian Nazis replied with disorders all over the country. With civil war threatening, Schuschnigg saw no recourse but to call for a plebiscite to ratify his policy. This drove Hitler to fury. He sent an ultimatum demanding postponement of the plebiscite, and when this was refused, he began to concentrate troops on the frontier. Finally Schuschnigg resigned, leaving the government to a Nazi minister who invited the Germans into the country.

Two problems are crucial in judging the origins and the consequences of the *Anschluss*. First, what was the attitude of the Austrians themselves? This is an extraordinarily difficult question which historians will doubtless be debating for decades to come. One might approach it by calling attention to the 99.75 per cent of the electorate which ratified the annexation in a plebiscite held in April. But this in fact meant very little: as in all Hitler's plebiscites, there was no real alternative, and pressure and terror were freely employed to obtain the desired results. Undeniably, Nazi and pro-German sentiment had been steadily growing in

Austria in the years immediately preceding the *Anschluss*. Before Hitler's advent in 1933, the Austrians had been almost unanimous in desiring union with their great neighbor whose speech and tradition were almost indistinguishable from their own. Then in the half-decade from 1933 to 1938, Chancellors Dollfuss and Schuschnigg had tried to stir to life an Austrian national consciousness, on a basis of religious and traditional values. But this was only partially successful; the whole Austrian Left, for one thing, had remained alienated. Most of the country's citizenry had sunk into apathy and had fallen away from political concerns. When the *Anschluss* came, a large minority were enthusiastic, and the majority accepted it with resignation.

The second question concerns the attitude of the other European powers. Why did none of them come forward to protect the independence of Austria? The answer is that not one both wanted to do so and was able to do so. Fascist Italy, which had mobilized troops on the Brenner Pass at the time of the first Nazi threat in 1934, no longer stood as the guarantor of Austrian independence. Since the establishment of the Rome-Berlin Axis in the autumn of 1936, Mussolini had aligned himself with Hitler instead. The Duce resented not being informed of what his German friend was planning in Austria, but when the annexation had been accomplished, he swallowed his humiliation and sent the *Führer* his congratulations.

What about Britain and France? In London, Foreign Secretary Eden, the chief champion of resistance to fascist aggression, had been dropped from Chamberlain's cabinet less than a month before the *Anschluss*, and under the prime minister's own leadership the British government was moving toward the policy of conciliation with Mussolini and Hitler that came to be known as "appeasement." Long before the Germans struck, Chamberlain and his chief colleagues had already accepted the absorption of Austria into the Reich. In Paris, the situation recalled what it had been two years before at the time of Hitler's remilitarization of the Rhineland. Once more the French had a weak government—indeed, this time they were between ministries and had no government at all.

Blum was about to make his last despairing effort to revive the Popular Front. He was to be followed, after less than a month in office, by a prime minister who promised a sterner policy. Edouard Daladier, the last prewar premier of France, had been burned twice in the past—once when he had ordered the police to fire against the rightist rioters of February 6, 1934, again two years later when he had led the faction within the Radical party that had endorsed the Popular Front. As a result, Daladier was well-liked neither in the country nor in his own party, to which the memory of participation in Blum's government had grown highly distasteful. But he had a reputation for tenacity and force of character. In April, 1938, Daladier put together under technically Radical auspices a government that in fact was both conservative and nationalistic. By serving simultaneously as minister of defense, he gave notice that he put the highest priority on France's preparation for war.

The next great crisis was to test whether Daladier meant what he said—whether he would really stand against Hitler when the showdown came.

The Problem of the Sudetenland

Hitler had scarcely finished with Austria when he began political operations against his other small neighbor to the southeast, Czechoslovakia. Czechoslovakia was a far stronger state than Austria: it was almost twice as populous; its industries were busy and up to date; and among the small nations of East Central Europe, it alone had maintained its post-1919 democratic institutions.* This relative success reflected the high level of education and efficiency among the Czechoslovak people; it also reflected the wisdom of its statesmen, more particularly the founder-president, Thomas G. Masaryk, and his faithful coadjutor, Eduard Beneš, who had succeeded to the presidency on Masaryk's retirement in 1935.

But Czechoslovakia had one grievous problem. The Paris Peace Conference, in one of its less happy decisions, had awarded to the Czechs the Sudetenland, a mountain rim of territory around the Bohemian and Moravian borders which was inhabited by three million German-speaking people. Masaryk and Beneš had maintained most convincingly that this was the only logical solution: the new Czechoslovak state, they argued, needed a natural mountain frontier for its defense, and Bohemia and Moravia formed a historical and economic unit which should not be broken up. It would have been impossible, moreover, to draw a boundary along clear linguistic lines, since in many areas Czechs and Germans lived mingled together. Masaryk and Beneš won their case, for in this instance, as in so many others, the conference in the end decided against the vanquished.

In the first decade and a half of Czechoslovakia's history, the Sudeten Germans created little trouble. They received far better treatment than did most national minorities in East Central Europe, and in comparison with what occurred in other countries, their grievances were distinctly minor. But after Hitler came to power, these grievances suddenly flamed into life. As had happened in Austria, local Nazi agents went busily to work, and they soon had won over most of the German-speaking population. For here, as opposed to Austria, there was no competing national loyalty to restrain the inhabitants of the Sudetenland from ardently seeking annexation to the Reich.

Once Austria was safely annexed, Hitler felt free to espouse the Sudeten grievances. In concert with the local Nazi leadership, he took up the demand for Sudeten autonomy within the Czechoslovak state. Autonomy was all that he openly sought; but the way in which he

---

* For a general discussion of East Central Europe between the wars *see* Chapter Fourteen, II.

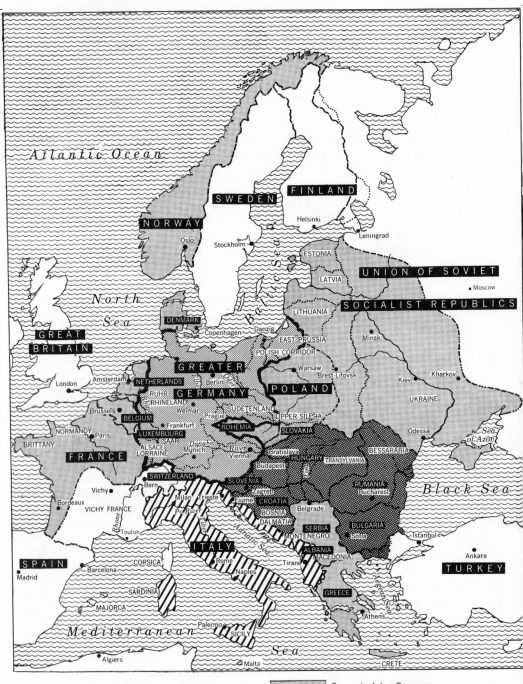

Hitler's Europe in 1941

Occupied by Germany

Occupied by Italy

Hitler's Balkan partners

phrased his claim left no doubt that annexation was his real objective. President Beneš and his colleagues knew it; hence they resolved to resist German pressure even to the point of war.

The Meetings at Berchtesgaden, Bad Godesberg, and Munich

The Sudeten issue first flared up in late March, scarcely more than a week after the annexation of Austria. There followed consultations between the French and British governments which set the pattern for everything that was to come thereafter. The French were prepared in theory to honor their treaty obligations by going to Czechoslovakia's defense, but in practice they were far from ready to do so. In this attitude, they were greatly influenced by the advice of their military chiefs, who warned them that the French army was in no condition to fight a war beyond its own borders, since it had put all its trust and most of its resources into the row of fortifications called the Maginot Line along the country's northeastern frontier.

The British, who, unlike the French, were not bound to Czechoslovakia by treaty, had no desire to fight at all. In their discussions with Daladier and his colleagues they found allies in the members of the French cabinet who were already in favor of appeasement. Thus the tacit result of the meetings between the two governments was an agreement that they could go no further together than the British would consent to move alone. In fact, this meant an abdication of French responsibility. In the spring of 1938, the relationship was established which was to persist until the outbreak of the Second World War: the power less involved in continental affairs took the lead, while France—whose concern for what went on in Central Europe was far more direct—meekly followed in Britain's wake.

The events of the summer and early autumn of 1938 showed how far this process had already gone. As tension and disorder mounted in the Sudetenland and Hitler's tone grew more violent, Prime Minister Chamberlain took diplomacy increasingly into his own hands. First he sent to Czechoslovakia a special mediator whose pro-German sentiments soon became obvious. Next he began to reveal the way his own thought was tending by insisting that the Czechoslovak government make concessions. Finally, when in mid-September it became apparent that Hitler was preparing an armed attack and that Beneš and his colleagues were resolved to resist, Chamberlain suddenly decided to go and see the *Führer* himself.

The spectacle of an elderly and peace-loving man, armed only with his inevitable umbrella, getting into a small plane to make the first flight of his life, stirred the imaginations and the sympathies of democratic-minded Europeans. It was quite evident that Chamberlain was prepared to grant Hitler anything within reason in order to preserve the peace. And this he apparently accomplished: he returned from Berchtesgaden with a formula of "self-determination" for the Sudeten Germans which he forced first on his own cabinet, then on the French, and lastly on the Czechs themselves. By September 21, when Beneš had finally bowed to British and French pressure and consented to the amputation of thousands of square miles from his country, the crisis seemed to have passed.

But next day, when Chamberlain went once more to see Hitler, this time at Bad Godesberg on the Rhine, everything had changed. The *Führer*, dumbfounded at the acquiescence of the French and British in his demands, felt defrauded of his triumph. For the past two weeks he had been stirring his people to a fever of patriotic excitement; his troops were massed for action on the Czech frontier; and now he was being asked to forego the military occupation of the Sudetenland. This he refused to do. He insisted that his soldiers must march into the German-speaking districts of Czechoslovakia at once.

Here at last the long-suffering Chamberlain called a halt. Even he would not submit to this sort of bullying. Deeply discouraged, the British prime minister returned home to report failure to his colleagues and to the French. For the first time the two great democracies began seriously to face the possibility of war. The French started to mobilize—the British to dig protective trenches against air raids and to distribute gas masks to the civilian population. But on neither side of the Channel was there a real conviction that war was coming. To nations who had lived for twenty years at peace the prospect of armed conflict was still unthinkable.

Both cabinet ministers and ordinary people were ready to grasp any last straw of salvation from whatever source. The savior was Mussolini—suitably prompted by the German government. In this moment of almost total despair, the Italian Duce stepped forward with a renewal of his old four-power proposal. He stood ready, he told his German partner, to meet with Hitler, Daladier, and Chamberlain to settle the Sudeten issue. All three quickly accepted. Their deliberations were equally brief: on September 30, 1938, in the city of Munich—where the Nazi movement had begun—the four leaders agreed to Hitler's maximum program. The only modifications of the *Führer's* Bad Godesberg demands were face-saving clauses providing for the occupation of the Sudetenland in stages and for the final delimitation of the frontier by an international commission. Hitler had won, but the peace had been saved for another year.

V

THE LAST YEAR

The Aftermath of Munich

The Munich settlement is notorious in history: it has become synonymous with capitulation, appeasement, and treachery to small allies. But this verdict is a judgment of hindsight. At the time, the vast majority of the

British and French welcomed the agreement with relief and jubilation. When Chamberlain returned to London, bearing with him the document promising "peace in our time," he was received with intense enthusiasm by a vast crowd waiting at the airport. For the first time in his life he was really popular. The same was true of Daladier. The French prime minister, who had fewer illusions than Chamberlain and knew very well that he had signed away his country's whole alliance system in the East, expected to be all but lynched at his return. Instead he was greeted as a savior. Only a minority of leaders in either country, such as Winston Churchill, bitterly criticized the Munich settlement and foresaw its consequences.

In defense of Munich, it can be said that it gave people in the Western democracies another year in which to prepare their minds for war. In September, 1938, they were completely unready for the horrors of conflict; a year later, although they still loathed the idea of war, they finally knew what they confronted and, in the case of the British at least, were prepared to face the facts. They had been pushed to this sober estimate of international realities by months of mounting evidence that Hitler's word meant nothing and that he and Mussolini were bent on further and apparently unlimited conquests.

The basic premise of the Munich agreement had been that Hitler would now be satisfied and would consent to live at peace with his neighbors. But the very implementation of the settlement proved that this was not so: on the international commission delimiting the German-Czech boundary, the Nazi representatives were stubborn and overbearing, and the frontier as finally established was far more unfavorable to the Czechs than had originally been contemplated. Meanwhile, Mussolini had begun to threaten France: at the end of November, he mounted a great propaganda offensive for the annexation of the French territories of Nice, Corsica, and Tunisia. As a feeble gesture in reply, Daladier's appeasement-minded foreign minister in early December signed a mutual guarantee of France's frontier with Germany. The proof that German agreements were worthless came the following March— Hitler's favorite month for action—with the destruction of what remained of Czech independence.

The Second Czechoslovak Crisis and Its Consequences

The annexation of the Czech parts of Bohemia and Moravia was carried out in characteristic Nazi fashion. Hitler summoned to Berlin the elderly, ineffective figure who had succeeded Beneš as president,* and with the

---

* Beneš, whose personal position had been destroyed at Munich, had retired and left the country the previous autumn.

protracted tongue-lashing he had given Schuschnigg just a year earlier, bullied him into submission. Thus in March, 1939, the rump Czechoslovak state that had remained after Munich ceased to exist; with their mountain defenses gone, the Czechs had no capacity to resist. The Czech lands became a "protectorate" of the Reich; Slovakia achieved independence under a clerical and authoritarian government; and the Hungarians added a further slice of the country to the territory they (and the Poles besides) had acquired in the wake of the Munich settlement.

This second Czechoslovak crisis differed in two important respects from the earlier crises which Hitler had precipitated. First, it showed that the Nazi annexationist drive was now extending to non-German peoples. Until then, Hitler had claimed that he sought only to incorporate *German* territories into the Reich, and this argument seemed unanswerable to people who, like most of the British, had always had their doubts about Germany's Versailles boundaries. Now Hitler threw off the mask; after the annexation of the Czech lands it was apparent that he wanted far more than mere reunion with the Germans who lived outside the Reich.

Secondly, Hitler was caught in a flagrant breach of his word. He had broken the Munich agreement less than six months after its signature. This rankled in Chamberlain's mind. The British prime minister believed in doing things in businesslike fashion. To him the pledged word was the foundation of commercial intercourse, and hence, of civilized society. He was deeply and sincerely (if perhaps naively) shocked that the statesman whose promise he had trusted should have betrayed him.

In the weeks after the demise of Czechoslovakia, Chamberlain—with Daladier in his wake—swung around sharply to a policy of resistance to Hitler. Thus the British and French prime ministers were not at all willing to compromise when the *Führer* began his next annexationist move, this time seeking to incorporate the last major group of Germans outside the Reich, the inhabitants of the Free City of Danzig and the Polish Corridor. Indeed, Chamberlain and Daladier did the contrary: they pledged military aid to Poland and later to Rumania and Greece, and they notably speeded rearmament. In April, for the first time in their history the British instituted a program of peacetime conscription.

Danzig, the Polish Corridor,
and the Nazi-Soviet Pact

Meantime the Spanish Civil War had ended in triumph for the fascist powers. Ten days later, on April 7, Good Friday, Mussolini annexed the small Balkan country of Albania, which had long been a veiled Italian dependency. Throughout Southern Europe the forces of militant

fascism seemed to be sweeping everything before them. These, however, were only sideshows: the real point of danger lay on Germany's
eastern frontier, and during the next four months the crucial and agonizing problem for the British and French was to provide aid to Poland
in a form that the Poles themselves would accept.

For Britain and France to make their stand for Poland rather than for
Czechoslovakia was logical from neither the military nor the ideological
standpoint. Poland merely happened to be the next issue which arose
after Chamberlain's and Daladier's patience was exhausted. Without
natural protection for its frontiers, Poland was far more vulnerable than
Czechoslovakia; its army was less modern, and its armaments industry
less important. Furthermore, it had long since ceased to be a democracy,
even in theory. Ever since Marshal Pilsudski seized power in 1926—and
after his death in 1935—Poland had lived under an oligarchic dictatorship, with real power in the hands of a narrow military and political
clique. In its quasi-feudal pattern of landholding and social relations,
Poland ranked with the most reactionary countries in Europe: Spain
and Portugal and Hungary.

In the 1920's, Poland, like Czechoslovakia, had been bound by a military alliance to France but, after 1934, as France faltered and Nazi Germany grew steadily stronger, the Polish government had tried to steer a
tortuous course between a tie to France which seemed less and less
significant and conciliatory gestures toward Hitler. Yet the Poles were
unwilling to do what would have made either of these policies effective.
On the one hand, they refused to give up any of the German-inhabited
districts in their Corridor leading to the sea. On the other hand, they
never for an instant entertained the idea of putting teeth into their alliance with France by supplementing it with a similar understanding
with the Soviet Union. For if there was one thing on which nearly all
Poles were agreed, it was in their hatred for Russia.

At the time of Munich, Stalin had offered to come to the aid of Czechoslovakia, and he had taken his exclusion from the four-power meeting
as a serious rebuff. It is doubtful whether and how the Soviet Union
could have made this offer good. Lacking a common frontier with the
Czechs, the Russians would have been obliged to ask transit rights from
the Poles or the Rumanians, who hated the mere thought of having the
Red Army on their soil. This was again the problem the following spring
and summer. How could the British and French persuade the Poles to
accept the Russians as their protectors?

Chamberlain and Daladier carried out this assignment in the half-
hearted and dilatory manner to be expected of men whose own minds
were divided. As a good conservative, Chamberlain detested the idea
of casting in his lot with bolshevism, and Daladier was scarcely enthusiastic about implementing his country's alliance with the Soviet Union,
which had been allowed to languish ever since it had been signed four

years before. So quite literally, they sent low-ranking officers on a slow boat to negotiate a military agreement with the Russians. Meanwhile, Stalin had grown suspicious. He accused the British and French of wanting to embroil him in a ruinous war with Hitler, while the Western democracies let the two great authoritarian powers destroy each other. (And this was what many Western conservatives would have liked to do, although they represented only a minority view within the Chamberlain and Daladier governments.) Stalin decided that his five-year-old policy of international respectability and support for collective security had failed catastrophically. As a clear warning of what was to come, in early May he dismissed his foreign minister, the Western-oriented Litvinov, and replaced him with the tougher and more provincial Molotov.

Stalin's suspicions deepened during the negotiations in early August with the British and French. The Western spokesmen still gave no sign of considering the matter as urgent, and they clearly did not wish to grant what the Soviet leader really wanted—a position of dominance or control in Finland, the Baltic states, and eastern Poland. Meanwhile, Hitler had determined to seek an understanding with the Soviet Union, as Stalin's mind also began to turn toward a dramatic reversal of alliances. In mid-August, he informed the *Führer* that he was ready to start political conversations.

Once the German foreign minister, Joachim von Ribbentrop, arrived in Moscow, events went at a rapid pace. He and Molotov talked as one realist to another, and it was not hard for them to agree to carve the spoils of Poland between their two countries. On August 23, the greatest diplomatic bombshell of the century exploded over a stunned Europe. The Nazis and the Soviets announced that they had composed all their differences. The impossible had happened: the two ideological systems sworn to eternal enmity had signed a nonaggression pact and agreed to live at peace with one another. Most fascists throughout Europe accepted the Nazi-Soviet pact in cynical fashion as a clever bargain. To Communists it came as a shattering blow: from this moment on, true believers in Western Europe began to desert the party in droves.

Now that he was protected from the Russian menace, Hitler felt free to strike. The Nazi-Soviet pact made war inevitable. The next day, the local Nazis took over control of Danzig. In the Corridor also, the Germans redoubled their agitation. Meantime Britain and France began to mobilize. On the last day of August, the Germans presented their final demands to Poland. These were merely for the record: Hitler did not even wait for an answer. In the small hours of September 1, the German planes launched the attack, and the armored columns began their advance. On the morning of September 3, Britain declared war. In the afternoon, France followed, after the appeasers within Daladier's cabinet lost their last-ditch campaign for conciliation. Mussolini stayed neutral. The Second World War had begun.

Readings

The general diplomacy of the period is covered in Craig and Gilbert (*see* readings for Chapter Six) and in Bullock's *Hitler* (*see* readings for Chapter Nine). The alignment between Hitler and Mussolini is traced in Elizabeth Wiskemann, *The Rome-Berlin Axis* (1949), and the diplomacy of the Ethiopian War is narrated in spirited and polemical fashion by Gaetano Salvemini in *Prelude to World War II* (1953). A. J. P. Taylor's *The Origins of the Second World War* (1961) presents the "revisionist" argument that the conflict can be blamed in great part on Anglo-French blundering and that Hitler had no conscious intention of going to war.

For the Spanish Civil War, Salvador de Madariaga, *Spain: A Modern History* (1958), and Gabriel Jackson, *The Spanish Republic and the Civil War, 1931–1939* (1965), present the background and a general account of the struggle from the standpoint of moderate liberals; Gerald Brenan, *The Spanish Labyrinth* (1943), similarly deals with social and cultural factors in terms sympathetic to the Republican cause; Hugh Thomas, *The Spanish Civil War* (1961), is the best full-scale history and tries to be fair to all parties; whereas E. Allison Peers, *The Spanish Tragedy* (1938) and *Spain in Eclipse* (1943), are more favorable to Franco, David T. Cattell, *Communism and the Spanish Civil War* (1955), is a detailed and judicious analysis of Communist influence on the Republican side.

For the annexation of Austria, see the personal account by Kurt Schuschnigg, *Austrian Requiem* (1946). J. W. Wheeler-Bennett, *Munich: Prologue to Tragedy* (1948), and Keith Eubank, *Munich* (1963), are the standard works on the crisis of 1938, the first highly critical of the diplomacy of "appeasement," the second more sympathetic to Chamberlain and Daladier. For an explanation of the falterings of French policy, see Charles A. Micaud, *The French Right and Nazi Germany* (1943).

The Second World War

Chapter Thirteen

I
ILLUSION AND BLITZKRIEG

For the democracies of the West, the Second World War opened on a paradoxically sour note. From the moral standpoint, their cause was blameless. Britain and France had gone to war to defend a threatened ally and to stop the spread of fascism; they sought nothing for themselves, and the sympathies of the neutrals were overwhelmingly on their side. From the beginning, the Second World War was what the first war had become only after Wilson had redefined it: a war for democracy.

Yet most of the French and British felt otherwise. They went into the conflict without conviction, quietly, even sullenly. From one point of view, their lack of enthusiasm was a sign of maturity: the days of bands and flag waving were over, and people faced soberly and without illusion the suffering that lay ahead; even the Germans showed no real eagerness for the conflict until they had experienced the intoxication of Hitler's first victories. But this absence of martial ardor also revealed a deep-seated *malaise* among the French and British people. They were going into the war under leaders tainted by past appeasement, whose present public statements gave no evidence of profound belief in their own cause. The disillusionments of the Spanish Civil War and the betrayal of Czechoslovakia brooded over them—why, people asked themselves, were they fighting to defend reactionary Poland rather than the democracy of Spain or Czechoslovakia? Beyond this there was a sense

*German infantrymen move under cover of tanks
and field guns as they attack along the main street
of a small Polish town southwest of Warsaw in 1939.*
COURTESY BROWN BROTHERS.

of danger and disappointment because France and Britain were fighting alone—the other Western democracies of Scandinavia, the Low Countries, and the United States were not with them. Finally there was the sickening suspicion that the West had declared a war which it could neither properly fight nor fully win—an unreal struggle which seemed to have no logical end. This became evident as the Germans disposed of Poland in less than a month and the war in the west settled into a weary winter of waiting.

The Conquest of Poland

Against Poland the Germans for the first time tested their tactics of *Blitzkrieg*, or "lightning war," which they were to use again and again in the next two years. For this sort of fighting, Poland offered almost ideal terrain: the country was one vast plain—from northern Germany to the swamps and forests on the Russian border there was scarcely a natural obstacle to stop the advance of an invading army. The new German strategy aimed at taking the enemy everywhere by surprise: while massed aircraft raided his cities, ammunition dumps, and communications centers, columns of tanks raced ahead of the infantry, cutting supply lines and spreading confusion and terror in his rear.

The *Blitzkrieg* tactics worked with speed and efficiency: a German army of a million and three-quarters overwhelmed Polish forces only a third as large. By mid-September the Germans had advanced so far into the country that the Russians took alarm. On September 17, Stalin ordered the invasion of Poland by the Red Army, which moved forward almost without opposition until it met the Germans two days later. After a further week of fighting, Polish resistance ended with the capture of the capital city of Warsaw. The government fled—eventually to take refuge in London, where it became the first of the continental governments-in-exile which existed throughout the war under British protection.

With Poland completely crushed, Hitler and Stalin proceeded to divide the spoils in the amicable spirit of the nonaggression pact they had signed five weeks earlier. Hitler took the larger share. He annexed outright the former Free City of Danzig, the Corridor, and a number of additional districts in the west. The central part of the country he set up as a German protectorate—as he had done with the rump of Bohemia-Moravia—to be called the Government-General. For his part, Stalin annexed eastern Poland up to (and slightly beyond) the frontier that Lord Curzon had originally proposed in 1919. This area, which had a majority of Ukrainians and White Russians rather than Poles, the Soviet leaders had always regarded as rightfully their own, and they claimed that they were only rectifying a twenty-year-old injustice when they joined it to the Ukrainian and White Russian Soviet Republics.

The French and British stood helpless as the Poles reeled under the German attack and Poland disappeared from the map. They had gone to war to save Poland's independence, but now they found themselves half unable, half unwilling, to go to its aid. It was impossible for them to send ground troops overland; their navies could not enter the Baltic, which the Germans had effectively closed; their air power lacked the means to traverse the entire Reich. Their inability to help the Poles made the French and British feel guilty from the outset and gave them a first taste of how the war was to prove entirely different from what they had imagined.

They might have staged their own attack against the German defenses in the west—the so-called Siegfried Line—or bombed German cities, but they took neither measure. After a few tentative advances to secure better defensive positions, the Allied commander in chief, General Maurice Gamelin of France, decided upon a stationary war. Obsessed with memories of the First World War, too much convinced of that war's lesson of the superiority of the defense over the attack, he decided to sit it out in his Maginot Line fortifications. Similarly the French and British chose to husband their aircraft rather than to bomb the Reich. At the beginning of the war, they had expected massive Nazi bombardments and even gas attacks: people had left the cities by the thousands, and children had been systematically shipped to safety. But when the bombs did not fall, life returned to normal: those who had fled the cities came back, and gas masks were discarded. Since Hitler did not bomb France and Britain, Daladier and Chamberlain responded in kind. A tacit and informal truce reigned on the Western Front.

But this truce was profoundly demoralizing. As the French soldiers —who accounted for the bulk of the Allied ground troops—waited through the late autumn and winter in the Maginot Line, they began to wonder why they were at war. The Germans, facing them in equal inaction on the Siegfried Line, knew that sooner or later their *Führer* would give the order to advance. The French had no such consolation. This *drôle de guerre*, this *Sitzkrieg*, this "phony" war, as it came to be called, seemed less and less war than a long succession of wet, dreary days of meaningless boredom. Under these circumstances, it was not surprising that the soldiers lost confidence in national leaders who themselves appeared to have so little idea of how they proposed to win.

There was, of course, the blockade, but this revival of a successful expedient of the First World War was far less promising under the conditions of 1939, for the understanding between Nazi Germany and the Soviet Union opened a yawning gap toward Asia and the Near East. Month after month the British and French leaders cast about for some way to stop the leak. Yet every plan they devised proved to be still more dangerous than what it sought to remedy. There was an abortive scheme to cut off the German source of motor fuel by bombing the Caucasus oil fields from Allied bases in the Near East. There was also a proposal to extend the scope of the war to Northern Europe by going to the aid of the embattled Finns. But when the French and British were ready to help Finland, it had already succumbed to Soviet arms.

The Winter War in Finland

The Winter War between Finland and the Soviet Union was fought apart from the main conflict and was only tangentially related to it. In its origins and its ultimate effects, however, it was closely linked to the German career of conquest, for Stalin's understanding with Hitler permitted him to put pressure on the Finns, and their resentment of the treatment they received in the winter of 1939–1940 drove them to side with Germany against the Soviet Union in 1941.

By the Nazi-Soviet Pact, Stalin obtained from Hitler what he had sought in vain from Chamberlain and Daladier—a free hand to strengthen his defensive position by expanding into Poland and toward the Baltic, in brief, to restore Russia's boundaries to approximately what they had been under the tsars. First came the Soviet annexation of eastern Poland. Then came the signature of treaties establishing Russian bases in the three Baltic states of Estonia, Latvia, and Lithuania—an obvious preliminary to political penetration and, eventually, to annexation. In November, Stalin made similar demands on Finland; he was flatly refused.

Finland could offer tougher resistance to the Russians than could helpless Poland—caught as it was in a vise between the two great authoritarian states—or the Baltic republics which, during the past two decades of European history, had been no more than minor links in the *cordon sanitaire* against bolshevism. Finland, like Czechoslovakia, was a proud and efficient democracy, related by ties of history and tradition to Scandinavia, more particularly to Sweden. The Finns were thoroughly Western in orientation, and they rejected out of hand the idea of falling once again under Russian overlordship. They had a justified confidence, moreover, in their army and in the strength of their own defenses.

Thus when the Red Army attacked at the end of November, the Finnish troops held firm. The Soviet forces tried to advance both in the center and at the extremities of the country, along the Arctic Sea to the north and through the Karelian Isthmus west of Leningrad. On all three fronts, they were stopped. The Finnish terrain, heavily wooded and studded with lakes, offered far less room for maneuver than did Poland, and when Stalin decided to strike, the northern winter had already set in. The Finns were well provided and thoroughly trained for warfare in the snow. In contrast, the Red Army was catastrophically undersup-

plied with warm clothing and equipment that could function in arctic
temperatures.

As the Finns held the Russians at bay from December through February, hope and sympathy for their cause rose steadily in the West. The Swedes did all they could short of actually sending troops; supplies of every sort arrived by way of Scandinavia from Britain and France and the United States. But as Soviet reinforcements mounted and the weather turned slightly warmer, the Red Army was able to move again. By early March, it had breached the main defensive line in the south, and the Finns were overwhelmed by numbers. The peace treaty gave Stalin what he had demanded all along—the Karelian Isthmus, the city of Viipuri, and a naval base at Hangö. By thus moving the Soviet frontier 70 miles to the west, the settlement with Finland provided protection for the highly exposed city of Leningrad, but at the cost of incurring the unforgiving enmity of the Finnish people.

The Conquest of Denmark and Norway

The French and British, meanwhile, had finally prepared an expeditionary force to go to the aid of the Finns. But before it could sail, the Winter War was over, and a new campaign in the north was calling far more urgently for whatever reinforcements the Western Allies had at their disposal.

Throughout the late winter Norway had been the scene of a quiet but intense struggle for position between the British and the Germans. With its long Atlantic seacoast deeply indented by fjords, Norway would offer a deadly threat to Britain if it fell into German hands: it could provide the German navy with protected submarine bases and with the wider scope the fleet required for operations beyond the confined shores of the Reich. The British sought to prevent this and also to stop the shipment of Swedish iron ore down the line of fjords to Germany.

On April 8, 1940, the British and French announced that they were about to mine Norwegian territorial waters to cut off the passage of German ships. As the Norwegians were protesting this violation of their neutrality, the Nazi forces struck. Sweeping through Denmark before dawn, the Germans made simultaneous landings in the major seaports of Norway. In most places, the defenders were too surprised to offer much resistance. But in the Oslo Fjord the guns of an old Norwegian fortress sank a German heavy cruiser. Elsewhere three more cruisers were sunk. Still the German landings maintained their relentless momentum, as additional Nazi forces kept coming in by sea and air. By April 20, when the Anglo-French expeditionary force arrived, it was already too late; within another ten days the Norwegians and their allies were forced to evacuate the south and center of the country. In the north, around the seaport of Narvik, resistance continued for another month, but by the end of May, France itself was in supreme danger and the Anglo-French forces were urgently needed at home. In early June, the Allied expeditionary corps sailed away, accompanied by the Norwegian king and government, who, like the Poles before them, took refuge in London.

At this point, the fate of Norway and Denmark diverged. In Norway, the Germans imposed the rule of Vidkun Quisling, a Nazi sympathizer whose treason had aided them in their invasion. In Denmark, where German occupation had come so swiftly that the king and his ministers had no choice but to stay, the democratic government continued to function as before. Sweden was spared—the only one of the Scandinavian states to succeed in remaining neutral throughout the war.

The Fall of the Low Countries and France

The Netherlands and Belgium had also tried to stay neutral. But their turn was soon to come. On May 10, again without warning, the German army and air force descended upon them.

Resistance in the Netherlands lasted only four days. Like Denmark, the country was flat, and its frontier lay completely exposed to its great neighbor. Moreover, for a century and a quarter the Dutch had stayed out of war: they had lost their military tradition, and their army was equipped to maintain no more than a token defense. Their cities lay helpless: on May 13, the German air force blasted the center of Rotterdam—the first of the great terror raids which were shortly to give the war a new and sinister character. Next day Queen Wilhelmina and her government took ship for London.

Belgium was a different story. Here the experience of German invasion and occupation in the First World War had left bitter memories, and throughout the interwar period the army and the defensive forts along the eastern frontier had been kept in a state of readiness. From 1920 to 1936, Belgium had been allied with France. Then, with Hitler's remilitarization of the Rhineland and the signs of French faltering that it revealed, the Belgians decided to act alone: the following autumn, they denounced the French alliance and returned to their pre-1914 policy of neutrality, to which Hitler himself gave a solemn guarantee.

This decision proved fatal to both the Belgians and the French. The former took the precautionary measure of mobilizing on the outbreak of the war, but they refused to compromise their neutrality by coordinating their military plans with those of their neighbors to the south. Thus when the German attack came, nothing was ready: strategy had to be improvised from day to day. The Belgians manned their forts and prepared to resist, while the French and British advanced into Belgium to take up new and unfamiliar defensive positions.

From the start, almost everything went wrong. The key Belgian fort,

Eben Emael, withstood attack for only one day; on the day following, May
12, the main German attack broke into France itself at Sedan. In this place of tragic memory—where the French had sustained their decisive defeat in 1870—the new German strategy gradually revealed itself. Again as in 1914, the invaders were avoiding the French fortifications in the northeast by swinging around on the right flank, but this time Hitler had decided to cut in much farther east—in the broken and wooded country of the Ardennes, which the French had dismissed as impassable for a modern army.

Despite the lesson of Poland's fall, General Gamelin and his aides still did not grasp the nature of the German *Blitzkrieg*. They were taken completely by surprise when the German tanks overcame all natural obstacles and broke through at Sedan. Nor did they realize the full import of this breakthrough until it was too late. The French continued to think in terms of fixed lines and of holding the Germans along one of the northern rivers as they had done in the First World War. They did not appreciate the fact that once the decisive breach had been made, the German armor was free to fan out behind their lines and thoroughly disorganize their rear.

In the third week of May there was no stopping the Nazi armies as they drove relentlessly south. The French staffs were overwhelmed: accustomed as they were to the sleepy routines of the phony war, they could not adapt to the lightning speed of this new type of conflict. Officers and men packed up as well as they could for the great retreat; they would pause briefly in a new defensive position, then start the weary move again as they learned that they had already been outflanked. Soon confusion and something like panic prevailed: it was impossible under these circumstances for one unit to keep in regular communication with its neighbor or for the higher headquarters to maintain an orderly chain of command. The Germans dominated the air: their fighter planes strafed the roads at will, scattering the retreating French columns and the millions of refugees, French and Belgian, who were pouring south. Meantime, further east the Maginot Line remained intact; in a few more days it would be useless, since the Germans could attack it from the rear.

The *Führer*'s goal was Paris. He had overruled his generals in concentrating on the Sedan breakthrough and now he wanted to be sure not to lose momentum as had happened to Moltke in 1914. Hence he failed to capitalize fully on the parallel successes that his armies had scored in driving west to the Channel at Abbéville and Boulogne.

By May 25, this subsidiary drive had succeeded brilliantly: it had caught the defenders of Belgium in a trap from which there was no escape. Two days later, the king of the Belgians, in his role as commander in the field, ordered his soldiers to lay down their arms, while the civilian government fled to London. Both the French and the British felt betrayed—particularly the British because the bulk of their small expeditionary force had gone to the aid of Belgium. But Hitler's concentration on Paris gave them a few days' grace; the Germans paused for forty-eight hours before closing the trap along the Channel. The French and British used this respite to good advantage: they maintained constant harassing attacks, in one of which an intrepid French brigadier general, Charles de Gaulle, proved that he too knew how to mass his tanks and handle them to maximum advantage. Simultaneously the British assembled every floating thing at their disposal: at the end of May an incredibly varied array of naval vessels, yachts, small pleasure craft, and fishing boats began to cross the Channel in the greatest rescue operation of all time. Nearly half a million men were waiting for them, closely packed on the beaches of Dunkirk. The British experts had thought they could save twenty to thirty thousand: the rescue fleet finally carried back to England 215,000 British and 120,000 French. Their equipment remained behind, but the men themselves had been snatched from death or imprisonment to fight another time.

With the completion of the Dunkirk evacuation on June 4, the agony of France began. A week later Mussolini declared war, belatedly and ignominiously, so as to be in at the kill and pick up what spoils he could. In mid-June Paris fell—undefended and abandoned by the government. General Gamelin had disappeared from the scene long since, but his successor, General Maxime Weygand, had arrived too late and was soon caught up in the mood of despair that had begun to grip both military men and civilians. One by one they abandoned the successive plans for further resistance—a stand south of Paris, a "redoubt" in the Breton peninsula, finally even the thought of fleeing overseas, as the Norwegians and the Dutch and the Belgians had done, to continue the war from bases in the colonies.

The prime minister, Paul Reynaud (who had succeeded Daladier in late March), originally wanted to move his government to North Africa, but although chosen as a man of decision who would prosecute the war with more vigor than Daladier, he too succumbed to the prevailing defeatist mood. He allowed himself to be overruled by the appeasers within his cabinet, whose former accommodating attitude toward Germany had been revived by the experience of defeat. Since the beginning of June they had acquired a distinguished spokesman in Marshal Pétain, whom Reynaud had accepted as vice-premier. The hero of Verdun, now eighty-four, was the sole survivor of France's great leaders in the First World War: he had become the symbol of patriotism, of rectitude, of the solid traditional virtues. When he spoke, it was difficult for a mere civilian to resist his immense moral authority. On June 16, weary and discouraged, Reynaud resigned the premiership to Pétain. The next day the marshal sued for an armistice. On June 22, the Germans, who already occupied more than half of France, imposed their will on the vanquished in that very same railroad car at Compiègne in which Foch had handed his armistice terms to the Germans in November, 1918.

The fall of France came as the greatest shock that Western democracy had ever sustained. In Britain, in the United States, and among the smaller neutrals, the news was greeted with incredulity and anger. How was it possible, people asked, for the army that was supposed to be the finest in the world to succumb after scarcely more than a month of fighting? Treachery and cowardice seemed to be the answer.

In fact there had been very little treachery—except among a few Communists and extreme rightists. Nor did cowardice explain the bad performance of the French army. Rather, the incompetence of its chiefs had sapped its morale—this and the bewilderment brought on by the confusion of the great retreat. The French had been outnumbered and overwhelmed by superior equipment, but only in aviation had German superiority been decisive. The French command had not known how to use what men and materiel it had, and as this realization filtered down to both soldiers and civilians, the French lost heart and finally resigned themselves to defeat and occupation. Like the citizenry of the smaller democracies to the north of them, the French never had time to awake to their peril.

With the fall of France, Hitler thought that victory was his. As he received the news of the capture of Paris, the photographers caught him in an improvised dance of triumph: he exulted vulgarly and shamelessly at the end of more than twenty years of German "dishonor." Now France was gone, he calculated, surely Britain would see reason and come to terms as well. But Hitler had failed to reckon with the British people —and with Winston Churchill.

II
"THEIR FINEST HOUR"

Churchill's Leadership

On May 7 and 8—just before the Nazi storm broke over the Low Countries—Neville Chamberlain had sustained a furious attack in the House of Commons. The ostensible subject of discussion was his bungling of aid to Norway, but the debate soon extended to his whole conduct of the war. Like Daladier, Chamberlain had not known how to put his country on a war footing: profoundly and stubbornly a man of peace, he had neither mobilized the energies of his people nor given them a clear vision of the task before them.

His successor was Winston Churchill, a born fighter and a maverick by nature. Raised as a Conservative, then a Liberal minister in the great days of the party before 1916, Churchill had finally become an unreconstructed Tory. He had served as chancellor of the exchequer under Baldwin, but he was obliged to withdraw from the Conservative leadership for his criticism of the policy of conciliation with India in 1931. This again was characteristic of him: he was always an imperialist at heart. Thus deprived of official influence, Churchill became the most redoubtable foe of the Baldwin and Chamberlain governments: with only a handful of followers, he denounced the policy of appeasement and demanded more energetic preparation for war. The event had proved him right: thus in May, 1940, he was the logical person to assume leadership. He was also the one whom Labor preferred. The parliamentary leader of the Labor party, Clement Attlee, agreed to serve under him as deputy prime minister, and the other Labor chiefs followed Attlee into the government. Thus from the beginning, Churchill's war ministry was what Lloyd George's had never been, a true coalition and a true expression of national unity. It was strengthened by the return to office of Conservatives like Anthony Eden whom the public associated with the rejection of appeasement.

Churchill was an incomparable war leader. A descendant of Marlborough and the grandson of a duke, Churchill gloried in his distinguished heritage. His rich prose and the measured cadences of his speeches gave the British a sense of the majesty of their history and of the great task that had devolved on them, now that they stood alone. When Churchill told them bluntly that he could offer them nothing but "blood and toil and sweat and tears" they welcomed the grim prospect with gratitude: now at last all illusion had been stripped away and Britain knew what lay ahead.

The Battle of Britain

The mood of England in the summer of 1940 was epitomized by the remarks attributed to an apocryphal cockney on a London bus: " 'Ere, wot ye grousin' about? We're in the finals, ain't we? We're playin' at 'ome, ain't we?"

Indeed, the British seemed almost happy to be alone. They had never had much regard for their French ally, and now that this vexation was eliminated, the war had become blessedly simple. It had been reduced to a question of national survival. Realistically, it appeared impossible for the British to hold out. Only the intervention of the United States or the Soviet Union could give them hope of victory. Meanwhile they went about the business of defending their country with brisk self-confidence. They were quite prepared, as Churchill had warned them, to fight on their beaches, in their cities, and eventually—if their whole island should be lost—in the dominions overseas. These had been with them from the start, and if the British government should be forced to fall back on Canada, it seemed almost certain that the United States would enter the war.

To be sure, isolationist sentiment still predominated among the American people but President Roosevelt, who was already nudging his countrymen toward war, had responded to Churchill's urgent pleas by sending large quantities of old rifles and ammunition to replace the materiel lost at Dunkirk. It was with obsolete equipment of this sort that the British army—half raw recruits, half veterans of the expeditionary force that had seen service in Belgium and France—was preparing to resist the impending Nazi invasion.

Hitler himself was far less sure of his next step. The rapid fall of France caught him by surprise: it put him ahead of schedule, and he had no plans ready for his next move. Thus his military chiefs were obliged to improvise a plan for invasion on short notice. Operation "Sea Lion"—surely the most transparent code name ever devised—called for an initial assault in September by 90,000 men, who were to be transported by a flotilla of more than a thousand craft of all sizes, to be assembled at Ostend in Belgium, and in the area between Cherbourg and Le Havre.

The German navy, however, which had had no experience or training in amphibious operations, was far from enthusiastic about "Sea Lion." And even Hitler realized that it would be successful only if preceded by a thorough preparation from the air. So he ordered Reichsmarshal Hermann Goering, his right-hand man and the commander of the German air force (*Luftwaffe*), to soften up the British defenses. Goering was full of confidence: indeed, he was certain that he could subdue Britain by air attack alone without resort to the hazardous expedient of invasion.

But Goering did not know the high level of combat efficiency that the Royal Air Force (RAF) had attained in the past year. The British had used to good advantage the year's respite they had gained at Munich. By 1939, they were producing more than six hundred aircraft a month and had almost equaled the German rate of output. Their fighter planes were better: the British had gone into mass production a couple of years later than the Germans, and their new models, the Spitfires and the Hurricanes, were more advanced than the *Luftwaffe*'s. Finally, the British had invented radar: at the beginning of October, they were able to put into operation their first radar warning system.

Still, the German air force outnumbered the British by almost two to one. If it had concentrated its attacks on the RAF fields and fighter forces, it might have broken Britain's power in the air. Instead the *Luftwaffe* kept shifting its target: in late August, it struck at British ports and shipping; then it attacked airfields; finally (in early September), it launched its great *Blitz* against London, Coventry, and other industrial centers. Night after night, it struck at the British capital: each day, it seemed as though government and inhabitants could not hold out much longer in the burning and heavily damaged city. But the Londoners reacted with calm and fortitude: most of them filed patiently into cellars and subways to get what sleep they could, while those who had jobs to do—antiaircraft crews, fire fighters, and air-raid wardens—manned their posts with quiet efficiency.

Meanwhile, the weather itself was helping the British. During the six decisive weeks from mid-August until late September, there was an abnormal amount of fog and rain. Goering never got the fortnight of clear weather that he needed to mobilize his force with maximum effectiveness. As September wore on, his losses of aircraft grew more and more alarming. By the end of the month, it was obvious that bombing alone would never bring the British to their knees. On October 12, "Sea Lion" was postponed until the following spring. In fact, although no one dared tell Hitler so, the project of an invasion of Britain had been shelved forever. A few thousand intrepid pilots of the RAF had saved their country: they had won the Battle of Britain. As Churchill was to express it with his customary felicity: "Never in human history have so many owed so much to so few."

Hitler's Diplomatic Offensive: Mussolini, Pétain, Franco

In the autumn of 1940, then, Hitler was left without a war to fight. The conquest of Britain had eluded him, and Churchill was turning a deaf ear to his feelers for peace. He could try to cripple British trade with his submarines—and here he was scoring a notable success—but this was not enough to bring final victory within his grasp.

Frustrated in the west, Hitler turned south toward the Mediterranean. Here he had to deal with three Latin powers, all, in one form or another, allied or subjugated to him. If he could weld these together into an effective military bloc, then at least he might be able to strike at Britain overseas, at the powerful bases of Gibraltar and Malta and at Egypt—formally independent but now occupied by the British army—which held the key to the Near East and India.

Unfortunately for the *Führer*, the three dictators of Italy, France, and Spain were proud men and strong nationalists who had no intention of subordinating their countries' aims to Hitler's military needs. In Italy, Mussolini felt angry and humiliated by his own role in the war: his army's record in its single week of fighting against France had been mediocre, and his navy and air force in the Mediterranean were being battered by far smaller detachments of the British, who were also holding off his attempts to advance from Libya into Egypt. Hitler, therefore, saw no reason to give his tardy ally any substantial reward. He merely permitted the Italians to remain in the small area of southeastern France they had occupied in June, while postponing indefinitely the award Mussolini really wanted—Nice, Corsica, and Tunisia.

The *Führer*'s cavalier treatment of Mussolini reflected his concern for what was going on in France. Here Marshal Pétain—or rather his hatchet-man, Pierre Laval—less than three weeks after the armistice had bullied the French chambers into voting him full powers to govern and to alter the constitution as he saw fit. Armed with this grant of power, Pétain and Laval had replaced the democratic French Republic with an authoritarian and quasi-fascist "French State." It was referred to as the *Vichy government*, from the resort city in central France where it established its headquarters. This change of capital had been necessitated by the armistice terms: pending the conclusion of a final peace, the Germans were to remain in control of an Occupied Zone which included Paris, the north, and the whole Atlantic coast; although, in form, Pétain was the ruler of this part of France too, his effective power was limited to the Unoccupied Zone in the center and southeast.

Despite defeat and occupation, France still held a few trumps: most of its navy was intact; its vast colonial empire in Africa also remained beyond the reach of the Germans. These assets Pétain and Laval intended to exploit as astutely as they could in order to achieve for France a respectable place in the new Europe dominated by nazism. The marshal was reluctant to throw in his lot with Hitler; Laval was far more convinced that "collaboration" was the only sensible course. For his part, the *Führer* was ready to spare French sensibilities if he could win France as a true ally: potentially, he realized, Pétain had more to offer than Mussolini.

But when he finally met the marshal at Montoire on October 24, Pétain proved evasive. No substantial promise of collaboration was forthcoming. The same had been true of Hitler's conversation with Franco the day before at the frontier city of Hendaye. The Caudillo had been polite, even courtly. He had listened for nine long hours to the *Führer's* urgings that he enter the war; but he had refused to be dazzled by the proposal of a joint Nazi-Spanish attack on the fortress of Gibraltar, which for more than two centuries had dominated the entrance to the Mediterranean, a continued British taunt to Spanish sovereignty. Franco summoned all sorts of objections: the Spanish economy had been shattered by the Civil War; its Catholic people detested the German pact with the Soviet Union; he himself had no desire to play host to a foreign army. Hitler had at last met his match: the mild-mannered Caudillo had talked even the eloquent *Führer* into exhaustion. "Rather than go through that again," Hitler lamented, "I would prefer to have three or four teeth taken out."

So Hitler failed in his efforts to construct a Latin fascist bloc and to seal off the Mediterranean. In retrospect, this failure was to appear one of the major mistakes in his whole conduct of the war, for it left French North Africa at liberty and vulnerable to the maneuvers of his enemies.

The Conquest of Greece and Yugoslavia

Less than a week after the Hendaye and Montoire meetings, Mussolini set off on his own, as if to prove once and for all that he was something more than Hitler's satellite and to reassert his old claim to the Mediterranean as his private preserve. On October 28, he attacked Greece from bases in Albania. He had informed the *Führer* of his decision only at the last moment, thereby neatly repaying the Germans for the similar treatment they had so often given their allies in the past.

The attack on Greece was an act of rash folly. Mussolini's armies, as their record in France and North Africa had already shown, were far from ready for combat: their equipment was inferior, their morale was low. By early December, the Greeks had chased them back into the mountains of Albania. There the hapless Italians remained throughout the winter—until they were rescued in the spring by a great German offensive down the Balkan Peninsula.

This campaign was the sequel to a major reorganization of East Central Europe that had been proceeding ever since the previous summer. With the fall of France, the small states of the area which had looked west for protection found themselves at the mercy of their great neighbors. Once more Germany and the Soviet Union took parallel action. Stalin continued his program of restoring the Russian frontiers of 1914 by seizing Bessarabia from Rumania and annexing the Baltic States. Hitler added no more territory to the Reich, but he brought three more countries under his control as dependent nations. First he undertook to protect Rumania against Russia; in return he ordered the Rumanians to give up additional territory to their neighbors—half of Transylvania to Hungary and a smaller area south of the Danube to Bulgaria.

Such was Hitler's cruel and cynical policy of divide and rule. The revised boundaries of 1940 satisfied none of Germany's three new satellite peoples. On the contrary, both "haves" and "have-nots" found reason for grievance. The former victor in the First World War—Rumania—was left smarting at the loss of territories containing four million inhabitants. The defeated states—Hungary and Bulgaria—were still far from having attained the frontiers they regarded as rightfully theirs. All, then, hoped for better things; all realized that the nation which proved itself the most reliable German satellite would emerge in the best position at the conclusion of this second war. Hitler held them in his power through the hope of further gain and the fear of further loss. Earlier, by buying up their agricultural surpluses in the depression years, the Nazi Reich had put these countries in a state of economic dependence: now it had them in a state of political dependence as well.

Hungary was the most conservative nation in Europe—still semifeudal in its patterns of landholding and society and guided by its regent, Admiral Nicholas Horthy, in the closest possible conformity to the spirit of the old regime. Rumania and Bulgaria were peasant countries which, after a post-1919 experience with parliamentary democracy, had evolved into corrupt dictatorships, with their kings playing an active political role. The same was true of Yugoslavia. But Yugoslavia was also torn by the enmity between Serbs and Croats. In 1918, the Serb leaders had made it quite clear that they intended to govern the new state as an enlarged Serbia. Through most of the interwar period, the Croats had deeply resented the Serb domination under which they lived, and in the 1930's, they turned to Mussolini for help. The Duce had been delighted to oblige: it was a terrorist in Italian pay who assassinated King Alexander and Louis Barthou in 1934.

Less than a week before the outbreak of the Second World War, the Croats at last achieved an arrangement for internal autonomy that satisfied their minimum demands, but this was too recent to have had much effect in unifying the country. Thus Hitler found Yugoslav leadership weak and divided when, in the spring of 1941, he put the same sort of pressure upon them that he had earlier exerted on the Rumanians and Hungarians. On March 25, the regent, Prince Paul, adhered to the German-Italian alliance, which since the previous September had included the Japanese as well. Yugoslavia seemed to be safely in the Nazi orbit. But next day Belgrade began to stir: a conspiracy of high-ranking Serb army officers overthrew the regent and his prime minister and established the boy king, Peter II, in his place. The new government repudiated the German alliance and, sustained by a great wave of patriotic enthusiasm, prepared to resist the invasion that was sure to come.

Hitler's retribution descended swiftly and relentlessly. On April 6, the German attack began, both from the north and from Bulgaria. Once more, *Blitzkrieg* tactics worked with precision. In eleven days, all was over with Yugoslavia. Meantime, Greece too had been invaded. Hitler had come to the aid of his bungling Italian allies by attacking their Greek adversaries from the rear. A week after the capitulation of Yugoslavia, Greece signed an armistice.

The Greek king fled to the island of Crete, where the British had sent reinforcements the previous autumn. Surely, people thought, Crete at least would be able to hold out, since it was 60 miles from the mainland and protected by the British navy. But on May 20 Hitler began to despatch airborne troops; these, pouring in by parachute and glider, soon secured firm footholds in several parts of the island. Against this steady growth of German strength, the Greeks and the British found themselves powerless. At the end of the month, they were forced to evacuate Crete entirely. The Germans had obtained a magnificent air base for further operations in the eastern Mediterranean. They had also won complete domination over the Balkans. Two more governments-in-exile were added to the four already living under British protection.

The End of the Nazi-Soviet Pact

Yet Hitler's triumphal march through the Balkans had one fatal consequence: it delayed for a precious month the attack on the Soviet Union he had decided on the previous December.

This dramatic rupture of his pact with Stalin would doubtless have occurred in any case. Hitler never had really buried his hostility to bolshevism: he had merely concealed it for strategic reasons in order to protect his rear while he dealt with France and Britain. Eventually—as he had announced in *Mein Kampf*—he was resolved to eliminate the power of Russia once and for all, but he intended to do this only when he had forced the West to make peace. At all costs, he wished to avoid what he considered the supreme mistake of his imperial German predecessors—a war on two fronts. His timing, however, was disturbed by two untoward circumstances—Britain's failure to admit that it was beaten and the Soviet Union's refusal to accept the Nazis' ideas on the division of the world.

On November 12, 1940, Foreign Minister Molotov arrived in Berlin for political consultations. Hitler proposed a gigantic assignment of spheres of influence, based on the assumption of Britain's collapse and the carving up of its Empire. To the Russians he offered a chance to expand south "in the direction of the Indian Ocean." This proposal impressed Molotov not at all. The Soviet foreign minister made it quite clear that he was not interested in hypothetical gains from a still undefeated Nazi enemy with which his country was not even at war; he wanted a delimitation of spheres of influence within Europe itself. He also implied that his minimum requirement was a strong position in the Balkans, including the domination of Bulgaria and the Straits.

Thus the two great authoritarian states were much too far apart to reach a settlement, and Molotov returned home with nothing decided. Shortly thereafter Hitler determined to attack the Soviet Union the following spring. Almost certainly, Stalin must have known something of this decision, but if he did, he gave no sign of it. All his actions in the first half of 1941 suggested an exclusively defensive orientation—he was playing for time, hoping that by avoiding all provocation of his fearful adversary and by giving him no excuse for retaliation, he could postpone the attack for a few more months.

In January, the Soviet leaders renewed their trade agreement with the Germans, quite as though nothing were amiss. Three months later, they stood aside while their Slavic brothers in Yugoslavia went down to defeat. They gave the latter moral encouragement—but that was all, and the evidence strongly suggests that even this was only a gesture to put themselves in a favorable light before the Russian people. Shortly thereafter, on May 6, Stalin himself revealed how gravely he viewed the situation by assuming the Soviet premiership for the first time in his nearly two decades of unofficial national leadership. Still he refused to make any public admission of Russia's peril. As late as June 13, when the German troop concentrations on the Soviet frontier had been almost completed, an official press communiqué vigorously denied any deterioration in relations between the two countries.

Incredible as it may sound, Stalin and his colleagues seem to have deceived *themselves* as to the imminence of Hitler's attack. They did not even listen to the friendly warning that the German ambassador gave them on the eve of the onslaught. And when, on June 22, the greatest invasion of all time began to roll, they were still not fully prepared.

Now at last the war had entered on its major phase. Hitler had fallen into the trap he had sworn to avoid—a war on two fronts. And the British were no longer alone. They had survived their year of supreme peril—"their finest hour," as Churchill called it. The Russians were with them —and in less than six months the Americans would be fighting too.

III

THE WAR IN THE BALANCE

The German Invasion of Russia

For his reckoning with the Soviet Union, Hitler had massed a total of nearly 150 divisions, a large number of them armored. Once more overruling the advice of his military chiefs, he had decided to advance all along the line, rather than to concentrate his forces for a single decisive blow. Three army groups were to invade the Soviet Union on a front that would eventually extend for 2,000 miles. Their commanders were the same aristocratic generals, now field marshals, who had won the victory in France: Leeb in the north, with Leningrad as his objective; Bock in the center, headed toward Moscow; Rundstedt in the south, with the endless wheat fields of the Ukraine stretching before him. They were accompanied by satellite forces from Hungary, Rumania, Slovakia, and Italy. And in the north the Finns took up arms again to avenge their defeat in the Winter War.

At first it appeared as though the Germans would sweep everything before them. The wide encircling operations they had planned proceeded with deadly accuracy: parallel columns of tanks drove forward through open country, meeting little resistance, and then, when they were far in the enemy's rear, wheeled toward each other to close the jaws of a vast trap. Again and again, the Nazi armored divisions ambushed the Russians in this fashion. The latter seemed paralyzed with fear or astonishment: encircled and bewildered, they surrendered by the tens of thousands.

From July to September, nothing seemed able to stop the German advance. In early July, the northern drive reached Riga on the Baltic; a month later, Army Group Center completed the conquest of White Russia and captured Smolensk, the last major city before Moscow, less than 200 miles to the east; by mid-September the southern attack reached the Ukrainian capital of Kiev on the Dnieper. In the north, meanwhile, the siege of Leningrad had begun: it was to continue for thirty months under horrifying conditions of civilian misery and starvation.

In retrospect, military observers were to ascribe the great Soviet retreat to a calculated strategy of "trading space for time." The Red Army, they explained, had fallen back in order to lure the invader deep inside Russia, where it could destroy him at its leisure, as Kutuzov had done with Napoleon in 1812. It was undeniable that the precedent of the national struggle against the French invasion a century and a quarter earlier helped to kindle patriotic emotion for this new ordeal. Stalin consciously played on the memory of 1812 for propaganda purposes, and in his public utterances he began to subordinate Communist slogans to patriotic themes inherited from the Great Russian past. At the same time, in more private statements, he frankly admitted that the Germans had achieved a series of enormous tactical surprises. The Red Army—which was not greatly outnumbered by the invaders—had shown itself inferior to them in leadership and strategy. Its retreat had been dictated by necessity, not calculation: it was simply fortunate for Stalin that his annexations of the previous two years had extended the covering territories through which his armies could fall back. He was also lucky in having time to dismiss his high command, including such heroes of the civil war as his friend and political ally, Voroshilov. Only when Stalin gave the Red Army new and younger leaders did it learn how to meet and counter the Nazi onslaught.

The invasion thus reached its autumn climax. By the end of October, the Germans had entered the Crimea, they had virtually completed the conquest of the Ukraine with the capture of its greatest industrial city, Kharkov, and they were closing in on Moscow. But here Hitler's two earlier errors began to tell: he desperately needed the month of fighting weather he had lost by his offensive through the Balkans the previous spring; he also needed the tanks he had failed to concentrate before Moscow and had used instead in the conquest of the Ukraine. Hitler's initial delay and his subsequent scattering of his forces gave the Red Army exactly the reprieve it required—a six weeks' breathing space in which to build up its defensive strength in the center. By October 2, when Bock was at last in a position to make a full-scale advance on Moscow, it was too late. The defenders of the Soviet capital were ready; their communications lines were short, while his were being stretched to the limit; and the snows of an abnormally early winter were soon to begin.

Nevertheless it was a perilous time for Russia. The Germans, halted by heavy rain and snow in late October, returned to the attack in mid-November as soon as the ground had frozen. This time, their advance parties reached the suburbs of Moscow, where riots broke out in the city streets and the Soviet regime itself seemed about to topple. The main government offices had been evacuated to the east. Stalin alone remained in the capital as a grim symbol of resistance to the last; he had taken the conduct of the war into his own hands, and legend was gathering once more around the man of steel. On the day of crisis, December 2, the defenders of Moscow held firm: the supreme danger was over.

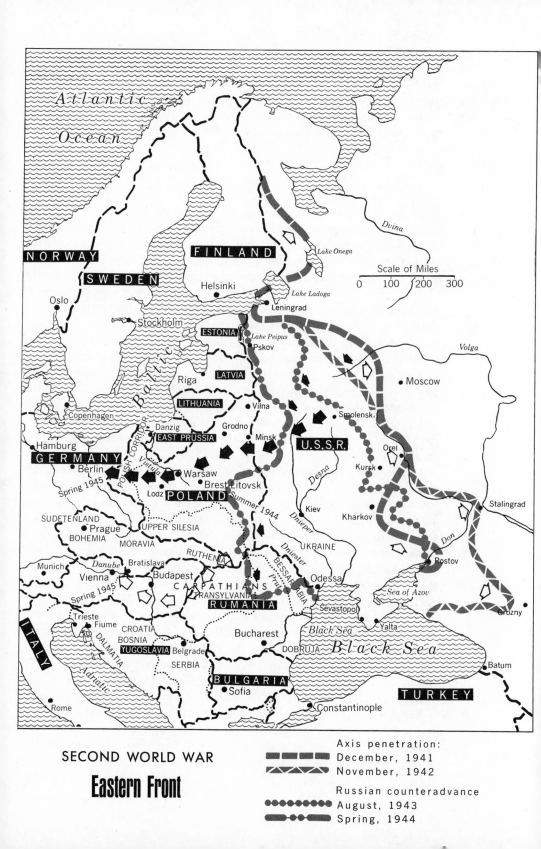

SECOND WORLD WAR

Eastern Front

Axis penetration:
December, 1941
November, 1942

Russian counteradvance
August, 1943
Spring, 1944

By this time, full winter had arrived; the German soldiers were huddling miserable and half-frozen in their advanced positions. On December 8, even Hitler was obliged to bow to realities and announce the suspension of operations. Two days earlier, Stalin had ordered a counter-offensive. And on the seventh of the same month, the Japanese attack on Pearl Harbor had brought the United States into the war.

The Intervention of the United States: the Great Coalition

With the American intervention, the Second World War attained its final form. It became a coalition struggle of the two greatest democracies of the West in declared or tacit alliance with the homeland of communism. These ill-assorted bedfellows had been thrown together by a series of historical accidents. Britain and the United States shared with the Soviet Union a common enemy in fascist terror and aggression, but there was little else to hold together two such radically different types of society, whose history during the previous quarter-century had been marked far more often by hostility than by friendship. On both sides, a massive legacy of distrust barred the way to harmonious cooperation. At the end of 1941, it was an open question whether the colossus of the East and the Anglo-Saxon powers would succeed in sinking their differences and in forming a solid fighting front. The next three years were to be punctuated by unremitting and constantly disappointed efforts on the part of Churchill and Roosevelt to establish with Stalin a true comradeship in arms.

At the outset the British served as the connecting link between the Russians and the Americans. The average Englishman was far more convinced than was his American counterpart of the advantages of an alliance with the Soviet Union—for one thing, he owed more to the Russians: with the German invasion in June, the *Luftwaffe*'s attacks on British cities had come to an abrupt end. Hence Churchill voiced the sentiments of the overwhelming majority of his fellow citizens when, on the morrow of the Nazi attack, he pledged Stalin all the aid he could spare. In so doing, he did not repudiate his anti-Bolshevist past; he merely admitted frankly that to him the necessities of warfare overrode everything else. In the months that followed, he was generous in sending supplies—most of them going by the long, exposed sea route around the North Cape, where German aircraft based in Norway took a fearful toll of British convoys. With the signature of a mutual aid pact in mid-July, Britain and the Soviet Union became formally allied.

Roosevelt was unwilling to go that far. He well knew that an influential segment of the American people would never countenance an alliance with a Communist state. But even before Pearl Harbor, he had agreed to ship supplies to the Soviet Union, using as precedent the lend-lease arrangements which had been made with Britain the previous spring. These marked a major turning point in the successive steps that had brought Roosevelt's policy into ever-closer alignment with Churchill's war effort: in the summer of 1940 there had been the deal by which Britain conceded the use of overseas bases to the United States in return for fifty overage destroyers; a year later the American president had met the British prime minister at sea off Argentia in Newfoundland to sign the Atlantic Charter; and in September, 1941, the American navy had all but gone to war, when it was ordered to "shoot on sight" at submarines or other naval vessels threatening its convoy operations.

Still the American people continued to be profoundly divided: on the eve of Pearl Harbor, a clear majority opposed armed involvement on Britain's side. The Japanese attack rescued Roosevelt from a cruel dilemma by forcing his hand: now the country had no alternative. The president was also spared the dangers of a congressional debate over whether to declare war on Germany and Italy as well as Japan; the two fascist states themselves took the initiative by inaugurating hostilities with the United States in conformity with their Tripartite Pact with Tokyo.

Roosevelt and his military advisers made their crucial decision within a month after Pearl Harbor when they determined to give the defeat of Germany priority over dealing with Japan. Although this meant that some sort of coordination with the Russians was essential, the American government was resolved to limit such coordination to the military sphere. It would make no political or territorial commitments. Thus the British were left to deal with Stalin on the diplomatic front. From the beginning, he showed himself a tough negotiator. In late December, Anthony Eden, once again British foreign secretary, flew to Moscow to find out what the Russians wanted: he was astounded to learn that Stalin —who had barely saved his capital a fortnight before—insisted on retaining nearly all his gains from his pact with Hitler; the Soviet Union's rightful boundaries, he claimed, were those which existed at the time of the Nazi attack.

Temporarily, the British were able to put Stalin off by explaining— quite honestly—that the Americans would never consent to such a deal. To agree to the expanded Soviet boundaries of June, 1941, would be a direct violation of the Atlantic Charter, which promised self-determination to enslaved peoples. It meant consenting to the forced annexation of territories containing millions of Finns and Estonians, Lithuanians and Letts, Rumanians and Poles. Stalin's claims against Poland created a particularly embarrassing situation for Churchill and Roosevelt. Britain had gone to war in order to help the Poles, and now the Soviet leader was insisting on keeping the lands he had annexed at their country's fall. True, he had signed an agreement with the Polish government-in-exile shortly after Hitler attacked him. This provided for the liberation of Polish prisoners whom the Red Army had captured in 1939 and their enrollment in a new army of liberation; but the agreement was vague on the question of postwar boundaries, and the Poles in London were displeased with the way in which the Russians were carrying it out.

Thus as early as the first month of American involvement in the war, the problem had arisen that was to poison relations within the grand alliance at its very end.

The War in 1942: the Soviet Winter Offensive
and the Anglo-American Air and Sea Campaigns

When the Red Army finally halted the German invasion in December, 1941, the situation of the Soviet Union seemed all but hopeless. It had lost its richest lands and more than half its industrial resources: the territory occupied by the Germans contained two-fifths of its population, its grain, and its railroad lines, plus two-thirds of its coal and iron. Over-all industrial production had fallen by more than half, and famine in the cities was beginning to take a dreadful toll.

Yet Stalin went on with his winter offensive. From December to May, the Red Army pushed forward, disengaging an ample protective zone before Moscow and dislodging the Germans from their advanced positions in the Ukraine. This campaign showed how much the Red Army had learned from the Winter War against Finland two years earlier: the Russians were now warmly clothed; they traveled light; and they knew how to operate in dispersed formation in the snow, infiltrating past the German outposts and cutting them off from their supplies and their escape routes to the rear.

This resiliency of the Russians—this ability to fight back after the terrible defeats of the summer and autumn—amazed and delighted their well-wishers in occupied Europe and in the West. It seemed to betoken some peculiar strength in the Soviet peoples, or in the system of government under which they lived. Thus the winter of 1941–1942 marked the beginning of a new wave of pro-Soviet and pro-Communist feeling in Europe. Stalin's pact with Hitler in 1939 had completely deflated his country's prestige. Now the rupture of that pact and Soviet resistance to the Nazi invasion brought a sharp and steady rise in Russia's standing: the years between 1941 and 1944 saw Soviet prestige higher than ever before.

From the perspective of the ordinary citizen who was no expert in military affairs, it looked as if Russia were doing all the fighting, while Britain and the United States were standing idly by. For nearly three years, the war in the east dwarfed the struggle in the west. The Nazi-Soviet conflict was without precedent in history. In the extent of territory it covered, in the forces engaged, in the ruthlessness displayed on both sides, certainly no modern war was comparable to it. Against the 150-odd divisions that the Germans and their satellites had sent to Russia, the Red Army had mobilized more than twice as many. These Soviet divisions were smaller and lighter than the German units, but as the war continued, and as Russia's population advantage began to tell, the weight of numbers fell ever more heavily on Stalin's side, despite the frightful losses that the Soviet peoples suffered. These again were without precedent: at the end of the war, total Soviet deaths—civilian and military— were estimated at twenty million. Millions had died in combat; millions more had starved or frozen to death. The Germans had slaughtered countless others among the civilian population behind the lines or worked them to death as prisoners of war. The Soviet Union was not a signatory of the Geneva Convention, and the Nazis saw no purpose in conforming to its provisions in dealing with enemies whom they regarded as subhuman. On neither side, then, had a prisoner much chance of humane treatment: in most cases, imprisonment meant brutality, hardship, and a lingering death.

With the Soviet Union carrying the brunt of the fighting, there was mounting pressure on the British and Americans to come to the aid of the Russians by opening a second front on the European continent. Stalin pleaded for it in terms that alternated between polite suggestion and peremptory demand. Public opinion in Britain and the United States clamored for it—here once again the average citizen could not see why his country was taking so long to do the obvious. Neither the Russians nor the Anglo-American public understood that the Western Allies were *already* contributing mightily to the common war effort, but this contribution was more dispersed and harder to grasp than the Russian, reflecting the complex and wide-ranging commitments of a truly global struggle.

The Red Army faced a comparatively simple situation in strategy and supply. It was fighting close to home, in the great "heartland" of the Eurasian continent. Its supply lines were short, and its soldiers required little beyond food, clothes, and war materiel. It had a clear and comprehensible task: to expel the invaders from its country. Thus when it had turned the tide and begun to advance, its strategy followed a simple pattern: it pushed on for about 300 miles until its supply lines were stretched to the limit, then it paused to consolidate and regroup for another advance. Only when the Russians reached their own frontiers in the summer of 1944 were they faced with the perplexing choices that had plagued the British and Americans from the start.

The Western democracies were fighting not one war, but several. In Asia and the Pacific, they were fighting a war against Japan, which in the early part of the year 1942 was a series of unbroken defeats. In this struggle, they had no help from the Soviet Union: Stalin, fully occupied in defending himself in Europe, was not anxious to engage another enemy, and he maintained a strict neutrality in the war with Japan. The British were also fighting in the Mediterranean, and they were mounting a constantly increasing air offensive against the Reich itself. This had begun even before the diversion of the *Luftwaffe's* major strength to the attack on Russia gave the British air superiority in the west: in

November, 1940, Molotov's conversations in Berlin with the Nazi leaders had been rudely interrupted by an RAF raid. In late 1941 and 1942, the British bombing attacks extended steadily in scope: the great north German cities of Berlin, Cologne, Hamburg, and the Ruhr were assailed repeatedly. By the beginning of 1943, the Americans were ready to give full-scale assistance. With the addition of American strength, the air offensive against Germany went into a new phase. Hitherto the British planes had restricted themselves to night attacks; the American bombers —the B-17's or Flying Fortresses—which were more heavily armored, could strike in daylight as well.

The Americans on all fronts, and the British on most of theirs, were operating at the end of supply lines that were thousands of miles in length. Hence they could not put the bulk of their military manpower into combat units, as the Russians could do so readily. Throughout the war a discouragingly high percentage of the Anglo-Americans in uniform remained absorbed in manning supply lines. It was over such far-flung communications lanes that the Red Army received the tanks and trucks and jeeps that alone enabled it to fight on. Some came around the North Cape, some by the longer but safer route via the Persian Gulf that was opened in the autumn of 1942.

In either case, the trip by sea took weeks and tied up a whole flotilla of cruisers, destroyers, and corvettes in convoy duty. For the British and Americans had still another war to fight—the war at sea. Although Germany was primarily a land power with an army that had proved itself the finest in the world, it was also a formidable naval power. In over-all naval strength Germany now ranked fourth—after the United States and Britain and its own ally, Japan—but in certain strategic classes of vessels Germany had no peer. Its two great battleships, the *Bismarck* and the *Tirpitz*, were the strongest afloat. The *Bismarck* kept half the British Home Fleet immobilized simply in watching it, until one day in May, 1941, it eluded its guard, spreading terror through the North Atlantic and sinking Britain's largest warship, the *Hood*, before it was itself destroyed by combined air and naval attack. The *Tirpitz* remained in a Norwegian fjord, a constant source of anxiety to the Royal Navy, which failed time after time in its attempts to sink it from the air. The German submarine fleet was a still greater menace: at the end of 1942, Hitler had 400 submarines, which destroyed more than six million tons of merchant shipping in the course of the year. For many months, the German submarines sank ships faster than the Americans and British could build them. It was only in the autumn of 1942 that the Anglo-American production rate outstripped monthly losses.

Finally, the critics of British and American strategy forgot that all the prospective operations in the west involved an amphibious assault against a heavily defended coastline. Here history offered no precedents. The great democracies had almost to invent the technique of amphibious warfare: the Germans had not dared to launch "Sea Lion" against Eng-

land; the Russians had no need for, or experience in, major landing oper-
ations. These were to become the Anglo-American specialty—their great contribution to the art of modern warfare. But the Western Allies could make their supreme attempt—a major cross-Channel invasion of France —only after gaining experience in the Mediterranean and in the Pacific. They also needed time to construct a great fleet of landing craft: again and again during 1943 and 1944 a shortage of landing craft was to be the crucial limitation on offensive operations.

Nevertheless, Churchill and Roosevelt did mishandle the issue of a second front. Their confusions and hesitations on this score were only natural, since their military advisers disagreed: the Americans were eager to land on the Continent as soon as possible; the more reluctant British were attracted by the possibilities of less costly operations in the Mediterranean. When Molotov came to Washington six months after the American declaration of war, the dispute was still unresolved: the communiqué issued at the end of his visit spoke in guarded terms of the "urgent tasks of creating a second front in Europe in 1942." This the Russians—and the Anglo-American public—in general interpreted as a commitment to act within the current year. Hence it was with some trepidation that Churchill set out for Moscow in August to explain to Stalin that the second front must wait until 1943; for the present, the British and Americans could do no more than land in French North Africa. It was the first time the two war leaders had met, and considering the tension of the moment and the memories of mutual antagonism that lay between them, their encounter was relatively harmonious. Stalin bowed to the inevitable, but his patience was to be tried still further the following year when the new front promised for 1943 proved to be a secondary operation in Italy rather than a major landing in France. The true second front was not to materialize until the very last year of the war.

The Nazi "New Order": Racism and Collaboration

The pressure for a second front did not come solely from Stalin and his advisers. It came also from all those in the Western camp who were concerned with delivering the populations of occupied Europe from their Nazi oppressors.

At the end of 1941, Hitler had conquered the most extensive empire that European history had ever known. Directly or indirectly, he ruled over all the former democracies of Western Europe, except for neutral Sweden and Switzerland; he held the whole of the Balkans and East Central Europe, the Ukraine, and a vast zone in European Russia. Italy was closely allied to him, Spain more loosely. Except for minor bits and pieces, all the Continent lay in his grasp.

As master of Europe, Hitler enjoyed a great historic opportunity. More powerful than either Charlemagne or Napoleon, he could follow in their footsteps and give Europe the unity it had so long sought. As Spengler had predicted, he might be the "Caesar-figure" who would defend the West against the onslaughts of "Asiatic bolshevism." Nor was this merely a German dream: it was also the aspiration of millions of non-German Europeans who believed that the treaties of 1919 had been mistaken, that the Wilsonian ideal of self-determination and the League of Nations had failed, and that some more realistic form of supranational authority was needed to take their place. In the weary and disillusioned Europe of 1940 and 1941, an influential minority both of leaders and of the led was willing to accept German hegemony. The Germans were the most numerous and the most industrially advanced of the major peoples of Western and Central Europe, and after the collapse of France, leadership seemed to devolve on them almost by right.

Hitler offered the Europeans a "New Order." He promised them a stern justice under which each nation would be assigned its fitting role. But the reality of the New Order proved to bear very little resemblance to the promised ideal. By the beginning of 1942, at the very latest, the vast majority of the populations of occupied Europe had turned against Hitler and the nation he led. In 1943, the Italians, too, were to become his enemies, and with them a small but resolute minority among his own people. By the end of the war, nazism was universally hated as the most dreadful tyranny that Europe had known since the Dark Ages.

What had changed men's minds? First, Hitler and his henchmen found themselves obliged to sacrifice their schemes for the reorganization of Europe to the necessities of warfare. The Nazi overlords of East Central Europe redrew the map in an illogical and temporary fashion in order to spur their satellite states to further exertion. More important, however, was the German need for labor. With the invasion of the Soviet Union in 1941, Hitler began to face a stringent manpower shortage. The Russians alone outnumbered the Germans—and the *Führer* could not send all his troops to the east, since he also needed to garrison France and Norway and the Balkans. Under these circumstances, his sole recourse was to take every able-bodied German out of agriculture and industry and send him to the front. The gaps this left in the Reich's productive force had to be filled, and the only manpower reserve lay in the occupied countries. Thus the Nazis began to resort to labor drafts abroad. Originally, these foreign laborers went to the Reich as "volunteers," but as stories of ill-treatment filtered back to the occupied countries, it became increasingly difficult to find workers who were willing to go. Gradually all pretense was dropped: by the last year of the war, the millions of foreigners working in Germany had frankly been degraded to an army of slave laborers. Young men fleeing from forced labor in the Reich had become the chief source of recruitment for the resistance organizations that were springing up everywhere.

Still worse was Nazi racial policy. In *Mein Kampf*, Hitler flaunted his ideas of German superiority and his contempt for most of the peoples

of Europe. Any honest effort to reorganize the Continent under German
headship immediately struck the flagrant contradiction of Nazi racial doctrine. This, more than anything else, ultimately alienated the Europeans from Hitler's New Order.

In treatment of subject peoples, the Nazis tried to adhere to a clear racial hierarchy. In the highest category ranked the fellow "Nordics" —the Dutch, the Norwegians, and the Danes—who were invited to join the Germans as "master races" in the New Order. The Danes alone showed even the slightest inclination to accept the honor—and this only because Denmark received preferential treatment as a Nazi showplace, a model dependency which was allowed to keep its institutions intact. Next came the French and the Belgians, "mixed" peoples who were rather perplexing to racial theorists. Immediately after them ranked the Slavs—the Russians, the Poles, and the Czechs—of whom the Czechs alone, who were peacefully inclined and vital to German war production, escaped the worst of Nazi brutalities. Finally, of course, in the lowest order, came those whom the Nazis regarded as pariahs—the Jews and the Gypsies. These were to be exterminated. In the spring of 1942, Hitler decided on a "final solution" of the Jewish question, and in the next three years his faithful SS detachments destroyed six million Jews in the gas chambers and crematories of Auschwitz and other concentration camps. Thus perished during the Second World War about three-quarters of European Jewry—two-fifths of all the Jews in the world.

Such treatment of the conquered was not only criminal—it was stupid, for it alienated even those who might otherwise have been favorable to the New Order. "Aryans" who themselves were safe from racial persecution were revolted by Hitler's systematic destruction of the Jews and frequently shielded them in their homes at the greatest personal risk. Other peoples who were themselves victims of persecution and had welcomed the Nazis as liberators, were disillusioned to find that they did not receive privileged treatment. For example, numbers of Ukrainian peasants had greeted the Germans in 1941 as deliverers from Communist tyranny. Many hoped for the reconstitution of the independent Ukraine which had existed for a brief period at the end of the First World War. But German occupation policy soon made it apparent that the Ukrainians were being confounded with the Great Russians in the common lot of "barbarian" Slavs.

Just as Nazi occupation policy—and the racial theory of which it was an outgrowth—were unprecedented in European history, so were the choices with which it confronted individuals among the conquered peoples. Earlier it had been assumed that populations who temporarily fell under enemy control in wartime would obey the orders of the invader; relations between the two might not be friendly, but they were supposed to be "correct." Even during the First World War, in occupied Belgium, officials like the mayor of Brussels were generally applauded for staying at their posts and doing what they could to help their fellow citizens.

In the Second World War, circumstances were quite different. At first, a great many local officials tried to conform to the older pattern, and some of them—who sacrificed their good names to what they regarded as their duty—rank among the unsung heroes of the conflict. But as Nazi occupation policy hardened, it became ever more difficult to reconcile German orders with the voice of the local officials' own consciences, and when they were asked to help herd Jews or forced laborers, most of them refused.

Under these circumstances, only a handful remained with the Germans until the end. The prototype of such true "collaborationists" was Vidkun Quisling of Norway, whose name was given to the whole species. But Quisling had few followers in Norway, and elsewhere in the west Hitler found no suitable leading figure to govern in his name. He organized Belgium and Holland as military commands—as Poland had been. In France there was Marshal Pétain, but he was no Quisling. On the contrary, the marshal was a perplexing borderline case, whose presence at the head of the Vichy government confused and divided the French through most of the war. Another—and more sinister—borderline figure was Ante Pavelich, the ruler of Croatia, which Hitler had separated from the Serbian lands of Yugoslavia in conformity with his characteristic tactics of divide and rule.

These special cases can be understood only in the light of that other phenomenon—counterpoise and deadly enemy of collaboration—the Resistance movements.

The Resistance: Tito and De Gaulle

Resistance meant sabotage and guerrilla warfare against the Nazi occupiers. It meant the establishment of shadow governments and shadow political parties to prepare the ground for the day of liberation. It also meant liaison with governments-in-exile, where such existed.

The different European countries reacted in varying fashion to the experience of occupation. In Poland and Norway and Yugoslavia, the Resistance began on the very day the country was conquered. In Denmark and Czechoslovakia—to cite the other extreme—there was virtually no Resistance until toward the end of the war: these countries were close to Germany, the early treatment they received was comparatively mild, their terrain was not suited to guerrilla operations—in short, they lacked the prerequisites for militant Resistance activity. France lay somewhere between: here the Resistance swelled as Nazi occupation policy grew sterner and disappointment with the Vichy government spread. In Italy, the war itself brought slow disillusionment: an Italian Resistance was ready to spring up almost overnight when the country changed sides in the war.

Throughout Europe, however, the conditions that stimulated such activity were much the same. Resistance grew in rural areas, where mountains or forests offered cover, and also in cities, where workers felt threatened by the labor draft. It sprang up where there were idealistic or desperate men whose hatred of the invader impelled them to leave their ordinary jobs to go underground or take to the hills. This hatred was partly ideological and partly national: Resistance was most intense and united in areas where patriotism and antifascism reinforced each other in a common hostility to Germans and Quislings.

The Resistance tended toward the left. Its recruits most frequently came from the working classes or from young intellectuals with a social conscience; it was strong at the extreme ends of the social scale—among the poor and among the upper classes, whose sense of adventure and martial tradition brought the Resistance a precious reinforcement of military talent. The great middle class and the richer peasantry generally stood aside: people of this sort, cautious by tradition and wedded to routine, hesitated to take the risks that Resistance activity entailed.

The inspiration of the Resistance was something like that of a revived Popular Front. As in the Popular Front, the Communists played a leading role. To European communism, Stalin's pact with Hitler in August, 1939, came as the cruelest blow: bewildered and disillusioned, the Communists of Western Europe and the Balkans hovered for a year and a half in ideological limbo, waiting for Moscow to clarify its stand. But in mid-1941, the German attack on the Soviet Union delivered them from uncertainty. They renewed their faith and reknit their cadres and undertook Resistance activities on an impressive scale. Soon in country after country, they had become the single strongest element in the Resistance. They had powerful assets that other groups lacked—unquestioning discipline, leaders experienced in clandestine activity and in the guerrilla warfare they had learned about in Spain—above all, their following had little to lose and was prepared to run risks and to endure suffering at which others quailed.

Their position as the spearhead of the Resistance gave the Communists a special prestige among the occupied peoples. They profited by and in turn strengthened the legend of the Soviet Union as the country that was doing all the fighting. Consequently, many people who usually distrusted communism and Communists were willing to cooperate with them during the war years. Others—more farsighted—realized that within the ranks of the Resistance, men were preparing the postliberation regimes under which their countries would live. The Communists, they discovered, were trying to engulf the whole Resistance and to put it under their own leadership. Thus certain of the more tough-minded Resistance chiefs determined to oppose communism at all costs—even to the point of armed conflict.

The Second World War on the continent of Europe has sometimes been called an international civil war. It was such a conflict in a double sense. First, it was a desperate struggle between resisters and collaborationists—between patriots who were trying to drive the invaders out of their country and the smaller number of traitors who put themselves at the service of Nazi Germany. This was a war without mercy: a Resistance fighter well knew that if he fell into the hands of the black-shirted SS, only torture and death awaited him. Alongside this avowed conflict raged another and quieter civil war, yet one which was scarcely less cruel—the war of Communists against non-Communists within the Resistance itself. The examples of Poland, Yugoslavia, and France may suggest how this latter struggle developed in three widely different settings.

The Poles very early organized a strong and united Resistance movement. Here collaborationists were virtually nonexistent: the cruelty of German occupation policy saw to that. The Poles were proud that they never produced a Quisling, but they were not exposed to the temptations that assailed the Scandinavians or the Dutch; Poland was never invited to collaborate in the Nazi New Order, and its people were immediately treated as inferiors. Nor was there a problem of Communist influence: in Poland, traditional hatred of Russia and of communism had only been intensified by Stalin's connivance with Hitler in the partition of the country. The Polish Resistance was both conservative in tone and supported by the overwhelming majority of the people. It carried on a regular underground government, with law courts, bond issues, even a rudimentary educational system, and, through a remarkable organization of clandestine couriers, it maintained contact with the Polish government-in-exile in London.

Stalin had no regard either for the government in London or for the underground regime in Poland itself. When the Red Army crossed the Polish boundary on its triumphal advance west, he chose to ignore both of them. Instead he set up his own puppet regime of Communists who had been indoctrinated in Moscow, and he let the authentic Polish Resistance fighters be destroyed by the Germans while making only the most perfunctory moves to save them.

Yugoslavia, in contrast, produced both a non-Communist and a Communist-led Resistance movement of major dimensions. Indeed, the Yugoslavs never really demobilized after their defeat in the spring of 1941. A number of Serbian army officers, under the command of Colonel Draja Mihailovich, fled with their weapons and continued the struggle in the country's mountain fastnesses, where they organized bands of guerrilla fighters called *Chetniks*. Mihailovich's exploits soon aroused widespread sympathy in the West. The Yugoslav government-in-exile appointed him minister of war and relied increasingly on him to assure its return home at the end of the conflict.

Meanwhile, however, Churchill and Roosevelt had begun to have grave doubts as to whether Mihailovich was mobilizing Yugoslav Resistance to the full, for the Chetnik leader was proving himself rather Serb than Yugoslav: he made no secret of his intention of enforcing Serbian supremacy on the country's liberation, and he neither tried nor desired to appeal to the Croats, Slovenes, and other minority peoples within Yugoslavia. This role fell to another resistance leader, Josip Broz, better known by his revolutionary nickname, Tito. Tito's movement began later than Mihailovich's but soon outdistanced it; for Tito was a Croat, and although he himself had long since cast off the ancestral Catholicism that characterized Croatia, he had no love for Serb supremacy, and he preached reconciliation and unity among the Yugoslav peoples. He condemned both the Serbian collaborationists and the Croat leader Pavelich, who was taking his revenge for the humiliations his people had suffered at the hands of the Serbians by slaughtering tens of thousands of them with Hitler's and Mussolini's blessing. Tito was also a Communist, and his bands of Partisans—as they were called to distinguish them from Mihailovich's Chetniks—were systematically indoctrinated by Communist political commissars. During the war, however, Tito kept his own communism in the background; it was rather the Popular Front formula that he followed when he organized a Yugoslav underground government in November, 1942.

Tito fought the Germans and fought them hard. By 1943, he was keeping at bay at least ten enemy divisions. Mihailovich, in contrast, remained quiescent, holding his forces in reserve for an eventual day of reckoning and even occasionally making agreements with local Serbian collaborationists. To Churchill and Roosevelt—anxiously watching from a distance the complexities of the Yugoslav situation unfold—it gradually became evident that Mihailovich was putting hatred for Croatia and communism before his desire for his country's liberation from the Nazis; actually he was waiting until the British and Americans were ready to help him install a Serbian nationalist government. This game the Western Allies refused to play. In 1943, first Churchill, and later Roosevelt, withdrew support from Mihailovich and gave their help to Tito instead.

In France, as in Yugoslavia—and as was to occur later in northern Italy —Communists played a very prominent part in the Resistance. But France found in Charles de Gaulle a military and nationalist leader who was far more successful than Mihailovich in counteracting their influence. An expert in tank warfare from whose books the Germans learned the *Blitzkrieg* tactics they were to apply so devastatingly against the French, De Gaulle had been a prophet without honor in his own country. Called by Premier Reynaud in France's hour of supreme peril to serve as undersecretary of war, he had come to office too late to stay his army's collapse. Yet he was able to use his official position to maintain the link with Britain after France's defeat. Refusing to accept Pétain's armistice, he flew to London, where on June 18, 1940, he broadcast a message calling for the adherence of all Frenchmen who wanted to continue the fight.

In Britain, De Gaulle established a Free French National Committee to serve as an embryo government-in-exile. Recruits arrived in a slow trickle: most of the French took a "wait-and-see" attitude—which was only natural since Pétain's government in Vichy still seemed to speak with the voice of legitimacy. Nowhere else in Western Europe were men's allegiances so cruelly divided. Churchill gave De Gaulle his support—although he found the general extremely difficult to deal with and complained that the Cross of Lorraine (De Gaulle's emblem) was the heaviest cross he had to bear. Roosevelt, on the contrary, distrusted the Free French leader as an authoritarian and refused to grant recognition to his National Committee. This distrust proved mistaken, but it was understandable in view of De Gaulle's excessive pride and his tendency to regard his country's destiny as incarnate in his own person.

By 1942, however, De Gaulle began to make definite progress. A sizable segment of the French overseas empire—including Equatorial Africa, the Pacific islands, Madagascar, and Syria—had come under his control. Pétain's regime was steadily losing prestige as its impotence to shield France against the German occupation grew more evident. It had also failed in its effort to justify its existence by bringing to trial Blum, Daladier, and Gamelin as responsible for the collapse of 1940: the trial boomeranged when the defendants courageously spoke out and turned the charge against their accusers; Blum in particular became a national hero as his final plea circulated clandestinely among the Resistance fighters. And these were rallying to De Gaulle. In early 1942, the vast majority of the Resistance organizations within France recognized the general as their chief. A number of their leaders joined him in London, including several prominent Socialists, whose arrival gave the Free French movement a more representative and democratic flavor. By the autumn of 1942—when the British and Americans were preparing for a landing in French North Africa—it was apparent to all except those irremediably prejudiced against De Gaulle that the active and militant element within France had deserted Vichy and had transferred its sympathies to the Free French movement.

IV
THE TURNING OF THE TIDE

In the autumn of 1942, the tide turned. For more than three years, events had moved in Hitler's favor. The war had been a long succession of German victories—the greatest the world had ever seen. The best his enemies had been able to do was to stop his advance in the air battle of Britain and before Moscow and to defeat his Italian ally in the Mediterranean. At the end of 1942, the trend was reversed: the Russians held firm at Stalingrad, the British broke out of Egypt, the Americans landed in French North Africa; in two widely separated theaters of combat, the Allies were preparing vast encircling operations that would bring the Nazis their first major defeats. From this point on, the victory of Britain and America and the Soviet Union was never in doubt: the only question was how long it would take—and the answer to that question depended on the great strategic decisions which the Allied leaders were to make in their efforts to fight a coalition war of unprecedented scope and intensity.

The Battle of Stalingrad

Hitler changed his military command after the failure before Moscow. His old field marshals, disappointed by the *Führer's* interference with their strategy, retired and were replaced by younger men, who were more pliable and closer to the Nazi party. And Hitler himself assumed the post of commander in chief.

Although the military amateur was now in charge, the plan for the campaign of 1942 showed a more coherent strategy than that pursued in 1941: the attack was to be on one front alone; the whole weight of German arms was to be concentrated in the south, where Hitler hoped to achieve the decisive results that had eluded him the previous year. In the north and center, his forces were to remain where they were: as the spring thaws set in, and military operations bogged down, Hitler could note with gratification that the Russian winter offensive had ended without dislodging his troops from any essential position. The Germans had been obliged to withdraw before Moscow, but they still had Leningrad in an iron grip. It was in the south, once the mud had dried, that Hitler was to make his supreme effort: he planned to drive from the Ukraine to Stalingrad on the Volga, and to the Caspian Sea, thereby literally cutting the Soviet Union in two. By seizing the Caucasus, he hoped both to deny the Red Army its major source of oil and to solve his own most urgent supply problem.

At first, the German tanks rolled forward as relentlessly as they had the previous summer. In early July, they took Sevastopol in the Crimea; at the end of the month, they were in Rostov and preparing to cross the Don. Once across the great river, they raced ahead almost without interruption: by late summer, they were just short of the oil center of Grozny in the north Caucasus, and their advanced patrols had reached the Caspian Sea.

Meanwhile, on August 22, the Battle of Stalingrad had begun. Stalingrad was a key city in every sense. It was dear to Stalin's heart: under its original name of Tsaritsin it was the place where he had first made a military reputation during the civil war. It was also a major industrial center—one of the new manufacturing complexes which had been built up safely remote from the Soviet frontiers during the Five-Year Plans. Finally, it was a strategic position of first importance: situated on the Volga just where the Don bends closest to its sister river, it stood farthest east of the great cities of southern Russia. Beyond Stalingrad lay little but open steppe: should it fall into enemy hands, communication between the south and the center of the country would be effectively severed.

Stalin gave the order to hold at all costs. With their backs to Asia, the city's defenders stood their ground. But the Germans—suffering enormous losses—still inched steadily forward. By mid-September they were in the city itself: attackers and besiegers fought desperately at close quarters in streets and factories. For a few days the position of the defenders seemed hopeless.

Once again Stalin kept his nerve. Already he had given the order for a great pincers movement that would catch the Germans in a trap. On September 21, the first Soviet attack began: crossing the Volga north of Stalingrad, it advanced into the open plain between the two rivers. Ten days later, the second attack moved from the south. The Germans were caught off guard. Isolated at the end of a dangerously stretched communications line, the besiegers of Stalingrad now had to turn to face a new threat to the rear. In October and November, the Russian pincers began to close. If the Germans were to escape it had to be before winter set in. But Hitler refused to give the order for evacuation: he had resolved that his quarter-million soldiers at Stalingrad should die at their posts. It was full winter when the two Soviet advances met; the trap snapped shut—the rest was one long German martyrdom. Hunger, frost, and typhus took a mounting toll. By the new year, the Germans were reduced to a ragged rabble of sick and half-crazed men. On February 2, 1943, when the final surrender came, only 80,000 remained alive to be led off to captivity.

So ended the greatest battle of human history.

The Battle of El Alamein

For two years, the desert war in North Africa had seesawed back and forth with no decisive victory for either side. The Italians had invaded Egypt from their own colony of Libya. Then in December, 1940, the British launched a surprise attack, driving the Italians back 500 miles and capturing 130,000 of them, with casualties on their own side totaling less than 2,000. At this point, Hitler saw the necessity of bolstering his groggy ally. He sent to Libya one of his ablest tank leaders, General Erwin Rommel, with reinforcements of German armored troops and instructions to supplant the Italians in command, which Rommel did with a vengeance. Exploiting to the full the decisive moment when the British ranks had been depleted to reinforce the Greeks, Rommel pushed his enemy back to the Egyptian frontier in the spring of 1941. But then he himself was obliged to give up his reserves to support Hitler's attack on Russia. Once more the initiative passed to the British, and once more they carried out a successful winter offensive. Finally, at the end of May, 1942, the pendulum swung back for the last time: Rommel nearly routed

his foe; only the determined stand of the Free French at the strong point
of Bir Hakeim saved the British from disaster. In mid-June, it appeared that Rommel would reach the Nile and that the whole Allied position in the Middle East would collapse.

On the last possible defensive line, the British called a halt. At El Alamein, only 70 miles from Alexandria, they dug in at the end of June and began to recover their strength. A new general arrived to take command—Sir Bernard Montgomery, lean, stern, and ascetic, whose flamboyant communiqués concealed the fact that he was a man of caution who refused to attack until every detail of the operation had been meticulously prepared and until he enjoyed superiority in both men and materiel. Throughout the summer of 1942, Montgomery husbanded his forces at El Alamein: he retrained his troops and re-equipped them with new and heavier tanks sent from the United States. In late October, all was ready. The British artillery opened fire with the heaviest barrage that the African continent had ever known, and the sappers began a cautious advance through a desert thickly strewn with mines.

For ten days the decision hung in the balance. Then Rommel's lines broke, and he was forced to retreat. For the next two months, the British pursued him along the Egyptian and Libyan shore. Nowhere could the Germans make a stand. Relentlessly, methodically, Montgomery dislodged them from every strong point. On January 24, 1943, he captured Tripoli, and the road to Tunisia lay open.

The Landings in French North Africa: Darlan, Giraud, and the Free French

The advance from El Alamein formed one claw of the great pincers movement which the British and Americans had devised to liquidate once and for all the Axis position in North Africa. The other was a series of landings in French-controlled Morocco and Algeria that Churchill and Roosevelt had decided in July was to be their major effort for the year 1942. Rejecting as too hazardous the project for a landing in France itself, they chose to descend on neutral ground—to exploit the gap which Hitler had left in his defenses when he failed to persuade Franco to seal off the Mediterranean.

The plan was primarily American in inspiration, and its commander was also to be an American: General Dwight D. Eisenhower. Joint landings were to be made on the Mediterranean coast of Algeria and United States troops alone were to disembark from the Atlantic in Morocco. Owing to Roosevelt's insistence, De Gaulle and his Free French were left out completely: they were told nothing of the projected invasion and assigned no part in it. The Americans were confident that they could succeed without De Gaulle's help: their clandestine agents in North Africa had been in direct communication with the anti-Vichy French of Morocco and Algeria, and they had found another military leader, a "nonpolitical" general, Henri Giraud, who they believed would rally North Africa to his side and persuade the forces stationed there to make only a show of resistance to the landings.

Roosevelt and his advisers were gravely mistaken. When, on November 8, the great invasion armada approached the African coast, and the untried American troops scrambled ashore, the French army and navy fought hard. Their commanders ignored Giraud's appeal and followed Pétain's order to oppose the invaders. In Morocco especially the fighting was bitter, and casualties began to increase on both sides—not at all what Eisenhower had been led to expect. Giraud had failed him, and now he had to improvise another solution. In this moment of anguished uncertainty, a fortunate accident came to his aid. Admiral François Darlan—Pétain's heir apparent and the third major figure in the Vichy regime after the marshal himself and Pierre Laval—happened to be in Algiers visiting his sick son. Darlan was a born intriguer: after three days of intricate maneuvering, he found what the situation required. In his role as commander in chief of the Vichy armed forces, he ordered an end to the fighting. In return, Darlan demanded that the Allies confirm him as provisional ruler of French North Africa. Eisenhower agreed: he had no other recourse. On November 11, an armistice was signed, and the fighting ended.

The "Darlan deal" was bitterly criticized in Britain, in the United States, and among the French Resistance. It was certainly an arrangement of pure expediency, confirming as it did the rule of reactionaries and quasi-fascists in French North Africa. From the moral and ideological standpoint, it had nothing to recommend it, but from the military standpoint, it brought results: it enabled the French to return to the fight almost immediately. Scarcely had the armistice been signed than they joined the British and Americans in the advance on Tunisia, where the Germans had flown in troops from Sicily and were preparing to make their final North African stand. Meanwhile the unfavorable political effects of the deal were gradually overcome. On Christmas Eve, Darlan was assassinated. He was replaced by the blameless Giraud, a stately figure who had no idea how to govern. A power vacuum was left which De Gaulle was eager to fill. Roosevelt was still prejudiced against him, but at Churchill's urging he finally consented to let the Free French leader go to Algiers in June, 1943, to share power with Giraud.

This was an unequal and unstable relationship from the beginning. Once De Gaulle arrived in Algeria, it became apparent that virtually all the drive and enthusiasm among the French were on his side. Soon the Gaullist pressure grew overwhelming. By the autumn of 1943, Giraud was out of power, and De Gaulle was heading what was in reality if not yet in name a provisional government of the French Empire. Nearly all the colonies now obeyed him; the Resistance was in his hands; the Vichy government had become a mere shadow, since the Germans had used the North African landings as a pretext for occupying the whole country. As the moment of liberation approached, all eyes turned toward De Gaulle.

The Conquest of Sicily, the Fall of Mussolini, and the Invasion of Italy

Meanwhile the pincers had closed on Tunisia. Its reduction had taken longer than the British and Americans had expected, but the delay brought additional Axis reinforcements and the prospect that a larger number of Germans would eventually be caught in the trap. In late March, 1943, Eisenhower began the final attack from the west, and Montgomery moved from the east. This time their advance proceeded steadily. On May 12, Axis resistance came to an end: 160,000 German and Italian prisoners were taken—a prize comparable to that at Stalingrad.

The next step was Sicily. Once more Churchill and Roosevelt had decided to give priority to clearing the Mediterranean. Meeting at the Moroccan port of Casablanca in January, they had determined to occupy the great Italian island which nearly divided the Mediterranean in two. Although they did not then realize it, this meant that the real second front in France was to be postponed for still another year, for the landing in Sicily led to further operations on the mainland of Italy which were inevitably to develop into the major Anglo-American effort for 1943.

The attack on Sicily began on July 10. It was the largest landing operation that the British and Americans had yet undertaken: 160,000 men participated—some coming in by parachute or glider, but most of them carried in the nearly three thousand ships and landing craft that made up the invasion fleet. After sharp fighting on the beaches, the conquest of Sicily proceeded rapidly. The Germans fought hard but the Italians, who constituted the bulk of the island's defenders, offered little more than token resistance. They were already sick of the war—disgusted by constant defeats, by the domineering of their German allies, and by the way Mussolini had lied to them about their nation's strength and its readiness for war.

For the Duce himself, the play had almost ended. On July 25, just after the fall of the Sicilian capital of Palermo, he was toppled from power: a combination of monarchist conservatives and Fascist dissidents persuaded the old king to dismiss him and make him prisoner. Mussolini's successor was Marshal Pietro Badoglio—the conqueror of Ethiopia and a very recent convert to antifascism, to say the least. Badoglio hoped to take Italy out of the war unscathed, and in this he faithfully expressed the longings of his people. In the month and a half that followed Mussolini's fall, the country lived in a strange euphoria; free political activity revived as though by magic, and the Italians cherished the illusion that they were entering on a new era of peace, liberty, and national harmony.

Actually their troubles had only begun. For Italy, the second phase of the war was to be still crueler than the first. As soon as Badoglio made overtures for peace, he discovered the harsh reality—the British and Americans would sign an armistice only under the formula of "unconditional surrender" which they had announced at Casablanca. Badoglio wriggled and squirmed: he tried to set conditions for his surrender and to deceive the Germans as to his intentions, but he succeeded in neither aim. In the end he was forced to make a simple capitulation to the Allies; meantime Hitler, completely undeceived, had been pouring troops over the Brenner Pass to hold in check his faithless ally.

On September 2, the British made an initial landing in Calabria on the toe of the Italian peninsula. A week later, the Americans followed with a more perilous attack at Salerno south of Naples. Simultaneously the armistice was announced. The Germans were already poised to strike: without a moment's hesitation, they seized the city of Rome—from which the king and Badoglio took flight—and occupied the whole northern and central part of the country. The Allies could do nothing to stop them: indeed, they were barely able to hold their own ground on the bloody beaches of Salerno. Subsequently, they liberated Naples and brought under their control Sardinia and the southern mainland but, when the autumn rains ended the fighting season, the British and Americans were still far from Rome.

For the next year and a half, Italy was to remain cut in two. In the north Mussolini, whom the Germans had dramatically freed from imprisonment, wielded nominal authority as a pathetic and powerless Quisling. The king and Badoglio, whom the Allies were supporting in the south, were scarcely less feeble and unrepresentative of the Italian people. Between the two hovered the uncertain mass of Italians—half-starved, half-frozen, and miserable in the damp Mediterranean winter.

Teheran and the Great Strategic Decisions

After its victory at Stalingrad, the Red Army swept on to further winter triumphs. It drove back the German besiegers before Leningrad,* cleared an additional zone west of Moscow, retook Rostov and began the liberation of the Ukraine. In the spring of 1943, however, as had happened the year before, the Germans struck back. In March, they recaptured the recently liberated city of Kharkov, and in early July they attacked 100 miles farther north in the region of Kursk and Orel. But this was their last effort; never again were the Germans to regain the initiative on the Eastern Front. In mid-July the Soviet summer offensive began to roll: it was the beginning of a colossal advance that continued almost

---

* The siege was finally lifted a year later.

two years and reached its end in the smoking ruins of Berlin. After freeing Kharkov once more, the Russians crossed the Dnieper and wrested
Kiev from German control. By the end of the year, they had liberated
more than half the Ukraine.

Victories such as these drew the two fronts closer together. With the
British and Americans at last ashore on the European continent and
with the Russians advancing relentlessly toward their own borders, a
new coordination had become urgent. So long as the campaigns in the
east remained widely separated from those in the west, it had been possible to treat them as two separate wars. Now it was essential to knit
them together, and this was the purpose of the first of the two meetings
that brought Churchill and Roosevelt into personal contact with Stalin
—the meeting held in November and December, 1943, at the Persian
capital of Teheran.

At Teheran, grand strategy was not the sole topic of discussion. Political questions were also touched on, and the outlines of an eventual settlement for Poland were sketched. Yet Roosevelt was still reluctant to make
territorial commitments for the future: he preferred to wait until the end
of the war, when the victorious Allies could deal with all major issues
at once. This postponement suited Stalin far better than the Soviet leader
was willing to admit: to delay a settlement meant to wait until the Russians had physical possession of the lands they demanded. Hence at
Teheran Stalin advanced his territorial claims in rather perfunctory fashion: eventually he agreed with Roosevelt's desire for postponement.
Churchill, rather, kept pushing for an early discussion of controversial
issues; with his longer experience of international dealings, he realized
better than Roosevelt that the time for bargaining was now, *before* the
Red Army had the spoils of war in its hands.

In the same almost accidental fashion, Russian and American views
on strategy coincided, whereas the British were more hesitant. For nearly
two years Stalin had been pleading for a major second front—preferably
in France—that would relieve German pressure on his own forces. This
was also the desire of the American military leaders, whose only purpose
was to find the shortest and speediest way to drive for the enemy's heart.
Churchill, on the contrary, was always doubtful about a cross-Channel
invasion: he dreaded a repetition of the fearful losses that the British
had suffered in France in the First World War. Hence he favored operations in the Mediterranean and the Balkans that would strike at what he
called the "soft underbelly of Europe." And—ever mindful of political
considerations—he hoped that in this way he could keep at least part of
East Central Europe free from Soviet control.

Roosevelt refused to listen to such arguments. The American president
was less of a military expert than Churchill or Stalin; he did not try to
run his war in the personal fashion they did, and he was far more dependent on the advice of his military chiefs. Hence he reflected their
military impatience with political considerations and their desire to win
the war in the shortest possible time by striking directly at Germany it-

self. This purely strategic reasoning—rather than any alleged "softness" toward Soviet communism—brought Roosevelt into agreement with Stalin about a cross-Channel invasion of the Continent.

Hence the great achievement of the Teheran Conference was to overcome Churchill's last lingering objections and to confirm the tentative decision the British and Americans had reached six months earlier—a major landing would be made in France in May of 1944. The commander of the operation was to be General Eisenhower. Stalin—much gratified —promised to open a simultaneous offensive on the Eastern Front. The strategy had been established that would bring total victory in the last year and a half of the war.

V

THE FINAL ASSAULT

The Liberation of Rome and Anti-Fascist Italy

The Teheran decisions had put the Italian campaign in a paradoxical position. It was to be both an active front and a secondary front. It was the only place on the Continent where the British and Americans were actually fighting, but its needs were constantly subordinated to the task of building up strength in England for the cross-Channel operation in the spring. Hence it was always short of manpower: again and again, a planned offensive dwindled and failed because of a lack of reserve troops.

These handicaps were already apparent in the first efforts to break the winter stalemate south of Rome. In January, 1944, the Allies made a landing at Anzio, only 30 miles from the Italian capital, and a simultaneous assault on the Germans defending the mountain abbey of Cassino. They hoped to catch Hitler's forces off guard by attacking them at two points at once and then to advance quickly to the liberation of Rome. Both expectations were cruelly disappointed. The defenders of Cassino could not be dislodged from their mountain positions, and the Anzio attack soon bogged down into a weary stalemate, with the British and Americans pinned to the low and marshy ground which the German artillery dominated from the surrounding hills.

The advance on Rome had to be postponed until spring. Meanwhile the Allied commander, Sir Harold Alexander, was collecting one of the most oddly assorted armies that Europe had ever seen. Its core remained British and American, but the contingents that were gradually added to it made it a truly international force. Every spare unit of soldiery that could be fitted in nowhere else seemed eventually to find its way to Italy as reinforcements. There were South Africans, Canadians, and New Zealanders; there were Brazilians and American Japanese from Hawaii; there was the Jewish Brigade from Palestine; there were the Poles whom

the Russians had freed and the British had trained in the Middle East.
Finally, and most important of all, there were the French from North
Africa, under the command of General Alphonse Juin. Of these, only
the officers and a minority of the enlisted men were of European origin:
the greater part were blacks from south of the Sahara and Moslems
from Algeria and Morocco.

The French colonial forces supplied what Alexander sorely lacked—
tough, seasoned mountain troops who could fight in the rugged country
of central Italy. It was these who were finally able to outflank the German positions at Cassino and begin the advance on Rome in mid-May.
A week later, the Poles took the abbey itself, and in another few days,
the British and Americans had broken out of the Anzio beachhead. Once
the mountains had been breached, the way to Rome lay open. The Germans did not try to defend the Italian capital: throughout the campaign
it was treated by both sides as an open city. On June 4, the Allies entered
Rome in triumph, to the wild rejoicing of its inhabitants.

Rome was the first of the continental capitals to be freed from the
Nazi grasp, and its liberation inaugurated a new era in European political history. It marked the beginning of postfascist politics—of the reconstruction of democracy on the ruins of authoritarian regimes. Six weeks
before Rome fell, Badoglio had been persuaded to reconstruct his ministry to include the leaders of the chief anti-Fascist political parties. Simultaneously the king announced that on the liberation of the capital, he
would retire in favor of his son, who was less tainted with cooperation
with Mussolini. In early June, the king relinquished his functions. Badoglio also had to go. The democratic political leaders insisted that they
would serve under him no longer and that the new chief of government
should be Ivanoe Bonomi—the next to the last pre-Fascist prime minister
of Italy—who had been chairman of the clandestine Committee of Liberation during the German occupation of Rome.

Thus after its entry into the capital the government of southern Italy
presented a much more democratic face to its own people and to the
outside world. In this it reflected the desire of anti-Fascist Italians to
get back into the war—to "work their passage home," as Churchill put
it. For the Italian surrender had been unconditional only in theory:
actually, it promised the Italians humane treatment and a just peace in
return for contributions to the Allied war effort which the anti-Fascist
leaders were only too anxious to make. The real limitation from which
they suffered was a lingering distrust on the part of the Allies and more
particularly of Churchill and his advisors. In view of the apathy toward
the war that most southern Italians had displayed, this distrust was only
natural.

With the liberation of Rome, however, the atmosphere changed dramatically. The Italian capital had produced a real Resistance movement,
and north of Rome the Resistance was strong and militant. When the
Allies reached Florence in early August, they found that its citizens had

already taken up arms for their own liberation. By the time the campaign had again frozen into a winter stalemate in the mountain chain running between Florence and Bologna, the military achievements of the Italian Resistance had been universally recognized. A new Italian army was being trained to take its place beside the British and the Americans and the French in the final push to liberate the northern cities. In the last six months of the war, the Italians had been all but accepted as full Allies in the common cause.

The Landings in Normandy and Southern France

The liberation of Rome was overshadowed by a greater event—the most dramatic of the whole war—which occurred only a day and a half later: the Allied landings in Normandy.

Through the winter and spring the great build-up of forces in southern England had mounted until, as the soldiers put it, the island seemed about to sink under the weight of men and materiel it was carrying. General Eisenhower had been obliged to revise the schedule originally agreed on with the Russians. The target date had been postponed for four weeks in order to take advantage of another month's production in landing craft and to coincide more closely with the Red Army's summer offensive. At the same time, the demands of the Italian campaign had necessitated the cancellation of a secondary attack in southern France which had originally been planned for the same month as the main invasion. Subsequently this second operation was restored—but it was to occur nearly ten weeks after the Normandy landing, when the same invasion fleet could be regrouped for a new effort.

As if these postponements were not in themselves enough to handicap the great enterprise, the weather of early June proved treacherous. The soldiers were already embarked, and tossing about the Channel in the agonies of seasickness, and still it was doubtful whether the landings could proceed. The portents remained unfavorable—the time was growing shorter and shorter in which moon and tide would permit a landing at all; too long a wait would mean postponing the whole operation for at least a fortnight. At this point, Eisenhower rose to the full height of his terrible responsibility: with the plans and hopes of the alliance dependent on him alone, he decreed that the invasion should proceed. At the last moment the weather changed for the better; the sea was choppy but not impossibly rough as the troops started to go ashore.

The landings began in the early morning of June 6 on a 60-mile arc along the broad indentation of the Norman coast between Cherbourg and Le Havre—close enough to the English coast to permit air fighter cover all the time. It was not the *Luftwaffe* that the invaders now had to fear; it was the Germans' artillery, their barbed wire, their underwater obstacles and mines—all the heavy defenses that they had been preparing for three years against just such an attack. Casualties were heavy

SECOND
WORLD WAR

Western Front

▨▨ German advances
⇨⇨ Allied advances
◄ Major aerial conflict

Scale of Miles
0   100   200   300

Atlantic Ocean

North Sea

IRELAND

GREAT BRITAIN

London

Coventry

Dunkirk

Calais

Abbeville

Cherbourg

Brest

Le Havre

Falaise

Paris

July 1944

Summer 1944

FRANCE

Bordeaux

Lyon

Marseille

Fall 1944

Nice

Madrid

SPAIN

PORTUGAL

Lisbon

Gibraltar

Narvik

NORWAY

Oslo

APRIL 1940

SWEDEN

Stockholm

FINLAND

Helsinki

Leningrad

U.S.S.R.

Riga

DENMARK

Copenhagen

Baltic

1940-1942

1941-1945

Hamburg

NETHERLANDS

Rotterdam

Arnhem

Ostend

RUHR

Eben Emael

Liège

Cologne

Bonn

Remagen

BELGIUM

ARDENNES

Sedan

LUXEMBURG

Winter 1944/45

Spring 1945

Stuttgart

SWITZERLAND

Spring 1945

Milan

Turin

Bologna

Florence

Winter 1944/45

ITALY

Fall 1944

Summer 1944

Rome

Anzio

Cassino

Naples

Winter 1943/44

Fall 1943

Palermo

Summer 1943

Malta

Potsdam

Berlin

Dresden

Prague

CZECHOSLOVAKIA

Vienna

AUSTRIA

Budapest

HUNGARY

Belgrade

YUGOSLAVIA

ALBANIA

GREECE

POLAND

Warsaw

Adriatic Sea

Mediterranean Sea

on D-day, and for long hours the outcome hung in the balance. Yet the invaders were able to profit by German indecision: the enemy commander—Rommel, the legendary "desert fox" of North African fame—was calamitously deceived about their intentions. Believing that the Normandy landings were only a feint, and that the main invasion would come in the Calais area, where the Channel was narrowest, he kept his armored forces in reserve until it was too late. When they finally began to move, the harassing attacks of the French Resistance held them to a slow crawl.

Throughout June and most of July, Eisenhower's forces consolidated their beachhead and steadily increased their strength. Within a week of D-day, more than 300,000 British and Americans were ashore, and through artificial harbors built off the beaches a steady stream of supplies began to flow in. The British under Montgomery were assigned the hard and unspectacular task of holding the main enemy attacks and hammering away at the city of Caen. The Americans, under General Omar Bradley, received the more attractive assignment of fighting their way out of the bridgehead and taking the Germans in the rear. On July 25, the American forces began the breakthrough at Saint-Lô. From there they went on to the cathedral town of Coutances, cutting off the enemy's retreat from the Cherbourg peninsula. By early August, the dashing tank commander, General George Patton, was out in open country, heading off on a great race across northern France.

With Patton's breakthrough, the campaign in France suddenly became fluid. In the next month and a half, nearly the whole country was liberated. On August 15 occurred the long-delayed descent on the Riviera beaches. Three American and seven French divisions—most of them withdrawn from the Italian campaign—poured ashore against light opposition. Within two weeks, they had taken Marseille and Nice and were beginning a triumphal advance up the Rhône Valley. Meanwhile central and southwestern France was liberating itself with its own resources; the Resistance fighters descended from the hills, harassing the frantic Germans who now had no thought but to escape from the enormous trap that was closing on them. Simultaneously, to the north Montgomery had beaten off the last German attacks and surrounded eight enemy divisions in a pocket near Falaise; the Americans were advancing through Brittany to free the vital seaport of Brest; and Patton's tanks, wheeling south of Paris, were already threatening to cut off the German forces in the capital.

At this point De Gaulle went into action. His prize armored division, under General Leclerc de Hauteclocque—which had been held in reserve for just such an eventuality—was given the order to advance on Paris. Here the Resistance had already risen: for ten days it fought bitter street battles with the occupying forces. Finally, Leclerc's tanks settled the issue. By August 26, the city was free. The day before, General de Gaulle —now universally recognized as the liberator and leader of the French —had arrived to take over authority: on a glorious summer afternoon

he walked in triumph from the Étoile down the Champs Elysées to the
Place de la Concorde, and then drove by car to Notre Dame, where the Te Deum of thanksgiving was interrupted by the desperate rifle shots of unyielding collaborationists.

In September, it seemed as if Germany might be defeated that very autumn. On the eleventh of the month the forces from the Normandy beachhead joined those coming up from the south to form a continuous front. During the next few days, they advanced together to reach the German border at several points. To the west, Montgomery's British and Canadians, after crossing the Seine and surrounding the frightfully devastated seaport of Le Havre, swept on to the Belgian frontier almost without opposition. In the first two weeks of September they liberated most of Belgium, and by the middle of the month they were advancing into the Netherlands. Now was the time to break the German defenses with one bold stroke. Yielding to Montgomery's eloquent pleas, Eisenhower decided to risk a great gamble on his left flank. An airborne operation—the largest yet attempted by either side—was to strike across the Rhine at Arnhem in the Netherlands, in an effort to leap the river obstacle and then carry the war into the heart of Germany.

The parachute attack at Arnhem began on September 17. The initial landings succeeded, but the operation was soon hampered by bad weather and the slowing of relief forces coming up from the south. The airborne troops held out for more than a week. Then the Germans closed in and the evacuation of the bridgehead became imperative; only a quarter of the original force reached the south bank of the Rhine alive. To the east meanwhile, Patton's tanks were running out of fuel, and the French and Americans who had come up from the south were meeting stern resistance in Alsace. By early October, it was clear that victory could not come until the following year.

The German Resistance and the Attempt on Hitler's Life

The Germans, however, knew that they were beaten. For four years, death had been raining down on them from the skies, and as the Anglo-American air offensive mounted in intensity, the German cities and communications system were steadily crumbling. The Allies had won unquestioned mastery of the air; the *Luftwaffe* had failed completely. With the collapse of his promise of victory through air power, Reichsmarshal Goering had retired into obscurity. By the last year of the war, he no longer ranked among the top Nazis. The real directors of the German war effort were now three: a politically moderate young architect, Albert Speer, who was reorganizing the economic front to make the most efficient use of the nation's resources; the SS chief, Heinrich Himmler, whose machinery of terror kept the population in line at home and whose black-shirted private army was trained to a ruthlessness and fanaticism that won for it an increasingly prominent role on the fighting fronts;

finally Josef Goebbels, book burner and rabble rouser, whose task was now to mobilize the energies of the German people for a last-ditch stand —the utterly faithful Goebbels who never wavered in his loyalty to his chief and who alone among the Nazi leaders chose to share Hitler's fate at the end.

The official propagandists had told the Germans that an Allied landing in France could never succeed—that it would be thrown back into the Channel with a staggering loss of life. By July, when it was obvious to all that the Normandy invasion had in fact succeeded, Hitler's subjects were left to draw their own conclusions. A courageous minority decided that the only recourse was assassination. They could see no other way to save their country from further destruction. On July 20, they planted a bomb in the temporary shelter on the Eastern Front where Hitler was holding a staff conference. The *Führer* escaped as if by a miracle: although a number of those standing around him were killed, and although he himself received injuries from which he never fully recovered, he lived to continue the war and to take frightful revenge on his enemies.

These enemies included a large group of late converts to the opposition—military men like Rommel who turned against Hitler only when they realized that the war was lost. But the core of the conspiracy consisted of dedicated and high-minded men—a few generals, diplomats, and civil servants, Protestant and Catholic clergymen, Social Democrats, and trade-union executives. Most of them were anti-Nazis of long standing. They were revolted by Hitler's tyranny, and they phrased their opposition in moral and frequently in religious terms. In embryo they presented the small, conservative, but extremely distinguished German counterpart to the Resistance movements that had sprung up in the occupied countries.

The failure of the July 20 bomb plot meant that the war was to continue until the total defeat of Hitler's Reich. It meant that the Germans would have no such escape from their bondage to a half-mad war lord as the Italians had found the year before with the overthrow of Mussolini. It also marked the last act in the gradual subjugation of the German army to Hitler's control: so many of his outstanding generals had been involved directly or indirectly in the plot that henceforth the military leadership was under a cloud. Finally, and most important, the failure of the assassination attempt brought the destruction of the flower of German antinazism. In the savage repression that followed it, at least three hundred oppositionists lost their lives—a political elite that was to be sorely missed when the Germans began the difficult task of building up a new democracy.

The Soviet Breakthrough:
Poland and Rumania

A month before the fateful bomb exploded, the Red Army had opened its promised summer offensive. In the spring it had completed the liberation of the Crimea and the Ukraine. Now it began advancing along an 800-mile front against enemies reckoned at two million—as compared to the one million facing the Allies in the west. It drove the Finns to sue for peace; it reached German soil at the border of East Prussia; it crossed both the old and the new boundary of Poland and seemed on the verge of delivering the capital city of Warsaw.

At this point, the Polish Resistance rose in arms. On August 1, it began to fight the Germans in the streets of Warsaw. The Red Army was just across the Vistula, but it refused to move. Despite anguished pleas from Churchill and Roosevelt—despite their efforts to send supplies to the fighters in Warsaw over an impossibly long air route—Stalin remained adamant; only at the very end would he offer even token help to the Polish insurgents, who could not maintain the unequal fight. After two months of hopeless struggle, they succumbed to German arms; thus ended the authentic and independent Polish Resistance.

The official reason for Stalin's inaction was that the Poles had risen irresponsibly and prematurely—before his army was ready to go to their aid. Most Western historians have found this argument unconvincing. They suspect that Stalin had ulterior motives in allowing the Poles to perish—that he was pleased to see eliminated a Resistance movement which would have proved extremely troublesome to him. It was only too evident that he had small regard for the Polish government-in-exile, to which the Resistance owed obedience. Indeed, his relations with it grew worse as the war continued and the Poles steadily refused to agree to the annexations of their territory that the Soviet Union had made in 1939. After the Red Army crossed the Polish frontier in late July, Stalin set up at Lublin a competing government, the Committee of National Liberation, which was dominated by faithful Communists. To this new and totally unrepresentative authority, the destruction of the Resistance fighters in Warsaw offered distinct advantages; the Polish Communists would now face little local competition when the Russians finally entered Warsaw.

From the merely military point of view, however, Stalin's strategic argument made sense, for it was true that the Red Army had no immediate need to push on to Warsaw: Poland could wait—it was already all but in Soviet hands. To the south, a greater prize glittered. In the late summer of 1944, the collapse of the whole German position in the Balkans began to loom on the horizon. On August 23, the Red Army reached the mouth of the Danube deep within the frontiers of Rumania. Among the Rumanians—the most listless and corrupt of Hitler's satellite peoples —panic and demoralization reigned. The time called for bold action, and young King Michael II seized the opportunity: he took his country out of the war and opened the gates of the Balkans to the advancing Soviet forces.

Thereafter—as had happened the week before in France—the Germans had no recourse but to get out of the peninsula as fast as possible. Following Rumania, Bulgaria sued for peace and re-entered the war alongside the Soviet Union. In early October, as the Germans began to evacuate Greece, the British arrived from Egypt almost unopposed and took up the thorny task of trying to persuade the Greek Resistance to accept the return of the government-in-exile. In Yugoslavia, Tito redoubled his attacks on the retreating Germans; slowly his Partisans advanced from the mountains into the Serbian plain until in late October they entered Belgrade in triumph. Tito had swept away the Serbian Quislings; he had driven out the Croat terrorist Pavelich; Mihailovich he had captured and held prisoner; only the Yugoslav government-in-exile stood between him and the undisputed power he craved—but to the exiled king and his government Tito was resolved to pay as little heed as possible.

As opposed to the Communist leaders in Poland, who were completely dependent on Stalin and the Red Army, Tito had done the job himself. He had received help from the Red Army only at the very end, when it marched through his country from Rumania on its way to attack the Germans in Hungary. This was to be the secret of Tito's stubbornness and strength in his subsequent conflicts with the Soviet Union.

In Hungary, the Red Army at last encountered a firm German stand. Here it was to be stalemated for most of the winter. Once more it shifted the focus of its efforts—this time back to the plains of Poland. It had already achieved the essentials of Stalin's purpose: virtually the whole of East Central Europe now lay under Soviet domination.

The Churchill-Stalin Agreement
on Spheres of Influence

It was this harsh reality that prompted Winston Churchill to pay a call on Stalin in early October. He was acting alone and he was fully aware of the risks he was taking, but he was convinced that there was not a moment to lose and that he should try to save what could be saved before it was too late. He could not wait for Roosevelt to accompany him: the American president was fully occupied with his own campaign for re-election and at least another month must pass before he would be free to exert his influence in the great political and territorial decisions that the vertiginous course of the war had raised.

Churchill himself has given the classic account of what passed between him and Stalin: "The moment was apt for business, so I said, 'Let us settle about our affairs in the Balkans. Your armies are in Rumania and Bulgaria. We have interests, missions, and agents there. Don't let us get at cross-purposes in small ways. So far as Britain and Russia are concerned, how would it do for you to have ninety per cent predominance in Rumania, for us to have ninety per cent of the say in Greece, and go fifty-fifty about Yugoslavia?' While this was being translated I wrote out on a half-sheet of paper:

Rumania	
Russia	90%
The others	10%
Greece	
Great Britain	90%
(in accord with U.S.A.)	
Russia	10%
Yugoslavia	50–50%
Hungary	50–50%
Bulgaria	
Russia	75%
The others	25%

"I pushed this across to Stalin, who had by then heard the translation. There was a slight pause. Then he took his blue pencil and made a large tick upon it, and passed it back to us. It was all settled in no more time than it takes to set down." *

In this simple fashion, Stalin and Churchill marked out their spheres of influence in the Balkans. On just such an issue had the Soviet understanding with Nazi Germany broken down four years earlier. Now Stalin had obtained from Churchill what Hitler had refused to grant him—a position of preponderance in the eastern part of the Balkan Peninsula.

It is easy to criticize the spheres of influence agreement of October 9, 1944. Indeed, the American government—true to its consistent refusal to make deals while the war was in progress—never accepted it. True, it was a calculated, realistic bargain in the old tradition of power politics. True, the minor percentages of influence were impossible to enforce; Churchill might better have written 100 per cent for Rumania and Bulgaria on Stalin's side, and for Greece on his own, rather than 90 per cent or 75. Still worse, the 50–50 agreement for Hungary eventually broke down completely, as did the similar understanding about Yugoslavia. Finally, the whole arrangement had the fatal weakness of omitting Poland—the country where the war began and which during all its stages was the source of bitterest contention between East and West.

Nevertheless, it is only fair to add that Churchill was playing from a desperately weak hand. He probably got the best agreement that could have been obtained in the existing circumstances—certainly one more favorable to the West than the situation that was to emerge at the end of the war. And—paradoxically enough—the 50–50 arrangement for Yugoslavia eventually proved to be far less a lost cause than it seemed in the first months of 1945: after Tito's break with Stalin three years later, this was about where Yugoslavia stood, precariously poised between East and West.

---

* The Second World War, Vol. VI: Triumph and Tragedy (Boston: Houghton Mifflin Company, 1953), p. 227.

But the most telling argument in favor of the spheres of influence agreement was its effect in Greece. Here, two months after the meeting between Churchill and Stalin, the Communist-led Resistance (the EAM-ELAS) rose in revolt against the newly returned government-in-exile. Fighting flared in the streets of Athens, and the situation grew so serious that the British prime minister himself felt obliged to fly to Greece to calm the storm. He curbed the Communists by military force, and he mitigated the country's internal differences by arranging for a regency under the archbishop of Athens. His task was immensely simplified, moreover, because the Soviet Union gave no support to the Communist insurgents. In this one instance at least, Stalin stood strictly by his word: Greece was treated as a British sphere of influence.

*The Ardennes Offensive
and the "Battle of the Bulge"*

On the Western Front, meanwhile, the advance toward Germany was continuing. Here, although progress had been slowed, operations were not broken off completely for the winter, as they were in Italy, but steadily gathered power for the final assault on the Reich. Eisenhower's forces were now organized into three army groups: in the northwest were Montgomery's British and Canadians; in the center, three American armies under Bradley; in the south and east, the American army under Patch which had come up from the Mediterranean and the French army commanded by the hard-driving and mercurial De Lattre de Tassigny. Since D-day the continuous arrival of troops from the United States had gradually increased the American contribution to the coalition forces: of the seventy-odd divisions poised to attack the Reich, approximately half were American, a quarter were British, and—something that few people realized at the time—the final quarter consisted mostly of French units, underequipped and short of supplies, but surpassing all the others in combative spirit.

Then in mid-December the unexpected happened: the Germans struck back, powerfully and with stunning effect. For this—his last offensive effort—Hitler called on his most experienced commander, old Field Marshal von Rundstedt. Rundstedt's plan was bold and well conceived: he tried to cut through the Allied armies at their weakest point and, by capturing the great supply base of Antwerp, to demoralize them and disorganize their rear. The place he chose to strike was the same rugged and woody Ardennes where the Germans had breached the French defenses four and a half years before.

Rundstedt's plan came uncomfortably close to success. Favored by a spell of cloudy weather which prevented Allied planes from reconnoitering his troop concentrations, he caught the Americans thoroughly off guard. Soon a whole sector of the Allied line in Belgium and Luxemburg was staggering back: a great "bulge" opened which had to be closed at all costs. Eisenhower hastily summoned reserves from the south: this necessitated further strategic withdrawals; indeed, orders were given to evacuate the newly liberated Alsatian capital of Strasbourg —orders which De Gaulle was able to get reversed only by threatening a complete rupture between France and the United States. It was a gloomy Christmas in Paris and Brussels: the victory which had seemed so close had once more been thrown into doubt. In London also there was fear as well as sorrow: the new V-missiles which the Germans launched from bases in the Netherlands were descending on the city with deadly accuracy.

By the third week of January, Eisenhower's forces had stopped the German offensive and pushed the attackers back out of the bulge. But the Battle of the Bulge, as it came to be called, had shaken the Allies and disorganized the timetable of their advance into the Reich. Once again it had made the Western war effort seem far less impressive than the Russian, for while the Americans and British were recovering from the shock they had received in the Ardennes, the Red Army was setting out on another spectacular winter offensive. Resuming the attack in Poland where they had broken it off five months earlier, the Russians captured Warsaw in mid-January, 1945, and then swept on 300 miles to penetrate deep into Germany itself. East Prussia and Upper Silesia were in their grasp: before them literally millions of Germans were fleeing in the bitter cold. The Red Army did not pause until it reached the Oder River, only 40 miles from Berlin.

This was the situation when the Big Three of the wartime alliance met on February 4 for the second (and last) time at the Crimean resort of Yalta. Their talks were overshadowed by the enormous Soviet successes and the partial Western reverse on the battlefield; to most prognosticators it seemed that the Russians would be in Berlin long before the British and Americans had advanced very far into the Reich: the Red Army's cannon could already be heard in Hitler's capital, while the Western Allies were still on the German frontiers more than 300 miles away. What Churchill and Roosevelt did not know was that the Ardennes offensive had exhausted the *Führer*'s last reserves—that in fact it had hastened rather than delayed the hour of victory in the West.

The Yalta Conference

The Yalta Conference has aroused more controversy than any other event of the whole war. In the United States it has been attacked in the bitterest terms: Roosevelt, his enemies have claimed, was "duped" by Stalin into "selling out" Eastern Europe and Manchuria to communism.

The Far Eastern clauses of the Yalta agreement are not relevant here. The decisions on Europe, moreover, must be considered in light of the atmosphere in which the conference was held and the grave limitations under which it did its work. More than a year had passed since the meeting at Teheran. In this climactic fourteen months, the character of the war had changed entirely: eight nations had been freed from the Nazi grasp, and final victory was now in sight. A multitude of problems stood in urgent need of immediate solution—problems to which the spheres of influence agreement of the previous October had offered only a partial and unsatisfactory answer.

Yet the participants were acutely pressed for time. Roosevelt, who had made the longest journey to reach the Crimea, was strictly limited in the time he could be absent from Washington, and the sessions of the conference could last scarcely more than a week. The procedure for reaching *strategic* decisions which had worked comparatively well at Teheran began to break down in dealing with the essentially *political* decisions that were the chief subject of discussion at Yalta. There was simply not enough time to argue them out to a clear conclusion. Hence the Big Three had recourse to loosely drafted formulas which gave a fallacious sense of an agreement that did not really exist. As soon as the conference adjourned, the deep antagonisms between East and West revealed themselves; each side had a conflicting interpretation of what it had agreed to do.

This was particularly true of the Declaration on Liberated Europe which the Big Three issued. It promised to assist the nations newly freed from Nazi tyranny to solve their problems through democratic means and by free elections. But in the outstanding case in point—Poland—certain other decisions of the conference implicitly violated these high-sounding phrases. For in substance, Churchill and Roosevelt agreed to what Stalin wanted to do with the Poles. The Western leaders consented to the frontier that he had been demanding all along—roughly corresponding to the Curzon Line—and to his proposal for compensating Poland by extensive annexations to the west at Germany's expense. Similarly in the contest for political authority, Stalin made good his claim that the nucleus of the future Polish regime should be the Communist-dominated government at Lublin rather than the London government-in-exile. The only concession that Roosevelt and Churchill could win from him was an undertaking to "reorganize" the Lublin government to include a certain number of "democratic leaders." This proved an empty pledge—as did a similar agreement to enlarge Tito's government in Yugoslavia. The Communists remained in control: when the Polish peasant leader Stanislaw Mikolajczyk and three others were added to the Lublin group, they could serve merely as a powerless and frustrated democratic opposition.

In the decisions on Germany, however, the West fared rather better. For one thing, the more punitive proposals for the postwar treatment of the enemy were nearly all abandoned. Although the conference decided in theory to break up the Reich into several separate states, it did nothing concrete about it, and in the succeeding weeks the idea was quietly buried. In more positive vein, the Big Three agreed to admit France to equal partnership in the future control of Germany, including a zone of occupation of its own. Moreover—largely at Churchill's insistence—the conference postponed for future discussion the Soviet demands for reparations, for an inter-Allied control of the Ruhr, and for a Polish-German frontier running along the Oder and western Neisse rivers.

In all these matters, it was Churchill who fought the battle both for France and for Germany—for the preservation of both as future bulwarks of the West against Soviet power. Roosevelt, on the other hand, seemed hesitant and unsure, siding now with Churchill and now with Stalin. He distrusted communism—but he also distrusted British imperialist aims (which was a perfectly valid suspicion, so long as Churchill was in power). Hence he failed to coordinate adequately with his British friend, and he was prepared to make large concessions in the interests of Allied unity. Furthermore, he was less vigorous in expressing his opinions than he had been at Teheran. Churchill thought him very frail just after the adjournment at Yalta: in two months he was dead.

In short—however the harsh reality might be covered by soothing phrases—Roosevelt conceded to Stalin the domination of East Central Europe which the latter had won by his pact with Hitler in 1939 and more recently by his spheres of influence agreement with Churchill. The American president gambled that the Soviet leader would respond positively to this kind of generosity—more particularly in the planned organization of the United Nations which was also discussed at Yalta. True, the Red Army already controlled the areas in question—including the Baltic States, whose reannexation to the Soviet Union the Big Three did not even discuss. Nothing could have been done to deprive Stalin of what he had conquered. The alternative was to refuse to recognize the *fait accompli*, as the United States was subsequently to do in the case of Communist China. This course President Roosevelt rejected. He was convinced that public opinion in his own country and in Western Europe would be grievously disappointed if the war leaders at Yalta failed to reach an agreement, and in this conviction he was probably right. To the veterans of the Resistance in particular it would have come as a stunning blow to learn that the unity of the great alliance had been broken before the war had even been won. That was how things looked at the time. Posterity has judged otherwise.

The Last Campaigns: Vienna, Berlin, Prague

Within three months of the adjournment of the Yalta Conference, the war in Europe was over. Roosevelt was dead. And the Red Army held all three of the major capitals of Central Europe as the result of an extraordinary sequence of events.

In early March Eisenhower's armies began a general advance toward the Rhine. When the forward units in the center reached the river, they discovered to their astonishment that the retreating Germans had failed to blow up one of the bridges—the railroad bridge at Remagen south of Bonn. This stroke of fortune changed the whole military outlook. Rather than having to wage a desperate and bloody struggle to cross the Rhine, the Americans were over the river at one bound.

They were followed within three weeks by the British to the north and the French to the south. From this point on, the campaign in western Germany became the swift chase of a beaten enemy. Montgomery moved toward the Danish frontier and the Baltic. De Lattre wheeled southeast to take Stuttgart. Bradley rolled up the German resistance in the Ruhr, trapping more than a quarter-million of Hitler's last troops. And when this battle came to an end, the Americans set off to the east to cut the Reich in two. On April 11 they reached the Elbe River, only 60 miles from Berlin.

Three days earlier the final offensive in northern Italy had begun. In little more than a week of intensive fighting, the Allies broke the Germans' mountain defenses and poured down into the north Italian plain. The Resistance fighters rose to meet them, as one city after another accomplished its own liberation before the Allies arrived. By the end of April, all Italy was free: the Germans laid down their arms. Mussolini, deserted by his protectors, tried to escape to the Swiss frontier, where he was discovered by a local Resistance detachment and summarily shot.

In the east, the Red Army had once again, as in the previous summer, shifted its main blow to the south. While Stalin was at Yalta, his commander in Hungary, Marshal Rodion Malinovski, was finally winning the long struggle for Budapest. In mid-February, German resistance ceased in the Hungarian capital. The road to Vienna lay open. And in eight weeks more the Austrian capital was also in Soviet hands. The race for control of Central Europe was already going in Stalin's favor.

Before Berlin, however, the greatest of the new Soviet commanders, Marshal Grigori Zhukov, had paused for two months, preparing his forces for the final assault. In front of him lay Hitler's last hope—the most desperate and fanatical of his soldiers, whom he had ordered to stand their ground and die in defense of the Nazi capital. Berlin was now a mass of ruins. Indeed in the last winter of the war the Allied air forces had roamed at will over the Reich; virtually every city had been blasted again and again. With legitimate strategic targets exhausted, the British and American aviators struck almost at random, ruthlessly obliterating the architectural monuments of Germany's past and rendering millions homeless. The fire bombing of Dresden in February, 1945, in which tens of thousands lost their lives, ranks among the most terrible events of the entire war.

Still Hitler refused to recognize the inevitable. He decreed that the German people should go down with their leader in a macabre *Götterdämmerung,* and he immured himself in the air-raid bunker below the Reich Chancellery as the battle for Berlin began to rage above him.

During Zhukov's two-months' pause, however, the military situation inside Germany had changed completely. The Americans had broken across the Rhine and now were almost as close to Berlin as he was. They were already on the Elbe, and the Red Army was still on the Oder. Between the two rivers lay the German capital. Toward the west Berlin was almost defenseless; its guardians were concentrated to the east against the threatened Soviet attack. The prize seemed to lie within Eisenhower's grasp. Why did he not reach out for it?

The answer is a mixture of strategic and diplomatic arguments, which seemed convincing at the time, but which in retrospect have been questioned again and again. From the strategic standpoint, the supreme Allied commander was worried about his supply lines, which had been stretched to the limit by his race across the Reich. He also felt the need of a clear line of demarcation between his own troops and the Russians, which the Elbe alone could provide. Finally he was constantly receiving reports that the Nazis were preparing to make their last stand in an Alpine redoubt in southern Germany and Austria, and he wanted to cut them off before they had time to consolidate this new position. Hence he ordered Bradley to stop at the Elbe and to wheel toward the south.

In fact the reports about the "redoubt" proved to be without substance. By mid-April, the German forces were far too disorganized to execute any such maneuver. There were also political aspects to the capture of Berlin which Eisenhower failed to appreciate: as a military man he had been taught that the fall of any particular city was always secondary to the main job of destroying the enemy forces. Churchill, on the contrary, fully understood the symbolic importance of capturing Berlin. He harried Eisenhower with ever stronger pleas to push on, but the supreme commander remained deaf to his entreaties. In Washington there was no longer the strong voice that might have supported Churchill. On April 12—the day after the Americans reached the Elbe—Roosevelt died, his last weeks overshadowed by mounting disputes with Stalin over Eastern Europe. With a power vacuum in Washington, Eisenhower was left to make his own decisions.

Vienna had already fallen to the Red Army on April 13. Here there was little that the Western Allies could have done, once they had rejected Churchill's reiterated proposals for an advance up from the Balkans or the Adriatic. Now before Berlin they chose to stand aside. On April 16, Zhukov opened his offensive. Nine days later he had the city surrounded. As the Russian tanks smashed into the capital, Hitler knew that the end had come. On the last day of April he shot himself, and his body was burned in the Chancellery courtyard.

The rest was a week-long mopping-up operation against scattered masses of German soldiery. As the American troops swung south, they had one more opportunity—the Czech capital of Prague, where the Resistance rose on May 5 and invited General Patton to enter. Eisenhower asked the Soviet command what he should do; the latter responded with a strong negative. Once again the American insistence on good relations with the Russians won the day. The Red Army did not reach Prague until May 9—two days after the German High Command, in a surrender ceremony at Eisenhower's headquarters at Reims, had finally brought the Second World War to a close. The six-year struggle with nazism had ended—but the new contest over the future of Europe had already begun.

Readings

Once again the most wide-ranging and spirited account by a participant is by Winston S. Churchill, *The Second World War*, 6 vols. (1948–1954). For one-volume histories, one can turn to Louis L. Snyder's *The War: A Concise History* (1960); to Chester Wilmot, *The Struggle for Europe* (1952), a highly stimulating narrative, inspired by admiration for Churchill and Montgomery, and concentrating on events after the Normandy landings; and to Gordon Wright, *The Ordeal of Total War 1939–1945* (1968), which deals far more with social, economic, and psychological questions than with the military campaigns and synthesizes recent scholarship with a notable judiciousness and breadth of view. Herbert Feis, *Churchill, Roosevelt, Stalin: The War They Waged and the Peace They Sought* (1957), and *Between War and Peace: The Potsdam Conference* (1960), analyze the diplomacy of the Allied coalition in balanced and understanding fashion.

Marc Bloch, *Strange Defeat* (1949), offers a highly suggestive interpretation of the fall of France. Raymond de Belot, *The Struggle for the Mediterranean* (1951), by a French admiral, chronicles the middle years of the war, when the question of the Mediterranean was paramount. William L. Langer and S. Everett Gleason, *The Undeclared War* (1953), traces the slow progress of American involvement.

For Hitler's "New Order," see Arnold and Veronica M. Toynbee, eds., *Hitler's Europe* (1954), and Alexander Dallin, *German Rule in Russia 1941–1945* (1957). Alexander Werth, *Russia at War 1941–1945* (1964), presents a magnificent panorama of the conflict on the Eastern Front. Norman Kogan, *Italy and the Allies* (1956), deals with Italy's change of alliance and subsequent activity as a cobelligerent of Britain and the United States.

Hans Speidel, *Invasion 1944* (1950), gives a professional military account of the Normandy landings from the German standpoint. For an analysis of the most important of the inter-Allied conferences, generally favorable to President Roosevelt, see John L. Snell, ed., *The Meaning of Yalta* (1956). H. R. Trevor-Roper, *The Last Days of Hitler* (1947), chronicles the macabre end of the Nazi Reich.

Eastern Europe: The Years of Revolution, 1945–1949

Chapter Fourteen

I

THE WAR'S END

The Second World War was never formally terminated. No peace treaty ratified the defeat of Germany, as in 1919. With the lesser belligerents —Italy, Hungary, Rumania, Bulgaria, and Finland—treaties were finally concluded, after several adjournments and protracted wrangles between the Soviet Union and the Western powers. These treaties embodied hard-won compromises on the questions on which technical agreement could be reached, such as boundaries, reparations, and the limitation of armed forces. They did not touch the wider dispute as to the character of the regimes under which the states in question should live. In dealing with Germany, disagreement between East and West on these larger issues was so great that it proved impossible to draft a formal treaty even for more technical matters. Instead, the postwar settlement merely developed gradually, as one practical decision led to another in the efforts of hard-pressed administrators to make postwar Germany a viable community.

To a lesser degree this was true of Europe as a whole. No great conclave of the powers, such as had met in Paris in 1919, drew up a blueprint for the reconstruction of the Continent. Rather, the postwar settlement emerged piecemeal during the half-decade 1945–1949. This process was notably different in Western Europe from what it was in the areas occupied by the Red Army. In the West there was a substan-

*Tito, while leader of the Yugoslav partisans
fighting the Nazis, arrives on the Dalmatian Island of
Vis to meet Dr. Ivan Šubašić, representative of King Peter's
government.* COURTESY BROWN BROTHERS.

tial—and rather surprising—return to the prewar or prefascist situation. In the East there occurred a major revolution imposed by the occupying power.

Neither in the East nor in the West did the years immediately following the war see the sort of spontaneous revolutionary outbreaks that had flared up in Central and Eastern Europe after 1917. The revolutions of the first postwar era had been less extensive and less successful than most contemporaries had anticipated: European society was less seriously shaken by the four years of conflict than Europeans themselves had hoped or feared. In 1945, the same thing proved true in even more striking fashion. Although the second war continued longer than the first, although the suffering it caused was greater and the passions it unleashed more tumultuous, it produced even less revolutionary effervescence.

Population Displacements

Three things at least held revolutionary activity in check. The first was the fatigue of peoples, which the very magnitude of the war had made still more overwhelming than in 1919. In the Second World War, the civilian population was even more heavily involved than in the first: constant bombardment from the air and the wide sweep of operations on the ground had brought the realities of war directly into the homes of tens of millions in Europe's population whom the first conflict had spared; the uprooting of peoples through flight, forced labor, or political persecution had been on a scale which dwarfed anything that Europe had experienced before.

In the first three and a half years of the war alone, thirty million Europeans had fled or had been driven from their original homes. These included a million and a half people deported from the Polish areas annexed by Germany, into the "Government General," which became one vast dumping ground; it also included 100,000 Alsace-Lorrainers expelled into Unoccupied France, and 400,000 Germans long settled in Eastern Europe whom Stalin insisted that Hitler move to the west as a token of fidelity to the Nazi-Soviet pact. Subsequently a large percentage of these went east again—as the *Führer* tried to set up German colonies in the occupied parts of Russia and the Ukraine—only to flee headlong back to the Reich in the great retreat of 1944.

Meantime, some twelve million Russians had left their homes for the interior of the country. In the Balkans and Hungary, as a result of Hitler's boundary changes, several hundred thousand more people had found themselves uprooted. And by 1944, eight million foreign workers were toiling in the Reich. These formed the bulk of the more than twelve million "displaced persons" whom the Allied armies and international relief agencies gradually returned home at the close of hostilities. By the end of 1946, the job had essentially been done. But there was still a hard core of more than a million—mostly anti-Communists from Eastern Eu-

rope—who refused to go home. These continued to eke out a wretched
existence in the hopelessly drab surroundings of refugee camps.
The result of all this reshuffling of peoples—and of the hunger and
cold and sickness that had gone with it—was a massive war weariness
which again was without precedent. In 1945 and 1946 most Europeans
were simply too tired to think of revolution.

The Restraints on Revolutionary Activity

Besides nearly universal fatigue there were specific political limitations
on revolutionary activity which did not exist in 1919. The chief revolutionaries—once again the Communists and their Soviet sponsors—had
become very different from what they were in the years immediately
after the Bolshevik Revolution. They were, of course, much stronger.
But at the same time they were more disciplined and more bureaucratized. They could be managed from Moscow with far more precision
than had been possible (or even intended) after 1917. In the years following the Soviet involvement in the Second World War, Stalin had
ordered them to play the game of moderation. The Communist slogans
called for national unity and a glossing over of ideological differences in
order to maximize the war effort. Once more, as during the Civil War
in Spain, Stalin and his colleagues dictated a line of policy that eschewed
revolution and was designed to reassure the middle class.

By 1946, this line had changed, and the Communists shifted to revolutionary militancy. By that time—at least in Western Europe—it was too
late: the forces of social conservation had regained their strength and
self-confidence. The Communist partisans had been disarmed and democratic parliamentary regimes re-established. The Western Allies had
remained in military occupation long enough to assure a substantial
restoration of the old order.

Military occupation was another respect in which 1945 differed from
1919. After the first war the occupying armies of the victorious Allies
had been stationed only in the Rhineland and in a few scattered areas of
Central and Eastern Europe; elsewhere there had been little organized
armed force to oppose the activities of local revolutionists. In 1945, on
the contrary, military power was everywhere: in the West, the British
and Americans had millions of men stationed in France, Italy, and Germany; in the East, the Red Army had six nations in its shadow. In both
areas, the military authority, either directly or by implication, frowned
on any sort of spontaneous revolutionary gestures. In the West, this was
obvious. In the East, it was less apparent, because the Soviet Union was
fostering the activities of local Communist parties—but in its own way
and at its own pace. It was *imposing* a revolution, a strange and novel
revolution—guided and bureaucratic—which was directed both against
conservatives and against indigenous revolutionary stirrings. The central
paradox of the great change imposed by Stalin on East Central Europe

in the years 1945–1949 was that it stifled in embryo the genuine and popular revolution for which all the elements were present when the Red Army arrived.

II
THE PRECONDITIONS

The six nations of East Central Europe which, in the course of the military operations of 1944 and 1945, came under Soviet influence or occupation had already passed through much common experience in the interwar years. To a superficial observer, these states appeared extremely heterogeneous. Two, Hungary and Bulgaria, had been among the vanquished in the First World War; two more, Rumania and Yugoslavia, had been with the victors and had been vastly enlarged as a result; two others, Poland and Czechoslovakia, had been revived in 1919, as new births of old nations which had disappeared long ago. In political structure, too, these states were very different: the three Balkan countries were kingdoms, the two new nations were republics, and Hungary was a kingdom with a vacant throne. Poland, Czechoslovakia, and Hungary were Catholic; Yugoslavia was divided in faith; whereas Rumania and Bulgaria were Eastern Orthodox. From the standpoint of language and cultural tradition, all were Slavic except Hungary and Rumania.

Underlying this tangled catalogue of differences, however, the six nations had in common their peasant character and the problems that character entailed. But this their rulers refused to recognize. With rare exceptions, the governments of East Central Europe in the period from 1919 to 1939 tried to behave as though they were ruling great powers in miniature: they concentrated their attention on questions of national prestige and neglected the more practical tasks of alleviating the poverty of their fellow citizens.

Nationalities, Minorities, and Politics

The chief public concern was the question of minorities and national frontiers. The treaty makers of 1919—by their own admission—had assigned a fifth of the population of the area to nations to which the people affected did not wish to belong. Approximately 22 million of the 110 million human beings in East Central Europe were officially considered as belonging to minorities and, at least in theory, were protected by special minority clauses in the peace treaties. But these were violated with depressing regularity and did not even apply to another category of people who also felt themselves aggrieved—members or offshoots of official "majority" nationalities who thought that their distinctive cultural traditions were not adequately respected. Such were the Slovaks, the Croats, and the Rumanians of Transylvania. In the first instance, the Czechs could argue with some justice that their sister people, the Slovaks, were not as "advanced" as they were, and hence needed to experience some period of tutelage; but for the inhabitants of Croatia and Transylvania, who had grown up under Austro-Hungarian rule and who considered themselves Western in culture and tradition, it was galling to live under the rule of people like the Serbs and the Rumanians of the "Old Kingdom" whose culture seemed more primitive and whose political tradition stemmed from centuries of Turkish rule. The pent-up loathing of Croats for Serbs broke out during the Second World War in horrifying mass atrocities.

In Hungary, which had suffered more than any other country at the hands of the treaty makers of 1919, the question of minorities and frontiers became the national obsession. Elsewhere feeling did not run quite so strong, but public absorption with the same problem was almost as intense. Nearly everywhere concern for national rights served to deflect interest from economic and social issues and from the possibility of attempting to solve them by work in common.

The same lack of realism characterized the political parties. These called themselves "liberal" or "radical" as the case might be, but for the most part, the parties actually consisted of cliques of city lawyers, who had acquired the manners of the West and knew little of the countryside and its problems. Nor were their broader political principles very solidly anchored. Most of them passed over quite easily to the service of the dictatorships into which the parliamentary regimes of these countries had evolved by the 1930's. The great exception, of course, was Czechoslovakia, where the political parties maintained their democratic allegiance until the disaster at Munich. Czechoslovakia—or rather its Czech lands of Bohemia and Moravia—was the exception in other respects also: in its level of education and industrialization, it seemed closer to the West than it did to the peasant societies of East Central Europe.

There were also Marxist parties, but these were not of first importance. In the countries which had a significant number of urban workers—Poland, Czechoslovakia, and Hungary—there existed Socialist parties on the Western model. In the Balkan peninsula, on the other hand, communism had begun to establish itself on a small scale, for in a predominantly agrarian society, where there were almost no trade unions to canalize the aspirations of the poor, Communist agitators found a free field. In such a society intellectuals were in an ideological vacuum in which political extremism could flourish unchecked. This was particularly the case in Yugoslavia, where in the 1930's, the University of Belgrade became a seedbed of Communist influence. It was from idealistic students of the Left—disgusted with the corrupt dictatorship under which they lived—that Tito recruited the young intellectuals who in the war years were to lead his Partisans to victory.

Generally, the leaders of "peasant" or "agrarian" parties were no exception to the usual Eastern European politician. Like "liberals" or "radicals," they, too, tended to be economically unrealistic and ideologically feeble. Most of them were of urban origin, and their notion of rural life was bucolic and sentimental; they idealized the peasants without making adequate distinctions between the problems of those who were desperately poor and those who were self-sufficient, and they failed to see the importance of industrialization in alleviating rural misery. Among the "peasant" politicians, however, there were a few leaders who had a wider vision. The left wings of these parties produced persons of stature, with a real grasp of peasant needs. Men such as these proved themselves the most impressive national leaders in the immediate postwar years—Stanislaw Mikolajczyk in Poland, Ferenc Nagy in Hungary, Iuliu Maniu in Rumania, and G. M. Dimitrov and Nikola Petkov in Bulgaria.

The Agrarian Dilemma

The more imaginative agrarian leaders at least dimly understood the problem of rural overpopulation. Here outsiders often misjudged the true situation: they thought in terms of the old stereotype of aristocratic dominance and the need for breaking up the great estates. In most parts of East Central Europe the concentration of landed property in the hands of the nobility was not a currently serious problem: only in Poland and Hungary had quasi-feudal conditions persisted similar to those that prevailed in southern Italy and Spain. Elsewhere, small peasant holdings were the rule. In Bulgaria and in much of Yugoslavia, this had been true even under Turkish suzerainty. In Rumania and Czechoslovakia, post-1919 reform measures had redistributed the land on an extensive scale.

The real problem, rather, was the misery and low level of productivity among the peasant masses, however independent in theory a great part of them might be. Almost everywhere, the peasants were the majority of the population: only in Bohemia and Moravia were they less than half, and in Bulgaria—the most rural and "primitive" of the six nations—they accounted for more than three-quarters of the inhabitants. But the peasants had little influence on the conduct of affairs: lacking the education or debating experience that would have equipped them to participate in politics and parliamentary life, they were ordinarily represented by city dwellers who had an inadequate understanding of their needs. These needs were those of any underdeveloped and depressed agrarian society—Russia, much of Asia, Latin America, and the Iberian Peninsula offered comparable examples—that is, better farming methods and the economic stimulation of an expanding industry.

In absolute terms, East Central Europe may not have been overpopulated. It had far fewer people per square mile than England or Belgium, but these were highly industrialized nations which had a very small percentage of their people on the land and whose population was remaining relatively stationary. In the peasant countries to the east, on the contrary, population was increasing, and the increase was pressing against

the available productive resources. The land was becoming overfrag-
mented: between two-thirds and three-quarters of the landholding peasants cultivated plots that were too small for their own needs. In addition,
there were millions of landless peasants working as farm hands—a reserve
of unskilled labor which kept agrarian wages permanently depressed.
Since so much cheap labor was available, there was little incentive to
improve farming methods. "On a given unit of land" in one Balkan country "four times as many people produced three times less wheat than
in Denmark." *

As a result, poverty was increasing and the peasants found few chances
to break out of the vicious circle of misery in which they were caught.
Educational opportunities were meager, as indeed were nearly all other
possibilities of self-improvement. The organization of cooperatives offered one vista of hope—but governments were not interested in encouraging them. Industrialization offered another, but here both ingrained
prejudice and lack of capital stood in the way. Realistically considered,
industry alone could break up the old routines in the countryside and
drain off the excess agricultural population to find new and productive
work in the cities and thus to raise living standards for all. This had been
the experience of Western Europe in the nineteenth century, as it was
to be that of Russia in the 1930's. But East Central Europe lacked the
hard-driving leadership which Stalin provided when he transformed his
country from top to bottom. This, then, was the problem which the interwar years left to the future—how could the peasant nations of the East
learn from Soviet experience while avoiding the barbarity and human
suffering which the great transformation of Russia had entailed?

The Legacy of Nazi Occupation

These problems were themselves sufficient to produce a revolutionary
situation. Beyond them, the demand for change was intensified by the
experience through which East Central Europe passed during the war
years.

From 1941 to 1944, the whole area was in the Nazis' grasp. This was
also true of Western Europe, of course, but German behavior in the East
differed markedly from German conduct in the West. There, the occupying power was dealing with peoples whom it regarded as relatively
superior: these peoples were assured of decent treatment most of the
time provided they did not try to resist German orders. In the East, it
was quite different: here the Nazis dealt with nations they considered
inferior both "racially" and culturally, and their concern with the conquered peoples was limited to making them serve the German war effort.

Hence in East Central Europe it was much harder to stand aside and

---

* Hugh Seton-Watson, *Eastern Europe between the Wars 1918–1941* (Cambridge,
Eng.: University Press, 1945), p. 98.

wait for the war to end as so many people succeeded in doing in the West. Of the occupied countries, only the Czech lands received even moderately good treatment, and of the peoples allied with the Germans, the Hungarians alone were dealt with in any sense as equals. Elsewhere the alternative was clear: one could either suffer as a whole nation, like the Poles, or accept the humiliating relationship of an alliance which actually meant subjugation. The latter policy was the more common. Willingly or coerced, the rulers of Hungary, Rumania, and Bulgaria and the new puppet states in Croatia, Serbia, and Slovakia became minor auxiliaries in the German war effort. Most people of property or standing in the community also "collaborated." Still worse, on the extremist fringe of profascist activity in Eastern Europe, violent outbreaks of anti-Semitism punctuated the war years. In short, the East produced far more home-grown fascism than did Scandinavia or the Low Countries or even France. Here also lay an impetus to revolution.

III

THE TWO REVOLUTIONS

At the very least one might foresee that the end of the Nazi tyranny over East Central Europe would produce three revolutionary changes: land reform in the areas where great estates still existed, industrialization, and a thorough purge of fascists and collaborationists. These were the elements of the spontaneous and indigenous revolution which began to appear almost everywhere once the Germans had left and the Red Army had taken their place.

The natural leaders of this revolutionary change were the respected figures within the peasant parties and those who had fought the Germans during the war as Resistance chiefs. Their natural adversaries were the Moscow-trained Communists who had quite literally arrived in the baggage train of the Red Army. The first phase of liberation from the Nazis was to be marked by a continually frustrated effort on the part of the indigenous leaders to realize their ideal of a spontaneous and democratic revolution as against the Stalinist concept of an orthodox Communist revolution imposed from outside.

"People's Democracy"

At first, the peasant leaders' cause did not seem utterly hopeless. In the early stages of Soviet occupation, the democratic parties in most countries of East Central Europe enjoyed some margin of liberty. Already, however, there were two great exceptions. In Yugoslavia, Tito's grassroots Communists had the local situation firmly in hand, and in Poland —which in international and strategic terms was the most important country of all—the Soviet puppets who had first established themselves in Lublin and then moved into the ruins of Warsaw, were desperately clinging to every shred of power they possessed. The Polish Communists knew very well that they had almost no backing in the country and that if free elections ever should be held Mikolajczyk's Peasant party would sweep the field. Hence they effectively quarantined the Peasant leader and the three colleagues he brought with him under the terms of the post-Yalta agreement for enlarging the Polish government. Mikolajczyk himself, after two years of political frustration, first within the government and then in open opposition to it, finally fled the country in despair.

These were two special cases at the two poles of Communist influence. In Yugoslavia, the Communists were so strong that they did not need to share authority with other political groups. In Poland, they were so weak that they did not dare permit anyone else to exert influence, and they relied unashamedly on the Red Army to keep them in power. Elsewhere coalition government was the rule. In Bulgaria and Rumania, the phase of true coalition lasted only a few months; in Czechoslovakia, it lasted nearly three years. There and in Hungary relatively free elections were held.

The formula of government was everywhere the same—what came to be called "People's Democracy." To the Communists and their Soviet sponsors it suggested a transition regime—something more proletarian than the "bourgeois" democracies of the West, reflecting a situation which was not yet ripe for true communism, since the old social structure and ways of doing things still persisted. To non-Communists, on the other hand, "People's Democracy" meant a Popular Front, distinctly leftist in tone, but with communism accepting the limited role of revolutionary vanguard. Obviously, these two concepts would not long be compatible. Yet for the short term, the disparate coalitions of Communists, Socialists, Agrarians, and miscellaneous democrats which governed the various People's Democracies were held together by an emergency program on which all could agree: the purge of fascists, land reform, and other acts of social equalization which the postwar situation urgently required.

In this unstable relationship, the degree of liberty permitted to the individual varied greatly from region to region and from one department to another of the national life. In most places there was considerable tolerance for free speech and free meetings, but at the same time people found it inadvisable to say anything openly derogatory about the Soviet Union and its representatives. What freedom they enjoyed was extremely precarious, and the power of communism behind the scenes was far greater than it appeared to be on the surface. Everywhere the Communists held control of three vital levers of power—the ministry of propaganda, the ministry of the interior (which directed the police and local administration), and the army general staff.

Was People's Democracy, then, a mere fraud from the outset? Or was it a form of government and society in its own right which might have lasted longer had historical circumstances been different? In operation, it showed itself both fraudulent and short-lived. But when People's Democracy was introduced, a number of leaders of unimpeachable democratic conviction—men like Eduard Beneš of Czechoslovakia and Ferenc Nagy of Hungary—believed in it and were willing to try it. If Stalin had died earlier, or if the declaration of the Cold War had been delayed, People's Democracy might have had a better opportunity to evolve in a tolerably free direction. Perhaps two of the six nations in question might have remained close to the Western definition of democracy. "The argument that Soviet domination was the ultimate objective of the People's Democracy phase does not in itself mean that the People's Democracy did not have content of its own, and it certainly does not prove that this phase had to last the three years that it did rather than one, five, or ten." *

The Return to Soviet Fundamentals

Within the Soviet Union, however, changes were already in process which spelled disaster for the democratic leadership of East Central Europe. During the war Stalin had somewhat relaxed the iron hold of Communist ideology and discipline in his own country. This respite was partly owing to necessity: the dislocations of wartime, the German occupation of the Ukraine and of the western part of Russia itself, and the mobilization for military service of trusted local Communists made it impossible to keep the people in the tight check characteristic of the previous decade. Moreover, the slogan of national unity in the war effort was applied at home as well as abroad, and this dictated the same moderation that was being imposed on the foreign Communist parties. In the desperate struggle he was waging to halt the German invaders and drive them out of the country, Stalin was willing to accept help from any quarter, no matter how alien to Communist principles: he not only appealed to the patriotic memories of the Great Russian past; he also mobilized the force of religion by granting small favors to the Orthodox clergy and encouraging them to make statements in support of his regime.

In the days of victory, the tide of patriotic emotion was at its height. The heroes of the hour were the military chiefs—first among them Marshal Zhukov, the conqueror of Berlin, who remained in Germany as commander of the Soviet occupation forces. Stalin was jealous of his generals. Although during the war he had put on a marshal's uniform and directed the course of military operations himself, he had not actually participated in the fighting. He never witnessed a battle, as Churchill so often did; he stayed, rather, within the Kremlin, as mysterious and shut

---

* Zbigniew K. Brzezinski, *The Soviet Bloc: Unity and Conflict* (Cambridge, Mass.: Harvard University Press, 1960), p. 47.

off from his own people as he had been during the prewar years. The
people themselves seemed to realize this; they spontaneously hailed as liberators the marshals who had led the Red Army to victory and who as military men and nonpolitical figures epitomized more suitably than Stalin the national spirit that had won the war.

The first sign that the regime was returning to a policy of rigor was the recall of Zhukov from Berlin, in March, 1946, and his reassignment to an obscure command in the Russian provinces. There followed a purge of the armed forces. Communist indoctrination was again imposed on the troops, and those who had become ideologically contaminated by contact with the West were systematically weeded out. The forced labor camps in Siberia began to fill up again as Stalin deported by the hundreds of thousands the minority peoples of the Crimea and the Caucasus who were accused of having collaborated with the Germans. On music, on literature, and even on science—upon all cultural life—the pall of Communist orthodoxy descended once again.

The leader in this reimposition of ideological control was a young favorite of Stalin's, Andrei Zhdanov. It was Zhdanov who, on the occasion of the twenty-ninth anniversary of the Bolshevik Revolution, in the autumn of 1946, called for internal indoctrination and discipline in the Cold War that was opening with the West. It was Zhdanov whom Stalin entrusted with the task of bringing to heel the writers who had permitted their fancy to wander during the war years.

Zhdanov was quite obviously a candidate for the succession to the aging Stalin. His rival was a man of the same generation—a leader of the new type who had never known anything but the Stalinist atmosphere of intrigue and terror—Georgi Malenkov. In Zhdanov, something of the spirit of Old Bolshevism survived: in ideological terms, he was a doctrinaire, and he believed in a policy of revolutionary militancy for the foreign Communist parties, both in the East and in the West. Malenkov, on the other hand, was the pure bureaucrat—an administrator with a natural bias toward caution. In the early phases of Soviet postwar initiatives in East Central Europe, Zhdanov's militancy predominated. The later phases were to be marked by the less imaginative and more routine imposition of Communist control through Soviet agents who bore the Malenkov stamp.

The Communist Crackdown

In Bulgaria and Rumania, assertion of Communist control began during the war itself, when the Soviet Union had not yet turned toward ideological rigor at home. As with Yugoslavia and Poland, where Communist domination had existed from the outset, the contrasting cases of the two eastern Balkan monarchies reflected the comparative strength of pro-Soviet elements in one nation and their total dependence on the Red Army in the other.

Bulgaria probably had more genuine pro-Russian sentiment among its population than any other country of East Central Europe. It alone among the Axis satellites had refused to contribute troops for the invasion of the Soviet Union. And in the coalition government, called the Fatherland Front, which was formed in the autumn of 1944 after Bulgaria changed sides in the war, the Communists very early began to take the initiative. By the following January, they already felt strong enough to start attacking the other parties. Striking at the one political group that could really threaten their power, they deprived the Agrarian League of its talented chief, G. M. Dimitrov, by forcing his resignation and driving him out of the country. Thereafter, Communist pressure was unrelenting: in September, 1946, the monarchy disappeared; the next month a manipulated election gave the Communists a majority in the Grand National Assembly, and by the end of the year the opposition parties had been reduced to utter impotence.

The Soviet representatives remained behind the scenes during the process of consolidating Communist control over Bulgaria. In Rumania, on the other hand, they played a leading role from the beginning. Six weeks after the Communist onslaught had opened in Bulgaria, in February 1945, the Soviet deputy foreign minister, Andrei Vishinsky, arrived unexpectedly in the Rumanian capital of Bucharest to give Stalin's orders on the spot. Here the coalition government had been working very poorly from the Soviet standpoint: it had neither proceeded with sufficient rigor against the old ruling classes nor contributed adequately to the prosecution of the war. Unlike Bulgaria, which was in a military backwater, Rumania lay directly on the main communications line to the fighting fronts. Hence Vishinsky forced King Michael II to dismiss his prime minister and to appoint instead a pro-Communist figurehead, Petru Groza. The British and Americans protested, to no avail. Indeed, the issue of the Rumanian government was one of the nagging conflicts with the Soviet Union that clouded Roosevelt's last weeks. With Soviet help, Groza and the Communists had come to stay. By the time the king himself was forced out at the end of 1947, all power was in Communist hands.

The experience of Hungary and Czechoslovakia was quite different: the formula of People's Democracy was something more than a mask for Communist control, and democratic political leaders were able to exert real influence for two or three years. In Hungary, the Soviet occupation authorities actually permitted free elections. In November, 1945, the peasant Small-Holders party led by Ferenc Nagy won a clear parliamentary majority, and Nagy himself became prime minister. In Czechoslovakia, where former President Beneš had returned to the leadership of his country with Stalin's blessing, a similar experiment yielded rather different results. The Czechoslovak parliamentary elections of May, 1946, showed no party the clear victor, and the Communists emerged as the single strongest group. It was natural, then, that Beneš should appoint their leader, Klement Gottwald, to head the government.

For the better part of the next two years, the Communists of Czechoslovakia behaved with comparative moderation, and the country continued on the democratic course to which it had become accustomed in
the prewar years. In Hungary, however, a storm was already building
up. The extent of the Small-Holders' victory had taken the Hungarian
Communists and their Soviet sponsors by surprise, and the latter were
resolved that this sort of thing should never happen again. They began
to bring pressure to bear on the majority party, seizing its secretary-
general and finally putting him to death. Meanwhile, Prime Minister
Nagy, harassed from all sides, was steadily losing control of the situation.
In May, 1947, the Communists took advantage of his absence on vacation
in Switzerland to force him to resign his office. The demoralization of the
Small-Holders followed, and with it the gradual imposition of Communist rule.

Nine months later, Czechoslovak democracy succumbed. In a bloodless coup d'état in February, 1948, the Communists seized power in
Prague. The following September, President Beneš died. With his disappearance from the political scene, the last glimmer of democracy
flickered out in East Central Europe. In one country after another, the
process had been the same. First, the authentic leaders of the democratic
parties had been forced out. Then these parties, under new and more
pliant leadership, were reduced to the role of mere façades, or—in the
case of the Socialists—were obliged to fuse with the Communists. Finally
the monolithic control of a single party was imposed on the country,
together with the distinguishing marks of Communist rule—a campaign
to collectivize agriculture, a speeding of the tempo of industrialization,
and an end to what vestiges of personal liberty still remained.

IV

THE SUPPRESSION OF OPPOSITION

The Communist suppression of organized opposition proceeded in three
stages. First, the democratic political leaders were attacked. Then came
a series of trials of prominent churchmen. Finally, the Communists began to purge their own ranks, as a deadly duel opened between the
"Muscovites" loyal to Stalin and the home-grown leaders accused of
"nationalist" deviations.

The Democratic Leaders and the Churchmen

During 1947, the democratic leadership of East Central Europe all but
disappeared. Mikolajczyk of Poland and Nagy of Hungary both escaped
abroad; Iuliu Maniu, the veteran Peasant leader in Rumania, was condemned to life imprisonment; Nikola Petkov, who had succeeded G. M.

Dimitrov as the chief figure in the Bulgarian Agrarian Union, was tried on false charges and summarily hanged.

With these people eliminated—and with the older conservative leadership either extinct or discredited—the Christian churches alone remained as possible centers of opposition. Communist rule was by very definition anti-Christian, but the rigor it displayed toward the church varied greatly from country to country. These local differences reflected both the strength of religious sentiment in the particular country and the degree to which church organizations themselves were equipped to offer resistance to Communist control.

Within the nations of Orthodox faith, the influence both of religious sentiment and of church organization was comparatively weak. In the three Orthodox areas of the Balkans—Bulgaria, Rumania, and the Serbian parts of Yugoslavia—the religious pattern resembled that of Russia before 1917; that is, the level of education among the clergy was low, and the people had little religious militancy. Nor was there any central leadership abroad, such as the Papacy offered in the Catholic world, to which the Orthodox faithful could look for encouragement in time of persecution. On the contrary, each nation had its separate church organization, linked to the others solely by spiritual ties, and with a tradition which emphasized national solidarity and obedience to the authority of the secular state. Hence it was not too difficult for the Communist rulers of Bulgaria, Rumania, and Yugoslavia to make their Orthodox clergy conform. Some priests and bishops merely bowed their heads and did what was expected of them; others gave active support to the new regimes. But in neither case did they present a serious problem to those in authority.

In the Catholic countries, it was quite different. Here—except possibly in the Czech lands—religious faith was strong and respect for the priests nearly universal. The Catholics of East Central Europe, moreover, enjoyed active support from outside: not only the Vatican but millions of Catholics in Western Europe and the United States gave them constant encouragement in their struggle to preserve their faith.

The Communists were wise enough not to proceed directly against religion itself. They chose rather to limit the church's role in education and to frighten the clergy into submission by striking at the chief figure, or primate, within each country. In Yugoslavia, Tito brought to trial the spiritual leader of the Croats, Archbishop Alois Stepinac, who was condemned in 1946 to a long prison term. A similar fate befell the primate of Hungary, Cardinal Joseph Mindszenty—whose trial in 1949 recalled the Soviet purges in the defendant's public admission of the most unlikely charges—and Archbishop Beran of Prague, who was deported from his see in 1951. All these proceedings bore a melancholy resemblance to one another, but the character and policy of the defendants were by no means uniform. Beran was a true democrat. Mindszenty was a popular figure and a personality of heroic stature; the son of peasants, he was a conservative of the old stamp who had opposed land reform because it would entail financial loss for church education. Stepinac presented a still more doubtful case from the standpoint of East European democracy: as primate of Croatia, he had countenanced the fascist regime of Ante Pavelich during the war years and hence, at least indirectly, shared responsibility for the mass murder of Serbs under this most sinister of Axis puppets.

However the moral justification of these trials might vary, the result they achieved was the same. By the early 1950's, the Catholic church in Croatia, Czechoslovakia, and Hungary had been terrified into submission. But the Polish experience was different. Among the Poles—who ranked with the Irish as the most profoundly Catholic people of Europe—it was impossible to take the same stern line that had succeeded among the Catholic peoples to the south. In Poland, solidarity between clergy and people was too strong, and religious feeling was too intense to yield to merely political pressure. Hence the Polish Communists moved warily: they did nothing to interfere with the succession to church leadership of Archbishop Wyszynski in 1948, and they allowed church-state relations to drift along with no clear victory for either side. This was one of the chief reasons why the Communist regime in Poland was to follow after 1956 a course which markedly diverged from that of its ideological partners in East Central Europe (see Chapter Nineteen, IV).

Tito's Heresy and the "Nationalist" Deviation

One other country had diverged still earlier from the model that the Soviet Union laid down: Tito's Yugoslavia, which in June, 1948, was expelled from the Stalinist camp and subsequently undertook to establish its own definition of Communist goals.

That Yugoslavia should be the first Communist nation to leave the common fold presented a most striking paradox, for in the early postwar years, Tito's regime ranked as the most advanced of all—the country where Communist control had proceeded the furthest and where People's Democracy came closest to Soviet standards. But for this very reason the Yugoslav Communists were under suspicion in Moscow from the start: they had been too successful; they had achieved power by their own efforts—aided rather by Britain and the United States than by the Soviet Union. Stalin never forgave Tito his wartime traffickings with the West, and as the Soviet leader grew older and more suspicious he came to detest the resilient self-confidence of the Yugoslavs and the feeling of national self-sufficiency which went along with it.

Tito, for his part, strenuously objected to Russian domineering and to the tendency of the Soviet secret police to treat his country as its own preserve. The issue between him and Stalin, then, was chiefly one of national independence. This was already evident five months before the break, in January, 1948, when the Communist official organ in Moscow rebuked Tito for the plan of a South Slav federation which he had been discussing with the Bulgarian Communist leaders. It was quite clear that Stalin wanted no competition from any secondary affiliations within the Communist camp. Hence it should not have come as a complete surprise when in the following June the newly founded association of Communist parties, or Cominform (see Chapter Seventeen, I), expelled the Yugoslav Communists on the patently false charge that they had faltered in the campaign to collectivize agriculture.

At first Tito seemed shaken by his expulsion. He kept insisting that he remained a loyal Communist, and he was slow to reply to the insults that the press and radio of the other East European countries poured upon him. Indeed, during the first year of Yugoslav isolation, it appeared that Tito's regime might not withstand the united onslaught of its neighbors. But gradually Tito's peculiar assets for such a struggle made themselves evident. His Resistance record had given him a position as a national as well as a Communist hero—and his break with Stalin immensely increased his popularity by putting the emphasis on this patriotic aspect of his past. The Russians failed in their efforts to turn the Yugoslav Communists against him: the army, the party cadres, the secret police remained Titoist. As he gathered confidence, the Yugoslav leader himself began to grope his way toward a definition of his new position: he stressed the Leninist purity of his doctrine, as opposed to Stalin's perversions of it, and he took the first steps toward reopening his contacts with the West and toward the liberalization of his regime at home.

The real influence of Tito's new form of Communism was to become apparent only in the 1950's (see Chapter Nineteen, IV). Meanwhile, two immediate consequences followed his dramatic rupture of relations with Stalin. The first placed the small and backward Adriatic state of Albania in a still more paradoxical situation than that of Yugoslavia. Before the war, Albania had been under Mussolini's control. It was from Albania that the Duce had launched his disastrous attack on Greece in 1941. In 1943, with the collapse of Italy, the Albanians developed a Communist-led Resistance movement, which resembled Tito's and waged its struggle under his protection. With the liberation of the Balkan Peninsula in 1944 and 1945, Albania became a Yugoslav dependency, and after the war it took its place as a satellite within another satellite's orbit—a Communist state managed indirectly by Moscow via Belgrade. The Albanian Communists evidently resented this dependence on Yugoslavia, for they took advantage of Tito's rupture with Stalin to break with Yugoslavia and to proclaim their direct fealty to Moscow. After 1948, Albania continued to exist as an isolated outpost of the Communist world, barely sustaining itself against the enmity of both the Greeks and the Yugoslavs.

The second consequence of Tito's success was the final round in the suppression of opposition to communism in East Central Europe. In the summer of 1948 Zhdanov died, his policy of revolutionary militancy discredited by the failure of the Cominform to bring Tito to terms. After

Zhdanov's death, his followers within the Soviet Union were system-
atically purged. At the same time, the Soviet leadership adopted a tactic of keeping a tight rein on the East European Communists. The Russian leaders urged them to follow Soviet example and purge their own ranks, in an effort to eliminate all those who might fall under suspicion of a "nationalist" or Titoist deviation.

In this purge, which extended from the spring of 1949 to Stalin's death four years later, several of the most responsible of the East European Communist leaders lost their lives. Of those accused, only Wladislaw Gomulka of Poland, who was merely imprisoned without trial, lived to play a prominent part in the post-Stalinist era. In many respects, this new purge resembled what Russia had experienced in the 1930's, but there was an important difference. In the Soviet Union from 1936 to 1938, Stalin's new men had purged the "Old Bolsheviks." Now it was the older men, the "Muscovites" trained to iron discipline, who were slaughtering the newer type of leadership which the war and postwar years had pushed to the fore and which thought at least partially in national rather than in Stalinist terms. In both cases, however, the results were the same—the stifling of talent and independent initiative and the imposition of a gray bureaucratic uniformity on the whole party.

The Balance Sheet

By the end of 1949, the five states of East Central Europe which still remained within the Soviet camp had brought their two revolutions to an end. In each, the power of the old ruling classes had been destroyed; the churches had been deprived of their influence and all but forced out of the field of education which they had earlier dominated; and by the same process, political democracy had also perished.

On the more positive side, all these countries had made enormous economic advances. The collectivization of agriculture was proceeding apace—although at a less rapid rate than had been true of the Soviet Union in the 1930's. Bulgaria alone offered an exception: here by 1951 nearly half the land had been collectivized. Although this was a doubtful expedient and stubbornly resisted by the peasantry, there was little question of the eventual benefits to be conferred by the parallel campaign for industrialization. In all the countries, basic industry was nationalized, and nearly all had embarked on five-year plans on the Soviet model. By 1953 these were to result in doubling the area's steel production and in a three-year increase of almost 100 per cent in over-all industrial output in both Poland and Czechoslovakia.

For the present, however, the people of Eastern Europe derived little advantage from this economic progress. The work week was long and factory discipline severe; in a few sectors of the economy, forced labor was being used. With the industrial labor force increased by about a third, overcrowding in the cities was becoming a grave problem. Highest priority went to heavy industry; consumer goods were in short supply. As the 1940's ended, East Central Europe was finally facing up to its basic economic problems. Yet, as the Soviet Union had done in the 1930's, it was advancing at enormous human cost and with the promise of a better life for the individual postponed to a remote future.

Readings

For the interwar background of social and political problems, see Robert L. Wolff, *The Balkans in Our Time* (1956), Henry L. Roberts, *Rumania: Political Problems of an Agrarian State* (1951), and Hugh Seton-Watson, *Eastern Europe between the Wars 1918–1941* (1946). All are highly critical of the pre-1939 regimes. Seton-Watson, in *The East European Revolution* (1950), also gives a general history of events from the collapse of Nazi power to 1949. For the subsequent course of Communist rule in East Central Europe, see Fred W. Neal, *Titoism in Action: The Reforms in Yugoslavia after 1948* (1958), and Zbigniew K. Brzezinski, *The Soviet Bloc: Unity and Conflict*, rev. ed. (1961), which traces both the consolidation of the bloc and its internal strains after Stalin's death.

Western Europe: The Years of Recovery, 1945-1949

In Western Europe, the postwar settlement—both social and political—emerged from a long struggle between two opposed movements. The first was the ideology of the wartime Resistance, an active force of renovation and change. The second was the entrenched power of old institutions and attitudes, which might seem no more than a force of passivity and inertia, but which in fact had behind it the bulk of inarticulate public sentiment. This was the basic contrast between the two. Those pressing for change were both articulate and devoted to the public welfare —but they were only a minority. Those who wanted to return to the old ways were for the most part silent and absorbed in their private concerns —but they were the more numerous. In the final amalgam, there was to be far more of conservatism than of innovation in the postwar West.

The quiet, largely undeclared struggle between these forces dominated the half-decade 1945–1949. By the end of the 1940's the issue was decided: the main lines of social and political settlement which were to persist through the whole subsequent decade had been firmly established.

I

THE MOMENT OF LIBERATION

The end of the war in Europe was greeted everywhere with an enormous sigh of relief. True, the war in the Pacific was far from over—and the general assumption was that it would continue longer than it actually

During the war cherries had been scarce and expensive in Europe. Now they are plentiful, and this woman has no difficulty in selling her stock. COURTESY PHOTOWORLD, INC.

did—but most Europeans were not much interested in the Far Eastern struggle. It had been from the beginning the Americans' war, and it was only the professional military men of Europe and people with a special concern for the colonies who had their eyes fixed on Asia in the late spring and summer of 1945. To the rest of the population, these imperial questions seemed remote and of little importance. Indeed, people already appeared to sense the outcome, that the former colonies would be reoccupied only temporarily and that they would very soon break away from the mother country. But this problem still lay in the future (*see* Chapter Eighteen). Both Britain and France were busily redeploying their forces for service in the Far East when the explosion of the atomic bomb at Hiroshima in August, 1945, brought the war against Japan to an unexpectedly early close.

In actuality, each city or country of Europe had ended its own war at the moment of its liberation. Its military forces might continue fighting until the final surrender, but the people at large were already turning to the rebuilding of their houses and their lives and had little thought or energy left over for the prosecution of the war. The end of the war, like the postwar settlement, came about piecemeal. Each community in turn experienced the supreme moment of liberation. Each in turn felt a nightmare lifting and a brief thrill of fraternity and human renewal. At this moment, the forces of the Resistance occupied the center of the stage.

The Ideology of the Resistance

The European Resistance movements tended toward the left. They included both Socialists and Communists, and also Catholics of advanced social views who usually called themselves Christian Democrats. A minority of Resistance leaders distrusted the Communists from the outset and tried to exclude them from positions which might entitle them to postwar influence but, for the majority of the Resistance fighters, particularly the rank and file, the Communists were comrades-in-arms like any others. Non-Communists gave them their friendship and hoped that in return the Communists would prove cooperative in the rebuilding of postwar democracy.

This was the vision of the Resistance—a vision both vague and generous. It resembled the ideal of the Popular Front, but it went beyond the prewar concept of a merely temporary expedient or a minimum program, to embody a whole new view of European society. To the Popular Front's goal of social justice it added the Christian Democratic ideal of class reconciliation. It sought to bridge the gap between Communists and democrats—and also the chasm which had so long separated Catholics from anticlericals—by creating a new and nonsectarian socialism. By the same token it strove to supplant the old political parties with a new movement which would bring to national leadership men who were both more public-spirited and more technically competent than the usual parliamentary politicians of the old stamp.

This vision—like the corresponding image of People's Democracy in Eastern Europe—was not wholly unrealistic. At the beginning, it corresponded to a yearning for political and social renewal which was widespread on the European continent: in 1944 and 1945, most of the more thoughtful people in France and Italy and Germany considered it impossible to return to the former routines of parliamentary democracy; they were convinced that something more active and vital and efficient was required. Even in their view of communism the optimists of the Resistance were not wholly mistaken: Western European communism *had* changed during the war years. The Resistance experience had brought to the fore new and younger men who tended to think first of their own country's needs, rather than of Moscow's orders, and who preferred a political system in which the essentials of personal liberty were preserved. But men of this sort seldom held posts of top command; the great question in the months immediately following liberation was how much practical influence they would be able to exert on the postwar activity of their parties.

In the end, they proved to have little influence. As the Cold War opened, Stalin brought the Western Communist parties to heel and reimposed the old discipline upon them through "Muscovite" leaders on whom he could rely. At the same time, the non-Communist Resistance chiefs, with a few notable exceptions, were finding it impossible to dominate the reviving parliamentary life of their respective countries. With the first postwar elections, the older—and presumably discredited —parliamentary leaders began to return in large numbers to positions of influence. In the unfamiliar conditions of peacetime, the Resistance chiefs were showing themselves no match for the seasoned politicians. Faced with the tricky infighting of the parliamentary arena, the veterans of the Resistance behaved like inexperienced amateurs. The only Resistance leaders who were able to make a permanent mark on the postwar scene were those who had very early joined some regularly constituted political movement.

The Purge of Fascists and Collaborationists

This failure to recast in a new form the party framework of continental democracy was the first great defeat for the Resistance. The second was the failure of the purge of fascists and collaborationists. At best it would have been an enormously difficult task to punish the guilty and to redress the grievances inherited from years of tyranny. In the atmosphere of 1945 and 1946, which was heavy with both weariness and political passion, it proved impossible for the new political authorities to find a judicial formula which could convince the average citizen that justice was being done.

In the moment of liberation itself, the Resistance fighters dealt out their own retribution. Mussolini perished at the hands of Italian partisans after the barest semblance of a trial. In all the countries which had suffered under Nazi oppression, the more extreme Resistance leaders took advantage of the interregnum between the departure of the Germans and the arrival of regular Allied authority, to settle old scores and to shoot down their enemies as they chose. This was particularly true of Communists and of criminal elements which had attached themselves to the Resistance late and for their own personal advantage.

Under these circumstances, it is not surprising that crimes were committed under the cover of patriotism. The number of suspected fascists and collaborationists shot out of hand is extremely hard to determine. In France somewhere between 10,000 and 20,000 were killed during the liberation in summary fashion. Nearly 800 more were executed after regular trials of one sort or another. For those guilty of lesser offenses, De Gaulle's government devised a series of penalties which ranged from discharge from public service to prison terms and temporary loss of citizenship rights.

In Italy, in the Low Countries, and in Scandinavia, the new democratic governments followed similar procedures. Throughout liberated Europe, both public administrators and the judiciary tried to carry out the purge in conscientious fashion, but nearly everywhere the results were disappointing. It proved impossible to establish exact gradations of collaboration; it was even difficult to determine with any precision who had been responsible for another man's death. As a result, the public soon lost interest; worse, the average citizen concluded that it was all a matter of politics and that one set of politicians was simply taking revenge on its adversaries. Thus, the postliberation purge almost entirely failed to accomplish the moral purpose which the Resistance leaders had intended: far from "purifying" the atmosphere of politics, as the Resistance had hoped, it poisoned it further through a massive injection of hatred and personal rancor.

This was particularly true in Germany. Here, where the anti-Nazi forces were weak and would have had great difficulty accomplishing the purge on their own, the Allied occupation authorities assumed the task of "denazification" themselves. But to "denazify" Germany was a far harder task than to rid France, for example, of fascists and collaborationists. In the latter country, only a small minority was involved; in Germany, the great majority of the adult population had been associated with the Nazi party in one form or another. Hence denazification proved to be an enormous and unmanageable operation: it bogged down in masses of paper, as millions of Germans filled out elaborate questionnaires; it foundered in quiet sabotage and a conspiracy of silence among the population at large. Frequently it proved simpler to try the lesser offenders first, since their cases were easier to untangle. This resulted in

an unanticipated injustice: as denazification degenerated into an un-
savory comedy, the only feasible course seemed the granting of amnesties on an ever wider scale—and these, naturally, were of greatest benefit to those whose cases had not yet come to trial. Thus many insignificant people who had been tried earlier received heavy penalties, while some important offenders whose cases had been postponed escaped scot-free. Finally, the simplest solution was to call a complete halt: denazification never officially came to an end; it just dwindled away.

The mass of the German people followed the denazification procedures with complete skepticism. From them, they gained no clear impression of justice being done or wrongs being righted. This was particularly true of the Allies' greatest effort to teach the Germans a lesson: the trial of the major war criminals held at Nürnberg from November, 1945, to September, 1946.

The Allies spared no pains to make the Nürnberg trial an impressive example: a Lord Justice of Great Britain presided over the eight judges sitting on the bench, and a Justice of the United States Supreme Court served as chief prosecutor. The case was meticulously prepared: the crime of waging aggressive war and the "crimes against humanity" for which the defendants were being tried were carefully defined and supported in great detail. The accused included all the leading Nazis, except for Hitler and Goebbels, who had taken their lives in the Chancellery bunker in Berlin, and Himmler, who had committed suicide just after his capture by the British army. But to the Germans as a whole the trial carried no moral message. The defendants' countrymen saw it as an act of revenge inflicted by the victors on the vanquished, and whatever signs of impartiality the court displayed were canceled out in the German mind by the fact that Soviet judges were participating along with the British, the Americans, and the French. The final verdict was received with apathy as a foregone conclusion. The only surprise, perhaps, was that three of the defendants, including former Chancellor von Papen, were acquitted. Seven received prison sentences, among them Albert Speer, Hitler's efficiency expert in the last year of the war. The remaining twelve were all condemned to be hanged, but Goering at the last moment escaped the noose by taking poison in his cell.

Elsewhere the major auxiliaries of the Nazis had been tried by their own people. In Norway, Vidkun Quisling was condemned to death and executed; in France, the same fate befell Pierre Laval. But Marshal Pétain, who had likewise received the death penalty, was granted clemency by De Gaulle and his sentence commuted to life imprisonment on an island off the Breton coast. The trials of Laval and Pétain had been far from edifying: they had been carelessly prepared and marked by outbursts of political invective. Here, as in Germany, the conclusion was the same: the punishment could not be made to fit the crime—the retribution exacted was inadequate for what had gone before. The wrongs committed in the Nazi era had been so vast and so diffused that no proper punishment could be devised. What the Resistance leaders had intended as a great moral lesson had degenerated into a series of spiteful attacks against a few thousand broken and bewildered human beings.

II

THE ECONOMIC PROBLEM

The Extent of War Damage and War Losses

When the war came to an end, vast stretches of Western and Central Europe lay in ruins. Although no one region was so terribly devastated as northeastern France had been in the First World War, the total damage done in the second war was far greater and spread over a far wider area. Nearly everywhere transport had been completely disorganized: bridges and railway stations had ranked as high-priority targets for Allied aviators and had been systematically bombed in preparation for the final advances. Port installations had suffered almost as much. Thousands of square miles of farmland lay devastated. In Germany, nearly all the great cities were in ruins, and even in France, which had escaped with less damage, such seaports as Brest, Le Havre, Saint-Nazaire, and Toulon were more than half destroyed.

In Britain, war damage was concentrated in the ports and industrial cities; in Italy, it lay chiefly in the two swathes of countryside where the Allies' advance had successively come to a halt in the two last winters of the war—the area between Naples and Rome, and that between Florence and Bologna. The Italian seaports were also grievously damaged, as were such industrial centers as Milan and Turin. In contrast, the northern countries fared rather better. Denmark had escaped almost without destruction; neither here nor in Norway had there been any regular fighting at the end of the war, which found the Germans still in occupation. Similarly, Belgium's rapid liberation had helped preserve its cities: Antwerp and the region of the Ardennes were the places most heavily damaged. But in the Netherlands, where the Germans had remained almost until their final defeat, devastation and human suffering had been very severe; at the end, the urban poor were close to starvation, and the Allies were obliged to send emergency supplies by parachute.

In France, half a million buildings had been completely destroyed, and another million and a half seriously damaged. Half the country's cattle had disappeared, along with more than three-quarters of its railroad engines. Only one-tenth of its trucks and automobiles were fit for service. Industrial production at the beginning of 1945 stood at less than half what it had been in 1938. But in Germany things looked far worse. In a city such as Frankfurt less than a quarter of the houses were still standing. As late as 1946, the output of German industry had risen to only one-third of its volume of ten years before. In Germany, however, appearances were deceptive. Under the surface of unprecedented destruction, a major share of the nation's assets remained intact. Large parts of the German countryside had been spared, along with most of its smaller towns and villages. Moreover, at least three-quarters of its industrial plant was still usable: the melancholy fact was that British and American aviators had been far more successful in destroying artistic monuments and workers' housing than they had been in crippling German industry. This was one of the chief reasons for the German "miracle" of economic recovery in the years after 1949.

Experts viewing the devastation of France and Germany estimated that it would take twenty years to rebuild. (Actually, the larger part of the task was completed in a single decade.) But this covered only the material losses. So far as human losses were concerned, it was harder to make an estimate, for here there had been intangible drains which only time would fully reveal.

Of the major belligerents in the West, Germany alone lost more men in the second war than it had in the first. More than a million and a half Germans had been killed in action, an additional two million were missing, and another million and a half were prisoners. Elsewhere—in Britain, in France, and in Italy—the numbers of those who perished in combat fell far below what they had been in the earlier war. But civilian losses were much higher. Two and a half million French men and women had been held in captivity in Germany as prisoners of war, forced laborers, or concentration camp inmates. Of these, more than two hundred thousand had been executed or had died of hardship and starvation. Countless others returned home crippled in body and in spirit. The six-year torment of the war eroded Europe's population both physically and psychologically. Once the first flush of joy at the coming of peace was over, it became apparent how much in fact the war had cost—how tired and depressed people were, and how few were fully capable of making the strenuous effort required to restore Europe's economy to a state of vigorous health.

Reconstruction, the Black Market, and American Aid

The initial pace of reconstruction was very slow. For the first few months, governments and people concentrated on the immediate tasks of restoring communications and essential services and reopening the coal mines, on which everything else depended, but they did not pursue these goals with any consistent policy. They wavered between an attitude of laissez faire and an effort to keep wages and prices strictly in line. Only in the Low Countries and in Scandinavia—particularly in Belgium and in Norway—were governments strong enough to take stern action to limit currency circulation and thereby to hold inflation and the black market in check.

In France and Italy, on the other hand, inflation and black-mar-keteering completely escaped control. Price regulation proved almost wholly ineffective: soon the black market became the real market, since goods were unobtainable at the official prices. Meanwhile, the value of money fell steadily. The French franc, which had been officially estab-lished at the rate of 50 to the dollar at the time of the Normandy in-vasion, stood at about 300 when it reached a temporary plateau in early 1948. The following year, the Italian lira, which Allied Military Govern-ment had valued at 100 to the dollar, was finally stabilized at 625. Yet these results had been achieved only at the cost of abandoning con-trols entirely and of letting prices outstrip the wage level. In Italy, the postwar lira had fallen to one-fiftieth of its prewar purchasing power; in France, the fall had been at least half as great. This inflation was not as ruinous as that experienced by Germany in 1923, but it was enough to destroy once again the class of small investors and to wipe out nearly all private savings.

Even this modest economic stabilization, moreover, occurred only with American aid. Such help had reached Western Europe in successive waves. First there had been the emergency aid in the form of food and essential supplies that Military Government had brought to Italy and the corresponding Civil Affairs officers had handled for France. But by the end of 1945, the American army in France and Italy had finished its work and gone home. The new funnels for aid were the United Nations Relief and Rehabilitation Administration (UNRRA) and a number of direct grants from the United States to individual countries. These expedients in turn proved entirely inadequate. Not until the American government —in the context of the Cold War of 1947—inaugurated the Marshall Plan, did Western Europe at last find its way out of the economic morass which had almost engulfed it (*see* Chapter Seventeen, I).

III

THE OCCUPATION OF GERMANY

In Italy, Military Government had been only a temporary expedient. In France, the Allied armies had restricted themselves to supply and civil liaison functions. In Germany, on the contrary, Military Govern-ment ruled the country for four full years. There seemed to be no alter-native, for here the unprecedented had happened: the German central government had disappeared. All that was left were local officials—and in the East even these were often lacking, since mayors and district administrators had departed along with the population fleeing before the advance of the Red Army. In his last statement, Hitler had delegated his powers to his naval chief, Admiral Karl Doenitz, and for a few days the admiral tried to run a semblance of government from his headquar-ters in Flensburg. But the Allies soon brought this to an end. By mid-

May of 1945, the slate had been wiped clean. The four occupying powers were left alone with their problems and with each other; they must both rule their separate zones of Germany and devise a common policy for the government of the country as a whole.

The Potsdam Decisions: the Oder-Neisse Line

The Western Allies had wavered back and forth between moderation and rigor in their planning for postwar Germany. In September, 1944, eight months before the end of the war, Roosevelt and Churchill had temporarily agreed on the extremely harsh scheme proposed by the American secretary of the treasury, Henry Morgenthau, Jr. The "Morgenthau Plan," as it was called, was based on the notion of a "pastoral" Germany: the Reich was to be stripped of its industrial potential. Its inhabitants, by returning to the bucolic conditions under which they had lived in the days of Kant and Goethe, were presumably to lose their taste—along with their capacities—for waging aggressive war.

The Morgenthau Plan was economic madness. None of the secretary's advisers who had drafted it ever explained how it would be possible for Germany to support its swollen twentieth-century population with an eighteenth-century economy. As this simple truth dawned on the British and Americans, they quietly shelved the Morgenthau proposals. By the time of the Yalta Conference, Churchill was pleading for humane treatment for Germany, while Roosevelt seemed irresolute and hesitant. Still something of the Morgenthau Plan attitude lingered. In the final directive issued to Anglo-American Military Government, the key formula specified a level of economic activity just sufficient to prevent "disease and unrest." This ambiguous wording was capable of two different interpretations. At first it was treated as a strict minimum which the Germans were not to exceed, but subsequently its interpretation was modified to allow them to raise their standard of living as far as their own resources permitted.

Stalin and his advisers were clearer about what they wanted from Germany. They were interested in a social revolution which would transform their zone—or preferably the whole nation—into a People's Democracy, and in receiving substantial reparations as compensation for the destruction their own country had suffered. Beyond that they wanted a boundary for Poland sufficiently generous to help the Poles forget what they had ceded to the Soviet Union and to tie them firmly to Russia's policy. These concessions Stalin had failed to obtain at Yalta. The final conference of the Big Three, held in Potsdam, just outside Berlin, the following July, gave him an opportunity to return to the attack.

Much of the criticism that Yalta generated should more properly have focused on Potsdam, for it was here that the British and Americans finally consented to the Oder-Neisse boundary for Poland and the sum of ten billion dollars in reparations for the Soviet Union which Churchill had succeeded at Yalta in having postponed for later decision. But Churchill was able to participate only in the first part of the Potsdam Conference; toward its end he was obliged to give up his seat to Clement Attlee, whose party had just defeated Churchill's Conservatives in the British parliamentary elections. Likewise, President Truman had taken Roosevelt's place. Of the original trio of wartime comrades-in-arms, only Stalin remained. It was certainly not without influence on the Potsdam decisions that the Soviet leader was facing two inexperienced Western negotiators.

The Oder-Neisse boundary—which put under Polish rule an area inhabited by nine million Germans—was never formally conceded by the British and Americans; they simply agreed to the *de facto* administration of the area by Poland, pending final decision by a regular peace conference. This proviso really meant very little: it did not prevent the expulsion by the Poles of the vast majority of the Germans within their new borders, to whom the Czechs added nearly three million more by driving out the Germans of the Sudetenland; the problem of absorbing twelve million expellees and refugees became the most agonizing difficulty that German administrators faced in the immediate postwar years. But on one matter at least Truman and Attlee held firm. They did not grant Stalin's third demand—an interallied control of the Ruhr that would have associated the Soviet Union in the administration of Germany's most important industrial area, and so given it an opportunity to spread Soviet ideological influence into the very heart of the country. The Western leaders thereby made certain that experiments in People's Democracy would be restricted to Russia's Eastern Zone.

The Partition of the Country

Just before the Potsdam Conference met, the four Allied powers moved into the occupation zones which had been formally assigned the previous spring. Earlier they had been administering on a temporary basis the areas that their troops had occupied during the course of hostilities. Now they redeployed their forces behind the definitive zonal demarcation lines—the Russians in the east, the British in the northwest, the Americans in the south, and the French in a smaller zone to the southwest bordering on their own country. In substance, this meant American withdrawal from such central German regions as Thuringia and Saxony and their reassignment to Soviet control.

At the same time, the occupation powers arranged for a similar four-way division of the City of Berlin—which was entirely surrounded by the Soviet Zone. This was an awkward arrangement and it was to cause repeated international crises in succeeding years, but the Allies hoped to mitigate the Berlin problem and to give a minimum of unity to the country by establishing in the former capital a number of central German agencies. These would have the task of ensuring uniformity in carrying out the less controversial of the Potsdam decisions—which included the level to which German industry would be limited, a pledge to treat the country as a single economic unit, and provisions for the demilitarization and democratization of German society.

Quite obviously, however—as Eastern European experience was demonstrating—the Russians interpreted the term *democratization* differently from the British and Americans. By it, they meant the unquestioned leadership of Communist and pro-Soviet elements. In accordance with this policy, in the spring of 1946, they forced the East German Social Democrats to merge with the Communists—a process in which the former party (which was originally much the stronger) almost entirely lost its identity. By the end of the year, the Soviet occupation authorities had firmly set their zone of Germany on the same course which the satellite states of East Central Europe were simultaneously following.

Similarly in economic policy the Russians went their own way. They took reparations not only by dismantling factories and shipping them to the Soviet Union—which was permitted by the Potsdam agreement—but also by tapping current German production—which had been expressly forbidden. By operating their zone as a self-contained economic entity, they violated the provision that Germany was to be treated as a unit for purposes of foreign trade. This behavior evoked retaliation from the West. In late 1946 and 1947, the British and Americans moved toward a separate economic policy of their own: they ceased dismantling factories, they raised the permitted level of German industry; in short, they began to shift from treating the Germans as enemies to preparing them for a role as future allies.

In December, 1946, the Americans and British agreed to fuse the economic administration of their two zones into what came to be called the *Bizone*—the nucleus of the future state of Western Germany. Meanwhile, a series of conferences between the Western and the Soviet foreign ministers had ended in total deadlock. In the same fashion, the Allied Control Council—which consisted of the four zonal commanders—had also broken down. It held its last meeting in March, 1948, when the Soviet representative walked out in protest against the invitation the British and Americans had extended to the French to join the Bizone. Three months earlier, the foreign ministers had adjourned their final conference without agreement. The rupture was complete. By the spring of 1948 the partition of Germany between East and West was an established fact.

The Establishment of State Governments, Political Parties, and the Bonn Parliamentary Council

In the winter of 1945–1946, Germany was at its nadir. Industry was languishing, millions were living in cold and squalor in cellars and temporary barracks; the old and infirm were dying of hardship, and the expellees from the East were receiving a chilly welcome as unwanted guests; social dissolution seemed imminent, as parents lost control over their children, and prostitution and black-marketeering flourished on the fringes of the occupation armies.

Yet at this very moment, Western Germany was taking its first steps toward political and moral revival. Toward the end of 1945, the British and American occupation authorities began the reconstruction of German administration above the local level. They established state governments within their zones—four in the British Zone and four in the American. These states did not exactly correspond to the former divisions of Germany. A few, like Bavaria, which was the largest in territorial extent, were revivals of the old middle-sized states of the Reich. Others, like North Rhine–Westphalia, the most populous, were formed from provinces of Prussia, which at last disappeared from the map. In general, however, this redrawing of administrative boundaries benefited the country: it tended to equalize the states in size and to group together areas with common interests.

With the organization of the Bizone, the state governments began to acquire a new political significance. Indeed, the bizonal Council of Ministers-President of the individual states became a West German government in embryo. These ministers-president—or prime ministers—had received their appointments from Military Government as trusted anti-Nazis: some had been imprisoned under Hitler; some had lived in exile; some had remained at liberty within the Reich but had succeeded in avoiding involvement with the Nazi tyranny.

The ministers-president and their ministerial colleagues gave tangible evidence of the revival of German democracy. Most of them were older men who had acquired political experience under the Weimar Republic, and the parties they represented were similarly reincarnations of Weimar models. Two parties dominated the field from the outset. Neither the right-wing parties nor the Communists were able to win much support: the former were discredited by their collusion with the Nazis, the latter by their association with the Russians, who were too close for comfort. The Social Democrats and the Christian Democrats, rather, found the postwar atmosphere congenial, and emerged almost equal in strength from the first elections to state diets, or parliaments.

The Social Democrats—who had kept alive their organization in exile —had never broken their ties with the Weimar years. They had found a new kind of leader, however, in Kurt Schumacher. Schumacher offered a striking contrast to the older type of bureaucratic, routinized Social Democratic leadership. A veteran of twelve years in concentration camp, he had emerged shattered in health, with both an arm and a leg missing, but with a passionate faith in the future of his party; by his intense, frenetic drive and his burning oratory, he steered the Social Democrats toward a more nationalist course and away from their former exclusive dependence on the trade unions.

German Christian Democracy was also for the most part a revival of
an earlier party—the old Catholic Center. The new name suggested a broadening of its base to include a substantial Protestant wing. Its leader, however, was a Catholic and a prominent Centrist from the Weimar years. Konrad Adenauer—whose personality and influence were to dominate a decade and a half of post-Nazi German history—had already ranked as an important figure in the late 1920's and early 1930's. But he had largely restricted himself to local affairs, serving as lord mayor of the Rhineland city of Cologne. Under the Nazis he had never compromised with the regime, yet at the same time he had been careful not to engage in the more dangerous kind of Resistance activities. Except for two brief periods in prison, he had simply waited out the twelve years of Hitler's rule. Then in 1945 he emerged from retirement—tough-minded, astute, astonishingly robust for his sixty-nine years—to become his country's guide and savior as it groped its way toward its second experiment in republican and democratic government.

It was largely under Adenauer's influence that the Rhineland university town of Bonn was selected as the place where a "Parliamentary Council" was to meet to draft a constitution for Western Germany. In September, 1948, after the French had accepted the Anglo-American invitation to join their smaller zone to the Bizone, representatives of the West German state diets convened in Bonn to establish at last a federal government. Three months earlier, the Western occupation powers had proclaimed a currency reform: by a conversion of old marks into new at a rate of ten to one, they cut the ground from under the black market and prepared the way for rapid economic revival. The Soviet Union, meanwhile, had precipitated the first great crisis over Berlin, in an effort to force the Western Allies to desist from their plan of establishing a federal government (*see* Chapter Seventeen, I).

The Parliamentary Council proceeded, undaunted, with its labors. In February, 1949, the constitution or "basic law" was substantially completed. Two more months were needed to alter it to suit the occupying powers. By summer, however, everything was ready for its ratification by the West German people and for the election of the first federal parliament. In these elections, the Christian Democrats scored a narrow victory over their Social Democratic rivals; Konrad Adenauer became the first chancellor of the new German Federal Republic, which was formally inaugurated at Bonn in September. Next month the Soviet Union, not to be outdone, proclaimed its puppet "Democratic" Republic in the Eastern Zone.

In essentials, if not yet in theory, the occupation was over. Although the Western powers reserved certain rights to themselves under an "Occupation Statute" and although their troops remained in the country, Germany had in fact become a sovereign nation once again. It was divided, true, but the Western portion contained the bulk of the coun-

try's industrial resources and two-thirds of its population—which gradually grew to three-quarters, as hundreds of thousands of refugees from
political oppression crossed the demarcation line from east to west.
Within a year after its foundation, the German Federal Republic was
being courted as an ally by the military coalition that the United States
was building against the Stalinist menace, and it was already taking its
place as a nearly equal partner in the councils of the West.

The Austrian Parallel

Post-Nazi Austria resembled a Germany in miniature. The Danubian
republic, whose independence the wartime allies had decided to restore,
also found itself partitioned into four occupation zones, with its capital
surrounded by the Soviet Zone and divided four ways. But there was
one important difference: from the beginning, the Austrians possessed
a central government at Vienna. Although this government had originally
been established under Soviet auspices, it soon received full recognition
from the Western powers. The Communists, who had played only a
minor part in its formation, eventually dropped out entirely. The federal
government continued as a semipermanent coalition of the People's
Party and the Socialists, who roughly corresponded to the two leading
German parties. Thus Austria was in an excellent position to take full
advantage of the possibilities for military evacuation and neutrality which
were to appear in rather surprising form ten years after the war's end
(*see* Chapter Nineteen, II).

IV

FRANCE AND ITALY:
THE ERA OF "TRIPARTISM"

Communism, Socialism, Christian Democracy

In the first general elections of the postwar era, held in France in October, 1945, and in Italy the following June, three parties clearly dominated
the field. Two of them were the old parties of the Left—the Communists
and the Socialists. The other was Christian Democracy. In Italy this
group was the heir of the Popular Party of the period of 1919–1922, but
in France it was almost a new creation. Together the trio of parties polled
nearly three-quarters of the vote, reducing their adversaries to mere
splinters or pathetic reminders of former greatness. In France, the three
emerged nearly equal; in Italy, the Christian Democrats outstripped
their rivals to the left.

Flushed with its victories in the combats of the Resistance, communism emerged for the first time as a major force in Western European

politics. This Resistance prestige was one reason for its new importance;
another was its control of organized labor, which it had wrested from the more moderate, Socialist-oriented trade-union leaders during the war years. Finally, the economic hardships of the years 1943–1946—particularly among the urban poor—encouraged the spread of Communist influence; economic desperation pushed whole classes of the population toward the extreme left. But poverty was never the chief reason for the appeal of communism. Its hold depended rather on what the French called its *mystique*—its power to inspire devotion and sacrifice among its adherents. This was especially true of intellectuals and of young people —the two groups of converts in whom Communist organizers took most pride, and who generally knew communism only in the moderate and patriotic guise it had assumed during the war years.

In contrast, socialism seemed tired and stuffy. It was true that old Léon Blum had declared, after his release from prison in Germany: "Socialism is the master of the hour." It was also true that the ideology of the Resistance movements was broadly socialist. But this was only in the sense of general goals: most Resistance veterans had little regard for the Socialist *party* as a regular political organization. The inability of the Resistance to effect a regrouping of Western European political forces was also a defeat for socialism: after its failure to become the nucleus of a wider and less doctrinaire type of movement—which was what Blum had in mind—the Socialists were thrown back on their old organizational base. With a cadre of aging leaders, they resumed the attitude they had maintained before the war. In the intervening years, however, circumstances had changed drastically. Socialism's new position as the middle group among the three mass ideologies was not as favorable as it initially seemed, for it cast the Socialists in a difficult role as mediators under pressure from both sides and made them appear far more "center" than "left." This was particularly true in their relations with communism: whatever the Socialists did proved wrong. Where they resolutely kept their independence from the Communists, as in France, they were accused of having a merely negative policy and of splitting the working class and the labor movement; where they cooperated closely with the Communists, as in Italy, they found themselves reduced to the position of helpless fellow travelers.

Christian Democracy was actually a more conservative ideology than socialism, but it had a fresher look—as a movement based on Catholic principles, it alone could challenge communism on the grounds of faith and personal devotion and compete with it for the allegiance of the young. Like communism, it was closely associated with the Resistance tradition. In France, the new Christian Democratic party—called the Popular Republican Movement (MRP)—was founded in November, 1944, by former Resistance leaders, chief among them De Gaulle's foreign minister, Georges Bidault, who had served as chairman of the clandestine Resistance directorate. The MRP also let it be understood that it had the general's secret blessing. This De Gaulle never confirmed, but the image of the French Christian Democrats as the "party of fidelity" to the national leader certainly helped them in the first postwar elections.

They were also helped by the fact that in France, as in Italy, millions of conservatives whose own parties had disappeared in the wave of revulsion against fascism voted for them as the least objectionable of the three mass formations. This influx of grudging support swelled the ranks of the Christian Democrats far beyond their leaders' most optimistic hopes. For the short term, it was a source of strength, but in the long run, it created difficulties by deepening the cleavage between conservatives and reformers characteristic of political parties whose common denominator was religion rather than a coherent social philosophy.

In the period 1945–1947, however, this problem still seemed remote. The most urgent questions for the reviving democracies of Western Europe were economic rather than political and, in solving them, a "tripartite" formula of government was far from ideal. Of necessity, the immediate postwar ministries in France and Italy were based on a nearly equal sharing of power by the three mass parties. Yet agreement on such a basis was almost impossible: the differences among the parties were too great. The split over economic policy found the Communists and Socialists, as Marxists and proponents of state action, allied against the Christian Democrats, who preferred free enterprise. On questions of personal liberty, on the other hand, the Socialists stood together with the Christian Democrats against the authoritarian Communists. Thus the tripartite governments were riven not by one cleavage but by two—with the Socialists in the uncomfortable middle position in both cases. Both conflicts needed to be resolved before postwar democracy in France and Italy could face its problems with any strength or coherence.

France: De Gaulle and the Politicians; the Welfare State

During the fourteen months after France's liberation, Charles de Gaulle governed his country as a benevolent dictator. Aided only by the advice of the Consultative Assembly—which had been enlarged with new members from the Resistance and the political parties following its move from Algiers to Paris—the general and his ministers directed the French war effort and took a number of long-range decisions on economic policy. De Gaulle sought to restore his country's great-power status by making a maximum contribution to the winning of the war; the first great success he scored was the decision of the Big Three to admit France to equal partnership in the occupation of Germany. He also inaugurated a welfare-state policy in order to associate the working classes in a new spirit of national unity and to deprive the Communists of their most telling propaganda points.

With the end of the war, however, and with the election of a Constituent Assembly the following autumn, De Gaulle began to feel more and more uncomfortable. An authoritarian by temperament, he had worked only reluctantly with the Socialists and the other political leaders who rallied to his movement in the war years. He never had liked politicians nor accustomed himself to their methods. The parliamentary leaders, for their part, had deferred to him during the war emergency only because they saw no alternative. With the coming of peace and the restoration of a popularly elected Assembly, a rupture was unavoidable. De Gaulle believed in a strong executive; the politicians wanted an executive of the old parliamentary type who would be strictly dependent on the legislature. For three months the general tried to adjust to the new situation. In November, he reorganized his ministry to take account of the proved electoral strength of the three mass parties, but almost immediately he began to dispute with the Socialists, who refused to approve a military budget of the size he demanded. De Gaulle saw no alternative but resignation. Unwilling to try a coup d'état—which would probably have succeeded—he abandoned his office in January, 1946, and retired to his home in the country.

With De Gaulle's resignation, the real era of "tripartism" began. It continued for a year and a half, under alternating Socialist and MRP leadership. With this succession of tripartite ministries, the regime of "politics as usual" returned to the Assembly. The governments lacked coherent direction; they postponed dealing with urgent problems or concealed their evasions of responsibility under meaningless compromise formulas. Almost overnight the Third Republic atmosphere of intrigue and behind-the-scenes maneuvering resumed its previous sway.

Yet for all its faults, the era of tripartism constructed one lasting monument, for on one thing at least, the three governing parties agreed: the welfare state. Resuming where the Popular Front had left off nearly a decade earlier—and building on what De Gaulle had already accomplished in the same direction—the tripartite ministries vastly enlarged the role of the state in French economic and social life. In the first six months of 1946, they laid the foundations of a welfare-state system which all subsequent governments accepted as an accomplished fact.

Among these reforms was the nationalization of the coal mines, gas and electricity, and major banking and insurance enterprises, as well as a system of additional pay for workers and employees with children, based on the principle of family allowances which was almost the only positive legacy left from the unhappy Vichy period. This latter measure formed part of a comprehensive body of social security legislation, which eventually covered more than half the population and absorbed about 16 per cent of France's total national income. The social security system was bitterly criticized as a "monster" strangling French economic life. No doubt it was excessively bureaucratic in its administration and employers did tend to pass on its costs to the consumer in the form of higher prices but, in providing protection against the worst forms of want, it acted as a powerful brake to social unrest during France's years of inflation and economic hardship.

Finally, in establishing a national planning office under Jean Monnet, the French government provided itself with a framework for future economic expansion which Italy and Germany completely lacked. The Monnet Plan was to be of immense benefit in canalizing the country's resources when production at last began to soar in the boom years of the next decade.

Italy: Parri, De Gasperi, and the Socialist Split

Originally, Italy seemed less fortunate than France in not having an unquestioned national chief like De Gaulle, but she finally acquired a leader whose tenure in office was to be far longer than that of the French general. The great paradox in the situation of France and Italy—whose course during the immediate postwar years ran so closely parallel—was that France lost her national leader at the very time that Italy was at last finding hers.

In June, 1945, the triumphant Resistance leadership of the newly liberated North forced a change of prime minister. They pushed the old and ineffective Bonomi out of office and substituted their own man, Ferruccio Parri. Parri had been one of the three main chiefs of the northern Resistance: an engineer by training and an anti-Fascist of more than twenty years' standing, he had served a period of detention on one of Mussolini's penal islands in the late 1920's. Subsequently he had helped establish a clandestine political formation, the Party of Action, which was dedicated to that nonsectarian form of socialism to which so many of the Resistance fighters aspired.

Parri was a man of towering moral stature, but as an administrator he was no more effective than his predecessor. His party soon proved to be one of leaders without followers: although it had played a Resistance role second only to that of the Communists, and although it included a large part of Italy's foremost intellectuals, it failed to win support among the wider public. The pressure of the three mass parties proved overwhelming. Far from attracting the Italian Socialists into its own orbit, moreover, the Party of Action was forced to stand helplessly by while the Socialist leader, Pietro Nenni, moved toward an alliance with the Communists which was to cripple his own party for more than a decade.

By the autumn this disastrous alliance was leaving Parri isolated in his own ministry. Yet it was the Right rather than the Left which finally torpedoed the experiment in government by militant anti-Fascists. In late November, a loose coalition of conservatives—who had been steadily regaining confidence during the past few months—brought Parri down. His successor was the Christian Democratic leader, Alcide De Gasperi.

As foreign minister under the two preceding governments, De Gasperi had gradually been strengthening his position and preparing for his advent to power. A supple parliamentarian and a man of quiet tenacity, he had already figured among the younger leaders of the Popular Party in its brief pre-Fascist history. After serving a prison term in 1927 and 1928, he had waited out the last decade and a half of Mussolini's rule as a librarian in the Vatican. During 1943, however, he had cautiously begun to reconstitute his former party and to add to it newer Christian Democratic elements from among the clandestine opposition to fascism. Two years later, he had done his work so well that he was leading the single strongest force in Italian public life.

De Gasperi's policy combined antifascism and moderate reform with a basic conservatism. Hence although his own record under Mussolini had been impeccable, he was sufficiently indulgent toward the holdovers from the Fascist past to reassure the politically apathetic or those with a slightly tarnished ideological background. Furthermore, he won the men of property over to his side by reasserting the authority of the state. De Gasperi's deeply ingrained sense of state power was exactly what was needed to bring order out of the chaotic conditions into which Italy was falling in the winter of 1945–1946.

In the course of the year 1946 the Italians realized that a firm hand was finally in control. Early the following year, this hand was strengthened by the secession of a minority of democratically minded Socialists from Nenni's pro-Communist leadership. With the Socialists split, the stage was set for a dramatic showdown between De Gasperi and the Italian Communists.

The Dropping of the Communist Ministers and the End of Tripartism

In early May, 1947, the Communist ministers were forced out of the French government. They were actually not too sorry to go: they were confident that they could prove the impossibility of ruling the country without them, and that the Socialists and the MRP would soon be obliged to consent to their recall. In fact, nothing of the sort happened; the departure of the Communists from the French government proved to be permanent. Later in the month, the same thing occurred in Italy, where De Gasperi now felt strong enough to dispense with his Communist aides entirely.

The Italian prime minister, like his French counterpart, had had his resolution stiffened by assurances of support from the United States. In the Cold War with the Soviet Union which was opening, the Truman administration was anxious to see the government of its allies in safely anti-Communist hands. The dropping of the Communist ministers ranked as one of the opening acts in the inauguration of the Cold War. It also settled the two issues which had plagued the postwar governments of Western Europe from the beginning: in the realm of economic policy, it meant a victory for free enterprise and conservative solutions; on the question of personal liberty, it meant that the traditional Western freedoms would be preserved and no compromises made with the more slippery definitions of People's Democracy. In the new political phase that was opening, the Socialists found themselves more and more pushed to the side; for the next half-decade the Christian Democrats, in Italy and France as in Germany, were destined to take the lead (*see* Chapter Seventeen, II).

V

THE BRITISH LABOR GOVERNMENT

In July, 1945, midway between the ending of the war in Europe and the armistice in the Far East, the British held the first of the European postwar elections. The result was a resounding defeat for Winston Churchill and his Conservative party. For the first time in its history, Labor emerged with a clear-cut majority. With 393 seats in the House of Commons to 198 for the Conservatives, it received an ample mandate to carry out its socialist program. Indeed, the Labor victory of 1945 was also the first time in history that a Socialist party had ever won a parliamentary majority in a major European country.

American observers, stunned by the news, interpreted it as an act of base ingratitude toward the peerless leader who had won the war. This was far too sentimental a reading of what had occurred. In fact the Labor victory was the logical outcome of the way the British war effort had been managed; it flowed almost inevitably from the economic and social legacies of the war itself.

The Postwar Economic "Imperatives"

Of all the major Western belligerents, the British had most thoroughly mobilized their people and their economy for war. Far more efficiently than the Germans, they had allocated manpower and womanpower and rationed the necessities of life for the whole population. The result had been a "semisiege economy," based on the principle of "fair shares" for all. In Britain, the black market had been almost nonexistent; rich and poor had fared alike. A nation profoundly united against the Nazi menace had expressed its solidarity in the first experiment in economic equality that a great Western democracy had ever made.

During the years of wartime austerity, the poor people of Britain had actually seen their standard of living rise. Both money wages and the workers' share of the total national product increased; infant mortality dropped to the lowest level ever known; milk for every child in Britain became the most striking symbol of wartime equality. Obviously this current could not be reversed once the war had ended. Whichever party

The Conflict Opens

A *bomb explodes in a Madrid Street (1937)
during the Spanish Civil War—a conflict that
was to prove a prelude to an even greater
struggle.* COURTESY WIDE WORLD PHOTOS.

Blitzkrieg: the German armies advance into Poland (1939). COURTESY BROWN BROTHERS.

The Second World War

The leaders of the Axis powers meet in a
triumphant mood at Salzburg, Austria.
COURTESY BROWN BROTHERS.

The Germans march into Paris (1940). COURTESY WIDE WORLD PHOTOS.

The turning of the tide: Stalingrad (1943). The spectacular Soviet defense of the city resulted in a disastrous Axis defeat. COURTESY WIDE WORLD PHOTOS.

Axis Triumph and Disaster

The beginning of the end: D-Day. COURTESY BROWN BROTHERS.

Era of Hope

The Big Three at Yalta (1945): Winston
Churchill, Franklin Roosevelt, and Josef
Stalin. COURTESY BROWN BROTHERS.

The end of the Third Reich
is foreshadowed in the ruins
of Muenchen-Gladbach,
captured during the Allied
drive to the Rhine. A month
later Berlin had fallen and
the war in Europe was over.
COURTESY BROWN BROTHERS.

*General Charles de Gaulle
of France.* COURTESY
BROWN BROTHERS.

Marshal Tito of Yugoslavia.
COURTESY BROWN BROTHERS.

*Robert Schuman, French
foreign minister (1948–1953).*
COURTESY BROWN BROTHERS.

Alcide de Gasperi, postwar prime minister of Italy. COURTESY WIDE WORLD PHOTOS.

Wladislaw Gomulka, postwar leader of Poland. COURTESY BROWN BROTHERS.

The leader of postwar Germany—
"Der Alte"—Konrad Adenauer.
COURTESY WIDE WORLD PHOTOS.

The spectacular postwar
recovery of Germany was
most clearly evident in the
rapid and impressive
reconstruction of its
devastated cities. At right,
Frankfurt (1952). COURTESY
BROWN BROTHERS

Jean-Paul Sartre, French philosopher and writer and principal exponent of the existentialist school. COURTESY BROWN BROTHERS.

Albert Camus, French-Algerian writer. COURTESY WIDE WORLD PHOTOS.

Harold Macmillan, British prime minister (1957–1963).
COURTESY BROWN BROTHERS.

Nikita Khrushchev, winner of the post-Stalin struggle for power in the Soviet Union.
COURTESY BROWN BROTHERS.

The Cold War

The growing unrest in Soviet satellites
erupted into open rebellion in 1953 and 1956.
Below, Soviet armored tanks move in on
street fighters in East Berlin.
COURTESY PHOTOWORLD, INC.

was to govern, it must continue the equalitarian policy, for there had
come into being during the war an "implied contract between govern- ment and people"—in return for doing everything the government de- manded for the winning of the great conflict, the British people were assured that their rulers would pursue an advanced social policy at the war's end. Three major "imperatives" for the future faced any postwar government.

First, it would have to take steps to divert an increased share of the country's current output of goods to the export market so that the balance of payments could be restored; second, it would have to find means of directing into investment a larger proportion of the national income in order to satisfy the necessity for greater and more efficient production; third, it would have to provide for a tre- mendous new outlay on the social services and, consequently, main- tain taxation at a high level.*

In short, Britain was faced with the necessity of pulling itself up by its own bootstraps. During the war it had consumed all its economic fat and liquidated all its overseas investments. Totally dependent on imports for its survival, it had to find a way to pay for these imports and at the same time provide for the social needs of its own population. This could be done only by increasing the export of finished products—and that in turn required heavy outlays for the modernization of Britain's antiquated industries in order to make them fully competitive. The British them- selves, meanwhile, must do without woolens and Scotch whisky and the other luxury exports which could buy precious dollars. And they must pay extremely high taxes.

On this policy of continued austerity combined with an extension of social services the two major parties were in agreement. Indeed, the Conservatives in Churchill's National Government had already con- curred in postwar plans for vastly increasing public educational facilities and for establishing a National Health Serivce (which in the United States would be called "socialized medicine"). But to the Tories such a policy was uncongenial. To Labor, on the contrary, it was the natural fulfillment of what the party had been advocating for decades. The voters of Britain seemed aware of this, and they cast their ballots for the party better suited to carry out the policy which was coming in any case; a massive defection of the middle class from the Conservatives to Labor suggested that millions among the electorate had understood the imperatives of the hour.

Finally, in explaining Labor's victory, it should be noted that the Brit- ish Socialists were in a far better campaigning position than their adver- saries. They knew it very well: it was they who broke up the wartime

* Keith Hutchison, *The Decline and Fall of British Capitalism* (London: Jonathan Cape, 1951), pp. 283, 285.

coalition and insisted on an early election, refusing to listen to Churchill's pleas that they wait until the war against Japan had been won. This favorable position again grew out of the role Labor had played during the war. In the allotment of ministries in the National Government, the Labor men had received the assignment of supervising the home front. Their leader, Clement Attlee, became deputy prime minister—in practice, the man who provided governmental continuity during Churchill's long absences overseas. Attlee's strongest associate, Ernest Bevin, applied his wide experience in trade-union leadership to directing the ministry of labor, which handled manpower allocations. The Conservatives, on the other hand, headed the foreign ministry and most of the military service ministries. The Tory assignment was to run the war on the fighting fronts, for which the Conservatives were fitted by tradition and temperament, just as Labor was fitted to manage the domestic economy. A large number of Conservative MP's served as officers in the armed forces, whereas the Labor people more frequently remained at home. Thus—as the Conservatives bitterly lamented—by going off to fight the war they had lost touch with their home constituencies. Labor had stayed behind, free to rebuild its political fences and to prepare its program for the postwar era.

The Labor Program: Nationalization and Its Consequences

The record of Labor in power during the six years 1945–1951 was very nearly unique in still a further respect: Prime Minister Attlee and his colleagues did what political leaders almost never do—they carried out to the letter the program on which they had been elected.

Some of these measures were contributions to the welfare state and showed the influence of Keynesian economics: the National Health Service, the extension of educational facilities, and an integrated program for new housing and for the rehabilitation of depressed areas. Such measures aroused little controversy. It was against Labor's more strictly socialist proposals that the Tories directed their fire. The controversial center of the Labor program was the series of nationalization acts which sought to bring the "commanding heights" of the economy into public ownership. Even here, however, opponents made distinctions. It was difficult to fight with much conviction against the nationalization of the coal mines, which had been a sick industry ever since the 1920's and which the government alone could provide with the capital needed for the urgent task of modernization. It was on steel, rather, that the Conservatives chose to make their stand. In Britain, as in any modern industrial country, the production of steel was the key to the whole economy, and Labor's success or failure in bringing it under public authority would be the touchstone of how far the ministry had actually progressed in conquering the "commanding heights."

The parliamentary struggle over the nationalization of steel was intense and bitter. In order to force the measure through before their mandate expired, Attlee and his colleagues felt obliged to alter the constitution itself. They used their crushing majority in the House of Commons to modify the Parliament Act of 1911 by reducing the power of the House of Lords once again; in the future, the Lords would be able to delay legislation for no more than a single session. By the time this hurdle had been surmounted, however, and the nationalization of steel had become law, Labor had only one year of power left. In 1951, the Conservatives returned to office, with the denationalization of steel as the first item on their agenda.

Nearly all the other nationalizations survived. The Conservatives did not try to reverse these any more than they sought to undo the Attlee government's welfare-state measures. In this sense, Labor accomplished a permanent, irreversible revolution in British life. But Labor's very success also presented it with an insoluble dilemma. By the end of four and a half years in office, it had almost completely accomplished its program. What was it to do now? The great change which Socialists had dreamed of for a century had come at last, but life continued much as before. The most glaring economic inequalities had been eliminated, class hatred had been enormously reduced, but still the intangible barriers of speech, education, and manners separated class from class. Nor did the workers themselves experience the qualitative change in the whole atmosphere of life that socialism had promised. The man in the coal mines or in the nationalized railroads did not feel that he now *owned* his place of work in his capacity as a citizen. This was partly because of faults in the nationalization acts, which had organized state enterprise in too centralized and bureaucratic a fashion and had made almost no provision for worker consultation. But it was also because of a special form of blindness in socialism itself, which, as Keynes had warned, had vested too much of its hope in the panacea of nationalization. Nationalization, people now saw, was not the final end and aim of economic policy; it was only one of a number of weapons at the disposal of the welfare state, partial and fallible like any other. The failure of nationalization in Britain to accomplish what had been hoped for was a major cause of the crisis of confidence which was to shake European socialism as a whole in the decade of the 1950's (*see* Chapter Twenty, III).

VI

THE PARLIAMENTARY RESTORATION

Throughout Western Europe parliamentary democracy was restored at the end of the war. It was a restoration in a very real sense, for the norms of parliamentary life had been overthrown or suspended everywhere, except in neutral Sweden and Switzerland. Even in Britain the system had not functioned fully, since no general election was held for ten years—the parliament elected in 1935 sat longer than any such body of modern times—and by-elections were not contested between the parties.

In the smaller countries, the governments-in-exile returned and picked up the threads of political life where they had dropped them in 1940. Norway, Denmark, and the Netherlands resumed their parliamentary systems unchanged; the only marked alteration was a shift in political influence toward the left which, as in Britain, reflected the austerity and the economic imperatives inherited from wartime. In Belgium alone real difficulties arose. King Leopold III, who, unlike the sovereigns of Norway and the Netherlands, had remained in his own country throughout the war, labored under a double suspicion: he was accused of having capitulated prematurely in May, 1940, and of subsequent acts of collaboration with the Germans. The "royal question" threatened to tear the country apart: the Flemings in general supported the king, whereas the French-speaking Walloons demanded his withdrawal. Not until 1950, when Leopold abdicated in favor of his son, did Belgium return to civil peace.

In Scandinavia and the Low Countries, the restoration of parliamentary democracy in its old form came as no surprise. More worthy of comment was the return of the major states of Western and Central Europe to their former constitutional patterns. In France, this was perhaps only natural, since the Third Republic from 1870 to 1940 had proved the longest lived of the recent political systems under which the country had lived, and the Vichy regime ranked as scarcely more than an interlude. But in the nations which had passed under fascist dictatorship—in the one instance for twelve years, in the other, for more than twenty —the restoration of parliamentary institutions in the old style was certainly not a foregone conclusion.

The Constitutions of France, Italy, and Western Germany

The surprising thing about the postwar constitutions with which France, Italy, and Western Germany provided themselves was that they showed so little trace of the criticism to which their earlier institutions had been subjected—even by democrats—during the years of dictatorial rule.

In France, both among the Resistance and among the more immediate followers of General de Gaulle the conviction had been almost universal that the constitution of the Third Republic would not do. Similarly the popular referendum held in October, 1945, had shown an overwhelming majority for giving the country a new institutional framework. But, as the Constituent Assembly (which had been elected at the same time) labored through the following winter, it became apparent that the new proposals which were taking shape only intensified the eccentric features of the Third Republic. The left bloc which dominated the Assembly—and whose historical memories went back to the Jacobin tradition of 1793—imposed its view that a single parliamentary body should concentrate nearly all power in its own hands. De Gaulle and the MRP were opposed and, by taking their case to the conservative mass of the French people, they assured the rejection of the new constitution by a narrow margin of the electorate in a second referendum held in May, 1946.

Thus it became necessary to elect another Constituent Assembly and to draft another constitution. In the new Assembly—although the "tripartite" character remained—the MRP increased its representation, and the two parties of the Left lacked the slight majority they had held in the earlier body. The second draft constitution was more conservative than the first. Indeed, when in the autumn it received the people's endorsement and the "Fourth Republic" was formally inaugurated with the first regular parliamentary elections, the representative bodies looked much as they had before 1940. The Chamber of Deputies was renamed the National Assembly, and the second chamber, now called the Council of the Republic, did not enjoy the full powers of the old Senate; but both of them met in their traditional halls and conformed to their old procedures, and soon the councillors of the Republic were referring to themselves as senators and claiming nearly all the prerogatives of the former body. Meanwhile, the only other major constitutional innovation —a new procedure for designating the prime minister—was operating in just the opposite way from what had been intended. It was supposed to make the appointment of the prime minister more straightforward and his tenure more secure. In practice it made his appointment harder; and his stay in office proved more precarious as ministries under the Fourth Republic lasted even a shorter time on the average than they had under the Third. No wonder that the citizenry soon grew skeptical about a constitution which had actually been accepted by only a third of them; the massive abstentions in the second constitutional referendum —more than 30 per cent of the eligible voters—already showed how little the French were satisfied with their new institutions.

In Italy, the old constitution was even more obviously in need of renovation than was the French. It had not only been in suspension for more than two decades; it was also nearly a century old and reflected an earlier age in its provisions for a monarch with more than nominal powers and for a Senate appointed by the king. In June, 1946, the monarchy disappeared in a popular referendum which was held simultaneously with the election of a Constituent Assembly. This Assembly labored for nine months. The new republican constitution it produced was a massive document specifying all sorts of novel human rights—most of which in practice proved inoperable. Except for making the Senate elective and substituting a president for the king as the titular chief of state, the Italian constitution which came into effect in January, 1948, reproduced with astounding fidelity the main features of its antiquated predecessor.

One change, however, was so little discussed that it passed almost unnoticed: women's suffrage. In Italy, as in France, women won the vote without a struggle. What had seemed scarcely within the realm of possibility in 1939, was accepted by nearly everyone at the war's end as the natural consequence of the changed role of women in economic and social life.

In Western Germany, the Parliamentary Council at Bonn labored under a handicap which did not affect the French and Italians. The Germans had to pay heed to the wishes of the occupying powers, which had reserved the right to request modifications in the completed document. More particularly, this meant an insistence on decentralization—which the Americans characteristically associated with the concept of democracy. The German constitution makers of 1949 simply bowed to foreign pressure when they gave more powers to the states than these had enjoyed under the Weimar system. For the same reason they renamed the Reichstag the Bundestag (or Federal Assembly). In other respects, the Bonn constitution followed the Weimar model fairly closely. There were, however, two significant changes in the federal executive. The emergency powers of the president, which had opened the doors to the Nazi tyranny, disappeared from the 1949 constitutional document, and the German president became no more than a ceremonial figure in the normal Western European pattern. In his place, the chancellor was assured of a more stable tenure through an ingenious device which permitted a vote of no confidence only when the opposition had already agreed on a candidate for the succession.

The Problem for the Future:
Legitimacy Against Apathy

In postwar Europe parliamentary democracy proved that it had become the normal and "legitimate" form of government. Its restoration was accepted by the vast majority of the population as a return to natural and well-tried forms of rule. Indeed, in some respects it appeared to have profited by its period of suspension: the party structure had become simpler, now that three major parties—as in France and Italy—or two—as in Britain and Western Germany—dominated the field. On the Continent, the old multiparty system seemed likely to disappear; in Britain, a two-party alternation in power was functioning properly for the first time in a generation.

Yet this simplification of the party structure meant that discipline within the individual parties was becoming tighter, and the resulting "tyranny of party machines" made the average man think that politics was a professional game with which he had no concern. Such was the more threatening aspect of the ease with which parliamentary government had been restored: the other face of general acceptance was public

apathy. One reason why people concurred in the return of the old practices was that they did not know what to put in their place. They were
not particularly enthusiastic about parliamentarism, but they could
think of no alternative. The paradoxical result of the effortless parliamentary restoration was a massive falling away from political interests.

With it went a parallel loss of concern for ideology. The Resistance
experience had been the last great explosion of the ideological fervor
that had characterized European political life for more than a century
and a half. The failure of the Resistance to recast the Continent's politics in its own image was also a failure of the whole ideological approach
to human society. As Europe returned to "normal" at the end of the
1940's, it became apparent that the old ideologies which had provided
the guiding thread for so much of its history no longer really counted.
To young people in particular they seemed stale and irrelevant. What
counted now was the split between East and West—the gulf between
the Communist way of looking at things and all the other points of view,
whose differences one from another were coming to seem less and less
important, since they shared the same enemy. The Communist–anti-
Communist cleavage immensely simplified the European ideological landscape. Indeed, for a while it seemed to have obliterated it entirely. It
was only in the middle and late 1950's, with the reduction in the intensity of the Cold War following Stalin's death, that true ideological debate
returned to European politics—but in a greatly altered form, with new
problems and a new vocabulary (see Chapters Nineteen and Twenty).

Readings

The rebuilding of democracy in the three major countries of the Western
European continent is dealt with in the following: for Germany, Gabriel A.
Almond, ed., The Struggle for Democracy in Germany (1949), John Ford
Golay, The Founding of the Federal Republic of Germany (1958), and Alfred
Grosser, Western Germany from Defeat to Rearmament (1955); for France,
Gordon Wright, The Reshaping of French Democracy (1948), Philip Williams,
Politics in Post-War France (1954), and Edward Mead Earle, ed., Modern
France: Problems of the Third and Fourth Republics (1951); and for Italy,
Muriel Grindrod, The Rebuilding of Italy (1955), and H. Stuart Hughes, The
United States and Italy, rev. ed. (1965). A highly sympathetic account of the
British Labor government is given in Keith Hutchison, The Decline and Fall
of British Capitalism (1951). For the concept and early history of the Marshall
Plan, see Howard E. Ellis, The Economics of Freedom (1950).

The following two collaborative studies deal with the conflict of ideologies
in the first half-decade of the postwar period: Mario Einaudi, Jean-Marie
Domenach, and Aldo Garosci, Communism in Western Europe (1951), and
Mario Einaudi and François Goguel, Christian Democracy in Italy and France
(1952).

On economic problems, besides Landes (see readings for Chapter Five),
there is a perceptive analysis by M. M. Postan: An Economic History of Western Europe, 1945–1964 (1967).

Cultural
Reconstruction, Chapter Sixteen
1945-1965

I

THE HERITAGE OF THE RESISTANCE

The Demand for Ethical Renewal:
from Silone to Camus

Postwar cultural life in Europe began with the Resistance to fascism. It began while the war was still in progress when, from their hiding places, from exile, or from concentration camp, the opponents of Hitler and Mussolini took up the task of defining the new cultural values. Even in the blackest hours of the war, this Resistance literature was a literature of hope. It was just as "committed" in the ideological battle as the writing of the 1930's had been, but it directed its struggle with tyranny less toward specific political goals than toward the renewal of Europe's humanist and humanitarian tradition, defined in the broadest possible terms. Christians and atheists, Marxists and liberals, could all find a place in the ethical vision of the Resistance years.

This was the message of Italy's leading anti-Fascist writer, Ignazio Silone, who had published in exile his novels, *Fontamara* (1930) and *Bread and Wine* (1937), chronicling the struggles of the south Italian peasantry to preserve their land and their lives from political and economic exploitation. It was also reflected in the work of Silone's countryman, Carlo Levi, whose *Christ Stopped at Eboli* (1947) similarly dealt with the poverty of southern Italy; Levi had been exiled by Mussolini's

*Pope John XXIII is carried through St. Peter's
Basilica, where he headed the procession of 13,000
Roman Catholic clergy which opened the Ecumenical
Council on October 11, 1962.* COURTESY BLACK STAR.

police to a remote village in the south, and here, in his years of forced retirement, the author had discovered an Italy unknown to cultivated northerners like himself—and whose existence as revealed in his book helped stimulate a widespread demand for social and economic reform in the postwar years.

In Germany, the most forceful protests against oppression took the form of explicit and harrowing memories of life in the concentration camps. Such were Ernst Wiechert's *The Forest of the Dead* (1946) and the more detailed analysis by the left-wing Catholic publicist Eugen Kogon, *Der SS-Staat* (1946), translated under the title *The Theory and Practice of Hell*. From these accounts there emerged an ambiguous and troubling view of human nature under unbearable stress: on the one hand, writers who had lived through the concentration camp experience gave countless examples of self-sacrifice and human solidarity; yet they also told without shame of the stratagems and compromises with the camp authorities essential to survival and of how, in the last stages of hunger and suffering, human feeling could disappear almost completely. This too had been the experience of the Allied soldiers who had liberated the camps in the spring of 1945 and had discovered with horror the spectacle of human beings descended to the level of beasts.

The most influential book to come out of France's wartime Resistance was the brief novel by "Vercors," *The Silence of the Sea,* published clandestinely in 1942. The story had shocked some French patriots by the sympathetic picture it gave of a German officer in occupation, but this attitude in fact marked the best in the Resistance spirit: it rose above national allegiance to pay homage to human quality wherever it might be found.

Such was one of the most attractive qualities in the work of Albert Camus, the most representative of the writers who first made their mark in the Resistance. Camus was Algerian French by birth—accustomed since childhood to life in a culturally mixed community where allegiances were unclear and ethical principles undefined. This Algerian background had suffused his first novel, *The Stranger* (1942), the portrait of a murderer indifferent to his crime and dissociated from the world around him. But an infatuation with the absurdities of existence—which showed strong traces of Gide's influence—was characteristic only of Camus' early work. His subsequent experience as editor of a clandestine Resistance newspaper gave him a more sympathetic understanding of humanity. Camus' masterpiece, *The Plague* (1947), marked a new direction in his writing: an allegory of man's struggle against disease and death, it carried echoes of the author's own wartime stand against the resurgence of a barbarism that civilized peoples were supposed to have outgrown centuries ago.

Before his untimely death in an automobile accident in 1960, Camus published one more book of primary importance—*The Fall* (1956), a meditation in the form of a monologue on human hypocrisy and guilt. It showed with quiet perfection the abiding qualities of Camus' work —its direct, classic style, its ethical scrupulousness, and its concern for the human condition in its widest sense. Camus was anything but a moral preacher: he detested merely rhetorical positions, and he believed that a single individual could do little more than "bear witness" against the evil he saw around him. But he felt at the same time—as he declared on receiving the Nobel Prize for literature in 1957—that he was serving as a representative of the new generation of Europeans born during the First World War, whose whole youth had been passed in political and social chaos, and who were now seeking to re-create the values of purposeful activity and human solidarity.

The Vogue of Existentialism: Heidegger, Jaspers, Sartre

Just after the war many people assumed that Camus was an existentialist because of his interest in the ethical problem of "absurdity" and his friendship with France's leading existentialist, Jean-Paul Sartre. But in 1950, the two parted company: Camus insisted on speaking out against the concentration camp system in the Soviet Union; Sartre refused, alleging in characteristic Marxist fashion that such revelations would only play into the hand of "reaction."

At the time of his break with Camus, Sartre ranked as the most frequently quoted figure on the French intellectual scene. In the previous decade, he had adopted the German philosophy of existentialism and given it a new twist and a far wider appeal. Existentialism itself traced its origins back to the nineteenth century, and more particularly to Kierkegaard and Dostoyevsky and Nietzsche. An anti-intellectualist philosophy, it was impatient of systems and of traditional categories and tried to go directly to the heart of human experience. Its first period of influence had been in Germany in the 1920's, where its two founders, Martin Heidegger and Karl Jaspers, had both published elaborate and "difficult" works which broke sharply with conventional philosophical style. Heidegger was a frank irrationalist, seeking in obscure and tortured fashion to create a new mode of discourse for encompassing the questions of dread, despair, and death which he felt to be central to human existence. Jaspers was more concerned with the meaning of history and with enunciating unshakable moral principles. It was characteristic of their differences that Heidegger accepted the Nazi regime, while Jaspers refused to compromise with it.

Sartre was a generation younger than these two—who were already elderly men at the outbreak of the Second World War—and he was far more concerned than they were with the ideological implications of existentialism. Therefore he joined to the ideas of his German predecessors both Marxism and his own brand of psychoanalytic theory. The result was a heady brew which was eagerly swallowed both in France and in the Western world as a whole in the immediate postwar years. Sartre's major philosophical treatise, *Being and Nothingness* (1943), and the spate of plays, novels, and essays with which he followed it, were cited constantly by people in the most divergent intellectual camps.

The sources of this appeal are not hard to find. Existentialism, as Sartre redefined it, focused its attention on human problems which the experience of war, collaboration with the enemy, or Resistance had brought to the consciousness of nearly everyone. It emphasized extreme situations and moral dilemmas—the freedom and the responsibility of every human being to make his own choices in ambiguous contexts where right and wrong were far from clear. By its linkage to Marxism, it urged the necessity of committing oneself in the ideological battle on the side of the revolutionary masses.

But although it claimed to be a philosophy of action, existentialism was actually a creed of despair: it betrayed a compulsive need to take a stand at all costs—even in violation of honesty or common sense, as Sartre showed in the matter of the Soviet forced-labor camps. As the years went on and the Cold War opened, Sartre's tone became shriller and the position he adopted on specific issues more and more unrealistic. Just as the special situation of the war and the postwar period had given his ideas their relevance, so in the new ideological atmosphere of the 1950's they began to lose their cogency. With Europe returning to something resembling "normal," the vogue of existentialism passed, and more traditional and academic philosophy resumed its sway.

II

THE NEW TALENTS IN LITERATURE AND THE ARTS

The Losses in the War

In the First World War, the European aristocracy suffered the heaviest losses as a single class; in the second war, it was the intellectuals who paid most severely with their lives and talents. A disproportionately high number of them were killed in the Resistance or perished in concentration camps. This was to be expected, since so many intellectuals were dedicated to the antifascist cause, and since Hitler—and Stalin too—made a systematic effort to "decapitate" subject peoples by depriving them of their intellectual leaders.

This "decapitation" operated in several different ways. First there were the concentration camps themselves, which deadened the intellect even when they did not kill (although in a few favored cases, political prisoners were able to make good use of their years of detention to write books of a notable sweep and moral elevation). Then there was the near-destruction of the Jews, who had supplied so high a proportion of the century's intellectual leaders. Finally there was emigration: of the thousands of European scholars and writers who fled to the New World during the 1930's or the war years, at least half remained in their new homes and were permanently lost to the European intellectual community.

In the initial flush of liberation, people did not quite appreciate how serious these losses had been, for the first effect of the war's end was to unleash a torrent of creativity: all the thoughts which had been dammed up for years suddenly began to pour forth. As wartime censorship ceased, as paper and printing facilities gradually became available, writers took out of their desk drawers the work they had labored on in secret during the era of tyranny. Now at last they could speak the truth; now at last they could relieve their minds of all the pent-up thoughts and emotions they had been obliged to hold back for so long. The result was a sense of new power, of variety, of a deeper truth: men and women were jubilant at the possibility of writing about human experience as it actually had been, free of the doubts and constraints that fascist domination had laid upon them.

Once this first outpouring was over, however, it became apparent that less was really new than had at first appeared. Once writers had had their say about war and tyranny—once artists had grown accustomed to their postwar freedom of expression—they began to feel other limitations and to find other reasons for doubt. They saw how thin were the ranks of those with major talent; as the younger men held back in hesitation, the older intellectual and artistic leaders resumed their sway. Thus there was no dramatic assumption of leadership by the avant-garde, as had happened following the First World War. There was hesitation, rather, and groping for new forms of expression and, with it, a great uncertainty about the new intellectual and esthetic direction. The United States was frequently the answer; one by-product of the Second World War was a shift of the center of gravity in a number of cultural fields to the other side of the Atlantic. Of the European countries, Germany, of course, had suffered the most irreplaceable loss of talent; here the tendency was to fall back on conventional models and on well-tried modes of expression. But everywhere in Europe, to a greater or lesser degree, the younger writers and artists needed time to find their way and to become conscious of their own claims as a new esthetic generation.

The Novel: Neorealism and Its Sequels

In the novel, the "old masters" were André Gide in France and Thomas Mann in Germany. At the war's end, Gide assumed a position of unquestioned pre-eminence as France's first man of letters which he held until his death in 1951. With Mann, it was different. Long years of exile had separated him from the life of his native country, and when he finally returned to Europe from his California home, he chose to settle in Switzerland rather than in Germany. Before leaving America, however, he had published his final masterpiece—*Doctor Faustus* (1948), an allegory of his own country's fate and that of its greatest creative artists, as expressed in the life of a composer who had in him something of Nietzsche and something also of Schönberg.

It was Italy which first produced a new school of fiction. Inspired by the Resistance against fascism and by the example of an already established novelist, Alberto Moravia—the author of a series of cool, detached, and melodramatic stories of Roman life—a group of younger men began to write in what they called the "neorealist" vein. They came from all parts of Italy, and they were only loosely linked to one another. Perhaps the best-known abroad were Elio Vittorini, who was Sicilian, Vasco Pratolini, a Florentine, and the north Italian Cesare Pavese. Despite their marked differences, they had in common a definition of goals which went beyond the merely photographic aim of nineteenth-century realism, with its pretense of absolute objectivity, toward a new art which would be more popular, more poetic, and more politically "engaged." The neorealists combined a concern for the sufferings of the poor with an optimistic faith in the future. They wanted to distill from the squalor of poverty an esthetic beauty which would prefigure the better life to come. Most of them, at the outset at least, were convinced Communists.

Post-Nazi Germany produced nothing comparable to Italian neorealism. Its first literary efforts after the great defeat tended to be memoirs of war and privation—a "literature of the ruins." But here also there was an effort to tell the full truth as people had actually experienced it. In a twisted and bitter form this was the goal of the sensational novel *The Questionnaire* (1951), by the former Free Corps fighter Ernst von Salomon, which exposed the farce of denazification and whose immense popularity revealed how much of the Hitlerite mentality still lingered. Not until the very end of the decade, with the publication of Günter Grass' *The Tin Drum*, did post-Nazi Germany finally produce a novel of first rank—surrealist in manner, corrosive in its treatment of moral clichés, and with a virtuoso range in its use of the German language.

In France the counterpart to neorealism could perhaps be found in the satiric novels, full of slang and inspired by a skeptical view of human nature, of Marcel Aymé and Raymond Queneau. In England there was the school of the "angry young men." These were usually writers of lower-middle-class origin, who had benefited by the postwar democratization of British life, but who at the same time were depressed by what they felt to be the drabness of the welfare state and enraged by the invisible social barriers that still persisted. The novel which seemed most representative of the whole school was Kingsley Amis' *Lucky Jim* (1954) —a half-hilarious, half-pathetic story of the mishaps of a young instructor at a provincial British university.

Just at the end of the 1950's there appeared in France a "new wave"

of novelists—among them Nathalie Sarraute, whose works suggested an
internal meditation on individual experience, expressed directly and without the old paraphernalia of "realism" or of psychological explanation. In Italy, too, younger writers of fiction like Italo Calvino began to turn away from neorealism and toward more fanciful themes, while an elderly amateur, the Prince of Lampedusa, produced the nostalgic Sicilian tale *The Leopard* (1958), which quickly became the most respected Italian novel of the twentieth century. In sum, the restoration of fantasy and of internal harmony to the novel seemed to be the new direction of the 1960's.

The Drama: the Poetic and the Experimental Theater

The evolution of the postwar drama roughly paralleled that of the novel. Here too there were older masters, whose works enjoyed general esteem even when they were not popular successes. In England, T. S. Eliot turned his poetic talents to the theater in *The Cocktail Party* (1950), whose title belied its religious theme; in France, Henry de Montherlant also invoked religious memories in his exalted, static, and rather pretentious plays, *The Master of Santiago* (1947) and *Port-Royal* (1954).

The two Germanies had their rival dramatists laureate. In the West, it was Karl Zuckmayer, who had written in exile in the United States his explosive anti-Nazi tragedy, *The Devil's General* (1945). In the East, Bertolt Brecht similarly returned from exile to become the chief literary luminary of the Communist world and Europe's most influential dramatist. As a popular writer, however, he never repeated the pre-Nazi success of his *Three-Penny Opera*. Brecht's later plays like *Mother Courage* (1945) couched their social protest in a more obvious and less amusing form.

Out of the French Resistance to the Nazis there emerged a number of powerful dramas whose purport was just sufficiently veiled to escape the censor. Such were Sartre's *No Exit,* Camus' *Caligula,* and Jean Anouilh's *Antigone.* In the immediate postwar period, Anouilh became the most prolific of France's serious playwrights, alternating light comedies with dramas of intense moral earnestness, which dealt obsessively on the theme of human innocence pitted against arrogance and cruelty. By the 1950's, however, Anouilh's great vogue was over. The new figures were foreigners who had lived long years in France and had become thoroughly assimilated to French culture—the Rumanian Eugène Ionesco, the author of a series of short, "experimental" plays in surrealist vein, and Samuel Beckett, who had once served as secretary to James Joyce and whose *Waiting for Godot* (1952) applied the master's stream-of-consciousness technique to the dramatic stage.

Waiting for Godot had only one rival as the most arresting play of the 1950's. This was *The Visit* (1956), by the Swiss Friedrich Duerrenmatt—

a chilling drama of greed, abiding hatred, and moral corrosion. Another noteworthy play was John Osborne's *Look Back in Anger* (1957), whose very title betrayed the fact that its author was one of England's "angry young men."

The Films: from Italy to Sweden

By 1945, the esthetically conservative no longer questioned that the cinema had become an art form at least the equal of the "legitimate" theater and even perhaps superior to it. In the first twenty years after the war, a greater share of original talent went into the producing of films than into the writing of plays for the stage. Indeed, the number of superior motion pictures was so great and their character so varied that it was extremely difficult to find the main trends among this embarrassment of riches. Along with a continued high level of excellence in France and Britain, films from Italy and Sweden, two countries which had made scarcely any contribution to the cinema arts during the prewar years, now moved into the front rank.

In Italy, neorealism in the novel had an exact parallel in the films, and the relationship between the two was very close. The war had not yet ended before a new generation of producers was trying to put on film the misery of the conflict and its sequels as the Italian people were still experiencing them. The results were the classics of the Italian postwar cinema—Roberto Rossellini's *Open City* (1944) and *Paisà* (1946) and Vittorio de Sica's *Shoeshine* (1945) and *Bicycle Thief* (1948). Like the neorealists of the novel, Rossellini and De Sica sought to show the reality of poverty and at the same time to tinge it with poetry and hope. Far more than was true of the novel, the character of these motion pictures derived from the physical limitations of the postwar years: wanting simply to film what they had seen, and lacking both studios and money, the Italian directors worked outdoors, using real streets and amateur actors and frequently improvising rather than following a formal script.

By the 1950's, the best days of the Italian postwar cinema had ended. Public apathy, clerical hostility, and official disfavor had nearly killed it. Most of the more interesting films of the decade were French—like the psychologically intense melodramas of Henri-Georges Clouzot—or British, like *Room at the Top*, which once again dealt with the problem of lingering class barriers that obsessed the "angry young men." Meanwhile in Sweden there appeared a new director of major talent, Ingmar Bergman. Bergman, like the postwar Italians, was something of an improviser. His films frequently lacked structure, and the philosophy with which they were embellished was vague and rambling. But at his best— as in *The Seventh Seal* or *Wild Strawberries*—Bergman's work had a haunting, poetic quality and a verve and expertness of acting, which immediately brought it international acclaim.

At the decade's end the advent of the "new wave" in the French and

Italian novel found its counterpart in a recrudescence of imaginative film production—in the work of Federico Fellini and Michelangelo Antonioni in Italy and of Alain Resnais in France. Renais' *Hiroshima Mon Amour* (1959) and *Last Year at Marienbad* (1961) set the tone for a whole series of films in the early 1960's whose slow pace and bewildering shifts of time-sequence tried to convey a new and more profound sense of emotional reality.

The Fine Arts: the Reconciliation of the Abstract and the Figurative

Although Paris still retained its traditional pre-eminence in painting, it was more and more challenged by other centers. The reputation of France in the arts was in great part owing to the continued activity of major painters surviving from the first quarter of the century—Matisse, Rouault, and Picasso. The younger men, however, in the late 1940's began to experience the influence of German Expressionism and American abstract art. The result was a great variety of styles, with non-representational art in the ascendant, but little pronounced change in direction.

As in the novel and in the films, so in painting Italy made the most dramatic leap from obscurity to the front rank, and for the same reasons: the end of Fascism and the lifting of its atmosphere of cultural mediocrity and formalism released new talent in the plastic arts. In comparison with the work of French painters, that of the postwar Italians tended to be warmer and more serene. It was also more figurative—in strong contrast to the dominance of abstract art nearly everywhere else in the Western world. The Italians tried to reconcile the new awareness of design, color, and balance, which non-representational art had brought to the fore, with the more traditional values—such as emotional evocation and a feeling for subject matter and recognizable shapes and forms—which linked them to the great art of the past.

Architecture: Postwar Reconstruction and the Engineering Influence

In literature—divided as it was by barriers of language—the influence of the New World on the postwar European scene was relatively limited, although a novelist like Ernest Hemingway enjoyed great prestige among the neorealists. In films, this influence was still less—since Hollywood productions were usually inferior to the better European work. In painting, Americans for the first time in the years after 1945 won real respect from the Europeans. But it was in architecture and music that the American effect on the Old World was most pronounced. In these fields—whose artistic idiom had always been highly international—the United States had begun to move into a position of leadership as early as the war years.

This was partly because influential architects who had emigrated from

Germany—such as Walter Gropius and Mies van der Rohe—chose to remain in their new home. It also reflected the character of postwar architecture, which made heavy demands on engineering, at which the Americans excelled. During the war years, moreover, when very little building was done in Europe, the modern style had been steadily advancing in the United States. Thus the Americans—who had learned their architecture from Europe in the 1920's and 1930's—could now turn and repay the debt.

By 1945 the triumph of the modern on both sides of the Atlantic was assured, and the vast job of reconstructing the cities which had been devastated during the war offered a unique opportunity for bold new design. But in general the results were disappointing. Although most of the rebuilding was in some variety of modern style—except where respect for traditional artistic monuments absolutely dictated the contrary—the individual buildings usually lacked imagination, and they tended to be erected in haphazard fashion. In most cases it proved too expensive and legally complicated to draw up a uniform plan for a city and to devise a whole new street layout. The pressure was for rebuilding as fast as possible with only secondary regard for esthetic considerations and the harmony of the whole. Where reconstruction was somewhat delayed, however, the results were more satisfactory. This was true in Coventry, in parts of West Berlin, and in the French seaport of Le Havre, where the patriarch of modern French architecture, Auguste Perret, designed what was virtually a new city with broad avenues and parks, heavy and conventional in detail, perhaps, but admirable in its over-all effect.

The Scandinavians, who had welcomed the modern style in the 1930's, maintained this allegiance in the postwar period. The Swedes in particular developed the style in new directions by using rough building materials, breaking up plain wall surfaces, and intricately interweaving the masses of individual structures. The British, who had resisted the modern longer than any others, turned to it more and more in the years after 1945, with an emphasis on the design of new school buildings, which became a kind of English specialty, and on establishing "satellite towns," as self-contained units rather than conventional suburbs, to take up the overflow from the cities. But the Italians once again showed themselves the boldest postwar innovators. And it was also in Italy that the engineering influence proved strongest. The Italians became particularly interested in industrial design—as in the new buildings constructed by the Pirelli rubber company at Milan and the Olivetti typewriter concern at Ivrea—and in the use of reinforced concrete. The master of concrete construction was Pier Luigi Nervi. In his employment of slabs and beams and shell domes, Nervi developed a whole new series of architectural possibilities. The results were buildings of an astonishing lightness which seemed to stand almost without support, such as the exhibition hall at Turin, dating from 1948–1949, and the stadium constructed for the Olympic Games in Rome in 1960.

Finally, Europeans continued to influence the course of modern architecture abroad, especially in the less developed parts of the globe. The
new capital cities designed for Pakistan by Le Corbusier, and for Brazil
by Oscar Niemeyer, showed the unbroken creativity of European architects in combining monumental vistas with intimacy of detail in a form
particularly appropriate to regions of strong sun and a warm climate.

Music: Shostakovich, Hindemith,
and the Heirs of Schönberg

After 1945, as had been true ever since the pall of Stalinist orthodoxy
descended, Soviet artists and writers lived under such tight restrictions
that they could contribute very little of importance to European cultural
life as a whole. It was only with the death of Stalin in 1953 that even the
most cautious sort of innovation became possible once again (*see* Chapter Twenty, II).

In music, however, despite the way in which Andrei Zhdanov brought
the Soviet composers to heel—along with everyone else who had strayed
from the narrow ideological path during the war—Russian work continued to command respectful attention abroad. The war itself had seen
the emergence of Dmitri Shostakovich as the Soviet Union's most influential composer. Less witty and original than Prokofiev, Shostakovich
specialized in the grander and more obvious musical effects, as displayed
to maximum advantage in his Seventh Symphony, written during the
siege of Leningrad. Chastened by having twice fallen into official disfavor, Shostakovich eventually learned to curb his more experimental
tendencies. The same was true of the Soviet Armenian Aram Khacha-
turian, who knew how to work folk melodies into an instrumental form
which gave them an extraordinary popular appeal.

In Western Europe, however, just the contrary occurred. Under the
influence of younger American composers and of major European composers who continued to live in the United States, the continental leaders
of the musical world turned toward bold experiment. Of the great Germans who had remained in America, the most important was Paul
Hindemith—the ultrascrupulous and powerful composer of the opera
Mathis the Painter, first produced in 1938—and, of course, Arnold Schönberg, the prophet of atonal music. Schönberg's greatest influence came
only after the Second World War, as the new generation began to adopt
his twelve-tone form of composition. Among the elders, Schönberg's
contemporary and fellow Californian by adoption, Igor Stravinsky, also
turned to experimenting with similar techniques. When Schönberg died
in 1951, he had finally won recognition as the most important musical
innovator of the century. At the Festival of Contemporary Music held at
Cologne in 1960, Americans joined with Europeans to celebrate the
triumph of the modern, which in music, as in painting and architecture,
had finally been assured.

III

REFORMS IN EDUCATION

The Influence of American Science

In science, even more than in the arts, postwar Europe was profoundly influenced by the United States. The wartime development of nuclear physics had been a joint Anglo-American effort, but in the public mind the Americans won most of the credit. A fairer judgment would also have emphasized the fact that a very large number of the leading nuclear physicists who had aided the United States—like the Italian Enrico Fermi —were refugees from fascist oppression.

The postwar prestige of American science did not derive solely from its wartime achievements. It derived also from the very realistic consideration that the United States alone—particularly in the years of hardship in Europe immediately following the war—had the money and the resources to build the great laboratories which the new demands of experimental science required. This material weakness faced European scientists with a severe crisis of self-confidence. They began to send their students in large numbers to the United States for advanced training; they argued strenuously for the introduction of laboratory exercises in the secondary school curriculum—which had always been a weak point of European education; at the same time, they tried to emphasize the theoretical aspects of scientific research for which they did not suffer under the same sort of material handicaps.

In social science also, American scholars overwhelmed the Europeans with their larger numbers and the more elaborate research facilities at their disposal. Here again the contrast was partly one of empiricism as against theory: in the United States, economists, sociologists, and anthropologists emphasized teamwork and quantitative method; in Europe there was a tendency to continue using the older literary and discursive approaches. In any event, the decade and a half following the war saw no major innovations in European social science. The British and the Swedes maintained their ascendancy in economics; the French continued to combine anthropology with sociology in the tradition of Durkheim; the Germans, in this as in so many other fields, were fully absorbed in recovering the ground they had lost during the twelve years of Nazi tyranny.

A final evidence of American influence was the spread of research institutes and new educational foundations which were jointly financed by the European countries and the United States and in which American and European scholars worked together more closely than in the past. Outstanding among these was the Free University of Berlin, founded in West Berlin in 1949 as a secession from the old university, which had passed completely under Communist dominance.

School Reform and the Church Question

In teaching as in advanced research, the postwar years found the Europeans at grips with a major crisis of self-criticism. The experience of war and tyranny—which nearly everywhere had lowered educational levels and even for brief periods closed down the schools and universities entirely—intensified and brought out into the open a number of long-range problems of European education which the previous generation of teachers had either minimized or denied.

First there was the problem of numbers. This came about through the combination of three separate developments which reinforced each other—a postwar population spurt; the educational interruptions of wartime, which frequently meant that two different age groups were crowding the schools and the universities at the same time; and the democratization of life, which prompted poor and lower-middle-class parents to seek educational advantages for their children that they would never have expected for themselves and which in turn induced governments to raise steadily the age at which adolescents could legally leave school. In Britain, the Labor government first set fifteen as the prescribed age, then raised it to sixteen. In France, in the late 1950's, the school-leaving age jumped from fourteen to sixteen.

The outcome of all these changes together was an unprecedented rise in the number of students. In Germany, the number of those attending universities was more than double what it had been before the war. In France, by the 1950's, one out of five adolescents was attending the elite high schools or *lycées,* whereas the prewar figure had been one in fifteen. Usually this swelling of numbers meant overcrowded classrooms and a shortage of teachers, whose pay often failed to keep pace with the rising cost of living. In a poor country like Italy, the schools and universities were overwhelmed, and the level of instruction fell correspondingly. Britain just barely kept abreast of the new demands, and France, which had always taken particular pride in its public educational system, found itself lagging behind.

With the vast increase of numbers—and with a different type of student now flooding the high schools—the question of the curriculum itself suddenly became urgent. European education, far more than American, had traditionally been literary and classical. It had put primary stress on the humanistic training of a comparatively small and privileged element within the population. In the postwar world, much of this teaching seemed antiquated and irrelevant, and it had little meaning for boys and girls from the poorer classes, who had but remotely shared in the cultural heritage of the aristocracy and the upper bourgeoisie.

This situation produced a series of reforms in school curricula directed toward strengthening natural science and contemporary subjects. There were also efforts to build "bridges" between classical and vocational schools, so that gifted pupils from the second group could move into the first and become eligible for admission to a university. Able and ambitious students from families with modest means were similarly aided by a vast increase in public scholarship funds. This process went further in Britain than in any other major country. By the 1950's, the extension of higher education to members of the British working class had drastically changed the student composition of the universities and was already beginning to transform the whole character of the national elite (see Chapter Twenty, III).

Still, on the Continent at least, public education was failing to keep abreast of student demand. Supplementary schools were needed, and these the church alone seemed in a position to provide. In the enormously changed educational conditions of the postwar years, the Catholics in particular made a powerful case for receiving aid from the state. This aid was a matter of urgent necessity, since church schools had suffered even more than state schools from economic stringency. In Germany, such religious pressure created no real problem; German state education was by tradition closely tied in with both Protestant and Catholic teaching. In Italy the church enjoyed the advantage of having a Catholic party in power—De Gasperi's Christian Democrats—which merely continued and intensified Mussolini's policy both of giving favors to church schools and of encouraging religious teaching in state institutions. In France, however, the question of state aid to Catholic schools gave rise to a major controversy; it stimulated the revival among Socialists and Radicals of an anticlericalism which the Resistance experience was supposed to have ended forever. In general, the Catholics won. In 1951, they secured the adoption of a law establishing the principle of indirect state aid to church schools; eight years later, under the new Gaullist regime, this principle was extended to give the Catholic institutions a position almost on a par with those operated by the state.

IV

THE CHURCHES AND SOCIETY

In the immediate postwar period, the Christian churches wielded extraordinary influence. The part that individual ecclesiastics and militant laymen had played in the Resistance gave them a new type of prestige, and in places where civil government had broken down, the clergy frequently became the sole rallying point of the forces of order. In East Central Europe the Nazi yoke had scarcely been lifted when the Catholic church was plunged into a bitter struggle with communism; here once again the opponents of tyranny closed ranks behind the clergy.

The Jewish Survivors and the Attraction of Israel

In Central and Eastern Europe, and to a lesser extent in the West also, a dreadful memory weighed on the consciences of all convinced Chris-

tians: the destruction of six million Jews. Hitler's mass slaughter had
permanently altered the religious map of Europe. In the West, the change was relatively slight: most of the French and Italian Jews had survived, and a large number of them owed their lives to the protection of the Catholic clergy; these small and well-assimilated Jewish minorities resumed their positions in society after the war almost as if nothing had happened. In countries like Germany and Poland, however, the change was catastrophic. Vast communities of Jews had been reduced to mere fragments—in Germany only 30,000 out of 600,000 remained—and the few who had survived Hitler's extermination camps frequently found it impossible to take up their former lives. Too many ties had been broken, and too many terrible memories lay between Jew and Christian. Although both the Communist governments in East Germany and Poland and the Christian Democratic government in Bonn officially frowned on anti-Semitism—and although the West German regime agreed in 1952 to pay three and a half billion marks in restitution for what the Jews had suffered—anti-Semitism lingered among the people. Consequently the surviving Jews felt that they could never trust their fellow citizens again; while the older ones returned to their former homes, the younger and more active decided to emigrate abroad.

Thus the Jewish emigration of the 1930's—which had mostly been from Germany and Austria to the New World—was followed in the postwar years by another wave of departures, this time primarily from Poland and Rumania. The goal was Palestine, which in 1948 became the independent state of Israel. The Soviet government generally refused to let its nationals emigrate; the Communist-dominated governments of East Central Europe pursued a more uncertain policy, sometimes permitting but more usually forbidding their Jewish citizens to leave. There was, however, much clandestine emigration. In all, perhaps half a million Jews were able to make their way from Eastern Europe to Israel in the decade 1945–1955.

As the state of Israel developed in its first two decades of independence, it became apparent that a new phenomenon had appeared in human history. Israel was an outpost of Europe: its laws, its economy, its educational system all followed European models. In a sea of Arab culture, it stood beleaguered as a small island of Western influence. In this sense, it resembled the colonies of European settlement—the United States, the British overseas dominions, and the countries of Latin America—which had become independent nations in their own right. But Israel was a colony with a difference: it stemmed from no mother country. It did not reproduce, as the other overseas settlements had done, the institutions and language of a *single* European nation. Since the Jews had been a minority wherever they had lived, they possessed no ready-made model for their new state. Hence Israel followed a variety of examples; its economic practices, for instance, were basically socialist, but derived from several different European traditions. The result was that the new nation bore a contrived and artificial character—it represented a triumph of human will over enormous odds—a source both of pride and of weakness to the Israelis as they faced the united hostility of their Arab neighbors.

The Rebuilding of Protestantism in Germany

It was on the consciences of German Protestants that the crimes of the Nazi era weighed most heavily. The church spokesmen who had resisted Hitler or refused to compromise with him were those who took the lead in purging German Protestantism of Nazi influence and in turning the churches away from association with authoritarianism and racism. Such were the Confessional pastors—chief among them Martin Niemöller, who emerged with enormous prestige from his eight years in concentration camp—and to a lesser extent the bishops of the "intact" state churches.

The most important immediate result of this movement of self-purification was to give German Protestantism an organizational unity it had never known before. Ever since the Reformation of the sixteenth century it had been broken up into separate state churches, closely dependent on secular authority. Now in the changed circumstances of postwar collapse and political disintegration, the Protestant leaders saw the need of tightening the bonds between the state churches and establishing an organization which could speak unequivocally for the members of the faith throughout the country; in the autumn of 1945 they formed an Evangelical Church Council for all Germany.

At first, the former Confessional pastors dominated this body, but as the years went by and Western Germany returned to the self-satisfaction attendant on prosperity, the influence of Niemöller and his associates began to wane. Their ethical strenuousness jarred with the new West German temper of complacency; in continuing to emphasize German guilt for Nazi crimes and in arguing against the rearmament of the country, they were opposing the main drift of public and official pressure. Furthermore, they were accused of not caring sufficiently for the fate of East Germany—an overwhelmingly Protestant area, as opposed to the nearly equal division between the two faiths in the West—which accounted for more than 40 per cent of the total German Protestant population. Thus moral leadership tended to slip from the hands of Niemöller and to fall to those who spoke for the Protestants of Eastern Germany in the same militant fashion in which the Catholic primates of Poland, Czechoslovakia, and Hungary had tried to defend their flocks against Communist domination.

Social Catholicism and the Worker-Priests

At the end of the war in Europe, the prestige of the Catholic church stood higher than it had for nearly a century. Pope Pius XII—who had come to the papal throne just a few months before the outbreak of the conflict—had cautiously begun to take a stand against the Nazis as the war progressed, and the emergence of Christian Democratic parties into positions of leadership seemed to mean that Catholic values would find able defenders at the very highest levels of government. These values in general were expressed in advanced social terms: when the war ended, both the Papacy and Christian Democracy were emphasizing the plight of the working classes and were interpreting the basic social documents of the contemporary Church, *Rerum Novarum* and *Quadragesimo Anno,* in a sense of uncompromising protest against the exploitation of one class by another.

Within Catholicism, however, as within German Protestantism, more conservative views soon prevailed. The Christian Democrats in power proved rather different from what they had been in the Resistance years, and social Catholicism gradually became reduced to the position of a barely tolerated left wing on the fringe of the official parties. This was particularly apparent in the case of the most imaginative experiment the church had ever made to win back the de-Christianized workers of the great industrial centers—the worker-priest movement in France.

The idea animating the worker-priests was that the only way to reconvert the hostile and the apathetic among the laboring classes was to offer dramatic proof that the clergy was not so separated from, and uninterested in, the life of the factories as its enemies had asserted. If the workers refused to go to church, then the church itself must come to them. Beginning in 1946 a few specially trained French priests began working—in ordinary laborer's clothes—in the factories of the Parisian industrial area. They were only gradually to reveal their identity and to begin their active mission, as little by little they won the confidence of those who worked alongside them.

By 1951, ninety worker-priests were in the factories, and the idea had received the enthusiastic endorsement of the French episcopate. But then the difficulties began: in Communist-led rioting in Paris, two or three of the priests fell into the hands of the police, and it was discovered that they had become infected by Marxist doctrine. The Vatican took alarm. Pope Pius XII forbade the further recruitment of worker-priests and severely limited the scope of those already active. For seven more years the dispute within the church dragged on—with the French cardinals constantly pleading for the continuation of the experiment. Finally in 1959, shortly after the installation of a new Pope, John XXIII, the Vatican rendered its final verdict: work in factories, it decreed, was "incompatible with the life and obligations of the priesthood."

Pope John XXIII and the Vatican Council

The decision concerning the worker-priests did not give an accurate guide to Pope John's own attitude. It was characteristic, rather, of his first two years on the papal throne, when he was proceeding with caution and following the advice of the elderly Italian cardinals who dominated the Curia, or central administration of the church. Although an old man himself, the new Pope was youthful in spirit and a bold reformer. Of peasant origin, with a simple, profoundly human approach, his whole style was in strong contrast to that of the aloof and aristocratic Pius XII. Pope John's unfailing affability and warm humor brought the Papacy close to the mass of Catholics—and to Protestants, Jews, and unbelievers, who came to love him almost as much as did those of his own faith. In his brief four and a half years of office, he made a greater change in the Catholic church than any Pope of the twentieth century.

The keynote of Pope John's policy was *aggiornamento*—bringing the church up to date by squarely confronting the problems of the contemporary world. Such ideas were embodied in his two great encyclicals —*Mater et Magistra* of 1961, and *Pacem in Terris,* published shortly before his death in the spring of 1963. The first, as its date implied, continued the series of social pronouncements begun in 1891 with *Rerum Novarum.* Just as *Quadragesimo Anno* had celebrated the fortieth anniversary of its predecessor by applying its message to the new problems that had arisen during the preceding generation, so Pope John's encyclical drew attention to the vastly altered situation that had emerged in the thirty additional years that had gone by; more particularly it pointed to the poverty of the underdeveloped world and the responsibility of Europeans and Americans to share their wealth with those less fortunate. *Pacem in Terris* was equally contemporary in tone: a stirring appeal for peace, coupled with a condemnation of thermonuclear war, it both reflected and reinforced the progress toward international understanding which had marked the preceding decade of European history.

Yet the most extraordinary of Pope John's innovations was the calling of a church council—the first since the Vatican Council of 1870 and the most important since that of Trent, in the late sixteenth century, which had met the challenge of Protestantism by laying the basis for a Catholic reformation. The council of the 1960's—Vatican II as it came to be called —brought together more than 2,500 cardinals and bishops from the entire Catholic world. Its agenda was enormous, so great in fact that observers frequently questioned whether it would ever be possible for so large and unwieldy a body to deal with more than a fraction of what it had undertaken to debate. Several times its machinery seemed to be grinding to a halt. Yet in four successive autumn sessions, lasting about three months each, it managed to inaugurate the most extensive reforms that the church had experienced in the modern era.

The first session, in the autumn of 1962, already showed where the council's center of gravity lay. In organizing their proceedings, the church fathers (with the Pope's evident support) gave preference to "progressives"—characteristically those from France, Germany, the Low Countries, North America, and the underdeveloped world—as against the conservatives who dominated the Curia and the Italian and Spanish hierarchies. This first session was necessarily preliminary: there was an exhilarating sense of renewal as the assembled fathers cast off the control of the Curia and engaged in a free debate that astounded non-Catholics accustomed to regarding the Church as a monolith; it was agreed that final decisions on the most controversial issues must be postponed to a further session. Then in the ensuing period of adjournment Pope John died, and the whole idea of the council seemed in danger. But the College of Cardinals elected as his successor the figure closest to the deceased pontiff among the Italian hierarchy—Giovanni Battista Montini, archbishop of Milan, who chose to be called Paul VI. Although in manner and in training Pope Paul recalled Pius XII, with whom he had worked for many years, in policy he tended to follow the line that John XXIII had marked out.

Yet the new Pope's guidance was less sure than that of his predecessor. When the council reassembled in September, 1963, hesitations appeared, and the one decisive achievement of this second session was the vote of the schema (or constitution) on the liturgy, which included an authorization for the use of vernacular languages in large portions of the Mass. Not until the third session, the autumn following, did conservatives and progressives clash head on. This time the debate was even more outspoken than before: such sensitive subjects as disarmament and birth control were broached with realism and frankness. The fathers voted that in the future the bishops should participate alongside the Pope in the government of the church; they completed the constitution on ecumenicism and pushed forward the one on the relation of Catholicism to the modern world. But on two of the most hotly debated drafts they were unable to have their viewpoint officially promulgated—a declaration absolving the Jews of responsibility for the death of Jesus (which had served so often in the past as a pretext for anti-Semitism) and a statement on religious liberty intended to inaugurate a new era of understanding with non-Catholics. Although there were overwhelming majorities for both these drafts—indeed, in the case of the declaration on religious liberty more than 1,500 of the church fathers made an unprecedented plea to Pope Paul to use his personal authority to bring the matter to a vote—the Pope refused to override the delaying tactics of the conservative minority. This check to the cause of reform was only temporary. When the council reconvened for the fourth—and final—time in September, 1965, one of its first acts was to vote by a vast majority the substance of the declarations on religious liberty and on the Church's relations with Judaism.

Quite apparently in the last session of the Council Pope Paul was trying to act as a mediator between the conservatives and the reformers. But this task proved almost insuperably difficult: the pontificate of John had released a flood of new tendencies within the Church which subsequently travelled under their own momentum. In some of them John's successor shared to the full: he broke with papal precedent by making dramatic journeys to Israel and to India, to South America and to Africa; he remodelled the Curia in Rome, retiring from its direction the more reactionary cardinals. He drew the line, however, at the notion of fully sharing his authority with the bishops, and he expressed his frank alarm at the widespread questioning of religious tradition and the malaise among the younger members of the clergy that led them to want to marry or even to leave the priesthood entirely. The clearest sign of the Pope's evolution to the right was the encyclical *Humanae Vitae,* issued in the summer of 1968, which reaffirmed the intransigent Catholic stand on birth control.

The reforming wing of the Church, despite the respectful tone in which it addressed the Pope, firmly maintained its own position. This tendency was particularly militant in the Low Countries, where the Dutch Catholics prepared a new catechism that redefined dogma in arrestingly contemporary terms, and where the Primate of Belgium, Leo Jozef Cardinal Suenens, emerged as the eloquent advocate of the right of the various national churches to adapt their practices to local conditions and needs. In the spring of 1969 Suenens precipitated a major controversy by calling for the end of the "centralized, formalistic, legalistic, static, and bureaucratic conception" of Church government which even after a decade of innovation remained entrenched at the Vatican.

The Cold War, 1947–1953

Chapter Seventeen

I

THE SPLIT BETWEEN
EAST AND WEST

*America's Postwar Role:
Preconception and Realities*

President Roosevelt had based his wartime policies on a few general ideas about what his country's position was in the world and what the postwar international scene would be like. Convinced that Woodrow Wilson had gone astray through lack of "realism," he wanted to avoid his predecessor's mistakes by making full allowance for the brute facts of power politics. His vision, like Wilson's, was "idealistic"—but its idealism was tempered by a recognition of the limits imposed on constructive statesmanship.

In retrospect, Roosevelt frequently appears to have been overcautious about these limits. He was sure, for example, that his countrymen would tolerate the stationing of American troops in Europe for only a very brief period, and it was partly for this reason—in order to get a settlement which would not need American policing—that he was accommodating with Stalin at Yalta. In other respects, however, Roosevelt was oversanguine: he saw good reason to hope that the wartime alliance of Britain, the United States, and the Soviet Union would hold together and that, by acting as a steering body within the newly formed United

*A view through barbed wire and across
the wall of the Brandenburg Gate between
East and West Berlin.* COURTESY FRITZ HENLE,
FROM MONKMEYER PRESS PHOTO SERVICE.

Nations, the three could give a clear direction to the making and the maintaining of the peace.

In this view of the future, each European power had its anticipated role. The Soviet Union would dominate Eastern Europe and would aid in controlling Germany; Britain would take the lead in the Mediterranean, France on the Western European continent, and the united power of the wartime partners would serve to keep Germany firmly in check.

One by one, as the postwar years went by, these preconceptions proved unfounded. First came the disputes with the Soviet Union over the government of postwar Germany. Then Britain confessed its inability to guard the Mediterranean. France meanwhile—deeply involved in colonial warfare and in domestic struggles both economic and ideological —was recovering its strength more slowly than had been anticipated. Soon Germany was to be split, with each of its two halves taken into rival alliance systems by its occupiers. By 1947 at the very latest, the preconceptions on which the American government had based its European policy had all proved erroneous. The central international drama of the next two years was the forging of an anti-Soviet alliance by the United States to cope with these new circumstances and the corresponding consolidation of the Communist world under the authority of the aging Stalin.

The United Nations: Unforeseen Weaknesses
and Unanticipated Strengths

The United Nations, like its predecessor the League, grew out of the victorious wartime coalition. Indeed, it was founded while the war was still in progress: the initial drafts for its organization were worked out by the four "sponsoring powers"—the United States, the Soviet Union, Britain, and China—at Dumbarton Oaks, in Washington, in the autumn of 1944, and its final Charter was signed by the representatives of fifty nations at the conclusion of the conference held in San Francisco from April to June of the following year.

At first sight, the Charter of the United Nations looked much like the old Covenant of the League. Like its predecessor, the new international organization aimed at nearly universal world membership: during the decade and a half after its foundation, it admitted about fifty additional members—some from among wartime enemies or neutrals, but the majority from the former colonial areas of Asia and Africa. Like the League, the United Nations had a General Assembly in which all its members participated with an equal vote; a Council, renamed the Security Council, on which the five Great Powers (including France) occupied permanent seats, with the smaller powers electing six from their own ranks on a two-year rotation basis; specialized agencies for economic and cultural affairs, whose functions had now been vastly enlarged; and a system for guiding toward nationhood the former colonies of defeated enemies—which previously had been called *mandates* and were now renamed *trusteeships*.

These changes in terminology, however, meant more than merely revising an old institution—just as the shift in the organization's headquarters from Geneva to New York symbolized a real change in its center of gravity. It was no longer a predominantly European enterprise; the membership of the United States and the Soviet Union made its claims to world jurisdiction far more real than had been true of the League. Moreover, this non-European character grew steadily, particularly after 1955–1956, when twenty new members were added, many of them from Asia and Africa, and 1960, when there came a further influx of sixteen African states. Finally, both of the United Nations' deliberative bodies were slightly different in character from what their counterparts in the League had been, and these differences were to become decisive in the first decade and a half of the new organization's existence.

Churchill and Stalin had agreed with Roosevelt that the United Nations should more frankly recognize the predominant role of the Great Powers in international affairs than the League had done. Hence they had strengthened the authority of the Security Council by conferring on it "primary responsibility for the maintenance of international peace and security," under the terms of Article 24 of the Charter. At the same time, in Article 27, they had assured that no great power could be put in a minority; on all major decisions unanimous vote of the Big Five was required. Stalin had insisted on this at Yalta, and Churchill and Roosevelt concurred—on the thoroughly realistic basis that if the Great Powers were in disagreement, the Security Council would not be an effective agency for enforcing the peace. But the events of the immediate postwar years once again changed these preconceptions: the government of China proved entirely unable to function as that of a great power, and in 1949 it lost control of the whole Chinese mainland to the Communists; the remaining four powers, as the cleavage between East and West widened, began to vote regularly three to one, with the Soviet Union casting its veto not merely in exceptional cases, as the Charter had anticipated, but almost as a matter of routine.

With the Security Council paralyzed, attention shifted to the General Assembly. Here the founders of the United Nations had again changed the former machinery of the League by substituting a two-thirds majority for the earlier rule of unanimity. Thus when the Security Council was unable to act, the Assembly could frequently muster the requisite majority. From 1950 on, this became the increasingly regular pattern of United Nations activity. There developed with this pattern a new importance for the non-European nations, the neutrals between the two great-power blocs, and the middle-rank states, whose voices grew ever more influential in the General Assembly.

For the settlement of *European* concerns, however, the United Nations proved almost powerless. Nearly all its major decisions—on the independence of Israel in 1947–1948, on the Korean War in 1950, on the Suez crisis in 1956, on the Congo in 1960—lay outside the confines of Europe. On the Continent itself, the gap between the Communist and the non-Communist world was too wide to be bridged by any international organization. Here the two power blocs went their separate ways, organizing their rival security systems independently and sometimes in defiance of the United Nations that they themselves had taken the lead in founding.

The Peace Treaties with the Axis Satellites

After their adjournment at Potsdam, the Big Three turned over to their foreign ministers the task of making the peace. Pursuant to this decision, the American secretary of state, Britain's new foreign minister, Ernest Bevin, and Molotov for the Soviet Union constituted themselves a Council of Foreign Ministers. They met first in London in September, 1945, then in Paris the following summer, where they were joined by the French foreign minister, and finally in New York at the end of the year, to work out the final details of settlement.

The outcome of more than a year of discussion was a series of peace treaties with Italy and with the four minor German satellites: Bulgaria, Hungary, Rumania, and Finland. Essentially, these treaties were the work of the Big Four alone, although the advice of the lesser allies was sought, and they signed the final documents. The treaties followed a common pattern: they imposed reparations, limited the armed forces of the defeated countries, and made a few territorial changes. Such changes were mostly minor. Except for the enormous alteration in the frontiers of Poland and the disappearance of the Baltic States—both matters which lay outside the sphere of the peace treaties—the boundaries of Europe returned substantially to those established at Paris in 1919. Once again, however, as at Yalta, the Soviet Union insisted on retaining the territorial gains it had made during the war: the peace treaties ratified its annexation of Bessarabia from Rumania, and of the Karelian Isthmus and the Arctic seaport of Petsamo from Finland.

In addition, the frontiers of Italy were reduced to conform more closely to ethnic lines. The question of Italy's eastern frontier was the most serious the peacemakers faced, for it brought the new anti-Fascist Italian regime into conflict with another product of the wartime Resistance, Tito's Communist government in Yugoslavia. Elsewhere the Italian territories in dispute proved comparatively easy to assign. France contented itself with four small Alpine areas; the Austrians of the South Tyrol remained in Italy, after having received the dubious consolation of a special autonomy statute. Tito and his Soviet backers, however, were far more intractable: they claimed not only Venezia Giulia—most of which the Western powers were quite ready to concede, since the bulk of its people were Yugoslavs—but also the seaport of Trieste, whose population was overwhelmingly Italian.

For Trieste, after long and bitter wrangling, the Big Four finally
reached a desperate solution reminiscent of Danzig in 1919—they established it as a Free Territory. In the case of Trieste the free-territory arrangement never really worked at all: both sides sabotaged it, and only after Tito had broken with Stalin—thereby losing his advocate in the councils of the mighty—did its solution become possible. In 1954, the Western powers, by unilateral decision, allowed Italy to annex the city itself, while the rural part of the Free Territory went to Yugoslavia. In the case of the Italian colonies, the Big Four again were eventually forced into a solution which satisfied nobody. After failing to agree among themselves, they referred the question to the United Nations, where the same disputes were renewed. Not until the end of 1949 did the United Nations decide on the final disposition of the three Italian territories in Africa: independence for Libya, federation with Ethiopia (which the British had liberated during the war) for Eritrea, and an Italian trusteeship, preparatory to independence, for the Somali coast. Quite against their expressed intent, the Western powers had been driven to accept a plan which inevitably stimulated the drive for freedom throughout the African continent (*see* Chapter Eighteen, III).

By this time, however, the peace treaties themselves had become obsolete. The fundamental assumption on which they were based—that of a wartime coalition imposing its will on the vanquished—within less than three years was thoroughly out of date. Italy had won full acceptance as a military ally of the West, and Bulgaria, Hungary, and Rumania were functioning as obedient satellites of the Soviet Union. Finland alone remained outside both of the two great-power blocs.

The Truman Doctrine and the Marshall Plan

This change of circumstances had already become amply apparent when the foreign ministers turned their attention to making a settlement with Germany. Twice during 1947—in March and April in Moscow, and in November and December in London—they tried to reach some minimum accord. Their efforts failed completely; the standpoints of East and West were much too far apart. By the end of 1947 it was apparent to everyone that a Cold War had replaced the process of international consultation.

Discord first erupted into actual violence in the eastern Mediterranean. The Greek Communists—in whose suppression Churchill had played an active role at the end of 1944—took up arms once again in September, 1946. This time they were aided by the fact that Greece's northern neighbors—Albania, Yugoslavia, and Bulgaria—were all under Communist regimes and were able to send them clandestine help across the border. They were also encouraged by the widespread popular dissatisfaction with the postwar Greek regime, in theory a parliamentary monarchy, but in fact a corrupt right-wing oligarchy, almost entirely dependent on British armed support.

In early 1947, however, this backing began to falter. The British Labor government, faced with the necessity of reducing its military budget, notified the United States that it could no longer support either the Greeks or the Turks, who were simultaneously coming under Soviet pressure. President Truman rose to the challenge. In March, he announced to the American Congress that in the future the United States would "support free peoples who are resisting attempted subjugation by armed minorities or by outside pressure." Shortly thereafter American military missions went to Turkey and Greece, where they re-equipped the Greek army for a more resolute assault on the Communist guerrillas in the northern mountains.

The Truman Doctrine became the cornerstone of a new interventionist policy of the United States in European affairs, replacing the inconsistencies and hesitations which had characterized the first year and a half of peace. Its counterpart in the economic sphere was the plan for European recovery first enunciated by Secretary of State George C. Marshall the following June. In its original formulation, however, the Marshall Plan was not, strictly speaking, a Cold War maneuver. It offered aid to *all* European countries, irrespective of ideology, provided they would coordinate their economic proposals to use American assistance to maximum effect.

Perhaps the clearest sign of how the cleavage between East and West was making impossible any over-all European cooperation was the manner in which the Marshall Plan gradually became transformed into an instrument of the Cold War. This process of perversion occurred on both sides of the great ideological divide. In the East, the outcome was at first uncertain. Most of the Soviet satellites held back, distrustful of Secretary Marshall's invitation. The Poles and the Czechs, however, were willing to accept until they were sharply called to task by their Russian masters. By mid-summer of 1947 it had become quite clear that the Soviet Union would permit no Communist participation in the Marshall Plan. The American president and his advisers were now free to continue the distortion of the original proposal by presenting it to Congress as the economic complement to the military program of the Truman Doctrine. When the Marshall Plan—or, to use its official name, the European Recovery Program—went into effect in early 1948, it had become exclusively a Western European enterprise.

The Cominform, the Italian Election of 1948, and the Insurrectionary Strikes in Italy and France

The forced refusal on the part of the Czechs and the Poles in July, 1947, to participate in the Marshall Plan inaugurated the decisive eighteen months in the split between the two ideological camps. Until the end of 1948, one event followed closely on another in tragic sequence.

In September, 1947, the Communist parties of the Soviet Union and its satellites, together with those of France and Italy—the only Western European affiliates of major importance—revived the Third International under a new name. The re-established Comintern was called "Cominform," to suggest that it was no more than a vehicle for the exchange of information. In fact, it did rather more: during the next five and a half years of intense Cold War it served to coordinate the ideologies and the economic plans of the East European Communist states, to reinforce their solidarity against the West, and to spur the militancy of the French and Italian parties. But it never achieved the prestige or importance of the Third International. In April, 1956, having outlived its usefulness, the Cominform officially disbanded.

The first fruit of its founding was a militant new line in the French Communist party. On November 12, the Communist leaders who dominated the general trade-union federation issued a "manifesto to the French working class" calling for an insurrectionary general strike in the factories, the railways, and the coal mines. For a month the very existence of French democracy seemed to hang in the balance as violence and sabotage spread, and non-Communist workers were systematically intimidated. But little by little, decisive government action brought results. The Socialist minister of the interior, Jules Moch, a man of cool resolve, did not hesitate to call out special police forces and even used the army against the strikers—who finally lost heart when they discovered that they were threatened with the loss of their social security benefits. By December 10, the crisis was over, and the French production index began to climb as the value of the franc held steady.

Two months later, the last bridgehead of Western democratic influence within the Soviet-dominated world was eliminated with the Communist seizure of power in Czechoslovakia. Then in April a parallel event occurred in the West. In Italy, which alone with France among the Western European nations had a Communist party strong enough to threaten the democratic regime itself, the electorate went to the polls to choose the first parliament under the new constitution. The voting was preceded by the most frenetic electoral campaign of postwar European history. The Communists, still smarting under their exclusion from the government ten months before, were trying to force their way back in by proving the hold they had on the Italian masses. In this effort they enjoyed the unstinting support of Pietro Nenni's Socialists, who had formed an electoral alliance with them called the People's Bloc. Prime Minister De Gasperi's Christian Democrats had made a similar alliance with three smaller democratic parties, among them the minority Socialists who had broken away from Nenni's leadership a year before. De Gasperi further profited by the backing of the Vatican and the American government, which for the first time in history tried to influence the outcome of a European election. Moreover, the memory of recent events in Czechoslovakia served as a warning of what might happen if the Communists should triumph. On April 18, 1948, the Italian people gave their verdict: De Gasperi and his allies swept the field. Together they won more than three-fifths of the seats in the Chamber of Deputies, and the Christian Democrats alone, who had polled 48.5 per cent of the vote, gained a narrow majority in that body. The Communists and their Socialist allies had been held to 31 per cent, a level of popular support which was to remain almost unchanged for the next decade.

The Italian Communists' bid for power had failed. They recovered their militancy briefly in July, when their leader, Palmiro Togliatti, was wounded in an assassination attempt, and they staged in protest a dramatic general strike. For two days an atmosphere of revolution brooded over the country as barricades went up in some of the northern cities, but the mere threat of military force was enough to bring about the movement's collapse. The Communist trade-union leaders, who had known all along that they were too weak to lead an insurrection, called off the strike with scarcely concealed relief. In the autumn the same thing happened in France: an eight-week strike in the coal mines directed against the Marshall Plan proved to be no more than a desperate repeat performance of the massive social unrest the Communists had unleashed the previous year. Nor did the Communist labor leaders have their followers as well in hand as in the autumn of 1947. In late November, when the strike formally ended, four-fifths of the miners had already gone back to work.

By the end of 1948 the economic and ideological offensive of the Western European Communists had been broken and the Soviet bloc had experienced a further defeat in its failure to bring Tito to terms. After being expelled from the Cominform the previous June, the Yugoslav Communists were now groping their way toward neutrality between the two power blocs. In the meantime, the architect of the Soviet policy of revolutionary militancy, Andrei Zhdanov, had died with his work in ruins. Had he won a free hand earlier, the Italian and French Communists might have come closer to success. As it was, the movement had started too late: with the United States now once again fully involved in European affairs, it was doomed from the start.

The Berlin Airlift

The last and most protracted crisis in this year and a half of constant alarms was the first great international conflict over Berlin. In June, 1948, having failed to dissuade the British and Americans from their plan of organizing a West German government, the Russians decided to put pressure on the weakest and most exposed point in the Anglo-American defensive position: they cut off railway and road access to the three Western sectors of Berlin and simultaneously tried to force the city government into line. But the Western powers would not be bullied.

They supported the democratic majority on the Berlin city council—
whose resistance forced the Soviet authorities to set up a separate administration for the eastern part of the city—and they mobilized every available transport plane to supply Berlin by air. All through the summer and autumn the great airlift went on. Then winter brought a new problem. Surely, the Russians thought, the Western aircraft could not bring in enough coal to supply the needs of the two million people in their sectors. But the Americans and British simply increased the number of their planes and added coal to the food and essentials they were already carrying. By spring the success of the Berlin airlift was evident to all. In May, the Russians called off the blockade. The Western position in Berlin was safe for another decade.

In Greece also the West was winning the Cold War. With Tito's defection from the Soviet camp, the Greek guerrillas lost their most important supply base. Hard-pressed by their assailants, they retired into an ever-smaller sector of the northern mountains. In the autumn of 1949, the last Communist guerrillas laid down their arms.

II

THE ATLANTIC ALLIANCE
AND THE GOVERNMENTS
OF THE CENTER

In the spring of 1949, the Western powers formally established the ideological and military alliance toward which they had been moving during the past two years. The Atlantic Pact, signed in April in Washington, brought together ten European nations, the United States, and Canada. It included France and Britain, the Low Countries, Italy, and the two Scandinavian nations, Denmark and Norway, which had fought in the war on the Allied side. Portugal and Iceland also joined, and subsequently Greece, Turkey, and Western Germany.

The Atlantic Alliance was, strictly speaking, no more than a military arrangement for mutual protection. Each member nation undertook to provide ground, air, or naval contingents in proportion to its means, with France supplying the largest number of ground troops and the commander of the central sector. The United States made the largest overall contribution of money and materiel; the supreme commander was to be an American. In addition, President Truman undertook to increase the American military commitment in Germany by permanently stationing combat troops along the Rhine. This was to be the keystone of Atlantic military policy—the defense of Western Germany, with a force which was eventually to consist of fifty Allied divisions. Such an army was obviously insufficient to stop a major Soviet advance; but it could fight a costly delaying action, and the Atlantic planners trusted that it would give Stalin sober thoughts about launching any probing attack toward the West.

In addition to its primary military function, the Atlantic Pact expressed the growing ideological solidarity among the Western democracies and provided experience in working out common policies which was subsequently to find expression in the movement for European unity. The Marshall Plan was already pushing in that direction; throughout the late 1940's and early 1950's, the American government constantly encouraged European initiatives for economic and administrative cooperation. Never in history had relations between the United States and the Western European democracies been so close and cordial. During the four years of his second administration—1949–1953—President Truman and his secretary of state, Dean Acheson, pursued a coherent policy of supporting and strengthening governments of the democratic Center. They hoped to stimulate the growth of a "Third Force" in Europe—a moderate parliamentary rule which would prove equally resistant to Communist subversion on the Left and to the revival of authoritarian doctrines among conservatives. This Third Force, they surmised, would at last provide a plateau of stability on which democratic government would gradually gain the confidence of the disaffected masses.

Government by Christian Democrats: De Gasperi, Adenauer, Schuman

From 1948 to 1950, this policy seemed to be succeeding. With the threat from the Communists checked and the inflationary spiral brought to a halt, democracy in Western Europe was finally beginning to function in an approximately normal fashion. The three chief nations, moreover, had leaders who understood one another and spoke a common ideological language. In Italy, after his sweeping electoral victory of April, 1948, De Gasperi remained in uninterrupted power for more than five years; although his own party followers formed the core of his ministry, the Christian Democratic premier preferred to give it a less clerical character by associating with them, whenever possible, the leaders of the three minor democratic parties who had fought the electoral battle at his side. Chief among these was Count Carlo Sforza, a veteran diplomat and a "good European" who, as foreign minister in the period 1920–1921, had tried to pursue a policy of international conciliation and who from 1947 to 1951, under far more favorable circumstances, returned to the same office with hopes undimmed.

In Germany, another Christian Democrat, Konrad Adenauer, began in September, 1949, the longest chancellorship in German history—indeed, the longest single tenure of power that any democratic statesman had held in the entire modern history of Europe. Adenauer's authority throughout his postwar political career remained still more unshakable than De Gasperi's. France, in contrast, with De Gaulle in the shadows,

found no single unquestioned national leader. Nevertheless the element
of continuity was provided by Christian Democrats—the MRP leaders
Bidault and Robert Schuman—who between them almost uninterruptedly
held the foreign ministry during the first postwar decade. Of the two,
Schuman was both the more responsible and the more imaginative. A
Lorrainer who had been a German citizen before 1918 and had even
served in the German army during the First World War, Schuman spoke
French and German with equal fluency and was admirably equipped
by education and temperament to act as mediator between the cultures
of his two homelands.

Adenauer had the reputation of being pro-French. As a fledgling politician in the early 1920's, he had been accused of sympathy with French
annexationist schemes for the Rhineland. The third member of the trio
—De Gasperi—had a similarly varied political past. Before 1914, as a
young "irredentist" from the South Tyrol, he had been elected to the
Austrian Parliament, and he spoke German fluently. Indeed, he is said
to have expressed surprise and pleasure at discovering that he and
Schuman had a second language in common. And this, in fact, was true
in both the literal and the figurative sense—De Gasperi, Adenauer, and
Schuman spoke a common language. They were "good Europeans" who
saw the urgent necessity of united action to preserve their Christian
heritage.

They also had similar ideas on domestic economic policy. All were
by nature conservative but willing to temper conservatism with cautious
reform. Only Adenauer and De Gasperi, however, enjoyed sufficient
continuity in office to permit them to undertake long-range programs.
By the end of 1947, when Schuman became prime minister of France,
the country had already completed its cycle of postwar economic change.
In his eight months of office, Schuman was able to effect no substantial
alterations in domestic social policy. It was rather in his subsequent
five-year tenure of the foreign ministry and in his European initiatives
that he made his permanent mark. During the period 1947–1951, France's
ministries changed too frequently and its parties were too evenly balanced to achieve much coherence in economic policy. Only in retrospect
were these years of uncertainty and flux to appear—ironically enough—
as the best the Fourth Republic had ever known.

In Italy and Germany, the tempered conservatism of Christian Democratic rule found expression in measures of social equalization. Although
these were in no sense socialist, they significantly altered the internal
balance of economic forces in favor of the laboring classes. In Italy, the
most pressing problem was agrarian poverty, for which De Gasperi had
promised remedial action during the election campaign of 1948. Another
year was needed, however, for the government to submit specific legislation to parliament, and still another eighteen months to carry an initial
measure for the redistribution to poor peasants of a million and a half
acres of land held in great estates. This reform measure fell far short of

De Gasperi's original proposal; it provided for the needs of only a small part of Italy's landless peasantry, whose standard of living remained depressed. But it started the long-overdue process of breaking the economic power and social prestige of the large landowners and lifting the economy of the backward southern part of the country to bring it closer to that of the industrial north.

In Germany, the most dramatic reform undertaken by the Adenauer government was the law voted in 1951 for "co-determination" in the factories. Although the idea of giving workers a share in management had originated among Catholic trade-union leaders and the left wing of the Christian Democrats themselves, Adenauer and his ministerial colleagues were reluctant to make so radical an innovation in the face of vehement opposition by employers. Only the pressure of the Social Democrats and the threat of a strike by the powerful metal workers' union finally ensured the passage of a law providing for worker representation on supervisory boards in the iron, steel, and coal industry. The following year, however, when it was proposed to extend co-determination to the rest of German industry, the conservative opposition was more successful. A second law, passed in 1952, significantly reduced the power of the workers' representatives on the boards. This retreat was partially balanced by a piece of legislation voted almost simultaneously—the act for the "equalization of burdens." The "equalization" measure aimed at a vast redistribution of wealth to compensate Germans who had suffered severe damage in the war, by taxing those who had been more fortunate. All properties of more than a thousand dollars in value were subject to the tax, and eventually nearly half the population was scheduled to profit in some fashion or other by the government-sponsored redistribution of wealth.

The Schuman Plan

By the spring of 1950, the economic aid which had been arriving from the United States under the Marshall Plan during the past two years was beginning to show substantial results. In France and Italy, production levels stood well above those of 1938. This was only a modest achievement, and the economic gains were partially canceled out by a 10 per cent increase in population, but it at least showed that Western Europe had emerged from its economic stagnation and made up the ground lost during the war years. Meanwhile the "miracle" of German industrial expansion had begun. At the beginning of 1949, less than a year after the Anglo-American currency reform had at last set the German economy moving, the production index stood at 85 per cent of the 1936 figure.

During the first two of the four years that the Marshall Plan was scheduled to run, American aid averaging four billion dollars a year had resulted in a thirty-billion dollar expansion of annual output. Over-all

production of goods and services had gone up by 25 per cent—an increase
of 15 per cent over the prewar figure. Industrial output as a whole had risen by nearly a third—with steel setting the pace with an increase of more than half. Thus, despite the slow start of postwar economic recon-struction—and despite the greater extent of devastation in 1945 than in 1918—recovery had proceeded more rapidly and more evenly following the Second World War than it had after the First, and Western Europe had gained precious experience in cooperative economic endeavor.

It was in this context that Robert Schuman in May, 1950, came for-ward with the most imaginative proposal that postwar Europe had yet heard and the one from which all subsequent progress toward European integration stemmed: the project for a European Coal and Steel Com-munity, which came to be called the Schuman Plan. The French foreign minister suggested a pooling of heavy industrial resources and an elimi-nation of tariffs in the "core" nations of Western Europe—France, Italy, Western Germany, and the Low Countries. The idea caught on quickly: by the following April, representatives of the six nations were ready to sign the treaty establishing the Community. They guarded themselves by providing that it was to come into effect only gradually during the five years following its ratification; a half-decade of grace was granted for all the threatened vested interests to adjust themselves to the new competitive situation.

Meanwhile, the international outlook had changed drastically. The European atmosphere in which the Coal and Steel Community treaty was signed was radically different from the one in which it had been proposed.

III

THE KOREAN WAR
AND THE GOVERNMENTS
OF THE RIGHT

In June, 1950, the army of Communist North Korea crossed the thirty-eighth parallel to attack the American-endorsed government of South Korea. The United States responded quickly: President Truman decided to send military aid to the South Koreans. Subsequently the United Nations voted to support the American intervention, and a number of Western European countries agreed to supply troop contingents for an international army under United States command.

This distant Asian war had immediate and profound repercussions in Europe: the quiet and undeclared conflict between the Communist and the Western camps which had been going on for the past three years had suddenly flared into open violence and no one knew if and when the struggle would spread to Europe itself. Many recalled how a local war in Spain fourteen years earlier had set the stage for a major international conflict. Most Western Europeans were relieved that the Americans had gone to the aid of South Korea; the prompt American response suggested that the United States was faithful to its allies, and that the year-old Atlantic Pact would stand the test of war. But once the crisis was past, and the North Koreans had been driven back, Europeans began to have second thoughts. When the American army in its turn crossed the thirty-eighth parallel and invaded the territory of the enemy —thereby provoking the intervention of the Communist Chinese—the Europeans feared that the war was being pursued beyond its minimum objective of saving the South Korean government and that it might become a global conflict. Thus the Europeans' original gratification that the United States had gone to the aid of a small ally was gradually transformed into anxiety lest they themselves be drawn into a struggle for power in Asia with which they had only a' very limited concern.

Moreover the continuation of the war meant that Europe must help pay for it in some fashion or other. By the end of 1950 it was obvious that the conflict in Asia was having widely ramifying effects on the economic, the military, and even the political life of the Western European democracies.

The Economic and Military Effects: the EDC

From the economic standpoint, the immediate result of the fighting in Korea was an increase in raw-material prices throughout the world which, in turn, set off a new cycle of inflation. For the statesmen of Europe, this was heartbreaking: they had scarcely finished establishing their countries on what seemed at last to be a secure economic plateau, when the whole weary spiral of price rises, social unrest, and wage adjustments began once again. Nor was American aid this time as unstinting and as free from conditions as it had been in the previous two years. With the outbreak of the Korean war, the emphasis in Washington changed. In the later phases of the Marshall Plan and its sequels, "military support" replaced economic aid as the basis of American appropriations for Europe. Thus the Cold War perversion of Secretary Marshall's original vision was pushed one step further.

From the purely military standpoint, the Korean war induced a mood approaching panic. With the threatened spread of the conflict to Europe, the American government expressed the fear that the existing strength of the North Atlantic Treaty Organization (NATO) would prove inadequate to withstand a Soviet attack on Germany. The United States began to insist that the West Germans be armed for their own defense. Without a German military contribution, the Americans argued, the protection of the West against a Communist assault would be perilously fragile.

For the Europeans in the Atlantic Alliance—and for the French in particular—this American demand raised a cruel dilemma. Most West European statesmen disliked rearming Germany only five years after Hitler's
defeat; they recalled that the demilitarization of the country had been
one of the few aims on which all the occupying powers had agreed. At
the same time the European nations were entirely dependent on the
United States for military and economic support, and they could not
afford to dispute the wishes of their great ally. In this major international
quandary, the French proposed a dramatic compromise solution: the
Germans would be rearmed—but only as the soldiers of a European army.
The sting would be taken out of a revived German militarism by making
certain that the country had no national army but only contingents in
a special force under international command.

This was the central idea behind the European Defense Community
(EDC), whose founding treaty was signed at Paris in May, 1952, by
representatives of the six countries of "Little Europe" which were already bound together by the Schuman Plan. From the standpoint of
European integration, the proposal seemed to be another step forward
along the path that the French foreign minister had already marked out.
In actual fact the new Defense Community was rather different from
the Coal and Steel Community which had preceded it. First, it was not
a pact between equals. Under its terms, West Germany alone was to have
no national army; France, Italy, and the Low Countries, on the contrary,
were to retain separate forces of their own in addition to those they contributed to the European command. Still more important, the EDC
leaped over a succession of stages which "good Europeans" thought
should logically have preceded it. The Schuman Plan had been intended
as only the first of a series of "communities" which were gradually to
link the economies of the six member states. Subsequently, as through
the years "Little Europe" grew accustomed to work in common, a joint
political authority would naturally and inevitably follow. The direct leap
to a military community—logically the very last stage in the succession
—meant the short-circuiting of this whole process. The Europeans were
in the paradoxical situation of having established an international army
with no international political authority to which it could report.

The final paradox of the EDC was that its initial sponsors, the French,
eventually proved to be the prospective members who were least enthusiastic about it. They had originally put it forward as a neat contrivance for avoiding an impossible obstacle. When the contrivance finally
became reality, they began to have grave doubts. While the other
national parliaments one by one ratified the EDC accord, the French
Assembly held back. For two full years, the question of the EDC hung
suspended over France's parliament, poisoning the political life of the
country and contributing mightily to the slow but already painfully apparent decline of the Fourth Republic.

The Political Effects: the Elections of 1951
and 1953; Gaullism and the Conservative Revival

In the political sphere, the Korean war encouraged a trend toward conservative government which had already been apparent in the two years between mid-1948 and mid-1950 when economic stability seemed to have been attained at last. With the return of something approaching "normal," social protest and the demand for change had begun to lose their edge. The outbreak of war in Asia greatly accelerated the conservative revival; the remilitarization of Europe naturally played into the hand of parties which had always stressed nationalism and the tradition of fighting "natives" overseas. Similarly, the Communists also took heart, hoping to exploit the new economic stringencies to their own advantage. But by 1950 their power had been broken: now they could only embitter the political atmosphere by their endless complaints and denunciations.

A series of national elections extending through the years 1951 and 1953 most dramatically showed this process at work. First France went to the polls, in conformity with the new constitution of the Fourth Republic, which had set the term of the National Assembly at five years. In the French election of June, 1951, the "tripartite" arrangement of 1946 was replaced by a "hexagon" of parties roughly equal in strength; in the redistribution of political forces, the two parties of the Center—the MRP and the Socialists—were the chief losers, whereas the great gains were made on the Right. At the end of the year, the British electorate also gave its verdict. The Labor party, which had secured only a narrow majority in the regularly scheduled election of 1950, felt obliged to reinforce its uncertain mandate. In new elections held in October, 1951, the Conservatives reversed the previous year's results by an equally narrow margin, and Winston Churchill returned to power for the last time.

In 1953, the Italian Chamber of Deputies—whose term, like that of the French Assembly, ran for five years—and the West German Bundestag —which was chosen for four years—both came up for re-election. On the surface, the results of the Italian election in June and of the German election in September seemed to be in complete contrast. In Italy, Prime Minister De Gasperi's Christian Democrats lost ground to the Right; in Germany, Chancellor Adenauer's followers gained. But the actual effects on the national life were much the same. In both countries, Christian Democracy in power had become a far more conservative force than it had been at the outset. The major reform acts of previous years—land redistribution in Italy, co-determination in Germany—had gradually been confined in scope by the pressure of the propertied classes. In Germany, however, the conservative revival expressed itself *within* the Christian Democratic leadership, whereas in Italy it spoke through revived parties of the Right which were openly backed by the larger businessmen and landowners.

The gradual triumph of conservatism was accompanied by a corresponding change in Europe's political leadership. Indeed, this sometimes happened even before the Center and moderate Left parties which
had governed in the period 1947–1951 were defeated at the polls. In
Britain, Aneurin Bevan, the leader of Labor's left wing, unable to stomach the new rearmament policy, resigned from the cabinet in early 1951.
In Italy, Count Sforza was forced out of the foreign ministry the following summer, and his French counterpart, Robert Schuman, was dropped
from the same office at the beginning of 1953. Half a year later, De Gasperi also departed: despite his followers' losses in the elections, Christian
Democracy was still by far the strongest party in Italy; yet when the
veteran prime minister tried to form a ministry based solely on his own
party, he was rejected by the Chamber. After more than seven years in
office, De Gasperi retired; he died the following year, pleading until the
last for the ratification of the treaty establishing the EDC.

One by one the "good Europeans" were being moved off the scene
and, in an effort to salvage something of their former position, they were
reduced to electoral stratagems that brought them only further discredit.
For the election of 1951, the French government modified the proportional system which had been instituted in 1945. The new electoral law
provided that a party (or coalition of parties) which won a majority of
the vote in any constituency was to be assigned *all* the seats for that area;
the coalition of parties that the framers of the bill had in mind was, of
course, the democratic Center which had governed for the past four
years. In Italy, which also operated under a proportional system, De
Gasperi and his colleagues devised a still more transparent maneuver;
here a coalition which had gained a narrow majority in the *whole country*
was to be rewarded with a bonus of two-thirds of the seats in the
Chamber.

In both cases, these electoral tricks disappointed the expectations of
their contrivers. In Italy the unpopularity of the "swindle law," as its
enemies called it, contributed to the decline of the democratic parties;
when the votes were counted, it was discovered that their coalition had
just missed its majority, and that hence the proportional system would
operate as before. In France, the electoral law of 1951 did in fact reduce
the power of the political extremes; but it failed to provide the reinforcement of Center rule which its sponsors had anticipated.

France most clearly showed what were to be the new tendencies of
the early 1950's. At first it seemed that the 1951 election had brought to
the fore a revived authoritarianism of the Right. In the new Assembly,
the strongest single party—which ousted the Communists from first place
by the narrowest of margins—was the Rally of the French People (RPF)
led by Charles de Gaulle. In the spring of 1947, the general, disgusted
by the weaknesses of the restored parliamentary regime, had emerged
from retirement to found his own political movement. It won support
very rapidly: conservatives and authoritarians of all sorts flocked to De

Gaulle's banners. But it reached its high point too early: in the first autumn of its existence it polled 40 per cent of the vote in municipal elections throughout the country. Then De Gaulle faced his usual dilemma: lacking a popular majority and with no general election scheduled for nearly four years, the Gaullists of the RPF could maintain only a sterile opposition which in fact benefited the Communists. De Gaulle, as at the time of his original retirement, was once again unwilling to undertake a coup d'état and allowed his movement to wither through lack of clear direction.

Hence the RPF electoral success of 1951—in the teeth of the special law which had been devised to hold it in check—came too late to save it. Those who really profited from the new parliamentary situation were the fifth and sixth parties, which, along with the Gaullists, had now joined the Communists, Socialists, and MRP as major forces on the French political scene. These were the old Radicals, now transmuted into frankly conservative representatives of small business, and the so-called Independents, who spoke for the larger propertied interests. Together these two parties replaced the Socialists and the MRP as the dominant influences in French political life. First the Socialists had lost ground when the withdrawal of the Communists in 1947 had put them in an exposed position on the left flank of the governing coalitions; after the election of 1951, they dropped out of the ministries entirely. Then the MRP began to slip, with the loss of half its following to De Gaulle and the perversion for military ends of its projects for European unity. In the election of 1951, it showed itself the weakest of the six major parties. Finally when the economic conservatives succeeded in hoisting their own man into the prime ministry, all the other parties went into a severe decline. The government of Antoine Pinay, a small businessman and an Independent, in the last ten months of 1952, gave postwar France for the first time a clear (if unambitious) economic policy: in an effort to inspire confidence among investors and tax evaders, Pinay pursued a strictly laissez faire strategy which postponed all controversial issues to an indefinite future.

The attractions of this policy proved too powerful for the loyalty of the Gaullist deputies. Most of them were mere conservatives who had ridden into the Assembly on the general's coattails and had no profound belief in Gaullism as an ideology. One by one they began to desert their leader and join the government majority. In the spring of 1953, De Gaulle realized that his party had failed; he gave his followers their "liberty of action" and retired once more to his home in the country.

In Italy and Germany, too, authoritarian appeals were failing to win favor. In the elections of 1953 in both countries, neo-Fascist and neo-Nazi forces made a poor showing. A revival of Hitler's or Mussolini's doctrines—or even the milder authoritarianism of De Gaulle—found little welcome in the early 1950's. By 1953, old-fashioned conservatism, rather, with a strong tinge of traditional nationalism, had emerged as the dominant political force in Western Europe.

IV

EASTERN EUROPE:
THE CLIMAX OF THE TERROR

Stalin's Last Years

At the end of his life Stalin sank into a state approaching paranoia. Life became a nightmare for those around him: the aging despot suspected everyone and one favorite replaced another with a capriciousness which defied explanation. Rumors circulated that Zhdanov's death in 1948 had not been accidental; the press announced a mysterious "doctors' plot" to poison the leaders of the Soviet state. A number of the doctors named were Jewish; one of the most sinister features of Stalin's last years was an appeal to the latent anti-Semitism among the populations of Eastern Europe.

In short, a new purge comparable to the great terror of 1936–1938 seemed to be threatening. This atmosphere of universal danger was intensified by the grim international outlook. Just as the West was concerned lest the Soviet Union extend the scope of the Korean war to Europe, so Stalin was equally afraid lest the United States pass over to the attack. If the "American imperialists," he reasoned, had gone to war for so little a thing as Korea, what was to prevent them from assaulting the Communist camp in Eastern Europe itself?

The Sequels to the Purge
of the "National" Communists

For the satellite nations of East Central Europe, this threat of war meant the intensification of Soviet pressure to step up heavy industrial production and to postpone still further the adequate provision of consumer goods. It also meant the decline of the Cominform; a process of anticipating Stalin's orders on the part of his satellite lieutenants, or of receiving indirect instructions through the Soviet ambassadors and "advisers" in the Eastern capitals replaced the formal consultations that this body had been intended to provide. Finally, it meant that the purge of leaders suspected of "national" deviations took a new and still more sinister turn.

This second wave of the purge appeared in its most intense form in Czechoslovakia. Between 1950 and 1952, the Czechoslovak Communist party was shaken by the most severe internal crisis that East Central Europe had yet seen. One reputation after another toppled, as accusers followed accused into the defendant's box. When the trials ended—in December, 1952—eleven top leaders were hanged, several of whom were Jews, for the new element in the Czechoslovak purge trials was a scarcely concealed anti-Semitism. Under the transparent euphemism of "cosmopolitan" tendencies, the Jewish Communist leaders of Eastern Europe were systematically accused of sympathy with Israel and with the West.

At the end of 1952 the Cold War reached its climax. Just as nationalist and conservative tendencies were gaining in the West, so in the Soviet sphere the narrowest and most isolationist definitions of communism were in the ascendant. At the very moment that "good Europeans" were losing ground in France and Italy, in the East the mere suspicion of "cosmopolitanism" was becoming sufficient to bring imprisonment and even death. With each month that passed, the two armed camps of divided Europe appeared to be drifting further and further apart. When 1953 opened, it seemed that only a miracle could save the old continent from a new and still more deadly world war.

Readings

On the Cold War itself, there are two general accounts, the first moderately pro-Western in orientation, the second very strongly so: André Fontaine, *History of the Cold War,* 2 vols. (1968, 1969), and John Lukacs, *A History of the Cold War* (1961).

For the individual Western European countries, besides the books by Grosser, Williams, and Hughes (*see* readings for Chapter Fifteen), one may consult the following: Francis Boyd, *British Politics in Transition 1945–63* (1964), and Giuseppe Mammarella, *Italy after Fascism: A Political History 1943–1963* (1964). The series of essays edited by Francis O. Wilcox and H. Field Haviland, Jr., *The Atlantic Community: Progress and Prospects* (1963), traces the growth of the Atlantic idea.

On Eastern Europe, besides Brzezinski (*see* readings for Chapter Fourteen), there are thorough, scholarly essays on Yugoslavia, Poland, and Hungary in the first volume of a collaborative study edited by William E. Griffith: *Communism in Europe: Continuity, Change, and the Sino-Soviet Dispute* (1964).

The Loss of Colonial Empire

Chapter Eighteen

In the fifteen years from 1945 to 1960, the European powers almost completely liquidated their colonial empires. Most of these colonies had been acquired in a mere decade and a half at the end of the nineteenth century and the decisive acts in their liberation came in an equally brief time span. By 1960, nearly all the more important of the formerly colonial areas of Asia and Africa were fully independent, and most of the rest had formal independence scheduled for a very early date. A decade later, colonial rule of the old type lingered on in only a few territories, the greater part of them in sub-Saharan Africa.

In some instances, this process of liberation occurred peacefully. In others, the European powers agreed to retire only after long and bloody wars. But almost everywhere, the departure of the Europeans was forced in one form or other. Only through the steady growth of local nationalist movements were the colonial powers led to realize that their days were numbered, and that it was wiser to grant independence with good grace than to continue a hopeless delaying action.

I

THE SETTING

Asia and Africa in the War Years:
the Loosening of Colonial Ties

In the Middle East, in Africa, and in Southeast Asia, the Second World War had been fought by the Europeans and Japanese with scant regard for the local populations. The major belligerents decided the "natives' "

The king of Laos signs a treaty with France at the Elysée Palace in 1949. President Vincent Auriol, center, looks on. COURTESY PHOTOWORLD, INC.

fate as the necessities of war dictated and rarely troubled to seek out the views of the leaders on the spot. Thus the British brought India into the war without consulting the spokesmen of the Congress party, Gandhi and Nehru. They agreed with the Russians to a joint occupation of the formally independent nation of Iran and, in Egypt, which was also supposed to be independent, they took advantage of their special treaty rights to set up at Cairo and Alexandria their main military bases for the Mediterranean. Nor were the French any more considerate of local feelings. The allegiance of one colony or another to Vichy or to De Gaulle depended almost entirely on the decision of individual French governors or military commanders; in Algeria or Morocco the French were as little concerned with what the local Moslem population thought about the war as the British were in Egypt.

Thus the Asians and Africans of the European colonies lived through the great conflict as passive spectators—except, of course, for those who were recruited into the Indian army, which fought for the British in the Near East, or the French colonial forces, which made so splendid a record in Italy and in the liberation of southern France. But although the colonial peoples were necessarily on the sidelines, they did not fail to see what was happening. The more acute of the local nationalist leaders realized how the war itself had undermined the foundations of colonial rule. The German defeat of France in 1940, and the Japanese defeat of the British and the Dutch in Southeast Asia in 1942, severely damaged the prestige of the European powers. This was particularly true in areas like Burma, Indochina, and Indonesia, where the Japanese were still in possession when the war in the Pacific came to an end. It was also apparent in more remote regions, where the presence of foreign armies—particularly the anticolonialist Americans—shook the local populations out of their age-old lethargy. Almost everywhere a similar lesson applied: after the shocks that the war had administered, colonial authority could never be the same again.

Even before the war ended, the British and French had reached this conclusion about the Arab countries of the Near East. The European conflict hastened the liberation of the territories which France and Britain had received as Class A mandates from the spoils of the Turkish Empire in 1919. Iraq had already achieved its independence from Britain in 1937. The French—after protracted squabbles with the British, whom they feared as postwar rivals in the Levant—in 1945 honored their prewar promise to free Syria and Lebanon. In 1946, the British, not to be outdone, gave independence to the small kingdom of Transjordan, which was enlarged two years later (and renamed Jordan), when it conquered the central part of Palestine that remained outside the new state of Israel. In 1954, with the British agreement to evacuate the Suez Canal Zone within twenty months—and thus to end the indirect control over Egypt which had been crucial during the war years—there disappeared the last traces of European suzerainty over the Arab nations of the Eastern Mediterranean.

The Attitude of the Remaining Colonial Powers:
Assimilation, Commonwealth, and Intransigence

The victors in the First World War had ended the colonial rule of one power, Germany. The victors in the second war similarly reduced the number of their rivals overseas by eliminating Italy. By 1945 there were only five significant colonial powers left: besides the two major nations, Britain and France, three small European countries—Belgium, the Netherlands, and Portugal—retained important holdings in Southeast Asia and Africa.

These five powers varied greatly in their attitude toward colonial rule. In general, the British faced the end of imperialism with the greatest realism and equanimity. Through their formula of a Commonwealth of self-governing dominions, they had developed a framework both for preparing colonial areas for nationhood and for retaining economic and cultural ties with them after their liberation. Nevertheless, the British had reasons for doubt and hesitation. It was not clear whether the Commonwealth formula—which previously had been applied only to areas of European settlement such as Canada and Australia—would work equally well for nations with Asian and African populations and governments. The British were divided, moreover, on the issue of the pace at which liberation should proceed. The Conservatives still had a strong imperialist wing, with which Winston Churchill himself was in sympathy. Indeed, the great war leader had declared quite bluntly that he had no intention of liquidating "His Majesty's Empire." Labor, on the contrary, stood united in its resolution to give independence to the colonies as rapidly as individual circumstances would permit. It was fortunate for the cause of colonial liberation that the British Labor party was governing the country during the decisive postwar years. When the Conservatives returned to power in 1951, their imperialist wing had been much weakened, and it was too late in any case to reverse a process which had by now become irresistible.

France's counterformula for colonial evolution—the assimilation of native elites to French culture—was far less flexible than that of the Commonwealth, for it depended on the actual desire of Asians and Africans to become Frenchmen, and it was incapable of rapid extension to whole populations. Should the majority of natives gain the vote, it would break down completely. This was what in fact happened after 1945. During the war, De Gaulle had promised the colonies which rallied to his Free French movement a democratic suffrage and the reorganization of France's Empire as a "French Union." In subsequent years, the Union proved generally to be a fraud. Although the new French constitution of 1946 provided for consultative institutions for the Empire, these never acquired real power, and the individual territories under French control continued to be governed from Paris much as they had been in the past. Yet the extension of the vote—despite official delays and chicanery—gradually became a reality. Both the Constituent Assemblies of 1945 and 1946 and the regular parliaments which followed them had about eighty overseas deputies, who vigorously defended their constituents' interests and who eventually came to regard themselves as the spokesmen and founders of future nations.

The smaller colonial powers were far less "enlightened" than Britain or France. All three proposed to keep their colonies while making an absolute minimum of concessions. In the case of Portugal, such a policy was practicable: its two vast but undeveloped colonies in Africa—Angola and Mozambique—gave almost no trouble in the postwar years. Initially it appeared that Belgium had the same advantage: the great Belgian colony of the Congo enjoyed an unexampled prosperity during the war and its aftermath—partly owing to the newly discovered importance of its uranium deposits—and its rulers carefully restricted the education of the natives to the essentials of technical training. Not until the very end of the 1950's did the liberation of the Congo suddenly become urgent.

The Dutch, in the Indonesian Archipelago, had one great colony which accounted for much of the wealth and prestige of the home country, but their postwar situation was less fortunate than that of the Belgians. Although they had pursued an equally stern policy of resistance to advances by the native people, they faced circumstances which were much more unfavorable to continued colonial rule. Indonesia was six times as populous as the Congo and infinitely more developed culturally. Furthermore, whereas the Belgian government-in-exile had held possession of the Congo throughout the war, the Dutch had lost Indonesia to the Japanese under humiliating circumstances. At the war's end, it proved impossible for the Netherlands to re-establish its control. The independence of Indonesia was to rank as one of the two key events of the late 1940's which decisively set the colonial world on its new course.

II
THE LIBERATION
OF SOUTHERN ASIA

The British Withdrawal: India, Pakistan, Burma, Ceylon, Malaya

The most important single act in the end of empire was Britain's liberation of India for, with its population of 400 million, India alone had as many people as all the rest of the colonial world together. It was the keystone of British overseas rule—the epitome and symbol of imperial authority.

India, moreover, was better prepared for independence than any other major colony. For half a century the British had been systematically

training its aspiring young men to staff the civil service and the judiciary,
and in the Congress party it possessed a reservoir of talented political
leaders. Although India had taken long strides toward self-government
in the interwar years, this process had not been rapid enough for the
nationalist spokesmen; they rejected the offer of quasi-independence
which Britain made in 1942 and, during the latter part of the war, Nehru
and his colleagues were in jail. When the conflict ended, it was obvious
that the Congress party would be satisfied with nothing less than complete independence.

This the Labor government was resolved to grant. The only obstacle
was the attitude of the Moslem League—the rival of Congress—which
insisted on the establishment of a separate state for India's Moslem
minority. The British were reluctant to do this, since there was no natural way to divide the country and in many areas Moslems and Hindus
lived closely intermingled. But eventually partition became unavoidable:
this crude and unpalatable solution—which had already been applied to
Ireland, which was occurring *de facto* in Germany and Korea, and which
was soon to be extended to Palestine and Indochina—proved to be the
only one possible. In the summer of 1947, India and the Moslem territories which took the name of Pakistan became independent nations
within the Commonwealth. The definition of the Commonwealth was
stretched one step further to permit the two Asian nations to participate
as republics in an institution which necessarily honored a monarch as
its symbolic head.

The island of Ceylon, on achieving independence, likewise chose to
remain within the Commonwealth, but Burma, whose conquest by the
Japanese during the war had decisively broken the tie to Britain, determined to cut the last link. Burma became a neutralist nation, torn by
internal strife during the first years following its independence and precariously poised between India and Communist China. Indeed, throughout Southeast Asia the victory of the Chinese Communists in 1949
brought the threat of extremist insurrections led by influential Chinese
minorities. This happened in Malaya—another dependency of Britain
which had fallen to Japan in 1942; here the British felt obliged to fight
a long and cruel jungle war against Communist guerrillas before they
considered it safe to offer self-government to the peninsula. Yet the
struggle with local Communist subversion could delay but not halt the
process of liberation. In 1957, a pacified Malaya became the fourth independent Asian nation within the Commonwealth.

The Struggle for Indonesia and Indochina

The French and Dutch did not give up their Southeast Asian possessions
so easily. Both Indonesia and Indochina had to fight for their independence against the dogged resistance of stubborn imperialists.

When the Dutch returned to Indonesia after the war, the local nationalists—who had developed their clandestine organizations during the years of Japanese rule—were already in substantial control. The only recourse was to negotiate with them for self-government short of independence. But the negotiations soon broke down, and the former colonial power shifted to an attempt at coercing the nationalists by force. For four years the fighting continued in desultory fashion. Finally, however, the Dutch realized that they lacked the military means to bring the Indonesians to terms. In 1949, Indonesia became an independent nation.

In Indochina the story was much the same, but here the fighting continued longer and the solution was less clear-cut. From the beginning, the situation of Indochina was extremely complex. It alone of the major French colonial territories had remained loyal throughout the war to the Vichy regime and hence neutral in the world conflict. For this reason, it was not until the very end of the war that the Japanese took over formal control. By that time, the clandestine struggle for power had become at least five-sided: besides the Vichy French and the Japanese, there were agents sent out by De Gaulle who were trying to establish their influence in preparation for the hour of victory; there were Chinese infiltrating in the north; and there was the Communist-trained leader Ho Chi Minh, who was organizing the native cadres for a republic of Vietnam in the eastern part of the country. The two western Indochinese protectorates, Cambodia and Laos, remained outside the power struggle.

When the war ended and the Gaullist agents were able to operate freely, their first inclination was to negotiate with Ho Chi Minh, who appeared to be at least partially independent from Moscow control and who was leading a nationalist movement with a broad popular base. This was also the view of the French ministry at home, which invited the Vietnamese leader to Paris for consultations on self-government for Indochina. But while Ho Chi Minh was away in France, a catastrophe occurred: a subordinate French commander precipitated fighting on his own authority. The government in Paris was too weak to resist—by the end of 1946 it had allowed itself to be pushed into war. Thus there was set the dangerous precedent of local French representatives literally blackmailing the more liberal ministries at home into support of their own uncompromising colonial policies.

The war in Indochina dragged on for more than seven years. It became a steadily increasing drain on France's military forces, its economy, and its national morale. In its worst years, it killed more young officers than the French national military academy could produce: for this was a war fought by professional soldiers; it was so unpopular among the French people that the government dared not send conscripts to Asia, as the United States was to do in Korea. It was a war that seemed without end and without possibility of a favorable outcome. As it continued and as the French were obliged to make more and more concessions to

the Indochinese who opposed the authority of Ho Chi Minh, the army
gradually found itself in the paradoxical position of the British in Malaya —fighting a Communist-led national movement in the name of non-Communist native nationalists who also laid claim to independence.

The victory of the Communists in China in 1949 intensified the struggle by providing Ho Chi Minh's forces with a northern supply base similar to that which the Balkan Communist states had offered the Greek insurgents two years earlier. By the same token, it put Ho's movement itself under firmer Communist control. The next year the Korean war broke out—followed in a few months by the intervention of the Chinese. The Chinese intervention at first seemed to improve the outlook for the French struggle in Indochina. It made that conflict a part of the Cold War, as it became apparent that the Communist Chinese were now supporting two parallel threats to Western influence, one on their northern and one on their southern borders. The result was a drastic alteration in American policy toward Indochina. The United States government, which had formerly condemned the French for adhering to a discredited colonialism, now shifted to support of the Indochinese war as a contribution to the joint Western attempt to hold the line against communism.

The change came too late to save the French. Although the American government poured money and supplies into Indochina, the French military position continued to deteriorate. When the Korean war came to an end in 1953, the Communist Chinese were free to increase their pressure toward the south. The Americans, on the contrary, sick of war in Asia, decided not to intervene in Indochina. At this point, the French command committed an act of supreme folly: it threw nearly all its remaining resources into the strong point of Dien Bien Phu near the Chinese border. The Vietnamese and Chinese Communists—fully aware of the fortress' symbolic importance—assaulted it unsparingly. In May, 1954, Dien Bien Phu was overwhelmed—and with it the last hopes of the French in Indochina.

The fall of Dien Bien Phu was the first of the great shocks that were eventually to destroy the Fourth French Republic. It swept into power Pierre Mendès-France, the most talented and courageous of France's political leaders, who had consistently declared that it was necessary for his country to cut its losses and make peace in Indochina (*see* Chapter Nineteen, II). In July, a conference of foreign ministers at Geneva settled the matter by partitioning Vietnam, as Korea had been, along the seventeenth parallel of latitude. To the north, Ho Chi Minh's Communists were to rule. South of the parallel, an independent Vietnam joined the states of Cambodia and Laos, which earlier had been granted their freedom, and these in turn found themselves linked to Burma and Indonesia in a perilous neutrality between East and West. French rule in Asia had come to an end. The renewed war on the part of the United States to preserve the pro-Western regime in South Vietnam still lay in the future.

III

THE AFRICAN AWAKENING

In Africa, the postwar change was even more dramatic than in southern Asia. The independence of the latter area, which had an ancient and advanced culture and strong nationalist movements, could not be denied after 1945; qualified experts had been almost unanimous in predicting what would happen if the Europeans tried to stand against the tide. In Africa, it was quite different. Here the process of liberation surprised the specialists themselves by its swiftness and irreversibility. Most of Africa was far less developed than Asia, and its nationalist movements were infinitely weaker. Once started, however, the drive toward liberation gathered its own momentum; colonial authority began to crumble in places where a decade earlier it had scarcely been questioned. Indeed, the Europeans sometimes seemed to be hustling the African spokesmen themselves toward independence when both sides knew that they were not ready. In this process, as in Asia, the British took the lead, while the French followed more reluctantly.

In 1945, the map of Africa was not much different from what it had been in 1914. Except for the transfer of the former German colonies to British and French tutelage, and the largely theoretical independence of Egypt, almost nothing had changed. The pockets of freedom were the same as they had been in the past—Ethiopia, Liberia, and the white-dominated Union of South Africa. Less than a tenth of the continent was even formally independent. As the 1950's opened, the map was still unaltered, but in the preceding five years pressure had been building behind the torrent which was to come. The independence of Libya in 1951 set the course for a decade of furious movement. By 1960, the colors on the map had been reversed: now only scattered pockets of Africa were neither already free nor well on their way to independence.

The British Example: the Independence of Ghana and Nigeria

The British Labor government had instituted an Africa-wide program of colonial preparation for independence by establishing plans for economic development and systematically turning over authority to native officials, but it was the Conservative ministries of the 1950's which actually presided over the course of liberation. The process began in 1954 with the termination of British treaty rights in Egypt. The logical sequel occurred at the beginning of 1956, with the liberation of the Sudan, which had been under joint British and Egyptian authority. The really decisive event, however—at least for Africa south of the Sahara—was the gaining of independence by the Gold Coast, which in 1957, under the new name of Ghana, became the first purely African nation within the Commonwealth.

The Gold Coast was a natural place to begin: it was prosperous, it was economically developed, and it had almost no European population. Indeed, the fact that West Africa had never been an area of European settlement greatly simplified the problem of its liberation, for the French as well as for the British. It was logical that the next British colony after Ghana to become independent should be the west coast territory of Nigeria—the continent's most populous country—which from the moment of its liberation in 1960 moved into the front rank of African power.

Britain's other West African territories, which were smaller and poorer than Nigeria and Ghana, progressed more slowly toward independence, but their future was no longer in doubt: they soon became African countries ruled by their own black leaders. British East Africa, however, presented a different picture. Here small but influential minorities of European settlers feared the government of native Africans and insisted on retaining their privileges. They had a model of stubbornness in the Union of South Africa, which pursued an unyielding policy of white dominance and strict separation of the races.

From 1952 to 1956, the East African colony of Kenya was torn by bitter racial strife. In protest against the whites' monopoly of the best highland farming country, the secret society of the Mau Mau swore to drive them out by a campaign of systematic terror. Here, as in Malaya, the British could see no alternative to a stern campaign of repression. Once the Mau Mau were beaten, however, the British turned almost immediately to conciliation. The liberation of British East Africa came a few years later than that of the west coast colonies, but the result was much the same. By the mid-1960's, not only Kenya had become independent but also its neighbor Uganda and the former territories of Tanganyika, Nyasaland, and Northern Rhodesia, which took the new names of Tanzania, Malawi, and Zambia. In the early stages of this process there had been talk of multiracial government—as opposed to the rule of the whites in South Africa, on the one hand, and on the other, to the West African formula of an all-black nation. This proved impracticable: those Europeans who chose to remain in the new East African states did so at their own risk and as merely tolerated partners in an economic development geared to the needs of the black majority. The one exception was (formerly Southern) Rhodesia, where the whites were numerous and resolved to maintain their racial supremacy. In 1965, after having rejected a settlement worked out in London that would have extended representation to the blacks by gradual stages, Rhodesia declared its independence, staving off a series of half-hearted British efforts to bring it to heel.

French North Africa and the Algerian War

French postwar policy in Africa made a bad beginning with the repression of two native revolts—a local one in Algeria in 1945 and a far more widespread and serious insurrection on the island of Madagascar two years later. In both cases, the revolts were put down with a brutality which effectively discouraged any further such attempts for another decade. In Algeria, as in Madagascar, the French were extraordinarily successful in keeping news of their operations from the Western press.

France's real difficulties began with the independence of the former Italian colony of Libya in 1951, for the freeing of Libya—the most backward of the five Arab countries on the southern shore of the Mediterranean—not only drew attention to the vestiges of British control in Egypt; it also, and rather more seriously, underlined the dependent position of France's three North African territories—Tunisia, Algeria, and Morocco.

These were the only areas of the continent comparable to South Africa in the extent of their European settlement. There were about 200,000 Europeans in Tunisia, 300,000 in Morocco, and a million—of whom roughly half were of French origin—in Algeria. Of these, the settlers in Tunisia and Morocco created the less serious problem. Besides being fewer in number than the Europeans of Algeria, they had been established on the land for a shorter period, and they were living in a society which even the French recognized as predominantly Moslem in character. Tunisia and Morocco were formally not colonies at all; they were protectorates, still in theory subject to their traditional native rulers, and both had well-organized nationalist movements under leaders who were moderate in temper and oriented toward the West—in Tunisia, the forceful orator Habib Bourguiba, and in Morocco, Sultan Mohammed ben Youssef.

Hence the situation in the two protectorates permitted a comparatively painless ending of imperial rule. After several years of repressive policies, the French struck off on a fresh course under the government of Mendès-France. In the summer of 1954, just after he had liquidated the Indochinese war, the new prime minister made a dramatic trip to Tunisia to begin the process of conciliation. A year later the country became fully self-governing. Meanwhile, in Morocco, however, the conservative predecessors of Mendès-France had made the catastrophic error of deposing the sultan—once more by simply ratifying a *fait accompli* of the French representatives on the spot—and replacing him with his uncle, who they hoped would be more pliable. But the result had been to transform the exiled Mohammed into a popular hero and to unleash a storm of nationalist violence which reached its climax in the late summer of 1955; by autumn, it was apparent that the only solution was the sultan's recall. Once back on his throne, however, Mohammed ben Youssef—soon to become King Mohammed V—would accept nothing less than full independence. On March 2, 1956, Morocco severed its ties with France. Tunisia logically had to follow: later the same month it too achieved nationhood.

Once the process of negotiation had begun, freedom ran a swift course

in the two protectorates. The French were ready for a rapid settlement
with Tunisia and Morocco partly because a major insurrection had broken out in Algeria, the territory which lay between them. Algeria was far more precious and important to France than were its neighbors. It was the chief area of French settlement overseas; indeed, in theory it was not a colony but an integral part of France. It had, however, operated on a double standard of citizenship; both in its economy and in its administration, the European settlers were all-powerful, and these, like the whites of South Africa, regarded themselves as having at least as much right to the country as the native population. Many of them had lived there for three or four generations and considered Algeria rather than France to be their homeland.

When revolt broke out in the autumn of 1954—less than four months after the end of the war in Indochina—the French were in no mood to treat with the rebels. They decided for military repression; and this remained their basic policy for the rest of the decade. The last governments of the Fourth Republic tacked and veered in their attitude toward Algeria; a move toward negotiation was invariably followed by a renewed resort to military action. Whatever the hesitations of the ministries at home, the French in Algeria never wavered: the army and the settlers agreed that the only possible policy was resistance to the last. In one sense, they were right: the negotiation of a solution for Algeria was like trying to square the circle. The rebels in the hills insisted on independence; the local French knew that this would result in a Moslem-ruled country and the end of their privileges. It was not clear how much of the Moslem population actually backed the rebels—the latter did not hesitate to murder and terrorize natives who refused to accept their leadership—but it was quite evident that between the French position and that of the Algerian nationalists there was little middle ground.

Under these circumstances, it soon became apparent that the war in Algeria would be still costlier and more cruel than the struggle for Indochina had been. It lasted longer; it absorbed far more manpower; and it undermined even more disastrously the nation's strength and self-confidence. By 1956, the French had 400,000 troops in Algeria, including the young conscripts who had never gone to Indochina; almost all the divisions assigned to NATO were eventually drained off to service in North Africa. The war these soldiers were called on to fight was a merciless struggle in which the French replied to the bestial cruelty of their adversaries by the use of physical torture in the interrogation of prisoners. Countless young Frenchmen were revolted by what they were forced to witness or participate in; at home the consciences of the intellectuals and the clergy were deeply troubled. The government found no better way to deal with its critics than by a resort to arbitrary arrest and a sporadic censorship of the press. After nearly four years of inconclusive warfare, the long-awaited explosion came: the impasse in Algeria precipitated the fall of the Fourth French Republic and the establishment in its place of a new and more authoritarian regime under General de Gaulle. But even the prestigious general was unable to reach a quick solution. In view of the profound divisions in French opinion at home, it took him nearly four more years to come to an Algerian settlement. The war had dragged on for the better part of a decade when it was finally brought to an end—and on the Moslem rebels' maximum terms. In mid-1962, Algeria became an independent Moslem nation. After a desperate last-ditch uprising against the inevitable in the cities of Algiers and Oran, about three-quarters of the European population of Algeria chose to "return" to France—if such a term could properly be applied to the migration of hundreds of thousands of people who had never before in their lives seen Europe (*see* Chapters Nineteen, II; and Twenty, III).

The French "Community" in Black Africa

South of the Sahara, as if to balance their stubbornness in Algeria, the French pursued a far more conciliatory policy. Indeed, for a year or two they seemed almost to be outstripping the British in their liberality to the black populations of West Africa. First came the enactment of a "framework law" in 1956—which ranked as the only substantial achievement of the Fourth Republic's last phase—granting representative institutions to the twelve West African territories under French rule and to the island of Madagascar. Two years later France made the greatest leap in its history of imperial policy: in the referendum on the new Gaullist constitution, the colonies were given the option of voting either for independence or for the status of an autonomous republic in the "Community" which was to replace the French Empire. Only one—the small territory of Guinea—chose independence. The rest were satisfied with autonomy in the framework of the Community.

Within two years, however, the Community itself was proving to be only a transition phase. By the end of 1960 all the new African republics had successfully negotiated their independence from France and all but one had become members of the United Nations. Of the seventeen states admitted in that year, eleven were former French African colonies. Earlier, a number of the local leaders had discussed West African federation into larger units, but in the end the planned federations either broke down or failed to gain significant powers. As a result several of the new nations found themselves too weak and sparsely populated to function successfully as independent entities.

Thus the French Community experienced a paradoxical fate. From a juridical standpoint, its former constituent parts had less cohesion and less recognition as an international entity than the nations of the Commonwealth. In practical terms, however, most of the former French colonies remained more dependent on the old mother country than did the territories liberated by the British. Their weakness made continuing

European aid a necessity of life, and the French were more generous than the British in supplying civil servants free of charge and in extending economic assistance—indeed in the 1960's France ranked second only to the United States in the aid it gave to the underdeveloped world. Moreover, the continued use of the French language in the administration and the educational systems of the new nations contributed more prestige to the home country than did the prevalence of English elsewhere in Africa; for French was the preserve of France alone, whereas English was rapidly becoming an international language not necessarily associated with the British tradition. Thus the African nations "of French expression," as they termed their cultural affiliation, looked more frequently to France for guidance than their English-speaking counterparts did to Great Britain. Most of them voted with France in the United Nations and lined up on the conservative side in the informal division of African states between the moderate and those oriented to the left.

However favorable such a situation might be for the maintenance of French influence, the proliferation of new sovereign states—the "Balkanization" of the African continent—was of questionable benefit to the Africans themselves. In these unprecedented circumstances, the term "nation" lost its old meaning: boundaries followed the lines of European conquest rather than of tribal divisions, and what national consciousness existed was largely confined to the narrow circles of the educated who monopolized political life. Indeed, a few of the states seemed to depend on little more than the personality of a single political leader to whom they offered a political base. At the same time, old tribal hatreds were constantly threatening to erupt into murderous violence. Friendly observers agreed that Africa needed larger and more logical national groupings, but no one knew how to go about redrawing the map of the continent.

The Independence of the Congo; the Portuguese Possessions

In the climactic year 1960, the former German colonies and French trust territories of Cameroon and Togo also became independent, as did the former Italian colony of Somalia, but the most dramatic and unexpected event of the year was the sudden decision of the Belgian government to liberate the Congo. By none of the usual criteria of nationhood was the Congo ready for independence. Its educated elite was very small, its nationalist movement of recent origin, and it was still riven by tribal antagonisms which threatened to tear the new state apart even before its foundation. But the example of the neighboring French colonies had suddenly galvanized into life its latent hostility to European rule. After the Congo capital had been shaken by nationalist riots in early 1959, the Belgians decided that a gradual approach was no longer possible. They decreed the election of a parliament and the proclamation of independence for June of the next year.

The result was chaos. As the Belgians began to depart, the native Congolese army mutinied and the new government proved unable to enforce its authority. At one point there were three different Congolese leaders competing for authority—and autonomist regimes in two of the Congo states. Through the greater part of the 1960's the country languished in a state of almost incessant civil war.

Beyond the perennial danger of an explosion in the heart of Africa, loomed the whole question of the southern third of the continent, rich in minerals, where European influence was still far from being a spent force. Here Rhodesia and the Union of South Africa remained as bastions of white domination. And here the Portuguese colonies of Angola and Mozambique continued as relics of an earlier era. These were special cases in a number of respects. They were ruled by an authoritarian nation rather than by a democracy; hence, the gap between the practice of government in the colonies and at home did not loom as large as in a state with free institutions. The almost total absence of racial discrimination among the Portuguese, coupled with the unusually strong influence of the Catholic church, had accustomed the natives to a sleepy paternalism. Finally, the Union of South Africa, which favored the status quo in Angola and Mozambique as a buffer against the spread of African nationalism, encouraged Portugal in its retrograde courses. But even here the independence of the neighboring Congo had an unsettling effect. In 1961 a revolt broke out in Angola which continued sporadically through the next decade, obliging the Portuguese government to promise local reform and to maintain 80,000 troops in its African dominions. Old-fashioned colonial rule in the Portuguese colonies might persist for a few more years or decades, but it would not last forever.

IV

THE EFFECTS IN EUROPE

By the 1960's the Europeans faced the prospect of retiring within the old frontiers from which they had set forth so bravely five hundred years before. It was a vast change for the nations of Western Europe, and one to which many people, particularly of the older generation, found it extremely difficult to adjust. For commercial companies and the national economy as a whole, it frequently meant the loss of precious overseas investments. For individuals and corporate groups, such as colonial administrators, financial middlemen, and army officers, it entailed a severe diminution of prestige and income. Besides these there were the settlers and planters who found themselves no longer welcome in the new nations and who returned by the tens of thousands to their unfamiliar home countries. Before 1960, these settlers came mostly from the Netherlands Indies and the former French protectorates of Tunisia and Morocco; they returned embittered by their losses, filling the ears of their

fellow citizens with the tale of their grievances. The Europeans unwill-
ingly repatriated from the colonies swelled the ranks of the remaining
imperialists at home, urging them on to make a final, stubborn stand
against the tide of Asian and African nationalism.

The Last Stand of Imperialism: the Suez Expedition

Thus the loss of the colonies brought a temporary reinforcement to the nationalist Right. In France, the two hopeless imperial struggles which between them spanned virtually the entire postwar era—the Indochinese war and the Algerian insurrection—reduced the army to a state of intense frustration: it felt betrayed by the politicians at home, who had given it inadequate support, and it resolved to accept no more humiliations and defeats.

In Britain, the imperialists were concentrated in the Conservative party and had considerable influence on the new prime minister, Anthony Eden, who in the spring of 1955 took over from the eighty-year-old Churchill. The Conservatives faithfully carried out their pledge of the year before to evacuate the Suez Canal, but they were outraged when the Egyptian nationalist leader, Gamal Abdel Nasser, seized possession of the canal itself from its European stockholders. They resolved to punish Nasser and to check the spread of extremist nationalism through-out the Arab world. The French were glad to cooperate in a joint ven-ture: they knew that Egypt was giving both moral and material help to the Algerian insurrection, and they hoped that by cutting off the in-surgents' source of supplies, they could begin to reduce them to terms.

On November 5, 1956, a British and French parachute attack swooped down on the Suez Canal. The expeditionary force suffered minimal casualties, and it seemed that nothing could stop its march on Cairo. But in the meantime worldwide indignation had been gathering. The British and French had let the best occasion for intervention slip by: they had not acted in September, when irritation against Nasser's move had been nearly universal, but had waited until mid-autumn, when the canal was functioning normally again, and Western European ships were passing freely. What had triggered the British and French action had been secret information that the Israeli government was planning its own attack on the Sinai Peninsula.

Even then, however, Eden and his associates across the Channel let precious days slip by. On October 29 the Israeli invasion began. Two days later the Anglo-French air force went into action against the canal. Nearly a week more passed before the parachute landings came. The date of the attack itself—one day before the presidential election in the United States—seemed a little too cleverly calculated to take advantage of a temporary paralysis in American policy. Meanwhile, the Soviet Union had sent an ultimatum calling on France, Britain, and Israel to desist from the attack.

Faced by complete lack of support from the United States and by the condemnation of a crushing majority in the United Nations, Eden and his French partners were obliged to retreat. A special United Nations police force replaced the Anglo-French expeditionary command in the canal zone. By the end of December, the final contingents of the invasion army had sailed for home.

The Suez Expedition was the last stand of old-fashioned imperialism. It surprised its own sponsors by the vehement reaction it provoked, creating overnight a solid front of opposition among the Asian and African nations. Suez showed that never again could Europeans coerce "natives" in the old manner. But the Suez incident was an episode, rather than a genuine reversal, in the process of freeing the colonies. Once its lesson had been digested, the course of liberation was resumed, and at a still swifter tempo.

The Economic Consequences: Oil and Prosperity

Even from Asia, however, the Europeans had not completely withdrawn their influence. The chief remaining area of imperial control was the Persian Gulf, where Britain still "protected" a number of sheikdoms with fabulously rich sources of oil. By the 1960's, oil represented the last great overseas investment of the Europeans, but even here conditions were slowly changing: Italy, which had been despoiled of its colonies, was successfully undercutting the established oil-exploiting nations by offering Middle Eastern governments far more favorable terms. The time was not far off when native rulers would be masters in their own lands again, and in control of oil resources.

Most Europeans believed that the continued exploitation of oil in the Middle East was essential to their prosperity. But economists were beginning to doubt this and advanced the persuasive argument that the enormous profits of European oil companies in Asia did not really benefit the economies at home, since they merely represented a higher price charged to the consumer. This, in broader terms, was true of colonial exploitation as a whole: *under contemporary conditions*, it enriched the small group of Europeans with investments or well-paid positions overseas while scarcely affecting at all the majority of the home population. In fact, it was beginning to be apparent that colonies no longer even paid for themselves—they were a drain on the European nations rather than a source of profit. The most telling case in point was the contrast between France and Germany: France, which had tried to retain its colonies, had lagged behind in economic progress; Germany, which had lost its colonies a generation earlier, had experienced a great industrial boom. By 1953, when Europe as a whole entered on a period of general prosperity, it was becoming obvious that the end of empire was a source of benefit rather than of loss to the economic expansion and social welfare of the old Continent.

Readings

Perhaps the most useful general introduction to the whole subject of colonial liberation is John Strachey, *The End of Empire* (1960), which deals more particularly with the British withdrawal from India. The two French colonial wars of the postwar era are analyzed in a critical vein by Ellen Hammer, *The Struggle for Indochina* (1954), and by Richard and Joan Brace, *Ordeal in Algeria* (1960).

On the emerging nations of Black Africa, one may consult the following: Robert I. Rotberg, *A Political History of Tropical Africa* (1965); Ruth Schachter Morgenthau, *Political Parties in French-Speaking West Africa* (1964); Richard Adloff, *West Africa: The French-Speaking Nations, Yesterday and Today* (1965); and Crawford Young, *Politics in the Congo: Decolonization and Independence* (1965).

For a spirited, scholarly, and highly critical account of the Suez expedition, see Hugh Thomas, *Suez* (1967).

Europe

Its Own Master,
Chapter Nineteen

1953-1960

I

THE CHANGE IN THE
INTERNATIONAL CLIMATE

The Relaxation of the Cold War

In the first eight months of the year 1953 there occurred four events whose joint effect was to reduce the international tension that in the previous half-decade had seemed to be mounting inexorably: Eisenhower replaced Truman in the American presidency; Stalin died; the Korean war came to an end; and the Soviet Union announced that it had perfected a hydrogen bomb. Once more Europe reached a turning point such as it had experienced in 1947 with the beginning of the Cold War, and in 1950 with the outbreak of the conflict in Korea. The events of 1953 did not end the international struggle between East and West—but they notably changed its character, adding to the previous exclusive concentration on preparing for war an alternative vista of peaceful "coexistence." This was what the neutralist states, the dissident Communist regimes in Eastern Europe, and the Socialist opposition parties in the West all wanted—and with them the vast mass of inarticulate public sentiment on both sides of the ideological divide.

The advent of the Republicans to power in the United States meant the rule of a party which was more detached from European concerns than the Democrats had been. President Eisenhower and Secretary of

A sniper looks down on a body lying in the street in Budapest during the Hungarian uprising of 1956. COURTESY BLACK STAR.

State John Foster Dulles were less understanding and sympathetic with the Europeans than were Truman and Acheson—indeed, Dulles aroused hostility nearly everywhere—but the result was the beginning of a "salutary neglect" of Europe by the United States and a new feeling of independence on the part of the Europeans. With the departure of an American administration which they had liked and trusted, European statesmen became more inclined to go their own way. They no longer deferred, as they had in the past, to the wishes of their great ally across the Atlantic. By the late 1950's, it was becoming apparent that the postwar subordination of the old Continent to America was ending and the Europeans were once more masters in their own house.

Moreover, Eisenhower and Dulles were able to accomplish what the Democrats could have managed only with the greatest difficulty—to make a compromise peace in Korea. The end of the Korean war in July eliminated the most serious single threat to the delicate international balance. It also meant that the American master demagogue, Senator Joseph McCarthy of Wisconsin, no longer enjoyed the vast unofficial power as self-appointed prosecutor of "traitors" which he had wielded during the years of the Korean conflict. With the coming of peace and the lifting of the national atmosphere of tension and frustration which had favored his rise, McCarthy began to lose influence; within another year his power had been completely broken. This also was reassuring to the Europeans, who had feared that McCarthy might be leading America to a new home-grown fascism.

Stalin's death brought to power in the Soviet Union younger leaders who were aiming at a "thaw" both in the international climate and in the dictatorship at home. In the succeeding years, this thaw progressed most unevenly: it was subject to sharp checks and reversals of course, particularly in the years 1956 and 1960. For Europe as a whole, however, the effects of the Soviet thaw were cumulative; by and large, the danger of war receded as the decade wore on. And—paradoxically enough—such also was the effect of the Soviet Union's announcement, in the very month following the Korean peace, that it possessed the secret of the hydrogen bomb. This did not make Europeans more nervous, as Russia's explosion of its first atomic bomb four years earlier had done. Rather it made them realize that the "balance of terror" was now complete—the United States no longer held a decisive lead in weapons and the preservation of the peace had become more urgent than ever.

The Failure of EDC
and the "Summit" Meeting of 1955

It was in this atmosphere of relaxed tension that in August, 1954, the French National Assembly, after more than two years' delay, finally voted on the treaty establishing the six-nation European Defense Community. Nearly everything had changed since the treaty was signed; the wartime

urgency which had originally stimulated it had now passed. The Korean
war was over and only the month before, Prime Minister Mendès-France had brought to an end the eight-year struggle in Indochina. The cause of EDC had become hopeless: Mendès-France simply laid it before the Assembly and without expressing his own opinion allowed the treaty to go down to defeat.

Next autumn the Western European powers contrived a substitute. Exhuming an almost forgotten five-nation treaty which had been signed in Brussels in 1948, they added Italy as well as Germany to the signatories—thereby reassuring the French, who felt they needed reinforcement against German influence in an international military force. The new treaty of 1954 did not organize an international army on the model of the EDC; it merely established within the framework of NATO —which Western Germany had joined in 1952—an inner circle to serve as a holding company for the German military contribution. Indeed, German rearmament materialized after the great pressure for it had already passed. Germany entered NATO just at the time that organization itself was beginning a long process of re-examining its basic assumptions. With the balance of nuclear terror now complete, the old concept of a defense of the West by conventional ground divisions was becoming obsolete, and the strategic substitute for it was far from clear.

The summer following the defeat of EDC saw the decade's most dramatic display of the new international atmosphere—the meeting at Geneva of the "Big Four." This "summit" meeting reached no tangible decisions, but it was the first time since the Potsdam Conference of ten years before that the leaders of the United States and the Soviet Union had come together. To Europeans, the mere fact that President Eisenhower and the new master of Russia, Nikita Khrushchev, had actually spoken with each other in an amicable fashion seemed to give a tenuous guarantee of peace. It was widely believed that the two leaders of the supernations had exchanged tacit pledges that so long as they were in power the Cold War would not be pushed to a final decision.

Hence in the mid-1950's Europe began to turn in on itself and to occupy itself with its own concerns. In 1953 and 1954, the economic boom, which previously had been restricted to Germany, spread to Britain and France and Italy. This in itself was a powerful incentive for concentrating energies at home. Another was the loss of colonial empire: except for France and Britain's desperate gamble at Suez and the running sore of the conflict in Algeria, the main trend of the decade was toward liquidating overseas commitments. The thaw in the East, moreover, was at last making possible a limited amount of cultural exchange between the Communist and the Western democratic world. This also strengthened the notion of Europe for Europeans—raising the hope that the sorely tried Continent, which had been torn by two fratricidal wars and a postwar ideological split that was very nearly as bitter, might finally recover its old cultural unity and with it its old self-confidence.

II

WESTERN EUROPEAN DEMOCRACY

In Western Europe, the years from 1953 to 1960 saw a reinforcement of the previous trend toward conservative government. By the end of the decade, the Socialist opposition parties were weaker than they had been for nearly a generation, and they were beginning to wonder whether they would ever again win a major election. Hence the dominance of the conservatives was far from being an unqualified benefit to Western European democracy. It suggested stability, it was true, and it expressed the satisfaction of material prosperity, but this satisfaction also meant complacency and absorption with private concerns. It carried one step further the public apathy and the drift away from political interests which had already begun to characterize the late 1940's. At the end of the 1950's, both Germany and France were living under "father figures" who lulled the electorate into a sense of security by keeping controversial issues from public discussion—in Germany, Konrad Adenauer, whose more than ten years of rule had profoundly altered the original intentions of the constitution makers at Bonn; in France, Charles de Gaulle, whose return to power had ended one French regime and installed another which was far more authoritarian in tendency.

Britain: the Churchill, Eden,
and Macmillan Governments

The return of the British Conservatives to power at the end of 1951 did not mean abandonment of Labor's postwar reforms. On the contrary, the Tories were emphatic in their claim to being a conservative party which was fully abreast of the times, and their chief spokesman for domestic affairs, R. A. Butler, proudly asserted: "The Welfare State is as much our creation as it is that of the Socialists." Gone were the days of a narrow businessman's party led by men like Baldwin and Chamberlain. In returning British Conservatism to the leadership of aristocrats, Churchill had broadened rather than narrowed its base, restoring its feeling for the interests of all classes of the population.

As prime minister from 1951 to 1955, Churchill limited himself to ending Labor's nationalization of steel and of inland transport and to reducing the expenses of the National Health Service by instituting a few relatively minor fees. In short, he and his colleagues behaved like responsible conservatives, rather than reactionaries, in accepting the great change which had gone before, while lopping off its more extreme features and improving its administration. They won back the confidence of the middle-class citizens who had deserted them in 1945 by ending the "austerity" and the war-born controls over economic life which Labor had prolonged beyond their period of maximum usefulness.

This return of the middle-class electorate to the Conservatives became amply apparent in the sudden and unexpected parliamentary election held in May, 1955. Although the previous parliament had still more than a year of life, the new prime minister, Anthony Eden—who after a decade of serving as Churchill's heir apparent, had finally come into his inheritance—decided to reinforce his slim majority. His calculation proved correct: the first real prosperity that Britain had known since 1914 brought votes to the party in power. The Conservatives returned 345 members of parliament to 277 for Labor, thereby securing a comfortable majority for the next half-decade.

Within less than eighteen months, however, they involved themselves in a major crisis. The Suez Expedition of November, 1956, brought down on Eden not only the condemnation of a majority within the United Nations but also the vehement opposition of the British Labor party. As the storm broke over his head, Eden's health collapsed; his failure at Suez ended his prime ministership, and he was obliged to give way to another protégé of Churchill, Harold Macmillan.

Macmillan, who was not an aristocrat like Churchill and Eden, but the heir of a Scottish publishing family with strong American ties, was exactly the leader the Tories' embarrassing situation demanded. Astute, tactful, calm in crisis—"unflappable," as his admirers called him—and possessing the confidence of all wings of the Conservative party, he was able to soothe the feelings of the die-hard imperialists, who were outraged by the withdrawal of the expeditionary force from Suez, while at the same time assuring the outside world and the moderate majority among his followers that he would embark on no more such adventures. In short, Macmillan healed the wounds of Suez in an astonishingly brief time and restored the Conservatives' unity and self-confidence for the political battles that lay ahead.

Within three years they were ready once more to risk an early election. This time they succeeded even more brilliantly than in 1955: in the election of October, 1959, Labor was totally overwhelmed; the Conservatives increased their majority once again, scoring their greatest popular triumph since their landslide victory of 1935. For the Labor party the electoral results came as a shattering blow. It was the third successive election in which they had been beaten, and the fourth in which they had lost seats—a situation almost without precedent in British parliamentary history.

Labor's 1959 defeat precipitated a major battle within the party. It called into question the moderate attitude of Hugh Gaitskell—who had replaced Clement Attlee as party leader after the 1955 election—which had reduced the traditional emphasis on nationalization and other socialist measures and differed only in detail from the Conservative foreign policy of reliance on the United States and nuclear deterrence. Labor's left wing was weakened by the death of its leader, Aneurin Bevan. Bevan's followers, however, were growing increasingly militant: in the course of the year 1960, there began to gather a ground swell of protest against Gaitskell's "me-too" political strategy, coupled with vociferous demands for Britain's renunciation of nuclear weapons.

Germany: the Adenauer System

In Western Germany also, the party in power reinforced its control in the late 1950's. Chancellor Adenauer's Christian Democrats—whose basic conservatism was by now quite apparent—in the election of 1957 once more increased their vote, receiving for the first time a clear popular majority. Like the Tories in Britain, German Christian Democracy had won three successive elections, each time raising its percentage of the national total.

Defeated in 1949 and 1953, and now once again in 1957, the Social Democratic opposition in Germany confronted the same necessity of re-examining its position as faced the British Labor party. Yet the German Socialists did not have quite so much reason for discouragement as their British counterparts. In 1957, they actually increased their vote; Adenauer's gains were not at their expense but at that of the minor right-wing parties, whose following Christian Democracy gradually absorbed as its conservatism deepened and Germany came closer to a two-party system. Hence the internal criticism within German Socialism took a rather different course from what it did in Britain: it concentrated on the routine leadership of Erich Ollenhauer, who had succeeded Schumacher on the latter's death in 1952, and on the party's tendency to continue its mechanical repetition of outworn Marxist slogans. In its new program voted in November, 1959, the party all but discarded its Marxist inheritance, reducing its emphasis on nationalization, accepting the re-militarization of the country, and renouncing the notion of class warfare as the basis of Social Democratic policy. The following year, the dynamic young mayor of West Berlin, Willy Brandt, replaced Ollenhauer as the party's official candidate for the chancellorship.

In this fashion, the German Social Democrats tried to accommodate themselves to the realities of life in postwar Germany. Two of these realities were basic: the Christian Democrats owed their long tenure of office first to the prosperity of the country, which initially had been restricted to the well-to-do but in which, by the mid-1950's, nearly all classes of the population were beginning to share; second, to the personality and influence of Chancellor Adenauer, particularly in the realm of foreign affairs. The Christian Democratic victories of 1953 and 1957 were endorsements of the laissez faire economic policy of the minister of economics, Ludwig Erhard, whose corpulent joviality expressed to perfec-

tion the joys of material prosperity; the electoral triumphs also amounted
to personal plebiscites on the rule of the old chancellor.

On passing his eightieth birthday, Adenauer did not retire, as Churchill had done. He continued to govern and to tower over his ministerial colleagues by his long experience, his indomitable will, and his vast prestige both at home and abroad. Not since Bismarck had a single individual so completely dominated a free German society. Adenauer's long rule began to alter profoundly the workings of the Bonn constitution: in place of a true parliamentary or cabinet system, it substituted the government of one outstanding personality which reduced the ministers to clerks and the opposition to impotent frustration. In this situation, the Bundestag became less and less important; the realities of power in Germany were more and more concentrated in the hands of a bureaucracy responsible in the final reckoning to the chancellor alone.

Meanwhile, Germany continued to be divided between East and West. As long as this was true, foreign policy necessarily dominated public discussion. In the diplomatic realm, Chancellor Adenauer—reinforced by the success of his party's policy at home—operated virtually as he chose. Like almost all other Germans, Adenauer refused to accept the partition of his country, but his attitude toward the Communist regime in Eastern Germany was so uncompromising that in effect it prolonged the East-West split. By insisting on free elections throughout the country—a position which the East German government and its Soviet sponsors could not possibly accept—the West German chancellor blocked any negotiated solution.

Italy: Christian Democracy in Flux

In Italy, as in Germany, the Christian Democrats maintained themselves in power throughout the 1950's and, as with the German party, their basic conservatism generally increased. But the Italian situation lacked the stability of the German. There was no unquestioned national leader: after De Gasperi's retirement in 1953, no single dominating figure emerged from the Christian Democrats' ranks. Furthermore, Christian Democracy was unable to regain the majority position in the Chamber of Deputies which it had temporarily won in the dramatic electoral battle of 1948. Ten years later, it reconquered some of the ground lost in 1953, but the election of 1958 still left the party obliged to find parliamentary allies to assure its tenure of power.

Thus Italy was in the paradoxical position of having a single party which was far stronger than all its rivals and which was alone able to supply a prime minister, but which at the same time was too weak to govern by itself and was profoundly divided by internal factionalism. In the seven years following De Gasperi's retirement, six prime ministers followed each other in office at approximately yearly intervals. They came from the left, the right, and the center of Christian Democracy's ranks. Sometimes they tried to govern in alliance with the smaller democratic parties, as De Gasperi had usually done; more often they acted alone as a single-party ministry dependent on the benevolence of a Chamber of Deputies in which they lacked a majority but which could offer no substitute for them. They experimented with all possible formulas of government and succeeded with none; no ministry lasted as long as two years.

The result was a situation of permanent flux underlying the apparent stability provided by the continued rule of the same party. As the 1950's wore on, Italian political life became increasingly concentrated within the confines of Christian Democracy itself. The real decisions in Italian politics were made not in the public competition among the parties but in the private factional squabbles of the governing group. These factions were legion. Two attitudes, however, dominated the rest and Christian Democracy would eventually be forced to make a choice between them. The most dynamic figure within the party, Amintore Fanfani, argued for an "opening to the Left" and a reinvigoration of social and economic reform. This viewpoint took on added cogency in the autumn of 1956, when —as a result of vast disturbances in Eastern Europe—Pietro Nenni led his Socialist party away from its alliance with communism. The growing strength of democratic forces within Italian majority Socialism—and its renewed understanding with the minority Social Democrats who had split off from it nearly a decade before—made two important changes in Italian politics: it meant that now there was another democratic party besides Christian Democracy which could make a real showing in an election; it also offered the Christian Democrats the possibility of a parliamentary alliance with a party which ranked third in strength in the country and which could give it a secure majority for a left-center reform program.

Christian Democracy's powerful backers, both in economic life and in the church, effectively vetoed Fanfani's idea of an "opening to the Left." Instead, they favored the other major tendency within the party, that of the Christian Democratic right wing, which preferred to govern without declared allies, but rather to accept the votes of the two reactionary parties, the Monarchists and the Neo-Fascists, to complete its majority. These latter were too weak to demand ministerial posts in return for their support. As a reward for their votes, they received the assurance that the government would continue its do-nothing attitude in economic and social policy.

By the summer of 1960 the influence of these reactionary forces had begun to threaten Italian democracy itself. The government's tolerance for neofascism and its preference for authoritarian solutions were becoming a public scandal. In July a series of left-wing demonstrations—which revived the memory of the wartime Resistance—brought about the ministry's fall. For the first time in twelve years a near-revolutionary atmosphere enveloped the country. In this crisis, the Christian Democrats and

the other democratic elements of the Center closed ranks. Fanfani put
together a new government in which three former prime ministers shared power with him. Such a ministry of "national concentration" actually settled nothing. It was no more than a temporary expedient—derived from French parliamentary experience—to tide over a grave emergency.

In the late 1950's, the winds of change were already blowing strongly through Italian political life. But the ruling party was still standing firmly against them. It was becoming ever more clerical and obscurantist, and it had almost forgotten its original goal of combining Christian values with moderate reform and a sturdy insistence on its independence from external direction of all sorts.

France: the Decay of the Fourth Republic;
Mendès-France and Mollet

While parliamentary conservatism was consolidating its position in Britain, West Germany, and Italy, in France the parliamentary system itself was going into a steady decline. The four years of the decay of the Fourth Republic, from mid-1954 to mid-1958, opened with one great crisis of confidence and closed with another. Between lay two abortive efforts at revival.

The fall of Dien Bien Phu and the collapse of the French position in Indochina inaugurated France's time of troubles. But it also brought to power Pierre Mendès-France, a statesman who had the courage to face at last the major international and colonial issues whose constant postponement had been poisoning the country's political life. The new prime minister liquidated the war in Asia and the EDC, and he began the process of conciliation with the North African protectorates; yet his real concern was not for foreign affairs at all, but for France's domestic welfare. His great goal was to modernize the French economy, to lift its retrograde sectors in agriculture and small industry to the level attained by the more advanced of the country's enterprises in the postwar years. The irony of Mendès-France's prime ministry was that during six of his seven months in office he was compelled to concentrate on diplomatic and imperial concerns which he believed to be secondary; he had scarcely turned his attention to his plans for economic modernization, when a motley coalition of his enemies—who hated him as a reformer, a Jew, and the "gravedigger" of the Empire and the EDC—brought him down.

With the fall of Mendès-France in February, 1955, French politics returned to the old game of compromise and delay, as the Moslem revolt in Algeria widened its scope. Parliamentary elections were due the following year, however, and these provided an opportunity for a second attempt to revive the country's energies. In preparation for the election of 1956, the reforming wing of the Radical party which followed Mendès-France made a coalition with the Socialists, who saw in this alliance an opportunity to recoup the losses they had suffered in the conservative electoral victory of five years earlier. The joint campaign conducted by Mendès-France and the Socialist leader, Guy Mollet, had something in it of the old Resistance spirit of social and moral reinvigoration on the democratic Left; it promised both reform at home and peace in Algeria.

In the election of January, 1956, this left-center coalition made the greatest gains. Hence it was logical that it be asked to form the government and that Guy Mollet, as the leader of the largest group within it, should become prime minister, with Mendès-France as his deputy. But the Mollet ministry proved itself unable either to revive the democratic Left or to carry out the program on which its supporters had campaigned. It had scarcely been installed in office when it was overwhelmed by reactionary pressure. On the one hand, a new party of authoritarian rowdies—a protest party of small tradesmen and peasants led by the demagogue Pierre Poujade, which had surprised everyone by electing more than fifty deputies—kept the Assembly in an uproar by its incessant tumult and obstruction. At the same time, the Algerian French resolved to block all plans for conciliation with the rebels. When the new prime minister visited Algiers in February, he was greeted by catcalls and rotten fruit from an angry mob; appalled by his experience, Mollet quickly abandoned the notion of a new departure in Algerian policy.

For the next fifteen months, then, France witnessed the extraordinary spectacle of a Socialist prime minister conducting a colonial war of repression. The Right was satisfied to have Mollet stay in office; it was far more convenient to allow the democratic Left to bear the onus of a reactionary policy rather than to apply that policy themselves. But Mendès-France could not stomach his colleague's actions; in May, he resigned in disgust. The idealists in the Socialist party became increasingly restive and several outstanding individuals withdrew or were expelled from its parliamentary group. In the autumn came the Suez Expedition—here once again Mollet was content to follow the lead of the imperialists. This travesty of a Socialist government eventually became the longest lived of all the Fourth Republic's ministries: with the support of the democratic Left and the tolerance of the Right, it had few declared enemies besides the Communists. But in the spring of 1957, when the government finally took up the task of revising the tax system in favor of the less prosperous classes, the conservatives decided that the time had come: they overthrew Mollet—and with him the last ministry of the Fourth Republic worthy of the name.

The last year of the regime was merely a long death agony. Mollet's two successors were young men of promise but little stature, who were chosen because neither had yet had time to offend anyone and because the more experienced statesmen were reluctant to accept the post. After eight months of walking a tightrope at home and trying to combine military action with half-hearted efforts at reform in Algeria, the government finally blundered into a major crisis. In February, 1958, a local commander, acting (in the now familiar pattern) on his own authority, bombed the Tunisian frontier town of Sakhiet, which was serving as a protected base for the Algerian insurgents. Once again, as at the time of the Suez incident, the Asians and Africans within the United Nations set up a great cry of indignation. The United States and Britain, in order to save something from the debacle, tried to serve as mediators between the French and the outraged Tunisians; but the Anglo-American "good offices" wounded the susceptibilities of the French Right. In April, the nationalists and conservatives brought down the last government of the Fourth Republic.

At this point a respected MRP leader, Pierre Pflimlin, tried to organize a ministry which would pursue a more coherent course. Rumors began to reach Algiers that Pflimlin intended to appoint a minister for Algerian affairs who was known to favor conciliation. This was more than the French settlers would endure. On May 13, a loose coalition of semifascist groups, acting in understanding with the local army command, seized control of the Algerian administration. Two years before, when Mollet had bowed to mob pressure, the Fourth Republic had suffered a shock from which it never recovered. The far more serious demonstration of May, 1958, finally killed it.

France: De Gaulle and the Fifth Republic

The insurrection of May 13 installed in power in Algiers a new and revolutionary authority in competition with the legal government in Paris. The North African "Committee of Public Safety" consisted of resolute and desperate men, both soldiers and civilians, who were determined to impose their own views on the home country. They wanted an authoritarian regime which would call a halt to the steady retreat from overseas dominion.

With the bulk of the French army in North Africa, the Algiers committee had the weight of military strength on its side. It also had many sympathizers in France, among conservatives and nationalists in general and the followers of De Gaulle and Poujade in particular. In contrast, the government in Paris that Pflimlin was trying to establish felt its power slowly slipping away as the month of May wore on, and this steady retreat turned into a rout when it became known that General de Gaulle himself stood ready to form an alternative government.

De Gaulle's candidacy was not what the insurrectionists in Algiers had originally intended; they had hoped for somebody more fascist and less conciliatory toward colonial aspirations for freedom, but they had no particular champion in mind. The Gaullists, on the contrary, knew exactly what they wanted. Once De Gaulle's name was launched by the small group of faithful followers who had remained loyal to him after the dissolution of his Rally of the French People five years before, the idea won favor quickly. Indeed, it soon became apparent that a government headed by the general was the only possible solution. De Gaulle—the liberator of his country—was still the "first citizen of France." His military background and his authoritarian preferences were congenial to the nationalist Right; his Resistance record and his known distaste for the tactics of a coup d'état made him acceptable to most of the democratic Left.

Meantime the insurrection had spread to the island of Corsica and was threatening the French mainland. It was becoming obvious that the army and police force were prepared to do nothing to stop it. On June 1, with a parachute attack impending on the defenseless capital, the French National Assembly bowed to the inevitable and invested De Gaulle as prime minister.

The general's return to power after his twelve years of retirement was, in form, a completely constitutional procedure—but, in fact, it was a revolutionary change imposed by a determined minority on a divided and irresolute majority, and it was so interpreted by both the French people and their elected representatives. As a sign of the gravity of the change, the latter, before disbanding forever, voted full power to De Gaulle's government to rule France as it chose for a period of six months, and to draw up a new constitution for the "Fifth Republic."

By September, the constitution was ready. In a popular referendum, it was accepted by 80 per cent of the French people with only the Communists and a tiny minority of doctrinaire democrats voting against it. Two months later, in elections for a National Assembly, the rightist parties won an overwhelming victory: a new and hastily formed Gaullist party, the Union for the New Republic, placed first; the old Independents of Pinay stood second; together these two secured almost three-quarters of the seats, while all the other parties were reduced to mere splinters. The Communists, handicapped by a new electoral system, fell to ten seats; the Poujadists simply disappeared.

The final act of establishing the new regime was the election of De Gaulle in December as president of the Republic by a specially chosen list of local "notables." The general's move from the prime ministry to what had formerly been a largely ceremonial office betokened the great change in the locus of power that the new constitution had effected. The Fifth Republic was not to be a strictly "presidential" regime like that of the United States. Its constitution provided for a hybrid organization—part presidential and part parliamentary—and it retained a prime minister, who was to be responsible to the Assembly, for the conduct of day-to-day business and for parliamentary liaison. But this Assembly had had its sessions shortened and its powers notably curbed. The weight of influence—which under the Third and Fourth Republics had fallen overwhelmingly toward the legislature—had been shifted to the executive branch and, within the executive, the final power of decision lay with the president rather than with the prime minister.

This, at least, was the way De Gaulle interpreted the new constitution, whose wording was frequently ambiguous. His prime minister, Michel Debré, was likewise content to act as his faithful lieutenant. Moreover, the other ministries, which at the outset were partly filled by leading politicians of the previous regime, one by one passed to technicians and civil servants. Thus the Fifth Republic gradually established its character as the rule of a bureaucracy presided over by a prestigious figure into whose hands a much-tried and much-divided people had delivered its fate.

In foreign and colonial affairs, De Gaulle behaved almost completely as a free agent. He took the conduct of the new "Community" in Black Africa into his own hands, as well as the still-vexed question of Algeria. Here he attempted a double policy: he prosecuted the war with vigor, and at the same time he promised the Algerian Moslems self-government, once he had reached a cease-fire agreement with the rebels in the hills. Against the French Algerian extremists who had originally precipitated his return to power, he took ever-sterner disciplinary action; when in January, 1960, the fanatic fringe of the settlers tried to repeat their successes of 1956 and 1958 by putting up street barricades, he brought them swiftly to terms. For the first time in four years, the government was master in the city of Algiers.

In this emergency, nearly the whole country rallied behind De Gaulle, but his very success in forging national unity against the French Algerian extremists revealed how thorough had been the collapse of political life at home. In the crisis of January, 1960, the general stood alone as his people's sole support. The old parties had been thoroughly demoralized —the Radicals, the Socialists, the MRP were torn between fruitless opposition and passive acceptance of the new order. The one democratic group which frankly opposed De Gaulle—the new Autonomous Socialists —were weak and untried. France was still technically a democracy: the essentials of free speech and free elections remained intact; the Fifth Republic's acts of arbitrary arrest and press censorship were no worse than they had been in the declining days of its predecessor. Yet the life seemed to have gone out of its democratic procedures. The nation was sinking into political torpor and conformity.

Rather than being recognizable as either a democracy or a dictatorship, the new regime began to assume an old-fashioned monarchical character. De Gaulle governed his country as a monarch—remote and benevolent at the same time—refusing to involve himself in the sordid details of politics and administration, but ready to intervene at any time to arbitrate differences among its citizens. It was in this role of national "arbiter" that De Gaulle preferred to regard his own office. He conceived it in such a way because he was interested above all in the "unity" of the people, and he insisted on the unity of the French because he believed that they had always been destined for "greatness"—which was the third of his trinity of central ideas. In pursuit of greatness for his country, De Gaulle sought a more independent French policy within the Western coalition: he protested against the favored position of Britain as the chief ally of the United States; he aligned himself with Chancellor Adenauer, whose position as a national leader in so many ways resembled De Gaulle's own; and early in the year 1960, he exploded an atomic bomb in the Sahara desert, thereby making France the fourth world power to have a nuclear capacity of its own.

Thus De Gaulle's regime presented a puzzling face to the outside world. On the one hand, it had efficiency and the modernization of the country for its objective, taking up the task of national renewal where Mendès-France had been forced to halt a half-decade earlier. On the other hand, the regime looked back to the past—with its notion of "greatness" which recalled an age when the national state was unquestioned and when the French still had the population and resources to play a major role in world affairs. In the 1960's, such a view of the position of any one European nation had become something of an anachronism.

The Neutralist Fringe: Finland and Austria; the Rapacki Plan

Of the twelve democracies of Western Europe, all except Sweden and Switzerland were members of NATO and formed part of the loosely knit ideological coalition of the West. The latter two carried over into the period after 1945 the traditional neutrality which they had preserved so successfully during both World Wars. Their cultural and ideological ties were completely Western, and in a more intangible sense than membership in NATO they also could be counted with the Atlantic Pact nations. Two other democracies, however, which directly bordered on the Soviet sphere, were confined by necessity to a stricter form of neutrality.

The first was Finland. Despite the fact that they had twice been at war with the Soviet Union in the years from 1939 to 1944, the Finns succeeded in keeping free of Russian domination and even in maintaining reasonably cordial relations with their great neighbor in the postwar period. At the same time they preserved their democratic institutions at home, gradually ousting the Communists from the positions of influence in the government and the economy that they had won at the war's end. To outsiders—viewing the fate of the other states of East Central Europe which had passed under the shadow of the Red Army—Finland's continued independence seemed a miracle. In fact, its explanation was comparatively simple. In their dealings with the Russians, the Finns proved themselves both tenacious of their liberty and punctilious in the fulfillment of their reparations and other obligations to the Soviet Union. For their part, the Russians were not sorry to have in the East a "show window" like Finland to display how tolerant they could be when they wished.

Austria was the second special case. In May, 1955, after ten years of four-power occupation, the Austrians won their independence from foreign control. Under the terms of the "State Treaty" signed by representatives of Britain, France, the United States, and the Soviet Union, Austria became, as its neighbor Switzerland had been for generations, a nation whose neutrality was guaranteed by the Great Powers. Within the country, political life proceeded much as before: the government continued to be a coalition of the two major parties—the Catholic People's Party and the Socialists—with the former, which was slightly stronger than its rival, regularly providing the chancellor. The Austrian economy, moreover, which had been so unstable following the First World War, also began to prosper, for with the development of light industry, the country finally found a secure financial base.

The Soviet Union's comparatively benevolent attitude toward Finland and Austria and the success of these two in preserving the essentials of their independence naturally inspired the idea that the same formula might be extended to other nations which lay along the great ideological divide. The most persuasive of such schemes for further neutralization was that of the Polish foreign minister, Adam Rapacki, who proposed the establishment of a nuclear-free zone in Central Europe to include his own country, Czechoslovakia, and both Germanies. The Rapacki Plan— which implied the withdrawal of Western Germany from NATO—was firmly rejected by the United States, and it was far from certain whether the Soviet Union—even in return for the neutralization of Germany— would accept the military loss of its Polish and Czechoslovak satellites. But as the 1960's opened and the nuclear threat became ever more obvious, the idea of a zone of "disengagement" in the middle of Europe was winning favor in the West, not only within the Socialist opposition parties but among wide strata of the inarticulate and unorganized citizenry.

III
THE IBERIAN DICTATORSHIPS

In one area of Western Europe, however, neutralist ideas were strictly banned. This was the Iberian peninsula, where authoritarian conservative regimes continued to exist after the defeat of fascism in the Second World War. Spain and Portugal were obviously not democracies, but in the rhetoric of the Cold War, Western propagandists counted them with the "free world." Portugal ranked as a member of NATO; Spain did not, for anti-Franco sentiment continued sufficiently strong in Britain and Scandinavia to keep the Spaniards from formal membership. But since Franco received military aid from the United States and permitted the establishment of American bases on his country's soil, Spain necessarily became a *de facto* partner in the Western coalition. Both here and in Portugal an uncompromising hostility to communism was one of the major ideological supports on which the regime rested.

By the 1960's, Prime Minister Salazar had become the senior ruler of Europe. He had been in power for more than a generation, longer than any other such dictator in the Continent's history. Yet he remained very little discussed. Quiet, ascetic, scholarly, Salazar hated publicity, and he effectively kept his country out of major ideological controversy during the crucial decade after the war's end.

While maintaining the essentials of his authoritarian control, the Portuguese dictator tried to modify its appearance so as not to offend the sensibilities of his democratic allies. In speaking of their economic institutions, the Portuguese dropped the term *corporate state*—which had a fascist ring—and referred to their *new state* instead. At intervals, moreover, Salazar lifted the censorship of the press and authorized something that resembled a free election. In 1953, the opposition was able to contest municipal elections in the three largest cities, polling 20 per cent of the vote, and again five years later there was a temporary relaxation of control for a presidential election campaign. But these sporadic acts of leniency scarcely changed the nature of the dictatorship. No real political life existed in Portugal. The regime had been in power so long that the political education of the people had never developed—its level was by far the lowest in Western Europe—and the opposition leaders had become elderly, cautious, and out of touch with their prospective constituents. Many were veterans of long jail terms, and occasionally one of them was sent back to prison after an unsuccessful electoral campaign. Still worse, in the spring of 1965 an opposition candidate for the Portuguese presidency was found murdered just across the Spanish frontier. It was only the military—who in the early 1960's attempted three armed coups against the regime—that could even remotely threaten Salazar's authority.

Portugal's greatest difficulties, however, were economic. Despite the stim. lus of indirect state control over the economy through Salazar's corporative institutions, Portuguese industry and agriculture failed to keep pace with the country's needs. The rate of investment remained low: economic expansion was far from adequate to cope with the needs of the nation's population, whose growth was one of the most rapid in Western Europe. As the 1950's passed, poverty and undernourishment became appalling. Salazar was careful to keep the center of Lisbon neat and clean to impress tourists, but elsewhere conditions were so bad that the Catholic hierarchy itself sounded an alarm. In 1954, the archbishop of Beja issued a pastoral letter in which he denounced the growing poverty and the regime's callousness to the misery of its people.

Finally Salazar decided that remedial steps were necessary. In 1955, he launched a five-year development plan. The initial results gave modest reason for encouragement: Portugal equipped itself with a steel industry, and the rate of economic growth began to average 5 per cent a year—which, however, was still far from adequate for a country with about two-fifths of its working population underemployed. Then, just after a second five-year plan had been inaugurated, revolt broke out in the African territory of Angola. Military expenses quadrupled, cutting deeply into funds for economic growth. By the mid-1960's it had become apparent that Portugal's problems were all of a piece: economic sluggishness, authoritarian rule at home, and repression overseas reinforced each other in the dubious legacy of nearly four decades of Salazar's paternalism.

Franco's Spain

In Spain, too, poverty was the central national problem, but Franco was less successful than his neighbor Salazar in keeping such matters from public discussion. Unlike Portugal, Spain was not a backwater protected from the main currents of European life. Its Civil War had made it of crucial interest both to Europeans and to Americans, and in the generation following the war's end Spain was never long absent from news and discussion abroad.

In 1945, many people assumed that the Franco regime would simply disappear, caught up by the same worldwide indignation which had swept away Hitler and Mussolini. Yet Franco did not depart from the scene. He maintained his power and, temporarily at least, even consolidated it. This paradox, which puzzled many Europeans at the time, was the logical result of the Spanish dictator's extremely clever wartime policy.

At the beginning of the war Franco's "nonbelligerence" was distinctly favorable to the fascist rulers of Italy and Germany who had helped him to power. But by the autumn of 1940 he had already become sufficiently skeptical of Hitler's victory to refuse to join him in an attack on Gibraltar. Two years later he took another step away from the Axis by adopting an aloof attitude toward the Anglo-American landings in French North Africa. By the end of the war his neutrality had turned to favor Britain and the United States. Yet this pro-Allied stand was never complete. Franco always made a distinction between the Western powers and their Soviet cobelligerent. He treated the war on the Eastern Front and that in the West as two separate conflicts, and to the German invasion of Russia he even contributed a Spanish "volunteer" division. This uncompromising anti-Soviet attitude at first caused difficulties for Franco with the Western democracies, but once the Cold War began, the Spanish dictator seemed vindicated. Now he needed only to point to his record as an anti-Communist crusader before the rest of the Western world had awakened to its peril.

Thus when the newly formed United Nations decided to quarantine Franco by imposing a partial diplomatic boycott, its effect was merely to reinforce his power: this interference from the outside consolidated Spanish sentiment behind him. The United States, which had never been enthusiastic about the boycott, soon veered to a policy of supporting Franco as a potential ally. By the time of the Korean war the Spanish regime seemed out of danger. During the first half of the 1950's, Franco's authority was secure.

In reality, however, the character of this authority had changed greatly in the years that had passed since the end of the Civil War. The Spanish fascist party, the Falange, which had originally served as the spearhead of the Nationalist coalition, had lost most of its influence; Franco was less and less inclined to play the role of its Caudillo. The old-fashioned conservative forces gained ascendancy, and it gradually became apparent that the Spanish dictator was at least as much their prisoner as he was their leader. Chief among these forces were the interlocking interests represented by the army, the landowners, the monarchists, and the church.

The army, of course, had produced General Franco himself and, like the dictator who had sprung from its midst, the army officers corps had no clear ideology: except for a generalized respect for strong authority, it was interested chiefly in its own privileges. Most of the great landowners were similarly nonpolitical and concerned only with keeping control of their estates. Insofar as they did have a political viewpoint, it tended to be monarchist. Some form of monarchism was the usual ideal of Spanish conservatives and, as the decade of the 1950's wore on, the monarchists became increasingly strong and self-confident. There emerged something resembling a two-party system within the authoritarian framework, as those loyal to the exiled pretender to the throne began to challenge the former political monopoly of the Falange. Even Franco seemed to be moving in that direction. In 1947, he issued an Act of Succession promising in vague terms that on his death or retirement the country would be ruled by a king once more. Seven years later he allowed the monarchists to contest the Madrid municipal elections and, in 1955, the pretender's son, Prince Juan Carlos, was permitted to return to Spain to study.

So far as the church was concerned, although the Civil War had largely been fought to preserve it from harm, its leaders were far from being uniformly satisfied with Franco's course. The Spanish hierarchy had traditionally been ultraconservative, and perhaps the majority of the bishops and archbishops remained in the reactionary mold. Ecclesiastics of this sort inspired the ascetic, semisecret laymen's organization called *Opus Dei* which was able to install a number of its members in high office when Franco reorganized his ministry in 1957. But a growing minority of bishops and priests took quite a different stand, preaching social reform and trying to dissociate themselves from the policies of the regime. The clergy of the Basque provinces were particularly militant;

some even went so far as to side with the workers in the illegal labor demonstrations that marked the decade's end.

At long last the poverty of the Spanish masses was beginning to arouse the conscience of the church. Spain had been ruined by the Civil War. Only help from the United States saved its economy in the postwar years, but this aid, although it stimulated the modernization of Spanish industry and transport, did little to narrow the yawning gap between rich and poor. Generally the rich grew richer and the poor grew poorer. In the big cities, corruption and profiteering were commonplace; in the countryside, misery reached unprecedented depths, as the great estates remained unimproved, and (in terms of buying power) agricultural wages fell. Despite all its propaganda about economic reform, the Franco regime remained anchored in the egoism and lack of business enterprise of the propertied classes.

Yet popular discontent stayed under control. The reasons for this stability were mostly negative. Spain's losses in the Civil War had been so frightful that almost nobody wanted to renew the struggle. Thus throughout the decade 1945–1955 the country was outwardly calm; opposition was restricted to grumbling (which the regime permitted), and although the vast majority of the people were dissatisfied, they remained inert and apathetic. Then suddenly at the end of 1955 a militant opposition flared up: there were strikes in Barcelona and the Basque provinces— the old centers of autonomist sentiment—and in Madrid the university students staged an impressive demonstration in honor of the recently deceased Ortega y Gasset, Spain's most influential thinker and an avowed opponent of the Franco regime; one of the student leaders was the nephew of Lorca, the great poet who had been slain by the Nationalists during the Civil War.

Both among workers and among students the new generation had abruptly and unexpectedly come into its own. The twenty-year-olds, too young to remember the horrors of the Civil War, had revived Spain's languishing political awareness. The police and the law courts bore down on the strikers and students and effectively curbed their unrest. Yet the lesson was already apparent: the trial of the student leaders, who received light sentences, became a courageous condemnation of the whole regime. Franco remained in power; but after 1955 he could never feel entirely secure (see Chapter Twenty, IV).

IV

EASTERN EUROPE AFTER STALIN

The death of Stalin in March, 1953, set in motion a whole series of interlocking changes in Eastern Europe. With the passing of the fearsome old tyrant, it was quite evident that the system of rule which had been so completely associated with his name and personality could not continue unchanged, either in the Soviet Union itself or in the satellite nations. Stalinism as such was no longer practicable, but the new formula which would replace it remained undefined. It required a full five years for the post-Stalinist system to establish itself. Only after the Soviet leadership had passed through five successive phases of adjustment to the realities of the mid-1950's did it reach something approaching a new equilibrium.

Phase One: the Malenkov Era

No single individual could replace Stalin. Obviously the succession would have to be divided among his heirs, and some form of collective rule was the only one possible. In the first post-Stalinist phase, an informal five-man directory governed the Soviet Union. Its members represented the main centers of power in politics and society—Malenkov for the bureaucracy, Molotov (minister of foreign affairs) for the old-line Stalinists, Marshal Bulganin (minister of defense) for the military, Lavrenti Beria for the secret police, and a more obscure figure, Nikita Khrushchev, for the party apparatus. Malenkov seemed to be the dominating figure: since the death of Zhdanov five years before, this pudgy, impassive manipulator had ranked as the closet approximation of an heir apparent to Stalin, and his assumption of the prime ministry suggested that he would take command over his four colleagues.

Within three months, the five-man directory had been reduced by one. In June, the others combined against Beria, stripped him of his authority, and executed him the following December. Beria was the most feared and hated man in the Soviet Union. His fall meant that the secret police was no longer to wield the almost unlimited powers that had made it the nightmare of the Russian people during the last years of Stalin's life. It certainly did not disappear from the Soviet scene—but it resorted less often to arbitrary arrest, and the average Russian citizen became less conscious of its existence. So far as the Soviet directory itself was concerned, moreover, the execution of Beria marked the last time in the decade that a disgraced leader paid for his mistakes with his life. The following years were marked by frequent purges and reorganizations in the Soviet political command; but the purge no longer meant physical extinction—it merely brought demotion and exile to a remote post.

With Beria's downfall, there occurred a number of small but significant changes in the Soviet machinery of control: anti-Semitism was curbed, as the "doctors' plot" which had epitomized the climax of the terror at the end of Stalin's life was revealed to have been a fabrication of the secret police itself; writers and artists were granted more freedom of expression; and conditions in the forced labor camps were slightly improved. Stalin's victims, meanwhile, had decided to test the extent of his successors' lenience. In June there was an uprising in East Berlin and other cities of the German "Democratic" Republic—the first open revolt against Soviet and Communist authority in the satellite world. The following month, a still more unprecedented event occurred: the prisoners in the forced labor camps of Vorkuta, a place of desolation north of the Arctic Circle, overwhelmed their guards and temporarily gained control of the camps.

Malenkov and his colleagues repressed both of these outbreaks by military action, but after the situation was under control again, they continued on their course of cautious retreat from Stalinist practices. More particularly, Malenkov sought to reduce the previous stress on heavy industrial production and preparation for war. Abroad, he relaxed the pressure of Soviet economic exploitation on the satellite states. At home, he shifted the emphasis to providing consumers with the goods they had been denied for so long: the new five-year plan he devised for the period 1956–1960 sought to double Soviet consumption levels, to provide housing for the seventeen million new people who had been added to the population of the Soviet cities during the last half-decade, and to cope with the permanent agricultural crisis by propitiating the peasant masses.

As this program unfolded in the course of the year 1954, the orthodox Stalinists found it too much to swallow and the military were even more recalcitrant. In February, 1955, after the greatest intraparty debate that the Soviet Union had seen for a quarter of a century, Malenkov resigned —alleging, in traditional Communist fashion, his own inability to cope with the problems his partial abandonment of Stalinism had called forth.

Phase Two: the Military Interlude and the Warsaw Pact

In the new directory which followed Malenkov's fall, the military naturally played a prominent role. Marshal Bulganin became prime minister, and Marshal Zhukov, the conqueror of Berlin, emerged from retirement as minister of defense. The influence of the military brought a new shift in economic plans and a return to an emphasis on armaments and heavy industrial equipment.

The major achievements of this change of direction were in relations with the Communist states of East Central Europe. In mid-May, 1955, the satellite nations for the first time were bound together in a formal military alliance with the Soviet Union. The Warsaw Pact, as the alliance was called, was the Eastern response to NATO and more particularly to the Western plans for rearming Germany; it also formalized the Soviet relationship to its satellites in a way which was less humiliating to the governments of East Central Europe than Stalinist practice had been. The Russians remained dominant, but they redefined their tie to their allies to make it appear more like one of equality.

Similarly, the Soviet leaders tried to improve their relations with Tito's Yugoslavia. Yugoslavia did not join the Warsaw Pact; it maintained the neutrality between the two great-power blocs into which it had finally settled in the early 1950's. But two weeks after the signature of the pact, Nikita Khrushchev, whose star was now definitely in the ascendant, journeyed to Belgrade to seek to end the seven-year-old quarrel with Tito. The talks were extremely amicable, and the final communiqué, which spoke of "mutual respect for . . . different forms of socialist [that is, Communist] development," suggested that Tito had been right all along.

Indeed, it appeared that under cover of a temporary alliance with the military, Khrushchev was advancing his own power and was returning to a lenient view of Soviet policy which was not too different from Malenkov's. As first secretary of the Communist Party's Central Committee, Khrushchev occupied the same position which had been Stalin's before the latter's rise to dictatorial authority. It was curious that the parallel did not occur to the other Soviet leaders and put them on their guard. Once more, as had happened a generation earlier, control of the party machinery proved to be the most direct avenue to dominance over the Soviet state. But Khrushchev's advance to power was more humane than Stalin's: he simply pushed his rivals out instead of crushing them completely. In October, 1955, the last of the Old Bolsheviks, Molotov, who had differed with Khrushchev over the reconciliation with Tito, confessed his errors —a sure sign of his impending resignation as foreign minister, which duly followed in summer, 1956.

The demotion of Molotov and the gradual revelation that Bulganin was no more than an imposing figurehead signalized the emergence of Khrushchev as the most important leader in the Soviet Union. This became clear when the new master of the Russians exploded a bombshell which rocked the whole Communist world.

Phase Three: "De-Stalinization"

On February 25, 1956, Khrushchev mounted the rostrum to address the Twentieth Congress of the Communist party of the USSR. With his customary ebullience and self-confidence, the first secretary launched into what gradually unfolded as the most important Communist statement of the postwar period. One by one and with mounting intensity, Khrushchev detailed the "crimes of the Stalin era." His audience followed him with breathless attention, alternately aghast and delighted. No doubt the speaker was carried away by his own eloquence and said rather more than he intended. But there was also calculation in his apparently extemporaneous outburst: all the pent-up hatred and fear of the deceased despot was crying out for expression, and there was no better way for the first secretary to consolidate his authority than by giving voice to it at last. Moreover, Khrushchev evidently hoped to win favor in the West by serving notice that he had definitely departed from the Stalinist path. The central thesis of his long, rambling utterance was that there were several possible ways to reach "socialism" besides that of Communist orthodoxy.

Khrushchev's address was supposed to be kept within party circles, but its text soon leaked out, both to the Communist and to the anti-Communist press. Nearly everywhere, its effects were immediate and thoroughgoing. Within the Soviet Union, it started a new ideological "thaw," of which the comparative leniency of the Malenkov era had given only a foretaste (*see* Chapter Twenty, II). Conditions were notably improved in the forced labor camps, writers and artists were again held in looser rein, and Khrushchev launched a program of cultural exchange with the West which included a number of official visits of his own. In the ranks of the foreign Communist parties, the "de-Stalinization" policy produced a minor earthquake. The hardened and experienced leaders whom the late dictator had promoted to power felt the ground trembling beneath them. The more patriotic and "liberal" Communists who had come to the fore during the wartime Resistance period raised their heads once more. Both in the Communist parties of the West and in those of the satellite states the most intoxicating perspectives seemed to be opening. Freedom from Soviet dominance was one aspiration, liberalization of the Stalinist ideological discipline another. All through the spring and summer of 1956 a vast soul-searching and examination of conscience within the Communist world mounted in intensity. Then in the autumn the explosion came.

Phase Four: the Polish "October"
and the Hungarian Revolution

This post-Stalinist ferment reached the highest pitch in Poland and Hungary. Along with Czechoslovakia, these were the most industrialized and Western-oriented of the Soviet satellites. Czechoslovakia differed from its two immediate neighbors in having a pro-Russian tradition and a Communist party which had purged itself of deviationists more thoroughly than any other during Stalin's last years. Poland and Hungary, on the contrary, cherished bitter memories of hostility to Russia, and their Communist parties harbored leaders who stood ready to guide them toward a new course.

In Poland there was Wladislaw Gomulka, the only major "national" Communist to survive Stalin's final purge. In Hungary there was Imre Nagy,* a comparative liberal and humanist in communism's ranks, who had served as prime minister in the Malenkov era and had left good memories behind him. In both countries, hope for a change from rigid Stalinist direction centered on a single individual, who soon became a symbol of the most varied aspirations for a freer life. These aspirations found their chief vehicle of expression in literary discussion groups which sprang up in the wake of Khrushchev's February speech and which soon entered into contact with the more articulate urban workers. In the spring and summer of 1956, Hungary's and Poland's courses ran

* Not to be confused with Ferenc Nagy, the Small-Holder prime minister in the period 1945–1947.

parallel. Not until the autumn did they diverge, the one to end in tragedy, the other in a cautious advance toward more liberal goals.

The signs of change first became evident in Poland. At the end of 1954, Gomulka had quietly been released from prison, and his ideas soon began to spread among the intermediate echelons of the Communist party. Then in June, 1956, a workers' uprising at Poznan (the former Prussian city of Posen) showed that the grip of the Polish Stalinists was weakening, and that a relaxation of discipline over both factory and intellectual life was becoming imperative. As the summer wore on, and as the talk in the discussion groups waxed bolder, the Stalinist leaders were forced out one by one. In early October, the last important one resigned; less than a week later, Gomulka, for the first time since his disgrace, attended a meeting of the Politburo, which he clearly intended to dominate. Faced with the prospect of a Gomulkaist Poland, the Russians took alarm. On October 19, a delegation of the major Soviet leaders, headed by Khrushchev, flew unexpectedly into Warsaw. Their arrival was accompanied by menacing Red Army troop movements toward the Polish capital. But though Khrushchev bullied and blustered, Gomulka and his colleagues held firm. The Poles insisted on proceeding with the election of the "national" Communist leader as first secretary of the party, which duly occurred on the twenty-first. After the Soviet delegation returned to Moscow, Khrushchev canceled the troop movements and accepted Gomulka as director of Poland's future course.

The decision had evidently been difficult and bitterly fought. So far as outsiders could tell, it was based on three major considerations. First, the Soviet leaders were convinced—and correctly so—that Gomulka was a good Communist who for all his apparent heterodoxy still intended to keep the party firmly in control. Second, the Poles agreed to stay within the Soviet orbit by maintaining their membership in the Warsaw Pact. Finally, the eruption of far more serious difficulties in Hungary counseled caution on both sides—to the Russians, it suggested the inadvisability of becoming involved in active intervention in two places at once; to the new Polish leadership, it gave an occasion to preach calm to their people lest they suffer the fate of their Hungarian friends.

In Hungary, as contrasted with Poland, there occurred no gradual shift of influence to Communist leaders who were more acceptable than the old Stalinists to the people at large. The die-hards at Budapest clung to power until the last and, when they did go, it was not through an intraparty change of authority, but through an explosion of popular anger. On October 23, a vast crowd of demonstrators—inspired by the events in Poland—was calling for the resignation of the government when the secret police opened fire. This event transformed into open revolution what had earlier been only a massive movement of protest. It swept Imre Nagy into the premiership, but it soon overwhelmed Nagy himself, driving him far beyond his Communist affiliations into a pledge of free elections and withdrawal from the Warsaw Pact. As the ten days of

Hungary's experiment in national communism proceeded, it became apparent that the party was no longer in control and that the revolutionists would not halt at the liberalization of the Communist system but were aiming rather at democracy of the Western type or even at a restoration of the old regime. It was symptomatic that Cardinal Mindszenty had been released from prison and was replacing Nagy as the most influential figure in the country.

After grave debates in the Kremlin, the Soviet leaders took a decision contrary to the one they had made in the case of Poland. They decided to intervene, sending back into Budapest the troops which they had withdrawn from the Hungarian capital, on Nagy's request, at the end of October. On November 4, the Soviet tanks brutally bore down on the revolutionists. The outside world stood aghast, but the Russians had chosen their time well: no one lifted a finger to save the Hungarians; the United States was fully occupied with its presidential election, the British and French with their expedition against Suez. Mindszenty took refuge in the American Embassy—Nagy in that of Yugoslavia. The Soviet Union returned the old Stalinists to power, as tens of thousands of Hungarians fled across the Austrian border, and the mass of the people submitted sullenly to their fate.

Phase Five: the "Refreeze" and the New Equilibrium in Yugoslavia and Poland

The suppression of the Hungarian revolution came as a shattering blow to Western Communists. During Stalin's last years, they had suffered under the deadening effects of orthodoxy imposed from the outside, and the life and the enthusiasm had gradually been drained out of them. Then the post-Stalinist "thaw" gave them a new hope and a new appeal. This brief revival of spontaneity made the succeeding disappointment all the more bitter: the shock of Hungary was the greater because of the illusions which had gone before. It bore particularly hard on intellectuals, who had followed the developments in Hungary with interest and sympathy, and who had learned that such figures as Georg Lukács, the most original theoretician in the Communist world, had thrown in their lot with the revolutionists. After the Soviet military action, both party members and fellow travelers began to desert communism in droves. Perhaps half the writers and artists who had ranked as the great ornament of the French and Italian parties abandoned the ideological allegiance to which they had clung for so long. After the autumn of 1956, communism still represented a major block of sullen discontent standing against the prevailing conservative temper on the Western European continent, but it had lost much of its idealism and self-confidence.

In Yugoslavia, too, the suppression of the Hungarian revolution meant a loss of ideological prestige. After a brief period of hesitation, Tito decided to endorse the Soviet intervention. Subsequently, he released his guest, Imre Nagy, whose execution in June, 1958, served as a grim warning to Communist leaders who might be tempted to stray beyond the borders of permissible deviation. These actions dimmed Tito's aura as the leader and model of national communism. At the same time, they only confirmed the course the Yugoslav regime had taken since its early years of unorthodox experiment. By 1954, Tito's initial period of innovation had come to an end. In the economic realm, he had decentralized his country's industrial direction and called a halt to agrarian collectivization and the compulsory delivery of crops. From the standpoint of individual liberty, he had strengthened the rights of the citizen before the courts and the secret police, granted a limited freedom of speech, reopened cultural channels to the West, and released Archbishop Stepinac (without restoring him to authority). Then Tito suddenly stopped the process of change. He reacted with a sharp negative when his former trusted subordinate, Milovan Djilas, proposed to establish in competition with Tito's special brand of communism a liberal socialist movement which would, in effect, have converted Yugoslavia into a two-party state. After repeated rebukes, Djilas was condemned to a long term in jail. The Communist monopoly of power remained unbroken. It is significant that the great intellectual ferment of 1956, which stirred Poland and Hungary so deeply, found few echoes among the Yugoslavs.

In Poland, the wave of popular protest which had swept Gomulka into power at first threatened to travel as far as the Hungarians had gone. In late October and early November there were anti-Soviet demonstrations throughout the country and a massive undercurrent of sympathy for Hungary. But Gomulka—who was a far more decisive figure and a more hard-bitten Communist than Nagy—succeeded in keeping his people under control. He was aided by the Catholic primate, Cardinal Wyszynski, who saw that Gomulka's rule was the best that Poland could hope for under the circumstances and who counseled his flock to vote for Gomulka-backed candidates in the elections to the Sejm (parliament) scheduled for January, 1957.

This tacit alliance with the church turned the elections into a personal triumph for Gomulka. According to Western standards, these were far from free, but they did result in the return of a minority of non-Communist deputies and the beginning of real debates in a body which earlier had been no more than a rubber stamp for the regime. Throughout the following winter and spring, the process of liberalization went on unchecked: the forced collectivization of agriculture came to an end; the workers' councils, which had sprung up before and during the great manifestations of the previous October, received official endorsement and the right to champion the grievances of the men in the factories and workshops; the secret police was curbed, and political prisoners were released. The intellectual ferment continued: the tone of the press became openly non-Communist or even anti-Communist, as the censorship collapsed, and the Resistance fighters of 1944, whom the Red Army had allowed to go down to defeat, were granted a posthumous rehabilitation.

Then Gomulka called a halt: striking out both against the remaining Stalinists within the ranks of Polish communism, and against the far more influential "revisionists" who were trying to push him into something resembling Western Social Democracy, he consolidated his authority over his party and his state. The danger signal that a reimposition of official control was on the way was the closing down of a militant Communist youth journal just under a year after the October effervescence had started. Thereafter one action inexorably followed another: intellectuals and writers were restrained, the powers of the workers' councils were reduced, the secret police began its spying once again, the old war of pinpricks against the church was resumed, and Gomulka lashed out ever more bitterly against his critics both on the right and on the left.

Still something had changed. As Poland in the course of the year 1958 settled into the Gomulkaist mold, it became apparent that the results were not notably different from the point that Titoist Yugoslavia had reached four years earlier. In both cases, the process of liberalization had disappointed the original expectations. Yet in Poland as in Yugoslavia there remained a residue of significant change which marked these nations off from their orthodox Communist neighbors. In both countries, the peasants were largely left to their own devices, and the urban workers enjoyed more individual and collective rights than they did elsewhere; in both countries, speech was freer, and the possibilities of contacts with the West more numerous and satisfactory. One nation had been forced to stay within the Soviet orbit; the other continued outside, but with a neutrality which, after 1955, leaned rather toward Russia than toward the West. In Yugoslavia there was more national independence—in Poland more intellectual and literary vitality. In both, the Communist party, as symbolized in the personality of one towering leader, refused to relinquish its monopoly of power. Together, however, they offered an alternative to the Soviet model of Communist rule, which served as a tenuous bridge between East and West and had a growing appeal for the newly liberated nations of Asia and Africa.

The Triumph of Khrushchev and the Uneasy Balance between Rigor and Leniency

Once he had swallowed the bitter pill of Hungary, Khrushchev continued to consolidate his control over the Soviet Union. In the summer of 1957, Malenkov and Molotov (who actually had very little in common and represented the two extremes of the Soviet leadership) were denounced as members of an "antiparty" group and exiled to obscure posts. The following autumn, Marshal Zhukov, whose popularity obviously competed with Khrushchev's own, was dropped from the defense ministry, on the charge of fostering a "cult of personality"—which since the dethronement of Stalin had ranked as the supreme error for a good Communist—and in the spring Khrushchev finally took the premiership from Bulganin. After 1958 the new master of the Soviet Union stood unchallenged. With the power of the secret police broken by the fall of Beria and that of the bureaucracy and the army curbed with the disgrace of Malenkov and Zhukov, the Communist party once more concentrated in its own hands all the major levers of authority.

Jaunty, full of earthy quips, and supremely self-assured, Khrushchev maintained an uneasy balance between ideological rigor and leniency. To the West he directed two years of soft speech, trying to repair the damage to his country's prestige which its intervention in Hungary had caused. But in the autumn of 1958, he shifted to a more provocative manner: once again the Soviet Union put pressure on the Western position in Berlin, inaugurating a period of renewed tension in international affairs which culminated in the complete failure of a "summit" meeting with President Eisenhower in Paris in May, 1960. At home the great "thaw" was over, but although sterner controls were again imposed, they fell far short of what had been common practice in the Stalinist era: too much had changed in Soviet society to permit a return to the situation of 1953. As contacts with the West continued and standards of living slowly but cumulatively rose, it became apparent that the ghost of Stalin had been laid to rest at last and that Russia had entered on a new phase of Communist rule whose outlines were still unclear but whose push toward a relaxation of tension and terror was unmistakable.

Readings

The new society and politics of Gaullist France are analyzed by Philip M. Williams and Martin Harrison, *De Gaulle's Republic*, 2nd ed. (1961), and by Stanley Hoffmann, *et al.*, *In Search of France* (1963); the former book is more critical, the latter more sympathetic, in tone. The course of the other Western European states, where the break with the earlier postwar era was less sharp, may be followed in Boyd and Hughes (*see* readings for Chapters Fifteen and Seventeen), in Alfred Grosser's brief but perceptive *The Federal Republic of Germany: A Concise History* (1964), and in a "provisional appraisal" of *The Adenauer Era* (1966) by Richard Hiscocks.

On Eastern Europe, besides Brzezinski and Griffith (*see* readings for Chapters Fourteen and Seventeen), Merle Fainsod, *How Russia Is Ruled*, rev. ed. (1963), traces the changes in institutions and economic practice since the death of Stalin; Ferenc A. Váli, *Rift and Revolt in Hungary* (1961), explains the great explosion of 1956; and Stephen Fischer-Galati, ed., *Eastern Europe in the Sixties* (1963), offers a series of essays by individual specialists on topics cutting across national frontiers.

On developments since the Spanish Civil War, Stanley G. Payne, *Franco's Spain* (1967), is compact and admirably balanced.

The New Society: Europe in the 1960's

Chapter Twenty

As the 1960's opened, Europe was definitely crossing the threshold of the new society which forty years before had been promised but not achieved. In the 1920's, there had been visible on the horizon an economy and a way of life which strongly resembled those of the United States—a mobile, mechanized society in which consumption levels were high and class lines were fluid. This great change had failed to occur: Europe's momentum had been lost, with the narrowing of economic vistas in the 1920's, the depression of the 1930's, and the war and the period of slow recovery in the 1940's. The first twentieth-century effort of reinvigoration had failed.

A generation later, however, Europe was ready to start again: a half-decade after the end of the Second World War the prerequisites existed once more, as they had in the mid-1920's, for an era of rapid economic expansion. This time, the promise did not fail. The five years after 1950, unlike those after 1924, brought more than disappointments and half-fulfilled hopes. And when another half-decade had passed, there was still no depression threatening.

In the interval between 1930 and 1960 something had been learned. The new generation of leaders in government, business, and the trade unions had widened their vision and their tolerance for experiment. They now knew both how to control the economy and how to project its development into the future. In this they had learned more from the example of the Soviet Union than most of them were willing to admit.

The imposing figure of Winston Churchill looks down on Prime Minister Edward Heath (left) and his predecessor Harold Wilson as they go to hear Queen Elizabeth address the opening of Parliament on July 2, 1970. COURTESY UPI PHOTO.

I

THE EUROPEAN POPULATION

The Postwar Population Spurt

In the period after the First World War, the slowing down of population growth—and its complete cessation in some places—had acted as a powerfully depressing force. The reverse happened after the Second World War: Europe entered on an era of rapid rise in population, and this growth was spread more evenly throughout the Continent than such spurts had been in the past. Thus Italy, which until about 1950 had had one of the highest rates of increase in Europe, after mid-century began to see its number of births slackening off. Conversely, Britain, whose prewar population had been almost stationary, experienced a slow but steady natural increase of about 0.5 per cent a year. Another highly urban country, the Netherlands, jumped to first place in population growth among the nations of Western Europe.

Yet the greatest postwar surprise occurred in France. The people which had ranked as the epitome of an old, stable, and even stagnant society suddenly began to multiply. In 1945, for the first time in a decade, France registered an excess of births over deaths. Nineteen forty-nine had the highest number of births that the country had seen for half a century. The nine years ending in 1954—a census year—showed a net population increase of 300,000 annually, and a total population gain of more than three million.

The result of such gains, however, was not to increase European pressure for emigration abroad. That pressure had existed only in the first postwar years, when the economy of Europe had not yet recovered sufficiently to absorb the new age groups looking for work. After the mid-century, there was less need to leave. The European economy itself was absorbing the population excess; of the industrial nations of the Continent, Italy alone had a continuing unemployment problem.

A Culture of Cities

As opposed to the population growth of the interwar period, which was concentrated in the rural societies of Southern and Eastern Europe and served merely to increase agrarian misery and discontent, the post-1945 spurt was confined almost entirely to the cities. Although the countryside still maintained a higher birth rate than the urban areas, it no longer kept its excess people on the land. Young men and women left the farms for the cities where industrial and clerical jobs awaited them. Thus in the 1950's the cities of Europe grew rapidly, while the population of the countryside remained stationary or even fell. This was just as true in the

East as in the West: in the satellite states of East Central Europe, the
forced industrialization program produced a massive influx of workers into the cities; in the Soviet Union, just under half the population of 1959 consisted of town dwellers. In nation after nation, the decade following the mid-century saw a loss of population from the country to the city, both in relative and in absolute terms.

For many peasants and rural dwellers, particularly of the older generation, this depopulation of the countryside was a source of grief and anxiety. The sense that a traditional way of life was departing prompted the rise of reactionary political movements, such as monarchism in southern Italy and Poujadism in southwestern France. Yet these political growths were only temporary. Their period of importance was confined to the mid-1950's, when the loss of influence on the part of the countryside first became apparent. In the longer view, the rural depopulation was a source of benefit rather than harm to the agricultural areas. It meant abandonment of marginal land and more intensive cultivation of what remained. It encouraged the consolidation of scattered plots and the elimination of "dwarf" holdings and, by reducing the excess of agricultural manpower, it tended to raise wages and to stimulate the introduction of tractors, reapers, and other types of mechanical equipment.

The new society was dominated by the cities. As in the past, the cities set the styles and the consumption patterns for the people as a whole, but no longer were there vast back-country areas which lay beyond the influence of urban attitudes. By 1960, almost all European society had been permeated by the culture of the cities.

The New Consumption Patterns

This urban culture was coming increasingly to resemble that of the United States: it was middle-class and white collar, rather than proletarian or aristocratic, and it was overwhelmingly oriented toward consumption. As the general prosperity of the 1950's gained momentum, the demands of European consumers became ever more pervasive and imperative. Entertainment was one need: scarcely had the thirst for motion pictures and radio been satisfied, when television began to spread. Private and individual transport was another: the number of automobiles in Europe more than doubled in the 1950's, and millions of motor scooters were circulating. This sudden multiplication of private transport effected what amounted to a class revolution. Before the war only the well-to-do had been able to afford motorcars and distant vacations; the mass of the population went to work by streetcar or bicycle and traveled very little. By the 1950's, all this had changed: even people of modest means had begun to buy automobiles, and a whole new class had been inserted between the bicyclists and the car owners—the intermediate stratum of those who traveled by motor scooter.

The European continent was simply too small for such mobility. Lacking the open spaces and broad highways of the United States, it began to crack under the strain. Crooked city streets which dated from the Middle Ages were hopelessly clogged with traffic; quiet vacation resorts had their peace shattered by massive arrivals from the cities. People fleeing noise and congestion moved out to the suburbs, as they were simultaneously doing in America, but nearly everywhere adequate housing was in short supply; this was the one important area in which by 1960 the losses of the war had not been fully made up. Wartime destruction had merely aggravated a problem of obsolescence in housing which was already apparent at the end of the 1930's: during the Depression far too few dwellings had been built; then had come the bombardments of the war; and finally, to cap all this, the post-1945 growth of population and the general rise in standards of living had enormously increased demand.

Cultural conservatives lamenting such social changes usually blamed them on American influence. True, American jazz, American styles, and American motion pictures held and even increased their popularity in the postwar period, but these were only the superficial manifestations of a deeper tendency. Actually Europe was not so much being influenced by the United States as traveling of its own will the same path that America had pursued a generation before. Consumption levels were rising and life was becoming democratized. The rest followed almost automatically.

Not all Europe shared evenly in this revolution of consumption and of class attitudes. It was most marked in the industrialized and otherwise "advanced" areas of Western and Central Europe—Britain, Scandinavia, the Low Countries, Western Germany, France, Switzerland, Austria, and northern Italy. As in the past, the Mediterranean world lagged behind. But the greatest postwar change was in Eastern Europe. Although Soviet consumption standards still remained far below what they were in the West, the difference was narrowing. The colossal effort at industrialization in the 1930's and the frantic pace of reconstruction in the 1940's were at last beginning to show results.

II

EASTERN EUROPE:
THE NEW MIDDLE CLASS

*The Later Five-Year Plans and the New Pattern
of Soviet Population*

In the postwar period, as had been true in the 1930's, the Soviet Union maintained the most rapid rate of industrial expansion in the whole of Europe. It continued its former practice of setting its economic goals in terms of five-year plans, which became both more precise and more flexible as the planners gained experience. Yet some of the old faults per-

sisted: the Soviet economists never allowed enough margin for error,
and when the unexpected happened, they could not adjust to the new situation. This was particularly true in agriculture which, by Khrushchev's own admission, was still lagging behind its targets in the late 1950's.

The Fourth Five-Year Plan (1946–1950) not only aimed to reconstruct war damage and to restore Soviet production to its prewar level; it also continued the earlier stress on heavy industry and on the economic growth of the eastern parts of the country. The Fifth Plan (1951–1955) marked a more decisive change in Soviet society. Previously, Russia had been an underdeveloped country in the sense that shortages of raw materials and equipment had limited industrial growth, while labor had never been lacking. After 1955, this ceased to be true; the countryside was no longer able to furnish manpower wholesale. The Soviet labor reserve had fallen—as it had earlier in the advanced economies of the West—and with this decline the life and productivity of the individual worker had become more precious.

This change reinforced the demand for consumer goods and a better standard of living that mounted to a clamor after Stalin's death in 1953. The Sixth Plan—which was scheduled to run from 1956 to 1960—precipitated both a great debate on economic policy and the fall of Georgi Malenkov. The coalition of Khrushchev and the military defeated Malenkov's scheme for satisfying consumer demand at last. Yet the new directorate was far from sure of its own intentions: the years from 1956 to 1958 proved to be a period of experiment such as Russia had not known since the 1930's. The most important innovations decreed by Khrushchev and his colleagues provided, on the one hand, for decentralizing the execution of the Plan, and on the other, for further concentration in agricultural management. In 1957 the Soviet leaders decided to delegate to regional economic councils the administration of the details of the Plan. The following year they agreed on the gradual transformation of the rural Machine Tractor Stations into Repair Technical Stations. This latter change was the logical sequel to a gradual consolidation of Collectives and State Farms into larger units which possessed their own mechanical equipment.

Then in November, 1958, the unprecedented happened. Khrushchev announced the decision to shelve the Sixth Five-Year Plan and to replace it by a Seven-Year Plan to run until 1965. This new plan, which aimed to increase over-all industrial production by nearly 80 per cent, was the first in which the Soviet leaders openly declared their intention of overtaking the Americans in per capita output. Moreover, the Seven-Year Plan at last struck a balance between the continued growth of heavy industry and the satisfaction of consumer demand, more particularly in the provision of housing, where fifteen million new apartments were called for.

One of the reasons for superseding the old plan was to take advantage of the information gathered in the general census of 1959. This census, besides documenting the massive growth of Soviet cities since the war, also revealed a number of significant changes in the general pattern of the country's population. Once more, as in the 1930's, the greatest industrial development had occurred to the east, in the Asian areas behind the Urals, and it was here that new cities had mushroomed from nothing. But this change, which was only beginning in the prewar years, by 1959 had decisively altered the distribution of the Soviet peoples. It had scattered the Great Russians throughout the Union, as skilled workers and administrators took employment in the newly developing parts of the country. In the census of 1959, 114.6 million of the Union's 208.8 million inhabitants declared themselves to be Russians. Only 97.8 million lived in the Russian Republic (RSFSR); the remaining seventeen million had migrated elsewhere, drastically changing the population pattern of some of the Asian republics. In Kazakhstan in Central Asia—the center of a boom in cotton growing—the Russians had become the largest single element (43 per cent) in the population. In the neighboring Uzbek Republic they numbered more than a million.

With Russians filling most of the responsible positions and setting the social tone in the Asian republics, it was small wonder that these were being steadily Russified. Although the official policy continued to provide for local autonomy and the fostering of indigenous culture, its practical application was becoming restricted to the realm of art and entertainment. The local literatures steadily lost in importance, as more and more people adopted Russian as their everyday language. And if these literatures strayed over into too proud a celebration of their independent past, they were sternly rebuked for errors of "bourgeois nationalism." This spread of Russian influence, however, was less a national change than a further example of the Europe-wide triumph of the city over the countryside and of advanced technology over the more primitive. For the far future it suggested a situation in which the term "Russian" could properly be used—as it had been for years by outsiders—to apply to the Soviet Union as a whole.

The other great change revealed in the census was the comparatively small size of Soviet families. The average number of children recorded was just over two—a figure which seemed incompatible with the annual natural increase of population of 1.75 per cent. The explanation, apparently, was a high marriage rate and great progress in cutting down childhood mortality. Broadly speaking, the small size of families reflected the fact that a very high proportion of Soviet women went out to work during the day and that the people as a whole were raising their expectations and hence restricting the number of their children, as parents had done in Western and Central Europe a generation or two before.

The Drive for Improved Living Standards

This rise in expectations was the most strongly marked feature of Soviet society in the 1950's. After more than a generation of denial and hardship, Russian consumers, like their counterparts in the West, were clam-

oring for the good things of life. For almost forty years, they had suf-
fered one calamity after another—time after time they had been urged on by their rulers to exertion and sacrifice in the Communist cause. First had come the World War of 1914–1918, then the still greater horrors of the civil war, and after that—following the brief breathing space of the New Economic Policy—the rigors of collectivization, the Five-Year Plans, and the great purge. Scarcely had these ended when the Soviet peoples had been plunged into the Second World War—with its frightful devastation and human losses, which seemed for a time to have canceled out all the gains of the preceding decade.

By 1953, however, when Stalin died, this ground had been recovered. Reconstruction was substantially complete, and the country was moving on to new heights of industrial achievement. The pressure of the Cold War was also lessening. For the first time since the Bolsheviks had come to power, there seemed to be no urgent reason for exertion, and the Soviet leadership began to give heed to consumers at last. As Khrushchev eventually realized, the deepest longings of his people were for a more comfortable life and an end to the fear of war. These two aspirations went together: the sentiment for peace was intense among a people whose every family had lost some member in the war and whose leaders for decades had justified their dictatorial rule by pointing to the danger of capitalist attack.

In the 1950's, such arguments were wearing thin. The Soviet population no longer consisted of an inert and inarticulate mass manipulated by its rulers at will, plus remnants of the old regime who were too frightened to protest. The new generation educated and trained in the 1930's had now come to positions of authority in the party and the economy. The census of 1959 revealed that illiteracy—which as late as the mid-1920's had accounted for nearly half the population—had been all but eliminated and that nearly four million people had received a university education. This new stratum of the intellectually trained demanded to be heard: its voice constituted at least a rudimentary public opinion, and its pressure was exerted both within and outside the ranks of the Communist party. By the end of the 1950's, the party, led by Khrushchev, was again in unchallenged control of Soviet society, but it was no longer the militant party of the prewar years driving a reluctant people toward the goal of a collectivized economy. By 1960, this goal had been achieved; the days of heroic exertion were over. The new aspirations for peace and personal comfort had affected the lower and intermediate ranks of the party itself, and the old separation between party and people was ending.

In brief, what had emerged in the Soviet Union was a new middle class, which was not notably different from its counterparts in the "capitalist" West. Like Americans and Western Europeans, the new stratum of Russian managers and professional people desired material well-being, private security, and a relaxation of tension. With the breaking of the power of the secret police, they were also beginning to long for freedom of expression and inquiry, both in ideological discussion and in the arts.

The Cultural "Thaw" and Its Sequels

In 1954, Ilya Ehrenburg, who earlier had ranked as a pillar of Communist orthodoxy, published a novel entitled *The Thaw*. Two years later, at the height of the excitement over Poland and Hungary, a less known writer, Vladimir Dudintsev, in his *Not By Bread Alone*, went still further in expressing the view that Russian writers should be free of ideological constraint and in attacking bureaucracy in state and party.

These two books suggest the sudden loosening of intellectual supervision which followed the death of Stalin. The earlier phases of the post-Stalinist era were marked by a revolt against the tyranny of "socialist realism" and a widespread search for a freedom that Russia had almost forgotten. Subsequently, this "thaw" was followed by a "refreeze." The limitations which were reimposed on Soviet writers and artists emerged most clearly in the case of Boris Pasternak's *Doctor Zhivago*.

Pasternak was an influential and respected poet of the prerevolutionary school who, after years of occupying himself mostly with translations, had finally written a novel, which he sent abroad to be published. It first appeared in Italy, but it was the publication of the English-language edition in 1958 which brought its author international fame. The novel became a best seller in the Western world—a success which was bound to displease the Soviet authorities, since the spirit of *Doctor Zhivago* was meditative and individualistic and sharply critical of the Bolshevik regime. This displeasure became open anger when Pasternak was awarded the Nobel Prize for literature. The author of *Doctor Zhivago* was not forbidden to go to Stockholm to receive the prize, but it was clear that such a trip would mean his permanent exile. After some hesitation, Pasternak declined the award, explaining in a letter to Khrushchev that he was "tied to Russia" by his "birth, life, and work" and that for him "to leave and go into exile abroad was unthinkable."

Thus Pasternak bowed to official pressure and continued to live quietly in the country house the Soviet state provided for him. In early 1960 he died, surrounded by the admiration of the more independent figures in the Russian literary world, and with hundreds of copies of his novel circulating clandestinely in Moscow and Leningrad. Pasternak's had been a voice from the past: that was one reason why his revolt had failed. But his lesson was not lost on the younger generation. Although the Soviet Writers' Congress of 1959 took a rigid position on the ideological commitment of literature, the signs of intellectual ferment continued. A number of younger authors began to experiment with new techniques and new themes, some of them deriving their inspiration from Italian "neorealism." In the realm of painting, a revolt against the old formalism and conventionality was in full swing; an exposition of Polish experimental art in the spring of 1959 gave occasion for repeated demands for shaking off "the yoke of slavish imitation."

The same oscillation from thaw to refreeze—and then back to a precarious balance between the two—was apparent in the field of science. In his last years Stalin had officially enforced the teachings of the biologist Lysenko, who had denied the Mendelian theory of genetics by reviving the early nineteenth-century notion of the inheritance of acquired characteristics. Such a position was obviously congenial to Marxists who insisted on man's ability to change the evolution of nature. In 1948, at the climax of the postwar reimposition of ideological control, Lysenko's scientific opponents were reduced to silence. For eight years the official theory held sway—as Soviet science separated itself almost completely from the mainstream of research in genetics. Then in 1956 the Russian scientists, like the writers and artists, declared their independence from ideological control. Their concerted opposition forced Lysenko's resignation as president of the Lenin Academy of Agricultural Sciences. By 1959, however, he was back again in official favor—only to fall once more (and this time apparently forever) when after Khrushchev's own departure he lost his key role as director of the Institute of Genetics in the Soviet Academy of Sciences.

On balance, the post-1956 control over Soviet culture was far looser than Stalin's had been. Most scientists were now at liberty to speculate as they chose, and the writers enjoyed more freedom than they had known since the 1920's. They could now write of Soviet society in terms of distinctions and shadings—as opposed to the black-and-white stereotypes on which Stalin had insisted—and they could depict communism as a faith that was changing and developing away from the monolithic orthodoxy of a former day. By the early 1960's the younger and more experimental writers were constantly getting into trouble—but they continued to publish nonetheless. Alexander Solzhenitsyn wrote of the forced labor camps in his *One Day in the Life of Ivan Denisovich* (1962); Victor Nekrasov published an honest and objective diary of his travels in America; and Yevgeny Yevtushenko captivated audiences both at home and abroad with readings from his own poems, one of which, "Baby Yar," castigated the anti-Semitism that remained so ugly a feature of Soviet society.

The younger writers and artists and scientists did not, like Pasternak, question Communist society as such. They accepted it as a fact of life —after all, they had never known anything else—with which they were satisfied and even proud, but they were striving for a more liberal type of communism, in which individual talent would enjoy the freedom it required for its full development. And this, in a wider sense, was the aspiration of the whole new middle class which the Soviet regime had raised to influence and authority.

The Satellites' Push for Economic Independence

Similar pressures for a fuller and a freer life also appeared in the satellite states of East Central Europe—more particularly in Hungary, Rumania, and Czechoslovakia, which had remained securely tied to the Soviet Union after the cataclysmic events of the autumn of 1956. Within half a decade of the suppression of the Budapest rising, the Hungarian government began to loosen the reins of police control; by the mid-1960's, personal conversation and cultural exchange with the West had become almost as uninhibited in Hungary as in Poland and Yugoslavia. Rumania soon embarked on a similar course of liberalization, but at a slower pace. Paradoxically enough, it was Czechoslovakia, the most "Western" and the most industrial of the Eastern European states, which adhered most closely to the old despotic model. The Czech Communist leadership remained more Stalinist than did other regimes; it lacked the imagination to see the benefits it might derive from appealing for cooperation to non-Communist technicians and intellectuals, as the Hungarians were doing.

Economic policy was the chief area in which the new drive for independence manifested itself. By the end of the 1950's, all the East European economies faced a knot of nearly insoluble dilemmas. The most serious was in agriculture. Here the Yugoslavs and Poles, who had brought collectivization to a halt, could point to the superiority of their productive record: the former announced an increase in farm output of 50 per cent in the three years 1956–1959, and the latter claimed a 10 per cent rise in the year 1961 alone. Elsewhere, with agriculture almost completely collectivized, stagnation threatened. The over-all population of the area was increasing at a rate of one million a year, while farm production was failing to keep pace, and the governments seemed able to propose only palliatives. They did almost nothing to conciliate the sullen opposition of the peasant masses. Still more, their agrarian policies were self-contradictory. Although the state planners stressed the importance of raising farm output, they starved agriculture of development funds and diverted its manpower to the needs of industry. By the mid-1960's, the old nightmare of rural over-population was a thing of the past; the new problem was one of an aging labor force—the average farmer was between forty and fifty years old—cultivating huge stretches of land with inadequate and outmoded equipment.

The needs of agriculture, then, were almost everywhere being sacrificed to industrial expansion. Yet even the industrial sector experienced vexing difficulties. In East Central Europe, as in the Soviet Union, the later 1950's brought the realization that an adequate provision of consumer goods could not be delayed forever and that to give the public some satisfaction in this respect was the surest way to reduce popular opposition to Communist rule. Beyond that, the economic planners began to recognize—as was simultaneously happening in the West—that further coordination within the bloc was necessary if Eastern Europe was to maximize its potential as an economic market.

So much could readily be agreed on. But the exact means of accomplishing it aroused heated debate among the Communist governments.

In 1958 Khrushchev decided to breathe new life into the COMECON
(Council for Mutual Economic Aid), which had been founded nine years earlier as the economic forerunner of the Warsaw Pact. At its meeting in Bucharest in June, the COMECON announced its intention to bring into harmony the major national economic targets up to the year 1975. On such an abstract goal, consensus was not hard to reach; already most of the national plans were trying to remedy past deficiencies by utilizing capital and labor resources more efficiently and keeping investment going up at a steadier pace. But when in the autumn of 1962, Khrushchev became more specific in his proposals for creating a "unified planning organ" to coordinate the national investment plans, his smaller allies began to balk. Those with less developed economies protested that their interests were being sacrificed in the name of a division of labor among the member nations of the bloc. The Rumanians in particular pointed out that it was unjust and illogical to build a "socialist" world on the basis of a division between "industrial and agrarian, developed and undeveloped" economies. In brief, Rumania served notice that it was not prepared to remain a grain and oil reservoir for the rest of the COMECON nations and that it was going to industrialize as Czechoslovakia, Poland, and Hungary had already done; nor was there any way that Khrushchev could prevent it. By the summer of 1963, Rumania had won its case; construction was progressing rapidly on a great new steel plant on the Danube. The Soviet leader had failed in his effort to bring the East European economies into line.

Rumania's defiance in the matter of economic coordination was only the most dramatic evidence of a growing independence on the part of the satellite countries. Although coordinated planning continued, it was no longer at Soviet dictation. In other respects also, the East Central European governments no longer automatically deferred to Moscow's wishes. They ran their own relations with the Christian churches: those with large Catholic populations had each worked out some kind of uneasy truce. Moreover, in the continuing struggle for power between "liberal" Communists and leaders in the Stalinist tradition, the individual parties reached their own tenuous balance with as much regard for local considerations as for the ideological weather in the Soviet Union. None of these regimes had yet become popular; but for the most part public hostility toward them was lapsing into indifference. And on the great new issue that was shaking the Communist world, all but one of the East European governments were aligning on the side of moderation.

The Sino-Soviet Rift and the Fall of Khrushchev

In the spring of 1960, a series of officially inspired articles in the Chinese press began to attack the whole basis of Khrushchev's foreign policy. The Soviet leader's efforts at international conciliation, the Chinese claimed, were totally mistaken: not only were they failing to bring results—they weakened the revolutionary militancy of Asians and Africans who looked to the Communist world for help and guidance and whose struggle for political and economic independence must be given first priority; Khrushchev's doctrine of coexistence with the capitalist world and his warnings on the dangers of thermonuclear war were nothing less than a betrayal of Communist first principles. In Chinese eyes, the Soviet Union and its European allies had joined the camp of the "haves" against the "have-nots." The same tendencies toward moderation that had been greeted in the West with relief and gratitude were condemned in China as ideological treason.

Khrushchev answered the Chinese polemics, at first cautiously, later with increasing asperity. And as the ideological duel continued throughout the next four years, all the East European countries except one supported the Soviet Union. Only Albania—weak, backward, and geographically isolated from the rest—aligned with China. After vainly attempting to force a change in Albanian leadership, Khrushchev broke off further relations. The result was to leave the small country on the Adriatic in a state of hostility with all its neighbors—with Western-oriented Greece and Italy, with neutralist Yugoslavia, and with Bulgaria and Rumania, which were still within the Soviet orbit. But if the vast majority of the European Communist leadership sided with Khrushchev, they were far from happy about the way he was conducting the exchange with the Chinese. A number of the East European parties thought that China should be dealt with more gently—that it was dangerous and unbecoming to air one's internal differences before the whole capitalist world—a point of view that was echoed by the powerful Italian Communist party.

Moreover, there was some truth in the Chinese contention that Khrushchev's foreign policy was not accomplishing its purpose. If it had been wholly conciliatory, it might have succeeded better. But the Soviet leader alternated soft approaches with truculent challenges. In August, 1961, he authorized the East German regime to cut off the flow of escapees to the West by building a wall between the two parts of politically divided Berlin, and a year later he installed medium-range missiles in Castro's Cuba. The first of these gambles succeeded: the Western powers were caught unprepared with no concerted response in mind. But in the Cuban case, the outcome was a Soviet defeat: after a tense week of Soviet-American confrontation, Khrushchev was obliged to withdraw his missiles. Indeed, the one significant instance of conciliation in practice —the treaty of 1963 prohibiting nuclear testing in the atmosphere—remained without a sequel, as Soviet and American disarmament negotiators found it impossible to overcome their mutual suspicions.

Meanwhile, Khrushchev was encountering similar difficulties on the domestic front. Here, although he radiated optimism and energy, his irruptions into the Soviet economic bureaucracy had an improvised quality that dismayed his subordinates. He kept tinkering with the planning machinery; he shook up factory management, first emphasizing local initiative, later returning to control from the center; most questionable of all, he tried to solve the perennial farm problem by shock tactics, ordering the ploughing-up of vast stretches of "virgin lands" in such barren areas as the Central Asian steppe. The result was a catastrophe: the harvest of 1963 proved disastrous, obliging the Soviet government to buy wheat from abroad, notably from the United States.

Beyond all this, there was the question of Khrushchev's "style." Although he had attacked the Stalinist cult of personality, his own rule had gradually become a one-man show. And there was much in this performance that offended the new "middle-class" generation of Soviet managers and political leaders. Khrushchev's manners were boorish, he talked too much, he favored his own family, he acted on impulse and sometimes irresponsibly. Still more, he was a living reminder of the unhappy past. Khrushchev, after all, had been raised to a position of influence by Stalin himself. Though he had repudiated the dead despot's legacy, he was tied to it by his own earlier career. A transition figure, Khrushchev might lead his people out of the era of unbridled tyranny, but he was neither by training nor by temperament the sort of man who could adequately represent the new forces at work in Russian society.

So, as Khrushchev's difficulties mounted, both wings of Soviet communism found reason to question his leadership—the old Stalinists because he had disgraced and humiliated them, the "liberals" and technicians because of his blunderbuss tactics. A temporary coalition between the two finally removed him from power. In the autumn of 1964, Khrushchev was preparing for a world congress of Communist parties which would offer irrefutable proof to the Chinese that the majority were against them; this was just the kind of showdown that so many party leaders, in Eastern Europe and in the West alike, were strenuously trying to avoid. The planned meeting, which was scheduled for mid-December, precipitated Khrushchev's fall. With the deadline only two months away, the Executive Committee of the Soviet Communist Party took advantage of his absence from Moscow on vacation to strip him of his state and party offices. In this thoroughly bureaucratic palace revolution of October, 1964, Khrushchev's nine years of undisputed power abruptly came to an end.

His successors were men of the new stamp—party-machine products, moderate in speech and colorless in personality—Aleksei Kosygin as prime minister and Leonid Brezhnev in the ordinarily more influential role of party first secretary. Aside from eliminating Khrushchev's flamboyance and cultivating a suaver style, the new leaders seemed to differ little from him in their concrete decisions. More than a year was to pass before a new course in Soviet policy became apparent.

The Swing to Rigor at Home and Abroad

The post-Khrushchev era began quietly enough with what appeared to be a further move in the direction of "liberalization." With the Seven-Year Plan due to expire in 1965, Prime Minister Kosygin sponsored a partial return to free enterprise methods. Without questioning the basic Communist premise of collectivized industry, he encouraged the individual plants to shift to a system which would emphasize profits and stimulate the initiative of managers. These reforms reflected the exchange of ideas between Soviet and Western economists which had taken place quite openly during the previous decade.

Then in early 1966 something more sinister happened. The writers Andrei Sinyavsky and Yuli Daniel—whose heterodox work had for a long time been circulating clandestinely and under pen-names—were brought to trial and sentenced to deportation. This time the pendulum swing from leniency to rigor went farther than it had done at any point since the death of Stalin, and a shudder of fear traversed the Soviet intellectual community. In countless small ways the pall of conformism seemed to be descending once again: conversation became less uninhibited, the secret police were more in evidence, and there were even signs of a partial rehabilitation of the fearsome tyrant whose name had apparently been discredited forever.

But the freer spirits refused to be terrorized. They would sometimes gather in the streets of Moscow and stage a tiny public protest—which the police would repress in a matter of minutes. Notable among those speaking out against the wave of conformity was Alexander Solzhenitsyn, who since Pasternak's death had emerged as Russia's greatest living writer. It had taken Khrushchev's personal intervention to ensure the publication of Solzhenitsyn's *One Day in the Life of Ivan Denisovich* two years before the former's fall from power. Solzhenitsyn's subsequent novels, *The Cancer Ward* (1966) and *The First Circle* (1968), enjoyed no such official protection; although they circulated underground among the Soviet intelligentsia, they could be published only abroad. The second of these created a literary sensation comparable to the appearance of *Doctor Zhivago* a decade earlier. An account of life at the end of the Stalinist era in an "institute" near Moscow, where highly gifted political prisoners worked on top secret projects, *The First Circle* recalled Tolstoy in its dense array of characters, its sweep of vision, and its warm humanity. The novel's success was more than the Soviet establishment could bear. In November, 1969, Solzhenitsyn was expelled from the Russian Writers' Union, with the strong implication that it might be wise for him to leave the country.

Solzhenitsyn continued to stand his ground, and a few of his literary peers such as Yevtushenko (who had described him as "our only living Russian classic") rallied to his support. For Solzhenitsyn was not a man who, like Pasternak, could be dismissed as a relic of the pre-Soviet period. He was a writer in the full vigor of maturity, a veteran both of war and of forced-labor camp, and an indomitable moral force. To the charge that he wrote in insufficiently positive terms about Soviet society, he replied with the countercharge that that society itself was "seriously sick."

Indeed, it had already become apparent that the new Soviet leadership was in grave trouble and that Brezhnev and Kosygin were facing a whole series of frustrations on a number of fronts—hence their readiness to unleash the Writers' Union against their most prestigious critic. It was also becoming evident that the process of "liberalization" which had begun under Malenkov and reached its heights in the Khrushchev era was not all of a piece: greater individual freedom at home, Kosygin's economic experiments, the détente in relations with the United States, holding the satellites in looser rein, and permitting increased contact between Eastern and Western Europe—these policies did not necessarily fit together into one coherent pattern of change. Moreover, all of them were getting out of hand and all were vulnerable to bitter criticism from the Chinese. This complex of Soviet difficulties reached the breaking point in a prolonged crisis over Czechoslovakia in the summer of 1968.

The Occupation of Czechoslovakia and the "Brezhnev Doctrine"

In January, 1968, there began a process of liberalization in Czechoslovakia which was to lead that country farther and faster than any Soviet satellite had gone in the whole post-Stalin period. In comparison to the Czech innovations, what Poland had done under Gomulka seemed cautious indeed. Still more, by the time the Czechs were ready to embark on their experiments, the Poles were already arrayed among their enemies. The Gomulka regime had become unrecognizable: most of the ground gained since 1956 had been lost, and a new wave of anti-Semitism had driven the greater part of the remaining Jewish population out of the country.

In early 1968, when a new and untried leader, Alexander Dubcek, took over the direction of Czechoslovakia's Communist party, that country was ready at last to assume the role of liberal example for which its democratic tradition and its high level of economic and educational development had so long fitted it. Dubcek's elevation to power came in the context not only of an almost universal longing for personal freedom, but of a languishing economy and a demand on the part of the Slovaks (among them Dubcek himself) for full equality with the Czechs. The new leader was a pleasant, unassuming, and mild-mannered man; he was also a superb tactician, whose outward appearance belied his inner determination. Scarcely had he been raised to authority than he began to speak in tones of quiet eloquence an unfamiliar language which his people found both delightful and intoxicating. He talked of "socialism with a human face" and of democratization—that is, an irreversible process of returning power to the people, as opposed to the sort of liberalizing familiar in the rest of Eastern Europe, which was granted from above and could always be revoked. By the end of February, when the Czech censorship simply ceased to function, Dubcek's had become the first truly *popular* Communist regime in European history.

Yet while Dubcek altered in revolutionary fashion the whole style of Communist government, he took care to do nothing that might alarm the leaders of the Soviet Union. He engineered the election as the nation's president of Ludvik Svoboda, an elderly military hero esteemed in Moscow. He also saw to it that the Communist "Action Program" issued in April, despite its permissive tone, should declare the party's intention of continuing to act as the main motor force in Czechoslovak society and of allowing no rival parties to compete with it on an equal basis. Most important, Dubcek constantly stressed his loyalty to the Warsaw Pact: mindful of what had befallen the Hungarians in 1956, he drew a sharp distinction between his domestic reforms and his foreign policy, which remained irreproachably orthodox.

Perhaps this careful balancing act—which the quick-minded Czechs seemed to understand almost intuitively—would have succeeded if the Soviet leaders had not been reduced to a state of extreme nervousness by a series of reverses abroad. First had come the quarrel with the Chinese, then the Cuban missile crisis, then Rumania's cantankerousness, finally the Arab-Israeli war of 1967 (*see* Section IV), in all of which the Russians had felt either humiliated or at the very least thrown off balance. In this perspective, Czechoslovakia's new course loomed as another potential Soviet defeat. And in the anguished discussions in the Kremlin, which began as early as March, the more pedestrian industrial managers, who could not stomach Kosygin's economic reforms, sided with the hard-liners on foreign and military policy.

In May Kosygin himself visited Czechoslovakia and apparently brought back a reassuring report. Yet the following month his government took the precaution of holding the staff exercises of the Warsaw Pact forces on Czech territory—an operation from which these troops were withdrawn with tantalizing slowness in the course of the summer. Almost simultaneously, at the end of June, a number of Czech intellectuals issued a manifesto entitled *Two Thousand Words* which, in addition to pledging loyalty to Dubcek's leadership, urged it to move even faster toward democracy and to resist Soviet pressure for a halt to reform. The hostility with which the Russian, Polish, and East German press greeted this manifesto suggested that Dubcek's carefully contrived policy was coming unstuck and that a showdown with the USSR might be in the offing.

Still the Soviet leaders hesitated before bringing their military power to bear. They agreed to the Czech contention that they discuss their mutual differences on Czechoslovak soil, and at a meeting held at the end of July in a small Slovak border town, Dubcek was able to refute their charges point by point. Hence it came as an almost total surprise when in the early morning hours of August 21 the Soviet Union, supported by four Warsaw Pact countries, occupied Czechoslovakia with ruthless swiftness. What had apparently tipped the scales toward intervention was the publication on August 10 of draft statutes for the Czechoslovak

Communists providing for an unprecedented range of freedom within the party itself, plus the announcement that a party congress to ratify the changes that had occurred over the past seven months would take place in early September.

From a technical standpoint the invasion was a total success. Approximately 175,000 troops—predominantly Soviet, but with contingents from Bulgaria, Hungary, Poland, and East Germany (and notably *not* from Rumania)—seized Prague and the other major Czechoslovak cities. It was the largest military operation that Europe had seen since the Second World War: by mid-September perhaps half a million men were occupying the country. Yet this military efficiency was matched by no corresponding political finesse. The almost total lack of advanced planning for an occupation regime suggested how late the Soviet leaders had made their decision and how bitterly the point had been contested in their inner councils. No "Quisling" emerged among the Czech Communists to collaborate with them. Faced with a spontaneous, improvised, non-violent, but extraordinarily successful resistance among the civilian population, the Soviet occupying authorities had no idea what to do.

At first they imprisoned Dubcek, threatened President Svoboda, and flew them both to Moscow. Within five days, the former was reinstated and brought to the Kremlin for negotiations. Dubcek kept his nerve; Svoboda resorted to the extremely effective threat of suicide. Returning to Prague as national heroes, the two resumed the direction of their country. Initially it seemed as if in fact they had conceded very little: they had merely undertaken to "normalize" the situation within Czechoslovakia and to dismiss a few prominent "liberals." In addition, however, they had called off the passive resistance, and this left them small leverage for withstanding further Soviet pressure. Month after month the process of wearing them down went on; piece by piece the structure of Czechoslovak democratization was dismantled. By April, 1969, when Dubcek himself was forced to retire, little was left of the brave reforms of the previous year. Yet at least Dubcek's successor, Gustav Husak, while compliant with Soviet wishes, was no Stalinist; the country had been federalized to give equality to the Slovaks; and in the smaller matters of life the memory of 1968 could not be erased from the consciousness and public procedures of a people that continued to cherish the memory of what might have been.

The Russians' invasion of Czechoslovakia naturally invited comparison with their suppression of the Hungarian revolt in 1956. Both produced the same shock of revulsion—with this time an almost total absence of bloodshed and a correspondingly mild response from the West. Yet from an ideological standpoint the events in Prague loomed larger than what had occurred in Budapest twelve years earlier. Imre Nagy had withdrawn from the Warsaw Pact; Dubcek had not. That the same treatment was given to both suggested that the "sins" of the Czechoslovaks were not foreign but domestic; it was liberal or democratized Communism itself that was in question. In retrospect the Soviet occupation of Budapest had seemed episodic and uncharacteristic: it had not halted the process of liberalization in Eastern Europe. The takeover in Prague had done precisely that.

In November, 1968, in a speech in Warsaw, the Soviet party secretary outlined what was subsequently called the "Brezhnev Doctrine." When "socialism" was threatened in any country, he declared, it became "not only a problem of the people of the country concerned, but a common problem and concern of all socialist countries." In short, Brezhnev both justified the invasion of Czechoslovakia on ideological grounds and gave warning that any Communist regime which was tempted to pursue a similar course would meet a similar fate. This interpretation of recent events did not go unquestioned. Several Communist parties—notably the Yugoslav, the Rumanian, and the Italian—had harshly criticized the occupation of Prague, and these remained unconvinced. When in June, 1969 the Soviet leaders were at last able to hold in Moscow a world conference of Communists to endorse their new line, the Yugoslavs ranked along with the Chinese among the absentees; the Italians signed only one part of the final communiqué; and the Rumanians adhered to it with grave reservations. Such unprecedented dissidence at a meeting which would ordinarily have functioned as a rubber stamp demonstrated the extent of dissatisfaction with the Brezhnev Doctrine. It also showed that the Russians were willing to settle for something short of full compliance. The result was an unstable situation in which the Soviet Union's insistence on its pre-1956 right to direct the whole "socialist" bloc was balanced by a realistic assessment of the tolerable range of dissent.

Moreover, in October the Soviet leaders finally sent a representative to Peking to talk with the Chinese. During the previous summer a series of incidents along their vast common border in Asia had mounted very nearly to the point of open warfare. Evidently alarmed that the decade-old exchange of insults was being translated into actions, the Russians were trying to defuse a desperately dangerous confrontation. And such also was the virtually unanimous wish of the European Communist chiefs outside the Soviet Union. Whether they ruled their countries—as in Yugoslavia and the nations of the Warsaw Pact—or led a powerful working-class opposition—as in Italy or France—Europe's Communists could see only damage to the common cause in the continuation of ideological strife between the two colossi of what had once been a united movement.

Meantime on the economic front at home 1969 had proved to be a bad year for the Soviet Union. Production had risen more slowly than at any time since the forced departure of Khrushchev in 1964. Since bungling in economic management had been a major reason for his fall, it was embarrassing for his successors to have to admit to similar difficulties. The shift to a quasi-profit system had not solved the long-standing problems of labor inefficiency and low rates of return on capital investment. The old-type bureaucratic managers remained unreconciled. On this front also, as in the realm of foreign policy, reformers and hard-liners remained locked in a perennial combat punctuated by phases of uneasy truce.

III

WESTERN EUROPE:
THE REDUCTION OF NATIONAL
AND IDEOLOGICAL DIFFERENCES

When, in May of 1965, Europeans paused to reflect that their continent had been at peace for twenty years, they could find reason for solid satisfaction in the road they had already traversed and in the prospects before them. More particularly, a comparison between the Europe of 1938 and that of 1965 was all in favor of the latter. Two decades after the end of the First World War, the situation had been bleak in the extreme: a society barely emerging from the Great Depression and riven by a three-cornered ideological struggle had just seen the peace saved at Munich—but with each passing week it was becoming more apparent that only a postponement had been gained and that a further great conflict was all but inevitable. In contrast, the twentieth anniversary of Hitler's defeat found Europe prosperous, confident, and no longer obsessed by the fear of war. The world was full of alarms—but the danger spots were beyond Europe's borders, in Asia, in Africa, or in the Middle East. An increasing number of Europeans were beginning to believe that should war erupt in one of these places, it would be possible for them to avoid involvement in it. This hope was reinforced by the informal détente—the tacit understanding to refrain from nuclear threats—which had characterized Soviet-American relations since the confrontation over Cuba in the autumn of 1962.

Almost no one argued that Europe's boundaries, as they had existed, virtually unaltered, since 1945, were entirely satisfactory. Yet at least they had acquired in the meantime the sanction of habit and resigned acceptance. The disappearance of the Baltic States was the most obvious violation of national sentiment—but there seemed not the remotest chance that this injustice would be rectified. Similarly, many Germans refused to be reconciled to their eastern frontier—but it was hard to imagine Germany dragging its allies into a war to recover the lost provinces from the Poles. In East Central Europe, as before 1939, half a dozen national minorities were dissatisfied with their lot—but they voiced their complaints less bitterly than in the interwar years, and their grievances were attenuated by the fact that all the countries in question were living under Communist regimes in which the pressure of economic and social adjustment dwarfed older and more sentimental issues. Indeed, the great remaining problem of Europe was its ideological division down the center; on both sides of the divide, people longed for the restoration of a continent-wide economy and culture. Even here, however, East and West alike saw reason for hope: as opposed to the steady exacerbation of ideological hostility in the 1930's, in the 1960's such hatreds and misunderstandings were diminishing, and the barrier that Winston Churchill two decades earlier had baptized the "iron curtain" had been punctured so often that in most places the term was no longer appropriate to the new realities.

Yet in one crucial area the iron curtain was still the dominant fact of life: a line of barbed wire and pillboxes still separated West from East Germany. This was the outstanding anomaly in a Europe which had settled into its mid-century equilibrium. Within the division of Germany, the wall across Berlin visibly symbolized the fact that here at least the Cold War persisted. The bizarre situation of the former German capital —the isolation of one-half of it as a beleaguered outpost of the West— was the last unresolved legacy of the Second World War. Khrushchev had been well aware of its importance: nearly his whole tenure of power had been occupied by an endemic Berlin crisis, as he kept urging the need for a permanent settlement. Yet though he mutliplied his threats and exhortations, he constantly postponed his deadlines and never pushed matters to a final showdown.

On Berlin an agreement between the Western powers and the Soviet Union seemed next to impossible: the former insisted on ironclad guarantees for their rights of access and freedom for the West Berliners to organize their government as they chose; the latter sought a way of reinforcing the East German regime, whose popularity was almost nil and which was transparently the weakest and most dependent within the Communist bloc. Between a West unyielding in its defense of the status quo and a Soviet leadership intent on tidying up a standing challenge to its prestige, the city of Berlin remained suspended in limbo.

Germany: the Succession to Adenauer

Such at least was the state of affairs as long as Chancellor Adenauer stayed in power. But in October, 1963, his fourteen-year tenure of office came to an end. His ever more restive subordinates had allowed him a final chance to lead his party to the polls: in the election of September, 1961, Adenauer's Christian Democratic Union had emerged victorious for the fourth time, but with a reduced percentage of the vote. Once more— as had been the case before 1957—the Christian Democrats were obliged to call on support from the parliamentary Right to make up their majority. These electoral losses suggested that the German public was growing weary of Adenauer's authoritarian leadership, and the succeeding year and a half was occupied by bitter party infighting, with the octogenarian chancellor trying to block the path of Ludwig Erhard, whose popularity as the architect of Germany's "economic miracle" made him the logical candidate for the succession. Eventually Erhard won: no other party leader had remotely as good a claim as he. In April, 1963, the Christian Democrats named him their candidate for chancellor, specifying that the change should take place in six months' time.

Erhard's style of government was very different from Adenauer's. Relaxed, affable, frequently irresolute, and unschooled in party intrigue, the new chancellor granted both the Bundestag and his ministerial colleagues a freedom to which they had long grown unaccustomed. Adenauer had treated his subordinates like schoolboys; Erhard gave them the sense of being his collaborators and equals. The result was a shift from one-man government to a more traditional cabinet system. Such a change had already been implicit in the outcome of the "*Spiegel* incident" the previous year. Franz-Josef Strauss, the minister of defense, had arbitrarily ordered the arrest of the editors of Germany's leading news weekly on the charge that they had published secret military information. After a vast outcry in the press and the universities, Strauss had been obliged to resign—a result that was generally interpreted as salutary in giving greater content and reality to German democracy.

A similar reinforcement of democracy was evident in the new self-confidence of the Social Democratic opposition. Under the buoyant guidance of the young and attractive Willy Brandt, the Social Democrats emerged greatly strengthened from the election of 1961; their vote had gone up by nearly five percentage points, which was almost exactly what the Christian Democrats had lost. Brandt was a man attuned to the 1960's, sturdily optimistic and pragmatic, with a notion of socialism that had nothing of Marx left in it and that was close to British or Scandinavian practice. Under his leadership, the Social Democrats strengthened their hold over West Berlin in the municipal election of 1963; they similarly controlled four of the nine West German state governments. After having made such gains in local influence, they were disappointed that the parliamentary election of September, 1965, pushed their vote up by only three percentage points, still leaving the Christian Democrats in control.

The moderation of the German Social Democrats reflected public satisfaction with the continuing prosperity of the country. At the same time the steady growth in the party's strength underlined the fact that a decade and a half of Christian Democratic rule had left many areas in Germany's economy and society woefully neglected. For one thing, there was the problem of absorbing nearly a million foreign workers, who after the Berlin wall went up in 1961 began to take the place of escapees from East Germany as recruits for the labor force. Still more important was a great backlog of unfilled public needs. Germany's highways were proving far from adequate for the new traffic; its lead in technology was slipping; and the construction of schools and hospitals was failing to keep up with the country's requirements. Erhard's economic policy was not quite so exclusively guided by free enterprise principles as some of his critics and admirers supposed: both agriculture and housing, for example, benefited from substantial government subsidies. But it was apparent by the mid-1960's that in Germany, as in the United States, expenditure for public welfare had been sacrificed to private affluence and that the Social Democrats had a mounting sentiment behind them when they blamed such deficiencies on Christian Democracy's unbroken tenure of power.

In foreign affairs, the difference between the parties was less noticeable. By the election of 1961, the Social Democrats had abandoned any thought of a neutralist stand and had aligned themselves on a position of loyalty to the United States and to NATO which was scarcely different from that of Adenauer. At the same time, they criticized him for having done too little about reunification. There was some justice in this reproach: by his rigid and uncompromising attitude toward the East German regime, the old chancellor had in fact ruled out any realistic progress toward reuniting the country.

At the beginning of 1963, nine months before his retirement, Adenauer —piqued by what he regarded as a cooling in relations between Washington and Bonn since President Kennedy had taken over from Eisenhower—had signed a treaty of friendship with France. This document might mean everything or nothing: its chief purpose was to codify for the future something of the cordiality and esteem that had grown up between Adenauer and General de Gaulle. But so personal a relationship could not be inherited by Adenauer's successor. And it was soon apparent that between him and De Gaulle relations were more distant than they had been under his predecessor. For Erhard was at the very least reluctant to support the drive for leadership in Europe and a world role overseas which the general had inaugurated after putting in order his own domestic difficulties.

France: De Gaulle's Claim to European Leadership

In the course of the year 1962, De Gaulle achieved two successes which marked a decisive turning point in his tenure of power: he brought the Algerian War to an end, and he reinforced his own office in a way that gave a new sense of permanency to the regime he had created.

The struggle in Algeria, of course, had been at the origin of De Gaulle's return to national leadership: the fear of the Algerian French that the politicians in Paris were about to "sell them out" to the Moslem rebels had precipitated the complex chain of events which eventually hoisted the general into power. Once in office, however, he disappointed the conservatives and nationalists who had hoped that he would pursue a policy of colonial repression. Equally dismayed were those of the center-left who had voted for him in the expectation that he would try to meet the Moslems' demands. De Gaulle did neither of these, following instead a zigzag course which alternated military action with vague conciliatory

gestures and ended by confusing both his friends and his enemies. It was
impossible to tell whether he was feeling his way without having a clear goal in mind or whether he knew all along what the outcome would be and was simply giving his people time to accustom themselves to the idea of letting Algeria go. In any case, in the nearly four years that he took to bring the war to an end, De Gaulle gradually eliminated all intermediate solutions. First he dropped as impracticable the idea of "assimilating" Algeria to France—that is, of making a reality of the Moslem Algerians' theoretical status as full French citizens. Next he tacitly ruled out the notion of an "association" of Algeria with France which would fall short of complete independence. Finally, in the spring of 1961, he began negotiations that ten months later were to bring about a solution earlier thought acceptable by only a handful of French intellectuals and leftists—the unconditional liberation of Algeria.

In the meantime, however, the long delay and the ambiguity of the general's statements had exasperated public opinion at home. By the autumn of 1960, scarcely any articulate French citizen seemed any longer to be a convinced Gaullist. The regime was apparently resting on an ever narrower base of support as it turned now this way, now that, to face a double and contradictory opposition. On the Right, the nationalist irreconcilables resorted to direct action. In April, 1961, the military leaders in Algiers staged the fourth insurrectionary demonstration to shake that effervescent city since 1956. This time, as he had done the previous year, De Gaulle sternly repressed the challenge to his authority; in France itself the army stuck by him, but it was quite obviously astir with discontent. No longer in a position to count on the military, the rightist opposition at home turned to conspiracy and terrorism: it alarmed the population of Paris with a succession of plastic-bomb explosions. These criminal acts, which were directed against prominent Frenchmen known to favor conciliation with the Algerian Moslems, actually claimed few victims; their main effect was to discredit the cause they were intended to serve by gradually convincing the mass of apolitical Frenchmen that the nationalist die-hards were both ruthless and irresponsible.

The democratic and leftist opposition, in contrast, stuck strictly to nonviolent protest. The furthest it went was a manifesto signed by 121 intellectuals—among them Jean-Paul Sartre—calling for civil disobedience in what they regarded as an unjust war. Most of those who objected to the prolongation of the Algerian conflict took a more moderate stand. The main target of their attacks was the barbarous behavior into which a war without mercy had led the special French units charged with the work of repression; first the Protestant clergy, later the chiefs of the Catholic hierarchy denounced the practices of torture, reprisals, and summary executions. Those who opposed the Algerian War could not understand the government's balancing tactics and the way it gave equal treatment to two oppositions so different in character: the police seemed at least as zealous in breaking up student or trade-union demonstrations against the war as in pursuing the authors of bomb outrages. In February, 1962—just one month before the negotiations with the rebels were successfully concluded—a Socialist-led protest against police brutality turned a million and a half people into the streets of Paris, the largest public manifestation that the French capital had seen since the Second World War.

Once the Algerian conflict was over, the nationalist opposition melted away. This was apparent in the results of the special election of November, 1962, by which De Gaulle sought to reinforce his authority.

The previous August he had barely escaped assassination by rightist fanatics. This—the closest shave he had yet had in the several attempts that had already been made against his life—convinced the general and his advisers that something should be done about the succession to the presidency. The provision in the constitution of 1958 that the head of state should be chosen by a list of local "notables" rather than by the people directly had assured De Gaulle's own election, but it was far from certain that in the event of his sudden death it would produce a president of similar views. With the Algerian War over—with the crisis that had originally brought him to power successfully surmounted—there was a real possibility that France would return to politics as usual. Most of the local officials who ranked as presidential electors were adherents of one of the old parties of the Third and Fourth Republics: what guarantee was there that they would not choose a politician of the same stamp who would be totally out of sympathy with the institutions and practices of the Fifth?

To meet this danger, De Gaulle instructed the new prime minister whom he had just installed in office, Georges Pompidou, to propose a constitutional amendment providing for the popular election of the president. The proposal in itself was enough to alarm the parliamentarians of the National Assembly; the form in which it was presented drove them to fury. For Pompidou bypassed the amending procedure specified in the constitution by announcing that the change would be submitted to a popular referendum for ratification. Faced with this violation of a constitutional document that had been purposely tailored to De Gaulle's own requirements, a large majority of the deputies closed ranks and girded for battle. They overthrew the Pompidou ministry—to which the general replied by dissolving the Assembly and calling for new elections.

Thus there were to be two "consultations of the electorate"—the constitutional referendum in October and a parliamentary election the following month. In this double struggle, De Gaulle seemed at a distinct disadvantage: virtually every political group except his own party was aligned against him. Moreover, the first electoral test produced only mediocre results: the constitutional change was adopted, but with a majority just slightly over 60 per cent and a high rate of abstentions. Then in the November election, De Gaulle turned the tables on his critics and detractors. His own party, the Union for the New Republic, did far better than it had four years earlier, scoring a landslide triumph that gave it in effect a parliamentary majority. The ultranationalist opposition virtually disappeared from the Assembly; even the conservative Independents, who had provided a qualified support for De Gaulle's ministers, were drastically reduced in strength; the democratic center parties barely held their ground; among the general's opponents only the Socialists and Communists made gains—and these were largely due to the emergency circumstances that in a number of constituencies had induced them, for the first time in fifteen years, to cooperate with each other.

The election of 1962 was the great watershed in the internal history of De Gaulle's rule. It brought a new type of man into the Assembly; nearly half of those elected had never served as deputies before, and most of these were political pragmatists, impatient with the guidance of the old party war-horses. More broadly, the election was a repudiation of the traditional parliamentary leadership: the voters, particularly the young, had shown that they were dissatisfied with old-fashioned politics —or, at the very least, bored by it. All this suggested that the Fifth Republic could no longer be regarded as the temporary expedient that its critics had called it.

The most telling issue against De Gaulle was the independent nuclear deterrent that the general was developing. Indeed, this was just about the only remaining question on which the opposition in the Assembly could mount a first-class debate and rouse the French public from its post-Algeria lethargy. The nuclear striking force cost a great deal of money; its critics could easily point to the way it diverted funds from such urgent purposes as education and housing. But De Gaulle refused to compromise his military program: the independent deterrent was central to his conception of his own role and that of the nation he led.

To American policy-makers the general's defiant stand frequently seemed mere cantankerousness: in his own mind it formed part of a logical and coherent view of the future. The United States, De Gaulle argued, could neither unite Europe nor be counted on to use its nuclear deterrent for the defense of the Continent. A master of *Realpolitik* and an unabashed exponent of national egoism, the general was skeptical of apparently generous or altruistic gestures in international relations. The Europeans, he contended, must rely on themselves. Of course, they must draw closer together; but they should maintain their separate national identities and defer to the leadership of the one power which by geography and tradition was equipped for the role—Gaullist France. This line of thinking further implied an indissoluble Franco-German understanding and a concerted effort to lure the states of East Central Europe away from their Soviet ties.

Once the Algerian War was over, De Gaulle began to put his long-range policy into effect. Now delivered of this albatross, he turned his energies toward the foreign scene. Besides trying to hold Germany in line and wooing such restive Communist countries as Czechoslovakia, Hungary, and Rumania, the general launched an ambitious program of making France a world power once more. He vented his sarcasm on the United Nations, cooperating with that organization only when he chose; he recognized Communist China, offering to mediate the disputes of Southeast Asia; he visited all ten republics of South America, promising Latin cultural solidarity and sympathy. Few if any of these initiatives brought concrete results—but they served to keep France and its leader constantly in the news. In the autumn of 1963, when Adenauer, Kennedy, and Macmillan all disappeared from the scene, De Gaulle—who already ranked as the sole great survivor among the allied leadership in the Second World War—was again left in lonely grandeur, literally as well as figuratively towering above his rivals.

De Gaulle's foreign policy bewildered both Frenchmen and other Europeans. The enthusiasts for European unity tended to distrust him; they disliked his nationalist language and regretted the passing of the Christian Democratic leaders whose vision of the future had been international and federalist. On the other hand, they recognized that a federal Europe could not be built without France, and that until that happy solution was reached, there was no alternative to playing along with France's ruler. One people, however, was almost uniformly hostile to De Gaulle's policy. British of all political persuasions saw it as a threat to their own position—for the general's notion of his country's European and world role challenged Britain almost as much as it did the United States. Whatever party was in power in London, distrust between De Gaulle and the British remained a constant in the international politics of the 1960's.

Britain: Labor's Half Decade of Power

The Conservatives had already governed Britain for more than a decade when articulate public sentiment finally began to turn against them. Elsewhere—in Eastern Europe, in Germany, in France—politics and the national economy seemed to be on the move as the 1950's came to an end. The British alone remained in the doldrums, apparently hypnotized by Prime Minister Macmillan's soothing rhetoric.

Yet under the surface of prosperity there was much to criticize in the Tory conduct of affairs. In comparison with the record of its neighbors across the Channel, Britain's economy was stagnating: inflationary pressures were not being absorbed by industrial expansion; investment was going into high-profit concerns rather than into those that could best aid the economy as a whole; and the excess labor force was unable or unwilling to move to the places where new jobs were available. Moreover, the years of Conservative rule saw a slow erosion of the welfare-state practices that the Labor government had installed and that the Tories had initially accepted: the National Health Service reinstituted charges for such medical help as prescriptions, eyeglasses, and dentistry, and the government freed certain categories of buildings from rent control; the latter measure encouraged a private construction boom at the expense of public housing.

Meanwhile British nationalists who had been incensed at Prime Minister Eden's knuckling under to the United States during the Suez crisis were further outraged when Macmillan apparently did likewise in the matter of nuclear arms. At the end of 1962, at a meeting with President Kennedy at Nassau in the Bahamas, he accepted a new arrangement which subordinated the small British nuclear force to American supply and production schedules. Indeed, the change was so drastic as to make people question whether Britain any longer ranked—although far behind the United States and the Soviet Union—as the world's third nuclear power. The contrast with the thoroughly independent fashion in which the fourth such power—De Gaulle's France—was readying its striking force was only too apparent.

It was neither economic nor nuclear policy, however, that at length discredited the Macmillan government. It was a series of internal difficulties within the Conservative party itself. First came a sensational sex scandal, complete with national security implications, which caused the resignation of the minister of war in the spring of 1963 and cast doubt on the judgment of the prime minister himself. The following autumn Macmillan found that he had to undergo an operation and promptly resigned—right in the middle of the Tories' annual party conference. The announcement could not have been worse timed, precipitating as it did an undignified and public scramble for the succession. The natural heir was the Conservatives' senior statesman, R. A. Butler, who had done so much to modernize the party's organization and policy. But his unconventional ways had never appealed to old-line Tories, and two younger party leaders of a similar reforming stamp divided Butler's following by also advancing their candidacies. As these declared aspirants canceled each other out, Macmillan from his hospital bed was urging another name—that of the foreign minister, the Earl of Home. And, in the end, it was Home whom the Conservatives settled on as party leader and whom the queen named prime minister. Taking advantage of a new law which permitted peers to renounce their titles, the noble earl converted himself into Sir Alec Douglas-Home; a vacant seat was found for him in rural Scotland; and he was duly elected to the House of Commons.

Despite the questionable feats of legerdemain that had brought him to power, and his old-fashioned aristocratic manners, Sir Alec was not the disaster in office that many had hoped or feared. He did his best to shake up the Tories' ranks, and he energetically propagated the notion that his was a party of economic expansion and reform. But the young Conservative modernizers had received the prime minister's encouragement too late. When Sir Alec came to power, there was less than a year to go before the general election scheduled for 1964.

This election campaign found the Labor opposition more united and confident than it had been since 1950. For a full decade, the Labor party had been shaken by factional strife; now it was the Conservatives who had publicly aired their internal difficulties as Macmillan's hold had weakened. What had torn Labor apart in the 1950's had been a great debate over nuclear arms. The party's left wing, supported by vast public demonstrations, had advocated the unilateral renunciation of Britain's deterrent. At the turn of the decade they had even persuaded the party conference to endorse this stand. Next year, in 1961, Hugh Gaitskell and the official right-wing Labor leadership had succeeded in reversing the vote. And in the following two years, the antinuclear movement had weakened, as it succumbed to its own factional disagreements, and the public began to lose interest.

Yet in January, 1963, when Gaitskell died, the wounds of the protracted nuclear debate were far from healed. His successor as party leader, Harold Wilson, was almost ideally equipped to restore unity in Labor's ranks. Originally a follower of Aneurin Bevan in the party left wing, Wilson had been careful to avoid an extremist label and had remained clear of identification with the unilateralists. As a tougher and more astute politician than Gaitskell, he knew when it was time to evolve toward the party center. Moreover, he was less clearly a product of Britain's aristocratic educational system than his predecessor had been. Although just as well-endowed mentally and far from being a proletarian, he was not so distinctively an intellectual; Wilson projected a "classless" image that was well suited to a party and a society impatient both with upper-class "Oxbridge" manners and with Labor's antiquated vocabulary of working-class solidarity.

Such was the appeal that Wilson made: he tried to bridge the gap between Labor's Right and Left—and at the same time to modernize the party—by calling on the new class of technicians and managers to cooperate in the great work of building a planned society. He stressed the need to expand educational opportunities, systematically outbidding the Tories, who had already endorsed a proposal for more than doubling university enrollments in the next generation. This was the great novelty of the election campaign—an appeal to the new middle class which went beyond the conflict between private enterprise and nationalized industry by offering a coherent program of industrial investment, realignment of private incomes, and the use of scientific knowledge under state direction.

The election was held on October 15—the very day on which Khrushchev was toppled from power. The journalists speculated that if the Soviet leader had fallen twenty-four hours earlier, the shock to the British public might have saved Sir Alec from defeat. As it was, Labor won by the extremely narrow margin of five seats; to enjoy a comfortable majority, Wilson had to depend on the nine Liberal party members. But once installed as prime minister, Labor's leader chose to behave as though he had received an unqualified mandate for change. He announced that his government would proceed to carry out its full program: it would curb speculation in land values and reinvigorate public hous-

ing construction; it would "intervene selectively" in the economy by
establishing public industries both in depressed areas and in "growth"
regions of technological advance; it would enlarge social security cover-
age and restore a full system of medical care without charge; it would
redistribute incomes by simultaneously raising pensions and taxes on
large earnings. Most imaginatively of all, it proposed the gradual fusion
of the vocational or "modern" schools and the more academically oriented grammar schools—into one or the other of which British children
were currently being shunted when they were not yet twelve years old—
by establishing a single system of "comprehensive" schools on the American model.

Paradoxically enough, Labor's greatest strides in carrying out this
program came in its initial period of rule, when its parliamentary majority hung on a handful of votes. In his first year and a half in office,
Wilson did in fact succeed in doing some of the things he had promised:
social services grew markedly; public housing and slum clearance increased sharply; "comprehensive" schools began to multiply. In short,
Labor made good on its pledge to shift resources from the private sector
to the public—and eventually even exceeded its announced goal on this
front. By early 1966 Wilson was confident enough to call an unscheduled
election. Taking advantage of a brief respite in the financial difficulties
that almost uninterruptedly plagued his government, he led his party to
a sweeping victory. The election of March 31 gave Labor 363 seats to
253 for the Conservatives—a more than ample margin which made the
support of the Liberals superfluous and sent that party once again into
a decline.

Yet Wilson's electoral triumph brought no respite from financial pressure. On the contrary, it was after 1966 that the central difficulty of
Labor in power became fully evident: social reform cost money, and
that money could be found only if the government produced a high rate
of economic growth. Such growth, however, was dependent on a favorable trade position, and Labor had inherited from the Conservatives a
balance-of-payments deficit and an overvalued currency. The obvious
answer was devaluation, but Wilson's government hesitated to resort to
so drastic an expedient; for a year and a half it tried to muddle through
with palliatives. Not until November, 1967, did it swallow the bitter pill
and reduce the value of the pound by 14.3 per cent on the international
exchanges.

One reason why Wilson had delayed so long was through fear of the
effects of devaluation on Britain's financial prestige. The pound was a
major international currency—second only to the dollar in its worldwide
influence—and in the wake of the British devaluation, seventeen other
countries, including Denmark, Ireland, Israel, and Spain, found themselves obliged to follow suit. To devalue the pound, then, meant to take
another step in Britain's slow, dignified abdication as a great power. To
this too Wilson and his colleagues saw no alternative: they announced

that their country would give up its military responsibilities east of Suez; for the first time in the postwar period they set the budget for education higher than that for defense. Thirteen years of Tory rule had masked the extent to which Britain had already relinquished its overseas commitments. The return of Labor to power put the final seal on the long-drawn-out end of empire.

Most of those at home were satisfied to let memories of glory fade. What bothered Labor's constituents were their own domestic concerns. The trade unions were restive as Wilson tried—mostly without success—to curb strikes and to hold wages in line. Intellectuals denounced the government's policy as unimaginative. Young people found it dispiriting and indulged in milder versions of the student disturbances that were simultaneously keeping the Continental universities in turmoil. In an obvious effort to win back Britain's youth, Wilson pressed through Parliament a bill lowering the voting age to eighteen, which went into effect on New Year's day, 1970. Under Labor Britain continued to offer the Western world a model of personal decency and political fair play; but it could not shake off the atmosphere of drabness and narrowed horizons that had clung to it ever since the heroic years of the early 1940's.

Despite these handicaps, the odds were heavily on the Wilson government when at the end of May the prime minister announced another early election, as he had done in 1966. Although he could have waited ten months more, the omens had suddenly turned favorable: the chronic balance-of-payments deficit had been converted into a surplus, wages were rising faster than prices—even a spell of glorious weather apparently confirmed Wilson's proverbial luck and consummate political skill. So he waged a "happy" campaign, talking little of the issues and leaving it to his opponent, the Tory leader Edward Heath, to warn of the economic dangers ahead. The result was voter apathy and a small turnout at the polls. In one of the greatest political reversals of the century, the election of June 18, 1970, swept the Conservatives into power, with 330 seats in the House of Commons to Labor's 287. As the new prime minister, Heath appointed an experienced team to serve with him, including Sir Alec Douglas-Home as foreign secretary. Its first order of business was to press on with the negotiations for Britain's entry into the Common Market, which in the meantime had at last become an attainable goal (*see* Section IV).

Italy: the Failure of the "Opening to the Left"

In Italy too the Socialists returned to power in the early 1960's. But here they were far from being strong enough to govern alone: they commanded less than 15 per cent of the vote, as opposed to the Christian Democrats' 40 per cent and the Communists' 25. Moreover, they were burdened by the memory of two decades of close cooperation with the Italian followers of Stalin. Not until the events of 1956 had shaken them

loose from this alliance were they in a position to offer a reinforcement
to Italian democracy—to participate in that "opening to the Left" which
Prime Minister Fanfani had so long advocated.

In the spring of 1962 the restless Fanfani was at last able to carry
out his design. The hesitations of his own Christian Democratic party
were resolved when it became apparent that the Vatican no longer opposed an understanding with Italian socialism; Pope John's policy of
coming to terms with the modern world was already having its effect.
For their part, the Socialist leaders agreed with Fanfani on the urgency
of reform and a planned economy: they realized, as he did, that the economic boom was hitting Italian society most unevenly, and that only
vigorous government action could redirect public and private investment into those sectors that were currently being neglected. Many of
the more old-fashioned or ideologically militant Socialists were reluctant
to go along with an economic program that owed far more to Keynes
than to Marx. But even these could appreciate the benefits that might
accrue to Italian workers by having some of their spokesmen in on the
planning process.

The original opening to the Left meant simply that the Socialists
would provide support to a revamped Fanfani government without
supplying any ministers themselves. By 1963, however, when parliamentary elections gave a 60 per cent majority to the parties which had
endorsed the new course, a closer alliance seemed preferable. At this,
an influential minority among both the Christian Democrats and the
Socialists began to balk. It took a summer and autumn of complex party
jockeying—and a colorless caretaker government—to convince the two
parties that there was no alternative. Not until the very end of the year
was it possible to put together a new ministry in which the Socialists
were full participants. In the process, Fanfani himself was sacrificed: his
hard-driving ways had aroused too much hostility on all sides. His heir
as prime minister was a younger and more agreeable Christian Democrat, Aldo Moro.

The Moro government had rough going from the start. It was difficult
at best to keep two such diverse parties working in harmony—and still
harder when economic troubles arose. In the winter of 1963–1964, Italian
prosperity got out of hand: with inflationary pressures mounting and
a balance-of-payments crisis threatening, the government was torn
apart by the contradictory remedies suggested. Two years later, when the
economy returned to prosperity levels, the life had gone out of the opening to the Left. The result of the anti-inflationary struggle had been a
postponement of the government's reform program: its proposals for the
regulation of urban growth, for massive aid to education, and for the
industrialization of the south had not advanced beyond the preparatory
stage.

From this point on, the well-tried devices of Italian politics began to
lose their potency. Moro stayed on as prime minister—there was no one

to replace him, and no one else whom the Socialists felt they could trust. Indeed, for a brief period it seemed as though the Socialists themselves, conscious of the gravity of the parliamentary situation, were ready to forget their internecine quarrels: in early 1966 they reunited with the smaller band of Social Democrats. But the reconciliation was superficial—the old party organizations were never fully fused—and it could not survive the shock of electoral disappointment. When Italy went to the polls in the spring of 1968, the Socialists lost heavily to the Communists and to the fringe formations of the extreme Left. A year later, the party split once more, approximately along the old line of cleavage, and therewith disappeared as a major force in Italian politics. With aging cadres and dwindling trade-union support, it lacked the human resources for a second try at revival.

In the wake of the Socialist electoral losses, Moro too had to go, after having stayed in power longer than any prime minister since De Gasperi. His successors were routine Christian Democrats, who simply tried to muddle along as best they could. For by now it was becoming apparent that the Italian administrative machine was unable to cope with the problems of a modern industrial society: underpaid, overstaffed, inefficient, and demoralized, the bureaucracy threatened to grind to a halt. Already in the autumn of 1966, when devastating floods hit such north Italian cities as Florence and Venice, the government had been bitterly criticized for its failure to foresee the danger and to take preventive action. Three years later a massive wave of strikes brought a further loss of public confidence. The northern industrial centers were shaken by sporadic but prolonged protests, sometimes violent in character, which had as their prime target the government's inability to provide adequate housing for the mass of newly recruited workers from the depressed and overpopulated South. It was symptomatic that this new proletariat proved particularly receptive to the appeals to violence emanating from wildcat union leaders with anarchist or "Maoist" sympathies.

By the end of the 1960's, then, Italian political life was sinking into a bog of discouragement. Factional strife had reduced party organization to meaninglessness; parliamentary debate seemed more and more irrelevant to the real issues confronting the nation. Increasingly Italians asked themselves whether electoral democracy itself could survive so dispiriting a state of affairs: nothing seemed to be working; all the old remedies had been exhausted. Memories of Mussolini suggested a resort to the rule of a "strong man"—but neo-fascism had ceased to be a functioning political movement, and despite rumors of military plots, no potential *duce* was lurking in the wings. The more realistic of the still untried alternatives was the gamble of an appeal to the Communists.

In the "swampy" situation of the turn of the decade, Italian communism could point with pride to its record of responsible behavior: its substantial independence from Soviet direction was apparent in the stand it had taken on the occupation of Czechoslovakia; it had given honest government to a number of Italian cities; it ran its cooperatives with quiet efficiency; its trade-union wing was striving to hold extremists in check and to direct labor agitation into constructive channels. Moreover, it was Italy's second largest party—Christian Democracy's only real competitor—and the strongest Communist party in the Western world. Along with the French, it was one of the two Western branches of communism which regularly made an impressive electoral showing. The Italian party not only held its ground; with each successive election it increased its vote. But these electoral gains, far from demonstrating a rise in militancy, reflected a steady drift from revolutionary propaganda to an emphasis on the party's "respectability." In the post-Stalin years, the Italian Communists, with the French following at a slower pace, had converted themselves into reformists who saw no reason why they should not share power in a reform-minded government. In 1970 it was still too early to tell whether such democratic professions should be taken at face value. Even the more daring among the Christian Democrats did not fully trust their Communist counterparts. Yet at the very least the profound change in Italian communism suggested that it could not remain forever in the state of political quarantine to which it had been consigned for more than two decades.

The New Technicians and the Maladjustments of Prosperity

By 1960, nearly the whole of Western and Central Europe was enjoying the most sustained prosperity it had known since the outbreak of the First World War. In France, which earlier had lagged behind its neighbors but had now suddenly advanced into the lead, production increased by nearly two-thirds during the period 1952–1958. Elsewhere, an annual rise in productivity of approximately 4 per cent had come to be taken for granted.

To operate this expanded industrial machine, a greatly increased staff of managers and technicians was required. These, like their counterparts in the Soviet Union, typified the changed society of the mid-century. They were realistic and matter-of-fact and they admired the efficiency of American methods. As opposed to the old type of educated European, whose culture was literary and humanistic, these people were better trained in science and economics and reflected both the postwar changes in educational curricula and the new democratization of the technical schools and universities.

Indeed, there had emerged what the British called a "meritocracy"— a class of highly trained specialists coming from all strata of the population and closely attached to none. Such men and women, who more and more frequently derived from lower-middle-class or working-class backgrounds, as they rose in the social scale, lost touch with their families and earlier associations. They advanced as individuals, leaving their original class behind them. This was not at all what European Socialists had had in mind when they dreamed of the future society; they had thought of whole classes rising, and of the leaders of these classes remaining with their own people as directors of political parties or trade unions. Before the war, to rise out of one's class was considered treason to one's comrades.

With the postwar democratization of life and education, however, the American notion of an individual ascent became accepted. The result was an impoverishment of the Socialist parties and trade unions, which saw themselves deprived of their natural leaders. The new class of managers and technicians—and with them a great part of the population at large—was impatient of all forms of ideological debate, which, in the new Europe of the mid-century, sounded old-fashioned, stuffy, and irrelevant and seemed to have little to do with the real problems of the Continent's economy and society. By 1960, a mixed economy was everywhere the rule; the welfare state and a large measure of official intervention in economic life were universally accepted. West Germany, Belgium, and Switzerland leaned toward free enterprise; Britain, Scandinavia, and the Netherlands were more tinged with socialism; France and Italy were somewhere in between; but the differences between one nation and another were of degree rather than of kind. For the new men of the mid-century the pre-1945 debates over the merits of capitalism or collectivism seemed academic and tedious: on the one hand, they were convinced that state intervention and state planning were essential; on the other hand, they were skeptical of the traditional socialist panacea of nationalization.

The result was widespread agreement on an implicit ideology that might be called "conservative socialism." As one skeptical but sympathetic critic put it, socialist doctrines had "begun to wear a somewhat antiquated look" for the very reason that "so many of their predictions" had "come true." * But this had happened in a *form* which almost no one had predicted and which disoriented the parties of the Left. More particularly, the decline of the cult of revolution as an end in itself and the decreasing public interest in such old issues as anticlericalism deprived political debate of much of its earlier moral fervor. The great new questions were technical: most of them did not lend themselves to impassioned advocacy and were dependent for intelligent discussion on the advice of experts.

Such was the outlook as the 1960's opened. As the decade progressed, however, and a new type of Socialist leader (like Harold Wilson) came to the fore, a second look at the newly emerging society suggested that matters were not quite so clearly on the road to a harmonious solution. Revolutionary spirit and class hatred might be greatly diminished, but status differences and large inequalities in wealth remained. A new

---

* George Lichtheim, *The New Europe: Today—and Tomorrow* (New York: Frederick A. Praeger, Inc., 1963), p. 182.

generation of democratic left-wing leadership—men who themselves could lay claim to being technicians and experts—began to search out the social anomalies and the pockets of backwardness which belied the over-all picture of a democratic and prosperous continent.

In a geographical sense, they found, the new prosperity was most unevenly distributed. It had attained its full development only in Europe's industrial heartland, stretching from Glasgow in Scotland to the north Italian city of Milan. Elsewhere—especially in Southern Europe—although the mid-century social changes had discredited the old ways of doing things, the standard of living had not risen proportionately. If Europe's own underdeveloped areas were more severely shaken by innovation than were the established industrial centers, they were still unable to keep up with the over-all economic advance; in Italy, for example, although the south made more progress in the decade 1955–1965 than in any other such period of its history, *in comparative terms* the gap between it and the north widened rather than diminished. Moreover, here, as in so many other backward parts of the Continent, excess manpower increasingly sought work either in the industrialized regions of its own nation or in more prosperous countries; by 1963, two and three-quarter million laborers were working in foreign lands. Almost necessarily, these people suffered from discrimination and difficulties in adjustment. And such social problems were compounded where, as in England, the immigrant workers were of another race. In the British election of 1964, the Labor party lost votes in more than one constituency for having championed the cause of nonwhites from the Commonwealth countries overseas who had been arriving in a steady stream since the Second World War.

Even in the more advanced areas, troubling residues of an earlier type of society remained. Old patterns of deference toward the wealthy and the educated persisted, as did the entrenched position of such people in the higher ranks of the civil service and similar elite bodies. To the new "postcapitalist service class" of managers and technicians, it was apparent that an open educational system could alone give access to the upper reaches of society. Yet the transition to a more democratic educational system was far from completed. Debate was still raging over whether the schools and universities should be primarily concerned with turning out specialists attuned to the world of the 1960's and 1970's, or whether they should continue to cultivate the old values of a "liberal" education. Similarly—as the British example showed—it was not yet settled whether preadolescent children should be routed into separate academic and vocational "streams" or kept together in a single school program. Over-all, both types of education were in short supply: experts estimated that university enrollments needed to be doubled and that advanced technical schools should be expanded even more rapidly to equal in size the traditional institutions of higher learning.

In the 1950's social criticism had focused on status differences. A decade later, economic questions had once more come into prominence.

For if educational reform promised eventually to break down caste barriers, there was no corresponding technique at hand to reduce disparities in wealth. As the years of prosperity continued, it became apparent that the continuing gap between the rich and the poor regions of Europe had its exact parallel in the difference between rich and poor members of the various national populations. Although the latter were improving their lot, they were not doing so as rapidly as the wealthy. In comparison with America, the basic items (such as food) in the budgets of the poor remained expensive, whereas the luxury items which the rich nearly monopolized were relatively cheap. Moreover, the wealthy tended to come from the same families as they had earlier; the higher business leadership recruited itself within very narrow circles. In the Europe of the 1960's, as in the United States, it was easier for someone without family backing to make his way in politics than in the world of business.

Social mobility, then, was not working as smoothly as some of the enthusiasts for the new society supposed. In the economic realm much of it was promise rather than performance. Even in the celebrated matter of American-type consumer goods, the comparative figures were sobering. Estimates suggested that 60 per cent of Britain's population could not yet afford to buy such things as washing machines, refrigerators, and automobiles; in Germany and France it was 70 per cent, and in Italy 80 per cent. Even by the 1970's, nearly half the families in Europe's wealthiest lands would still not own a car.

Such statistics indicated that social and economic conflict had by no means simply been relegated to an unhappy past. Indeed, in certain respects the new availability of mass consumer goods made matters worse; it underlined the difference between those who had them and those who did not. Thus, after the comparative quiet of the 1950's, unexpected sources of class tension appeared, and trade unions began to regain their militancy. This, however, was no longer narrowly ideological; the working-class demands of the 1960's were directed toward concrete economic goals. The most important strikes of the decade—those of the German metalworkers and the French coal miners in 1963 and the widespread industrial disturbances in Italy in 1969—were clearly inspired by the conviction that the ordinary workingman was not receiving his due share in the over-all prosperity.

The Common Market

Most of these new social and economic questions crossed national frontiers. Both prosperity and the maladjustments it entailed were Western European in scope. Trade unionists and managers alike could agree that the strict separation of one economy from another by national boundaries no longer made sense. With the experience of the United States and the Soviet Union in mind, they argued that a wider market was required for maximum efficiency. Hence the pressure for "integration"— a tighter concept than alliance but a looser one than union—which as

early as 1951 had manifested itself in the establishment of the European
Coal and Steel community.

Despite the failure of the next move toward integration—the EDC— the six nations of "Little Europe" had proceeded to organize further economic "communities." In 1956 came the pooling of their resources of nuclear energy in "Euratom," and in the following year, the establishment of a Common Market, which would eventually mean the elimination of all tariff barriers among them. A year later, De Gaulle assumed power in France. Despite the turn toward national assertion under the Fifth Republic, the Gaullist regime continued to honor the commitments of its predecessor toward its European partners.

These moves toward ever-tighter economic integration on the part of the "Inner Six" finally galvanized the other Western European nations into corresponding joint action. In November, 1959, the seven nations of the European periphery—Britain, the three Scandinavian states, Switzerland, Austria, and Portugal—signed a counteragreement for the reduction of trade barriers. This action was largely one of desperation; it arose from fear of the Common Market far more than from constructive purposes of its own. The nations of the "Outer Seven" (or European Free Trade Association) were geographically scattered and—except in the case of Scandinavia—their economies had little in common. The trade of Britain alone, moreover, exceeded that of all the others combined. The organization of the Outer Seven was not much more than a holding operation calculated to gain time in which to see how the Inner Six developed.

By January 1, 1958, all six had ratified the Treaty of Rome, establishing the Common Market, and the great experiment was launched. An area with a population of more than 170 million—comparable to that of the Soviet Union or the United States—was now associated in what was officially called the European Economic Community. From the start the new community aimed at something wider than a customs union: like its predecessor, the Coal and Steel Community, the Common Market had a supranational executive responsible to an intergovernmental council of ministers. Theoretically its powers were weaker than those of the earlier community, but since it shared with it a joint international assembly and court of justice, the procedures of the two inevitably tended to merge.

Between 1958 and 1962, industrial production within the Common Market went up at an average annual rate of 7.6 per cent—as opposed to 4 per cent in the seven nations of the European Free Trade Association—which in itself gave eloquent evidence of the success of the venture. During the same years, trade among the six nearly doubled. The original idea had been to reduce tariffs among the member nations very gradually so as to give the individual economies time to adjust to the change. But once the experiment was launched, businessmen began to lose their fears: many argued that it was better to get the transition over with as rapidly as possible and to start immediately to meet the new competition that tariff reduction implied. As a result, by mid-1963, the Common Market was two and a half years ahead of schedule, with internal tariffs down to 40 per cent of their previous level.

Five years later, on July 1, 1968, the full tariff union came into effect, as the last customs barriers fell. The great goal had apparently been achieved. Yet resistance to integration had by no means ceased. On the contrary, by the turn of the decade it was evident that a slowdown had occurred on a number of fronts: despite their engagements not to do so, the individual nations of the Common Market were still making commercial agreements on their own, they were still protecting a few favored monopolies, and they had yet to give full recognition to the professional credentials of each other's citizens.

The gravest problems that the community faced, however, were its relations with Great Britain and with the arbitrary and unpredictable ruler of the French. After nearly three years of hesitation, in the summer of 1961 the Macmillan government applied for membership. This proposition put the six before a cruel dilemma. Most of them wanted Britain in: the governments of the Low Countries in particular were mindful of their long-standing cultural and commercial ties across the Channel and eager for democratic reinforcement against the authoritarian pretensions of De Gaulle. At the same time, the British wanted to enter on terms of maximum benefit to themselves, while retaining their favored position within the Commonwealth. Such conditions gave pause even to those who endorsed Britain's membership: it seemed a one-sided bargain, and it threatened the prospects of political federation by, in effect, giving the community an open frontier. In the end De Gaulle settled the matter: after several months of a characteristic cryptic silence, in January, 1963, he vetoed the British application. Four years later, in May, 1967, he repeated the performance, replying in similar terms to a second British bid for admission, this time coming from Labor rather than the Conservatives and with fewer conditions attached; not until Britain had undergone a "profound economic and political transformation," De Gaulle maintained, would it be ready for partnership with its Continental neighbors.

When these words were uttered, the general's hold over his own people was already slipping. The Europe of the 1970's was in sight—and with it the possibility of unraveling some of the dilemmas that in the preceding decade had proved insoluble.

IV

TOWARD THE 1970's

In February, 1965, when the United States became fully involved in the Vietnam conflict, Europe found itself in a depressingly familiar situation. Once more, as in the early 1950's, the world's strongest power was at

war; once more, as at the time of Korea, the military ally of half the
Continent had embarked on a struggle to which it was impossible for Europeans, whether of the East or of the West, to remain indifferent. Moreover, the conflict in Vietnam recalled another set of painful post-1945 experiences. Unlike the Korean War, in which regular troops had fought each other along a recognizable front, the struggle in Southeast Asia was primarily of a guerrilla nature and one in which technological superiority failed to bring victory. Such had been the character of the two protracted and eventually hopeless wars that France had fought in its former overseas dependencies—Indochina and Algeria. Indeed, the Vietnam War in a number of respects was simply a continuation of the first of these; in the late 1960's the Americans were encountering on the same ground the same kind of agonizing difficulties with which the French had contended in vain a decade and a half earlier.

Under these circumstances it was understandable that Europeans should adopt an air of hard-learned wisdom and should advise their allies across the Atlantic to cut their losses and get out of Vietnam. Such, predictably enough, was the predominant view among the French—to which De Gaulle gave expression with his customary verve and irony. The Scandinavians were almost equally critical; but here the opposition to the Vietnam War sprang from humanitarian revulsion rather than injured national pride. In the countries that had close and crucial economic ties to the United States—Britain, Italy, West Germany—public criticism was muted by political realism, and the governments gave the American war effort their qualified support. Yet it was only in the nations under authoritarian regimes of the Right—Spain, Portugal, and Greece—that the United States found any enthusiastic backing. And in Eastern Europe even the leaders most independent of the Soviet Union—such as those of Yugoslavia and Rumania—found nothing good to say about America's Asian war. All in all, the struggle in Vietnam ranked throughout Europe as the most unpopular course the United States had pursued for a quarter of a century.

Yet although the conflict in Southeast Asia bulked as the dominant event of the 1960's, overshadowing the whole second half of the decade, its effects on Europe were less devastating than those of Korea. Its financial repercussions were less profound: while it brought the same kind of inflationary pressures, the European economies were now more self-reliant and better protected against outside shocks than they had been in 1950. Moreover, this time the Europeans themselves were far less worried that the conflict would spread; very few thought that the Americans and the Russians would actually come to blows. The Soviet Union had enough trouble at home already, and the support it gave the communist effort in Vietnam was undercut by its quarrel with China. The conflict in Korea had locked Europe into the frozen power relationships of the Cold War at its height: in contrast, the moral ambiguities of Vietnam merely intensified the Europeans' sense that they had entered an epoch of political fluidity in which the old guideposts were one by one being left behind. As the 1960's drew to a close, two substantial changes of power pointed the way to a new configuration—the end of De Gaulle's eleven-year rule in France and the passing of the Christian Democrats in Germany after a tenure of two full decades.

The End of the Gaullist Era

The first sign that De Gaulle's power was no longer what it once had been came with the French presidential election of December, 1965. Riding the wave of confidence that had been bearing him aloft ever since he had settled the Algerian war, the general, despite the fact that he was turning 75, decided to run for another seven-year term. At the start, the outcome seemed a foregone conclusion: faced with the novel situation of a presidential campaign in which the entire electorate would be voting, the opposition was divided and lacked a clear issue on which to concentrate its fire. Yet there were sufficient miscellaneous discontents throughout the land to offer an opportunity to a politician who could weld them into a new political movement. Such a man was François Mitterrand: supple, indefatigable, an experienced parliamentarian with a deceptively novel air about him, Mitterrand managed to rally behind him Socialists and Radicals and free-lance politicians like himself; he also won the tacit support of the Communists. Still more, Mitterrand converted the electoral campaign into a nationwide personality contest, in which, as in the United States, public "images" counted for more than political labels. The result was a spectacular humiliation for De Gaulle. In a field of six candidates, Mitterrand polled 32 per cent to the general's 44. Since no one had emerged with a majority, a second round of voting became necessary. This time, with only the two top candidates in the running, De Gaulle won—but with a margin of no more than nine percentage points. France's first presidential election by direct popular vote had dispelled once and for all the myth of the general's indispensability.

Mitterrand's success in forcing De Gaulle into a runoff was matched fifteen months later in the parliamentary election of March, 1967. The Federation of the Left in which the former had brought together the parties that had backed his candidacy functioned most effectively. For the first time since the Popular Front campaign of 1936, Socialists and Communists regularly voted for each other's candidates on the second round, reducing the government's support in the Assembly to a razor-thin majority. Yet the general himself learned no lesson from this second mishap. Haughtier than ever, he vetoed once more Britain's bid to enter the Common Market; he offered gratuitous advice to Israel, as he ended France's established policy of giving it military aid; and on a visit to Canada he embarrassed that country's government by demagogic appeals to the French-speaking dissidents of Quebec. It seemed apparent that at the very time De Gaulle's prestige at home was going into a decline, he was losing abroad his aura of diplomatic finesse.

All this suggested that the French Left could profit by his mistakes and that the successor to the general might very likely be Mitterrand himself —and even perhaps a Popular Front government with Communist participation. Then the unexpected happened: an astounding series of events that made the month of May, 1968, the strangest in France's postwar history both disoriented the Left and gave De Gaulle a year's reprieve.

It all started with student disturbances at Nanterre, the new, bleak suburban branch of the University of Paris. From here the agitation spread to the Sorbonne, the center of the old university on the Left Bank. The grievances of French students were of long standing: overcrowded conditions and the rigidity of the examination system were perfectly legitimate targets of dissatisfaction. What came as a surprise was the universality and the explosive force of the May protest. By the sixth, the students were fighting pitched battles with the police. The following week a large part of the Left Bank was ringed with barricades within which the students were masters. On the fourteenth, De Gaulle departed on a state visit to Rumania, leaving his government without clear directions for coping with the disturbances. In his absence the agitation spread to industrial workers, several factories were occupied, and the general was obliged to cut short his journey. Yet his return brought no respite—on the contrary, the strike movement intensified, as the students fraternized with the strikers, and the workers in the larger plants rejected the settlement that their union leaders had negotiated with the employers. By the end of the month the government's authority had apparently collapsed, and Mitterrand was openly advancing his candidacy for the succession.

At this point De Gaulle simply disappeared for the better part of a day. Having assured himself of the loyalty of his army commanders, he returned to Paris fortified by a new determination. He dissolved the Assembly, calling for elections within a month and summoning loyal citizens to rally behind him. In response, hundreds of thousands of conservative Parisians poured into the streets in a massive demonstration on the Right Bank. De Gaulle's declaration of May 30 marked the turning point. The initiative passed to the government, as the leaders of the democratic Left were caught unprepared for an election, and the Communists, who saw no profit to be gained from further agitation, urged moderation on their followers. By early June both the student movement and the strike movement were subsiding. In mid-June the police cleared the activists from the Sorbonne. At the end of the month, the elections gave De Gaulle's supporters the biggest majority they had ever attained. The Federation of the Left was crushed. Of the opposition parties, the Communists alone, despite heavy losses, came through with their prestige intact.

"The events of May"—as the French called them, at a loss to find a more precise term—certainly fell short of being a revolution. This the Communists had early discerned and taken their precautions by withholding their all-out support. Yet if it was not a revolution, what was it in fact? An eruption of pent-up discontent, a vast psychodrama, an intoxicating moment of fraternity—it was all these; but it lacked leaders and a program, and in the end the forces of law and order triumphed overwhelmingly. By late summer France looked as though the great movement had never occurred: the Gaullists had returned stronger than ever, and the general himself had been given a new lease on power.

Yet under the surface of restored calm, all was far from well. The wage increases that were granted to appease the industrial workers cost the country dearly, and De Gaulle refused to devalue the franc as his advisers were recommending. The parallel effort to conciliate the students and younger faculty by decentralizing and democratizing the structure of the universities was proceeding only haltingly. At the beginning of 1969 the general once more made a mistake that this time proved fatal. He announced a referendum on a proposal to reorganize the administration of the country on a regional basis. In itself the project had much to commend it: students of French government had long agreed that it suffered from over-centralization. Yet a large number of vested interests felt threatened by the proposed change, and the disparate cohorts of De Gaulle's enemies saw their opportunity when the general announced that he would treat the referendum as a vote of confidence. By mid-April several moderate and conservative groupings had joined a united Left in announcing their opposition to the proposal. On April 27, when the French went to the polls for the third time in as many years, the regional project lost by the narrowest of margins. The general resigned. The end of the Gaullist era had arrived more quietly than anyone had anticipated; the chaos that the general had warned against failed to materialize.

It now became necessary to elect another president, and the logical candidate was ready and waiting. Georges Pompidou had served De Gaulle as an able and efficient prime minister: he had kept his nerve the previous May when even the general had not known what to do, and his master, with the proverbial ingratitude of the powerful, had rewarded him with summary dismissal. Nine months later Pompidou grasped the chance for a political comeback; he managed his campaign with consummate skill; the demoralized forces of the Left were divided among four candidates. On the first round Pompidou's showing was almost exactly the same as De Gaulle's had been four years earlier; on the second round he actually did better, emerging an easy victor.

The election of Pompidou in June, 1969, proved that Gaullism could continue without De Gaulle. The new president had a solid parliamentary majority behind him, and he even enlarged it by inviting into the ministry some veteran non-Gaullists. Sober, realistic, technically well-staffed, the government took up the unfinished task of liquidating the legacy of the month of near-revolution. It devalued the franc by 12.5 per cent—too late to bring the economic gains that might have accrued if De

Gaulle had done so a year earlier; it announced a program of austerity; it pushed forward the reform of the universities and cast about for ways in which to propitiate the industrial workers. For what it sought above all was social peace and that reconciliation of the French which the general had preached so often.

Within the government itself there reigned a freedom of discussion that France's political leaders had almost forgotten. The new president did not lecture to his ministers like schoolboys, as his predecessor (in common with Adenauer) had done. Nor did he try to imitate De Gaulle's virtuoso performances on the international stage. With the general's departure, the bubble of Gaullist foreign policy burst; it became plain to all how little substance there was in the notion of France's "greatness," and that the country's international weight was approximately the same as that of any other country of comparable economic and human resources. Still more significantly, Pompidou lifted the French veto on Britain's admission to the Common Market. At a meeting of the Six in early December at The Hague, he acceded to the wish of his five partners to open negotiations both with the British and with whatever other nations had requested entry.

An additional reason for the change was that six weeks earlier a new German chancellor had come to power. From the start Willy Brandt dominated the proceedings at The Hague with the insistence that the British be extended a welcoming hand. For a half decade the French had bullied such gatherings; now leadership was passing to the Germans. This shift, and the new Social Democratic chancellor who incarnated it, marked an even more significant alteration on the international scene than the passing of De Gaulle.

The Advent of Willy Brandt

At the end of November, 1966, fretting under Chancellor Erhard's weak leadership and the unpredictability of the parliamentary allies on whom it depended for its majority, Germany's Christian Democratic Union had decided on the long-untried expedient of a "Great Coalition" with the chief opposition party, the Social Democrats. For the latter such a formula offered distinct advantages: weary of an exclusion from power that had lasted for more than a generation, German Social Democracy was obsessed with a desire to prove its responsibility and capacity to govern. Moreover, when it had shed its Marxist trappings in 1959, the chief impediment to its acceptance by the German middle-class public had disappeared. The Social Democrats knew how often in the past a coalition with a more conservative party had proved disastrous; but they were willing to run the risk in the interest of broadening their constituency.

The new chancellor, Kurt Kiesinger, an astute, urbane Christian Democrat in his middle years, was too young to have had a pre-Nazi political career. Quite the contrary, he was by his own admission a former member of the National Socialist party. This was a second innovation in postwar German politics, and it proved that a record of adherence to Nazism no longer posed an insuperable barrier to advancement. To German youth in particular, Hitler's era now seemed remote history: how was it possible, the young people asked, for their country to go on forever apologizing and atoning for the sins of the past? Along with such questions went a longing to "normalize" Germany's relations with the outside world—to be accepted as an ordinary European nation no different from the others.

Yet in Kiesinger's chancellorship normalization proved unattainable. Although the Social Democratic leader Willy Brandt had taken over the foreign ministry and announced his intention of advancing by small steps toward better relations with the East, Germany's policy abroad changed very little; nothing substantial was accomplished to put the West Germans in closer contact with those of the East or to bring down the wall that divided Berlin in two. This near-paralysis in foreign relations was matched by a lack of results at home. The collaboration of such dissimilar political parties made for a deadlock comparable to what the corresponding coalition in Italy had produced. The Social Democrats, as the weaker partners, naturally felt the greater frustration; but as the 1960's drew to an end, they began to sense that pressure for change was mounting and that it could be directed to their advantage.

In the spring of 1968, a month before "the events of May" in Paris, violent student demonstrations shook a number of German universities. A year later an unconventional and outspoken Social Democrat, Gustav Heinemann, was elected president of the Federal Republic. By this time, the quadrennial elections to the Bundestag were approaching. Brandt and his Social Democratic colleagues entered the campaign with vigor and confidence. They stressed the need for a change after twenty years of Christian Democratic rule; they proposed a more flexible and realistic policy toward the Communist states of Eastern Europe; they ran together as a team of seasoned experts. In contrast, the Christian Democrats seemed stuck in the familiar routines: reminding the voters of what had happened in Prague the previous year, they fell back on the Adenauer line of uncompromising resistance to Moscow, with the suggestion that Kiesinger, like the old chancellor, was the only man really up to the job.

What was most novel about the election campaign was a lively grassroots interest that the Social Democrats, as the party of movement and change, were able to exploit to the full. Particularly effective were the free-ranging discussions led by the novelist Günter Grass, which attracted throngs of people who had never before been tempted to vote for Social Democracy. When the electorate went to the polls on September 28, it was quite clear that Kiesinger's party would suffer losses and that Brandt's would make gains; all that was in doubt was the extent of the shift and the governmental formula which would result from it.

With 46 per cent of the vote and a loss of only three seats, the Christian Democrats still remained out in front; theoretically they might again have supplied the chancellor. But the third-ranking party that in Adenauer and Erhard's day had provided the margin they needed for a majority, the Free Democrats, was no longer interested in governing with its former partners. In the interval, it had evolved toward the left and now preferred to go into coalition with Brandt's Social Democrats. The latter's vote had risen by three and a half percentage points; they had gained more than twenty seats; they could scarcely wait to assume power. On October 21, 1969, Willy Brandt became Germany's first Social Democratic chancellor in nearly forty years.

Once installed in authority, Brandt acted with the decisiveness his followers expected of him. Besides opening the way to Britain's entry into the Common Market, he revalued the mark at a higher rate—thereby underlining Germany's true financial strength as against the devalued British and French currencies. Most significantly, he moved with speed and determination to carry out his pledge of improving relations with the East. To the Polish and Soviet governments, which had greeted his accession to power as a "positive" development, he offered the prospect of closer economic ties and an end to ideological polemics. In the case of the Poles, Brandt's policy pointed toward Germany's eventual acceptance of its post-1945 frontiers, and in the case of the Russians, toward a treaty in which both sides would renounce the use of force—a treaty that was in fact signed the following August.

Faced with these sudden changes, Walter Ulbricht, the old, hard-bitten, Prussian-style Communist who had ruled East Germany almost unchallenged for twenty years, saw that he too must begin to adapt to the world of Willy Brandt. Ever since 1961, when the Berlin wall had gone up, the lesser half of divided Germany had begun to make economic progress and to establish itself as a viable state. Before then, its greatest problem had been a steady population drain which had deprived it of nearly three million people, most of them young. With the chance of escape to the prosperous West cut off, East Germany launched its own modest version of an industrial boom. By the late 1960's, although manpower was still in short supply, and few East Germans owned such prime consumer goods as automobiles, the country's plants were working at a high level of efficiency, more particularly in the field of electronics, and an annual rise in productivity of 6 per cent had put East Germany among the world's foremost industrial powers, no small achievement for a state with a population of only seventeen million. These accomplishments had given Ulbricht's regime a new solidity and prestige—and a concomitant weight within the Eastern bloc. As director of the strongest industrial complex among the Soviet allies, the East German leader had spoken with a new-found authority in 1968, when he had urged on Brezhnev and Kosygin a tough line toward Czechoslovakia.

A year later the advent of Brandt threatened to upset what Ulbricht had achieved. The soothing words emanating from Bonn might leap over East Germany entirely, leaving it neglected by its own allies. So Ulbricht had little choice but to join in the Communist welcome to the new breeze from the West. Alleging his willingness to discuss "fundamental problems" with the Brandt government, he agreed to talks without preconditions and with an open agenda. In the spring of 1970, the West German chancellor met twice with his East German counterpart— apparently to no avail. Yet it seemed likely that Ulbricht would eventually drop his long-standing insistence on full international recognition in return for Bonn's willingness to admit to East Germany's existence at last. The day might still be far off when the barbed wire and pillboxes that divided the German people would disappear—but in 1970 it had for the first time become a real possibility.

Southern Europe: Echoes of War and New Forms of Authoritarian Rule

In April, 1967, a group of army colonels seized power in Greece. Faced with approaching elections that threatened to bring to power a center-left majority, the authoritarians of the Right had determined to forestall the popular vote. Democracy in postwar Greece had never functioned satisfactorily. Most of the time since 1949, when the struggle with the Communist guerrillas had come to an end, the country had been under conservative governments heavily dependent on support from the United States. The Right had been characterized by corruption and economic selfishness, the Left by demagogic behavior and periodic flirtations with communism. Yet for all the weaknesses of the parliamentary system, the younger leaders of Greek democracy were beginning to devise coherent reform plans when the *coup d'état* came. The rule of the colonels ended such hopes. A narrow, xenophobic, anti-intellectual tyranny descended on the country. The most prominent opposition leaders were jailed; some were later released under surveillance, and a few chose to go into exile. In December the King also fled abroad, after an abortive attempt at a counter-coup. By the turn of the decade the new Greek regime had entrenched itself in power; dissatisfaction was widespread, but no organized resistance had sprung to arms. Nor, despite a succession of promises, largely for American consumption, had the rule of the colonels been "liberalized" in any substantial fashion. While it might not be fascist in the strict interwar meaning of the term—it lacked both an explicit ideology and the support of a broadly based single party—it was unquestionably reactionary and suspicious of all forms of social and cultural innovation.

A month and a half after the Greek *coup d'état*, Israel and its Arab neighbors went to war for the third time in two decades. The "Six-Day War" of June 5–10, 1967, was a stunning Israeli victory. Yet it failed to

disarm the implacable hostility of the Arabs to Israel's very existence, 567
and it was followed by an almost uninterrupted succession of ground The New Society:
and air skirmishes that hovered on the brink of a fourth full-scale conflict. Europe
For the foreseeable future the Near East seemed destined to find no in the 1960's
peace.

The events in Greece and those on Israel's borders had no intrinsic connection—except for a tenuous link in the fact that both countries were closely tied to the United States. Together, however, they suggested that the Eastern Mediterranean had become one of the world's prime danger spots. Where a decade or two earlier Central Europe had been the focus of concern, now the Near East figured as the point of Soviet-American confrontation. Indeed, the Six-Day War had been the direct result of a more active Mediterranean policy on the part of the Soviet Union. It had marked the culmination of a naval buildup and a steady supplying of arms to Israel's Arab enemies. Not that the Soviet Union wanted war: it seems clear that it stumbled into encouraging Nasser's Egypt to make a show of force in the Sinai Peninsula that subsequently went far beyond what it had intended. Yet that such miscalculations could happen merely underlined the volatile and explosive character of power relations in the Near East.

Beyond that, the instability in the Eastern Mediterranean—coupled with the malfunctioning of democracy in Italy—impressed on Southern Europe's authoritarian rulers to the west the urgency of ensuring the continuity of their own systems. In both nations of the Iberian peninsula, the late 1960's saw the succession question settled at last: in Portugal as in Spain, the long-standing debate over who or what would follow Salazar and Franco was given a conservative answer. In the former country, after a stroke had incapacitated the aged dictator, one of Salazar's erstwhile collaborators, Dr. Marcelo Caetano, took over as prime minister. The advent of Caetano in September, 1968, could not fail to mark a few changes.* More cosmopolitan and modern-minded than his political mentor, he loosened up the censorship and gave greater scope to the opposition parties. Yet the broad outlines of Salazar's regime remained unaltered. The costly effort to hold on to the Portuguese holdings in Africa continued as before. And when parliamentary elections were held at the end of Caetano's first year in office, the results were much as they had been under Salazar: with the opposition divided and uncertain, and with most of the potential voters apathetic or not even on the electoral rolls, the official candidates swept the field. A generation-long tutelage had left the mass of the Portuguese incapable of exercising the limited political rights they now enjoyed.

In Spain, although Franco was ailing and in his late seventies, he refused to relinquish power. Instead, in the summer of 1969 he designated

---

* Salazar died 22 months later, in July, 1970.

the young Bourbon prince Juan Carlos as his successor, passing over the latter's father, who was the legitimate pretender to the throne. While this solution was technically monarchist, it in fact gave encouragement to those who wanted to see the regime go on as it was: in his speech of acceptance, Juan Carlos pledged his loyalty to Spain's existing institutions. Indeed, one of the curious features of the succession settlement was that it disappointed so wide a variety of people: the democratic opposition of Socialists and Christian Democrats saw its hopes for a liberal regime indefinitely postponed; the Falange likewise viewed the designation of Juan Carlos as the final step in its gradual decline from the prominent part it had played in the Civil War. Three months after his announcement of the succession, Franco confirmed these suspicions by naming a new ministry, predominantly of technicians and with a strong representation from the ranks of *Opus Dei*. This ministry was more homogeneous than its predecessors; it also promised to be more efficient and to guide Spain toward closer relations with the democracies of the West.

Such intentions epitomized the central problem that Franco's subordinates confronted in the twilight of his rule: how could they present an acceptable face to the outside world while retaining the essentials of authoritarian control? Many of them were younger men, alert to the criticisms of the political opposition, more particularly to those of the Christian Democrats, whose disparate factions were gradually coalescing and finding favor at the Vatican. Indeed, the reformers within the government had become almost indistinguishable from its moderate enemies. To preserve Spain's regime while liberalizing its attitudes and procedures—this squaring of the circle was the only course that made sense in the transition era between Franco and a restored monarchy.

The Tenacity of Ethnic Identity: Sweden, Belgium, Ireland

Several of the smaller democracies of Western Europe, whose internal affairs had aroused little general interest in the preceding two decades, in the late 1960's were thrust upon the attention of the world outside. In Scandinavia, the established tradition of Socialist rule found itself obliged to adjust to changed popular expectations. In Belgium and in Ireland, deep-seated linguistic and religious antagonisms flared into sporadic violence.

After a generation of almost uninterrupted power, the Social Democratic governments of Denmark, Norway, and Sweden began to appear routine and antiquated. The welfare-state experiments that in the depression years of the 1930's had seemed so novel had been accepted at home by their political opponents and had been widely copied abroad. As a consequence, the Social Democrats were voted out of office in Norway in 1965 and in Denmark three years later. In Sweden alone they managed to hold on to power and even to enlarge their following. This

achievement was a tribute to the astute sense of what the times required
of two successive prime ministers, Tage Erlander and Olof Palme. In September, 1968, Erlander, who had already been in office longer than any democratic premier of the twentieth century, led his party to a smashing electoral victory. The following year, after nearly a quarter of a century of directing Sweden's affairs, the veteran prime minister stepped down in favor of the 42-year-old Palme. Casual in manner and unafraid of controversy, Palme was not above playing a bit part in what later proved to be a highly sexual film or leading protest marches against America's Vietnam policy. Under his leadership the Swedish Social Democrats were determined to project the image of dynamism and sympathy with the forces of change that Willy Brandt and his colleagues were so successfully exploiting in Germany.

In Belgium the hostility between Flemings and Walloons, which had lain quiescent for two decades following the abdication of Leopold III, broke out once more in bitter contention over the "linguistic frontier" that in the meantime had been officially drawn across the country. The French-speaking Walloons, the erstwhile masters of Belgian business and culture and politics, saw minority status threatening, as their birth rate remained significantly below that of the Flemings. The latter, conscious of their growing strength, were resolved to resist the quiet process of education and social advancement that in the past had converted so many of their number into French-speakers. Thus it was not surprising that the focus of controversy should have been the old and distinguished University of Louvain, located a few miles on the Flemish side of the linguistic border, yet where the language of instruction had traditionally been French—a situation that militant Flemings found intolerable. In February, 1968, disputes over Louvain brought about the Belgian government's resignation; in the ensuing elections, splinter groups speaking for the two language elements made notable gains at the expense of the established nationwide political parties. In the end, the only solution the Flemings would accept was to divide the University in two and to move the French-speaking part to a new location on the other side of the linguistic frontier.

In Ireland it was religion rather than language that drew a cleavage dating back to the seventeenth century. The settlement of 1922 had left a large minority of Catholics in the Protestant-dominated North, which, after the liberation of the bulk of the country from British rule, had remained an integral, if self-governing, part of the United Kingdom. Subsequently the Catholics of Northern Ireland had suffered discrimination of all sorts—in housing, in education, and in job opportunities; still more, a shameless gerrymandering of election districts had assured the political preponderance of the Protestants. Meantime, as in Belgium, the culturally subordinated element of the population had steadily grown in numbers. Yet not until a group of student leaders became active in their behalf did the northern Catholics find a voice for their discontents. The agitation that rocked the country in 1969 had originally been based on a labor ideology and had been directed at all the poor, regardless of religion. It quickly became, however, a movement of Catholics, which by August had barricaded itself within the slums of the major cities and was engaged in an undeclared civil war with the Protestants. At this point Harold Wilson's government in London realized that it could no longer pursue the hands-off policy which had become customary in Britain's dealings with Northern Ireland; it found itself obliged to exert the overriding authority which in theory it had always possessed. Wilson sent British troops to restore order, and he promised to see to it that the grievances of the Catholics were redressed.

In Northern Ireland as in Belgium, the antagonisms inherited from the past seemed to be growing, rather than diminishing as most observers a few decades earlier had hoped and predicted. Faced with the new uniformity of a predominantly urban culture, Western Europeans held on stubbornly to the traditional allegiances that continued to make them different one from another. Threatened with homogenization, they clung to the language or religion that set them apart. Indeed, they sometimes stressed these distinctions more than ever or revived old ones that had almost disappeared. Even the Scots, although sharing their Protestantism and their language with the English to whom they had been indissolubly linked for two and a half centuries, began in the 1960's to feel the stirrings of a nationalist movement for home rule.

In the case of Scotland, resentment at economic subordination to London lay at the root of much of the nationalist discontent. This could be a third motive behind the tenacity of ethnic identity. Economic fears —frequently exaggerated—slowed the processes of integrating the six nations of the Common Market and of absorbing foreign workers into the life of the peoples among whom they dwelt. The workers' inferior economic status combined with ethnic differences to reinforce their sense of being outsiders; and hence they too found good reason to cling to their original identities. The minor languages of Western Europe might be on their way to disappearing—both Breton and Welsh seemed doomed, as the younger people saw no point in speaking them—but the more robust allegiances shared by millions proved even hardier than before. Religion, language, and economic level continued to divide the Europeans into clearly marked nations and sub-groupings. Thus there seemed no immediate danger that the infinite cultural variety which had given Europe its special charm might vanish forever.

The Revival of Ideology and the New Cultural Temper

The allegiances to which Europeans clung were also ideological. In the 1950's European and American observers had alike foreseen an end to ideology. By the late 1960's they were less certain. To be sure, party

programs had tended to become more and more alike: the real political
struggles went on over bread-and-butter issues which the trade unions were better equipped than the parties to handle. Yet ideological rhetoric did not wither away: it entered a new phase in which old terms took on unfamiliar meanings and in which youth played a larger part than ever before.

On the one hand, the traditional formations of the Left displayed an extraordinary tenacity. Or at least in each major country *one* of the two historical parties that claimed to speak for the working classes maintained its cadres and its electoral following. One could almost lay it down as a rule that where the Socialists were strong, the Communists were weak, and vice versa: in Britain and Germany, the Labor and Social Democratic parties continued to win elections and to lead governments, while communism remained a negligible political force; in France and Italy, the Communist parties, although excluded from power, displayed a strength and confidence that made many voters wonder whether it was worth while any longer to support Socialist formations riven by splits and factionalism.

Thus the ideological map of Western Europe was once again becoming simpler: the old antagonism between socialism and communism was being transcended not merely—as in France and Italy—by the growing tendency toward cooperation between them, but by the brute fact that one or the other was being shoved off the scene. Still more, in both parties entrenched bureaucracies and counsels of caution were clearly dominant. In the case of the Socialists this situation was of long standing: it was already half a century since they had ceased to be revolutionary in any practical meaning of the term. What was more novel was the spectacle of Communists running municipalities and cooperatives, as in Italy, or acting as a brake on spontaneous insurrection, as during the French "events of May"—in short, serving as the left flank of the national "establishment."

This at least was what the young thought, when they condemned Socialists and Communists together as pillars of the status quo. The parties of the old European Left, they felt, were incapable of speaking to the concerns of youth. The student movements which flourished throughout Western Europe in the late 1960's scorned the responsible leadership of the working classes: they appealed over the heads of these leaders to the individual workers or entered into alliances with splinter groups—sometimes Maoist or Trotskyist in orientation—which were similarly battling the official party machines. The students were determined not merely to reform the universities in which they were enrolled—to see the curriculum broadened and to share in its administration; they also saw themselves as the champions of a new cultural temper and the spokesmen of the oppressed masses, wherever and under whatever conditions these might live.

Faced by apathy or even hostility on the part of the workers in their own countries, the young people turned to the "Third World" as a source of ideological inspiration. With the European masses reluctant to act in a revolutionary fashion, examples of such behavior had to be sought in Asia or Africa or Latin America, where oppression and starvation—and armed protest against them—were undeniable. At its mildest, the concern of the students for the underdeveloped world sprang from an uneasy conscience at the privileged economic status that Western Europe now shared with the United States. At its more virulent, this sentiment turned to passionate hatred against an order which allowed the enormous disparities between the advanced western nations and the rest of the world to persist. The passing of old-fashioned colonialism, the young people argued, had been merely superficial: in the form of "neo-colonial" economic and cultural relationships the dominance of Europeans and Americans over non-whites remained unshaken. Of the anti-imperialist tracts that voiced the new temper, perhaps the most influential was the work of a black writer, Frantz Fanon, *The Wretched of the Earth*, originally published in French in 1961. A similar burning indignation suffused the passages on colonialism in the *Critique of Dialectical Reason* with which Jean-Paul Sartre summed up in 1960 his ideological progress to date. Sartre's restless energy had been increasingly absorbed by support for revolutionary movements in the Third World. This concern lifted him out of the shadows and uncertainties in which he had languished in the 1950's and gave his work a new relevance for the militant young.

Sartre's *Critique* was Marxist in vocabulary and derivation, but in tone it was highly personal. Try as he might to subject his thought processes to the discipline of an organized movement, his underlying temper remained individualist. And the same was true both of the embattled students and of those among Europe's older intellectuals to whom they looked as ideological mentors. The revolutionary young and the cultural critics who inspired them were alike more anarchist than socialist.

Anarchism as an active force had apparently died a generation earlier: its great days had come before 1914; it had flared up for a final, heroic moment in the Spanish Civil War. Now quite unexpectedly in the late 1960's the anarchist way of life and thought erupted once more on the European scene. What recalled the earlier anarchists in the new student movements was an emphasis on spontaneity, a doctrinaire insistence on "purity" of motive, and absolute, all-or-nothing distinctions between ideological good and evil. In terms of public behavior this temper led to sudden alternations between gentleness and violence or to bewildering combinations of the two. In the sphere of practical endeavor it meant a hatred of large organizations and a preference for work in small, close-at-hand communities in which the principles of direct democracy could be applied. Such unfamiliar juxtapositions disoriented those whose social situations were stable and settled; however straitened their circumstances, "respectable" citizens tended to regard the young activists with suspicion. As in the case of the anarchists of old, people wondered whether it was saintliness or terror that predominated among this new breed.

Index

Index

Aalto, Alvar, 204
Acheson, Dean, 460
Adenauer, Konrad, 413, 462, 494, 496-97, 565; as "good European," 461; gains in election of 1953, 466; succession to, 540-42
Adler, Alfred, 187
Africa: admittance of new republics to UN, 484; "Balkanization of," 485; Eur. settlers in, 482, 486; Fr. community in, 484; imperialism in, 24-27; impetus for independence, 455; insurrection of Eur. settlers in, 501, 502; liberation of, 480-86; multiracial govt., impracticability of, 480; preparation for independence, by Britain, 480-81; repression of native revolts by France, 481-82
Agriculture: crisis in, 144; improved methods of, 7, 134; in USSR, 262-65
Airplane: development of, 132; use in WWII, 333-34, 345-46
Albania: and surrounding hostility, 396; as dependency of Yugoslavia, 396; in Sino-Soviet rift, 532; in WWII, 335-36; It. annexation of, 318
Alexander, King of Yugoslavia, 173, 337
Alexander, Sir Harold, 362-63
Alfonso XIII, 303
Algeria: and Fr. intervention in Suez, 487; as integral part of France, 483; demands of the revolutionary authority, 501; efforts at reform in, by Fr. govt., 502; Egypt. aid to, 487; Eur. settlers in, 482, 500-503; war in, 484, 545, 559; independence of, 484; insurrection and repression in, 482-83; in WWII, 357
Allies (see also Triple Entente; World War I; World War II): and displaced persons, 382-83; and Fourteen Points, 115; and Nürnberg trials, 405; and Treaty of Versailles, 120-21; distrust of Italy, 363; division of Berlin, 410-11; military occupation by, 383-84, 410-11; plans for postwar Germany, 409; suspicion among, 73-74; WWI

Allies (cont.)
defense of channel ports, 45-47; WWI use of tanks, 72
Alsace-Lorraine: and Germany, 136, 155; and Treaty of Versailles, 121; fate of WWII civilians in, 382; Fr. acquisition of, 142; Fr. loss of, 32; problem of nationality, 30; WWI Ger. offensive in, 43-44
Amiens, Ger. attack on, 73, 74
Amis, Kingsley, 434
Amnesties, granting of in Germany, 405
Amphibious warfare, in WWII, 346-47
Amritsar massacres, 172
Anarchists: Ital., 552; new, 572
Anarcho-Syndicalists, 306, 309
Angola, revolt in, 486, 505
Anouilh, Jean, 435
Anschluss, 213, 311-13
Anthropology, development of, 189-90
Anti-imperialism, 527
Anti-Semitism: in Czech. purge trials, 469-70; in Eastern Europe, 388; in France, 253; in Germany, 249, 443; in Italy, 249; in Poland, 535; in USSR, 469, 512; in WWI, 250; in WWII, 349
Antonioni, Michelangelo, 437
Antwerp, WWII fall of, 45
Anzio, Allied landing at, 362
"Appeasement," 312
Arab-Israeli War, 536, 566-67
Aragon, Louis, 286
Arbitration treaties, escape clauses of, 11
Archbishop of Beja, the, 508
Architecture, 202-4; in Fascist Italy, 291; in Nazi Germany, 290-91; "International Style" of, 170, 222; in USSR, 291; in Scandinavia, 222; post-WWII, 437-39
Ardennes offensive, 372
Argentina, immigration to, 137
Argonne Forest attack, 75
Aristocracy: and liberalism, 13; evolution to democracy, 19; in Ger. army, 28; in 19th century, 19-21; in WWI,

Durkheim, Emile, 185, 189

East Central Europe (*see also* Bulgaria; Czechoslovakia; Hungary; Rumania; Yugoslavia): and Ger. war effort, 387-86; and Sov. pressure to step up industrial production, 469; agrarian dilemma, 386-87, 529-30; Catholicism and communism in, 394; collectivization of agriculture, 397; Communist purge in, 396-97; democratic parties in, 388; disappearance of democratic leadership, 393-94; economic advances of, 397; economic planning in, 530; end of democracy in, 393; evolution into dictatorships,385; experience of war years, 387-88; forced industrialization, 523; lack of leadership in, 387; land distribution in, 386; national frontier dilemmas, 384-85; nationalization of industry, 397; national minorities' dissatisfaction, 539; Nazi occupation of, 387-88; Nazi satellites in, 347; peasants in, 386-87; politicos and political mores, 385; population problems in, 137, 386-87; religion in, 531; reorganization of, 336; revolutionary changes in, after Nazi occupation, 388; and Sino-Soviet rift, 532; Sov. control of, 375, 411
Eastern orthodoxy, 384
East Germany, and occupation of Czechoslovakia, 536, 537; economic gains in, 565-66; escapees from, 541
Ebert, Friedrich, 167
Economic nationalism, 276
Economics: Keynesian theory of, 282-84, 422; post-WWII problems, 406-8
Eden, Anthony, 487-88, 497; and World War II, 332; as foreign minister, 301; conference with Stalin, 343; resistance to fascism, 321; retirement of, 497
Education: and aristocracy in 1914, 20; for peasants, 387; in Czechoslovakia, 385; post-WWII, 440-43; transition to more democratic system, 555-56; in Western Europe, 20
Egypt, 25, 356-57
Ehrenburg, Ilya, 528
Einstein, Albert, 181
Eisenhower, Dwight, 491; advance toward Rhine, 375-76; at summit conference, 493; attack on Tunisia, 359; final decisions in Germany, 377; lack of sympathy with Europeans, 491-92; Normandy command of, 362, 364-66; North Africa command of, 357-58
Eisenstein, Sergei, 292
El Alamein, Battle of, 357
Electoral laws, modification, 467-68
Eliot, T. S., 195, 435

el-Krim, Abd, 171, 303
Eluard, Paul, 286
Emigration: after WWI, 135-38; as a mass movement, 276; during 1930's, 276-77; Eur. pressure for, 522; of Jews, 240, 443
Enabling Act of 1933, 238
Entente (*see* Triple Entente)
"Equalization of burdens" (Ger.), 462
Erhard, Ludwig, 496-97, 540-42, 563, 565; and Bundestag, 541
Eritrea, federation with Ethiopia, 455
Erlander, Tage, 569
Erzberger, Matthias, 114, 166, 236
d'Espérey, Franchet, 75
Estonia, 98, 326
Ethiopia: and Italy, 298; expulsion of Italians, 25; It. occupation of, 299-301
"Euratom," 557
European Coal and Steel Community, 463, 465
European Defense Community (EDC) (*see also* Schuman Plan), 465; nonratification of, by France, 493; ratification of, by Eur. parliament, 465; substitution for, 493
European Recovery Program (*see* Marshall Plan)
Existentialism, 190, 431-32

Falange (Span.), 305, 508
Falkenhayn, Erich von, 48, 61, 65
Fanfani, Amintore, 498-99, 551
Fanon, Frantz, 572
Farben, I. G., 134, 142
Fascism (*see also* Germany; Italy; Nazism): advent of, 151, 190, 245-46; and birth rate, 276; and communism, 247; and industry, 247-48, 272; and *Quadragesimo Anno*, 287; and religion, 288-89; and youth, 234, 242, 246; attitude toward women, 249; action against, 250-51; culture under, 277-86, 290-91; foreseen by 19th century liberals, 14; Ger. vs. It., 248-50; leadership of, 224-25, 246; in Austria, 244-45, 249; in Belgium, 221; in Eastern Europe, 388; in Portugal, 173, 243-44, 349; persecution of Jews, 276-77; post-WWII return to, 382; psychological effects of, 278; purges of, 388, 389, 404-5; resistance to, and postwar culture, 429; tactics of, 230; tenets of, 173, 227-28, 230, 245-50
"Father figures," in Germany and France, 494
Fatherland Front in Bulgaria, 392
Fatigue, war, as checkrein on revolution, 382
Federation of Italian Industrialists, 232